D1752513

Nyanga

Ancient Fields, Settlements and
Agricultural History in Zimbabwe

MEMOIRS OF THE BRITISH INSTITUTE IN EASTERN AFRICA: NUMBER 16

Nyanga

Ancient Fields, Settlements and Agricultural History in Zimbabwe

BY

ROBERT SOPER

With contributions from

DAVID BEACH
INA PLUG
KATHERINE VERBEEK
JIMMY JONSSON

LONDON
The British Institute in Eastern Africa
2002

Published by

The British Institute in Eastern Africa,
c/o The British Academy,
10, Carlton House Terrace,
London SW1Y 5AH

Distributed by

Oxbow Books
Park End Place,
Oxford OX1 1HN

ISBN 1 872566 12 X

© The British Institute in Eastern Africa 2002

Printed and Bound in England by Short Run Press

Contents

List of figures .... *iii*
List of plates .... *vi*
Foreword .... *viii*
Preface .... *ix*

Section One

1. Nyanga and its Archaeology 2
The Nyanga complex 2
Preservation of the archaeological landscape 4
The British Institute in Eastern Africa/University of Zimbabwe project 4
History of archaeological research 8
Nyanga in the context of Zimbabwean archaeology 11

2. The Nyanga Environment 13
Topography 13
Geology 15
Soils 17
Climate 18
Vegetation 20

3. African Agriculture in Nyanga and Beyond 22
Agricultural practices and field systems in Africa 22
Traditional crops and plant use in Nyanga 27

4. Agricultural Works: Terraces, Ridges and Water Furrows 33
Terraces 33
Cultivation Ridges 55
Hydraulic works 61

5. Settlements, Homestead Structures and Other Features 86
Early hilltop settlements 86
Pit-structures 89
Enclosures 96
Other sites 102
Domestic structures 108
Homesteads and symbolism 110
Forts 112
Iron working 115

6. Livestock and Agriculture in the Nyanga Complex **124**
    Livestock 124
    Crops and cultivation 128

7. Nyanga Society in the Later Iron Age **131**

Section Two

8. Excavated Settlement Sites **140**
    Nyangui hilltop settlement 1732DD27 141
    Chirimanyimo Hill 148
    Mount Muozi 156
    Nyangui G7/1 ruined pit-structure 164
    Matinha I: Pit-structures and excavation 170
    Nyangui G1/21 pit-structure 175
    "Fishpit" pit-structure 180
    Ziwa MSE 17 stone enclosure 186
    Ziwa SN153 stone enclosure 193
    Stone enclosures in Mazarura and Nyautare and the Chirangeni excavation 198
    Chigura enclosures 208

Annex by David Beach

History and Archaeology in Nyanga **222**
    Appendix I to annex 235
    Appendix II to annex 236

    APPENDIX A Soil Analyses 240
    APPENDIX B Bones from Muozi Midden by Ina Plug 242
    APPENDIX C Identification of Plant Macrofossils by Jimmy Jonnson 249
    APPENDIX D Comparison of Pottery Assemblages from Excavated Sites 251
    APPENDIX E Glass and Copper Beads 257
    APPENDIX F Radiocarbon dates for Nyanga Sites 263

References and Annotated Bibliography **264**

Index **274**

Figures

1.	Map of the complex area with sample survey areas.	6
2.	Map of the Nyanga area.	14
3.	Simplified geological map of the Nyanga Area.	16
4.	Distribution of terracing identified from aerial photographs.	34
5.	Ziwa site SN113. Plan of terracing and enclosures.	36
6.	Ziwa site SN113. Section of the terrace transect.	38
7.	Ziwa Ruins, Mujinga A. Section of terrace transect.	40
8.	Ziwa Ruins, Mujinga B. Section of terrace transect.	41
9.	Ziwa Ruins. Profile of terraces on a north-east facing slope, c.1km north-east of the Site Museum, grid reference VQ622958.	42
10.	Maristvale. Plan and profile of terraces with drains at grid reference VR744133.	43
11.	Maristvale. Section of terrace transect at grid reference VR744133.	44
12.	Hypothetical sequence of terrace construction at Maristvale.	45
13.	Chirangeni. Plan of terraces and enclosure.	48
14.	Chirangeni. Section of terraces.	49
15.	Chirangeni. Section of "garden" terrace.	49
16.	Profile of terraces on the east side of the highland range north of Chirimanyimo at grid reference VR765310.	50
17.	Sections of terrace transects north of Chirimanyimo at grid reference VR763309.	51
18.	Section of terrace transect above Elim Mission at grid reference VR760532.	52
19.	Maristvale. Plan and profile of cultivation ridges in a vlei at grid reference VR744133.	56
20.	Maristvale. Section of cultivation ridges and ditches at grid reference VR744133.	57
21.	Mwenje, north side of basin. Cultivation ridges and terraces traced from an aerial photograph.	59
22.	Mwenje, centre of basin. Cultivation ridges and terraces traced from an aerial photograph.	60
23.	Mwenje furrow sections.	61
24.	Map of banked furrows in the northern part of the National Park/Demera Hill.	66
25.	Section of furrow NP1.	67
26.	Furrow sections.	70
27.	Pit-structures, hollows and ditches at Matinha IV, south of Chirimanyimo.	77
28.	Distribution of pit-structures, pit-enclosures and double concentric enclosures.	87
29.	Distribution of early hilltop settlements, forts and split-level enclosures.	88
30.	Pit-structure, Chirimanyimo.	90
31.	Distribution of ruined and well preserved pit-structures in Block G, Nyangui Forest Land.	94

32.	Pit-enclosure at Chirawu's Site 12, Ziwa Ruins, grid reference VQ625959.	97
33.	Double concentric enclosure, Chigura Hills.	99
34.	Two split-level enclosures north of Chirimanyimo, grid reference VR768310.	100
35.	"Simple" enclosure with houses and raised platforms around the perimeter. Ziwa Ruins, Mujinga.	101
36.	Muozi. General plan of the plateau.	102
37.	Muozi. Plan of the stone ruins on the western promontory.	103
38.	Muozi. Complete vessels from the surface.	105
38 (continued).	Muozi. Complete vessels from the surface.	106
39.	Sketch plan of Mujinga fort, Ziwa Ruins.	113
40.	Complex of fort, residential enclosure and pit-enclosure, with terraces and walled passages. Nyahava, Tanda, grid reference VQ321953.	114
41.	Iron-smelting furnaces.	116
42.	Location of excavated sites.	140
43.	Nyangui 1732DD27. General plan of the site traced from an aerial photograph.	141
44.	Nyangui 1732DD27. Plan of hollow A.	142
45.	Nyangui 1732DD27. Section of hollow A.	143
46.	Nyangui 1732DD27. Plan of hollow B and surrounds.	144
47.	Nyangui 1732DD27. Pottery.	145
47 (continued).	Nyangui 1732DD27. Pottery.	146
48.	Chirimanyimo Hill. Plan of the hilltop.	148
49.	Chirimanyimo Hill. General plan of the whole site traced from an aerial photograph.	149
50.	Chirimanyimo Hill. Plan of enclosure with Trench VIII.	152
51.	Chirimanyimo Hill. Section of Trench VIII.	152
52.	Chirimanyimo Hill. Pottery from Trenches I to IV.	153
53.	Chirimanyimo Hill. Pottery from Trench VII.	154
54.	Chirimanyimo Hill. Pottery from Trench VIII.	154
55.	Chirimanyimo Hill. Stone artefacts from Trench VIII.	155
56.	Muozi midden. Pottery from 0 to 30cm below surface.	158
57.	Muozi midden. Pottery from 30 to 60cm below surface	159
58.	Muozi midden. Pottery from 60 to 80cm below surface.	160
59.	Muozi midden. Pottery from 80 to 120cm below surface.	160
60.	Muozi midden. Metal objects.	162
61.	Nyangui G7/1. Plan of ruined pit-structure.	164
62.	Nyangui G7/1. a. Section of Trench II. b. Section of Trench III.	166
63*a*.	Nyangui G7/1. Pottery.	168
63*b*.	Nyangui G7/1. Pottery and iron arrowhead.	169
64.	Matinha. Map of ruined and well preserved pit-structures, with ditches and furrows. Traced from an aerial photograph.	170

65.	Matinha I/1. Plan of ruined pit-structure.	171
66.	Matinha I/1. Section of pit.	172
67.	Matinha I/1. Section of the entrance passage.	173
68.	Matinha I/1. Pottery.	174
69.	Nyangui G1/21 pit-structure. Plan and profile.	176
70.	Nyangui G1/21. Section of the basin below the platform.	177
71.	Nyangui G1/21. Pottery.	179
72.	Fishpit pit-structure. Plan.	181
73.	Fishpit. Plan of House A.	182
74.	Fishpit. Plan of House B.	184
75.	Fishpit. Pottery.	185
76.	Ziwa MSE17. Plan of the enclosure.	187
77.	Ziwa MSE17. Plan of House 1.	189
78.	Ziwa MSE17. Pottery.	191
79.	Ziwa MSE17. Iron objects.	192
80.	Ziwa SN153. Plan of the enclosure.	194
81.	Ziwa SN153. Pottery.	197
82.	Chirangeni area, west of Hambuka valley. Double concentric enclosures and an unwalled homestead.	199
83.	Chirangeni. Plan of the enclosure.	200
84.	Chirangeni enclosure, plan of House 1A.	202
85.	Chirangeni enclosure, plan of House 2.	203
86.	Chirangeni. Pottery from the enclosure.	205
86 (continued).	Chirangeni. Pottery from the enclosure.	206
87.	Chirangeni. Pottery from the garden terrace.	206
88.	Chirangeni. Iron objects and soapstone stopper from the enclosure.	207
89.	Chigura. Plan of the double concentric and residential enclosures.	209
90.	Chigura. Plan of House 1.	211
91.	Chigura. Plan of House 2.	213
92.	Chigura. Pottery.	214
92 (continued).	Chigura. Pottery.	215
93.	Chigura. Thick coarse ware.	216
94.	Chigura. Iron axe and washing stone.	226

Plates

Plate 1	Dense terracing on west side of the Hambuka valley, Mazarura.	3
Plate 2	Terracing and enclosures in Ziwa ruins, looking north from the summit of Mt Ziwa.	80
Plate 3	Ziwa SN113. Section of terrace 7.	81
Plate 4	Ziwa Mujinga A. Section through terrace wall and terrace above.	81
Plate 5	Terraces at Maristvale site SN51, from the south.	82
Plate 6	Chirangeni. Granite terracing.	82
Plate 7	Chirangeni. Stone-lined open drain through the terraces.	83
Plate 8	The Mwenje basin north of Mount Muozi. Virtually the whole basin is worked into cultivation ridges.	83
Plate 9	Demera hill. Footpath following furrow D1.	84
Plate 10	Demera hill. Reservoir below furrow D1.	84
Plate 11	National Park looking north-east. Furrow NP4 traverses the slope in the middle distance.	85
Plate 12	Low enclosure wall at Nyangui 1732DD27 early hilltop settlement.	118
Plate 13	Pit-structure with restored houses, National Park.	118
Plate 14	Grassy hollow of a ruined pit-structure. Nyangui G7/1.	119
Plate 15	Pit-structure with two radial walls. Nyangui Block G, group 1, pit 13.	119
Plate 16	Mount Muozi from the east side of the saddle. Two cairns in the foreground.	120
Plate 17	Mount Muozi stone walled site. House circles with the main group of complete pots.	120
Plate 18	Iron object from Mount Muozi.	121
Plate 19	Raised platform with plastered floor surface. Ziwa, Chirawu's site 12.	121
Plate 20	Lintelled entrance of a fort in Tanda. Grid reference VR360120.	122
Plate 21	Small fort with aloes south of Nyautare. Site 1732DC44, grid reference VR662225.	122
Plate 22	Furnace of type 2. Middle Pungwe valley, National Park.	123
Plate 23	Two hoes found in digging a pipe trench at Ziwa.	123
Plate 24	Nyangui 1732DD27, Hollow A. Grave cut through the cobbled floor.	217
Plate 25	Matinha I, 1. Pit and entrance passage with stone paving and revetment.	217
Plate 26	Nyangui G1/21. Mouth of the tunnel at the upper side of the pit.	218
Plate 27	Nyangui G1/21. Lower revetment of the main platform over the drain. Appended platform to right.	218
Plate 28	Ziwa MSE17. House 1 from the south.	219
Plate 29	Chirangeni enclosure. House 1A with H1B behind.	219
Plate 30	Chirangeni enclosure. East side of House 1A.	220
Plate 31	Chigura. North half of the inner enclosure of the double concentric enclosure	220
Plate 32	Chigura. Storage house H1 after excavation.	221
Plate 33	Cattle *tali* from Muozi compared with modern Nguni sample.	221

FOREWORD

Agriculture has been the mainstay of the population of most of Africa through the whole length of the Iron Age, the last two thousand years more or less. In a very real sense, then, African history is agricultural history, the crops and the methods of cultivating them being central to patterns of settlement and population expansion over the centuries. Obvious though this may seem, it has been only in recent decades that the historical significance of African agriculture, in its almost infinite variety, has come to be appreciated, as comparative linguistic studies and Iron Age archaeology have developed across the continent. Despite advances in understanding the repertoires of African crops, and the occasional archaeo-botanical identification of carbonised seeds recovered during excavations, less attention has been paid to the fields themselves, the cultivation techniques and farming strategies, because only very rarely do fields as such survive on the landscape.

Nyanga in the hills of eastern Zimbabwe is one of the exceptions, being a district where 'fossil' fields, in the form of stone terraces built on the slopes in series upon series, survive as a powerful testimony to a former farming community, and to the labour which it devoted to constructing, maintaining and hoeing these fields for the growing of sorghum and other crops. There are, it is true, some other mountainous districts of Africa where one finds abandoned agricultural terracing, but nowhere is it preserved over so extensive an area as it is on the escarpment and foothills of Nyanga. Some of those distant examples help by analogy in interpreting features of the old Nyanga system, not only the fields themselves but equally the farmsteads and settlements with which they were integrated. Equally relevant are existing terrace systems which are maintained and cultivated in remote hilly parts of various countries. The value of such comparative study of African farming systems of the present and past, especially those combining highly specialised or intensive techniques — notably furrow irrigation, manuring and terracing — is vindicated in this volume.

The recently completed archaeological research project at Nyanga, which Robert Soper has been directing and now reports here, forms therefore part of a broader concern with reconstructing the history of African agriculture, its fields and its farming methods. It is a subject in which I have to admit a special interest. When first working on archaeological remains in East Africa in the 1960s with the hope of locating examples of ancient fields, I became aware of the terraces, furrows and settlement complexes of Inyanga (as the district was then called) through the writings of the renowned field archaeologist, O.G.S. Crawford, and the publication of the work there by Roger Summers in the early 1950s — as well as the exciting general message which historians of the African continent at that time, above all Basil Davidson, were reading into those early research findings. Nyanga had to be on my itinerary, therefore, as soon as there might be occasion to extend my fieldwork so far to the south. But events in Southern Rhodesia, as it was then, intervened and precluded a visit to Nyanga for fifteen years.

When the opportunity for that arose eventually, in 1982, Nyanga more than fulfilled expectations with its vast areas of preserved hillside terracing, its grids of valley-bottom ridges for dry-season cultivation, its long contour furrows led off mountain streams, and its stone-revetted pit-structures and other visible remains of the homesteads of a former farming system. By this time, moreover, studies in other parts of Africa were leading to more sophisticated questions about the history of African agriculture and its techniques than had arisen at the time of Summers' pioneer research. Some of these new directions were articulated at a colloquium at Pitt Rivers Museum in Oxford in 1988, convened by the British Institute in Eastern Africa; this resulted in a special volume of the journal *Azania* (XXIV for 1989) on 'The history of African agricultural technology and field systems'.

That colloquium highlighted the need for a new and intensive round of research at Nyanga in view of the archaeological preservation, variety and extent of its agricultural features, this study to be part of the broader concern with fields and cultivation systems, both existing and abandoned, in East Africa and other parts of the continent. Accordingly, the British Institute approached the Rhodes Trustees, through the Trust's Secretary in Oxford, Sir Anthony Kenny, for support for a project to be directed by a suitably experienced archaeologist attached to the University of Zimbabwe. In the event the Rhodes Trust provided generous support for the entire research project and necessary equipment over five successive years, beginning in 1993. The project was directed by Robert Soper who was already a staff member of the University of Zimbabwe, and for whom the position of research fellow and the necessary academic and research facilities were provided by the University and its History Department. Equally important to the success of the project, from its planning stage to completion, was the encouragement and unfailing cooperation of the Zimbabwe National Museums and Monuments organization, at central, regional and local levels. At the end of the fieldwork the arrangement between the Institute and the University was extended for a sixth year (1998), thanks to special awards from the British Academy and the Smuts Fund, to ensure the complete analysis of the findings of the five seasons' work, including the numerous excavations which Soper had directed on selected sites, and for their writing-up. The results of that are now presented in this book, which will serve not only for reference but also for inspiring new endeavours towards revealing the history and archaeology of African societies and their agriculture.

This volume will be used and judged in the context of current knowledge of these subjects obtained through research undertaken over the years in various parts of Zimbabwe and other countries. Some of those contributions have already revealed outline sequences of Iron Age occupation, of which the successive stages and regional variants are defined by distinctive cultural features, by their pottery wares in particular. This Nyanga study is different in that it produces for the first time a sequence not merely of archaeological 'sites' and pottery types, but of the actual farming settlements and homestead structures, as well as modifications to their forms and locations, through an unbroken period of five or six hundred years. It is thus much more than an archaeological sequence since it documents the continuity and evolution of a rural community. The first stages of this, dating to the 14th if not the 13th century AD, are now identified on some of the highest peaks of the north Nyanga range — a rather surprising settlement phenomenon which was entirely unpredicted at the outset of this project, and which underlines the importance of a comprehensive archaeological survey such as Robert Soper and his teams have accomplished. Interestingly, the date of these complex hilltop settlements corresponds neatly with that of the most intensive activity and building at Great Zimbabwe, some three hundred kilometres distant to the south-west, and the question arises whether they represent in some way a local reaction to the power and expanding tentacles of the Zimbabwe state at that time.

That historical question is one for sober reflection and further investigation. More important, for an understanding of what was happening at Nyanga, is the highly distinctive nature of the early hilltop building complexes. Subsequent stages of settlement, from about the 16th century onwards, show a gradual downhill trend, associated in time with the intensification of terrace construction for cultivation, at altitudes below the restrictions imposed by the highland mists and frosts. Alongside the grain cultivation, livestock were kept for protein; the cows had to be confined within the homesteads and thus contributed essential slurry and manure for the intensively cultivated fields around. These cattle were of a dwarf variety, the result apparently of a process of local selective breeding, being small enough to pass through the low and narrow tunnels leading to the sunken stalls in the middle of the homestead structures — what were erroneously called 'slave pits' in old Rhodesian parlance. This recognition of the dwarf cattle, confirmed by archaeo-zoological study of their excavated bones, is one of the more remarkable revelations of this research project. Apart from helping resolve at last the 'mystery' of the stone-lined pits of the Nyanga hillsides, it underlines the integrated strategy of the old farming system.

The successive stages of this Nyanga sequence raise obvious questions about environmental changes and climatic fluctuations during the last millennium. More particularly they begin to reveal how the local farming community grappled with these changes, including those induced by its own intensive use of the land and its resources, by adapting accordingly its crops and its methods century by century, right down to the nineteenth and the limits of living memory. At that point the system eventually phased out so that it cannot be observed in action. But its signs, some of them highly conspicuous, survive across the Nyanga landscape and constitute an unparalleled archaeological resource from which to pursue yet further the investigation of African agricultural history.

J.E.G. SUTTON

PREFACE

The stone ruins of the Nyanga area of eastern Zimbabwe have intrigued observers since they were first reported to the outside world at the end of the 19th century. The early fanciful speculations about their meaning have been gradually tempered over the years by sober archaeological research, culminating in the recently completed project by the British Institute in Eastern Africa and the University of Zimbabwe. This book sets out the accumulated knowledge and understanding of the Nyanga archaeological complex as far as we now know it, in particular the significance of its agricultural works to which the landscape bears eloquent witness.

In Section One of the book, the archaeological and environmental background is presented in Chapters 1 and 2, and the general context of African agricultural history in Chapter 3. Chapter 4 covers the investigation of the ancient agricultural infrastructure — terraces, cultivation ridges and water furrows — and Chapter 5 deals with the successive settlements of the farmers who built them. Chapters 6 and 7 then seek to interpret the agricultural systems and the development of the society over six centuries.

Much of the interpretation relies on excavations of settlement sites and the analysis of the resulting data, the details of which would encumber and might even obscure the essential story. These are accordingly presented in Section Two — the excavation reports in Chapter 8, an Annex by the late David Beach on the available relevant information from documentary and oral sources, and a series of more or less technical Appendices. Finally an annotated bibliography of Nyanga archaeology is incorporated with the References.

Grateful acknowledgement is due to numerous bodies and individuals. The research on which the book is largely based was a joint project between the British Institute in Eastern Africa and the History Department of the University of Zimbabwe who have provided unfailing support. The project was made possible by generous funds from the Rhodes Trustees and the British Academy, with a supplementary grant from the Smuts Fund. Authorisation was granted by various bodies in Zimbabwe — the National Museums and Monuments, the Ministry of Home Affairs and Nyanga District Administrator, the Forestry Commission and the Department of National Parks and Wildlife — while the Office of the Surveyor General provided access to aerial photographs. Close cooperation was maintained with Mutare Museum, especially with the late Steve Chirawu and Paul Mupira who with P.Mufute participated in parts of the fieldwork; Paul Mupira also contributed a preliminary analysis of glass beads on which Appendix D is partly based.

I am indebted to numerous other individuals for support, advice and information. Bud Payne, for many years Director of the Nyanga Experiment Station, has been a valued friend, generous with his extensive knowledge of Nyanga and its archaeology. Paul Stidolph has provided information from his own aerial photograph survey and personal knowledge of parts of the Nyanga lowlands. At the University of Zimbabwe I am grateful for discussions with the late David Beach, Katherine Verbeek, Alois Mandondo, I.Mpofu, A.Mashingaidze, Anne Turner and Ngoni Nenguwo, and to Honours students in Archaeology — McEdward Murimbika, Munyaradzi Manyanga and Chris Chauke — who contributed to the research. M.Chifamba and J.Mukumburike provided technical assistance in the field and laboratory and numerous other students participated in some of the excavations.

Ina Plug analysed the faunal assemblage from Muozi; Jimmy Jonsson, Bob Drummond and the National Herbarium provided seed and plant identifications; the Department of Research and Specialist Services analysed soil samples; John Vogel facilitated the radiocarbon determinations; and the Oxford Forestry Unit identified a wood sample from Ziwa.

Many residents of Nyanga acted as informants, guides and excavators among whom particular mention may be made of John MacRobert, Claud Munditi and the staff of the Ziwa Site Museum, while Nelson Dzokoto was a regular field assistant. John Nyazanga, Bernard Sachota, Charles Mandikonza and Joseph Mukumbirike assisted with the questionnaire on crops and cultivation. I am also indebted for hospitality at various times to the Marist Brothers and Nyanga High School, Elim Mission, Nyangui Forest Station, St Monica's School, Chirimanyimo Madziwa School, Kagore School, Mr Martin Chikwiramakoma, and Mr Webster Mandikonza.

A succession of British Institute graduate students participated in field and laboratory work and drawing up of maps and plans — Nick Hanson-James, Alice Mayers, Biddy Simpson, Nicola Harrison and Vicky Barnecutt.

Lastly (and indeed firstly) I am grateful to John Sutton who initiated the project and has provided advice and constructive criticism throughout from his wide knowledge of African terracing and field systems. His review of the original manuscript of this volume offered many cogent suggestions for its improvement, but I remain of course responsible for the final version.

SECTION ONE

NYANGA AND ITS ARCHAEOLOGY

CHAPTER 1

NYANGA AND ITS ARCHAEOLOGY

THE NYANGA COMPLEX

The Nyanga archaeological complex presents an impressive landscape of stone-built features, extending over more than 7000 square kilometres in north-eastern Zimbabwe and constituting one of the largest agglomerations of stone structures in Africa. These features include widespread agricultural terracing and a variety of settlement structures and defensive works, as well as old water furrows and ridge-and-ditch cultivation works. These remains are the material manifestation of a later Iron Age society and its agricultural practices which developed over a period of perhaps 600 years from around AD 1300. As such, the complex has an important place in the history and achievements of the peoples of Zimbabwe, demonstrating their appropriate adaptation to a range of local environments. As a well-preserved record of ancient field systems and related works, it provides a significant example of African agricultural practices, which in general have left little clear trace on the landscape.

Coherent previous knowledge of the complex derived mainly from the important research directed by Roger Summers between 1949 and 1951 (Summers 1958). This concentrated mainly on the settlement sites to provide the general cultural background and a tentative development sequence in the relatively recent past. Interest in the history of African agriculture, which has developed over the last 20 years, focused renewed attention on the Nyanga terracing and inspired the project whose results are described in this volume.

The archaeological complex lies approximately between 17° 30' and 18° 45' south, and 32° 15' and 33° east, but the precise overall distribution is not easily defined as it tends to diffuse progressively to the edges and there is some variation in the distribution of different features. The core area of actual terracing as detected from aerial photographs covers around 5000 square kilometres on the flanks of the northern part of the Eastern Highlands of Zimbabwe and adjacent lowland areas to the east and, more extensively, the west (fig. 4). The southern edge of this core distribution seems to be the Pungwe valley. More sporadic occurrences of terracing are reported further afield: to the north across the Ruenya river, and in Stapleford Forest and Mkondwe 30km or more to the south. Summers (1958:9) believed that the terraces extend eastwards for a short distance into Mozambique but does not give the source or details of his information. There is also a written reference from the 1890s to terracing in the Chimanimani area 160km to the south (Beach 1988), but this case has not been relocated and it is not clear if it is directly related, there being no records for the intervening area.

Typical "pit-structures", another element of the complex, also extend south, at least to just north of Penhalonga, while stone-walled occupation sites with lintelled entrances which may be related extend westwards to Headlands/Mweya, accompanied by scattered occurrences of localised terracing. Total distribution is thus of the order of 7 to 8000 square kilometres, the greater part in the Nyanga, Makoni and Mutasa administrative districts.

The various elements of the complex are described in Chapters 4 and 5, with site reports on settlement excavations in Chapter 8. These comprise the terracing itself in ranges of up to 100 on escarpments, hills or valley sides below a maximum altitude of around 1700m (Plate 1); extensive areas of cultivation ridges; water furrows; mountain top settlement clusters; stone-built homestead sites of various types with different altitudinal and areal distribution; defensive structures or "forts"; and iron smelting sites. Some of these elements are still imperfectly dated and the relative combinations of different features may have varied over time. Not all of these features of course are peculiar to the complex. For example, hilltop stone enclosures, often roughly built, are common in many areas of Zimbabwe and there is no reason to associate most of them with the Nyanga complex. Some of those in Mount Darwin 150km to the north-west have affinities with the Nyanga examples in the presence of lintelled entrances and "loopholes", but there is no terracing there and no link has been traced.

The recent research has provided a better idea of the chronology and internal development through typological studies supported by radiocarbon dating. The total time range so far established is from about AD 1300 to 1900 and it is possible to trace continuity through this period in spite of substantial changes in the settlement pattern and domestic structures. It is not however yet known exactly when actual terrace construction started.

An earlier occupation of parts of the area in

the first millennium AD is represented by sites with Early Iron Age "Ziwa ware" pottery. This bears no resemblance to any of the pottery associated with the later complex and a hiatus in occupation is probable, with completely unrelated populations responsible for each. However, Summers (1958:233) considered that some crude terracing of granite slopes was associated with the Early Iron Age pottery; this has not been conclusively confirmed or disproved, but remains quite possible. Some terminological confusion is involved here. The Early Iron Age pottery was first discovered by Randall-MacIver (1906) at a site at the foot of Mount Ziwa, 20km north-west of Nyanga town, and Summers (1958) later formally named it after the mountain. At that time the major concentration of stone terracing and structures in the vicinity were known as "Van Niekerk Ruins", but after Zimbabwean independence this name was felt to be inappropriate and they were renamed "Ziwa Ruins", or the "Ziwa National Monument" for the area of 33 square kilometres now protected as an archaeological reserve. (A site museum was built here in 1993.) There is thus no association between the pottery and the stone ruins, although both bear the same name. The Early Iron Age lies outside the scope of the recent research except for the recording of such sites when encountered.

The survival of the complex (or several of its elements) into the 18th and 19th centuries places it within the time-range of the present inhabitants of the area, as discussed by Beach in his review of the documentary and traditional sources in the Annex towards the end of this volume. As Beach points out, there are no indications of any major migrations or population replacement, so we must attribute the complex to relatively recent ancestors, even though little direct memory of the archaeological remains seems to be preserved. The core area of the complex north of Nyanga town falls within the territory of the Nyama people under Chief Saunyama; extensive terracing and other structures west of the Nyangombe river fall within the Maungwe territory of the Makoni chiefship; while the typical pit-structures and scattered terracing to the south are within Manyika under Mutasa (compare Figures 4 and 95). There appears to have been little basic change in the distribution of these political units for several centuries and the genealogies of their ruling dynasties extend at least well back into the 18th century in the case of Saunyama, and considerably further for the others (Annex). It is thus difficult to attribute the complex to a single socio-political group. These populations now speak languages of the broad Shona group (in spite of an earlier attribution of some of them to a separate, non-Shona, Barwe cluster – see Annex). However this Shona identity is not entirely consistent with the archaeological evidence for the earlier stages of the complex as discussed in Chapter 7.

Plate 1. Dense terracing on west side of the Hambuka valley, Mazarura

Preservation of the archaeological landscape

Much of the archaeological landscape has survived with little disturbance, though this is now increasing. As noted in Chapter 3, it is mainly in areas considered marginal by subsequent agriculturalists that extensive evidence of old agricultural works survives undisturbed by later cultivation activities using different methods and technology. The Nyanga area is hardly marginal in terms of climate, having good or moderately good rainfall. Topographically however, the terrace agriculture used steep slopes and/or very stony areas not exploitable by other less labour-intensive methods. Agriculture in colonial times and since has increasingly been based on the ox or tractor plough which is impracticable on the terraces and favours the less stony, usually sandier soils; it is thus affecting in particular some areas of old cultivation ridges, though their distribution is still visible on aerial photographs.

Much of the area north of Nyanga town was depopulated at the end of the 19th century owing to succession conflicts over the Saunyama chiefship (see Annex); it has only been extensively repopulated since the effects of the Land Apportionment Act of the 1940s when many people were relocated from areas designated for white farming and other purposes. Significant population pressure has only developed even more recently. Further south and west, habitation by Manyika and Maungwe and others has been more continuous but in the south at least there is less terracing to be affected (except perhaps in Stapleford Forest – Summers 1958), though stone homesteads are often less well preserved. This southern area has not been examined in any systematic way during the present research.

Current traditional attitudes to the terraces and their resources within the local ecosystem have been documented and analysed in two studies by Matowanyika (1991) and Matowanyika & Mandondo (forthcoming). The studies were carried out in Kagore below the highlands to the north-east, and in Nyautare and two other areas below the highlands on the west. The authors have nothing to say on local beliefs as to who built the terraces and when. However, traditional land-use practices have injunctions against settlement on areas with terraces and other stone ruins and restrict their exploitation to non-destructive activities such as firewood and wild fruit/plant collection and grazing (though the latter causes some damage in Nyautare). In some cases stones may be collected from terraces and used in burials. Local modes of resource management comprise both sacred and pragmatic controls which are mutually reinforcing. The sacred controls are largely related to the concerns of ancestral spirits and, while the stone structures appear to have little sacred significance *per se*, they are often associated with sacred places, especially some hills and water resources, as well as with certain tree species of sacred significance. Mount Muozi is specially sacred in its significance for the Saunyama chiefship. Population pressure is eroding some of these controls, especially among more recent immigrants in resettlement areas. Some terraces are being modified into wider units suitable for plough agriculture, notably in parts of Nyamaropa and Chitsanza near Nyanga town, while terraces are also being reused for cultivation in Bende. These beliefs and controls clearly have been and are an important factor in the preservation of the terraces and other stone structures.

White farmers usually left structures alone in this area apart from clearing the occasional pit-structure, but resettlement of some of these farms has occasioned some damage through reuse of the stone. A major factor in higher areas has been afforestation, first by wattle and then by pine plantations, which have blanketed large areas in which there must be many pit-structures; some terracing has also been affected. Afforestation is still spreading rapidly northwards in Nyangui Forestry Commission land, and is affecting pit-structures and associated features such as the water furrows which served some of them. In the Troutbeck area in particular, archaeological remains have been swamped by holiday cottages and attendant landscaping and vegetation.

Some areas have been administratively protected thus far from much disturbance. These include Nyanga National Park, the Ziwa National Monument and areas at the foot of the escarpment falling within Nyangui Forestry Commission land but not exploited by them, being unsuitable for pine trees.

The British Institute in Eastern Africa/University of Zimbabwe project

The research project from which this volume derives, entitled "Agricultural History and Archaeology in Nyanga and Adjacent Districts of Zimbabwe", derives from the initiative of the British Institute in Eastern Africa and its then director John Sutton, who examined the terraces as part of his research on ancient and traditional field systems in the eastern half of Africa (Sutton 1983, 1988). The Institute obtained generous funds for a five-year project, 1993-97, from the Rhodes Trustees; this was extended for a sixth year (1988) with a grant from the British Academy and supplementary funding from the Smuts Fund. From its inception, this was a joint project with the History Department of the University of Zimbabwe, with the author as field director, and this has been carried out in close cooperation with the National Museums and Monuments of Zimbabwe. It is worth noting here that Cecil Rhodes was himself closely associated with Nyanga, and that the original Rhodes Estates purchased in the 1890s were given to the nation as the basis for the Nyanga National Park, now a major recreational attraction for Zimbabweans and visitors alike.

The project was conceived as a contribution to the history of African agricultural systems. As the name implies, the main aim was to elucidate the agricultural remains and the systems represented in the context of the cultural background of the complex as a whole. Thus it was intended to amplify previous work to trace the development of the complex and to study the construction, soils and potentiality of the terraces and cultivation ridges and their relationship to the cultural sequence, with deductions on cultivation practices.

At a general conceptual level the project has been pursued as an exercise in landscape archaeology, guided by empirical principles. The settlements and agricultural practices of the Nyanga complex people have modified the landscape to varying degrees, from scattered homesteads now supporting dense thickets (doubtless combined with less obvious effects on the local environment); to more extensive hilltop sites; to the total transformation of very extensive tracts by terracing and cultivation ridges. The approach has been to seek patterns of relationship with geology, soils and topography, including altitude, and where possible to trace how these have varied through time. Parallel to this is the study of settlement sites and spatial patterns of distribution, dispersal or concentration, and relationship between cultural features. The limitations of such morphological evidence are acknowledged, especially the difficulties of sufficiently precise dating and the danger of simplistic inferences and unwarranted associations (Roberts 1987:88). With these reservations, interpretations of these initial data allow inferences on environmental preferences and some hints of social organisation and agricultural systems, but do not at this stage attempt to go much deeper into the social, or even less the cognitive environment.

Research began with the examination of vertical aerial photographs for an area of some 12000 square kilometres, on the basis of which a number of sample areas were selected for ground survey (fig. 1). These areas were chosen to represent different parts of the highlands and lowlands and varying geological/soil conditions; further areas were added as a better idea of the complex and its local distribution was gained. Incidental observations outside the sample areas added to the overall picture. Focus was mostly on the area from the National Park northwards, where the greatest concentrations of terracing are found and where the highland evidence has been less obscured or disturbed by afforestation and more recent settlement. This research strategy, concentrating on the ubiquitous stone structures, may have missed sites without such structures, possibly introducing a bias in the data. The ensuing excavation phase included terrace transects and small-scale excavation of occupation sites. Soil samples were taken from terraces, and phosphate samples from occupation sites in the hope of confirming the use of certain structures as stock-pens. Information on traditional crops was also sought by means of a questionnaire.

Aerial photograph survey

Since most of the features and sites are represented by stone structures and modifications to the surface relief, they are potentially identifiable from the air and a systematic examination of aerial photographs was undertaken for the entire area potentially covered by the complex. Aims were to define the overall distribution of terracing; to correlate detailed distribution with geology, topography and drainage; to study the relative distribution of different types of features so far as they were identifiable; and to select sample areas for ground survey.

The photographs available are the blanket coverage of vertical photography carried out for the Surveyor General's Department at a scale of 1:25000 for mapping purposes. This coverage has been repeated at intervals over the last fifty years and the most recent series from 1986/87 was used as giving the best correlation with the 1:50000 map sheets and offering the most up-to-date configuration of roads, buildings and other features for planning access and identifying geographical features on the ground. Recent developments, in particular afforestation and residential development, have certainly obscured or destroyed archaeological features before (and since) 1986, so that earlier series of photographs were consulted in some cases. Each successive stereo-pair, amounting to over 1500 in all, was examined with a 2x or 3x stereoscope and any information noted and plotted on the 1:50000 maps*. Photographic coverage of the selected sample areas was purchased for more intensive examination

---

* Special thanks are due to the Surveyor General's Office for providing facilities and access to the aerial photographs and in particular to Eddie Daniels for his help and advice

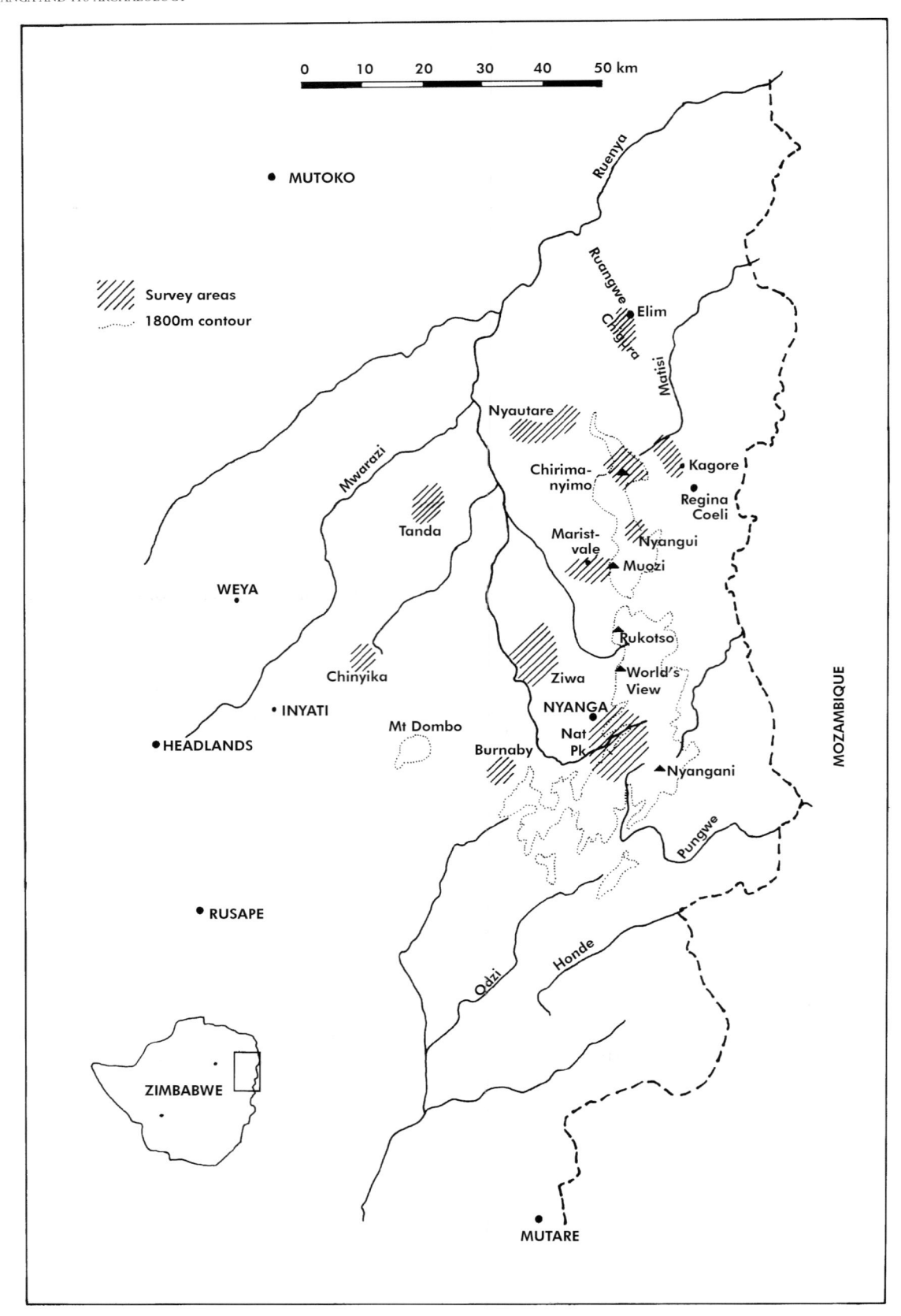

Fig. 1. Map of the complex area with sample survey areas

and use in the field, and enlargements of small areas at scales of up to 1:2500 were obtained where necessary.

Terracing, cultivation ridges, water furrows and various homesteads and stone walls are identifiable but not invariably, so that the data cannot be taken to be comprehensive or even representative without ground control. In the highlands, clumps of trees or bushes commonly indicate the presence of pit-structures, some of which are confirmed by traces of stone walls, but others may be natural outcrops or simple thickets. In many cases enclosures or stone walls identified on the ground could be seen as faint indications on the photographs once their position was known, although not initially detected; in other cases they were not visible on the photographs, especially when obscured by vegetation. Buried features or sites without surface relief are not detectable as crop or soil marks at this scale. Some modern or natural features resemble archaeological features but it was usually possible to distinguish these by their configuration or associations.

Ground survey

Initially seven to 12 days were spent in each sample area and visits were repeated in some cases. Sites or blocks of terraces identified on the aerial photographs were visited and recorded together with other sites encountered en route, but with no formal sampling strategy. Sites were recorded on a series of data forms designed for different structures – pit-structures, enclosures, water furrows – with a general form for other features. Sketch plans were drawn and selected sites were surveyed by plane-table, notably terraced areas and homestead structures. Chapters 4 and 5 detail the information derived from these ground surveys, amplified later in the project by excavation results.

Site locations could be determined very precisely from the aerial photographs in most cases; attempts to use a GPS (Geographical Positioning System) instrument for this purpose gave less accurate and inconsistent results. Geographical Information Systems were not employed since the relevant technology and digitised geographical information were not readily available at the start of the project. It would have proved helpful in the preparation of distribution maps. A GIS project on the correlation of terracing with geology and topography for a sample map sheet was attempted by Nehowa (1994), but the available computer memory proved inadequate to process the digitised data.

Excavation

Transects of ranges of terraces were excavated to investigate construction methods and soil depth and to obtain soil samples. Five areas were selected representing different altitudes and geology. These are described in Chapter 4.

For occupation sites, the main aim was to establish a broad cultural and chronological outline for the complex by means of small-scale excavations, to elucidate individual structures and obtain cultural material and dating evidence. Most sites except Muozi appear to represent single phases of occupation so that the procedure was to uncover structures with attention to details that most previous excavators apart from Summers (1958) had ignored. Examples of the main homestead types were selected, in most cases with attention to relatively easy vehicle access for transport of equipment; the Muozi and Chigura sites however were sufficiently important to merit 30 to 40 minutes' walk from the nearest vehicle approach. Excavation was by teams of six to ten students or local hired labour under the direct supervision of the writer, in some cases aided by a technician from the University of Zimbabwe or staff from the Mutare Museum. All spoil was screened through 6mm and usually 3mm sieves and samples for floatation and phosphate analysis were taken from potentially promising deposits. Floatation procedure was simple, involving stirring in a bucket and scooping with a fine sieve; in no case was water available on site and samples were carried back to base. Excavation reports are given in Chapter 8.

Dating

A chronology of the development of the complex is necessary for its understanding and interpretation. This has been achieved through a combination of approaches, none in itself very precise and even in combination offering only a broad outline.

Classification of homestead types reveals a number of distinct groups. Where distribution of these overlaps as in the highlands, probable relative ordering can be intuitively deduced from comparative state of preservation; distribution in the lowlands however is mutually exclusive.

Pottery analysis, covered in Appendix D, has shown general trends, some chronological and others probably geographical. These, though identified on the basis of preconceived cultural and chronological groupings rather than an independent seriation, do help to support the relative chronology, and the earlier stages are confirmed by the only stratigraphic sequence, that of Muozi. Glass beads from excavated sites, discussed in Appendix E, can be divided into earlier and later assemblages dating broadly to the 16th/17th and 18th/19th centuries respectively; samples however are mostly small and give no finer precision within these brackets, while some sites have yielded none.

Thirty radiocarbon determinations listed in Appendix F generally support other indications and in particular establish the earliest excavated sites at around AD 1300. Charcoal samples were taken where possible from carbonised posts *in situ* or from burnt destruction levels which had formed part of a structure. Where these were not available, resort had to be made to disseminated fragments in cultural deposits; such samples are assumed to have resulted from contemporaneous cultural activities, but in a few cases the deposits may have post-dated the occupation of the structure. The determinations are mostly "high precision" dates from the Pretoria laboratory, quoted at one standard deviation and calibrated for the southern hemisphere according to Talma and Vogel (1993), the precision relating to the sample itself and not necessarily to the context. The precision is in any case obviated, for all but the seven earliest dates before 400 BP, by the alternative calibrations occasioned by wiggles in the calibration curve. Six determinations give results of 100 BP or less and, while consistent with other indications of recent date, the "most likely" calibrations of AD 1900 should not be taken at face value. At least two determinations are inconsistent with other indications, while for two others only the very earliest end of the calibrated range would be accepted as probable. Nevertheless the broad dating framework appears consistent.

Site terminology
The official site designations allotted by the Archaeological Survey Section of National Museums and Monuments of Zimbabwe consist of the number of the relevant 1:50000 map sheet followed by a serial number – e.g. 1832BA36. These designations are given in the site descriptions in Chapters 4, 5 and 8, but to aid intelligibility sites are referred to by name or a more easily distinguished code. The local name for the immediate area is used when known. Others merit an explanation: "Fishpit" has no direct association with fish but derives from its vicinity to the National Parks fisheries staff housing compound. SN113 and SN153 at Ziwa are the provisional survey numbers used in the current research, while Nyangui G1/21 and G7/1 are the twenty-first and first pit-structures in groups 1 and 7 respectively in Block G of Nyangui Forestry Commission land (see Chapter 5 and Chapter 8). Only Nyangui 1732DD27 reflects lack of imagination and uses the official designation.

Neither this nor Block G are especially close to the hill known as Nyangui itself, a high but not very prominent point towards the northern end of the forestry reserve.

HISTORY OF ARCHAEOLOGICAL RESEARCH
Published references to the Nyanga remains may be characterised as belonging within three broad categories – primary archaeological fieldwork and excavation by professionals and amateurs; descriptions and allusions by travellers and officials; and speculative interpretations, often fanciful; the latter categories often overlap.(A full list of such allusions is given by Beach in the Annex of this volume and the Annotated Bibliography cites all the references.). We are here concerned mainly with the primary archaeology. Much of this was localised to single sites or small areas, only Summers (1958) attempting a wide synthesis; a number of secondary accounts in broader regional syntheses have been based on this. Until the 1980s, most interest had focused on the settlement sites and few people apart from Summers had considered the terraces and economic base of the society in any detail; even he was mainly concerned with establishing the cultural background, a necessary priority in view of the very incomplete knowledge at that time. In the 1980s, Sutton (1983, 1988) initiated a fresh perspective from the angle of the terraces, their conformation and use. The recent project derives from this approach.

Initial reports from the 1890s drew public attention to the Nyanga ruins (*Rhodesia Herald* 1894; *Umtali Advertiser* 1894; Edwards 1898; Schlichter 1899; Peters 1902). The first archaeological accounts were by Richard Hall and David Randall-MacIver. Hall, a journalist and first curator (and despoiler) of Great Zimbabwe, produced a description and plan of Nyangwe Fort (1904; not entirely accurate) and in 1905 he duplicated this and added the results of the first "slave pit" (pit-structure) excavations. Randall-MacIver was a competent archaeologist who visited Rhodesia at the instigation of the British Association for the Advancement of Science and worked at Great Zimbabwe and other sites, among them Nyanga. He spent some time at Ziwa (Van Niekerk) ruins and gave a quite detailed narrative description of these (1906). He excavated a number of sites there but recorded few details of stratigraphy. He recognised a "medieval" date and rejected any foreign influences, but erred in thinking that the Early Iron Age material was contemporary with the stone ruins; moreover he regarded the terracing as defensive in purpose and the whole as related to Great Zimbabwe. The latter two ideas were convincingly demolished by Hall (1909) and Randall-MacIver subsequently retracted the defensive theory in 1927. He also described and excavated forts and pit-structures on Rhodes Estate in the highlands, providing a more accurate plan of Nyangwe. The remainder of the material on Nyanga in Hall (1909) duplicates his earlier papers.

There are no further archaeological accounts until the 1930s, but Taylor (1924) and Lloyd (1926) recorded oral traditions relevant to the ruins, and Norton (1926) described an ancient road through the Bende Gap and some stone enclosures below the eastern escarpment. Lloyd's paper quoted a very circumstantial account of the keeping of small cattle in the pit-structures, an explanation which most subsequent writers have been reluctant to credit. (The function of these pits has been a recurring subject of speculation as discussed in Chapter 5. Their interpretation as pens for small cattle is important in the understanding of the Nyanga complex).

Advances in knowledge, particularly of pit-structures, were made during the 1930s and included for the first time formal descriptions of material culture. Frobenius (1931) covered the work of his expedition in 1929 and described terraces and pit-structures with sketch plans. He recognised the association of terraces with dolerite soils and attributed them to rice cultivation. Wieschoff (1941), a member of the same expedition, gave a detailed description of pit-structures and a lucid discussion of their function, reluctantly agreeing with Frobenius that they were sunken dwellings. Neither seriously considered the possibility of pits as cattle pens, although citing oral traditions to that effect. Wieschoff also excavated the site of Niamara, a stone ruin of the Khami phase of the Great Zimbabwe tradition across the Mozambique border east of Nyanga, an excavation subsequently republished by Gerharz (1973).

An excellent paper by York Mason (1933), from the University of Witwatersrand, described the stone structures of Mkondwe north of Penhalonga and his excavation of a typical pit-structure, including the associated pottery. He recognised the presence of houses around the pits and that the pits could be flushed out with water from artificial furrows, but deliberately refrained from speculating on their function. Mrs Martin (1940, 1941), wife of the owner of Mkondwe farm, described old glass beads of the Manyika and current Manyika pottery, distinguishing it from that found by Mason. She also (Martin 1937) recovered two burials from Mason's pit-structure, buried in passages between houses on the platform, which are still the only burials directly associated with pit-structures, although she concluded that they were probably secondary and not related to the occupants. Galloway (1937) described these human remains but diagnosed them as having predominant Bush-Boskopoid features, echoing his misclassification of skeletons from Mapungubwe (Galloway 1959). Fripp and Wells (1938) also excavated a pit-structure on Rhodes Estate, and compared the pottery with that obtained by Mason.

There are few publications from the 1940s with the notable exception of that of Mrs Finch (1949), an amateur archaeologist who provided a full and perceptive account of remains on the edge of the Inyanga Downs north-east of Troutbeck. These included various stone enclosures and forts, pit-structures, water furrows and ditches, and hollowed "dams", together with their inter-relationships. She, at least, had no difficulty in accepting the pits as pens for small cattle and even attempted population estimates. Stead (1949), Native Commissioner for Nyanga, recorded a few traditions about pits and classified terraces as earth, stone-faced and heavy stone, reporting that some were in use at that time. He also despatched an assistant to an area where small cattle were reported, but the resultant measurements are not especially diminutive.

Up to this time, knowledge of the Nyanga remains was fragmented, with little clear conception of the complex as a whole or of its dating. In the late 1940s the "Inyanga Research Fund" was launched to finance a visiting archaeologist of international repute to conduct a systematic research project. In the event, however, insufficient money was raised for this and the work was placed in the capable local hands of Roger Summers of the National Museum and Keith Robinson of the Monuments Commission. Three seasons of work were conducted from 1949 to 1951, comprising reconnaissance and excavations at 36 sites, published by Summers (1952, 1958). Concentration was mainly on the cultural evidence of the settlement sites, although the terraces were also described. The bulk of the investigation was at Ziwa ruins, both the stone structures and the "pre-ruin" Early Iron Age, but they also excavated sites in the Nyabombgwe (Nyautare) area of the lowlands to the north, and sites in the highlands south and south-west of Nyanga town, including pit-structures and Nyangwe Fort. Notable aspects of the work were the recovery of seeds from some of the Ziwa sites and the attempt to relate the archaeological findings to climatic evidence then available. Dating evidence was sparse (mainly glass beads and an attempt to age trees growing on the terraces) but a time bracket of AD 1500 to 1800 was proposed and a development sequence from highland sites, to Ziwa, to the northern lowlands, correlated with supposed climatic events. Some understanding of the settlement sites was also gained and he was able to synthesize the evidence into a coherent account of the complex. The preliminary report (Summers 1952) appeared to attribute the ruins to the Manyika, but the 1958 volume was more inclined to relate them to the Nyama people. It was an outstanding piece of work for the time and many of the conclusions have been borne out by the recent research.

Subsequent to Summers' work, Whitty (1959) contributed an architectural analysis of stone structures in Mashonaland in general, in which the Nyanga ruins were included. He clearly established the basic difference in conception between the Nyanga structures and those of the Great Zimbabwe tradition, noting the surprising sophistication of the former in catering for the everyday needs of the general population, as opposed to the role of the latter in only sheltering the residences of the elite.

Bernhard, a farmer at Nyahokwe adjacent to Ziwa, published a series of short papers (1959, 1961, 1962, 1963, 1964) mainly concerned with the Early Iron Age Ziwa tradition. Otherwise there was little work in the '60s and '70s apart from Garlake's excellent small guide book (1966); Huffman's (1975) reporting of a radiocarbon date on a wooden locking-beam from a fort near Ziwa; and a brief report by Storry (1974) on a pit-structure excavation in the Pungwe gorge.

Work was also slow to resume after Zimbabwe's independence in 1980 but a new departure was initiated by two papers by John Sutton (1983, 1988). He for the first time approached the complex from the perspective of the terraces and cultivation ridges and the agricultural systems they may represent, rather than the "cultural" approach to the settlement sites. The 1983 paper provided a thoughtful and full description of the terraces and their variation, pointing out that the vast majority could not have been irrigated, and considered the possible role of *tsenza* (*Plectranthus esculentus*) as an important crop associated with the cultivation ridges.

> "...the terraces....may doubtless be seen as the result of extensive agriculture over several centuries, this being one of the rare parts of Africa where, precisely because of the need to build terraces, the fields which were successively used and abandoned may be recognised and studied....it is not necessary to imagine a large population in the district at any one time."

Sutton's 1988 paper took another look at the terraces and other ruins and suggested the possibility of a more intensive system, using manure accumulated from the stall-feeding of cattle and small stock kept permanently in the pits/enclosures for at least part of the year. Other papers viewed the evidence in the broader African context (Sutton 1984, 1985, 1989a & b; Grove and Sutton 1989). These papers initiated the present phase of research in which Sutton has continued to advise.

Secondary, more or less summary accounts have appeared in a number of books or papers — Schofield 1942 (a brief section on beads); Clark (1959); Paver (1957); Whitty (1961); Fagan (1965); Petheram (1974). Summers (1971) revisited his Nyanga data in a wider regional context, attempting to fit the ruins into a general classification of stone structures, resulting in a rather fragmented presentation. He also tried to support his dating with a couple of radiocarbon dates which had been obtained from Lekkerwater (Tsindi) ruins near Marondera and the walled village of Chitakete at Harleigh Farm near Rusape (see below) and ascribed the concept of terracing to Arab influence.

There have been a few relevant historical studies mentioning stone structures in the context of pre-colonial history, notably Storry (1976) on the history of the Manyika chiefdom of Mutasa, Mukaronda (1989) on the Nyanga area, and Nyabadza (1989) on northern Maungwe, while Beach (1995 reproduced here as Annex) deals specifically with the historical background to the ruins.

The present project started in 1993 and a number of papers and a dissertation have been produced, the material of which is largely covered in this volume. The present writer's reports (Soper 1994, 1996) presented the progress of the project and preliminary results; Soper (1999) dealt with water furrows (described more fully in Chapter 4), mainly for the benefit of readers in Zimbabwe; Soper & Chirawu (1996, 1997) gave reports on two sites (also included in Chapter 8); an analysis of a faunal assemblage from Mount Muozi (Plug *et al* 1997), established the presence of dwarf cattle; and Chirawu's dissertation (1999) is a detailed description and analysis of settlement structures at Ziwa, with comparative data from the St Mary's/Maristvale area.

Parallel to the archaeological work have been a number of speculative or fanciful interpretations with little archaeological basis, attributing the remains to various immigrant groups of more or less remote antiquity. The earlier examples of this genre could speculate freely on the remains in the absence of much excavated archaeological evidence. Gwatkin (1932) interpreted the Mkondwe structures as an integrated military defence system built by foreign invaders, while Rossiter (1938) envisaged Egyptians overseeing local slaves. The later examples ignored or misinterpreted excavated evidence, harking back to the ideas of early settlers, now largely but still not entirely laid to rest, that ancient foreign civilizations must have been responsible for Great Zimbabwe and other stone ruins; they proved to their own satisfaction that the terraces were an agricultural enterprise to support Great Zimbabwe. Bruwer (1965) showed reasonable observation in a narrative style but was fixated on a Phoenician colony; Mullan (1969) misunderstood Summers' archaeological evidence and plumped for Yemeni Arabs; Gayre (1972) had less on Nyanga but blatantly misquoted Summers to establish that the builders were not "Bantu".

Nyanga in the context of Zimbabwean archaeology

The Nyanga complex falls within the time bracket of the later Iron Age. This started in Zimbabwe around AD 1000 with a number of regional ceramic traditions which replaced the Early Iron Age of the first millennium: in the south and south-west are the Gumanye and Leopards Kopje traditions attributed to early Shona speakers; in the north are the Harare and Musengezi traditions, originally also attributed to Shona speakers (Huffman 1978) but later seen as having closer relationships with some Zambian pottery traditions whose makers could not have spoken Shona (Huffman 1989). The Great Zimbabwe state developed from the Gumanye tradition around the 12th century, spreading its influence over much of the Zimbabwe plateau, including Harare and Musengezi areas, by the 15th century. At around that time it developed into two successor kingdoms, Torwa/Changamire represented by the Khami phase initially in the south-west, and the Mutapa state in the north (the latter known mainly from Portuguese written sources). This basic picture is being refined with the recognition of other traditions as research progresses (e.g. Pikirayi 1993).

How does the Nyanga complex, whose beginnings we can now trace to around AD 1300, relate to this picture? The first obvious consideration is its relationship to Great Zimbabwe and to the extensive and politically powerful state which was centred there. The early hilltop settlements of Nyanga, around the 14th century, are contemporary with the rise of Great Zimbabwe itself and the extension of its influence evidenced by the spread of other sites of this phase into northern Zimbabwe. The nearest documented sites are Harleigh Farm, 14km north-east of Rusape (Robins and Whitty 1966) and Tere ruins at Mutoko (Wieschoff 1941), respectively at the western and northern limits of scattered terracing, and the "Altar Site" at Mutare. Radiocarbon dating for Harleigh Farm places it around the 14th century. Later Nyanga phases would be contemporary with the Khami phase of the Great Zimbabwe tradition, to which the site of Niamara (Wieschoff 1941; Gerharz 1973) would appear to belong; this is in Mozambique "two and a half days walk" east of Nyanga town.

The stone architecture of the Great Zimbabwe tradition is very different in basic conception from that of Nyanga structures. As Whitty (1959) pointed out, the latter represent a folk tradition, part of the everyday life of common people, and reflect an attitude to building which was surprisingly sophisticated and realistic. There are indications of larger or special sites, which may suggest the existence of local chiefs but not a strongly stratified society. The Great Zimbabwe walls on the other hand are expressions of prestige, surrounding the residences of a relatively small elite of the relevant community, and are "conceptually more primitive" in Whitty's phrase. While there are terraces on some Great Zimbabwe sites, especially of the Khami phase, these are residential in function as opposed to the far more numerous agricultural terraces of Nyanga. *Dhaka* (mud-built) houses within the enclosures also contrast; those of the Great Zimbabwe elite (but not necessarily of the lower classes) commonly have solid *dhaka* walls and well plastered floors, while those in Nyanga have thinly plastered walls on a wooden framework. While both may have dividing cross walls, the parallel is superficial, those of Great Zimbabwe often interpreted by Huffman (1996) as audience chambers, and those of Nyanga separating the small livestock from the kitchen area (see Chapter 5).

In material culture, there is no resemblance between the respective ceramics, *pace* Summers (1971:101) who claimed that pottery from Nyangwe Fort was almost identical to that from Lekkerwater (Tsindi) Ruins near Marondera. Rudd (1984), the excavator, however attributed the Tsindi pottery to the Harare and Great Zimbabwe traditions, a diagnosis borne out by her illustrations.

As mentioned above, the romantic imagination of Bruwer (1965) and Gayre (1972) conceived Nyanga as an agricultural complex manned by slave labour, supplying the urban-industrial complex of Great Zimbabwe, while Mullan (1969) had a similar idea. These speculations have no archaeological basis and in any case cannot be sustained in face of the lack of any indication of dwellings of a controlling elite (whether Phoenician, Arab or African), and the absence of any items beyond a few beads which could have been exchanged for agricultural produce. The sturdy stone homesteads hardly suggest the dwellings of abject slaves.

There are thus very basic cultural differences between the Nyanga complex and the Great Zimbabwe tradition. That there was at least some contact between them, however, is indicated by the presence of rare Great Zimbabwe sherds as surface finds on a few Nyanga sites (e.g. "Ziwa Acropolis"), and some punctate-decorated sherds and "washing stones" common to Nyanga highland sites and Niamara (Gerharz 1973, figs 18,22).

The archaeology of the Mutapa state of northern Zimbabwe, also contemporary with most of the Nyanga complex, is poorly understood and most information comes from Portuguese historical sources. Some Great Zimbabwe tradition sites such as Zvongombe (15th century) have been attributed to an early stage of this and the above discussion applies to these. Pikirayi's work (1993) in the Mount Darwin area almost certainly located the important Portuguese trading station of Masapa with which the 16th/17th-century capital of Mutapa was closely associated, but provided little material evidence of the latter. Certainly one might have expected Nyanga to fall at least marginally within the Mutapa sphere of influence but there is no archaeological evidence of this as yet, apart perhaps from the few sherds mentioned above which could belong to this phase. Political influence, direct or indirect, may have contributed to the "Shonaisation" of Nyanga communities discussed in Chapter 7. As noted by Beach (Annex), there are no known Portuguese references to the area of the Nyanga complex.

There should be a chronological overlap between the beginning of the Nyanga complex and the end of the Harare and Musengezi traditions of northern Zimbabwe, but their distribution does not extend far enough east to be contiguous and there is no suggestion of any relationship in the ceramics.

More relevant may be the later remains in the Mount Darwin area, called the Mahonje tradition by Pikirayi (1993). These are characterised by "loopholed forts", some with lintelled entrances, which have at least superficial affinities with some of the Nyanga forts. The radiocarbon and luminescence dates are equivocal but the bead evidence places them later than the Masapa site of Baranda, probably in the 18th century. The pottery, like that of Nyanga, has little decoration (which however includes some incised cross-hatching) and shapes are not very distinctive, so that comparisons are inconclusive. The commonest vessels however are hemispherical bowls, often rare at Nyanga, and there are some carinated pots, absent in almost all Nyanga assemblages. Little is known of the archaeology of the intervening area so possible links cannot be traced. Any direct relationship however seems doubtful and the loopholes could be explained as parallel derivations from observation of Portuguese fortifications.

Closer to Nyanga are the later stone structures forming Whitty's "walled village zone" with lintelled entrances, overlapping with the distribution of pit-structures and extending westwards at least to the Rusape area, a zone which also has cultivation ridges and scattered terracing similar to Nyanga itself (Whitty 1959). Some relationship is thus probable. The only excavated site is Chitakete (Harleigh Farm 2) investigated by Crawford (1967). According to tradition this is a former capital residence of a Chief Chipadze of Maungwe in the 17th century and there is a radiocarbon determination consistent with this (280 BP, uncalibrated: SR-35) from the fill of an early pit. Summers (1971) compared the Chitakete pottery with that of Ziwa ruins and, while Crawford does not illustrate any of this, an examination of the museum collection supports a relationship; the range and broad frequency of vessel types and lip forms are similar and the commonest motif among the rare decoration is also single incision on the shoulder, although there are some differences in other decoration.

The conclusion must be that the Nyanga complex represents a tradition distinct from other later Iron Age traditions further afield in Zimbabwe, apart from relationships (probably comparatively late) extending immediately to the west. Unfortunately there is little or no archaeological information from adjacent parts of Mozambique to the east or north. Arguments for a possible origin from this direction were put forward by Summers (1958:267), based on a linguistic classification by Doke (1930) which assigned the dialects of the Nyanga area to the Barwe linguistic group. This issue is discussed by Beach (Annex) who casts doubt on Doke's conclusions, but relationships in that direction remain plausible.

CHAPTER 2

THE NYANGA ENVIRONMENT

The complex lies athwart the northern part of Zimbabwe's Eastern Highlands. Here a broad plateau narrows northwards into a high range flanked by steep escarpments to east and west, with lower, drier plains either side.

TOPOGRAPHY (fig. 2)

South and east of Nyanga town is a broad dissected plateau at around 1800m above sea level and about 15km wide. This is largely occupied by the Nyanga National Park and extends south-west to Juliasdale and west to Sanyatwe. Thence it declines relatively gently to the west past Triashill to merge with the main watershed between the Zambezi and Sabi basins at around 1500m, continuing through Headlands and Macheke. To the south the plateau is terminated by the Honde and Odzi valleys but the country rises again to a further plateau at 1600 to 1800m declining south to Mutare; on the east side of this Stapleford Forest reaches 2000m. The main plateau rises to the east to Mount Nyangani, at 2592m the highest point in Zimbabwe, while beyond the land drops steeply to the Mozambique border.

North of Nyanga town the plateau narrows somewhat through the Nyanga Downs to form a narrower plateau only a few kilometres wide at around 2000m, and this continues northwards for about 50km, broken by the Bende Gap, a lower pass at about 1750m. This narrow plateau tilts gently to the east and is crowned along its western edge by a series of peaks at 2200 to 2400m – Worlds View, Rukotso, Chinyamaura, Nyangui, Chirimanyimo and Chipawe. It is bordered to east and west by steep escarpments, often with near vertical cliffs, the western escarpment around 600m high. A number of major spurs project to east and west, of which the most prominent is Muozi (Plate 16). The Ruangwe range extends for another 25km northwards at a lower altitude of 1100 to 1200m, with a steep escarpment on its eastern side; it is described in more detail under the Chigura site report in Chapter 8.

To the west of this high range are relatively flat lowlands broken by granite inselbergs and kopjes (often large features such as Dombo, Ziwa, Muchena and Nani), and lesser dolerite features. The base level of the broad Nyangombe valley declines northwards from about 1200m to 900m. This landscape continues across the Nyangombe through Tanda and Chinyika Communal Lands. Thirty five kilometres north of Nyanga town a series of granite hills, of which the main one is Muchena, extend across the Nyangombe into Tanda, and a further 15km north a broad ridge of granite and dolerite runs down to the Nyangombe from Mica Hill. East of the high range the country drops to the Gairezi river and declines northwards in the Matisi basin, generally flat country with granite kopjes.

Drainage radiates from Mount Nyangani where most of the main rivers rise. The Pungwe runs steeply south and then east to the Indian Ocean. The Nyangombe drops west off the plateau and then turns north parallel to the highland range, becoming the Ruenya and joining the Zambezi. The Gairezi falls steeply to the north-east, then turns north along the Mozambique border to join the Ruenya. The Odzi rises further to the south-west and flows south-west to join the Sabi. The main tributaries flowing west and east from the highlands to the Nyangombe and Gairezi are perennial. The western tributaries of the Nyangombe, the Mwarazi and Nyangadzi, are more seasonal.

In his archaeological study of 1950/51, Summers (1958:3) divided the Nyanga complex area into two zones, Uplands and Lowlands, at the 5000 foot (1525m) contour, observing that typical pit-structures occur only above this level with rare exceptions. This is a useful concept followed in the present work (using "highlands" rather than "uplands"; "lowlands" is of course a relative conception since much of this zone lies above 1000m). However a division at 1400m is considered more appropriate to the topography, coinciding approximately with the base of the escarpments either side of the northern range, while the recent work shows that pit-structures do occur down to 1400m in the Maristvale and Burnaby areas. There is thus some cultural distinction at around 1400m which remains to be explained. The foot of the escarpments may be significant in the northern areas, but there does not appear to be a correlation with any obvious topographical or present vegetational distinction elsewhere. Since temperature and rainfall vary mainly with altitude, there may be a relationship with past climatic differences discussed below, possibly heavy winter frosts or drier conditions which may have prevailed around the 18th century in the final phase of what has been called the "Little Ice Age".

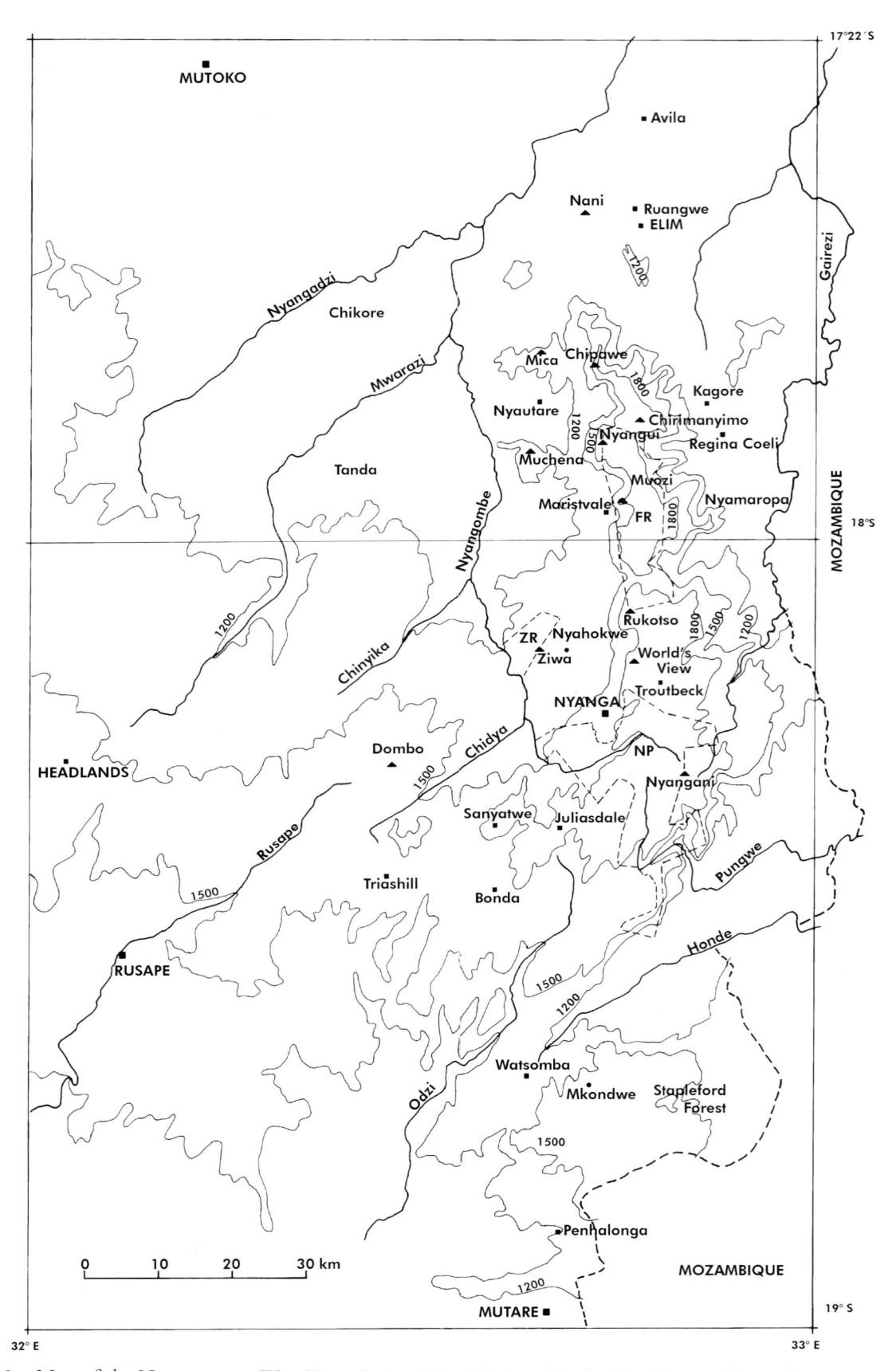

Fig. 2. Map of the Nyanga area. ZR= Ziwa Ruins; NP= National Park; FR= Nyangui Forest Reserve

GEOLOGY (fig. 3)

This area of the Eastern Highlands is composed of granites overlain by sedimentary rocks and dolerites. Agricultural terracing and settlement are found on all three rock types, but the terracing at least favours the dolerites as analysed in Chapter 4.

Much of the core area of the archaeological complex, from 32°30' to 33° east and 17°15' to 18°15' south, is covered by two geological maps and reports (Stocklmayer 1978, 1980). The southern map covers the Nyanga highlands north of Nyanga town, extending west just across the Nyangombe river, while the northern map includes the Ruangwe Range and extends north into Mutoko District. Information for areas to the west and south is far less detailed.

The granitic rocks, sediments and dolerites are of Precambrian age. The granitic rocks of the Basement Complex are the most extensive and form most of the western lowlands, often relatively flat but broken by granite dwalas. Stocklmayer (1978) divides the granitic rocks into older tonalites and gneisses, intermediate granites, adamellites, post-adamellite granites, and granites of indeterminate age, but for the purposes of this volume they will be loosely termed granites. Granites may be extensively terraced on parts of the lower slopes of the escarpments. Terracing is found on adamellite (Ziwa) and on intermediate granodiorite (Chirangeni, Bende Gap) at least, but no detailed correlation with the different granite types has been attempted.

The granites are unconformably overlain by sedimentary rocks of the Inyanga and Gairezi facies of the Umkondo group, and both granites and sediments are extensively intruded by dolerite dykes and sills. The Inyanga facies, intercalated with dolerite sills, caps much of the highlands north of the Bende Gap and forms the northward extension of the Ruangwe range. South of the Bende Gap are only minor outcrops, such as on Rukotso peak. These sedimentary rocks comprise calc-hornfels, sandstones, argillites, siltstones and shales. In the main highlands these are almost horizontally bedded and lie above the altitude of most of the terracing. In the Ruangwe range to the north they are folded with the intercalated dolerites into a series of parallel ridges and valleys with a steep eastern escarpment. Here both are extensively terraced. The Gairezi facies along the eastern border of Zimbabwe comprises similar sediments and dolerites but these are heavily folded. The aerial photographs show very little terracing on the latter formation and little of it has been examined on the ground.

Dolerite dykes are relatively common west of the highlands but are rare to the east. The larger ones may form narrow discontinuous ridges within the flatter granite terrain, and terracing is often concentrated on these. Dolerite sills or sheets cover about 20 per cent of the southern geological map. Almost the whole of the main Nyanga plateau south of the Bende Gap is capped by a major sill which reaches a thickness of 300m. North of the Gap, the dolerite distribution is more erratic among the sedimentary rocks. West of the highlands, dolerite sills form low boulder-covered hills or flatter pavements within the granite terrain and most of these are terraced.

There is alluvium on the banks of the larger rivers, especially the Gairezi and Nyangombe, but the only extensive alluvial deposits are in the area of the Nyamaropa irrigation scheme in the Gaerezi valley and the Nyarawaka basin to the north west of this.

Iron ore in the form of black magnetite sand weathered from the dolerite can be clearly seen at Ziwa Site Museum and is probably widespread. This is a relatively pure ore with high iron content and was probably used in the furnaces in the Ziwa/Nyahokwe and Nyanga town/National Park areas (Chapter 5) which appear to have produced very little slag. Other smelting sites such as above Kagore and near Elim Mission have more slag and may have used different ore, such as the laterite which Stocklmayer (1978) reports as forming on the dolerites, especially in higher rainfall areas.

Mineral exploitation apart from iron does not appear to have been an important feature of the complex. There is little correlation between the complex area and occurrences of other metallic ores, except at the fringes. Gold is not even mentioned by Stocklmayer for the main Nyanga area on the southern geological map sheet, but it is common in the Makaha Gold Belt to the north of the research area in Mutoko District, where almost every one of the more than sixty colonial period mines was pegged on ancient workings (Stocklmayer 1980:2). Three such mines occur south-east of the Ruenya river near Nyanzindwe Hill east of Avila Mission. Sporadic terracing and stone ruins occur in the Makaha area (Stidolph, pers.comm.) but these have not been examined in the present research and it is unclear how they relate to the Nyanga complex. There is also some copper and traces of tin in the Makaha Gold belt, while Inyati copper mine north-east of Headlands falls within the western extension of sporadic terracing; however within the main terrace distribution there are only minor traces of copper.

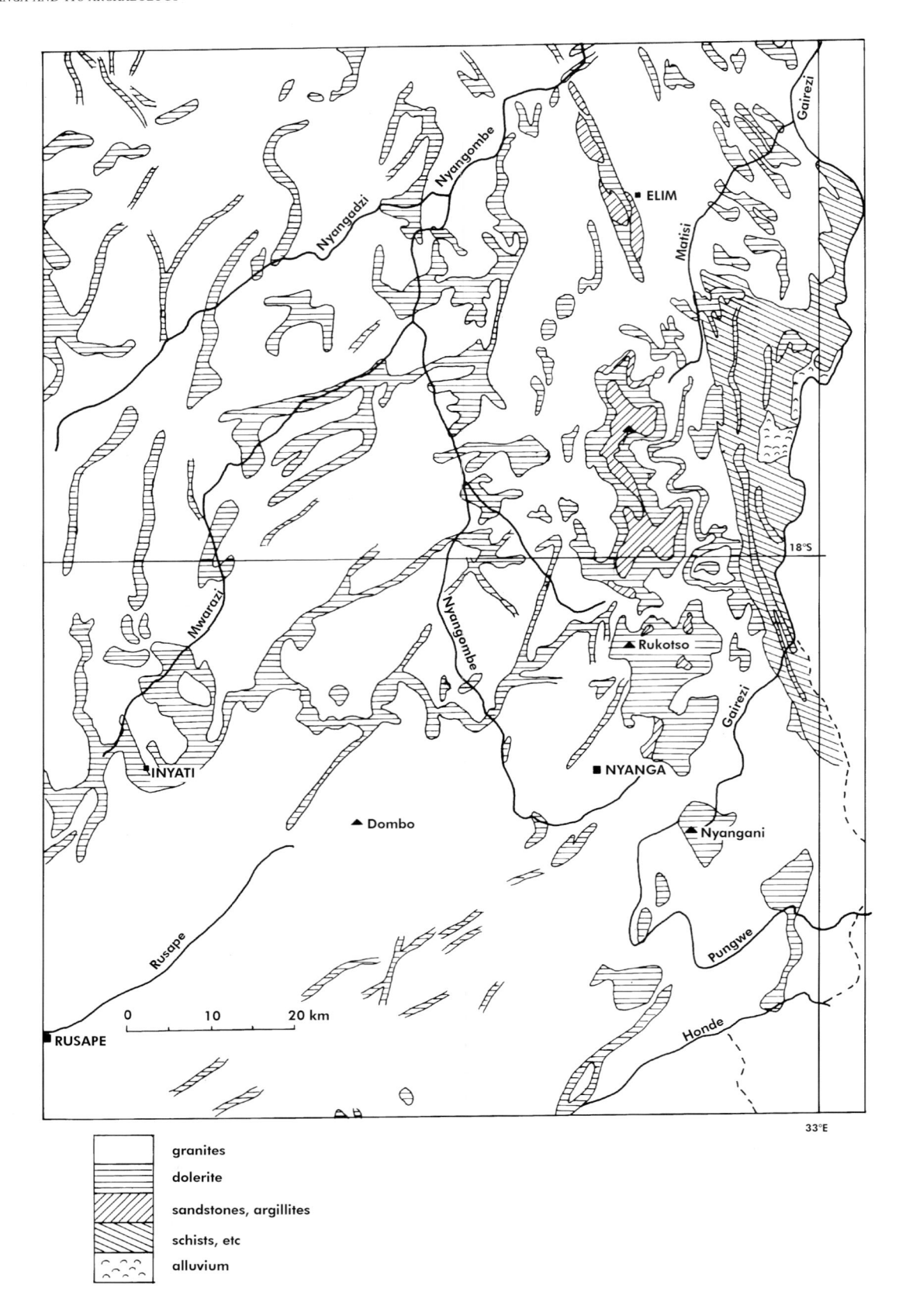

Fig. 3. Simplified geological map of the Nyanga area

SOILS (by Katherine Verbeek, Department of Soil Science and Agricultural Engineering, University of Zimbabwe).

Soils and their inherent fertility are a controlling factor in the distribution and viability of agricultural production. They thus form an essential background to a consideration of terracing and other agricultural works. In Nyanga, as elsewhere, the nature and distribution of soils are strongly dependent on both the composition of the parent material and the climate. Also topography (the catenary succession) has a large impact on soil formation through changes in drainage conditions. These factors control the mineralogy, the texture, the amount of leaching, and the physical and chemical properties of the resultant soil.

Rainfall in the Nyanga terraces varies considerably, from the highlands with mean annual rainfall above 1000mm, to the lowlands where mean annual rainfall can drop to an irregularly distributed 750mm. The soil types will therefore also be different.

Comments on the soils of individual sites are given under the site descriptions in Chapter 4, and results of detailed analyses of stratified samples in Appendix A.

Highlands (e.g. Appendix A: Nyangui G1/21; National Park below furrow NP1)

Within this rainfall zone the soil profiles are moist most of the year and the major soil process is ferralitization, characterised by intense weathering and leaching. Therefore the regolith is deeply weathered and the effect of the parent material is minimal due to "total hydrolysis". Also catenal effects are minimal and hydromorphy only occurs in the valleys. The mature soils which result are deep, red, clayey and permeable, with stable structure on convex slopes, extremely weathered and leached (typical clays are kaolinite, gibbsite and oxides of iron).

Highly weathered soils are characterised by less than 10% weatherable minerals and have thus a limited capacity to supply essential nutrients such as phosphorus, calcium, magnesium, potassium and sulphur. Moreover the storage capacity of nutrients expressed by the cation exchange capacity (CEC), is very low, either due to sandy textures with low clay content or dominant clay minerals with very low CEC like kaolinite. Low chemical fertility is also expressed by the high to very high acidity (low pH) and the low base saturation (BS%), indicating that the soils are deficient in all major nutrients and micro-nutrients. Strongly inactivated phosphorus and aluminium toxicity are linked to the low pH. The nutrient storage capacity of these soils is thus mainly concentrated in the organic fraction and they are otherwise chemically infertile. Virgin soils have a high content of organic carbon (up to 5%) due to the wet climate, but clearing land of its natural vegetation breaks the natural organic and nutrient cycle. Maintenance of organic matter through manuring, mulching and fallow periods is thus essential for conserving productivity.

Physical fertility is normally good in natural conditions as micro-granulation is well developed, allowing good drainage. Slopes are often steep but erosion is not widespread, predominantly again due to the structural stability and the high organic matter content. The formation of micro-aggregates reduces moisture storage at field-capacity and these soils have therefore a limited water holding capacity (10mm per 10cm soil depth) and are sensitive to drought.

The soils are classified in the Zimbabwe soil classification system as ortho-ferralitic (7G, 7E) soils. 7G soils represent the most leached soils on granites with less than 5% weatherable minerals. Clay content can be variable due to the mineralogy of the parent rock and position in the topography. Clay activity is low and pHs are in the acid range but aluminium toxicity is rare. 7E soils are the most leached soils derived from mafic rocks like dolerite. All these soils are distinguished by bright red colours with 2.5YR and 10R hues. Profile depth may be up to several metres. Soils are highly weathered and clay activity is low, but those with high clay and silt contents are subject to soil creep on convex slopes.

Lower lying areas

In these areas a distinct wet and dry season occurs and the rainfall becomes more erratic and variable as the altitude decreases. The major soil processes are moderate weathering and clay illuviation. There is both a strong catenal effect and a strong relation with the parent material in soil development.

The mature soils are less weathered and leached than in the highlands. The clay mineralogy is mixed and besides kaolinite other clay minerals like montmorillonite can also occur. This is reflected in higher values for CEC, CEC clay (E/C value), pH and base saturation than is the case for the highland soils. These soils have thus both a higher storage capacity for nutrients and a higher amount of nutrients available for plant growth. In the Zimbabwe soil classification system these soils are classified as fersiallitic (5E, 5G) and para-ferralitic (6G) soils.

On mafic rocks the soils are deep, red and clayey (5E) and are probably the most productive soils in Zimbabwe. Permeability is good for a soil with such a high clay content and is in the range of 9 - 20 mm/hr. This is due to the moderate to strong micro-granular structure in the subsoil. Chemical fertility is good. The lower members of the catena consist of vertisols.

On granitic rocks, soils are highly variable, both because of position in the catena and because of variable mineralogy of granitic parent materials. All are characterised by a good distribution of the various sand fractions with a significant amount of coarse sand (Nyamapfene 1991). Mostly soils are coarse sand, but texture in the subsoil can range from coarse sand (<5% clay) to clay (up to 50% clay). Clay contents are also variable within a single climatic zone and can vary between 15 and 35% over distances of a few kilometres. Clay content is thus more related to mineralogy of the rock than to the amount of rainfall responsible for weathering. Besides mineralogy of the rock, slope also has a marked effect on clay content as lateral movement of clay in suspension is a common process during the wet season.

The chemical fertility is dependent largely on the clay content, and for the sandy soils largely on the organic matter content as the sand fraction consists predominantly of inert quartz minerals (SiO_2) containing no nutrients. The organic matter content is also highly dependent on the clay content and the red clayey soils can contain up to 3% of organic carbon. However the sandy soils often have less than 1%, so that unless fertilisers or manure are added, yields will already decrease after one year of cropping due to declining soil fertility.

Soils of the agricultural terraces

Farmers in general are very aware of soil diversity and favour soils with the least constraints. The main constraint in Nyanga, especially in the highlands, is fertility, and the slope soils, not being subject to deep weathering, are immature and thus retain a higher proportion of mineral nutrients. Stoniness is not so critical for crop production and here is partly alleviated by terracing, which also concentrates the shallow soil; in addition, continuing decomposition of the parent material contributes significantly to ongoing fertility, especially on dolerite. Thus the more fertile soils on steep slopes are likely to have been preferred to the infertile oxisols of the adjacent plateaus, since the latter are characterised by low inherent fertility especially on sandy soils.

These terraces have been fallow for a century or more, so that the soil with its chemical properties should have reverted back to a more or less virgin situation and indicators for agricultural use and abandonment will have disappeared. Fertility indicators are pH and base saturation, exchangeable potassium and organic carbon content. Organic carbon content, an important indicator of soil degradation, is a property that regains equilibrium values in a short time; 100 years can be sufficient.

The effect of the parent material varies between dolerite and granite. Dolerite is an intrusive rock consisting of fine to coarse-grained mafic minerals, such as pyroxenes, amphiboles and some feldspars which all weather fairly easily to clay minerals. The mature upland soil (e.g. Appendix A: Chirimanyimo) is therefore normally a deep red clayey soil with more than 40% clay and little to no coarse sand fraction because all minerals weather easily and no quartz is present. The coarse sand fraction which occurs in the terraces needs to be mineralogically analysed to assess erosion and deposition versus *in situ* weathering, because it either (a) consists of coarse-grained rock minerals not yet weathered, indicating *in situ* formation and constant rejuvenation of the parent material through the slope effect and erosion; or (b) consists of quartz resistant to weathering, indicating soil formation in transported material. Dolerite soils from the piedmont slopes and lowlands are represented by Maristvale and Ziwa SN113 (Appendix A).

Granite is a coarse-grained rock consisting of quartz, feldspar and some mica, and will weather to sandy soils on terraced slopes. The sand fraction contains mainly quartz which is highly resistant to weathering. (Appendix A, Ziwa Mujinga).

Key chemical properties used to assess fertility status and erosion of the soil samples from individual sites are clay %, coarse sand %, CEC clay (E/C value), pH, base saturation %, exchangeable potassium, total phosphates, and organic carbon content.

A number of general conclusions may be drawn from the analyses in Appendix A:
1. There is a clear weathering and leaching sequence in line with the altitudinal change in rainfall regime from Elim to Ziwa to Maristvale to Chirimanyimo. CEC clay, pH and % base saturation decrease.
2. None of the soils have a restrictive soil fertility for plant growth although some imbalances occur especially in exchangeable potassium.
3. Organic carbon results seem to indicate that Maristvale was abandoned later and had a shorter fallow period than the other sites.
4. Soils are generally shallow in accordance with their topographic position and infilling behind terrace walls must have alleviated this to some extent.
5. There are indications that the soil layers except for the lowest ones in most terraces, have been transported and deposited. This is a geomorphological issue which a mineralogical study would clarify.

CLIMATE

Nyanga enjoys a moderate climate with fair rainfall, but with marked seasonality and a long dry season in the middle of the year. Almost all rainfall occurs between November and March, with December to February the wettest months. The highest areas may also receive some precipitation in the form of mist or drizzle in the winter months. Average annual (i.e. seasonal) rainfall varies largely with altitude between about 650 and 1500mm, but areas to the east of the highlands and more particularly to the south-east are significantly wetter, reflecting the direction of the prevailing south-easterly winds. Lowland averages decline northwards. There is wide seasonal variation, not uncommonly up to plus or minus 50 per cent of the average, and there may be considerable localised differences in any one season. In most seasons rainfall and temperatures are favourable for cultivation even in the lower areas, but uneven distribution through the season may be critical.

Table 2.1 gives results from a number of stations in order of altitude:

thus short term trends may affect comparability. Records for Nyangui Forest Station, Maristvale and Elim at least are not continuous, these stations having been abandoned during the war of independence. However the general picture is clear.

The highest recorded figure for the area seems to be 4689mm in 1974/5 for Nyazenga just south of Mt Nyangani at c.2000m (Brinn 1987). Ziwa Site Museum at 1300m in the western lowlands recorded 884mm in 1996/7, 890mm in 1997/8 and 1455mm in 1998/99, the latter a very wet year not included in any of the above figures, when Nyanga Experiment Station received a record 1787mm and Rusape 1161mm. The Ziwa figure for 1997/8 may be a slight underestimate as the rain gauge was eaten by a hyena at the end of the season, but little significant rain was subsequently received.

Higher altitudes experience very cold winds

Table 2.1

Station	Alt.	Years	Ave.	S.D.	Max (yr)	Min. (yr)	Position
Nyangui FS	1940	12	1450	477	2487(73/4)	742(93/4)	N highland ridge
Juliasdale	1920	30	1078				Highland plateau
Nyanga ES	1870	53	1156	298	1708(80/1)	411(91/2)	Highland plateau
Triashill	1760	40	940				SW highlands
Bende Dip	1760?	8	1558	489			Bende Gap
Nyanga Pol.	1680	82	956		1524(80/1)	364(91/2)	Nyanga town
Pangana	1410	9	680	297	1142(84/5)	257(91/2)	SW lowlands
Rusape	1400	91	804				W edge of complex
Maristvale	1350	29	926	300	1535(80/81)	346(67/8)	Western piedmont
Nyajezi	1080	25	643	169			Western lowlands
Nyamaropa S.	1000?	27	1076	341			Eastern piedmont
Regina Coeli	920	30	847	340			Eastern lowlands
Nyamaropa IP	890	31	895	300			Eastern lowlands
Elim 1	860	16	696	277	1451(84/5)	296(91/2)	NE piedmont
Elim 2		31	730	217			
Avila	750	24	640	207			Northern lowlands

Sources: These vary from official Meteorological Office stations, to institutions such as missions and schools, to private individuals: Nyangui Forest Station – 1971/79 Met.Office, 1992/98 pers.comm.; Nyanga Experiment Station, Nyanga Police Station, Rusape – Met.Office; Bende Dip, Nyamaropa Sereka, Nyajezi, Regina Coeli, Nyamaropa Irrigation Project, Elim 2, Avila – Brinn (1987); Maristvale, Elim 2, Pangana Ranch – pers.comm.; Triashill, Juliasdale – Bassett (1963). Number of years is given in the table but not all of these terminate at 1997/98 – e.g. those taken from Basset and Brinn end by 1967 and 1987 respectively;

and hard frosts in winter but below about 1500m these are not a serious problem for most areas. The wet season cloud base gives dense mists above about 1800m which may persist for days at a time and this was probably a factor constraining higher settlement zones.

Any variations in climate which may have occurred over the last seven centuries, that is the period represented by the Nyanga archaeological complex, would doubtless have affected occupation zones and agricultural practices. Although no specific data on long-term climatic trends have been collected from this particular area, a body of evidence is accumulating for changes over recent centuries for southern Africa as a whole. This is reviewed by Tyson and Lindesay (1992) who detect relatively clear indications of the world-wide "Little Ice Age". Evidence of this is clearest for temperature. For the second millennium AD they identify generally warmer conditions of the "Medieval Warm Epoch" from c.900 to 1300 AD; the 'Little Ice Age' from 1300 to 1850, though interrupted by sudden warming from 1500 to 1675; and an amelioration from 1850 to the present. Evidence for trends in rainfall over the same period is less clear, but in general indicates that in this summer rainfall region drier conditions obtained during the cooler periods. This view is supported further north by a major recession of Lake Malawi to at least 120m below its present level, ending about 1850; that implies a decline in rainfall by perhaps as much as 30 to 50 percent (Owen *et al.* 1990). Cold and probably drier conditions would have spread from south to north across southern Africa and climatic amelioration in the reverse direction, with some suggestion that warming may have begun in the north-east and progressed towards the south-west. Cold and dry conditions in the Nyanga area were thus probably less persistent and severe than further south, but still doubtless significant over the period in question.

Vegetation

There is a considerable range of vegetation types as might be expected from the variation in altitude, climate and soils. A useful review is given by Bassett (1963) for the "Inyanga Intensive Conservation Area" (land alienated for white farming and other purposes), complemented by Brinn (1987) for the "communal lands". Six broad vegetation types are distinguished by Bassett, largely the result of altitude and rainfall, while there are variations within them according to soils.

1. Tropical valley and lowland forest in the south-east and east in the Pungwe and Gairezi valleys with rainfall from 3300 to 1250mm. The commonest species in the wetter areas is *Albizzia gummifera* and in the drier areas are *Parinari curatellifolia, Uapaca kirkiana, Brachystegia boehmii* and *Julbernardia globifera*. There is particularly abundant growth of *Upaca kirkiana* on sedimentary soils of the Gairezi Facies.
2. Evergreen mountain forest in the high rainfall areas south and east of Mt Nyangani and the Pungwe Gorge, but probably largely cleared in other areas of comparable altitude and rainfall to leave types 3 and 4. This is probably the climax vegetation for large parts of the highlands and remnants survive as on Chirimanyimo. Common species are *Ilex mitis* and *Macaranga mellifera*.
3. Bracken scrub in western areas of the National Park and the southern plateau, much of it now covered with pine plantations. Apart from the bracken there is coarse tufted grass, woody shrubs and small trees, with clumps of forest, especially in and around old pit-structures. Common grass species are various species of *Cymbopogon, Setaria, Hyparrhenia* and a broad-leaved *Eragrostis*.
4. Short open grassland in the eastern parts of the National Park and northwards through Nyanga Downs and along the northern highlands (Plate 11). This has a dense grass sward around 50cm high with a variety of herbs and few trees. Dominant grass species are *Loudetia simplex* and *Themeda triandra* on granite and dolerite soils respectively (Rattray 1957:201). Large areas of the northern highlands are now covered by the pine plantations of Nyangui Forest.
5. *Brachystegia-Julbernardia* woodland to the west of the bracken scrub above about 1400m, and northwards fringing the short grassland and on the escarpments. The main constituents are *B.spiciformis* and *J.globifera*. In northern exposed parts of the National Park the *Brachystegia* is stunted.
6. Mixed woodland in the Nyangombe basin and other lower areas below about 1400m. This is generally sparse on arable land but is quite dense on hillsides and rocky areas. Tree species are variable but include *J.globifera, Parinari curatellifolia, Terminalia* spp, *Piliostigma thonningii, Gardenia resiniflora* and *Ficus* spp, and dominant grasses are *Hyparrhenia* spp and *Heteropogon contortus* (a painful accompaniment to field work in the early dry season). Baobabs, *Adansonia digitata*, become increasingly common north of Maristvale as conditions get drier.

No archaeological fieldwork has been done under the recent project in the area of type 1 and little in type 2. Stone walls do occur in dense forest but are hard to trace; it may be assumed that the forest has regenerated since abandonment. Pit-structures are common in areas of types 3 and 4 where terraces are rare or absent. Terracing is common on the escarpments and lower areas (types 5 and 6), with pit-structures associated with type 5 and various other kinds of stone-built homesteads with type 6.

Grasses are almost all perennial throughout the area and constitute "sour" grazing which loses palatability and nutritional value after early growth from May onwards until the new flush appears the following season; this may be a constraint to pastoralism, especially in the high grasslands where there is little supplement from browse. Rattray (1953) notes that cattle weights begin to drop from the beginning of June. Bassett (1963) estimates carrying capacity for cattle at three to eight hectares per beast for Type 4, eight to twelve hectares for Type 5, and six to seven hectares for Type 6, depending on the tree cover and the state of the grass cover. This appears to refer to European rather than indigenous cattle.

There is some debate on whether the high grasslands and bracken scrub are a long-standing climax vegetation or have been modified and maintained by human action. The weight of opinion seems to lie with several authorities who postulate that the climax vegetation here would be evergreen forest which was cleared by human action, with the present vegetation types maintained by fierce grass fires (Gilliland 1938; Bassett 1963; Challenger 1964). A contrary opinion is expressed by Tomlinson (1973) who obtained five pollen cores (with three radiocarbon dates) from wetland contexts in Nyanga National Park. All showed a dominance of Graminae pollen, interpreted as indicating that this area has been covered by grassland communities for a very long period, at least 5000 years in one core and possibly nearly 12000 years at the base of another, though the depositional context is not clear in the latter case. Tomlinson also concludes that there is no evidence for any regional change of climate of great magnitude and that the distribution of *Brachystegia* has in the past not been significantly different from that of the present day. However there are serious methodological problems with this study. Sedimentation is tacitly assumed to have been continuous and there is no discussion of its nature, though deposits range from peat to a variety of more or less organic clays. Tree pollen is said to be rare throughout, but the only specific identification is of *Brachystegia,* with no mention of mountain forest species which Gilliland and the others postulate to be the climax vegetation. Nor is there discussion of the possible pollen dispersal range of such species. One core produced pollen apparently of cultivated grasses towards the top at a date estimated at c.1500 to 1700 AD, but this date is obtained by extrapolating the rate of accumulation of peat in another core to that of "organic clay" in this one and so must be suspect. Reservations must thus be expressed on Tomlinson's conclusions and even if valid they are not necessarily relevant to the high grasslands further north.

If the clearance hypothesis is correct, human action, grazing and fire have had a drastic affect on the landscape and ecology. Archaeological evidence for occupation of the highlands from around AD 1300 provides an agency for forest clearance but as yet contributes no botanical data. The regeneration of rain forest over stone structures south-west of Mt Nyangani and also on Chirimanyimo would appear to support the forest climax view, at least under climatic conditions similar to the present.

There is a common belief in some circles that non-indigenous plants were introduced by foreigners responsible for the stone structures and are still associated with the ruins. This goes back at least to Hall (1909:203) who lists "wild Tonge mangu cotton of Indian origin, ... a bean Cajanus Indicus known in India as the Doll Plant (Kirk), Indian figs, also olives, lemons, grape vines and many other non-indigenous plants, shrubs and trees." Hall considered that this supported his attribution of the ruins to Arab influence, and Rossiter (1938), who favoured Egyptians, believed Hall and quoted this passage. Even the more responsible Mason (1933:580) claims that many of the plants associated with the ruins are not indigenous. The present author, has not observed any of these plants and botanists disagree. Gilliland (1938) specifically refutes that any plants connected with the ruins are not indigenous and K.E.Sturgeon, a government botanist, wrote "in most cases I have examined the present plant inhabitors of these sites have no direct connection with the people who once lived there except perhaps with the figs and even those are not introduced but are common indigenous species" (letter to C.B.Payne dated 2nd September 1954).

CHAPTER 3

AFRICAN AGRICULTURE IN NYANGA AND BEYOND

AGRICULTURAL PRACTICES AND FIELD SYSTEMS IN AFRICA

The Nyanga terraces, cultivation ridges and hydraulic works constitute substantial and unusually well preserved evidence of old field systems – probably the most impressive and extensive in Africa – and offer an opportunity for some reconstruction of the agricultural systems they represent. However the archaeological remains in the landscape, including the settlement sites, are only the material manifestation of a whole agricultural and social system, one in which the former rural community, its livestock, crops, husbandry practices and their social context are not immediately apparent. Some insights into this missing realm may be gained from a more general consideration of African agriculture and, in turn, the Nyanga data contribute to the broader understanding of its history.

African agriculturalists have adopted new crops from different parts of the world at various times over perhaps two millennia, and have developed appropriate methods for their cultivation. This process has been greatly accelerated in the 20th century and older "traditional" cultivation practices have been much modified or superseded by the introduction of more "advanced" methods and technology from temperate regions, notably the use of the plough. While less labour-intensive, these methods have often proved more deleterious to the maintenance of soil health than the older methods, being less sensitive to local conditions. Some examples of older practices do survive, albeit modified by changed socio-political circumstances, while accounts of varying detail and reliability by ethnographers, administrators and others document many other examples which are now in decline or abandoned.

"Traditional" practices cover a whole range from extensive "slash-and-burn" to the highly intensive; notable among the latter are Ukara Island in Lake Victoria (Allan 1965; Ruthenberg 1976), Mandara and Kofyar in Nigeria (White 1941; Netting 1968) and parts of Ethiopia (Straube 1967; Hallpike 1970). Most exhibit some form of soil and water conservation methods adapted to local conditions of climate, soils and topography for the individual needs of a variety of crops. Much of the range of technical measures adopted is illustrated by Reij *et al* (1996) and Adams (1989).

Physical soil and water conservation methods include: an almost infinite variety of ridging and mounding techniques suited to different soils, water needs and maintenance of fertility; terracing of steep slopes which modern methods have been unable or unwilling to exploit; and water management by drainage, furrow irrigation, control of run-off (water harvesting) and flood utilisation. In addition, cropping systems commonly include rotation, intercropping and protection of nitrogen fixing trees, while manuring and mulching are practised in some cases. Almost all traditional methods rely on simple hand tools and hence are labour intensive, but bestow an intimate familiarity with local microenvironments. The use of hand tools may also provide significantly higher yields than the plough, as noted by Dodshon (1994b:89) in the very different environment of Scotland, where advantages of a quarter to a third over the plough are estimated.

African agricultural systems are thus no less dynamic than those in other parts of the world and have adapted to changing physical, social and demographic circumstances. As Sutton (1984) eloquently argues, they should not be conceived as having been fixed in a sort of "ethnographic present". Archaeology can provide time depth and document earlier systems and techniques against which to assess the processes of change. This evidence however, as Brookfield (1986) points out, is essentially provided by the remains of "landesque capital" works, modifications to the landscape, which only provide a partial and biased inventory of past practices. Such archaeological evidence is only likely to have survived – or at least to be directly identifiable – in more or less marginal situations, wet, dry or steep, where it has not been destroyed by later, different practices. It could therefore be said to be atypical of its period and broader region, but given the wide range of systems, each adapted to its own peculiar environment, there can be no "typical" and any surviving evidence is significant. (For further exploration of these issues see Sutton 1989a, 1989b.)

Relevant to the Nyanga case are examples of terracing, ridging, water control and the use of manure.

Terracing and soil conservation

The sustained cultivation of steep slopes requires soil conservation measures to minimise erosion, and terracing is an appropriate (and obvious) response.

Erosion is determined by slope length and gradient, rainfall intensity and duration, soil structure and permeability, and vegetation cover. Under cultivation, there will necessarily be a period between land preparation and the establishment of a crop cover when the soil is exposed and vulnerable. Soil conservation principles thus entail the reduction of slope length and the control of run-off to non-erosive velocities suited to local soil conditions, while allowing maximum infiltration for water retention (Hudson 1973; Greenland and Lal 1977; Morgan 1986).

These general principles may be achieved by terracing, which in its broadest definition can be defined as any method which artificially breaks the slope to improve conditions for cultivation. The simplest form is trash lines of cut vegetation laid on the contour. Various forms of earth terracing with varying spacing, profiles and drainage provision are recommended for different physical, economic and technological parameters. In Zimbabwe for instance, compulsory erosion control by means of contour ridges has been imposed since the 1930s, although with little regard to local climate and soil conditions; these break the slope at intervals and tend to divert rather than retain run-off and cannot be used on steep slopes. The most effective measure for soil conservation is bench terraces which modify the slope into a series of steps with more or less horizontal ledges and near vertical risers, usually revetted. They may be graded laterally to divert excess run-off to a suitable outlet (diversion terraces), or levelled to retain water (retention terraces); the latter must have sufficient capacity to avoid overtopping and consequent damage to the risers (Morgan 1986:226). Bench terraces thus provide maximum soil conservation and erosion control as well as a level cultivation surface. Nowadays they may not be considered economic on steep slopes because of the prodigious labour requirements of the close spacing, but they are the main form of the old Nyanga terraces as described in Chapter 4.

One factor only rarely mentioned in the general publications on soil conservation is that of stone clearance, since stony slopes would not be considered viable in conventional agriculture. It is however a major concern in much African terracing and particularly so in the Nyanga case, where stones had to be cleared from the surface and beneath it to concentrate the often thin soils. The resulting stone of course provides material for the solid revetment of the risers, though in extreme cases the width of the riser may equal that of the cultivable surface of the step.

It is not necessary to attempt a comprehensive listing and review of African terracing here. Grove and Sutton (1989) provide the most recent review for sub-Saharan Africa, summarising its distribution and considering its implications. They postulate that terracing can only be adopted within a fixed and locally dense (though not necessarily large) population. Terracing with its requirement for constant and intimate attention may come to control the lives of its practitioners and constrict their activities severely. This parallels the point made by Brookfield (1972), that reluctance to abandon investment in landesque capital may inhibit stimuli towards further intensification – or disintensification – of cultivation methods.

Direct comparisons can be made between the Nyanga terracing (described in Chapter 4) and still existing practices in the Konso area of Ethiopia (Amborn 1989) and western Darfur in Sudan (Hale 1966). Published accounts from other areas give inadequate technical details. The terracing of both Konso and Darfur appears consistent with that of Nyanga in dimensions, gradients, conformation and construction, reflecting common problems and solutions. Amborn describes a range of types of terrace-riser construction, most of which are also recognisable in Nyanga. He implies however that, unlike Nyanga, all are retention terraces, with a front lip 20 to 40cm high; the fields are carefully levelled to hold water when it rains, with provision for drainage over or through the wall. Few terraces are directly irrigated though there are seasonally irrigated basins on the valley sides. In Darfur, terraces have frequent cross walls or earthen banks, some of which form property lines. (Similar divisions are evident in some Nyanga terracing). There is direct manuring by cattle grazing in the dry season and by application of collected droppings. Rainfall is substantially lower than in Nyanga and some irrigation is practised, although Hale gives no details. Construction and maintenance is, or was, usually by individuals or small parties, usually family, on a piecemeal basis.

The nearest documented extensive terracing to eastern Zimbabwe is in Mpumalanga (Eastern Transvaal) in South Africa, some 850km to the south. Published references to this deal primarily with the associated stone enclosures and have little or no description of the terraces (Collett 1982; Hoepen 1939; Jones 1935; Maggs 1995, 1997; Marker and Evers 1976; Mason 1962; more information was kindly supplied by Tim Maggs with whom the author briefly visited the area in July 1998). The terracing extends in a belt some 120km long and 10 to 20km wide along the eastern edge of the highveld, from Carolina in the south, through Machadodorp and Lydenburg to Ohrigstad. In two areas visited (a small valley in sandstone near Lydenburg and a dolerite ridge some 20km to the south), terraces are in a comparable size range to Nyanga. Risers appear to be generally flush with the terrace surface and are formally built rather than simply piled along the contour; most are probably single faced revetments. Walled pathways traverse the fields as they do in Nyanga, with branches leading directly into the stone enclosures; some such pathways run down through the terraces, the lower edge of which is often defined by a higher "foot-dyke" so that stock were excluded from the fields. The latter feature is not seen in Nyanga, while the design of the stone homestead enclosures is also different. The complex appears to be broadly contemporary with that of Nyanga and there are generic similarities in the terraces and trackways. However, the contrasts in enclosure design and associated pottery (Collett 1982) indicate no direct cultural relationship.

As a general observation, the various occurrences of terracing in Africa, or further afield, can be adequately explained as parallel responses where the cultivation of steep stony slopes was desired for whatever reason. There is a limited number of ways in which terraces can be built and it is unnecessary to postulate direct cultural relationships unless provable in specific cases. Irrigation may or may not be associated according to the potential provided by topography and water sources and the adequacy of rainfall.

Cultivation ridges
Very extensive systems of linear cultivation ridges, often covering many hectares, are a feature of the Nyanga archaeological complex as described in Chapter 4, while somewhat comparable ridges on a smaller scale are still used in the cultivation of seasonally waterlogged "vleis" in many parts of Zimbabwe today. A useful review and classification of "raised fields" in general is provided by Denevan and Turner (1974), who define them as "any prepared land involving the transfer and elevation of soil above the natural surface of the earth in order to improve cultivation conditions". This includes a multiplicity of forms of ridging and mounding. Form, group pattern or spatial arrangement, density, dimensions, and subsidiary features such as tie ridges, allow for tremendous diversity, reflecting the local interplay of environmental conditions, crop requirements, cultural tradition, technology and population pressure. Raised fields in general enhance fertility through pulverisation and aeration of soil, increased soil depth, concentration of topsoil and organic matter including manure, modification of microclimate, and control of weeds and erosion; they may also facilitate the harvesting of root crops. Ridges and ditches in particular adjust the crop root-zone to moisture availability, by drainage where there is permanent or seasonal waterlogging, or by retention under drier conditions.

The design of ridging and mounding and their effect on crop yields vary with the type of soil, topography, total rainfall and its distribution, and the crops grown; cultural factors however will control the precise measures adopted. A wide variety of crops can be planted on raised fields but root crops are by far the most common.

As noted at the beginning of the chapter, there is an almost infinite variety of raised fields in sub-Saharan Africa, though none seem to closely resemble the ridges described in Chapter 4 in form or scale. Sutton (1969) reviews a range of examples in East Africa, of which the closest resemblance to Nyanga is in Uhehe and neighbouring areas of the Southern Highlands of Tanzania. Here relatively narrow ridges (*matuta*) are built up on the gentle valley sides and broader flat-topped beds (*fyungu*) in the valley bottoms, the purpose being to allow sufficient moisture to seep into the cultivation soil and at the same time prevent waterlogging by carrying off excess. For Zimbabwe, the common recent or current form used in the cultivation of wetlands are *mihomba*, described below.

Irrigation
Hydraulic works associated with the Nyanga complex, including furrows and storage facilities, are described and discussed in Chapter 4. A consideration of irrigation practices in other parts of sub-Saharan Africa assists in their interpretation, even though not all the Nyanga works were for direct watering of crops.

In recent decades it has been fashionable to advocate irrigation as a means of increasing agricultural output in many parts of Africa. Many large-scale, more or less capital-intensive schemes have been initiated but have failed to achieve their potential due to problems of management which has been imposed from outside and often conflicts with the needs or perceptions of the farmers themselves. In reaction to this a body of recent research has been devoted to small-scale, farmer-managed irrigation systems, many of them indigenous and operating without outside intervention, from which lessons may be drawn on how they operate within the relevant societies (e.g. Adams *et al* 1994, 1997; Bolding *et al* 1996; Fleuret 1985).

A broad definition of "irrigation" is proposed by Adams (1989), including essentially any form of water usage, from flood recession cropping to groundwater pumping, and including water harvesting. Within this range, the Nyanga furrows and associated works fall generally within "hill furrow irrigation", which may be described as the leading of water under gravity from a convenient source to the place of utilisation.

Hill furrow irrigation may in rare cases be essential to successful agriculture where low rainfall makes regular cultivation unviable, such as the case of the Njemps near Lake Baringo in Kenya (Anderson 1989) and the archaeological example of Engaruka in the Rift Valley in northern Tanzania (Sutton 1998). However in most documented indigenous systems it acts as a supplement to normal rainfall, giving insurance against poor rainfall years and extended dry periods within a normal wet season, as well as giving the potential to extend the growing season before or after the rains. It may thus be employed even where average annual rainfall is as high as 1500mm, as in parts of Ethiopia and on Kilimanjaro, or near that amount in highland Nyanga. It is usually coordinated with dryland farming, and when combined with or facilitating the cultivation of varied crops, it smooths labour peaks of land preparation, planting, weeding and harvesting.

On any but the most minimal scale, irrigation requires social cooperation beyond the level of the individual household. Furrow construction and maintenance must be shared by all users, and provision made for equitable water distribution and resolution of conflicts. Thus for effective operation, management must be integrated with the socio-political organisation, as indeed is the case in the ethnographic examples cited in Chapter 4. Normally in Africa, this management is not imposed by any central authority but is inherent in the clan or lineage-based social organisation.

Irrigation is widespread in Africa wherever appropriate water sources and topography occur, subject to socio-economic motivation. Indigenous irrigation systems are very diverse in the environments in which they exist and the ways they exploit them (Adams *et al* 1994:18). Since such environments are often hilly areas appropriate to terracing, irrigation can be associated with terracing, though the terraces themselves may not be irrigated. Irrigation has often been seen as a symptom of intensification as discussed below.

Enhancement of fertility/Manuring

Land clearance and preparation is one of the heaviest tasks involved with cultivation, so that measures to improve and prolong fertility are desirable in order to realise the maximum return for the investment of labour. This is particularly important where investment in major capital structures such as terracing is concerned.

The main method of fertility enhancement is the provision of extra nutrients. Almost all added nutrients in indigenous African systems derive from vegetation – grass, shrubs, trees – either burnt as ash or rotted as compost, or from nitrogen-fixing legumes, or processed via animal dung or human faeces. Probably the most widespread is ash from the burning of cleared vegetation. Application is commonly by incorporation in various types of ridges and mounds, but some may be applied as mulches. (See Reij *et al* 1996).

Apart from nitrogen-fixing legumes and the rare African cases of the use of green manure, most practices involve a nutrient flow from uncultivated to cultivated land, and in the case of animal manure involve the integration of animal husbandry with cultivation. Where available land is limited, this constitutes a "nutrient trap" (Dogshon 1994b) whereby expansion of cultivated land reduces the pasture to maintain the animals required to fertilise it. This may be less relevant in most African situations but does seem to have been significant on Ukara Island (Allan 1965). However the use of crop residues and other vegetation for animal fodder and other purposes may limit their use for mulch, seen as a desirable measure for soil conservation.

The use of collected animal manure does not seem to have been generally practised in more extensive African agricultural systems, although grazing of crop residues after harvest may have provided some direct application. However, it is a frequent practice in the more intensive systems discussed below, where dung from animal kraals is accumulated and rotted for application during land preparation. A more specialised method is that of stall-feeding, whereby animals are kept permanently penned for a large part of the year and fodder is brought to them by hand. Large quantities of manure from dung, surplus fodder and bedding material is thus accumulated. This is documented for Mandara in Nigeria by White (1941) and for Konso in Ethiopia by Hallpike (1970), while Netting (1968) for Kofyar in Nigeria gives figures: a goat enclosure 4.75m in diameter and 2.30m deep produced 388 basket loads, spread over 1620 square metres, a rate of 25 litres of manure per square metre, or 250cu.m per hectare, if the enclosure was full to the top. There seems to be little information on the relative value of cattle and goat manure for Africa, but in lowland Scotland, sheep dung was most highly prized, followed by that of fowl, horses and cattle (Shaw 1994), and maybe goat is similarly superior to cattle.

Where manure is or was used, its application is graded outwards from the homestead, with heaviest application on the homestead garden, less on inlying fields and little or none on outlying fields (White 1941; Amborn 1989). A similar distribution is documented for present-day peasant farmers in north-eastern Zimbabwe (Scoones and Toulmin 1995).

There are features suggesting the use of "slurry" in some of the highland pit-structures of Nyanga. This consists of diluted dung and urine washed from animal pens, and is normally a product of modern stock rearing. It can only be produced where stock are penned in a solid-floored enclosure and water can be brought to the pen to flush it out. Such special circumstances are present in Nyanga but do not appear to be documented for any "traditional" husbandry practices. The advantage of slurry is that it makes maximum use of the high nitrogen content of urea, much of which is lost by volatilisation in normal farmyard manure.

Cropping

Cropping strategies are probably impossible to reconstruct from archaeological evidence. They are however an important element of cultivation systems, especially the more intensive ones. They have been widely appreciated by indigenous African agriculturalists (see for instance Reij *et al* 1996) and the Nyanga peoples must have been familiar with the principles. Different crops with varying growing seasons and soil requirements can be adjusted to locally varying conditions and can spread labour bottlenecks and climatic risks. Intercropping brings added advantages – staggered planting and harvesting, maintenance of ground cover to inhibit erosion and evaporation, and interplanting grains with legumes to exploit nitrogen fixation. Crop rotation from more to less demanding crops gives some compensation for declining fertility in more extensive systems. Carefully propagated crop varieties with different moisture requirements provide some insurance against irregular rainfall from year to year. Trees may also be important, whether planted or conserved, in consolidating terraces, providing fruit, shade and foliage for fodder or compost, as well as fixing nitrogen in the case of leguminous species.

Intensification

Irrigation and major capital works such as terracing, which are epitomised by the Nyanga structures, are often seen as evidence for agricultural intensification and many of the African examples quoted above have been characterised as intensive systems. It is not intended to go deeply into the theory of agricultural intensification, but some background is needed for the interpretation of the Nyanga evidence in Chapter 6.

Intensification is essentially conceived as a relative process, defined by Farrington (1985) as an increase in food productivity per unit of land and/or labour, while disintensification is a reduction in productivity. Thus the term may be applied at any point along a scale from the most extensive to the most concentrated system, without regard to the point at which a system may be regarded as actually "intensive". Almost all traditional agricultural systems that have been characterised as intensive in Africa, and probably elsewhere, in fact show graded zones of intensive methods: more or less permanent cultivation near the habitation achieved by manuring often aided by irrigation; and a decreasing application of intensive methods as distance from the habitation increases, culminating in extensive shifting cultivation of outlying fields. An "intensive" system may then best be defined as one in which the whole system is sustainable in the long term under conditions of high population density.

Debate on the stimulus to intensification was initiated by Boserup (1965) who considered that it was principally a response to increasing population pressure on available land. This seminal argument has since been criticised as too narrow by other writers who have introduced other factors (see Brookfield 1972, 1984, 1986; Grigg 1982; Farrington 1985; and Häkansson 1989). While the attainment of perceived food security may be the primary motivation, other factors such as social aspirations, taxation or the maximisation of production for profit in response to outside demand may also be important.

Brookfield (1984) identifies "innovations" as the mechanism for intensification. These may include increased labour input, new crops, new techniques or tools, and investment in "landesque capital" infrastructure such as terraces, earthworks and irrigation. With simple technology, "capital" investment in fact translates into labour. Many or all of these innovations entail modifications to the social system for mobilisation of extra labour and control of resources, and land tenure is also likely to be affected. Environmental conditions, technological expertise, investments already made and the social costs of change may be significant barriers to change (Brookfield 1972). Disintensification is normally a result of reduction of population and decrease in available labour.

Perhaps parallel to Brookfield's innovations is the concept of "specialisation" by Sutton (1985), in the choice of crops, development of new varieties and cropping systems, in field systems, and in storage and culinary habits; terracing and irrigation are the most obvious in the landscape. This concept can take us beyond the innovation stage and Sutton suggests a vicious circle of technological effort and economic dependence, whereby in isolated situations optional techniques or devices may become ultra-specialised to the point of irreversibility, prone to eventual disaster by land degradation or outside factors.

Stimulus to intensification has in many cases been seen as promoted by a refuge situation in which a population becomes rather isolated in difficult territory owing to fear of aggression or environmental circumstances. In the case of terracing, this line of thinking seems to be influenced by the common assumption that people would not voluntarily undertake the heavy labour involved unless obliged by circumstances to do so. Something in this vein is suggested for Nyanga by Grove and Sutton (1989), as also by earlier writers such as Summers (1958). A contrasting hypothesis is proposed by Widgren (1999) who plays down the isolation factor and indeed argues that intensive systems can only exist where neighbouring groups or markets are available for exchange of products, arising from a complex interaction of ecological, social and historical factors. An extreme modern example is the intensification by the Kamba of Kenya (documented by Tiffen *et al* 1994) under the stimulus of the Nairobi market, but here the resources for development have come mainly from wage remittances from labour migration, making this example hardly relevant to traditional situations – or to the Nyanga case. Brookfield (1986), however, points out that many difficult environments have countervailing advantages such as wetness or fertility, whereby a quantum leap in productivity can be achieved by relatively simple initial innovations, these stimulating and providing surplus resources for further innovation and investment in landesque capital. Focus should thus be on the opportunities offered by the natural advantages of such situations, with no need to assume that people were necessarily forced into difficult situations by pressures elsewhere. The relative fertility of unweathered soils on steep stony slopes may be one such advantage in the Nyanga case.

Whatever the stimulus, adequate labour and transmission of knowledge are critical factors in the maintenance of intensive or specialised cultivation systems. In colonial times in Africa, political stability and the reduction of raiding have often initiated out-migration of population from hill "refuge" areas, with a consequent "disintensification" to more extensive cultivation methods (e.g. White 1941 and Fricke 1996 for parts of Nigeria); in some cases the original nucleus settlements may survive in parallel (Widgren 1999). A case of more drastic (and earlier) disruption is that of the Dullay area of Ethiopia, where almost the entire warrior grade of young men was eliminated in battle, reducing the labour force and interrupting the transmission cycle of knowledge and responsibility (Amborn 1989).

Direct archaeological study of past intensive systems necessarily concentrates on landesque capital works. These tend to survive in marginal lands no longer considered viable for agriculture because they are too steep, wet or dry, either through environmental change to which the earlier system could no longer adapt, or because of a change in the perception of the value of the land and whether it is worth the labour to exploit it (Farrington 1985). The same factors probably led to the abandonment of these areas in the first place. Farrington has also pointed out the difficulties of identifying an intensive agricultural system and the causes of change from archaeological evidence alone. The problem can be approached by the study of field remains and settlement patterns, plant and bone remains and palaeoenvironments, provided that a fairly precise chronology is available, but such factors as cropping frequency, fertiliser and yields are almost impossible to identify. While labour investment is readily apparent from landesque capital, it is difficult to quantify population size, density and pressure or carrying capacity. The level of intensity, processes of change and causes of change will remain difficult to assess.

Traditional crops and plant use in Nyanga

Peasant agriculture in the Nyanga region, as elsewhere in Africa, has undergone considerable changes in the 20th century, with the introduction of new crops and cultivation methods. The former include numerous "European" vegetables (potatoes, tomatoes, brassicas and the like) and the great expansion of maize (already known by the late 19th century at least), partly for home consumption at the expense of the traditional millets and sorghum, and partly as a commercial crop. New methods include the plough, ox- or tractor-drawn, monocropping and contour ridging, under the influence of government extension workers.

Dryland plough agriculture is the norm at the present day in Zimbabwe generally. Wetland cultivation of vleis – seasonally waterlogged areas in stream headwaters – used to be an important element in indigenous horticulture, but was banned by the colonial authorities on the assumption that it prejudiced the dry-season flow of the streams and caused environmental degradation (Whitlow 1983; Owen *et al* 1995). It has however persisted in many peasant farming areas. One common method of cultivation of vleis or waterlogged stream banks is the use of cultivation ridges – *mihomba*. These are relatively short (c.20 - 30m), straight, cambered, parallel linear ridges, usually angled directly downslope for drainage. Indigenous crops grown on such *mihomba* in the Nyanga region are, or were, *tsenza* (*Plectranthus esculenta*), cucurbits, *majo* (a plant similar to, or a variety of taro or cocoyam *Colocasia esculenta*), and various vegetables; rice is also reported in some areas. These *mihomba* are shorter, generally narrower, and more localised in areal extent than the cultivation ridges described in Chapter 4, and may in most cases be distinguished from them on the ground or on aerial photographs. They are also widely distributed throughout the country, whereas the older ridge systems are restricted to Nyanga and Makoni Districts.

Information on the main staples in the early colonial period is given in varying detail in district reports from the 1890s (reviewed by Madya 1989 and discussed below). A few other crops are mentioned in oral traditions recorded by Machiwenyika (Appendix I to the Annex to this volume). There were and are however numerous other cultivated or semi-wild plants, some of which were of considerable importance. Information on many of these has been assembled by Tredgold (1986) for Zimbabwe in general, but there is no account specific to the Nyanga region. Archaeological data is also sparse and documents only the main staples (Summers 1958:175-7 and a few seeds from the recent research: see Chapter 6 and Appendix C).

It may be assumed that most crops and other plants cultivated and used in the local area early in this century would have been available to the people of the terrace complex, while cultivation practices at field level may be little changed apart from those associated with new crops. For direct information on these a questionnaire was drawn up and administered by enumerators to a total of 37 elderly informants, male and female, in different areas – Matema/Tangwena and Chirimanyimo in the highlands, Ruangwe and Mazarura in the northern lowlands, and Dzimbiti in the western lowlands. Emphasis of the questions was on cultigens and semi-domesticated weeds; some information was also forthcoming on wild plants and trees but this cannot be considered at all comprehensive. In some cases specimens were collected and identified by the National Herbarium. Recent introductions such as European vegetables, cassava, sugar cane and groundnuts were excluded.

Questions covered local and Shona (Manyika) names; parts of plants used and what for; time of planting and harvesting; where grown (in garden or fields) and who by (husband or wife); use of manure or ridging; intercropping and propagation. No attempt was made to distinguish crop varieties though these certainly exist. Some confusion was encountered between local and normal Shona names; in several cases there seem to be variant local names for the same plant and this may have led to some duplication of plants not clearly identified. Some confirmation and amplification of information was obtained from Tredgold's gazetteer of Zimbabwean food plants (1986) but she does not give most of the local names used in this area.

The plants and some information about them are listed in Table 3.1 which demonstrates the wide variety of species exploited.

Comments on results of the questionnaire

Roots

A number of rhizomes, domesticated and wild, were used. *Madhumbe*, the present variety of *Colocasia esculenta* (taro), is acknowledged as a recent introduction, but a specimen said to be *majo* was also identified as *Colocasia* by the Herbarium and is presumably a variant of earlier introduction. Both it and the similar wild plants, *manzongo* and *erera* are toxic unless properly processed by extended boiling. The use of *Zantedeschia aethiopica* (*manzongo*) is documented in South Africa, the young leaves and petioles as a vegetable and the root as food or source of starch, the toxicity destroyed by roasting or boiling (Watt and Breyer-Brandwijk 1962). The same source also gives the toxic *Colocasia antiquorum* as used in the same way. Alois Mandondo (pers.comm.) contributes the following comments on *majo, manzongo* and *erera*: The leaves of all these are used to prepare a slimy form of relish called *dowe*. When the male household head dies, *majo* is used in a ritual called *kudyiswa mbeu dzabambo* (literally eating the seed of the father), *majo* being one of the ingredients in the *mbeu* concoction administered to all the deceased's sons. *Majo, manzongo* and *erera* were also used to poison Nguni/Ndebele raiders in the 19th century. They would half-process it and leave it out in the open for the hungry raiders to consume. Some locals still appease the avenging spirits of raiders who died in this way. The appeasement ceremonies are called *madzviti* or *mangoni* in which people go into trance and start communicating in a Ndebele-like language.

Table 3.1

Local name	Shona name	Botanical name	English name	Parts used	Used for	Harvest	Comments
Grains							
mapfunde	mapfunde	*Sorghum bicolor*	sorghum	grains, stalks, stem	staple, beer	April-May	red & white varieties, height limit c.1800m
mhunga	mhunga	*Pennisetum americanum*	bullrush millet	grains	staple, beer, fodder	March-June	height limit c.1800m
rukweza, njera	rapoko	*Eleusine corocana*	finger millet	grains	staple, beer	April-June	red & white varieties, height limit c.1800m
njeke, mumanyika	magwere	*Zea mays*	maize	cobs, grains, stem	staple, beer, cash	April-May	njeke is old type growing up to 2100m
mupunga	mupunga	*Oryza sativa*	rice	grains	staple	April-May	
Legumes							
fendokoto	nyemba	*Vigna unguiculata*	cowpea	seeds, pods, leaves	staple, relish	March-May	height limit c.1800m, largely replaced by beans
nyimo	nyimo	*V. subterranea*	ground bean	seeds, leaves	staple, relish	April-May	height limit c.1800m
Roots, tubers							
madhumbe	madhumbe	*Colocasia esculenta*	cocoyam, taro	root, leaves, stem	staple, relish	from March	recent introduction
majo	?	? *Colocasia* variety	? none	root, leaves	staple, relish	from April	toxic. Used in funeral rituals
gogoya	?	? *Colocasia variety*	?	root, leaves	staple, relish	from April ?	
tsaya	tsenza	*Plectran thus esculentus*	Livingstone potato	tubers	staple, snack	Feb-May	eaten raw or cooked and mashed
Cucurbits							
mutikiti, munhikiti	muboora	*Cucurbita maxima*	pumpkin	fruits, seeds, leaves, flowers	Staple, relish	April-May	
mbudzidoko, kambudzi	muboora	*Cucurbita* variety	pumpkin	leaves, stem, seeds	relish, oil	Nov-March	highland variety
mushonja	magaka	*Cucumis metuliferus*	spiny cucumber	fruits, seeds	snack	May	
muferefere	manyani	*Citrullus lanatus*	melon	fruits, seeds	staple, snack	March-April	semi-wild
Other							
mono	?mono	*Ricinus communis*	castor oil	seeds	oil	April-July	
mushaba	?	?	?	seeds, leaves	smoking, snuff	April	mixed with tobacco for snuff
Useful weeds							
bupwe	derere	*Corchorus sp*	'okro'	leaves	relish	Dec-Feb	
nyatando	derere	*Hibiscus sp*	okro	leaves, pods	relish	Dec-Feb	
suza	nhungunira	*Bidens pilosa*	blackjack	leaves	relish	Dec-Jan	

mowa	mowa	*Amaranthus sp*	amaranthus	leaves	relish	Dec-Jan	
nyevhe	nyevhe, rune	*Cleome gynandra*	?	leaves	relish	Dec-Jan	
mutsema-tsema	?	?	?	leaves	relish	Dec-Jan	
mharupwa, mutsungura	mutsungu-tsungu	*Solanum nigrum*	common nightshade	leaves, fruits	relish, snack	Dec-March	
mabheni	mubheri	*Physalis angulata*	wild gooseberry	fruits	snack	March-May	Shona name suggests recent
tsuwa	?	?	?	roots	staple	Oct-Nov	kind of grass or sedge
nyonyo	?	?	?	roots	snack	Feb-April	eaten raw

Wild trees and plants

tsombori	mutsamberi	*Lannea edulis*	?	fruits	snack	Feb	
maonde, tsvita, tsamvi	makuyu	*Ficus spp*	fig	fruits	snack	Oct-Feb	
hute, hototo	hute	*Syzygium cordatum, S.guineense*	waterberry	fruits	snack	Jan-March	
nhenzvera	nhenja	*Vangueria infausta*	wild medlar	fruits	snack	March-April	leaves medicinal
musika	musika	*Tamarindus indica*	tamarind	pod mucilage	relish, snack	June-July	
muuyu	muuyu	*Adansonia digitata*	baobab	pith, seeds, leaves	relish	Oct-June	
muzhanje	muzhanje	*Uapaca kirkiana*	wild loquat	fruits	snack, relish	Nov-Feb	
maroro	muroro	*Anona senegalensis*	wild custard apple	fruits	snack	Jan-March	
nzambara	mudzanbara	*Carissa edulis*	carissa	berries	snack	Nov-Jan	
tsubvu	tsubvu	*Vitex sp*	chocolate berry	berries	snack	Apr-Jun	
matunduru	matunduru	*Garcinia huillensis*	Garcinia	fruits	snack	Nov-Jan	
matohwe	mutohwe	*Azanza garckeana*	snot apple	fruits	snack	Feb-Sept	
matamba	mutamba-muzhinyu	*Strychnos cocculoides*	bitter bush orange	fruits	snack	March-Aug	
nhengeni		*Ximenia caffra*					
hunzuru	?	*Trichilia sp?*	mahogany	seeds	relish, snack	Dec-March	
tsomho	?	?	?	fruits	snack?	Feb-April	
komva	?	*Ensete ventricosum*	wild banana	seeds	staple	dry season	
hokora-mutanda	?	?	?	fungus	relish	wet season	grows on old *msasa* logs
manzongo	?	*Zantedeschia aethiopica*	calla lily	rhizomes, leaves	staple, relish	Dec-June	toxic without extended boiling
erera	?	?	?	rhizomes, leaves	staple, relish		toxic, little used now
ndiya	?	*Dioscorea bulbifera ?*	yam	tubers	staple	Jan-March	

Other unidentified wild plants mentioned are: nyamupfu (roots, staple); nawa (roots); ruhwato (fruits "strawberries"); mhoriro (fruits).

The confused taxonomy and distribution of *tsenza*, *Plectranthus esculentus*, is reviewed by Sutton (1984) and Blench (1994-5). This used to be more widely grown in eastern Zimbabwe and is still popular in the Rusape area. It may be eaten raw or boiled as a rather mushy staple. Recent cultivation ridges (*mihomba*) are still sometimes referred to as "*tsenza* beds" and Sutton (1983) speculates that it may have been a major crop on the old cultivation ridges described in Chapter 4. That it was grown on such raised beds is recorded in the traditions reported below, but *majo* is likely to have been equally important on the wetter ridges. *Tsenza* is subject to serious nematode infestation and colonial authorities discouraged its cultivation for this reason, especially in the vicinity of potatoes.

Grains and legumes
The indigenous African grains, sorghum, eleusine and pennisetum, would certainly have been important staples grown on the Nyanga terraces, with varieties tailored to different altitudinal and rainfall conditions. The red varieties of sorghum and pennisetum are reported to be better for making beer and the white varieties for eating, while both make better beer than maize. One informant living at 2100m says that the indigenous grains do not do well at that altitude, though one old variety of maize is more successful. Maize does not appear to have been an important crop in pre-colonial times (see below). Rice was mentioned by very few informants but was certainly grown in precolonial Zimbabwe. The legumes, cowpeas and ground beans, were more widely grown in the past but have been largely replaced by beans. Their contribution to fertility by nitrogen fixation was clearly appreciated and exploited in intercropping with cereals. Curiously the name of Chirimanyimo hill means "cultivation of ground beans" but present inhabitants of the area are unable to explain the origin of this, having moved there only from the 1940s.

Other plants
The semi-wild weeds of cultivation, *Corchorus*, *Bidens pilosa*, *Amaranthus*, *Cleome gynandra* and *Solanum nigrum*, are encouraged and widely appreciated for their leaves, used for relish when still young and tender in the early to mid-summer rainy season, and sometimes dried for later use. The wild plants listed are mainly fruits, eaten raw or processed in various ways; the pith of the large ensete seeds is said to have been a valuable resource among the Tangwena people when forced from their homes during the independence war.

Cultivation
Almost all the questionnaire informants had gardens with water available from streams or wells, as well as the rainfed fields. Crops grown in such gardens are or were maize, rice, *madhumbe*, *majo*, *tsenza*, pumpkins and cucumber, while field crops are maize, sorghum, finger and bullrush millet, *nyemba*, *nyimo* and pumpkins. Crops grown on ridges are or were the root crops, *madhumbe*, *majo* and *tsenza*, as well as tobacco and sometimes maize. Alois Mandondo (pers.comm.) reports that in the Tangwena/Tombo area of the highlands *njera* finger millet is grown under shifting cultivation, woodland being felled and burned to clear fields commonly referred to as *tema*; in other areas it is grown in permanent fields

For intercropping, sorghum is only planted with the legumes and pumpkins, while maize, finger millet and bullrush millet may be grown together, also with legumes and pumpkins. *Madhumbe* is only grown with pumpkins, and rice was not reported as intercropped at all, though there were very few records. *Tsenza* was always grown alone.

Other Information
Early official reports of African crops for Inyanga and surrounding districts are reviewed by Madya (1989). The earliest report for Inyanga is from 1902 and notes bullrush millet in the Gaerezi valley; red millet on the highveld; sorghum in the Pungwe and Honde valleys; maize and *rapoko* on "the second plateau in the west" with beans, peas, groundnuts and other vegetables; little rice in the district; and bananas and lemons in the "lowveld" in the east. The specific identity of "red millet", mentioned frequently in all district reports, is unclear – it was probably a variety of sorghum. There is no mention of *tsenza* in this or any subsequent reports for Inyanga District, but it is recorded for Makoni District from 1900 to 1907 and for Umtali (Mutare) in 1902; it may have escaped the attention of the Inyanga Native Commissioner. Considerable rice in favourable seasons was reported for Mutoko in 1900. Maize was increasing in popularity in Umtali in 1906 and by 1909 the original hardy type of round flint maize, well established in the 1890s, was largely replaced by larger introduced varieties. The cultivation of maize increased rapidly in Inyanga in 1913/1914 and threatened to replace red millet as the main staple. Maize was grown extensively in most districts in response to commercial demand especially during the first world war, but declined in popularity with falling prices from 1919.

Some information on crops and cultivation is also given by Mukaronda (1988). Probably quoting from the original Shona version of Machiwenyika (Annex), he says "the people of Nyanga then grew maize, pumpkins, majo another type of the yam family, ndodzi and shushururu". He also quotes an elderly informant on the earlier cultivation of *tsenza, majo*, beans and maize in ridged gardens and of maize, beans, *njera, mapfunde*, sweet potatoes and a little groundnuts in the fields (see Chapter 4).

CHAPTER 4

AGRICULTURAL WORKS: TERRACES, RIDGES AND WATER FURROWS

TERRACES

Terraces present the most substantial and enduring modification of the landscape in the Nyanga region, the main distribution covering large parts of escarpments and slopes below an altitude of around 1700m within an area of at least 5000 square kilometres (fig. 4; Plates 1, 2). Constituting the dominant feature of the archaeological complex and chief witness to its agricultural activities, they were a main focus of the recent research. Direct considerations were the range of variation and technical details of construction and soils, few details of which are given in most archaeological or ethnographic accounts of terracing in Africa. Less direct but equally important are their cultural context and the interpretation of their significance and usage in the agricultural economy of the societies which built them.

As noted in Chapter 1, the distribution was determined from aerial photographs and provided data for a geological correlation. Preliminary ground survey gave a broad impression of the range of variation and a number of sample areas were then chosen for detailed examination, representing different geological conditions, areas and terrace types. Cross-sections were excavated, soil samples collected, and detailed plans made in several cases. The areas selected were:

Ziwa ruins, SN113 (1832BA83), 1300m, dolerite
Ziwa ruins, Mujinga, 1280m, granite
Maristvale, 1732DD34, 1440m, dolerite
Chirangeni, 1290m, granite
Chirimanyimo, Madziwa School, 1760m, dolerite
Elim Mission, 1040m, argillite

An initial distinction was made between single and double-faced revetment of terrace risers. The former have a simple often roughly built riser of facing stones, a relatively steep terrace surface of up to 10 degrees or more, and are generally on non-dolerite soils. The latter are diversion bench terraces as defined in Chapter 3, with a relatively horizontal surface in profile, graded laterally for gentle drainage and not infrequently with stone-lined drains to carry excess run-off down through the system. The risers in this type are more formally built, with a facing of large stones front and back and a fill of smaller stones; they may be on granite or dolerite. The wall-top may be flush with the terrace surface above, or rise above it anything up to a metre or more, depending presumably on the amount of stones to be cleared for cultivation. The higher walls may have drains built through them as at Maristvale but this is not very common; for instance high walls near Ziwa Site Museum do not have drains. In the case of flush-topped risers it is not always possible to tell whether they are single or double-faced from surface examination, and excavation has shown in some cases that where the outer face is of large stable stones, excess stones may be simply piled behind it without a formal inner face, as at Madziwa School, Chirimanyimo. The single/double-faced classification is thus not entirely satisfactory.

A further type of terrace was noted by Summers (1958) on rocky granite slopes at the foot of Mount Ziwa and Hamba hill in Ziwa ruins, and on the escarpment on the south side of the Bende Gap. These are extremely roughly built, usually of large stones. Summers (p.48, 96) found "Z2" Early Iron Age sherds on the surface on and in the vicinity of such terraces and considered that they could be associated. This association would be difficult to prove since even sherds incorporated in the terraces could derive from earlier occupation. However, in the case of the Bende Gap there are large sections of Early Iron Age vessels in adjacent rockshelters which might hardly have survived unscathed if there had been much subsequent activity in the immediate area. There is thus some suggestion that the Early Iron Age inhabitants initiated some terracing, although there is no reason to suppose any continuity from this to the later complex.

Terracing and geology
The view has often been expressed (first by Frobenius, 1931) that the terrace builders favoured dolerite rocks and soils and the data from the aerial photograph survey was used to check this. Geological mapping is not available for the whole area; however, two of the available half-degree sheets (spanning 32° 30' to 33° east and 17° 15' to 18° 15' south; Stocklmayer 1978, 1980) cover the larger part of the Nyanga terracing, except for some outlying areas to the west and south. The terrace distribution

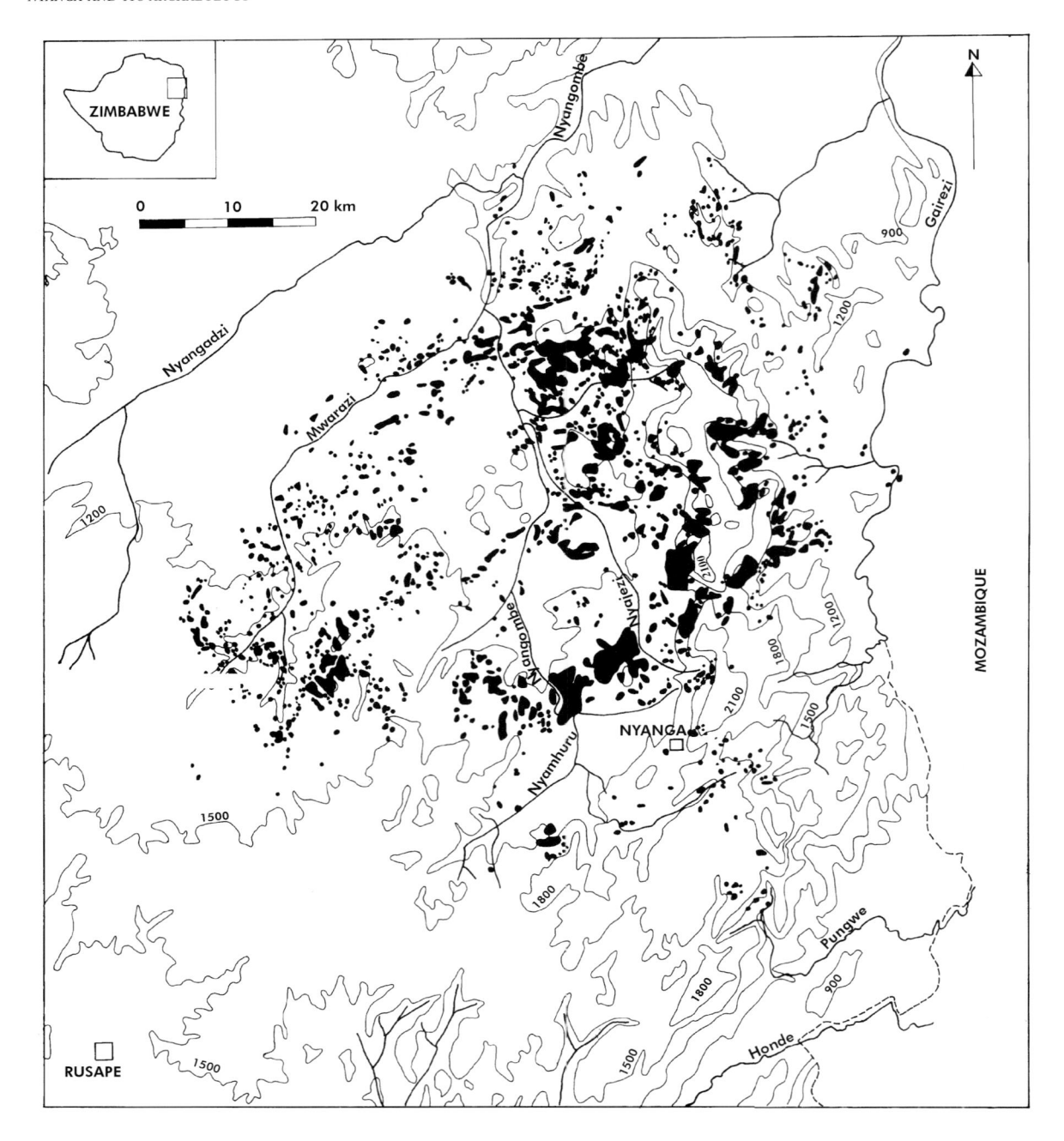

Fig. 4. Distribution of terracing identified from aerial photographs

extends only a short distance onto the northern of the two adjacent map-sheets (see below), and the main analysis is restricted to the southern sheet.

All terracing which was visible on the aerial photographs was plotted on an overlay for the geological maps at the same scale (1:100000). As noted in Chapter 1, not all terracing is visible on the aerial photographs so this is a minimum distribution which should however be representative. There could be some bias to dolerite terraces since these tend to be larger and hence with greater potential visibility, but, as will be seen, plenty of terracing was identified on granite areas.

The granites are extensively subdivided on the geological map, but for the purposes of this analysis only broad distinctions have been made between dolerite, "granite" and other (fig. 3). The last category here consists almost entirely of sedimentary rocks of the Umkondo Group, mainly the Gairezi Facies of schists and siltstones down the eastern border and the Inyanga Facies of sandstones and argillites capping the highlands north of the Bende Gap. The dolerites also crown much of the highlands such as the Nyanga Downs and the northern highlands where they are intercalated with the Inyanga Facies. Dolerite sills and dykes also form some of the foothills to the west of the highlands and carry the densest concentration of terracing of the whole complex.

Estimates of area were made on a one-millimetre grid, each square representing one hectare. This introduces an element of approximation at the edges of defined areas, especially where areas of terracing are fragmented into small plots. However, overall the relative proportions should bear a significant relationship to reality.

The total area of terracing plotted within the area of the southern geological map sheet is 19,262 hectares which constitutes 7.5% of the total area. This is a minimum distribution as noted above. Of this, 42.1% is on dolerite, 56.8% on granite and 0.9% on other. This however should be considered in relation to the relative area of different rock types, taking into account the altitudinal distribution of terracing. Little terracing occurs at higher altitudes so the area above 1675m (5500 ft), most of which is dolerite, was excluded from the analysis. In fact only 794 ha or 4% of the terracing occurs above this contour, almost all of it on dolerite, and when this area is excluded the plotted terracing covers 8.2% of the landscape.

Of the area below 1675m, dolerites make up only 12.7%, with granite accounting for most of the rest ("other" is not estimated separately since the amount of terracing on it is insignificant). Of the 18468 ha of terracing, dolerite comprises 40.3%, granites 59.3% and other 0.4%. However comparing this with the extent of the rocks we find that 25.8% of the dolerite below 1675m is terraced against only 5.5% of the granites. Again these are minimum figures, representing only the terracing identifiable on the air photos. The preference for dolerites however is clear. In addition, much of the terracing appearing on granite on the geological map is more or less closely adjacent to dolerite occurrences. Often the boundary between dolerite and granite is not as clear-cut as the geological map implies, especially at lower altitudes where the edges of dolerite sills have been subject to slow erosion, leaving residual dolerite rocks and soils among granite outcrops. Another phenomenon which may be envisaged is the expansion of terrace construction from nuclei on dolerite tracts of limited extent as the available area was used up. One might go on to speculate on the possibility of complementary crop and farming regimes on different soils but this would be extremely difficult to demonstrate.

Terracing continues some 20 km northwards on the next geological sheet, mainly in and around the Chigura section of the Ruangwe Range which forms the northward, lower extension of the highlands. This range is formed by rocks of the Inyanga Facies (including dolerites), which is reflected in a much higher proportion of terracing on "other" rocks, especially argillites. There is a total of 2481 hectares of terracing with the following percentages: dolerite 42.2%, granite 41.0%, other 17.8%.

The soils deriving from dolerites are of greater inherent fertility than those from granites, except where they are deeply leached under the higher rainfall of the highlands (see Chapter 2). The terrace distribution shows clearly that the terrace builders were aware of this.

Case studies

Ziwa SN113

This area, nearly 2.5 hectares in extent, is 650m south-west of Ziwa Site Museum at an altitude of 1300m, at grid reference VQ 611946 (fig. 42, no.12; officially designated 1832BA83). It is situated near the north-eastern end of a north-trending dolerite ridge and terracing continues to south and north. The local road to Tawengwa and Nyatate passes the foot of the terraces on the east side, and below this bare dolerite rock is exposed above the incised bed of a seasonal stream, a tributary of the Nyangombe river which flows two kilometres to the south-west.

The area provides a fairly coherent set of terraces on a relatively even slope, avoiding too many complications from local variations in topography. The aim was to survey a significant area of terraces and enclosures to show their relationship, and to excavate a transect across a series of terraces to study their construction and soil profiles. The survey was carried out by plane table at a scale of 1:200, using an EDM alidade which measures heights as well as horizontal distances. Contours were interpolated by hand from the recorded heights.

The area planned (fig. 5) covers c.2.33 hectares, comprising a maximum range of 22 terraces and all or parts of five stone enclosures, four of them pit-enclosures. There is a total fall of 26m from SSW to north-east and the upper slope continues for a short distance to the top of the ridge to the west, with a higher rocky kopje at its northern end. There is a shoulder north of centre of the plan, on which is a rather incoherent enclosure (A) with a small sunken enclosure just to the south. The area immediately west of the enclosure is almost level. Elsewhere slope gradients vary: 15° below the shoulder to the north-east; an average of 11° up the excavated transect from terraces 5 to 11; and 5 to 9° up the southern edge of the plan.

Terraces were numbered upwards from the road, each terrace taken to comprise the wall of the riser and surface above. Walls are mostly a little over one metre in thickness, usually with a lip on the upper side of about 10 to 20cm, occasionally more or less (fig. 6). Width between front and back wall varies from 1 to 10m, commonly between 2 and 5m. Height varies with slope, from about 20cm to 1.50m. Wall-tops sometimes slope due to the collapse of stones from the upper part of the outside face. A walled passageway ascends across the south-west edge of the plan, serving two pit-enclosures (B and C) on its north-east side. A smaller stone-lined path or drain crosses this and descends through the terraces to the WNW; this must have been built before the terraces as the terrace alignments are discontinuous across it. There is a further pit-enclosure (D) 20m below the first two, the pit entrance being blocked at the mouth and both pit and enclosure entrance passages unlintelled. There is another pit-enclosure (E) at the north-west corner of the plan. Enclosure A on the shoulder has no pit and the walls form no regular plan. The atypical sunken enclosure to the south abuts the upper side of the wall of T12; it measures 3 by 3.50m inside and is sunk 80cm below the surface, with walls rising a further 50 to 90cm and a narrow entrance on the upper west side. The floor is on fractured bedrock, up to 40cm of which has been

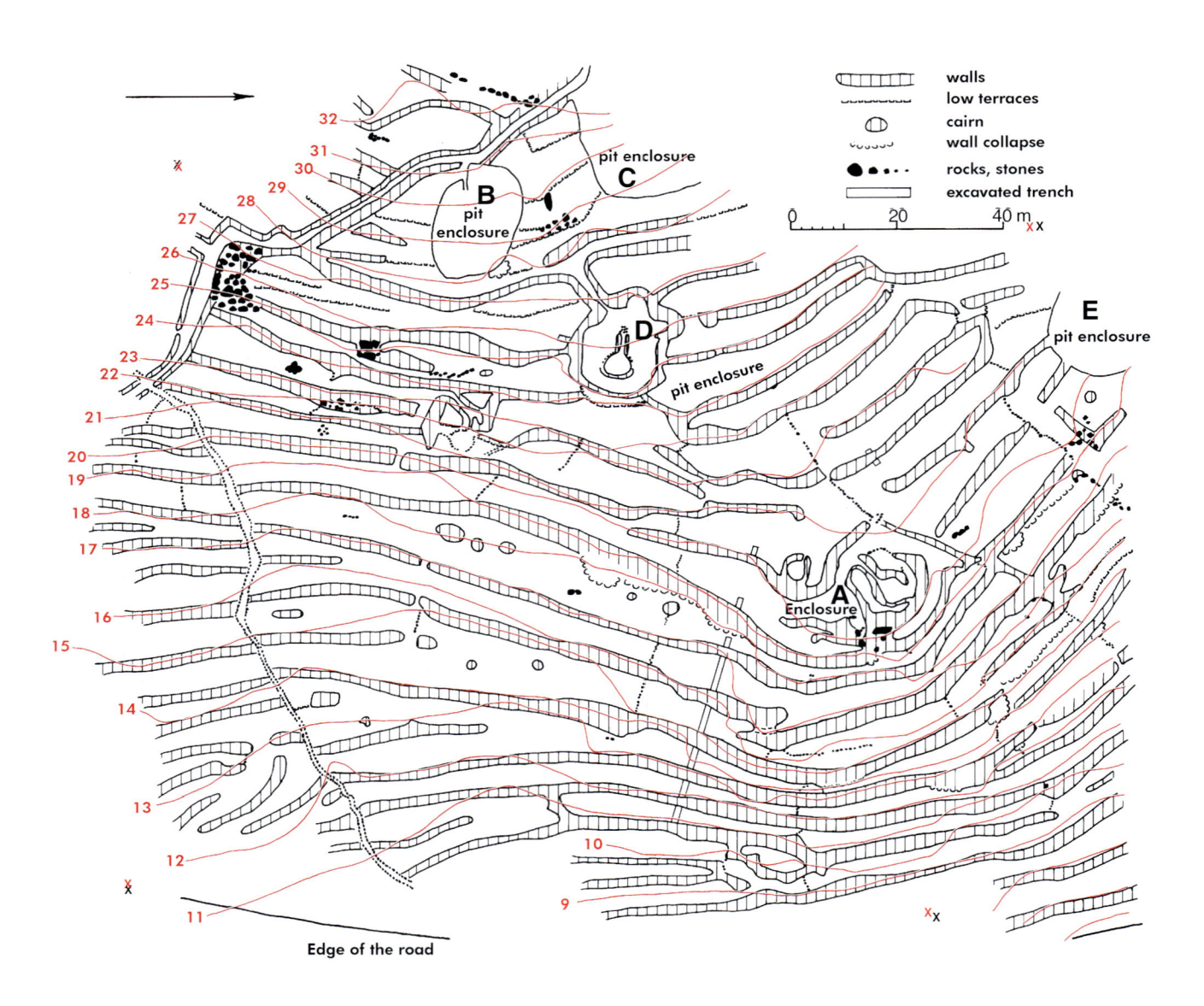

Fig. 5. Ziwa site SN113. Plan of terracing and enclosures. Vertical interval of contours is one metre

dug out on the west side to level it.

Lines of stones across terraces are frequent. A few of these may have been designed to check erosion where the terrace surface slopes laterally, but in a number of cases the lines cross several consecutive terraces and must mark boundaries (fig. 5). One such line parallels the excavated transect 12m to the south and defines the southern side of a roughly triangular area around the enclosure on the shoulder. The north-west side of this triangle is formed by further lines of stones and walls, the area thus enclosed being at least 0.275 hectares, depending on how far the divisions may have continued downslope. There seems to be a subdivision descending from the point of the shoulder. A second continuous line 40m long roughly parallels the north-west side of the triangle at a distance of 22 to 30m and may define space belonging to the north-western pit-enclosure. The area between the south side of the triangle and the path/drain may belong to the upper pit-enclosures and is about 0.8 hectares; a possible subdivision within it is marked by odd lines of stones and gaps in the walls.

The terrace transect (fig. 6)

A trench one metre wide was dug across all or parts of eight successive terraces, T5 to T12, and through the wall of T8. In addition one-metre squares were dug either side of the wall of T14, 13m north of the transect line.

T14 had only c.5cm of grey-brown gravelly soil on the upper side of the wall and up to 15cm of reddish brown loam on the lower side, over decomposing dolerite fragments. The wall is 40cm high on its upper side and 75cm on the lower.

Terraces 5 to 11 have widths between walls of 3.20, 2.0, 3.50, 5.40, 6.0, 4.40 and 8.0m respectively. Rises between surfaces are: T6 0.80m; T7 1.40m; T8 1.50m; T9 1.15m; T10 0.85m; and T11 1.50m. Surface gradients are: 0° for T6, 0.5° for T8 and T9; 2° for T5, 7, 10 and 12; and 3° for T11.

It is not clear how much soil may have been lost through erosion. Surfaces mostly look to have suffered some sheet erosion, with topsoil remaining only on T12 and part of T11, and rather thicker humus on T5 and 6 where there is tree growth on the walls. Terrace walls are generally 10 to 20cm high at the lower edge of the terrace surface, with the exception of T8 which is flush and T10 which is here 65cm. Probably relatively little soil has been lost at the lower side but the surface gradient may originally have been steeper, with greater soil loss from the upper side. Certainly some has been washed into the interstices of the walls as shown in the wall of T8.

Soils are generally shallow and profiles more or less similar throughout. Around 10cm of brown to dark brown slightly gravelly sandy loam grades into reddish-brown sandy loam also slightly gravelly. The gravelly elements consist of small fragments of yellow decomposing dolerite. The undisturbed subsoil is a dense accumulation of dolerite stones with yellow altered surface in a matrix of red clay-loam, with occasional fractured bedrock beneath sometimes rising to the surface, as in T7 and T11 (Plate 3). The sections in Figure 6 show that excavation has penetrated into the subsoil in T6, 7, 8 and 9.

Soil depths are uneven, depending on the configuration of the subsoil. They are deeper towards the lower side of the terrace, thinning towards the upper side. Maximum and minimum depths were: T5 25/15cm; T6 40/20cm; T7 30/0cm, T8 28/4cm; T9 30/12cm; T10 30/12cm; T11 25/0cm; T12 55/?cm. Terrace 12 is anomalous, having a few potsherds throughout, presumably derived from the adjacent enclosure, and 10cm of grey-brown topsoil; the unusual depth of 55cm at the lower wall face thins to 22cm at the other end of the 2m trench with the rising subsoil, here with a purplish brown matrix.

There were no surviving traces of any ridging or mounding which might have increased soil depth for cultivation.

The wall of T8 which was sectioned is 2.40m thick at this point, double the normal size. The lower face was built on the natural subsoil and had collapsed on the southern side of the trench, only two courses remaining at the base. On the northern side of the trench, the large stones of the face, 85cm high, had subsided outwards leaving a space behind filled with loose grey humus. The core of the wall consisted of stones of varying size from quite large to very small, in a matrix of loose brown loam which must have filtered in among them. As the stones were removed, a second vertical face emerged on the southern side of the trench but did not show clearly in the north section. This face is 1.20m behind the outer face and indicates that the original intention was to build a wall of standard thickness. This face also rests on the stony subsoil but at a level about 60cm above the surface of T7. This sloping subsoil would have been exposed before the thickening of the wall but this probably took place immediately, perhaps even before the completion of the original wall.

The upper wall face is only two or three courses high and seems to have been built on the original ground surface since a wedge of red-brown matrix with fewer stones passes beneath it.

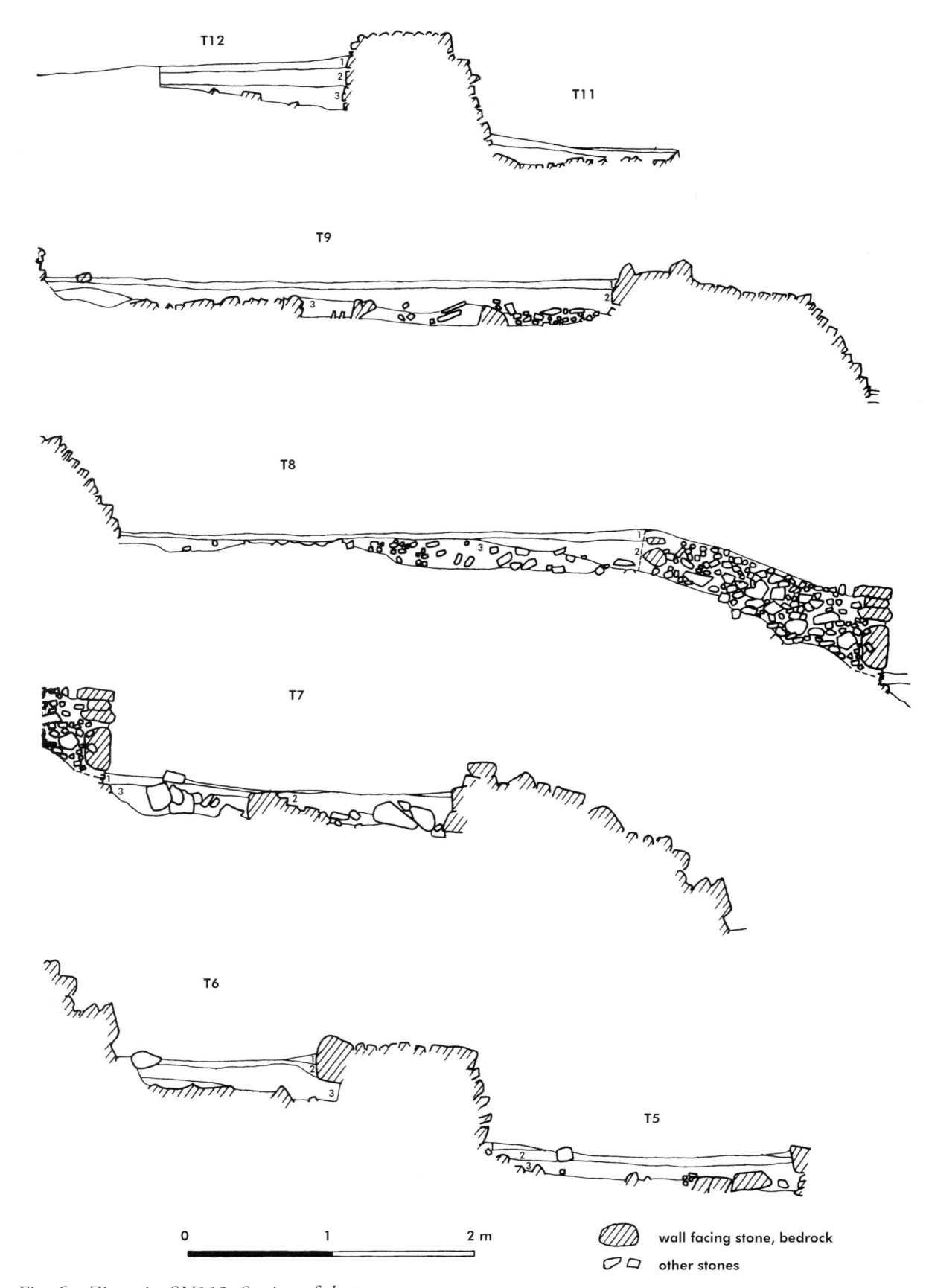

Fig. 6. Ziwa site SN113. Section of the terrace transect

Evidently the slope was cut back for each terrace and the stones removed, the larger ones for the wall faces and the smaller ones for the fill. The surface beneath the wall was left sloping and the soil salvaged before construction.

Comments on soil analyses (by K.Verbeek)
The area has relatively low rainfall (average around 800mm per annum) and soils are expected to have undergone only moderate weathering and leaching, with high CEC clay (E/C) values, pH and base saturation. Samples were analysed from T6 (Appendix A) and T12.

T6: Texture: Sandy loam to sandy clay-loam, clay increasing with depth to a maximum of 21%. Sand fraction distribution seems to indicate uniform parent material for the three horizons but there is an important coarse sand fraction. The parent material is therefore either slightly weathered or has a different origin and has been transported on top of the dolerite.

Weathering: slight weathering because E/C value (CEC clay) indicates montmorillonite. This seems inconsistent with the very high free Fe (12-14%), but this is plausibly due to parent material very rich in iron (there is surface concentration of magnetite sand at Ziwa Site Museum not far away).

Fertility: pH and % base saturation are optimum for plant growth, but there is a total absence of exchangeable potassium (optimum value > 0.2 meq%). Organic carbon % is high throughout and consistent with the fallow period.

T12: Very similar to T6 in all aspects with a few exceptions. Texture: maximum 26% clay at base of profile. Weathering: E/C values (CEC clay) decrease with depth indicating a more weathered clay which is inconsistent with soil formation; laboratory errors might be the cause. Fertility: exchangeable potassium is very low (below 0.07 meq %), except for the topsoil in correlation with the high organic carbon content.

Ziwa Mujinga
Mujinga is a large hill situated some 1500m north-west of the Ziwa Site Museum. It is mainly of granite, with some overlying dolerite; much of its slopes are terraced, with the exception of its northern and eastern sides. At the southern end of its fairly level crest is a small kopje on which is a fort (site 1832BA25, fig. 39). From the steep slope below the fort a long gentle spur descends to the south with a small narrow valley on its western side. This spur is all of granite and most of it is terraced, with a series of stone enclosures down its crest.

Two points were selected for excavation near the head of the small valley. Area A at grid reference VQ603955 (fig. 42, no.13) is a series of four substantial terraces on the eastern side of the valley above the stream bed. Area B is 75m to the east on the gentle western slope of the ridge top. A is wooded, mostly with *msasa* trees with a little grass and undergrowth; B is more open with only scattered trees. There is a stone enclosure a few metres south-east of B (fig. 35). The site as a whole is c.1200m north-west of SN113.

At Area A (fig. 7) a transect was excavated through the four terraces (numbered from the top) and through the wall of T1 (Plate 4). The general slope gradient is 12°, steepening to 14° towards the lower end of the transect. The existing surface gradients of the terraces are: T1 2.3°; T2 2.6°; T3 5.2°; T4 4.5°, and lateral inclination varies from level to 2°. Terrace widths between the walls are 3.0m, 3.50m, 6.80m and 3.50m for T1 to 4 respectively, and wall widths are 1.20m, 1.60m and 2.70m for T1 to 3, the outer face of T4 having collapsed into the stream if it ever existed. Falls between surfaces are 0.75m for T1; 1.10m for T2 and 1.30m for T3. Terrace surfaces are generally flush with the tops of the walls.

Stratigraphy is similar for all terraces: 1 - grey-brown sandy humic topsoil 5 to 10cm thick. 2 - light brown sandy loam with some gravel elements up to two or three centimetres in size, becoming more stony with depth (2a). The subsoil is red grit (3) from decomposed granite with some rotted granite in places. Total soil depth increases from the upper to the lower side over the sloping subsoil and maximum and minimum depths are: T1 15/52cm; T2 14/66cm; T3 12/76cm and T4 15/54cm. Depth is thus considerably greater than at SN113, although the sandy granite soil must be of lesser inherent fertility.

The average gradient of the subsoil is 8.5° for T1, 10.5° for T2 and 3 and 14° for T4, while beneath the wall of T1 it is around 17°, showing that the terraces were cut back into the slope to some extent during construction.

The faces of the wall of T1 include some large stones, up to 65 x 53 x 25cm in the upper face and 74 x 55 x 25cm in the lower face. The long axis of some stones is parallel to the wall face but others are laid into the wall giving good stability. The core of the wall has much small rubble but also larger stones up to 30cm, thrown in at random. There is a loose matrix of fine brown loam which has silted right down to the base, with some humus in the upper 15cm.

Construction is thus very similar to the

dolerite terraces of SN113. The original surface must have been rocky with some sizeable stones but a reasonable depth of sandy soil. Loose stones would have been used to start the lowest wall and then the soil scraped down behind, removing contained stones to build the wall faces and core. The decomposed subsoil must have been partially cut back to the line of the future upper wall and mixed with the soil. The soil was also removed from the new wall site the upper side flush with the surface or up to 10cm high.

The stratigraphy is similar to Area A but shallow: sandy grey-brown topsoil with some gravel over light brown sandy loam with gravel. The subsoil is again red grit or rotted granite. Soil depths are: T1 25/8; T2 35/6; T3 34/12. The average slope of the subsoil is slightly less than the general gradient, showing some cutting back.

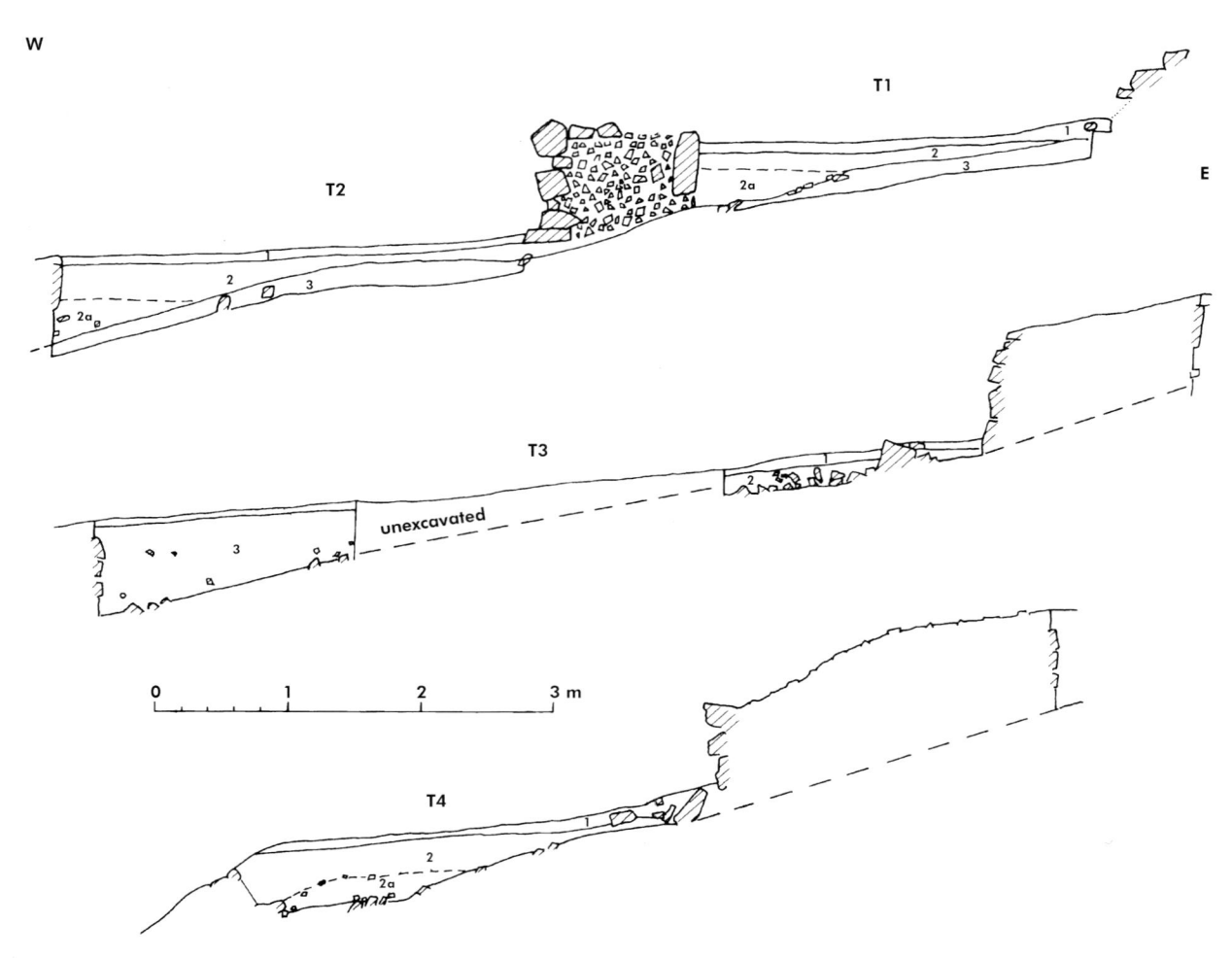

Fig. 7. Ziwa Ruins, Mujinga A. Section of terrace transect

down to the subsoil, on which the new wall was built.

Area B was a transect of three terraces (fig. 8). Seventeen metres and two further terraces northeast of T1 is the low wall of a "simple" stone enclosure described in Chapter 5 (fig. 35). The general slope here is only around 5° and the terrace surface profiles are more or less level, with lateral slopes of 1 to 2°. Terrace widths are: T1 (upper) 5.20m; T2 3.60m; T3 2.40m. Falls between surfaces are: T1 34cm; T2 54cm; T3 20cm. Walls are low and poorly preserved,

Comments on soil analyses (by K.Verbeek)
Samples were analysed from Area A T2, 3 and 4 and the wall matrix, and from Area B T3. Full results for A T2 are given in Appendix A.
Texture: coarse loamy sand to coarse sandy loam, with marginal clay increase with depth. Sand fraction distribution seems to indicate uniform parent material for all horizons in all terraces.
Weathering: E/C values (CEC clay) are relatively high indicating moderate weathering and a mixed clay

mineralogy. However in soils with low clay content E/C values are relatively meaningless as they are prone to large errors. Free Fe content is low as expected for granitic soils.

Fertility: pH and base saturation are not limiting for plant growth. Exchangeable K is good in AT2 but very low in AT3, AT4 and BT3 (below 0.07 meq %) except for the topsoils. This is difficult to explain because normally the opposite trend is

Site Museum (fig. 9). The slope extends from a valley bottom to the crest of the hill on which there is an enclosure. There are 25 terraces with a vertical range of 34m in a horizontal distance of 93m. The lower terraces are on granite, grading through mixed rock to the overlying dolerite on the upper slope. Terrace surfaces become increasingly inclined on the dolerite towards the top, but much of this is due to more collapse of the risers as the slope steepens from around

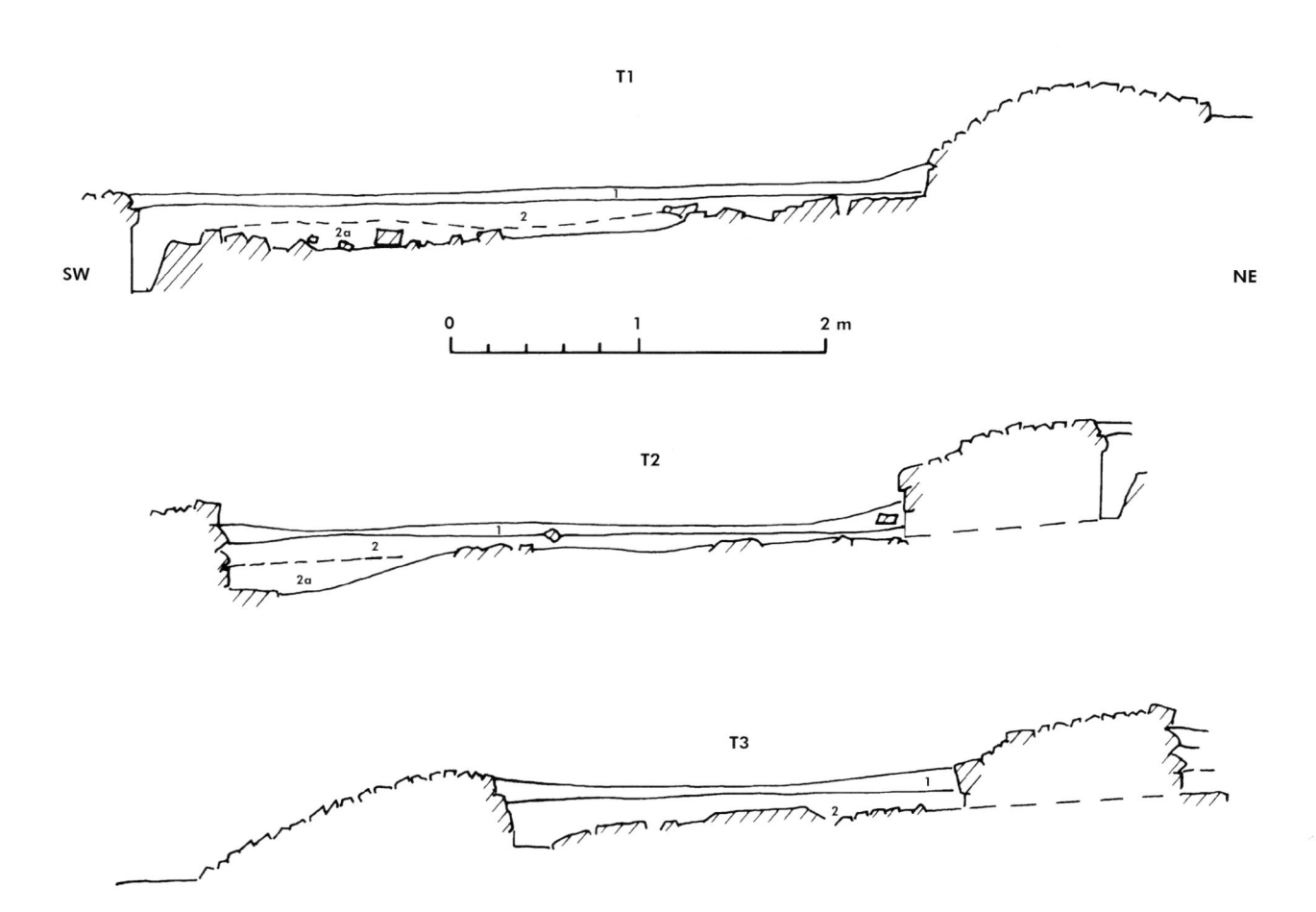

Fig. 8. Ziwa Ruins, Mujinga B. Section of terrace transect

expected through leaching and accumulation. Also in Zimbabwe granitic soils normally have a relatively high K content because of the high K-feldspar content. Organic carbon content is high for the topsoil on all terraces.

The wall matrix samples are consistent with those from the terraces.

* * *

In addition to the two sample areas excavated at Ziwa, a profile was measured of a fairly typical terraced slope about one kilometre north-east of the

15 to 25 degrees.

Terraces near Maristvale

Maristvale and Nyanga High School lie some 40km north of Nyanga town along the Nyanga North road below the western foot of the escarpment of the Nyanga highlands. Here two major peaks project like peninsulas from the main escarpment enclosing a deep embayment some 3.5km wide and 2.5km deep. The country rises from an altitude of around 1200m along the main road to 1350m at Maristvale on the foothills. Thence the land in the embayment

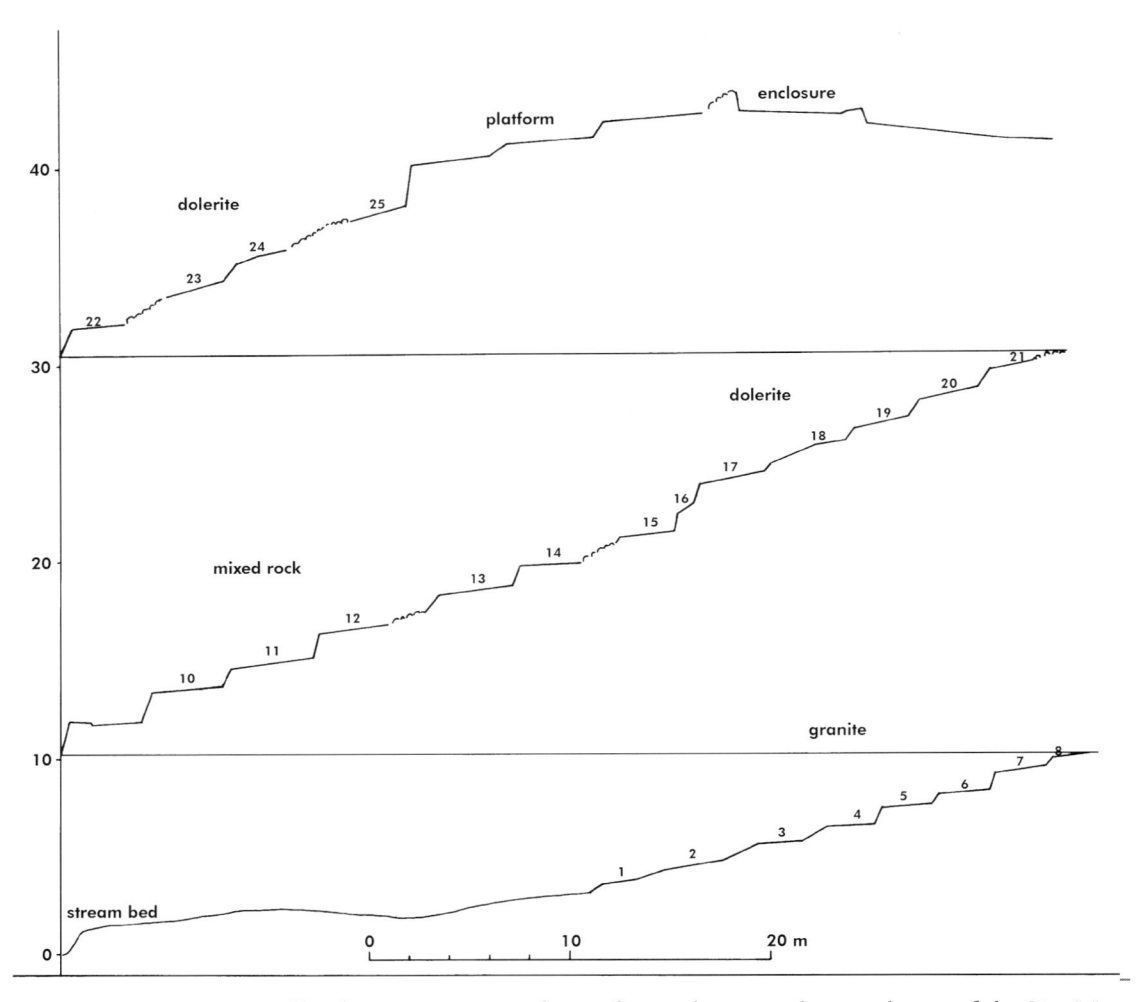

Fig. 9. Ziwa Ruins. Profile of terraces on a north-east facing slope, c. 1 km north-east of the Site Museum, grid reference VQ622958

rises relatively gently to 1600m and then steeply, often precipitously, to the peaks and plateau at over 2000m, the northern peak of Mt Muozi being about 2100m. To the west of the main road is a series of lower kopjes.

Geologically the underlying rock is granite but the peaks and highlands are formed by overlying strata of dolerite, calc-hornfels and felspathic sandstone (Stocklmayer 1978). Dolerite sills form the foothills on which Maristvale stands and kopjes west of the main road. Within the embayment is a further dolerite sill and a more extensive scatter of residual dolerite rocks with some sandstone, and occasional small kopjes and large boulders of granite.

A number of permanent streams descend the escarpment converging on the Pendeke and Nyahuku rivers, tributaries of the Nyajezi. Much of the area of the piedmont slope within the embayment is open grassland with scattered bushes and clumps of trees on rock outcrops. Denser *msasa* (*Brachystegia spiciformis*) woodland occurs towards the northern side in a system of steep rocky valleys, while there is also denser vegetation along the streams. Perched vleis have formed in areas of impeded drainage.

The visible archaeological features within the embayment comprise extensive terracing, pit-structures, small stone enclosures and walled pathways, with cultivation ridges in the vleis. Pit-structures are quite common down to 1400m and represent the homesteads of the previous inhabitants; below this level they are replaced by various types of stone enclosures among which are a few "forts" (Chirawu 1999).

The site here described (fig.10) lies 1.75km east and slightly south of Nyanga High School and Maristvale Mission, at 1440m above sea level (site number 1732DD34, grid reference VR 744134; fig. 42, no.14). Here a vlei has formed in a shallow valley which is partly blocked by a large granite outcrop; the whole of this vlei has been worked into cultivation ridges and ditches as described in the next section of this chapter. At the north end of the vlei and immediately adjacent is a set of terraces on a south-west trending slope with a gradient of 8 to 10°. There are about 30 more or less regular terrace walls in a distance of 90m (Plate 5), with less regular terracing continuing above for about 30m as the slope levels out. There are more terraces across a shallow reentrant to the south-east on the east side of the vlei.

In the main set of terraces (fig. 10), the terrace surfaces are generally narrow, often less than 2m, and slope laterally to the south-east at an average gradient of around 5°, there being occasional cross barriers of lines of stones, presumably to check erosion. Terrace walls are substantial, usually over a metre thick and sometimes up to two metres. They stand commonly up to 60 to 80cm above the terrace surface on the upper side and it is clear that their main function was to dispose of stones, leaving soil for cultivation. Wall faces are built of larger stones up to around 40cm in maximum dimension and the fill consists of smaller stones down to only a few centimetres in size. Stone shapes are very irregular and considerable skill has been exhibited in fitting them securely together. There appears to be little solid bedrock in the area, the nearest being the granite outcrop at the mouth of the vlei 125m to the south. The bulk of the stone is dolerite, ranging from small fragments to massive immovable boulders, but there are occasional granite boulders and a general scatter of pieces of light grey silicified sandstone many of which had been flaked in antiquity. These include massive cores and flakes of different sizes, and the presence of occasional rough bifaces and cleavers in the general area indicate an Early Stone Age date, though Middle Stone Age material is also present. The exposed dolerite is in irregular subangular weathered pieces with a dark grey-brown patina, but below ground they have a more or less deeply altered yellow surface; many of the small stones of the wall fill preserve this yellow patina. The sandstone is largely fresh and unaltered even when buried, apart from a thin patina.

The terraces are somewhat unusual in that the walls are pierced by numerous drains, either

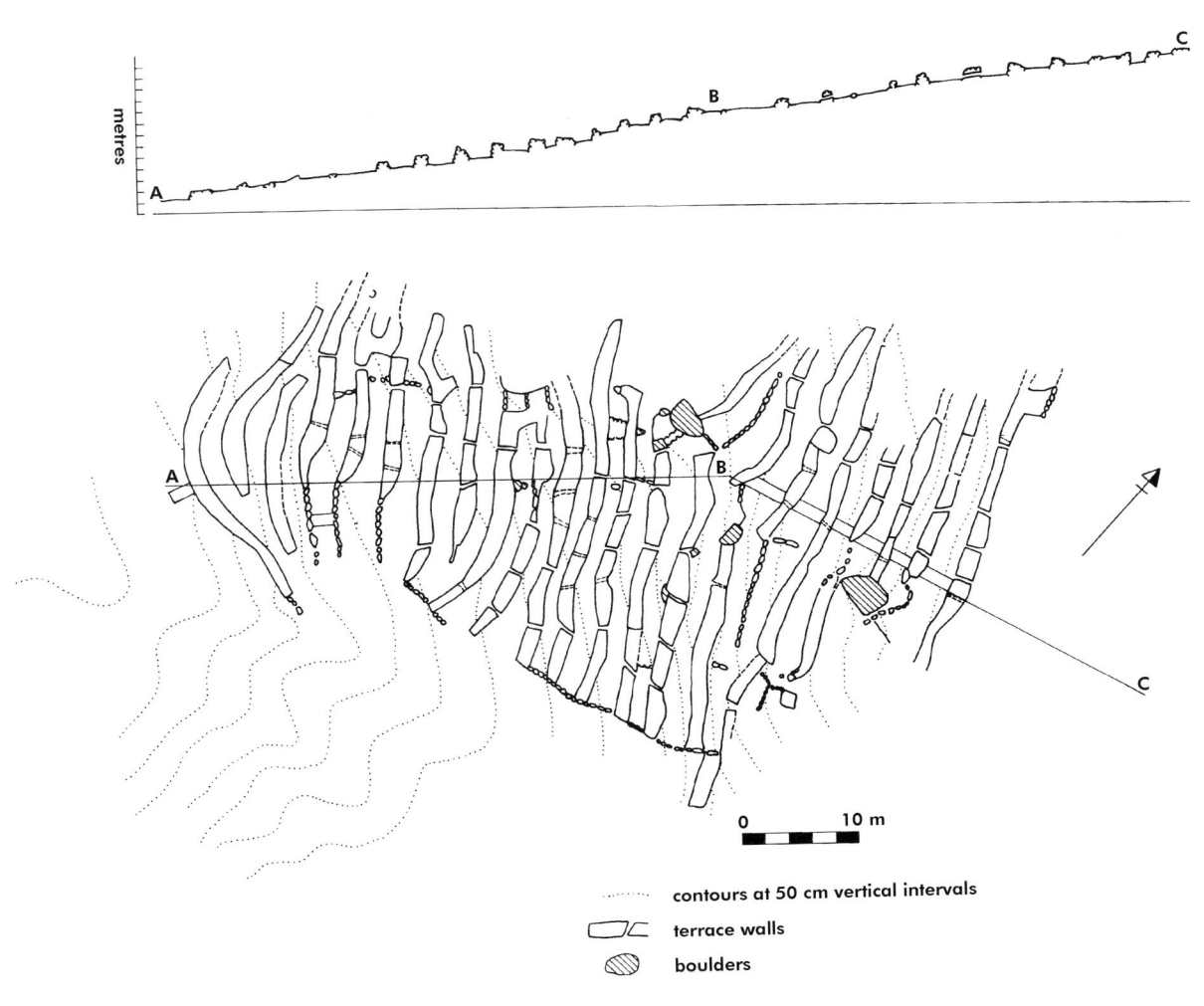

Fig. 10. Maristvale. Plan and profile of terraces with drains at grid reference VR744133

covered holes around 20cm square or simple gaps in the wall of about the same width. Some walls have drains spaced fairly regularly at around 3m intervals, while the distribution of others is less regular and was doubtless controlled by the immediate topography and the presence of immovable rocks. Some drains may have collapsed, while in other cases low walls may have made them unnecessary. While such drains do occur sporadically elsewhere, it is unusual to find so many and it is conceivable that they were to do with irrigation. The site was thus considered of special significance. Part of the terraced area was planned, together with the ridges in the adjacent area of vlei, and sections were excavated across some of the terraces and ridges to study their construction and soil profiles.

A series of six consecutive terraces (T16 to 21) and one of the intervening walls (T17) were sectioned by a one metre wide trench on the upper part of the slope, together with one terrace near the bottom and a trench below the lowest wall. A test pit was also attempted in a small unterraced stony area further up the slope to get an undisturbed profile, but the lack of terracing was quickly explained by the exiguous amounts of soil between the stones.

The terraces were numbered in sequence from the base of the series, each terrace being taken to consist of the wall and terrace surface above.

The stratigraphy was broadly consistent in all cases (fig. 11) except below the bottom wall where there was little soil:

1. Grey-brown humus topsoil at the upper east side of the terrace, wedging out to the west. Probably deposited or formed since abandonment.
2a. Grey-brown clay-loam with a few small stones <3cm in size
2b. Brown to red-brown clay-loam with few small stones, becoming redder and more clayey with depth in the deeper sections, e.g. T18, 20 and 21.

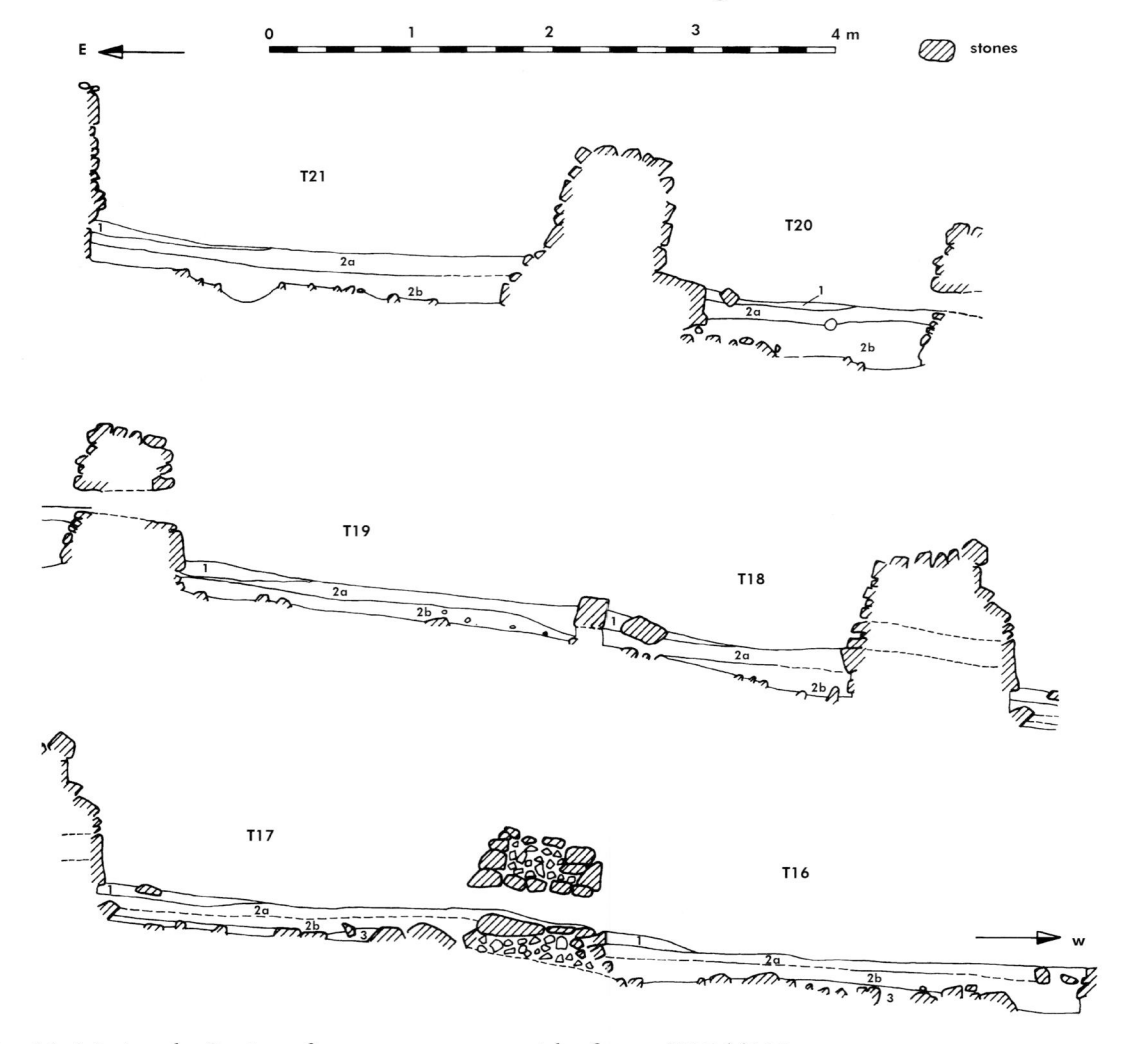

Fig. 11. Maristvale. Section of terrace transect at grid reference VR744133

3. More or less continuous spread of dolerite stones with yellow altered surface in red clay matrix. Undisturbed.

No vertical interfaces were observable to indicate foundation trenches for the walls, and it appears as if the soil was deposited against the wall faces after their construction.

Soil depth against the lower wall of the terraces ranges from 29 to 44cm with an average of 33cm and in most cases could hardly have been deeper, being graded to the drains. Against the upper wall depths range from 20 to 34cm with an average of 28cm, but 6 to 10cm of this is topsoil which is likely to have accumulated since abandonment; if this is excluded, the range is 12 to 26cm with an average of 19cm. As postulated below, soil depth may originally have been more even, with a sloping surface gradient which could have been levelled by erosion from the upper side.

The undisturbed surface of layer 3 preserved a fairly even slope and the terrace walls were built directly on this, except for the T19 wall. This wall is low at this point and consists of little more than a double line of boulders which appear to rest within the clay loam of 2a; this is likely to be a subdivision subsequent to the main construction, though the wall becomes more substantial and typical to the north.

A section was cut, or rather dismantled, through the wall and drain of T17. Before commencement of this work the facing stones on both sides were numbered and sketched, and the wall was rebuilt to its original state after completion. The facing stones were relatively large, up to c.40cm in maximum dimension, while the core fill stones were smaller, up to around 15cm but mostly smaller, down to only a few centimetres. There was a very loose fine light brown matrix between the fill stones of the upper part of the wall, becoming firmer and filling most of the interstices below the level of the upper terrace surface. The upper matrix was probably wind-deposited and the lower silted in. There appeared to be a thin lens of brown clay-loam between the basal wall stones and the undisturbed surface of layer 3 below.

The base of the drain was formed by one large and two smaller slabs. The sides were rather loosely built of smallish stones and the roof consisted of five parallel stones, 30 to 35cm long.

In at least one case, the upper face of T20 wall, the facing stones below ground level had a deeply altered yellow patina. This may have formed *in situ* since construction, but it seems more likely that these stones had come from original subsurface contexts.

A hypothetical sequence of construction fitting the observed data could have been as follows (fig. 12):
1. Virgin slope with loose surface stones weathered but unaltered; patinated subsurface stones in clayey loam matrix becoming stonier with depth.
2. Burn (?) the vegetation and cut the trees for timber/firewood.
3. Work along the base of the slope, cutting a step c.1.20m wide as deep as practicable. Turn the soil down slope and use the surface and subsurface stones to build the foundation of wall

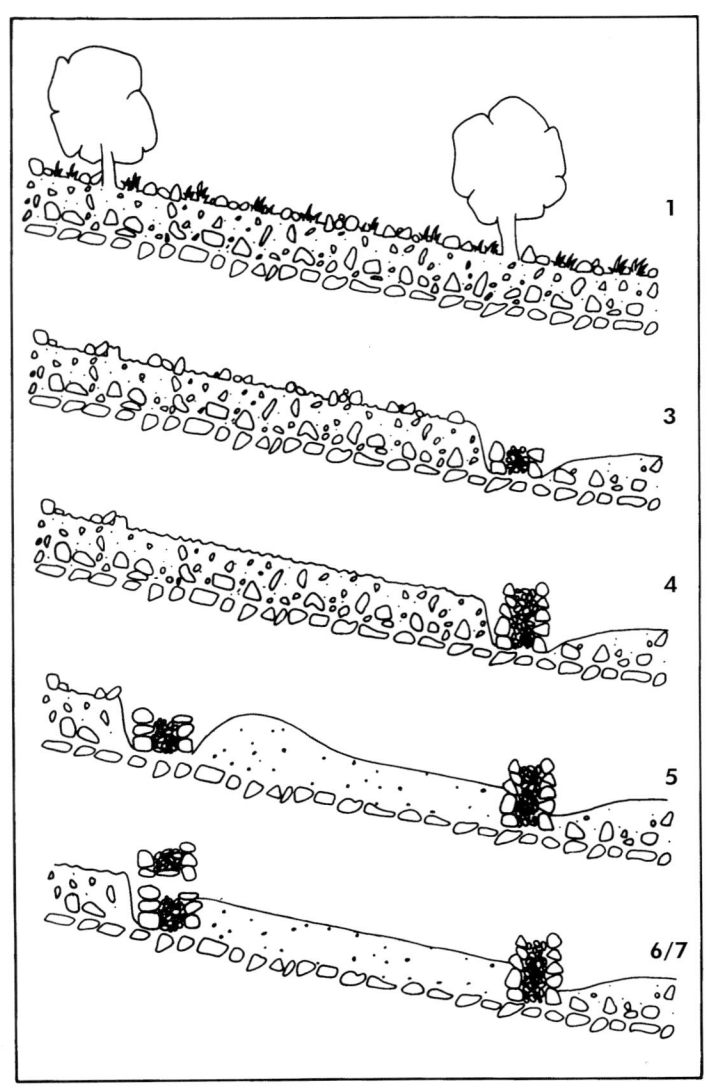

Fig. 12. Hypothetical sequence of terrace construction at Maristvale

1 behind the advancing front.
4. Clear the stones from the surface to above the future line of wall 2 and use them to build the upper part of wall 1.
5. Work along the cleared strip, extracting the subsurface stones and turning back the soil behind. Leave a bare strip of subsoil for the site of wall 2, piling the soil from here just below. Use the larger subsurface stones for the foundation of wall 2 on the bare strip; take the smaller stones to the fill of either wall.
6. Clear the surface stones from a parallel strip to above the line of wall 3 and use them to build the upper part of wall 2, putting in covered drains or leaving drainage gaps.
7. Smooth back the piled soil against the lower face of wall 2. The terrace soil is now almost stoneless with relatively even depth and a sloping surface.

Repeat 5, 6 and 7 *ad infinitum*.

Perhaps during use and certainly after abandonment, the upper part of the terrace surfaces erodes to more or less horizontal, the lower edge remaining graded to the level of the drains.

Comments on soil analyses (by K.Verbeek)
The site is higher in altitude than Ziwa, with a somewhat wetter rainfall regime so that more weathered soils are expected with higher clay content, lower CEC clay values, lower base status and pH, and higher content of iron oxides. Samples from T20 and the wall matrix of T17 were analysed, the wall samples being consistent with those from the terrace.

T20 (Appendix A): Texture: Sandy loam to clay, clay content increasing with depth to a maximum of 47% for the unworked subsoil. Sand fraction distribution shows a much lower fine and medium sand content in the subsoil layer 3 than in the upper layers, suggesting a difference in the parent material with some transportation of the upper deposits. The clay content at the base is also higher in line with *in situ* soil formation. The coarse sand fraction is much lower than at Ziwa SN113 which could be explained by more weathering.

Weathering: Moderate to well weathered soil expressed by a lower E/C value (CEC clay), indicating an illite clay mineralogy. This is inconsistent with the much lower free Fe (4-7%) than in Ziwa (12-14%). Also exchangeable calcium levels are much lower. A difference in dolerite mineralogy could be the reason.

Fertility: pH is below optimum for plant growth indicating a fair amount of leaching, also expressed by the % base saturation below 100%. Exchangeable potassium levels are higher than in Ziwa, moderate in the subsoil but high in the topsoil and 2a. Organic carbon % levels should be higher than in Ziwa because of a higher rainfall regime, but are in fact lower which might be explained by more recent abandonment.

Chirangeni
The Chirangeni area lies some 6km north-east of Nyautare business centre. North of Nyautare a range of relatively high hills extends westwards to the Nyangombe river, the altitude declining from nearly 1500m at Mica hill to around 1200m nearer the river. The southern part of this range consists of heavily terraced dolerite and the northern part of less terraced granite. The eastern end of the range is separated from the foot of the main highlands by a narrow valley in which the Hambuka stream flows northwards and a tributary of the Kumbu/Nyabomwe southwards, the watershed at 1260m being just north-east of Chirangeni hill itself. The geology here is largely granite, with a band of dolerite narrowing northwards on the east side of the valley, and localised occurrences of serpentine on the west.

From the valley the land rises eastwards, at first in spurs and plateaus and then in a steep escarpment to the distinctive flat-topped hill of Chipawe at 2000m. West of the valley a ridge declines northwards from Chirangeni hill, and a saddle separates this from Mica hill and the western range. A rough track from the main road at this saddle winds down into the Hambuka valley and across the low watershed.

The area was first visited in 1993 when a number of enclosures were recorded, and some planned, on the higher ground north of Chirangeni hill and on the plateau east of the valley. In 1996 an area of the eastern slope of the valley was selected for a detailed survey of terracing and enclosures (fig. 13), for comparison with Ziwa SN113. After the survey had been carried out, this very area was recognised as having been illustrated in Plate 2b of Summers (1958), an aerial photograph captioned "Typical area of Lowland Ruins" – a startling coincidence that we should have arrived by different routes at the same few hectares out of the vast area of lowland terracing. Finally in 1997 excavations were carried out in the main enclosure of the surveyed area (see Chapter 8), with some testing of the terraces.

Both sides of the north/south valley north of the watershed are heavily terraced (Plate 1), as is the dolerite area further south on the east side. The granite terraces tend to be relatively low and single-faced, but in the surveyed area, also in granite, many of them are more substantial.

The survey (fig. 13) was carried out over five days using a plane table and EDM alidade to plot both positions and heights. Contours were interpolated from spot heights. The area is east of the valley watershed and approximately 50 to 85m above it altitudinally, at grid reference VR 675344. It covers about 100m north/south by 125m east/west with a total fall of about 35m from ESE to WNW. Rocks are granite throughout and the soils are light coloured and sandy. The regularity of terracing is broken by local variations of slope and outcrops but a maximum range of about 50 terraces can be counted. On a slight shoulder is the large residential enclosure described in Chapter 8. A walled passageway crosses a reentrant from the north, curves up past the north-eastern side of the enclosure and continues east up the slope, subsequently curving back to the north-east to a small plateau above. Terraces abut the south side of the enclosure and both sides of the passageway and continue below the enclosure. In some areas, notably north-east and south-west of the enclosure, outcropping rocks confuse and interrupt the terracing and 10 to 15m south of the enclosure is a steep rocky unterraced slope. There is one small enclosure below the main enclosure c.15m north-west, and a couple of walled semicircular bays above to the east. Outside the enclosure entrance is a small level "forecourt".

There are no other residential enclosures on this spur, suggesting that it represents a single social unit, probably a relatively important one given the size and complexity of the enclosure. On a subsidiary spur across a fairly deep reentrant some 80m to the south-west, is a group of three small circular stone walls 1.5 to 3m in internal diameter which may represent a small unenclosed settlement. There are a number of enclosures down the next spur beyond the northern reentrant, one of them with a shallow pit with a sloping entrance passage (no tunnel). It may be suggested that the main drain in this reentrant forms a boundary; there are two cairns of truncated cone shape just south of the top of the main drain below the plateau rim which could also be boundary markers.

Terraces (Plate 6) broadly follow the contours but are not precisely levelled longitudinally. In profile most terrace surfaces are more or less horizontal. Fall between terraces varies with the slope from about 20cm to over 1m, heights of 50 to 70cm being common. Width between wall risers also varies from about 1 to 6m, the majority being between 2 and 3m. The edges of most terraces are more or less flush with the surface and revetments are probably single-faced with a thickness of perhaps 30 to 40cm. Some however are double-faced with upstanding walls up to a metre or so thick.

Stone-lined drains traverse the terraces following lines of natural drainage (Plate 7). These are generally around 40cm wide, normally lined with a single course of stones. They are not for irrigation or water spreading since the ends of most of the terraces are graded towards them; and not paths as there is a small culvert through the wall of the passage where the south-eastern branch of the main drain intersects it. They can only have served to drain excess run-off from rainfall, though a few terraces on the south side of the main drain do in fact slope away from it so that some of the run-off could have been directed along them. Terrace alignments are usually discontinuous across the drains and walled passage.

A section was dug across two terraces above the walled passageway (fig. 14). These terraces are 2.20 and 2.60m wide, separated by a double-faced wall flush with the upper terrace surface. A wider double-faced wall separates the lower terrace from the passageway and the upper wall is probably double-faced as well. The upper terrace shows grey sandy soil (1) over lighter grey-brown sandy soil (2), resting on more or less decomposed granite, with a depth of 25cm at the upper end and 45cm against the lower wall. The lower terrace has a similar section with the upper layer a finer grey-brown sandy soil and depths of 25 and 60cm at the upper and lower ends respectively. The base here is a hard gravelly subsoil with solid bedrock at the lower end against which the foundation of the passage wall may have been cut back.

A special structure is present in the north-west of the surveyed area in the angle of the main drain and walled passage. This is an area of about 20 by 18m almost surrounded by a relatively massive wall, with three broad terraces across it and a smaller terrace in a bay in the upper south-eastern corner. The terraces have partial or complete upstanding walls. There were a few sherds on the walls but no broken *dhaka* or signs of structures to suggest that it was residential. It seems best interpreted as a walled garden and a section excavated in the lower terrace (see below) supports this. The terraces slope towards the drain and water could not have been spread from it. There are at least two similar but smaller features at the same level on the next spur 100m or so to the north, with small house circles adjacent to them; some of these house circles have "cupboards" within the thickness of the wall, similar to those described in Chapter 8 in the enclosure in the surveyed area.

Two adjacent trenches 2.50 by 1.00m were dug against the wall at the lower edge of the bottom terrace of this walled garden (fig. 15). These showed

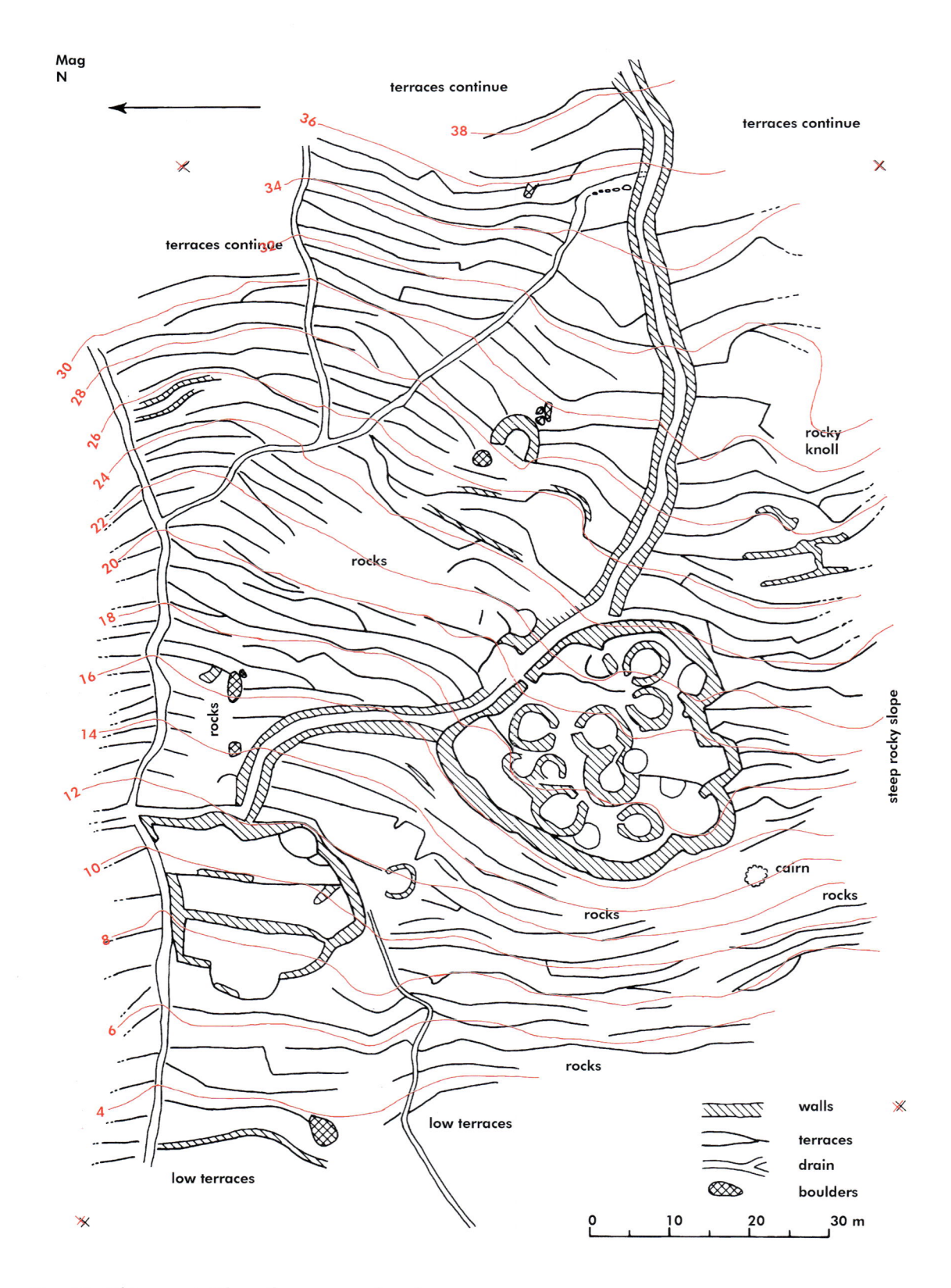

Fig. 13. Chirangeni. Plan of terraces and enclosure

two phases of terrace construction. Around 10cm of grey sandy topsoil (1) grades into a light grey-brown sandy gritty soil up to 30cm deep (2). This overlies a line of stones across the first trench representing

charcoal flecks in the absence of residential structures could indicate the use of domestic refuse for manure and could support the idea of a homestead garden, perhaps linked to the enclosure and distinct from

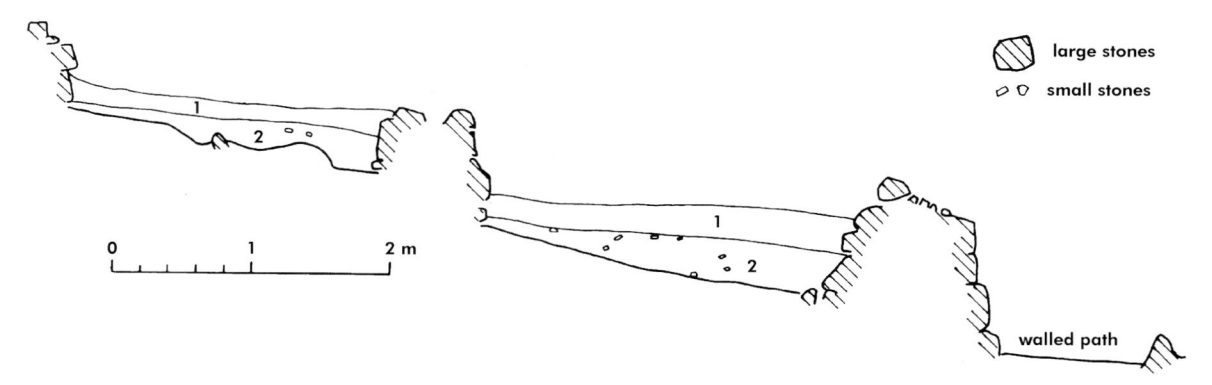

Fig. 14. Chirangeni. Section of terraces

an earlier terrace; behind these stones is up to 35cm of darker grey-brown sandy soil (4) containing a few small stones and charcoal flecks and a bone fragment. Between this earlier face and the later wall was lighter brown sandy soil (3). The apparent continuation of the earlier terrace in the second trench forms a rough diagonal wall leaving little deposit behind it within the trench. Small potsherds are scattered through all layers. The base is decomposed granite at the upper end grading to a hard gravelly subsoil which appears to have been hollowed out to the earlier terrace. There was thus a first single-faced terrace about 30cm high represented by the stones and layer 4. Subsequently the much larger double-faced wall was built below and filled with the lighter coloured sandy soil (2), the grey layer 1 having formed by soil formation since abandonment. The paucity of stones indicates that the soil was deliberately worked over to remove them, as suggested in the case of terraces at Ziwa and Maristvale. The presence of small sherds and

the open terraces. However the pottery, which is described and discussed under the enclosure site report in Chapter 8, is somewhat different from that of the enclosure and could come from an earlier site destroyed in building the terraces.

A charcoal sample was collected from the second trench at a depth of 40 to 55cm and should belong to the second terrace phase, though perhaps deriving from occupation associated with or antedating the first. It has been dated to 200 ± 50 BP, calibrated to anywhere between AD 1669 and 1878 (Appendix F: Pta-7601). The small fragments of which it is composed do not provide a very satisfactory sample and the wide range of calibration is also regrettable.

Chirimanyimo, Madziwa School
The aim here was to sample high-level terracing on dolerite. The area is on the eastern slope of the northern highlands, 4km north of Chirimanyimo

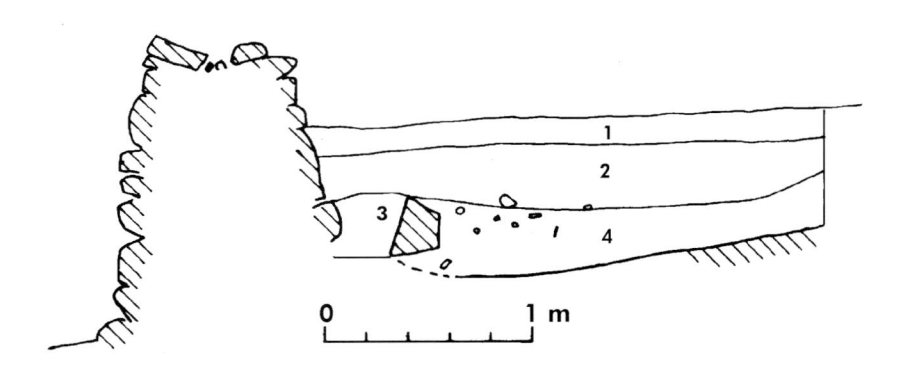

Fig. 15. Chirangeni. Section of terraces

hill and c.300m ENE of Madziwa Primary School, at grid reference VR763309 (fig. 42, no.15). It is at an altitude of 1760m, close to the upper limit of the terracing on the northern side of a spur running ENE. Above is a broad gently sloping shelf to the school, behind which the ground rises steeply to a plateau at around 1900m. Average annual rainfall here is probably around 1000mm. There are no obvious settlement sites in the immediate vicinity, the nearest pit-structure being c.300m to the south at a slightly higher elevation, with a split-level enclosure c.400m to the north at the foot of this range of terraces at 1700m. There are scattered protea bushes and clumps of small *msasa* trees near the site, with denser more mixed woodland towards the valley to the north.

Terracing here is quite variable. The excavation consisted of two parallel transects, A and B, 15m apart, each sectioning two terraces. There is some discontinuity of wall alignment between the transects. Here the tops of the riser walls are flush to the terrace surfaces, but shortly to the north the terraces are narrower with walls up to a metre high on the upper face and some outcropping boulders. Lines of stones across several successive terraces divide this area from the excavated transects. About 30m to the south, the walls are again more substantial, up to 1.50m thick and up to one metre high on the upper face, with a few cases of drains built through them. A profile of terraces 200m north of the excavated site is illustrated in Figure 16 and shows similar upstanding walls.

The general slope gradient at the excavated site is around 15° and heights of risers faces are 40 to 80cm. Transect A (fig. 17a) sectioned two terraces and the wall between them. Terrace widths between walls are 3.40m and 3.10m and surface gradients are 3 and 4°, banked up to 15° against the upper wall. Fall between them was 60cm before excavation.

The stratigraphy in both terraces showed: (1) reddish brown clay-loam 10 to 12cm thick, thicker against the upper wall, with a few plain potsherds;

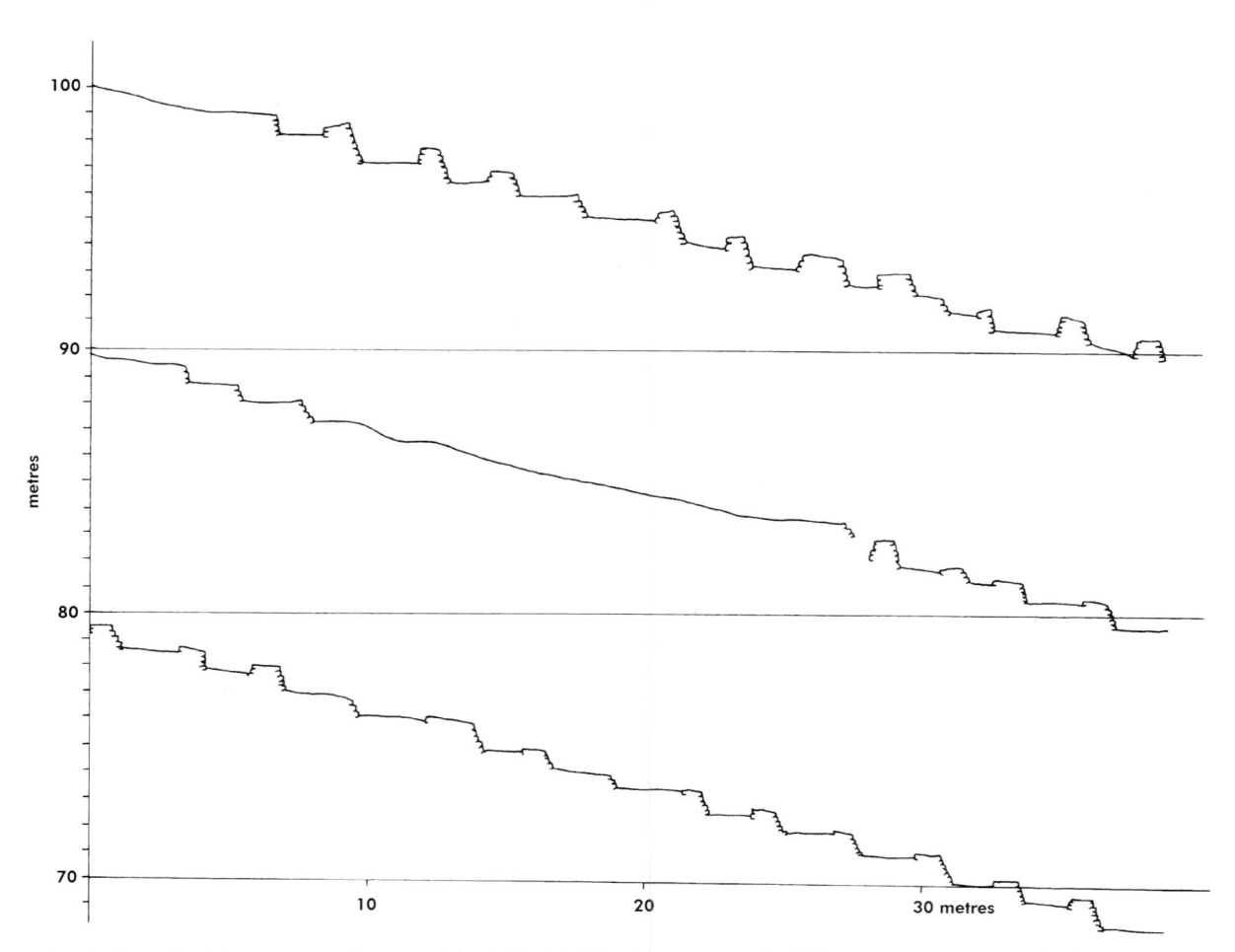

Fig. 16. Profile of terraces on the east side of the highland range north of Chirimanyimo at grid reference VR765310

(2) red-brown more clayey loam to 30 to 40cm below the surface, grading into (3), a similar matrix with more stones of yellow decomposing dolerite. This rests on (4), subsoil of dense similar stones in a red clay matrix. Layer 3, which is 15 to 20cm thick, passes beneath the walls but is not undisturbed subsoil as there are occasional small fragments of charcoal at the base. The gradient of 3 and 4 corresponds to the surface at around 15 degrees. Total soil depth, including layer 3, is 49 to 60cm in the upper terrace and 40 to 65cm in the lower.

The presence of the charcoal is unexplained and insufficient was recovered for dating. Layer 3 seems unlikely to have been worked over during terrace construction which thus did not reach the solid subsoil. The excavated wall has a good outer face of large stones but smaller stones are piled in behind it (2a), with only one or two courses of larger stones at the top. There is a fine brown earthy matrix between the wall stones, with signs of insect activity. The wall of the terrace below has only a single face, again with smaller stones piled behind. The clay-loam soil is quite cohesive but there has probably been some erosion from the lower side of the terraces and deposition at the upper side. The distinction between layers 1 and 2 would be due to root action and soil formation.

The terraces of transect B (fig. 17b) are narrower, 2m and 1.70m respectively, with a fall of 70cm and surface gradients of 0 to 15° and 1 to 4° on lower/upper sides. Stratigraphy is the same as in transect A, but in the upper terrace rests on large boulders with only a pocket of layer 3. Soil depth, including layer 3, is 2 to 40cm in the upper terrace and 35 to 60cm in the lower.

Comments on soil analyses (by K.Verbeek)
At this altitude and rainfall the real ortho-ferralitic soils are expected. Samples were analysed from terrace A T2 (Appendix A) and from beneath the wall, the latter consistent with the sample from layer 3.

Texture: clay as expected with high clay content increasing from 50% near the surface to 61% for the subsoil. The coarse sand fraction is much lower than in Maristvale and Ziwa and is consistent with

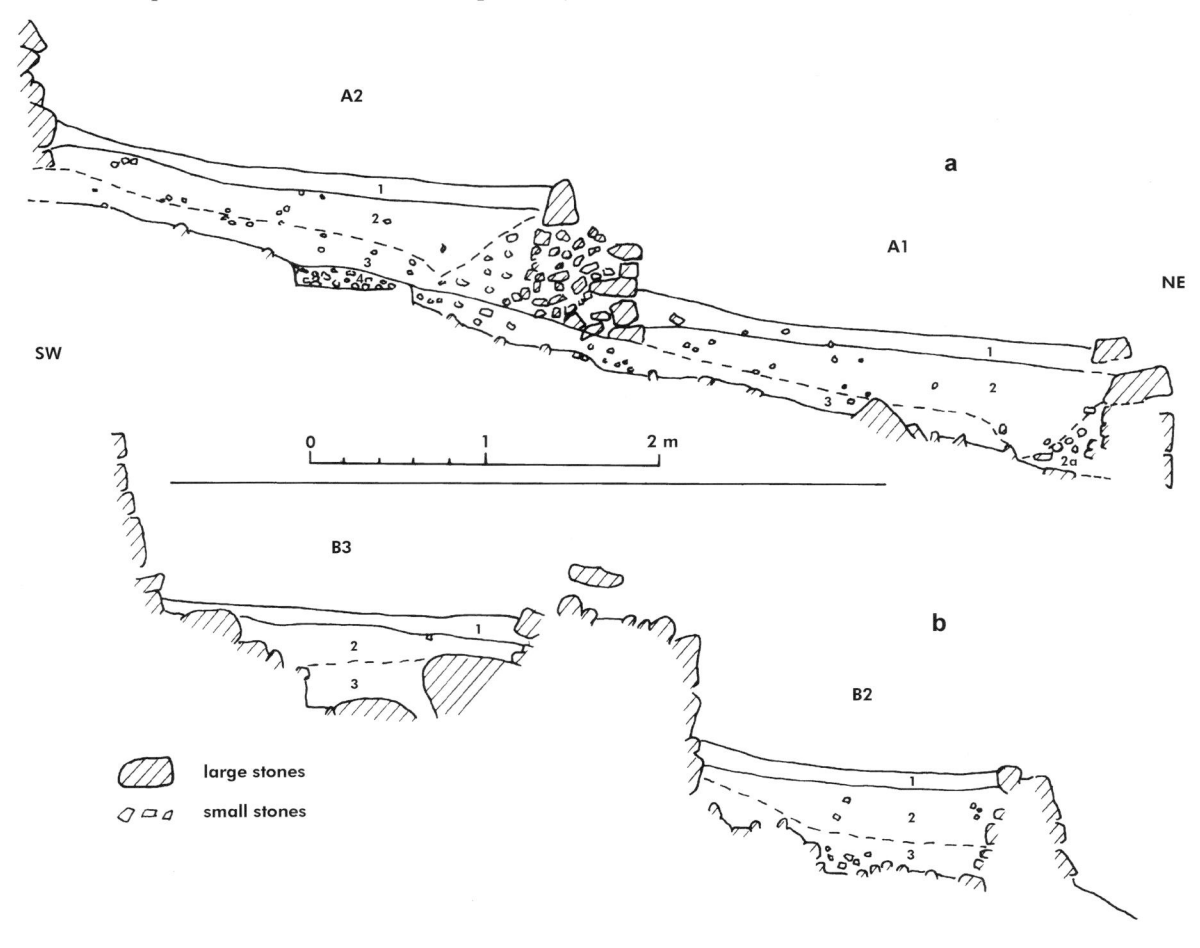

Fig. 17. Sections of terrace transects north of Chirimanyimo at grid reference VR763309

more weathering.

Weathering: deeply weathered ortho-ferralitic soil as expected, with a very low E/C value (CEC clay), indicating kaolinite clay. Free Fe (10 to 18%) is similar to Ziwa (12-14%), except for layer 4 which has very low content (5%) in total contradiction to the highly weathered state as seen by the E/C value of 6; a laboratory error is possible.

Fertility: pH and % base saturation are indicative of a leached soil as expected in this rainfall zone. They are low but not extremely so and not restrictive to plant growth; exchangeable potassium levels are in fact higher than in Ziwa. The high organic carbon % levels in the upper layers are in line with the higher rainfall regime, while those only slightly less high in the lower layers would support the interpretation of layer 3 as an old buried surface.

Elim Mission, Ruangwe

Elim Mission, near the northern limit of the main terrace distribution, lies at the foot of a steep escarpment which rises from 900m at the base to 1100m at the crest and is here broken by the Manjanja river. The scarp is in fact a sharp ridge formed by folded strata of calc-hornfels, argillite and dolerite with an almost vertical dip, and a tributary of the Manjanja runs parallel behind it. The investigated terraces are on the western reverse slope of the ridge just south of the Manjanja gap, at an altitude of 1040m at grid reference VR760532 (fig. 42, no.16). The scree rock here is argillite and calc-hornfels and the general slope gradient is 20 to 25°. Vegetation is fairly open woodland.

The transect (fig. 18) sectioned four terraces, numbered T2 to 5 from the top. Horizontal widths between risers are 1.60m, 2.20m, 3.20m and 1.70m respectively, with wall heights of 40 to 48cm. T4

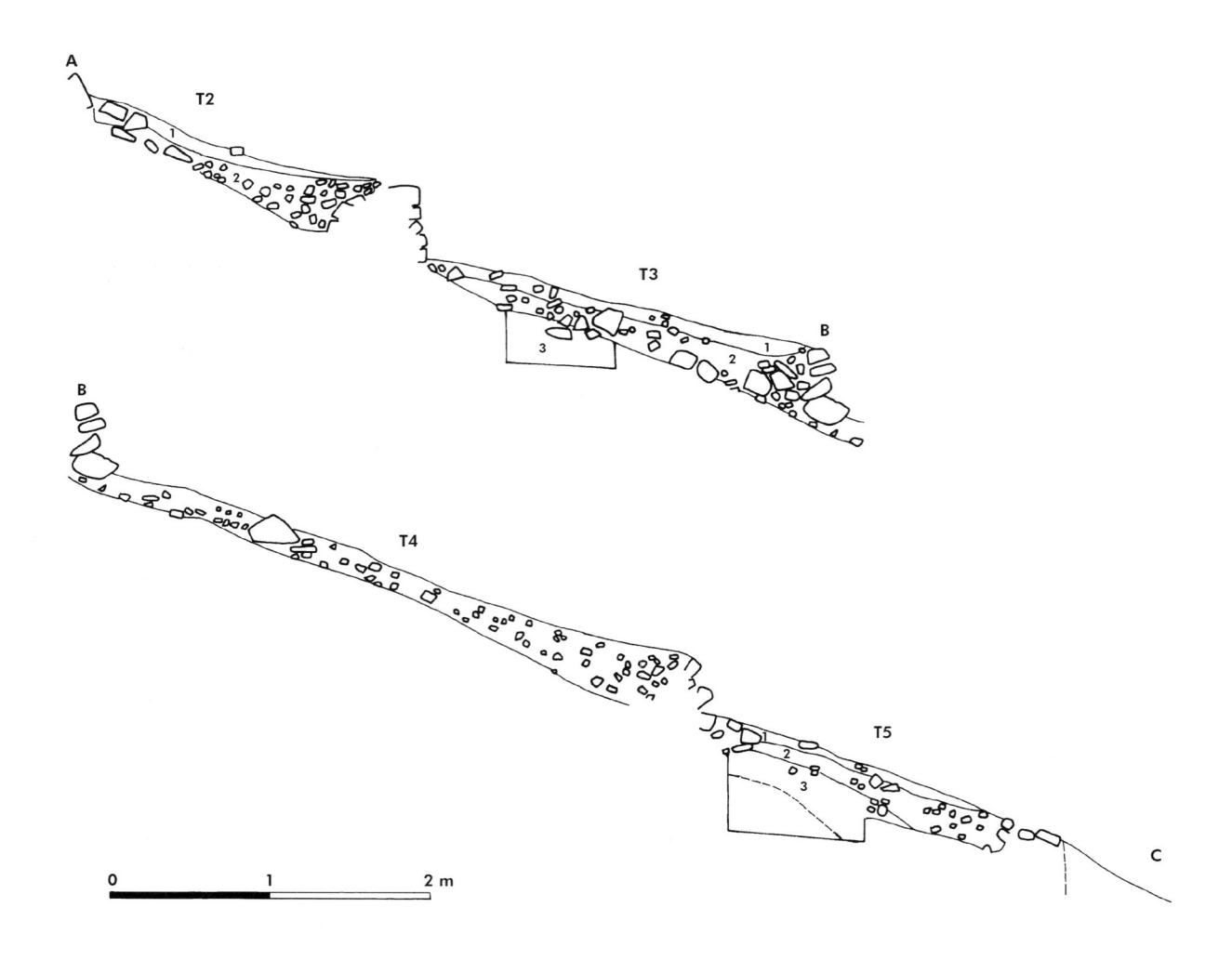

Fig. 18. Section of terrace transect above Elim Mission at grid reference VR760532

has traces of an intermediate terrace either side of the transect. Surface gradients are c.20°, 15°, 18° and 20°, so that only T3 has significantly modified the natural slope and even that remains steep.

The sections show 5 to 10cm of darkish brown loam (1) with numerous stones up to 10cm in size, over redder brown loam (2) tending to be very stony at the upper end and less so towards the lower end. This rests on a surface of yellow patinated stones in a cleaner red-brown gravelly matrix, forming a thin stone line on decomposed bedrock of red-brown clayey matrix with few stones (3). Total soil depths are: T2 8 to 30cm; T3 10 to 35cm; T4 15 to 40cm; and T5 12 to 30cm, but almost all are very stony.

Terrace walls are single-faced, irregularly built of largish stones up to 50 by 25cm, with smaller stones piled behind in a loose brown matrix. The procedure seems to have been to build a rough low wall with the larger surface stones, throw in the smaller stones behind, and scrape down the soil from above without much attention to removing the contained stones. Some soil has then filtered in among the smaller stones at the base. Erosion must have been considerable on the steep slope and some stones have probably been dislodged from the tops of the walls, so soils would have been somewhat deeper originally. Even so, conditions can hardly have been favourable for any sustained agriculture.

Comments on soil analyses (by K.Verbeek)
Located lower in altitude than Ziwa. Because of a different parent material, soils will be difficult to compare but the values of the key chemical properties may be expected to be similar to Ziwa. Analyses for T3 are given in Appendix A.

    Texture: Sandy loam to clay-loam, maximum 38% clay, with an abrupt clay increase between layer 2 and 3 (subsoil). This change is also visible in the sand fraction distribution and might indicate transport of the surface layers above the *in situ* third layer.

    Weathering: as in Ziwa, slight weathering with E/C value indicating montmorillonite and low free Fe%.

    Fertility: pH and % base saturation are optimum for plant growth with a high content of exchangeable potassium related to the different rock type. Organic carbon % is high in the topsoil and consistent with a fallow period.

DISCUSSION

Terraces in general are a response to the necessity or desire to cultivate steep slopes, either because the practitioners are constrained by political or environmental pressures or through a realisation that the young slope soils have greater inherent fertility than older more leached soils above or below. As argued in Chapter 6, the latter explanation seems more probable in the Nyanga case. Here stone clearance was an important, if not primary factor, since vast amounts of stones had to be cleared from and beneath the ground surface to provide enough soil for cultivation. The stones thus removed were often in excess of requirements for the terrace risers and in many cases entailed the building of upstanding walls. This is particularly noticeable in the vicinity of the Ziwa Site Museum, even where the vertical fall between terraces may be only of the order of a few centimetres.

The terrace soils are often seen to be shallow and it is unclear how far this is due to erosion during use and after abandonment. A soil crust has formed through raindrop action on almost all terraces; this has some stabilising effect but promotes rapid run-off. During use, cultivation would leave soils more vulnerable before the establishment of a crop cover but would facilitate percolation and reduce run-off. Some erosion has doubtless taken place and will have varied with local circumstances and terrace configuration. Aggradation of soil in the vlei at the Maristvale site (see below) indicates substantial soil loss from above, but as Verbeek suggests this may long precede any cultivation. Wall drains at the same site preclude any great erosion of the lower edge of terraces, though there may have been some levelling by loss from the upper sides. The general impression is that there has been little major soil loss in the case of reasonably well preserved double-faced terraces.

Terrace construction involved the extraction and moving of large quantities of stones, many of substantial size. In the absence of modern pick-axes, an appropriate instrument for this would be a stout small-bladed hoe, capable of working around and between the stones and providing firm leverage. A chance find from Ziwa of two such tools is illustrated in Plate 23, but complete hoes have not been found in archaeological excavations. Wooden levers might have aided in extracting and moving large stones, and digging sticks could have been used in subsequent cultivation.

The timing of the commencement of terracing is uncertain since dating thus far relies on association with the settlement sites described in Chapter 5. The earlier sites in the highlands – early hilltop settlements and ruined pit-structures of the 14th to 16th century – are above the upper limit of terracing and no direct association has been established. The early hilltop sites are two or three hundred metres higher than any terracing, even though some are not far away horizontally from terracing on the western escarpment. This seems a little remote for convenience and control, although there could have been undetected satellite settlements lower down. Some at least of the ruined pits are not far from terracing at the top of the eastern escarpment; however a relationship to the later pit-structures of the 17th/18th centuries is perhaps more probable from their more consistent propinquity. Lower pit-structures in the terraced zone on the western escarpment may be more confidently associated, while there is structural association with the lowland enclosures. Terracing was thus established by at least the 17th or early 18th century but an earlier date remains to be demonstrated.

There is no mention in the early written accounts of the 1890s and 1900s of any cultivation of terraces at that time and most had clearly been abandoned. Informants in the Hwesa area northeast of the Ruangwe Range state that the terraces were already there and abandoned prior to the establishment of the Katerere polity probably between 1750 and 1800 (Maxwell 1999:19). There are however some hints of more recent local use, for instance in or near the Bende Gap (Stead 1949:81):

> The stone-faced earth terrace is to be found on steep breath-taking slopes on the road to Nyamaropa Native Reserve via Bende. The steep slopes have been cut out into earth terraces about two feet wide and these have been faced with small flat stones which form the sub-strata of the hills. The shortage of rain in 1946-47 caused the crops grown on these terraces to be poor, but in normal seasons the crops are good.

These very narrow terraces are hardly consistent with the majority of terraces described above, while the isolated report suggests only localised use, perhaps a reuse of old terraces. Some informants in the recent survey acknowledge having sometimes cultivated on old terraces, while Chiro (1989) reports two cases of limited modern terrace building in Nyamaropa at the foot of the eastern escarpment; these terraces are poorly built compared to older examples, with quite steep profiles, and are designed mainly for stone clearance. One family had been forced to relocate to the top of a stony slope by heavy rains in 1980-81 and the terrace cultivation supplemented valley cultivation. In the same area, along the main road south of Regina Coeli, the current modification of old narrow terraces can be observed, forming wider terraces suitable for a plough; here both series appear to be single-faced with sloping terrace profiles.

Recent terracing has been initiated by peasant farmers in the Biriwiri area of Chimanimani in the southern Eastern Highlands since the 1950s (van der Zaag n.d.). Oral accounts on the stimulus to this are conflicting but there is no hint of the reuse or copying of old terraces. However this case offers some instructive parallels. The environment here is comparable to many terraced areas of Nyanga, having dolerite rocks and soils and steep stony slopes mostly in the range of 11 to 22° degrees but up to 40°. Terrace construction, unlike that inferred for most of the Nyanga terraces, is a cumulative process, starting with the dumping of surface stones along the contour and adding the stones which appear during cultivation over a number of years until a proper bench terrace is achieved with risers of 50 to 175cm. The risers are thus more roughly built than formal walls and presumably more stones remain in the cultivated soil, offering a contrast from the formal walls and stoneless soils of the Nyanga terraces.

Van der Zaag discusses soil fertility, pointing out that the slope soils are relatively young and more fertile than the weathered and leached valley soils, an advantage appreciated by the farmers themselves. Verbeek also makes this point above. The weathering of the fragmented parent dolerite is also an ongoing source of nutrients helping to sustain fertility, and farmers claim that yields have been stable for up to 20 years under interplanted maize and beans, with some application of chemical fertiliser and manure if available.

Labour input

One case study by van der Zaag gives a very approximate estimate of the labour involved: c.550 person/days spread over four years to terrace one hectare on a steep slope of around 22°. The height and number of terraces is not stated but must be considerable on such a steep slope. If terraces were an average of three metres between risers and the whole hectare was terraced, an overall construction rate of around 6m of terrace per person/day can be estimated. Clearly labour requirements will vary with the slope gradient and amount of stones and it would be unjustifiable to extrapolate this figure to the different and probably more laborious techniques of the Nyanga terraces, but it may suggest an order of magnitude.

For Nyanga itself, an alternative conservative estimate of the labour involved may be made based on data much of which are admittedly little more than guesswork. As noted earlier in this chapter, a total of nearly 22000 hectares of terracing was identified from aerial photographs in the main area of the complex – a minimum figure as some would not be visible. The density of terracing and the actual area worked within each hectare varies considerably, as would the labour input which depended on the gradient and amount of stones. However taking an average of 50% terraced area and an average spacing of five metres gives a total length of terrace of 22,000km. If for the sake of argument we take a period of 200 years and and average of 2000 workers involved, each person would have built the equivalent of 55m of terrace per year, a fair workload but not unreasonable. In practice the rate of construction would have varied over the time-span – there would have been a steady increase in tempo from initiation to a sustained period of maximum activity, and probably a piece-meal tailing off rather than a catastrophic abandonment; this fluctuation might reflect the number of people involved rather than the individual workload.

CULTIVATION RIDGES

The stone-faced terraces are not the only archaeological traces of old agricultural activity in the research area. Traces of extensive systems of ridges and ditches are also frequent in relatively stoneless areas below the stony slopes and in the valleys. Their distribution is wide and extends from the foot of the highlands at least as far as Headlands some 60 or 70 km to the west, while lesser occurrences are found to the east of the northern highlands. Their extent is most easily appreciated on the aerial photographs and must be comparable in total area to that of the terraces, although no quantification has been attempted. There is of course no direct physical overlap with terraces but in some cases they are immediately contiguous and are likely to be contemporary, although that is not demonstrated conclusively.

The ridges are roughly parallel, 7 to 10m wide between the bases of the intervening ditches, whose depth may reach up to a metre. Length depends on the topography and can be up to several hundred metres. Variations occur according to the local soils, topography and water-table. The flatter, wider examples have weathered at the edges to a gently rounded shape, but in wetter situations ridges tend to be more cambered due to the greater height and somewhat closer spacing needed for effective drainage. (The recent equivalent, the smaller *mihomba* ridges, are described in Chapter 3; these are also found in the Nyanga region but are more widely distributed throughout Zimbabwe.)

Siting in relation to topography and probably function are not homogeneous. Some occur in vleis, areas of impeded drainage which are seasonally or more or less permanently waterlogged; here the purpose was doubtless to provide drainage and to raise the cultivated beds above the water-table while providing moisture to the plant roots. However they are equally common on gently sloping areas with reasonable drainage where the purpose may have been to retard run-off and aid percolation. In some cases at least there seems to have been provision to distribute water diverted from streams or natural sponges.

An apparently first-hand tradition from an old woman in Nyatwe in the Manyika area of Nyanga may relate to these cultivation ridges. She reported that gardens called *gowa* used to be cultivated in water-logged areas (*matoro*). These were like modern gardens but had very long and narrow beds unlike the relatively wide beds of modern gardens. They grew *tsenza*, *majo*, beans and maize in these beds (Mukaronda 1988:12). "Modern gardens" presumably refers to recent *mihomba*, whose length is certainly shorter than the old ridges; however, as noted in Chapter 3, the latter tend to be wider, rather than narrower.

There has been considerable work on vleis and their cultivation in Zimbabwe (e.g. Whitlow 1980, 1983; Owen et al 1995). In general they are low-lying, gently sloping areas, usually seasonally waterlogged by run-off, seepage and rainfall. However they are heterogeneous and complex in nature, influenced by varying topography, geology, hydrology, soils and vegetation. They are the result of past as well as present environmental conditions, especially climate but including human action (Whitlow 1980)

An extensive ridge and furrow system in vleis on Rusape Source Farm north-east of Rusape, which falls within the area of distribution outlined above, is described and illustrated by Whitlow (1983). This system, which he notes is only an example of many vleis between Rusape and Nyanga, covers around 450 hectares and patterns within it range from fern-like arrangements of linear ridges in the heads of the vleis to somewhat rectangular patterns in the lower portions, with long well-defined ridges in the axes of the valleys. Some of the ridges extend outside the limits of the present-day vlei. He notes that these features are not typical of conditions in the rest of Zimbabwe, where localised patches of ridge and furrow [i.e. *mihomba*] are more common. The description is consistent with the Nyanga systems studied, though the measurements he gives appear to be rather narrower – two to four metres in width with a spacing (presumably the ditches) of two to three metres. Whitlow has no direct information on the age of the Rusape Source example, but speculates that the possible date could range from about 50 to 300 years, and that abandonment was due to the displacement of indigenous farmers by the early white settlers. The last point might perhaps be consistent with the Nyatwe testimony reported above, but would not hold for the area below the Nyanga escarpment which must have been abandoned earlier.

Under the recent project, two contrasting areas were selected for study in the Maristvale area below the foot of the western escarpment.

Area 1

The first, at grid reference VR 744134, is the small perched vlei immediately adjacent to the Maristvale terracing described above. The vlei is in a shallow valley partly blocked by a large granite outcrop and has a total area of c.275 by 200m (including the outcrop), part of which is a northern branch c.125 by 60m bounded on the west by a low dolerite ridge. The whole vlei has a series of ridges and intervening ditches, those in the northern arm forming a dendritic pattern converging to drain between the granite outcrop and the end of the dolerite ridge (fig. 19). At the time of study in August 1994 only the lower end of the vlei was waterlogged, but in July 1997 after a good rainy season all the ditches still retained water.

A trench 12m long and 1m wide was dug to test the stratigraphy and soil profile of the ridges and ditches. This was situated about the middle of the northern arm of the vlei towards the south-eastern side (fig. 19) and sectioned one and a half ridges and two ditches. It was dug to solid clay in the centre of the ridge at the north-western end and across the ditches, but to a lesser depth over the south-east ridge. The western ridge is c.8m wide and the eastern ridge 7m wide between the centres of the ditches, and the vertical distance from top of ridges to base of ditches was around 40cm before excavation in each case. Unfortunately an auger was not available to extend the stratigraphical information gained. The section is shown in figure 20.

The surface layer (1) throughout is a dark grey

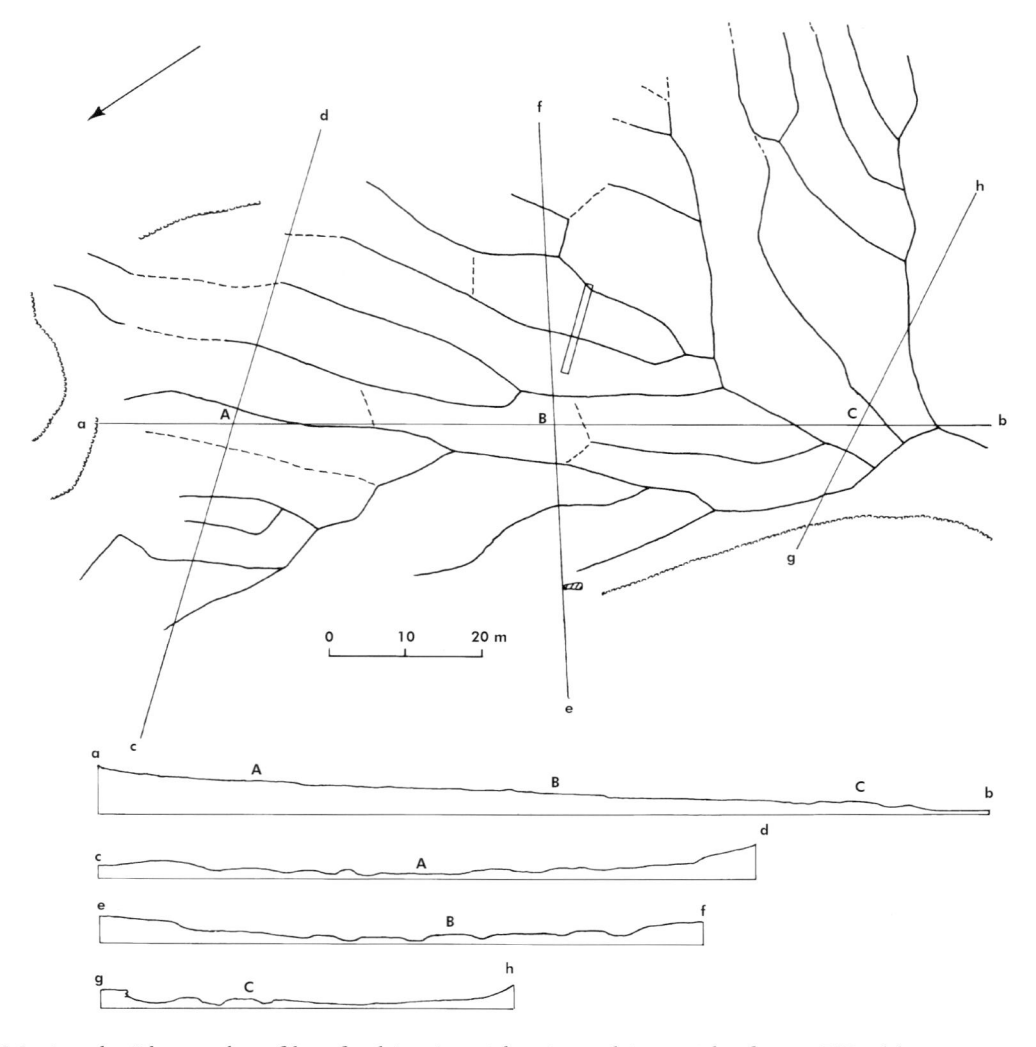

Fig. 19. Maristvale. Plan and profiles of cultivation ridges in a vlei at grid reference VR744133

sandy humus topsoil between 2 and 10cm thick. On the ridges this overlies a grey-brown sandy clay (4) with white flecks and rusty orange staining, the staining being less in the centre of the north-west ridge. There was some vertical cracking as the section dried out, especially on the south-east ridge. At the middle of the north-west ridge the grey-brown sandy clay overlies a reddish brown similar deposit with more cracks (5), mottled with light grey sandy material dropping down the cracks. This becomes more clayey with depth and at a depth of 100cm rests on grey-brown clay (7) around 6cm thick with a grey sand lens (6) on its surface. Below this again is a dense black clay (8) which was not further excavated at this point.

Below the north-west ditch is the same black clay (8) at the base, at least 20cm thick and continuing below the base of the trench; the surface of this slopes up gently to the south-east. Over this is light brown sandier clay (5a) with light grey sand mottling and a few small stones and with grey sandy lenses (6) near the base. The ditch was cut through this and the grey-brown sandy clay (4) above it. The primary ditch fill, up to 25cm deep, was of grey-brown clay (3a), interdigitated with light grey sandy clay (3b) on the western side. The final ditch fill consisted of up to 20cm of dark grey clay (2).

The section below the south-east ditch shows some differences owing to the vicinity of the valley side. Here the underlying clay (8a) is brown and rather sandier than the black clay (8), with extensive vertical cracking on exposure and a depth of around 50cm, overlying dolerite stones and boulders. Above this is a thin band of grey to grey-brown clay (7a) sloping down to the north-west, overlain in turn by a wedge of very sandy clay (6a), and by the upper grey-brown sandy clay (4). The ditch was cut through this into the top of the brown clay (8a). In the base of the ditch is a thin layer of light brown sandy clay (3c), overlain by light grey more or less mottled sandy clay (3b). The final fill is again dark grey clay (2) similar to the north-west ditch.

The basal clay must be an original vlei deposit, perhaps water-laid, of purely natural origin. It is browner with more silt content towards the edge of the vlei where it rests on the tail of the rocky slope. The surface gradient of the clay is less than 2° between the ditches, steepens to almost 3° below the north-west ditch and levels out again to c.1.5° to the north-western end of the trench. Sandy grey lenses (6) above the black clay, and the wedge of very sandy clay (6a) over the brown clay, should represent early deposition incidents of eroded material. The general cover of grey-brown sandy clay with white feldspar flecks and occasional small stones (4) and a probable original depth of around 50cm, has been deposited by erosion from the slopes above. Verbeek (see below) deduces that this deposit is of similar age to the terrace soils and is unlikely to have been formed by erosion resulting from cultivation before, during or after the construction of the terraces. The orange staining is due to annual

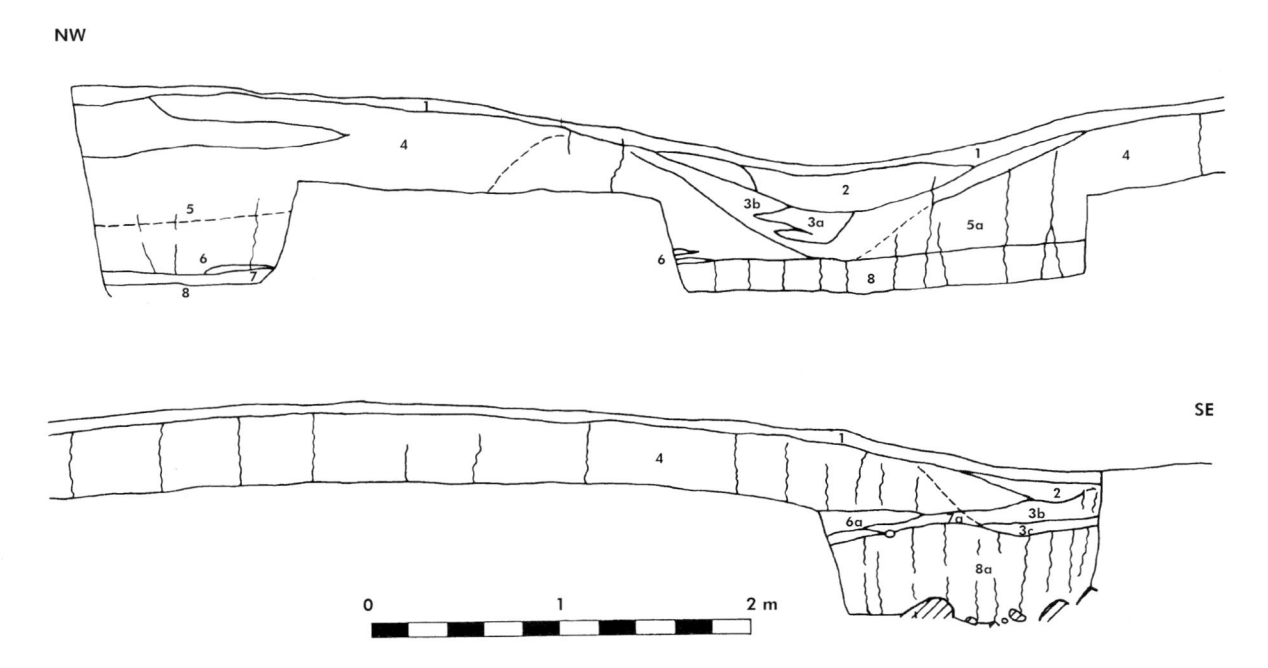

Fig. 20. Maristvale. Section of cultivation ridges and ditches at grid reference VR744134

waterlogging since deposition. The reddish brown to light brown less sandy clay (5,5a) which underlies this could represent the initiation of the same erosional phase, or an earlier deposition following a climatic change subsequent to the basal clay deposition.

Subsequent to the deposition of the grey-brown sandy clay, the ditches were dug, presumably for drainage to facilitate cultivation. Material from the ditches would have been piled on the ridges and the interdigitation in the north-west ditch indicates repeated back silting and recutting. The final ditch fill of dark grey clay was probably deposited after abandonment and the reestablishment of natural vegetation which would have inhibited the transport of coarser sediments.

Comments on soil analyses (by K.Verbeek)
The ridges are located in the vlei which is the zone of accumulation for all substances such as clay, bases, and silicic acid in solution or suspension. Here the topographic position or catena effect has the strongest influence on soil formation. In comparison with the terraces above, the soils are poorly drained (lower free Fe content) and are expected to be less weathered and to have a higher CEC clay (E/C value), pH and base saturation. Analyses are given in Appendix A.

Texture: Sandy loam to sandy clay, with a maximum of 43% clay in layer 8 but otherwise no clay increase with depth. Sand fraction distribution indicates a difference in the parent material between the basal clay and the layers above, comparable to that in the terraces. In both places the bottom layers could therefore consist of the *in situ* weathering, with the material above having been transported.

Weathering: Moderately weathered soil expressed by CEC clay higher than on the terraces as expected. Free Fe % (2-4%) is lower than on the terraces, also as expected through the reduction processes occurring in a poorly drained environment. The cracking is also indicative of an active soil.

Fertility: pH and % base saturation are optimum for plant growth, but exchangeable potassium levels are very low which is inconsistent with the other bases. This could indicate longer or more intense utilization which is consistent with the organic carbon % levels; these should be higher than on the terraces because of the wetter environment in the vlei but are in fact about the same.

Area 2 - Mwenje
The second area is some four kilometres north of Maristvale Mission, centred on grid reference VR 725175 at an altitude of 1360m. Here there is a second broad bay in the escarpment about 2.5km wide, bounded by Mount Muozi to the south and by the Nyangui massif to the north (Plate 8). Streams descend from the highlands and converge in the Mwenje river, with relatively gentle interfluves between, their gradient declining steadily from the foot of the escarpment (figs 21; 22). The aerial photographs show all these interfluves to be seamed longitudinally with cultivation ridges, with a total area of over 700 hectares. There is an especially clear set of ridges on one interfluve in the centre of the basin and this was chosen for study.

This interfluve (shown in Soper 1996, fig.8) provides an area some 1750m long and around 500m wide, with an overall longitudinal fall of about 120m and a maximum height of about 10 to 12 m above the bounding streams towards the lower end (fig. 22). Most of the area is covered by ridges which trend longitudinally down the spur, presenting a broadly parallel alignment, sometimes rather braided. There are some patches of low terracing along the higher stonier north-eastern crest which trends south-east/north-west parallel to the northern stream. A minor rocky spur towards the south-east at VR737175 has a concentration of stone homestead enclosures, with terracing on the steeper south side, and other enclosures are scattered the length of the interfluve where outcropping rocks or smaller colluvial boulders provided material for their construction. There is a pit-structure just above the base of the escarpment at VR743173.

Two linear features on the aerial photograph interrupt the lines of the ridges towards the lower western end of the interfluve. One crosses the ridge from side to side and is likely to be an old trackway. No modern path is evident here on the photograph taken in 1986, but a path has since developed, used by villagers from Village 5 of Nyajezi Resettlement Area travelling to the seed potato farms in the highlands south of Chirimanyimo hill.

Augering on three sample traverses of around 16m each parallel to the line of this feature shows:
- on the southern flank of the interfluve, up to 1m of light brown to greyish sandy silt, becoming somewhat mottled with depth and slightly coarser beneath;
- near the crest, around 60cm of light brown sandy silt on the ridges, mottled in its lower part, underlain by a lens of clean yellow fine sand over a sheet of consolidated rounded quartz gravel;
- on the northern flank, up to 1m of grey-brown sandy silt similarly mottled, underlain by either gravel or hard orange sand. The general impression is of an old outwash fan overlain by

Fig. 21. Mwenje, north side of basin. Cultivating ridges and terraces traced from an aerial photograph

alluvium.

The second linear feature is an old furrow. It crosses the ridges from ENE to SSW and converges with the first feature at a constant low downhill gradient. It would have carried water to the crest of the interfluve from a series of particularly deep ditches which clearly still carry water after heavy rain, as shown by occasional headward erosion and flow lines of bent grass. From here it could have been directed down the north-western ditches but is more likely to have served a group of stone enclosures at VR734175.

A section was excavated across this furrow (fig. 23b). The base of the section is a continuous compact gravel horizon, mostly quartz with stones up to 20cm in size. This is overlain by light grey-brown fine silty alluvial sand. The furrow was cut through this into the surface of the gravel and is revetted with stones on the lower side. The channel fill is of slightly coarser grey-brown sand and the uppermost deposit is slightly darker grey-brown fine silty sand, apparently washed down from the slope above.

The set of ditches from which this furrow originates, while not constituting a formal furrow, can be traced continuously for the whole length of the interfluve, and could have provided downhill

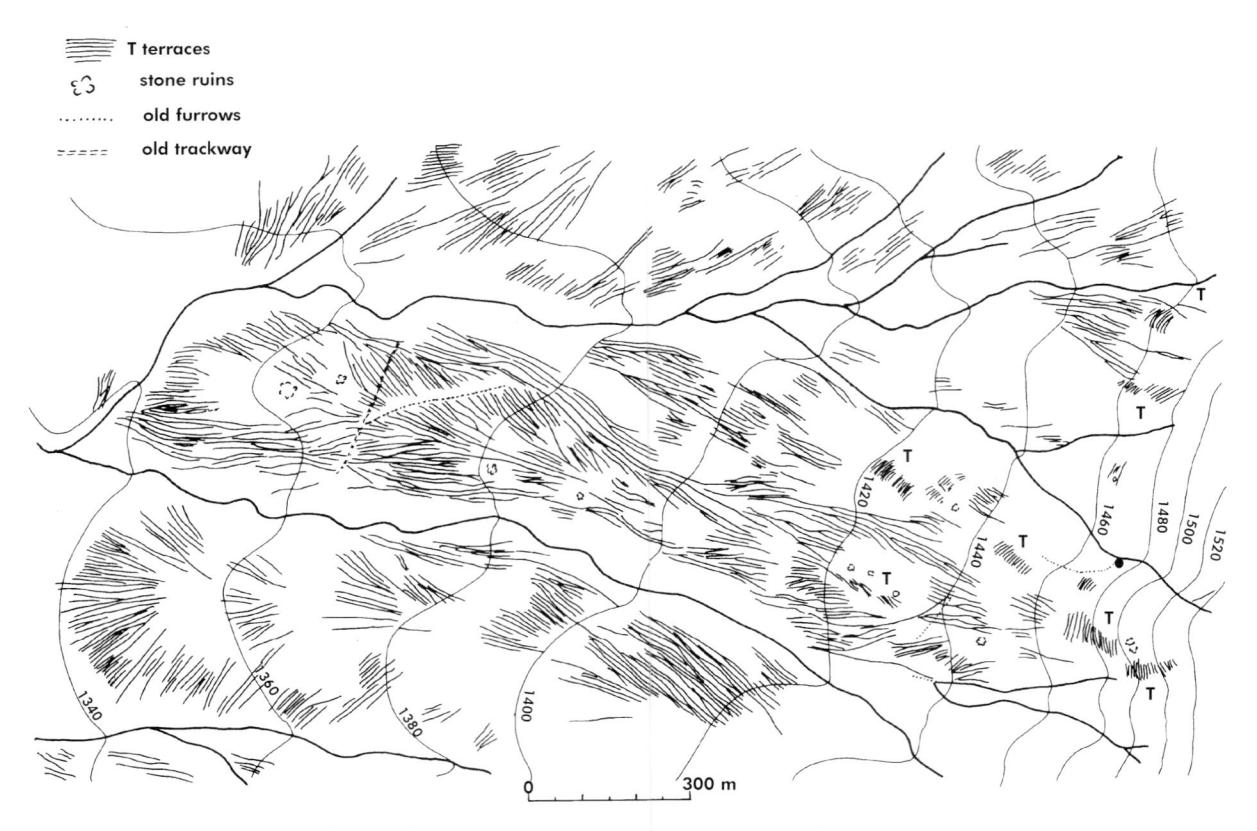

Fig. 22. Mwenje, centre of basin. Cultivating ridges and terraces traced from an aerial photograph

flow from the small northern stream at the foot of the escarpment. At this point (VR 742176) the stream is conveniently dammed by a pair of large waterberry trees (*Syzygium cordatum*), over whose roots is a fall of 80cm. The south bank of the stream is neatly revetted with stones for some 20m below. A rather exiguous line of stones diverging from above this revetment proved on excavation to be the lower edge of a shallow furrow 80cm wide (fig. 23a). The stream in July 1997, after preceding good rains, had sufficient flow to supply an artificial channel, but could be less adequate in a bad year.

Water from this point could reach most of the interfluve and there is a probable channel line on the aerial photograph passing above the spur with the enclosures, which could have supplied the ditches along the southern flank. The southern stream is too low to provide a feasible source of water for this interfluve, but there are some indications of a furrow feeding the next parallel interfluve to the south.

An area of about 1.7 ha between and to the west of the linear features was surveyed to provide data on ridge/ditch size and gradients. Most ridges are from 7 to 10m wide between the ditch centres, and the height of ridge above ditch varies from 5 to 20 centimetres at the crest of the interfluve where most natural levelling has taken place, to a maximum of about 70 cm near the base of the northern slope. The ridges slant slightly from the longitudinal slope of the interfluve at average gradients of around 2° 30' to 3° 30', the average longitudinal and lateral slopes being both around 2° 30'. The gradient of the furrow varies between about 40' and 1°.

The purpose of these ridges is clearly different from those in Area 1. The soil is not permanently waterlogged except near the southern stream, so there was little need for drainage or for raising the cultivated beds above the water-table. Rather the intention seems to be to slow run-off and direct it the length of the interfluve, allowing it to percolate into the bases of the ridges. In addition the growing season could be extended for at least some of the area by diverting water from the stream and directing it down the ditches. The present volume of the stream might have sufficed for perhaps a couple of months, though hardly throughout the dry season. The homesteads along the interfluve could also have been served, and their distribution indicates cooperative effort for the maintenance of the system and the allocation of water rights to those lower down.

This system is admirably placed at the foot of the highlands to benefit from such supplementary irrigation. For most other non-vlei ridge systems away from the escarpment to the west, diversion of water would probably have been impracticable and supplementary irrigation is unlikely.

homesteads and in some cases irrigating open fields. Water manipulation will thus be approached here from the angle of the furrow technology rather than as irrigation *per se*, leading to a discussion of the usages to which the water was actually put.

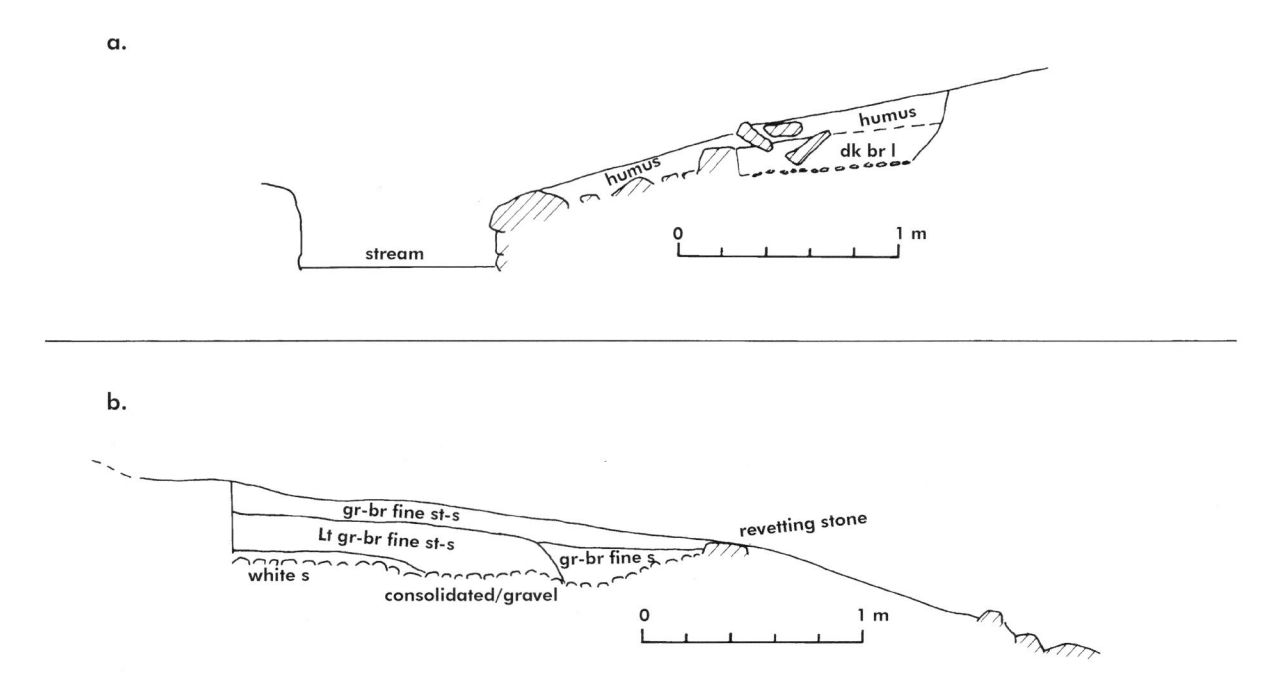

Fig. 23. Mwenje furrow sections: (a) immediately below take-off point of upper furrow; (b) lower furrow. s = sand; st = silt; l = loam; gr = grey; br = brown

HYDRAULIC WORKS

The manipulation of water through artificial furrows under gravity, using simple technology and locally available materials, is a widespread practice where appropriate water sources and conditions of topography exist. Much of Nyanga District, and indeed the Eastern Highlands in general, is well suited to this technology, since there are many permanent streams, often with steep gradients, susceptible to relatively easy diversion. Extensive evidence of old hydraulic practices shows that this potential was appreciated and exploited.

It often seems to be assumed that irrigation is a constant concomitant of terracing, this misconception perhaps based on spectacular pictures of rice cultivation in south-east Asia. However, in the Nyanga case very few of the terraces appear to have been artificially irrigated, although there is considerable evidence of old furrows serving

Reports of old water furrows in the western lowlands and Nyanga Police Post/Rhodes Estate areas go back to the early years of European settlement (Schlichter 1899; Peters 1902). Furrows reported as actually operating at that time appear to have been reconditioned abandoned examples (e.g. Mare furrow in the National Park; Nyanga Police Station/ Administrative Offices; Dutch Settlements [Peters 1902; Stidolph, pers. comm.]). Descriptions indicate that old furrows were still well preserved and could not have been long abandoned: "They are all about 16 to 24 inches [40 to 60cm] wide and about 2 feet [60cm] in depth. They have no paving or built sides" (Hall 1905:102); "... simple trenches about one metre in depth. The earth taken out of the trench is piled on its lower side and supported by boulders embedded in it" (Randall-MacIver 1906:12).

Take-off dams in streams were also described: "... well and strongly built of unworked stones without mortar" (Randall-MacIver 1906.12); "... made of huge boulders which have been placed in position. Some of these dams are from 30 yards to 50 yards in length, one at least being nearly 100 yards across" (Hall 1909:183 – some exaggeration may be suspected; for such rough estimates yards may be read as metres). Such dams have not been reported since Wieschoff (1941:24 but observed in about 1930) and they must have been washed away.

It was assumed by several of these early writers that the innumerable terraces of Nyanga and adjacent districts were irrigated and that the furrows were for this purpose (e.g. Hall 1909:183; Wieschoff 1949:24). Sutton (1983) however discussed at some length the association of furrows with terraces and cultivation ridges and the possible role of irrigation and he included some description of several furrows in the Demera hill and National Park areas. He concluded that most of the terraces were not irrigated but that some supplementary watering was possible for the cultivation ridges. There are a few cases where furrows do traverse terraced slopes and here irrigation of the terraces below the furrow is a possibility, although traces of distribution channels have not been observed and the association may be coincidental. Examples are Demera hill immediately east of Nyanga town and two furrows on the lower slopes of the escarpment in the Maristvale area described below. In most cases however, terraces and furrows do not appear to be associated. In the lowlands most of the terraces on the detached foothills away from the escarpments are too elevated above the streams to be accessible to gravity irrigation (although supplementary water could have been directed through some areas of cultivation ridges). In the highlands most of the observed furrows are above the upper limit of terracing (c.1700m). In one case where terraces do occur above this level in the National Park, an adjacent furrow (NP4) runs *below* them; as discussed below, irrigation of unterraced fields is probable in this case.

There is a more consistent association between highland furrows and pit-structures. This was noted by Peters (1902), and in more detail by Mason (1933) for Mkondwe near Penhalonga and by Finch (1949) for Inyanga Downs; the latter both provided maps/sketch plans. Summers (1958:20) gave a general description of interlinked furrows, pit-structures, ditches and "dams" in the Matinha area but otherwise had little to add to Finch. None of these give any technical details.

It may be questioned whether an artificial water supply was really necessary, especially in the highlands where average annual rainfall is well over 1000mm and permanent streams quite frequent. However annual and local rainfall variation is very great so that dry years are often experienced, while rainfall is markedly seasonal and dry periods may occur during the wet season. Furrows would thus provide an insurance in unfavourable years and extend the growing season, as well as providing convenient water for domestic purposes and livestock.

While most of the furrows can be attributed to the old terrace complex, the technology has continued to recent times. One informant who was born on Rhodes Estate in 1922, remembers building furrows in his youth. Finch (1949) records:

> [the] natives still use the numerous old furrows for irrigating, but they are in poor repair now. The present occupiers show no skill in rebuilding or repairing the furrows, merely scratching out mud gutters to lead the water from the older stone furrows to their gardens.

This criticism seems hardly justified, for clearly the furrows were adequately maintained and the "gutters" would be the normal device for distributing the water from the main furrow.

A relevant tradition was recorded by Machiwenyika in the early 1920s (see Appendix I to Annex):

> There is also something interesting which used to be done by Manyika people in the north. They used to hoe their fields early in winter, in places where they knew water can reach easily. The fields were hoed along the rivers, and from these rivers they dug small furrows, which aided them in leading the water to the fields. Some of the furrows came a long distance to their fields. Thus irrigation began before the coming of the Europeans. They carefully irrigated their fields in which they sowed these crops: peas, beans, pumpkins, mealies and other roots. The water ran through them rapidly and in a great volume. The countries in which irrigation was carried on are these: Nyatwe, Karombe, Nyamhuka, Bonda, Nyanga and surrounding countries.

Machiwenyika also records that men were brought from Nyanga to dig a furrow in Umtali in 1895.

Small furrows are still in current use by peasant farmers in some areas such as Chirimanyimo and the Kumbu area of Nyautare. Here they are used for irrigating gardens, household and livestock use, and in the latter case for fish ponds. This may indicate continuity from precolonial times or be a re-exploitation of the same potential.

Visibility

Furrows in use in the mid-1980s are visible on the 1:25000 aerial photographs as fine dark lines in areas devoid of too much tree cover. Most of these are narrow channels with little in the way of supporting banks or revetment, and gradients are often quite steep. Where abandoned furrows involved substantial banks, as in many cases in the National Park, they are clearly visible in grassland. Narrower examples of old furrows, such as those serving groups of pit-structures in the highlands, are less easily detectable on the photographs so that few are recorded in detail below. In lower areas without perennial grass cover, abandoned furrows are more likely to have been eroded away or silted over or may be obscured by trees.

Most of the furrows studied are now totally silted to a horizontal profile. Though some in the National Park retain some concavity in places, none offers much hint of the original dimensions of width and depth without excavation. They thus present themselves as a continuous step in the cross-slope, frequently utilised as a game trail or footpath as offering an easy route to traverse the valley side (Plate 9). They can be confidently identified by observation of a constant downhill gradient. The step varies from a very narrow feature for some of the smaller furrows leading to pit-structure, to a massive bank up to 7m wide and 2 to 3m high at the outer edge. Smaller ones may be obscured by hillwash or destroyed by erosion, and a line which starts out clearly and confidently often fades out and may not be recoverable by casting around along the probable gradient line. Some stone revetment may be seen in awkward places, notably in the Nyanore furrow below the Troutbeck road (see below NP6). More or less continuous stone reinforcement of the lower side may sometimes be visible but much has probably been buried, as revealed in most of the excavated cross-sections. Furrows can usually be traced to the vicinity of the parent stream where a small waterfall often forms a likely take-off point, but no dam structures appear to survive.

Abandoned furrows were studied in the Maristvale area at the foot of the western escarpment, in Nyangui Forestry Reserve in the northern highlands, in the Nyanga town/National Park area, and a single example near Troutbeck. The survey mainly involved the examination of furrows identified on aerial photographs with respect to source, course and apparent destination. Distances were generally measured by pacing, and gradients with a hand-held Abney level; a theodolite traverse was used in one case but provided little additional information commensurate with the effort involved. Some augering was done in the National Park and a number of cross-sections were excavated.

DESCRIPTION OF FURROWS

Maristvale

The most likely location for irrigation in the Nyanga terrace complex might be expected to be the lower slopes of the escarpments and the piedmont slopes, where perennial streams descending from the highlands could be relatively easily tapped and lower rainfall would make irrigation desirable. One area of terracing and cultivation ridges above Nyanga High School at grid reference VR744134 has been described in detail above. While it would be quite feasible to bring water to this site, no clear signs of any feeder furrow have been detected even when the area was denuded of grass cover by fire, and there were no channels for water spreading among the terraces themselves; numerous apertures through the terrace walls could equally well have been for drainage of excess run-off from normal rainfall.

Four other areas in the general vicinity of Maristvale were examined with reference to water furrows.

Mwenje: The first is the semicircular reentrant basin of the Mwenje river and its tributaries between Muozi and Nyangui, two to five kilometres north of Maristvale, extensively marked by cultivation ridges as described in the preceding section.

Within the basin is a modern working furrow some 4km long which originally served Summershoek farm and now serves Mwenje resettlement Village 5. This was not measured but from the map has a total fall of 60m giving an average gradient of about 0° 50'. It is not clear whether it follows the line of an older furrow, but Peters in 1902 (p.168) recorded that at least one farm of the Dutch Settlements had reused an old furrow. At the north-western side of the basin another recent but now abandoned furrow can be traced on the aerial photograph following a south-westerly trending spur for at least 3km with a fall of 120m. This was also used by Summershoek farm (Stidolph, pers.comm.) but again it is not clear if it followed an older line.

The take-off of an old furrow (M1) has been described above in the discussion of the Mwenje cultivation ridges. This is on a stream at the foot of the escarpment on the eastern side of the basin, at the head of an interfluve at an altitude of c.1460m (VR742176). No main furrow seems to be fed from this but the water could have been directed down any of the ditches between the ridges. Towards the bottom of the spur a furrow did in fact carry water from a set of deeper ditches to the crest of the spur, probably serving a series of stone enclosures and perhaps the north-western ridges. There are also traces of a possible silted furrow on the next spur to the south.

At the north-eastern side of the basin an old furrow (M2) was identified near the head of the piedmont slope below the steeper slopes which rise to the plateau of Nyangui Hill. This furrow is relatively steep and takes its source in a permanent stream at VR 727194 at an altitude of 1520m, the actual take-off point having been washed away. It runs south-west above the stream with some stone revetment for 100m at an average gradient of just over 3° before curving to the west around the spur for another 160m at an average gradient of 2°50', thence dipping somewhat to fade out between some low terraces. Most of this stretch runs on a low earthen bank. The total length is 300m and the average overall gradient is 3°7'. The furrow is totally silted and no cross sections were dug.

South of Maristvale two areas of terracing in valleys close to streams were examined for possible signs of irrigation. One of these is c.3.5km south of the High School above Doornhoek at VR 726732 where there is intensive terracing around a stream confluence, with a number of pit-structures and two "forts" associated with a walled trackway on the ridge to the west. No signs of channels could be detected here in the dense grass/shrub cover. The second area is c.2km south-east of the school at VR 737129 where another walled trackway crosses a stream. On the south side is another area of terrace walls but again no signs of irrigation were noted in the thick grass.

About one kilometre to the east of the School, a more convincing furrow (M3), visible on the aerial photograph, was found on the south side of the ridge on which a modern water-tank stands. It starts from a stream at VR741140 at an altitude of c.1490m and follows an artificial ledge with some stone revetment for the first 150 m at a gradient of around 3°. Thence it skirts the side of the ridge with terraces above and below for another 500 m, marked by a footpath with a constant downhill gradient averaging 1° 25' (range 20' to 5°), fading out at the end of the spur about 150m east of and 40m above the Maristvale water tank, at VR734141. It could have continued around the north side of the spur but no trace of this was seen. For most of the lower stretch it runs along a slight ledge with some supporting stonework below, but this is not noticeably different from the single-faced terraces parallel to it. The total length measured was c.670m with a fall of c.27 m,

an average gradient of 2° 18' overall. No possible sluices were seen which might have directed water to the terraces below, though such would not necessarily have been permanent features. There are at least two stone enclosures on the end of the spur below the last point traced and these could well have been the destination. This is a quite convincing feature but requires confirmation by augering. It is not a modern furrow associated with the Dutch Settlements or the Mt Mellary/Maristvale mission.

Nyangui

Traces of furrows are fairly common in Nyangui Forest Reserve in areas not yet planted with pine trees. Some of these are clearly recent, dating from "squatter" occupation up to the 1980s and two of these are mentioned in the site reports for 1732DD27 and Matinha I (Chapter 8). Older ones are hard to trace but there seem to be a fair number serving pit-structures on the eastern slopes of the highland ridge towards the northern end of the reserve. One of these was measured.

NY1. VR742237 - 748236. Altitude c.2080m. Length measured 810m, fall 29.50m, average gradient 2° 5'. This starts from a rock sill in a small stream flowing south-east and traverses a slope with a cross-gradient of 10 to 14° to the ESE at an average gradient of 1° 38' for 430m, passing well above two pit-structures. It then rounds a rocky spur and the head of a steep reentrant for 155m at 2° 32', and another rocky spur beyond for 165m at 2°, swinging ENE to north-east. It then appears to dip to the north over the spur for another 60m at 4° 20' where the line is lost. There are pit-structures lower down the spur 250m to the east probably served by a lower furrow, and two more 300m to the NNE, but the probable destination is a group of pit-structures, hollows and ditches c.950m to the north (Matinha IV, see below and Figure 64). Much of this distance is covered by a footpath with a steady downhill gradient on a fairly level plateau but no clear line has been traced down to this from the last point measured. Most of the surveyed course runs on a narrow ledge and there is a clear line through the rocks of the first spur.

Nyanga Town, south end of Demera hill

There are two furrows, D1 and D2, on the southern end of Demera hill east of Nyanga town, visible from the main road to the south (fig. 24)

D1. VQ 735835 - 729839. Measured by Abney and pacing. Altitude around 1780m. Length 770m, fall 18.20m, average gradient 1° 22'. This starts from the Rochdale stream in a deep steep-sided valley and traverses the steep slope to the south for 265m at 1° 44' on a narrow well revetted shelf; a steep wash-out here has been repaired with two tiers of revetting about 3m high. It then swings west to north-west around the hill (Plate 9) between substantial but irregularly spaced stone terraces for another 265m at 1° 14' to a pit-structure immediately below. Thence the line is less obvious between terraces above and below, but a probable course, passing immediately below another pit-structure, can be traced along a more or less continuous terrace for a further 250m at 1° 5', to fade out c.30m before the modern waterworks where a belt has been largely cleared of stones. There is no trace of any continuation at the appropriate level on an open slope beyond the waterworks.

About 100m after swinging north-west on the second stretch, just before the fire-break of the National Park boundary, there is a side furrow marked by a raised bank which drops down about 20m to a reservoir. This is 12m long and 7m wide, cut into the slope with a stone-reinforced bank below (Plate 10). From this reservoir a furrow parallel to the main line is traceable to the north-west for 80m across the fire-break, passing above a small enclosure with a smithing furnace and another with a fairly well preserved smelting furnace (see Chapter 5).

The main furrow almost certainly served the lower pit-structure and may well have been used to irrigate the terraces below its line, though no traces of distribution works were seen. In addition part of the function of the storage reservoir and parallel furrow may have been connected with the iron working enclosures.

D2. ?VQ 733833 - 726837. Altitude around 1740m. Most of this is marked by a substantial bank up to 3m high, towards the base of the same slope as furrow D1. This bank is 625m long with an overall fall of 2.80m, an average gradient of only 15'. Parts appear to have been reduced by sheet erosion since some individual gradient measurements go slightly uphill. The upper end of the bank starts at a swampy side valley at the fire-break at 730833, but there is a second bank a short distance above which continues to the head of the side valley and is here followed by a modern furrow. The latter runs back around the head of the side valley and originates at a concrete dam on the Rochdale stream at 733833; the old furrow may be assumed to have followed the same line. (The modern furrow diverges above this upper bank soon after swinging north-west above the end of the main bank.) Proceeding "downstream" the two banks overlap for some 150m before the upper one fades out 35m from the lower with a vertical interval of 2m. There is no obvious surviving connection between the banks but water could have been run down at any point. For much of the lower stretch of the main bank, there is a narrow shelf up to 60cm below the crest on which the actual furrow must have run; this is similar to a number of furrows in the National Park described below. The bank is traceable as far as a spur with gum trees at the edge of Nyanga town where a road turns up to the waterworks, but no attempt has been made to follow it through the gardens beyond.

Just beyond this point and immediately above the road is a further probable reservoir traversed by the modern furrow. This is cut into the slope with an earth bank on the lower side and is c.27m long, widening to 6m at the lower end. It resembles two features described below for National Park furrows 7 and 9, but could be a relatively recent feature associated with Nyanga town. About 200m before the end of the bank there is a small silted basin 3m in diameter immediately below, where augering showed c.45cm of silting. There is a broad area around 100m wide below much of the course of the bank, sloping at around 6 to 8°. There are no obvious side ditches or take-off structures, but from parallels with the National Park furrows this is likely to have had irrigated fields. There is a pit-structure on the spur above the end of the bank, and more at a lower level among the gardens of Nyanga village which the furrow could also have served.

Nyanga National Park

There are relatively numerous furrows visible on aerial photographs in the northern area of the Park between Mare Dam and the Troutbeck road (fig. 24). These generally show as broad banks traversing relatively gentle slopes. There are a few smaller examples further south in the Pungwe valley (NP10-12) but only one is visible further east towards Mt Nyangani, on the south side of the upper Nyangombe valley (NP13). A number of these furrows were measured or recorded under conditions of heavy grass cover in 1996 and were reexamined in October 1998 after a major fire when more details were visible.

NP1. VQ749784 - 747787, about 500m north-east of the housing compound for the fisheries staff. Altitude c.1850m. Length 585m, total fall 23.40m, average gradient 2° 11'. This derives from a small stream in a steep-sided valley, probably at the head of a small waterfall. The first 180m is along a shelf

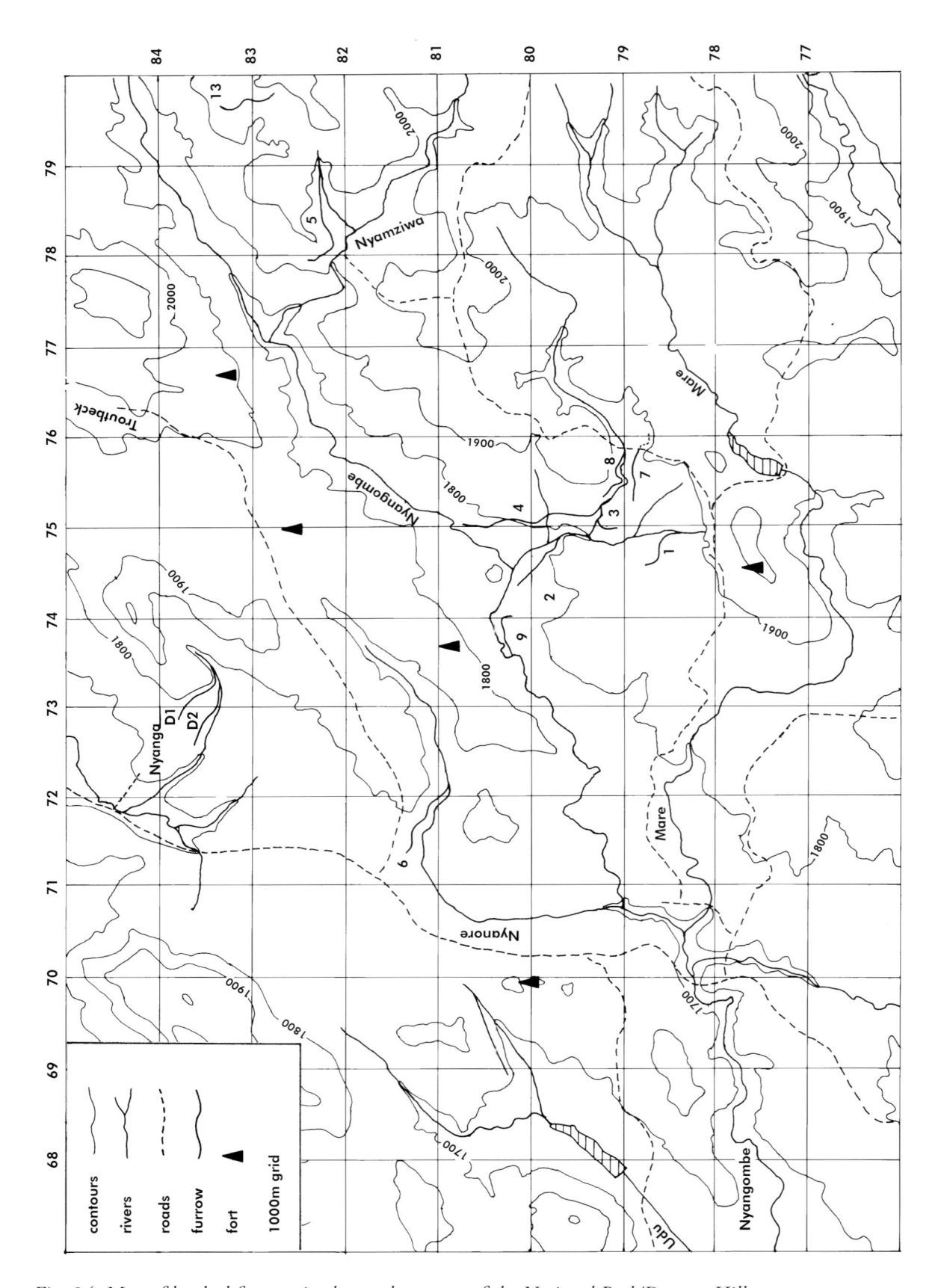

Fig. 24. Map of banked furrows in the northern part of the National Park/Demera Hill

1.50 to 5m wide along a valley slope with a cross gradient of 15 to 25°. It continues for c.90m on a shelf up to 7m wide above a gentler slope, then dips more steeply to cross a broad gentle reentrant with a cross gradient of 5 to 7°; it fades out on the far side of this. Gradients average around 3° in the upper valley course and 1° 56' after emerging from the valley, though individual stretches may be as little as 30'. There are four pit-structures within 20 to 50m on the upper side of the furrow, one of which has surviving *dhaka* house walls (see Fishpit, Chapter 8), but there are no obvious (i.e. stone-built) occupation sites which it could have served directly. One pit-structure on a spur immediately above the furrow has been reused and contains a couple of small raised platforms, two almost complete pots and some sherds. On the shelf of the furrow below this pit, here c.5m wide, is a small low-walled basin 3.50m in diameter into which effluent from the pit would have drained, the furrow itself running along the edge of the shelf below the basin. The furrow must be contemporary with construction of the pit-structure since if it were later it would have destroyed the basin.

There is a broad gently sloping area up to 300m long and 200m wide in the broad reentrant between the furrow bank and the river below, which could have been irrigated. Here a number of shallow gullies or ditches run more or less straight downhill. Three of these are 12 to 14m apart and around 50 to 60cm deep, with a rounded profile. A fourth similar ditch starts 30m to the south and converges with the others. The ditches start immediately below the bank and there are no corresponding drainage lines above; they are therefore likely to be side-furrows, although no signs of any stone take-off structures were seen.

A cross-section was excavated about 80m from the source, where the gradient is three to four degrees, the cross-slope 22° and the shelf c.2.50m wide (fig. 25). The section shows no clear outline of the furrow and consists mainly of a series of lenses or tip lines ranging from loose sand to fine silt, from light brown to grey in colour. The natural soil here is a light brown sandy loam and crumbly granite is exposed above. In view of the fairly steep gradient, the furrow profile would have been relatively small. The horizontal sand and silt lenses towards the upper side may represent shifting positions of the furrow and the sloping deposits lower down may be material from regular desilting.

NP2. VQ748797- 745800 marked on map sheet 1832B4. Altitude c.1780m. Length 840m, total fall 17.65m, average gradient 1° 12'. This starts from a strong stream at the top of a substantial waterfall; traverses a steep slope at an average gradient of 2° 30'; circumvents a reentrant at 1° 25' where a number of *mihomba* cultivation ridges have been dug across it; rounds a low hill at 0° 16'; and then traverses a broad gentle reentrant at 0° 25' for 160m on a bank up to 3.50m high to a low spur, and on across another similar reentrant for another 280m on a lesser bank at 1° 30'. The first broad reentrant slopes at around 7° and provides an area of c.200 by 150m below the furrow. Here a number of shallow ditches c.20m apart run down for about 150m from the furrow, and a take-off with probable remains of a stone lining feeds three of these. There are traces of cross furrows between the ditches. In addition a shallow diagonal furrow is traceable across the slope at gradients between 2° and 3° 40' to a saddle behind a rocky kopje above the parent stream close to its confluence with the Nyangombe river. Shortly before the broad reentrant a steeper slope of 10 to 12° has suffered some erosion and a number of small cairns perched on pediments indicate a soil loss of 30 to 40cm. There is a pit-structure on the crest of the

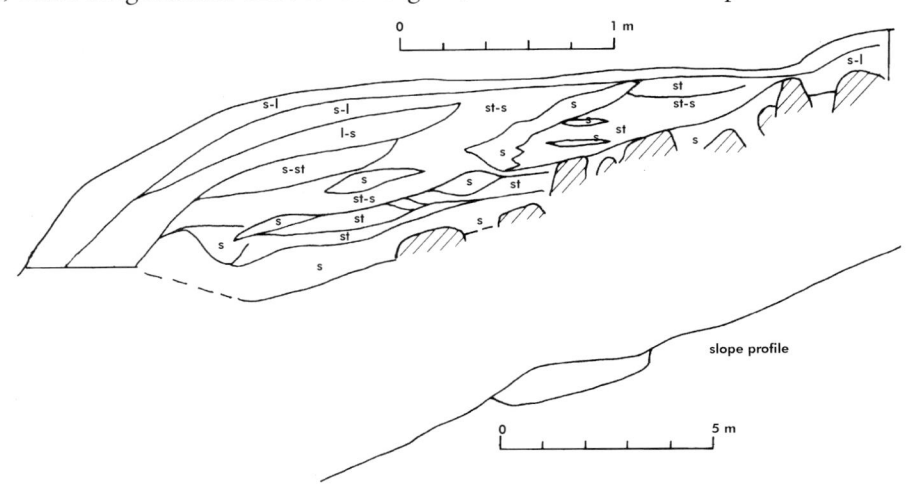

Fig. 25. Section of furrow NP1. s = sand; st = silt; l = loam

spur above the end of the furrow, and remains of a colonial period school abandoned in the 1940s (C.Payne, pers.comm.) in a tall eucalyptus grove immediately south of this.

NP3. VQ753792 - 750807 marked on map 1832B4. Altitude c.1830m. Length at least 350m, fall 5.7m, gradient 20' to 1° 30', average 56'. The first 80m are on a narrow alluvial terrace on the south side of a small valley, thence on a wide banked shelf revetted in places up to 1.60m high, around a broad spur with a gentle slope of c.10° below. It is then lost in a wattle grove, 100m before the edge of a major erosion gully. There are no obvious settlement sites in the vicinity but some recent contour ridges occur above and below the line. The irrigable area is c.120 by 100m and some shallow gullies are again visible down this slope on the aerial photographs.

NP4. VQ753791 - 750807 marked on map (Plate 11). Altitude 1850 - 1760m. Total length 2200m, fall 87m. This probably started 440m up the same side valley as the previous furrow below the foot of a waterfall, on the north bank; the actual line is not now visible here in the alluvial deposits but the average gradient would be 1° 10'. It emerges from the valley on a shelf c.6m wide c.7m above the stream and swings north on top of a broad bank for 300m at 1° 40'. From here the bank continues but the furrow follows a narrow revetted shelf about one metre below the crest for another 240m at 2° 30' into a reentrant where there is a small cross-stream. This is negotiated on an aqueduct of piled rocks c.5m wide, the stream trickling through the rocks about 2m below. There is a diverging upper bank before the stream which goes slightly uphill and may be an abortive line. For the next 330m after the stream there is a broad bank 2 to 3m high but the furrow again ran on a narrow ledge below the lip of this, eventually grading to the crest. The line then rounds a spur below a grove of *msasa* (*Brachystegia spiciformis*) and after a further 300m the bank divides into diverging lower and upper branches, with a lesser bank between. Concave furrow lines are visible on both the lower and middle banks. These banks fade out at a rock cross-dyke on the side of a spur within c.200m of the Nyangombe river, the average gradient from the stream crossing to this point being 2° 13'. Another bank continues to the end of the spur at a lower level (vertical interval 8.70m) across an increasingly steep slope at a gradient of 3° 50' and appears to end here above the Nyangombe river. From the cross-dyke, a stone-lined furrow drops diagonally across the slope for 120m at 7° 40' to the lower bank.

There are a number of areas of well-built stone-faced terracing, some pit-structures and an iron-smelting furnace above the furrow before the stream, and more pit-structures on the spur towards the end, but no settlement sites were seen below the furrow. There are some four hectares of potentially irrigable land before the stream crossing and around 10 ha below the lower course. Below and beyond the *msasa* grove are several more or less clear side take-offs from the bank. The clearest of these is stone-lined and runs diagonally down the bank and the area below this is heavily eroded, in some places to bedrock. There are occasional shallow depressions below these take-offs but not the clear straight ditches of furrows 2 and 9.

In both potentially irrigable areas there is some apparent terracing visible on the aerial photographs, but with the removal of grass cover by the fire of September 1998 this was clearly seen to be contour ridging of recent origin, while there is more contour ridging above the furrow before the stream. The contour ridges have a gradient of 1°. This contour ridging must postdate the construction of the furrow and may be associated with a colonial period site c.350m above the furrow before the stream. A number of circular revetted house platforms are discernible here, together with sundry iron-work, a broken bottle embossed "Spa Food Products Ltd" and a heavily corroded air rifle (identified as an American Daisy .176 pre-1940 model by Don Heath). Aerial photographs from 1950 show no settlement here and it must have been abandoned by that time. Another complete Spa bottle was found near a contour ridge below the furrow.

A cross-section of the furrow was excavated 150m beyond the stream crossing on the lower ledge of the shelf (fig. 26a). At this point, augering at one metre intervals above the lip of the main bank showed no trace of any furrow, but only homogeneous brown, slightly sandy loam. This became more clayey and redder in colour at depths ranging from 130cm at the edge of the shelf to only 55cm at the base of a steeper slope 13m above. The greater depth of brown loam towards the edge of the shelf suggests that soil was moved downslope to create the shelf as might be expected. The excavated section on the ledge shows an original furrow about one metre wide and 50cm deep cut into brown clayey loam and reinforced with some stones (which do not show in the section drawing). Lenses of silt and sand and some coarser gravel accumulated in the base of this furrow. The level was then deliberately raised by about 50cm with brown clayey loam similar to the material of the original shelf. Again a series of silt and sand lenses accumulated which are truncated on the outer side by later soil formation on the bank below. These lenses were covered by more brown sandy loam washing down from above after disuse, and dark grey humus topsoil filled in the remaining depression. The longitudinal gradient of the ledge at this point is around 2°. Using calculations provided by Elwell (1977) it has been roughly estimated from the gradient and cross-section that the furrow could have carried 65 or 160 litres per second at water depths of 20 or 30 cm respectively. This would be adequate to irrigate the potential irrigable land of approximately 10 hectares below and beyond this point.

NP5. VQ786823 - 779824 on the north side of the Nyamziwa river. Most of the course was measured by theodolite traverse except for the first c.200m, much of which is in dense bush. Altitude c.1950m. Length c.1000m, total fall c.15m. The measured section has a fall of 5.90m in 790m giving an average gradient of 43', with individual stretches all less than one degree and some almost horizontal. The upper course is considerably steeper. It starts in a narrow tributary valley of the Nyamziwa, crosses a steep bushy slope and an open spur to the edge of a major erosion gully 45m wide and about 10m deep. The line continues beyond this around a broad gentle spur and along the crest of a steep slope above Nyamziwa Falls. It then crosses a narrow rocky spur and continues on a bank for 120m to an eroded area, across which it can be traced dipping down at an average of 2° 50' to a group of three pit-structures, one of them above the furrow line. The large central pit, to which the furrow leads directly, is 9 by 8m in diameter with four or five large house bays on the platform (see Chapter 5 for pit-structure features); about 10 and 40m below are two basins walled on the lower side which would have caught effluent from flushing the pit, though no connecting ditches survive on the eroded slope.

An excavated cross-section above Nyamziwa Falls (fig. 26b) shows a width of c.120cm and maximum depth of 25cm which had silted to c.15cm. The gradient here is 30' which might have given a flow of between 30 and 70 litres per second, depending on the depth of water. The furrow appears to have been cut into the slope, whose cross-gradient is around 11°, and been banked on the lower side with sandy loam in which at least one stone was embedded, though no continuous lining was evident in the narrow trench. The dark grey loam above the primary silting suggests a period of disuse before further silting occurred. A lens of coarse red-brown sand above this probably represents a localised deposition event of material eroded from above, while the sandy loam overburden is likely to derive from more generalised slope wash.

Some of the land below the middle course would appear to be suitable for irrigation but there would be little scope for this towards the end, apart perhaps from the now heavily eroded area before the pits. The main destination would thus seem to have been the pit-structures; this is the only case observed of a direct association between pits and a heavily banked furrow, apart from NP1 above. (As noted above there are quite numerous cases in which pit-structures were served by smaller furrows.) The association provides a valuable indication of date, missing for the other large banked furrows. The pit-structure is well preserved and probably belongs within the 19th century, possibly a little earlier, but certainly precolonial (pit-structure dating is discussed in Chapter 5). This in turn gives a maximum date for the large erosion gully which interrupts the upper course and cannot be older than the furrow, even though it seems to be no longer active. Such erosion gullies are common in the National Park and adjacent areas and are likely to have been initiated by human activity, in this and a number of other cases probably by broken water furrows as discussed below.

NP6. VQ 721809 - 714814, on the north side of the Nyanore river, below the Troutbeck road. Altitude c.1780m. Length 1000m, overall fall 9.30m, average gradient 35'; gradient range 10' to 2° 50', mostly 30' or less. This a well graded, well built furrow, revetted below for most of its length and crossing several steep rocky slopes and stretches of bare rock with cross-slopes of up to 50°. It originates in a small spring above the right bank of the Nyanore, rounds a first spur on bare rock, skirts a reentrant, and crosses a steep rocky slope where it is revetted up to 2m high; crosses a flat plateau, skirts another reentrant, then traverses another steep rocky slope for c.250m to the beginning of the broad gentle reentrant in the angle of the Nyanga and Troutbeck roads, across which it is traceable for a further 100m. Here the gentle slope below was probably irrigated, though no clear traces were observed. Again there are no obvious settlement sites below the furrow, although there is a pit-structure c.80m above the end. There are at least ten apparently fairly recent graves on top of the final spur. There are some areas of probably recent *mihomba* cultivation ridges above the river at the lower edge of the final reentrant.

NP7. VQ ?763789 - 753788. Traceable from 758788 on the west side of the north circular road c.1200m from the junction with the Mare dam road, about 150m before a stream crossing. Altitude c.1880m. Measured length 600m, fall 13.55m, average gradient 1° 10'. The source is uncertain. East of the road there are suggestive traces on the 1950

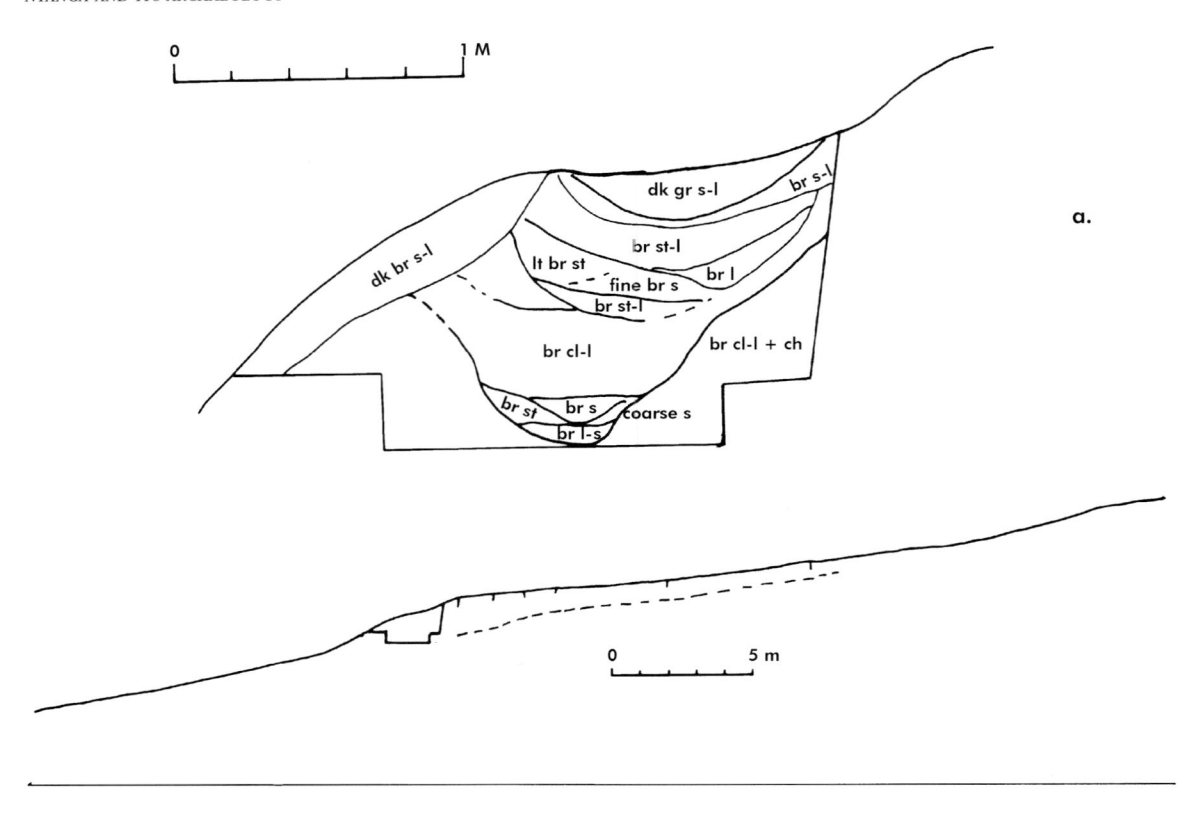

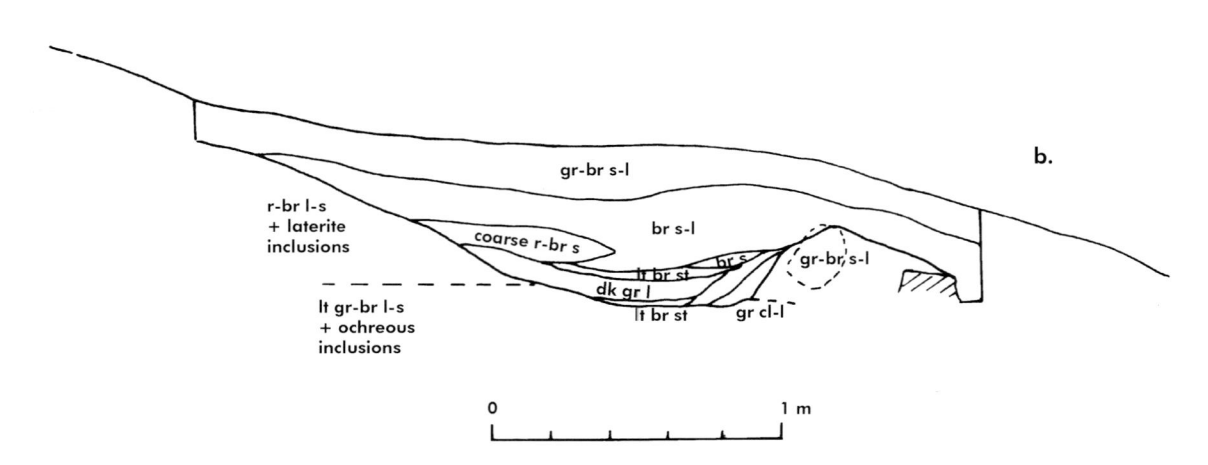

Fig. 26. Furrow sections: (a) Furrow NP4; (b) Furrow NP5.   l = loam; s = sand; st = silt; cl = clay; r = red; gr = grey; br = brown; lt = light.

aerial photographs skirting two low vleis and then taking a serpentine course into and out of a broad erosion gully to a marshy basin beyond, a total length from the road of around a thousand metres (although the straight line distance is little more than half that). This course has not been traced on the ground. Failing this source, the only explanation would have been the collection and channelling of run-off from the gentle slope above. Beyond the road there is a clear line with a concave channel above a low bank, along the north side of a gentle ridge, round a rocky spur to skirt the edge of a deep erosion basin. The average gradient to here is 57'. Thence it continues for 230m still near the top of the ridge at 1° 25' and dips into a reservoir. The latter is 16m long by 4.50 to 14m wide, cut into the slope, with an earth bank around 60cm high on the lower side and a lower bank across the middle. Augering showed only about 10cm of silting.

This furrow is of earth throughout with few signs of stone reinforcement. It resembles a contour ridge, and indeed there are contour ridges above and below it, but it is more continuous and its termination in the reservoir indicates a different function. Beyond the reservoir on the south and south-west slopes of the ridge there are quite extensive ranges of contour ridges, visible from the Mare dam road from just beyond the Nyangwe Fort junction. These were considered possible earth terraces before the fire revealed their true nature. About 40m west of the reservoir is a pit-structure with secondary usage indicated by the destruction of the tunnel and two small raised platforms in the bottom, while adjoining it are three or four revetted house-platforms c.5m in diameter; these are probably recent, having fragments of barbed wire around. This furrow gives the impression of being quite recent, contemporary with the later occupation which is clearly shown on the 1950 aerial photographs.

NP8. VQ 758790 - 753792. North side of the valley opposite NP7. Walked but not measured. Altitude c.1880m. Length c.600m, fall perhaps 20m. The end of this furrow is truncated by a fairly fresh steep erosion scarp immediately above the presumed upper course of furrow NP4. The course runs back on a quite eroded narrow shelf, winding around a more or less steep slope for c.400m as far as a steep recently eroded bluff cut back by the stream. It is not traceable above here but should have originated at about the bridge below the start of furrow NP7. Near the end, shortly before the truncation, is a stone-lined off-take dipping steeply across the slope to the top of the bluff above the stream terrace which the top of furrow NP4 should have crossed. It thus could have fed into the latter, although it is hard to discern the purpose.

NP9. VQ 7405 801 - 735802. South side of Nyangombe river at the end of the track past the Fisheries staff compound. Walked but not measured. Altitude c.1740m. Length c.530m, fall less than 20m. Starts in a small tributary stream with little flow at present, just west of the abandoned school mentioned under furrow NP2. Rounds a stony spur and runs north-west on a substantial bank (or rather on a narrow ledge below the crest of the bank as in furrow NP4) for c.200m to the end of a low spur. Here it enters a reservoir similar to furrow NP7, 15m long and up to 6m wide with an earth bank on the lower side, silted to c.20cm. From this it continues, swinging west around the end of the spur, still on a narrow ledge below the lip of a lower bank, just above a track parallel to the Nyangombe. Here there are several straight ditches running down from below the furrow, three about 15m apart, then two more about 30m apart. Passes just above a high bluff above the river and crosses the end of the main track to the edge of a bluff directly above the river terrace. This furrow has the typical features of the banked furrows as well as the straight ditches below probably for irrigation distribution, but also incorporates a reservoir similar to the probably later furrow NP7.

NP10. VQ 789748 - 787749, on the east side of the Pungwe valley. Length 240m, fall 5m, average gradient 1° 30'. Altitude c.1850m. This starts from the north side of a tributary stream of the Pungwe, skirts the side of a shallow reentrant on a low bank about one metre high and fades out at the end of a broad spur. Slope cross-gradients are up to 16°, 10° on the spur at the end. Augering at one point shows a width of c.80cm and a depth of 10cm. There is a largely ruined pit-structure c.40m above the apparent end and a broken iron-smelting furnace just below and beyond. It could have served the furnace and/or irrigated the gently sloping broad spur.

NP11. VQ 771701 - 774701, on the west side of the Pungwe valley, about 5km south of NP10, just west of a track down to the Pungwe from the Temburatedza Falls track. Not measured. Length c.300m, fall slight. Altitude c.1830m. It starts from the north side of a tributary stream of the Pungwe, rounds two spurs and reentrants to a small area of gently sloping land within a further reentrant above the stream. No sign of any stone-built settlement sites was noted in the vicinity.

NP12. VQ 772693 - 773694, c.600m south of NP11, south of the same track, on the western face of a hill, c.600m west of the Pungwe. Altitude c.1860m. First reported by Lorraine Swan. This appears to originate in a slightly spongy but not now very wet area and could also have collected run-off from more or less bare neighbouring rock. It traverses the side of the hill to NNE with no substantial banking to the head of a watershed diverging to the north-west. The length to here is 155m with an average gradient 1° 23'. From here it runs more steeply down the south-west side of the watershed to a pit-structure and could have continued to other pit-structures beyond, though it was not traced. A second furrow from the same point is visible on the aerial photograph and from across the valley to the west but is hard to trace on the ground. This runs SSE for about 500m, passing above two pit-structures. These are apparently domestic furrows serving settlement sites and could have had no irrigation function unless for limited homestead gardens.

NP13. VQ 797827 - c.796833, on east side of small southern tributary of the upper Nyangombe. Measured length 475m, fall 14.70m, average gradient 1° 47'. Altitude c.2050m. Starts in a small sandy valley, curves around a slight spur and shallow reentrant on a relatively slight sandy shelf revetted in places. Lost at junction with a disused motor track and not traceable round the end of the spur beyond, though there is some indication on the aerial photograph. There are two pit-structures immediately below the upper course and the probable destination was a line of six further pit-structures. Each of these and one of the first two has a large walled "paddock" above, the wall radiating from the pit platform and looping uphill to join the upper corner of the neighbouring "paddock", enclosing an area 30 or 40 metres wide. Such paddocks have not been observed anywhere else, although shorter radial walls are not uncommon as described in Chapter 5. Six of these eight pits have basins below their drains to impound effluent.

Troutbeck
There is a furrow (T1) c.4km north-east of Troutbeck on Tuscany Farm which is comparable to the banked furrows of the National Park. This is at the edge of the area described by Finch (1949) and is in fact shown on her map although she does not mention it in the text. It is close to and west of the Tsanga river and runs from VQ 827932 to 830933. Altitude c.1750m. It is visible as a marked feature on the 1986 aerial photograph but is now largely obscured by dense bush and young self-sown pine trees making it difficult to follow on the ground. The source is in a boggy tributary valley of the Tsanga and it is represented by a large bank up to 3m high and 8m wide, merging into a solid stone revetment 1.80m high towards the lower end. Total length from the aerial photograph is about 400m and the map gives a fall of around 20m, a gradient of just under 3°. It skirts the lower side of a spur and appears to end at the north-eastern end of this, where there is a dense local thicket but apparently no stone settlement structure. For much of the length the area below slopes initially fairly steeply, perhaps around 15°, but then levels out to a more gentle gradient. Between the lower end and the Tsanga river is a bog. Other furrows mentioned by Finch do not show as comparable banks and could not be traced with confidence on the 1986 aerial photographs.

Discussion
The furrows here described are not necessarily a representative sample for several reasons: area coverage is limited, the different types of furrows are not equally visible and identifiable, and many furrows have certainly been obscured or destroyed by forestry plantations, residential developments and other factors. Even so, they provide a nice problem in landscape archaeology, presenting varying technological responses to the potentials of water availability and topography according to perceived needs over perhaps several centuries.

A broad classification of furrow types is suggested, based on configuration, construction and apparent primary function, even allowing that some furrows cross-cut the proposed classes, others may not be comfortably covered, and further types may exist in areas not yet surveyed. The classification is necessarily based on the present research since published reports of specific occurrences (e.g. Mason 1933; Finch 1949) provide few or no details of construction.

Class 1. Narrow furrows of varying gradient and length, directly or plausibly associated with pit-structures or other settlement sites (NY1; NP12, 13).

Class 2. Generally well-graded furrows on relatively narrow revetted shelves, traversing ranges of terraces, probably for irrigating terraces below but also often serving settlement sites (M2, 3 D1).

Class 3. Furrows associated with cultivation ridges (M1).

Class 4. Well-graded furrows involving more or less massive earthen banks, rarely serving identifiable settlement sites but with potentially irrigable open areas below, occasionally with recognisable sub-furrows or ditches (D2; NP1, 2, 3, 4, 5, 9, 10(?), 11; T1; Udu).

Class 5. Furrows without major banks or stonework (NP7).

Class 1 would have served multiple functions, including domestic use, livestock and watering homestead gardens. Pits served by furrows could have been and probably were flushed out regularly, with the effluent in many cases impounded in basins or hollows below (see Chapter 5). If, as is argued there, the pits were used for livestock, this effluent would have been slurry or liquid manure, for use on the homestead gardens or adjacent fields (see Chapter 6).

Class 2 is the only type which may partially support the popular conception of irrigated terrace cultivation, but the serving of settlement sites may be an equally important consideration. They form a relatively small proportion of the furrows described above and, while doubtless more remain to be identified and recorded, the irrigation of terraces does not seem to have been a common practice as discussed at the beginning of this section.

It is not possible to generalise on Class 3, of which only one occurrence has been recognised, and even that may have primarily served settlements rather than the apparently associated cultivation ridges. Further work on ridge systems in appropriate situations may reveal more examples.

As far as the present research reveals, Class 4, although locally common, is of limited distribution, mainly in the northern part of the Park/Nyanga town/Troutbeck area. Sutton (1983:14) notes another example in a tributary of the Udu river at VR 6980 at an altitude of 1660m, also with straight ditches below, while there is a further example in the Burnaby area a further 9km to the WSW (VQ 595754-7, 1520m). There is no association of this class with terraces and little with settlement sites. It seems safe to conclude that their purpose was the irrigation of unterraced fields and the traces of distribution ditches support this. The soils however, like most of the mature highland soils, are extremely leached. Samples from below furrows NP1 (Appendix A) and NP4 are sandy clay-loams with very low pH, CEC, base saturation and potassium, only the organic carbon offering any fertility. Manuring would thus have been essential. The side ditches are parallel, spaced at 15 to 30m, and have doubtless been deepened somewhat by erosion (or aggraded so as to be unidentifiable). The areas between are generally flat-topped, defined by the depressed channels, and are clearly different in character from the narrower raised banks of the cultivation ridges described in this chapter. From recent practice, it might be expected that irrigated fields were fenced for protection from wild animals.

Class 5 is probably of recent origin, for domestic use or irrigation. There is another possible example, also resembling a contour ridge which may have served the abandoned school above NP2.

The proposed classes imply varying levels of organisation and cooperation for construction, maintenance and operation, according to the area or settlements served. Class 1 serving individual homesteads or groups of homesteads would have had relatively limited labour requirements and straightforward water allocation, and suggests nuclear or extended family ownership and organisation, perhaps up to the level of a small village. Class 2, if used to irrigate terraces, might have required more formal control in the allocation of water rights and the organisation of construction and maintenance. The single example of class 3 may also imply control above the family level for the sharing of water from a limited source, whether this was for supplementary irrigation of a large area of cultivation ridges or only for a number of scattered homesteads. The large earthen banks of class 4 must have involved a far higher degree of labour cooperation for construction and some institutionalised control of water allocation to irrigated fields, at least at the level of a large village. However none of the furrows described need imply any more centralised social or political organisation and it may be noted that the ethnographic examples below are all practised by acephalous societies where ownership and control is generally exercised by elders of one or more lineage groups.

Design and Construction
Technical data on channel design provided by Elwell (1977) enable rough estimates of flow for the National Park furrows to be made, given sufficient excavated information on width, depth, shape of cross-section and gradient, though other parameters such as surface roughness and vegetation would be difficult to allow for. Doubtless the original builders worked by eye and gravity without benefit of complex equations to establish specifications. Gradients are generally tailored to the terrain and determined by the desired destination in relation to the source. Initial courses in side valleys are generally relatively steep to achieve adequate flow of water where furrow width is often restricted by steep cross-slopes. Gradients may similarly be increased to achieve a viable line and flow through obstacles such as rocky spurs. Elsewhere gradients are rarely more than about 1° 30' and may be as little as 10' or 20' where it was necessary to maintain maximum height. One can only speculate on the methods used to maintain the minimum gradient. In this steep and varied terrain the eye is often deceived so that furrows may appear to run uphill, although instruments indicate the contrary. The furrow builders would certainly have developed better judgement through experience and probably managed without any form of levelling device in most cases. In less stony situations, the flow of water under gravity would give sufficient indication, but it is hard to see how this would have sufficed in the case of the Nyanore furrow, NP6, where the lower portion of the furrow maintains an average gradient of only 30' for nearly 300m across a steep and very rocky slope, while further back it is revetted across a bare rock slope of up to 53° at well under one degree. This could however be a recent construction if it was contemporary with the graves above. Here volume of flow must have been sacrificed for minimum fall, since width is greatly restricted

by steep slopes and rocks.

All furrows except class 5 have some degree of stone reinforcement of the lower side. On more gentle, less stony slopes this may be a single line of stones, not always continuous, set in an earth bank, and these stones may have had to be carried some distance. On steep and stony cross-slopes more formal revetment was necessary. The best example of this is again NP6, where a revetment 2m high was built up to carry the furrow across steeply sloping bare rock. In some cases it was necessary to cross small side streams or drainage lines. In the case of NP4 the stream course had been filled with large boulders through which the side-stream could filter, while in some of the Nyangui furrows advantage was taken of natural rock sills. Such crossings would have been liable to wash-outs after rain and would have needed at least annual repair. A current furrow in the Kumbu valley near Nyautare is carried across a stream on a hollowed log (Soper 1996, fig.11), and doubtless this expedient was used for relatively small spans in earlier times.

The large banks of Class 4 represent a massive movement of earth which appears grossly excessive for hydrological effectiveness, since even quite a large furrow could have been retained by a much lesser embankment. Possibly the broad shelf was cultivated and irrigated by water lifted from the furrow. The banks can hardly be natural features such as old river terraces since some run 40m or more above the parent stream and could not have survived intact for the long period implied by such down-cutting. Again it is hard to conceive of any cumulative process deriving from the use of the furrow which would occasion the growth of such banks from lesser beginnings. One is forced to conclude that enormous labour was expended in the construction of the banks, involving the shifting of many tons of earth from up-slope over distances of 20m or more in the case of the gentler slopes. This requires further investigation and quantification by measured profiles and augering. Bank construction must have taken place before the furrow itself was inserted, so that water flow could not have been used to maintain gradient. The diverging upper bank before the stream on NP4 could suggest that occasional errors were made.

In a number of cases described above, the furrow ran on a narrow shelf on the outer face of the bank, a metre or so below the crest. The first case observed was on NP4 below the stream crossing, where augering at one metre intervals across the top of the bank at two locations showed no trace of any other furrow. It was conjectured that the builders had been unable to raise the level high enough across the aqueduct to reach the top of the previously constructed bank. This explanation would not however apply to NP4 before the stream crossing where adequate height was available, nor to D2 or NP9. Possibly the bank was originally wider with a high lip on the outside giving a very deep furrow, but it is unlikely that this would have peeled off so neatly and consistently over quite long distances, while the ledge is often seen to be reinforced with stones forming a substantive edge. This feature thus remains unexplained.

Reservoirs are another feature not previously recognised in the Park area. The four examples described above are associated with furrows of Class 2 (D1), Class 4 (D2: NP9) and Class 5 (NP7). Their function is clearly for water storage and it may be significant that in all these cases the water source is relatively exiguous, making storage desirable. Storage may have been temporary accumulation to provide sufficient volume for specific usage events, or more long-term to assure a more substantial regular supply than provided directly by the furrow. Water could have been lifted out for use or tapped by cutting and deepening a channel through the bank. Assuming the reservoirs to be contemporary with the original furrow construction, the practice of water storage is of some antiquity. It also continues to the present: some farmers in Chirimanyimo dig cisterns above their gardens, fed by small furrows, and run a hose pipe from the base, the head of water providing pressure for spray irrigation.

As mentioned at the beginning of this section, take-off structures from parent streams have not been observed and may be assumed to have been washed away since Hall, Randall-MacIver and Wieschoff apparently saw some earlier in this century. Such structures would in any case have required constant maintenance and renewal. Bolding *et al* (1996) note that modern indigenous take-off dams in Chimanimani are permeable and specifically designed not to capture the whole flow of the stream. The same is the case for traditional furrows of the Marakwet in Kenya (Soper 1981) where dams are often constructed of brushwood, impeding the flow sufficiently to direct water into the head of the furrow; these dams have to be rebuilt every year.

Informal furrows in the Chimanimani area described by Bolding *et al* (1996) offer parallels in physical details and some information on social context. They imply that the furrows have only been developed since early colonial times, although one might expect that the possibilities would have been recognised and exploited earlier.

Technically speaking, the furrows are simple and straightforward earth constructions. The adequately laid out furrows, nicely meandering along the hill slopes, reveal that [the] irrigators have sufficient knowledge of topography, contours and hydraulic laws ..... Furthermore there are some ingenious structures such as stone paths or road crossings and an aqueduct ..... Clearly, the use of local knowledge and skills and of local materials implies that at any moment irrigation structures can easily be repaired and maintained without outside technical assistance ..... The individual furrows are not known by 'names', nor do they have an organised management structure, nor do acknowledged leadership positions exist (p.212).

Most furrows have a simple infrastructural set-up with temporary stone weirs diverting water from the river and earth furrows to convey the water to the fields. This puts no heavy demands on required construction and maintenance skills. In most cases the flow of water under gravity is used as a means to level furrows and locally available materials are used to construct aqueducts, bridges and canal lining at vulnerable places. The furrows serve multiple purposes of which irrigation is the main one ..... Water is perceived to be owned by no-one (p.215).

Dating and associations
The furrows provide imprints of specialised human activities on the landscape over an appreciable period of time. In view of the variety of types recognised, it may be questioned whether these represent an evolutionary trend in design and function or merely reflect varying practical or culturally regulated responses by local communities to their various needs.

Class 5 has been plausibly assigned to the colonial period and needs no further discussion. Classes 1, 2, and 3 seem to represent straightforward technical responses to physical circumstances and needs and hence might be regarded as generalised and not time-specific. Class 4 however stands out from the others in its scale, technology, limited distribution and apparently specialised function for open field irrigation, suggesting attribution to a limited group of people, probably over a limited time period.

All the furrows described, with the exception of Class 5 and the possible exception of NP6, are almost certainly older than the end of the 19th century, from the negative evidence of early European accounts. Some are probably not much older than that, as noted at the beginning of this section. Class 1 is directly associated with pit-structures whose primary occupation would surely have been reported by the early observers had they seen it. On the other hand, the state of preservation of some pit-structures (e.g. Fishpit) and a few radiocarbon dates suggest that they had not been long abandoned, indicating that these furrows should have been in use some time in the 19th century. How much earlier they were constructed must remain an open question for the time being, but it is not unlikely that the builders of the earlier ruined pits also built furrows as far back as the 17th century. Classes 2 and 3 are present along the foot and lower slopes of the western escarpment, an area which was apparently depopulated in the 1890s, and some (of uncertain class) were available to be reopened by the early Dutch Settlements. The terraces and cultivation ridges with which they are associated are undated but are likely to go back at least into the 18th century. Class 4 has few direct associations, but in the apparent absence of other settlement sites it may be suggested that these furrows were built by the inhabitants of the pit-structures more or less close above them, and this view is reinforced by the link of NP5 and NP1 with such pits. A 19th century date again seems probable. Some cultural distinction from other pit-structure occupants may be implied, since pits in this immediate area do not seem to be directly served by furrows and one wonders why no pit-structures were built *below* the furrows; although substantial stretches are relatively stoneless, at least some suitable sites were available. These furrows must have been used by Manyika people who were in this area at that time, as they were in the Mkondwe area near Penhalonga; areas further north were occupied by Unyama people.

Some furrows were reopened in early colonial times and are still in use. Others described here may also have been reused, though there do not seem to be any reports of this apart from that of Finch (1949). This might apply especially to those which still exhibit some concavity, such as parts of NP1 and 4. This reuse could plausibly be associated with the reuse and modification of neighbouring pit-structures and the late site above NP4. Aerial photographs taken in 1950, when many "squatters" were still resident in the northern part of the National Park, do not show any furrows in active use, apart from large resuscitated furrows such as that from the Mare river serving the Rhodes Hotel. However, that photography was in winter when there is unlikely to have been any cultivation and small furrows may have been grassed over. At that time a series of small rectangular plots below NP3 and fields below NP1 suggest that those two furrows were being used, as were NP7 and possibly parts of NP4 and the Udu furrows. The rest were certainly abandoned, as were D1 and D2.

It may be concluded that there was a general appreciation of hydrological principles and the potentialities of furrow construction among the people responsible for the terrace complex, and that this was put into operation where physical circumstances permitted and the need was felt. The technology adopted was usually the simplest appropriate to the circumstances, but in the case of Class 4 was developed to a much higher degree.

Furrows and erosion
In the National Park and surrounding areas there are numerous very large erosional ravines cutting the slopes, most of them with little active erosion at the present day. The subsoil here, as shown on the geological map, consists of coarse-grained adamellite granites, here deeply weathered. Most of these ravines follow lines of natural drainage for small catchments but others seem to be independent of this. The larger ones may be up to 250m long, 30m or more wide and 10m deep. A few are associated with old furrows which may have played a part in initiating them. The case of the Nyamziwa furrow NP5 is mentioned above, the ravine having eroded back for about 100m above the furrow. The case of furrow NP8 had been noticed and photographed by C.Payne in 1959 and he has also provided information on two accounts of actual gully formation.

He learned from Don Purdon via Doug Watson, how in the mid-1930s a gully was created on the right bank of the Mare river below Nyangwe Fort when the furrow which led to the Rhodes Estate manager's house burst its bank. The gully is probably that visible on the aerial photographs at grid reference 745770 which appears to be about 20m wide and 60m long and is now stabilised by vegetation. The second case is related in the unpublished memoirs of a Mrs Filmer who lived near Chapungu Falls, 6km SSW of Pungwe Falls, for 10 years from 1937. Her breakfast was interrupted one morning by a loud roar from the spontaneous creation of such a gully, the result of a modern furrow having been diverted on to the grass for cleaning, apparently overnight.

It is thus clear that these ravines can be rapidly initiated by furrow breakage. However this would not appear to be the cause of the majority of the ravines, though human agency may well have been a contributing factor through disturbance of the vegetation cover and soil by the activities of the pit-structure inhabitants.

"Dams", ditches and pit-structures
It has been noted that groups of pit-structures were often served by furrows where a source of water was available and the topography permitted, and it has been suggested that the water was used for domestic purposes, livestock housed in the pits, irrigated gardens and for flushing out the pits. Small dams below such pits to impound the effluent have also been noted in connection with furrows NP1, 5 and 13, and one linked to Nyangui G1/21 is described in Chapter 8. In some cases however there is a more complex system of ditches and hollows associated with the pits. Sites of this type have been described for Nyanga Downs (by Finch 1949:51-5) and for northern Nyangui (by Summers 1958:20). The latter site seems likely to be the extensive group of pit-structures in the vicinity of the old Chirimanyimo dip tank some 4km south of Matinha, which was not examined in the present work.

These accounts note that pit-structures are served by furrows, and ditches run from the pit drains to open, apparently unlined hollows, or in some cases to the usual dammed basins. Other similar hollows may be fed directly by the furrow, providing an unpolluted water supply. Ditches may be quite long and the hollows often have "spillways" with further ditches below. The hollows may be quite large, up to 10m or more in diameter and 2m deep, or relatively small, 3 or 4m in diameter. Many if not all of the former are likely to be old ruined pit-structures of the type excavated at Nyangui G7/1 and Matinha I, whose stone revetment has either been largely robbed or has collapsed and been buried; they could of course have been reused as dams. Finch suggested that the hollows might have been "pond gardens" for the cultivation of rice, but many would seem to be too small or deep for this. If, as Summers and Finch imply, the smaller hollows and some of the larger ones were for water storage for irrigating fields below, it is hard to see how the water could have been subsequently extracted.

A site of this type (fig. 27) was surveyed in northern Nyangui at grid reference VR750243 and is designated Matinha IV on Figure 64. This is in fact the site at the presumed destination of furrow NY1. Here there is a group of three pit-structures, three large hollows and a complex of smaller hollows in an area of c.7000 square metres, and the larger pit-structure and the two upper hollows are presumed to have been fed from the furrow. A long ditch runs down from the drain of the pit for about 100m, either through one of the large hollows or bypassing it, to just above a group of six small hollows, and thence onwards another 120m to the edge of a steep slope. Ditches also run from the two upper large hollows, that from the southern one for 70m to two small interconnecting hollows and thence to join the ditch below the other small hollows; that from the other hollow could not be traced so far. A paved floor was encountered in the southern large hollow while collecting a phosphate sample, showing it to be a ruined pit-structure.

The ditch from the pit-structure would have led the effluent to the small hollows below, and if desired into the lower large hollow, something like a sewage farm. There is a fairly level shoulder below the small hollows to the north-east where slurry or precipitate collected in them might have been used on gardens. The other large hollows with their ditches may represent a separate water storage and distribution system operated by the occupants of the pit-structures. Alternatively, and assuming that they are indeed old ruined pit-structures, the ditches may be contemporary with the hollows and represent an earlier system for collecting effluent, unconnected with the later pit-structures but used in the same way.

Eight samples were taken for phosphate analysis from the positions marked on figure 27 with a view to testing whether there could have been any concentration of animal dung.

1. base of the large NW hollow, in the top of brown clay below 20cm of topsoil - 5500 ppm
2. base of the large SW hollow between the paving stones, below 20cm of topsoil and 10cm of brown loam - 12500 ppm
3. the upper small pit on the ditch from no.2. Brown clay below 15cm of topsoil and 5cm of gravelly deposit - 450 ppm
4. the western small hollow of the line of four. Brown clay below 10cm of topsoil and 5cm of brown loam - 450 ppm
5. the eastern of the two lower small hollows. Greyer brown loamy clay with stones, below 25cm of stony topsoil - 13500 ppm
6. the ditch 7m above no.3. Brown gravelly loam below 17cm of topsoil - 12500 ppm

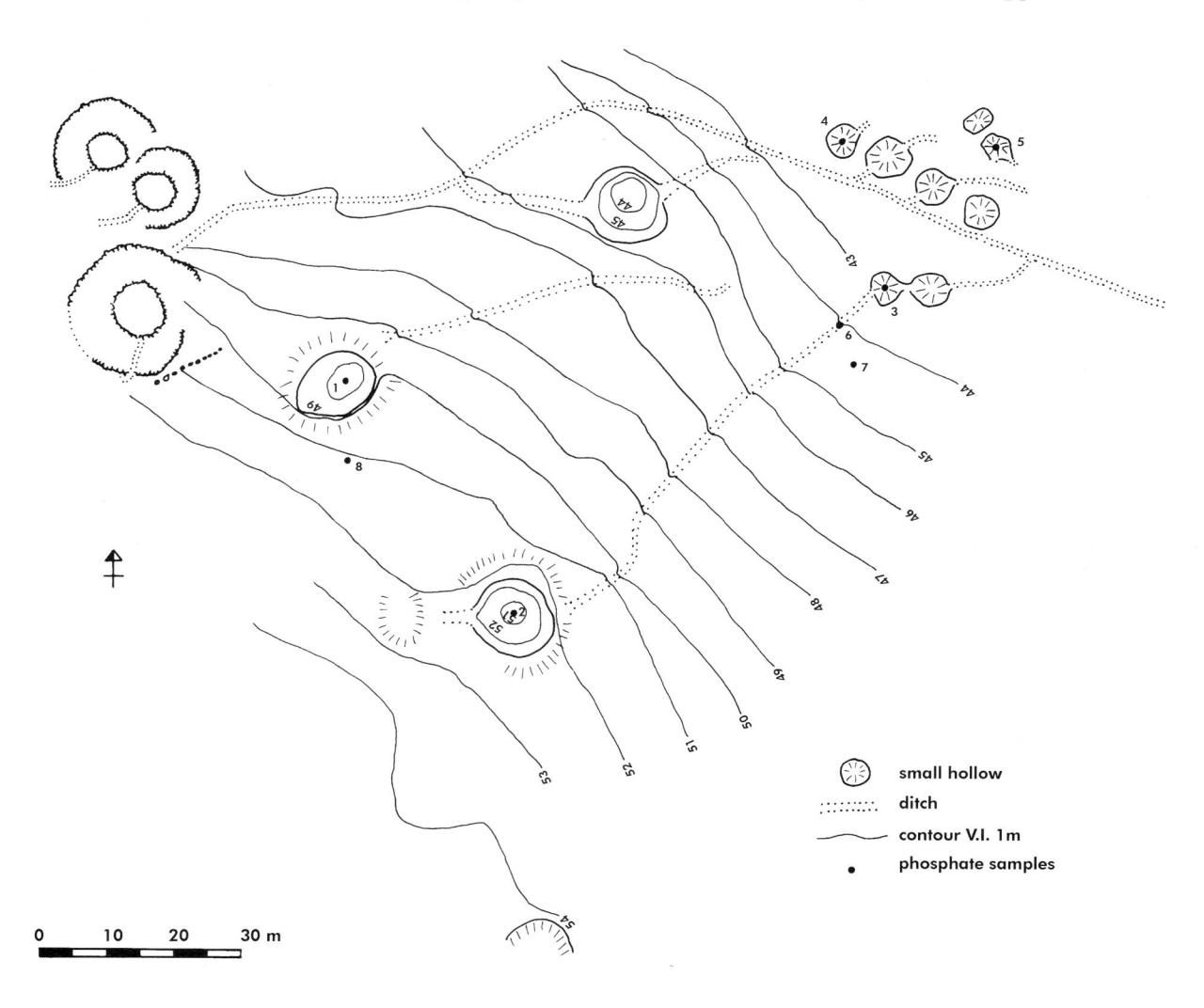

Fig. 27. Pit-structures, hollows and ditches at Matinha IV, south of Chirimanyimo

7. open ground 6m south of no.6. Brown gravelly loam below 17cm of turf and brown loam – 8000 ppm
8. open ground 10m south of no.1. Clean brown loam below 20cm of topsoil – 25500 ppm.

Values for the paved SW large hollow and the third small hollow are high and for the NW large hollow moderately so, consistent with the dung/slurry hypothesis for the hollows as ruined pits. However, samples 7 and 8, located away from the features to provide a background count, are also high, while samples 3 and 4 from two of the small pits are very low. Possibly these pairs of samples were transposed in the laboratory, in which case the pattern would be quite consistent.

A comparable ditch with small hollows is described in the site report for Matinha I in the valley north of the site (Chapter 8, fig. 64), but there does not seem to be any adjacent level ground suitable for cultivation.

The ditches and hollows represent the same principle for impounding effluent as the small dams immediately below many pit-structures, but removed to a greater distance below. This may reflect greater fastidiousness but is more likely to reflect the location of suitable sites for the homestead gardens. These features are different in character from the reservoirs of the National Park and do not seem to be related.

Indigenous irrigation in eastern Africa: some examples for comparison
Traditional water management systems are widespread in Africa where local conditions allow, and many of these involve hill-furrow technology. Published ethnographic accounts largely approach the subject from the point of view of irrigation and the management of the systems, often with little attention to the technological details. They do however provide useful comparative material from which it may be possible to suggest aspects of the Nyanga systems not directly observable in the archaeological evidence.

Hill furrow systems are quite diverse in the environments in which they exist and the ways in which they exploit them (Adams *et al* 1994). There are however limited options for leading water under gravity with simple technology. Some form of dam is required to divert water from the stream, while provision for flow control is needed to ensure that the furrow capacity is not exceeded, with consequent damage from erosion or washouts from overtopping. Furrow gradients and construction must be tailored to the slopes and soils traversed, and structures provided to cross gullies or streambeds where necessary. The devices for tapping the water for use can range from purpose-built structures to simple temporary holes cut in the furrow bank as circumstances require. With such limitations and ranges of options, inevitably certain generic similarities will be observable when making comparisons between hill-furrow irrigation systems in different places.

Useful published information is available for several systems still operating: the Marakwet in the Kerio Valley on the western side of the Rift Valley in Kenya (Soper 1971; Ssennyonga 1971; Adams *et al* 1997; Watson *et al* 1998); the Sonjo in northern Tanzania (Adams *et al* 1994); the Taita on the Taita Hills in south-western Kenya (Fleuret 1985); and the Konso in highland Ethiopia (Amborn 1989). A historical account of the Njemps near Lake Baringo in northern Kenya in the 19th century is given by Anderson (1989); while the archaeological site of Engaruka not far south of Sonjo in Tanzania also provides comparative information (Sutton 1986 and 1998 are the most comprehensive reports).

Environmental situations vary. Marakwet and Sonjo are situated in semi-arid lowlands below better watered highlands from which permanent streams descend. Rainfed cultivation is practised but in many years is only marginally viable so that irrigation is a useful supplement (the Marakwet also cultivate rainfed fields on the escarpment above). Njemps irrigation was on a flood plain within a semi-arid environment and was developed in response to outside demand from trading caravans, being abandoned early this century as demand declined; irrigation was used to start a sorghum crop well in advance of the rains. Engaruka, occupied around the 16th and 17th centuries, is in an even drier situation at the foot of the Crater Highlands, where reliance on irrigation would have been more essential. Taita and Konso are in better watered highlands where irrigation is applied to garden plots, and to extend the growing season for staples in the case of Taita. In all cases except Njemps, cultivation is, or was until recently, for subsistence.

In Nyanga, the lowlands below the escarpments are in a somewhat comparable topographical situation to Marakwet and Engaruka but average rainfall at 800 or 900mm is higher. The highlands are more comparable to the Taita and Konso environments. Irrigation in both highlands and lowlands would have served to extend the single rainy season and to span dry intervals within it but would not be critical to viability in most years.

Descriptions of technical details of the East African furrows and their engineering are uneven. The best studied system, and one of the most impressive, is that of the Marakwet. Permanent rivers and streams descending the Rift Valley escarpment are tapped for irrigation of unterraced fields and supplementary uses on the piedmont slopes and floor of the dry Kerio valley. There are over 40 furrows, the largest over 14km in length with a fall of 1400m. Permeable take-off dams are of brushwood, boulders and logs and have to be reconstructed each year. The head of the furrow is controlled by a sluice to regulate flow, vertical rockfaces are negotiated on aqueducts supported by log scaffolding, and one furrow may cross another or a streambed by hollowed logs or structures of stone slabs. Gradients are generally steeper than with most Nyanga furrows as there is normally ample difference in altitude between source and destination. Rapid flow can thus be sustained of up to 200 litres per second, but this entails adequate lining to combat erosion, daily monitoring and regular maintenance.

At Engaruka main feeder furrows were taken off at the head of outwash fans and led for considerable distances along the footslope of the escarpment. Stone-lined side furrows distributed water among shallowly terraced levelled fields which cover a total of around 2000 hectares.

Details for other systems are more sparse. Furrows may be up to a kilometre or more in length in all cases and are stone-lined where necessary, unlined in the case of Sonjo and Njemps. Permeable take-off dams are noted for Sonjo and Taita, in the latter case designed to wash away after heavy rain to avoid overloading the furrow. Aqueducts of hollow logs or banana stems are used by the Sonjo and Taita. The Taita exploit very small streams by use of storage dams or cisterns (Wandera and Soper 1986). These have a capacity of up to 100 cubic metres and are filled overnight and drained for irrigation the next day by means of a pipe at the base, in the past made of a hollowed log; here is a possible parallel for the Nyanga reservoirs described above.

Apart from Engaruka, irrigation of terraces among these examples is only practised by the Konso. Some terraces near the settlements may be carefully levelled with a raised edge so that fields can be flooded by irrigation or rain to allow maximum infiltration, and measures to drain excess water are provided. Unterraced riverside plots are also irrigated by the Konso but more distant terraces are not. Sonjo fields are divided into small basins through which water is distributed in turn. Marakwet and Taita direct water with a hoe through their sloping fields. Tapping of water from the furrows, where mentioned in these accounts, is by cutting a simple hole in the bank, but formal stone sluices are identifiable at Engaruka.

Residence at Engaruka was in nucleated villages with terraced house sites above the main feeder furrows, a pattern similar to the Sonjo in the recent past. The Konso also live in (walled) villages, but for Marakwet and Taita residence is more dispersed within lineage-based territorial units

Irrigation systems require direction and social cooperation, for the mobilisation of labour, for construction and maintenance, for the allocation of water rights and the resolution of disputes. The examples described here are all practised by acephalous societies with no central authority. Among the Marakwet furrows are constructed, owned and managed by individual lineages which are also territorial units. In the case of smaller rivers where available water is limited, a furrow may be jointly owned by several lineages who have an annual rotation of primary usage rights. In Sonjo organisation is by an institutionalised group of elders for each village, labour being provided by the young men. In Njemps organisation and control were by a council of elders on which senior members of specific clans had greater influence. In Taita furrows are controlled by elders of lineages which are territorial as well as kinship units. Here principles of water allocation are embedded in fundamental social forms and processes but are not egalitarian: users closer to the source, in addition to the physical advantage, are usually more influential socially and politically than tail-enders.

Within the common factors imposed by the technicalities of water control, all these examples reflect appropriate but differing adaptations to varying conditions of topography, climate, altitude and water availability. While none are directly comparable to the Nyanga systems, they offer some hints for the reconstruction of missing elements and interpretation of usage. Take-off dams from streams would almost certainly have been permeable, capturing only a part of the flow, while even the best constructed dams would be readily destroyed by flood waters, leaving little or no trace. The apparent lack of formal sluices where furrows of Class 2 traverse terraces does not preclude their use for irrigating the terraces, and the postulated irrigation of sloping fields from furrows of Class 4 finds parallels in Marakwet and Taita.

Some aspects of the Nyanga furrows are not seen in the examples quoted, notably the heavily banked furrows of Class 4 and the linking of Class 1 directly to homesteads, with their use for flushing livestock pens. This serves to emphasise the variety of individual adaptations.

From the point of view of organisation and administration, the way in which this is commonly integrated into wider kin-based institutions of social control in the ethnographic examples suggests a similar hypothesis in the Nyanga case, outside any direct intervention by the Manyika or Saunyama chiefs.

Clearly human intelligence can anywhere appreciate the potential for channelling water for perceived needs and has the capability to realise this, even with relatively simple technology. Whether or not this potential is developed to achieve some degree of agricultural "intensification" depends on interacting factors, including subsistence needs related to population pressure, political and social requirements and outside demands for produce.

The evidence presented above for furrow technology and for the agricultural works as a whole demonstrates the competence of the Nyanga farmers in exploiting the potentials of their environment. The stimuli behind this exploitation and the ways in which these agricultural works were utilised are discussed further in Chapters 6 and 7.

Plate 2. Terracing and enclosures in Ziwa ruins, looking north from the summit of Mt Ziwa.

Plate 3. Ziwa SN113. Section of terrace 7

Plate 4. Ziwa Mujinga A. Section through terrace wall and terrace above

Plate 6. Chirangeni. Granite terracing

Plate 5. Terraces at Maristvale site SN51, from the south

Plate 7. Chirangeni. Stone-lined open drain through the terraces

Plate 8. The Mwenje basin north of Mount Muozi. Virtually the whole basin is worked into cultivation ridges

Plate 9. Demera hill. Footpath following furrow D1

Plate 10. Demera hill. Reservoir below furrow D1

Plate 11. National Park looking north-east. Furrow NP4 traverses the slope in the middle distance

CHAPTER 5

SETTLEMENTS, HOMESTEAD STRUCTURES AND OTHER FEATURES

This chapter defines and describes the different types of settlements and homestead structures belonging to the Nyanga archaeological complex. These comprise: early hilltop settlements; pit-structures (ruined and well-preserved); various forms of enclosures – pit-enclosures, double-concentric enclosures, split-level enclosures and "simple" enclosures; and forts. The excavation of individual examples of most of these is reported in Chapter 8. Some typical structures within homesteads – divided houses and raised platforms – are also described, as are iron-working sites. The distribution of the different types of settlement structures is more or less mutually exclusive in time and space and they characterise different periods or areas within the complex as discussed in Chapter 7.

The maps, Figures 28 and 29, illustrate the areal distribution of sites recorded during the project, as well as from previous records in the Archaeological Survey index of National Museums and Monuments. Some of the latter are unconfirmed reports, including a few "slave pits" below the normal altitudinal range. Broad distributions are clear from the positive records, but negative indications of apparent gaps in distribution should not be taken as reliable so that the full extent of occurrence of any particular type is not necessarily portrayed. Where concentrations of records make it impossible to plot sites individually, the size of symbols gives an indication of numbers. On Figure 28, the symbols indicate the number per 5km grid square, though isolated examples are shown in their actual location. "Simple" enclosures, more or less ubiquitous, are not shown, nor are miscellaneous sites regarded as 19th century Manyika "refuge" sites, relatively common in the southern half of the area.

EARLY HILLTOP SETTLEMENTS

These occur at high elevations all along the northern highland range, including most of the highland peaks (fig. 29). Chirimanyimo Hill, Nyangui 1732DD27 and Muozi are described in Chapter 8. They are characterised by scattered small walled hollows, usually densely vegetated, among boulder formations, and larger low-walled enclosures on the surrounding open slopes. Terraced house platforms also occur on several sites. Total site size often reaches 300m or more in maximum dimension. These sites had not been recognised as a distinctive class prior to the present research and they are called "early hilltop settlements" for want of a more descriptive term. They are distinct from the "forts" described below or the less formal but probably defensive walled hilltops such as Demera Hill above Nyanga town.

The following sites have been identified and it is likely that more remain to be discovered.

Grid.ref	Name	Elevation	Size	Situation
VR 760270	Chirimanyimo Hill	2180m	c.700 x 500m	Mountain top
VR 742308	N of Chirimanyimo	2080m	>100 x 50m	Ridge top
VR 764174	Nyangui 1732DD27	2050m	c.300 x 120m	Ridge top
VR 760155	Nyangui For.Res	2100m	c.180 x 70	Spur
VR 741154	Mount Muozi	2100m	c.250 x 75m	Isolated plateau
VR 771135	Chinyamaura Hill	2190m	? (smaller)	Mountain top
VQ 778994	Rukotso shoulder	2170m	c.75 x 50m	Top of spur
VQ 754996	Rukotso peak	2400m	c.150 x ?100m	Mountain top
VQ 762927	Worlds View	2380m	?230 x ?80m	Mountain top

No comparable sites have as yet been recorded south of World's View and distribution appears to be limited to the northern range

The walled hollows are common to all sites. They range in diameter from about three to seven metres and are sunk up to a metre or so below the surrounding surface. In sloping situations the wall may be freestanding on the lower side and more of a revetment on the upper side. It is possible that some of the smaller examples could have been sunken houses, but a larger one at 1732DD27 (Chapter 8) could not have been roofed and they are more likely to have been for livestock. They appear to be a prototype for the pits of the later pit-structures described below.

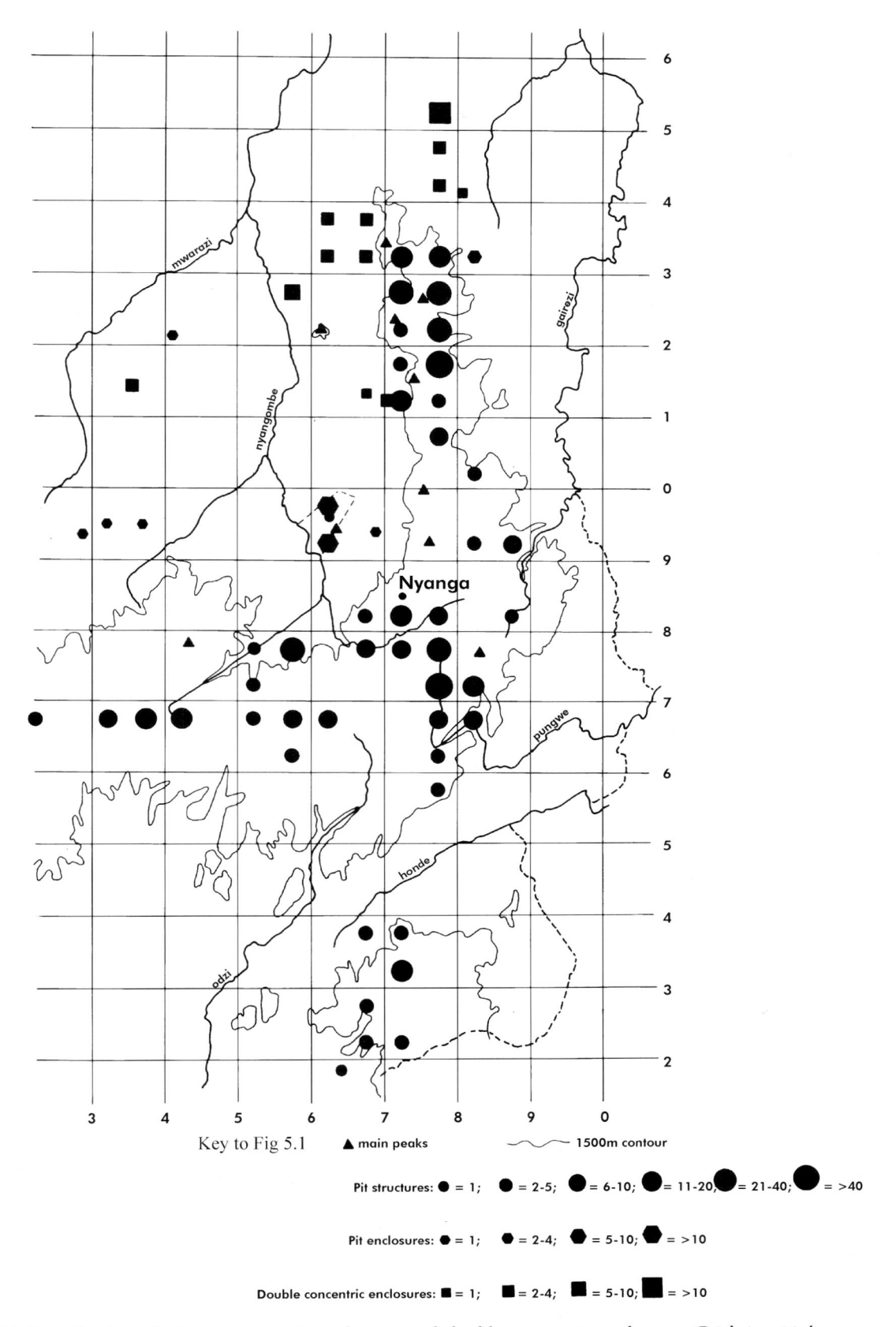

SETTLEMENTS, HOMESTEAD STRUCTURES AND OTHER FEATURES

Fig. 28. Distribution of pit-structures, pit enclosures and double concentric enclosures. Grid size 10 km

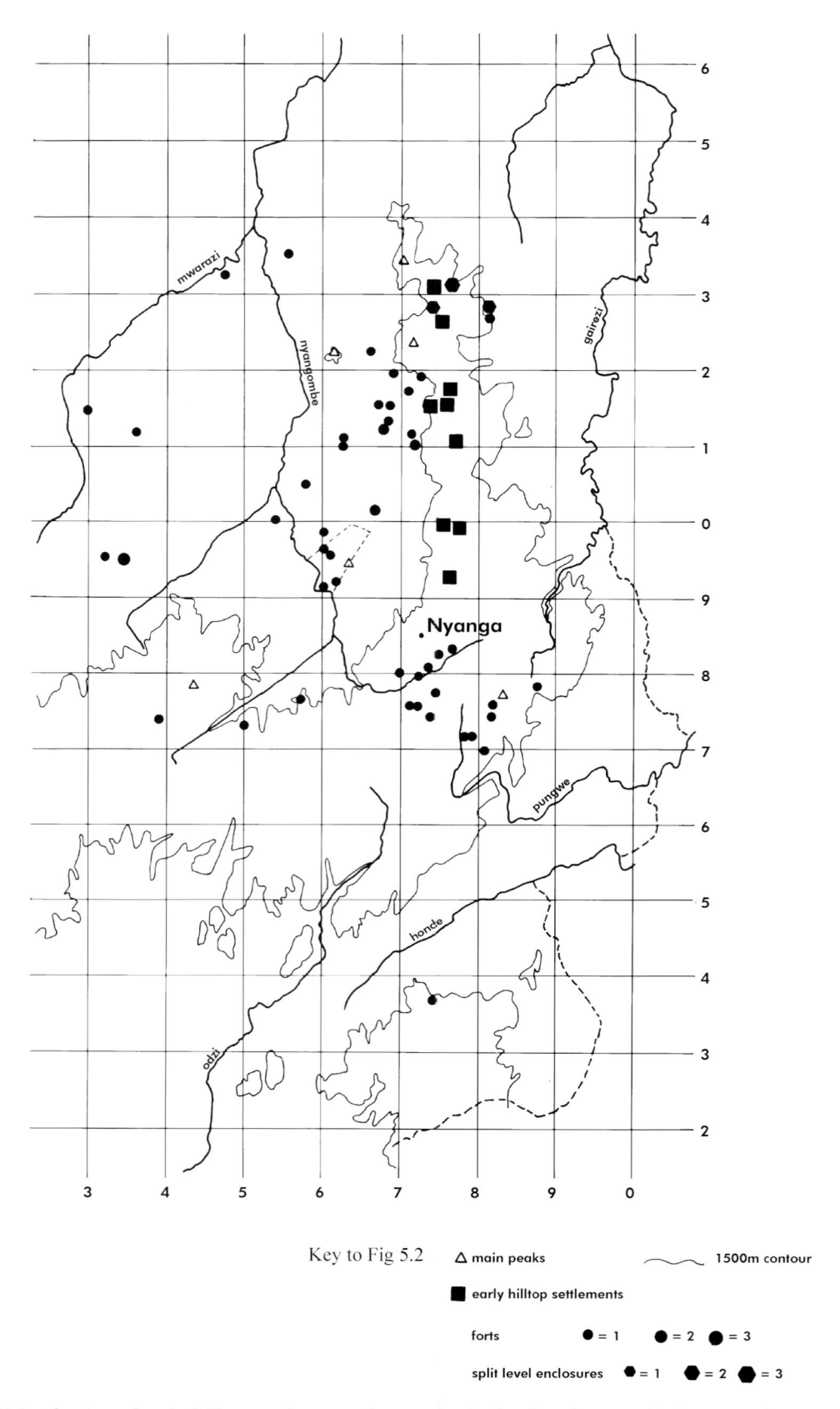

Fig. 29. Distribution of early hilltop settlements, forts and split-level enclosures. Grid size 10 km

The larger enclosures are around 20m in diameter and have low walls usually formed by a double line of large vertical stones, originally with an earth fill (fig. 50). The width of the walls is around one metre and height is 30 to 40cm; they probably formed the base of a quickset hedge (Plate 12). These may have been hedged homesteads or could also have been for livestock; none have been excavated. These larger enclosures are absent at the Muozi site where the isolated plateau provided no immediately accessible grazing. However the site across the saddle to the east of Muozi on the root of the same spur (VR760155) has an unusual long wall and could arguably have housed the cattle of the Muozi residents. Muozi is also unique in having a large ash midden (see Chapter 8).

Terraced platforms on steep slopes are present at Chirimanyimo Hill, Muozi and on the north side of Rukotso peak; they are at least partly residential, some with provision for livestock (Chapter 8: Chirimanyimo).

Potsherds, virtually all undecorated, are prolific at the excavated sites and quite common on the surface at other sites where vegetation permits observation, but no potentially datable imported items such as glass beads have been found in spite of careful search, with exception of one bead from Chirimanyimo Hill.

Chirimanyimo Hill is the largest and most impressive site. It also differs from the others in that part of the hilltop itself is surrounded by a wall, within which are irregular walled enclosures, while there are substantial terraced platforms below the crest of the hill. It is suggested that this site was of greater relative importance than the others as discussed in Chapter 7.

The excavations and dating evidence (especially the radiocarbon determinations – Appendix F) show that these are the earliest of the Nyanga stone structures so far recognised and investigated, dating to the 14th and 15th centuries AD. There is no direct association with agricultural terracing since all these sites lie above the upper altitudinal limit of this, so they do not contribute to the discussion of terracing or help to establish the date of its beginning. However, the pottery analysis (Appendix D) indicates cultural continuity to the early ruined pit-structures of the 16th or 17th century (see below and Chapter 7), showing that these settlements belong to an early phase of the Nyanga complex as a whole. It should be noted that even these ruined pits are not directly associated with terracing.

No clear antecedents for this occupation have been identified, locally or in areas further afield for which archaeological evidence is available. It may well have emerged as an idiosyncratic adaptation to rather special conditions. Implications of the hilltop locations and dating are discussed in Chapter 7.

Pit-structures

Two categories of pit-structures have been recognised from the recent research: well preserved and clearly recognisable examples (known in colonial times as "slave pits"; Plate 13), and examples which have been reduced to open grassy hollows with little extant sign of stonework, here distinguished as "ruined pit-structures" (Plate 14). The former, although later in time, will be discussed first to describe the characteristic features. Pit-*structures* are distinguished from pit-*enclosures*, the latter occurring in a limited area of the western lowlands (see below).

Well preserved pit-structures are a common feature of the Nyanga archaeological complex, found in their hundreds, if not thousands, in the Eastern Highlands from beyond Chirimanyimo hill in the north at least as far as the Penhalonga area in the south (fig. 28). Excavated examples described in Chapter 8 are Nyangui G1/21 and Fishpit, while others have been excavated by earlier workers (see below).

These features are remarkably standardised in their basic features throughout their distribution (fig. 30; 69; 72). They take the form of an artificial platform built out from a slope so that the upper edge is at about ground level, sometimes slightly raised or dug into the slope. The sides and lower edge are revetted with stone facing which may be stepped back in two or more tiers to give the necessary height on steep slopes, the lower edge being commonly 1.50 to 2m high. The platform is roughly oval, 15 to 25m in diameter, and in larger examples often has an irregular plan through the addition of extensions. In some cases a radial wall extends outwards from the platform up to 25m or more (Plate 15); this is interpreted as sheltering a homestead garden. In one, possible unique, case in the National Park, the radial walls of a line of pit-structures had been extended up-slope to enclose large "paddocks" 30 to 50m wide (see Chapter 4, furrow NP13).

Within the platform, more or less central, is a large stone-lined pit, usually four to nine metres in diameter and 1.80 to 3m deep (Plate 13). The base of this pit is at or sometimes below the original slope profile and is graded in the same direction as the slope. If not on bedrock, it is paved with flat stones. The walls of the pit would have been built up as the platform was constructed. They are neatly built of irregular-shaped stones cunningly fitted and wedged to form a vertical face; no batter (backward slope) is required for stability as they are locked together by the compression of the solid platform fill of earth and rubble. The largest stones were reserved for the coping around the top and may measure up to a metre or more in length and 40cm in height, weighing several hundred kilogrammes; levers must have been used to move these. No evidence of roofing has ever been noticed.

Access to the pit is through a curved tunnel from the upper side. In the great majority of cases this curves to the right from the pit, but in rare cases a left-hand curve is imposed by rock formations; however, in some (but not all) examples in the southern part of the National Park and to the west it appears to curve left from choice. Tunnels are neatly walled, and roofed and paved with flat slabs. Entrances at either end have remarkably consistent measurements, 1.10m high and 50cm wide with a variation of about 10cm; walls at the entrances often have a slight batter so that the top is wider than the bottom. Internal headroom may sometimes be greater. Length of the tunnel varies but is commonly around seven metres. The exterior entrance usually has an open revetted passage sloping down from ground level.

At the lower side of the pit is a small sump at the mouth of a drain about 20cm high and 25cm wide which leads through the platform to emerge on the slope below, or into a sunken ditch if the base of the pit is well below ground level. In some cases this ditch leads to a small dammed basin or hollow.

On the platform around the pit are walled bays for houses or other structures, the walls being around 50cm high. One house is invariably sited above the tunnel and has a slot near the middle of the floor, through which logs could be dropped vertically to close the tunnel (as recorded by Lloyd 1926). Up to about eight other house-bays may be arranged on the platform around the pit, and a narrow walkway may be left most of the way around the edge. In many cases one or more of the houses has a low dividing cross-wall, one half being roughly paved with stones and the other having a clay floor, presumably to provide shared accommodation for people and small livestock (see Chapter 8: Fishpit

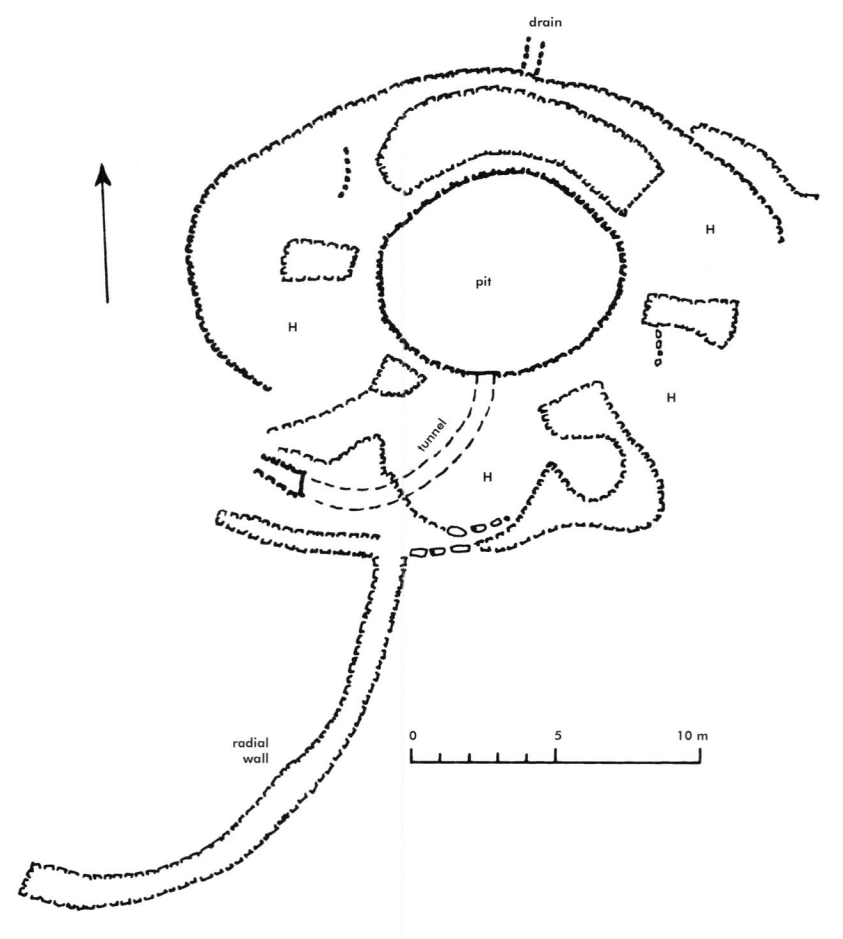

Fig. 30. Pit-structure, Chirimanyimo

for excavated examples). Such houses have two entrances, one from outside the platform to the paved half and the other from the floored side to the pit surround. This type of house, common to the highland pit-structures and the lowland enclosures of Ziwa ruins, is discussed in a separate section below.

Adjacent to the house over the tunnel there is often a smaller bay two to three metres in diameter with a higher floor; at Nyangui G1/21 (Chapter 8) this has a floor laid on stone slabs with a cavity beneath. Such bays may have contained storage huts. Some pit-structures also have the normal type of raised platforms (also discussed below) for storage huts as commonly seen in the lowland enclosures. Some pit-structure platforms are too narrow to support houses as noted by Summers (1971:33); these appear to be normally adjacent to larger examples to which they are probably ancillary.

The function of the pit is most plausibly interpreted as accommodation for livestock, almost certainly small cattle. The central defended situation within the heart of the homestead indicates valuable property and no other explanation is consistent with the observed facts. In addition, this is recounted in a number of recorded traditions (Lloyd 1926; Wieschoff 1941:28). The hypothesis of the penning and stall-feeding of cattle for the accumulation of manure was advanced by Sutton (1988), but archaeological evidence of beasts small enough to enter the tunnels was lacking. This was eventually provided by the excavation of the Muozi midden (see Chapter 8, Appendix B and Plug *et al* 1997) which yielded bones of dwarf cattle only a metre or so in height.

One might expect that the kraaling of livestock in the pits and their regular passage through the narrow tunnels would have led to abrasion of the stone walls, and that this would indicate the size of the stock. Details for Nyangui G1/21 are described in Chapter 8 but are inconclusive. Examination of a number of other pits and their tunnels built in both dolerite and granite has also shown no clear signs of such abrasion; some stones are smoother than others but with little consistent pattern, and these appear to be stones that had been softened by weathering prior to use. Small projections which might have been attractive for scratching are not noticeably worn, and fresher surfaces appear to have resisted abrasion. It might be concluded, very tentatively, that cattle in the pits were not very crowded and may have been kept there semi-permanently, supporting the stall-feeding hypothesis. It may be noted that the tunnel of the granite pit-structure reconstructed for display in Nyanga National Park (Plate 13) shows considerable smoothing and polish around the entrance due to the passage of thousands of visitors each year.

Pit-structures were thus residential units for people and their stock, with the cattle stalled in the pit where they would have been sheltered from the cold winds of winter and protected from surreptitious theft; goats and probably calves were kept within the houses. The apparent lack of any other common contemporaneous occupation structures in the highlands shows them to be family homesteads for the general population. They are often loosely clustered in the landscape in groups of anything up to 30, and such groups or individual examples may be served by artificial water furrows as noted in Chapter 4. Water from these could be led through the pits themselves and there are occasional structural indications of this (e.g. Brand 1970); the impoundment of slurry effluent flushed from the pits through the drain has also been mentioned in Chapter 4 and is discussed in Chapter 6. Pit-structures are found consistently above an altitude of 1400m; lower examples within this range are associated with stone terracing, but most are above the upper limit of terracing, between about 1700 and 1900m.

These well preserved pit-structures appear to date from the 18th to mid-19th centuries, consistent with the sparse bead evidence (Appendix E). Those on Rhodes Estate, some of the best preserved, had been abandoned some time before the 1890s, but hardly earlier than the mid-19th century since the survival of *dhaka* features and three recent radiocarbon determinations indicate a late continuation. (The 17th century date from Fishpit is not consistent with the well preserved *dhaka* structure with which it is associated and must be anomalous.)

These features have fascinated observers over the past century and a number have been excavated (Hall 1905; Randall-MacIver 1906; Mason 1933; Fripp and Wells 1938; Summers 1958; Brand 1970; Storry 1974). The published reports provide a wide sample which is useful for comparison with the results of excavations undertaken in the present project, namely at Nyangui G1/21 and Fishpit described in Chapter 8. A particular shortcoming of several of the earlier excavations, however, was that details of the houses which stood around the central pit were often neglected or misunderstood.

Earlier explanations for the pits, reasoned or fanciful, may be of some interest to the curious. Most observers were reluctant to accept the cattle explanation, mainly because of the size of the tunnel. Early writers saw them as dungeons for slaves employed in building and working the terraces, and the term "slave pits" is still current in some circles. Other improbable explanations have been mine shafts and gold-washing tanks (Peters 1902); refuges for women and children in time of danger (Randall-MacIver 1906:29); defensive bunkers (Gwatkin 1932); water storage tanks (van Hoffen 1966); grain silos as a symbolic representation of Astarte's womb (Bruwer 1965); or play pens for keeping the children out of mischief while their mothers were busy (tongue-in-cheek by Mears 1969). Less fanciful explanations for the pits have been sunken houses (Wieschoff 1941) or for grain storage (Stead 1949). The argument that they were for small cattle is not entirely new. It was accepted by Finch (1949), while Summers (1958) postulated that they were for small stock or possibly pigs.

Ruined pit-structures
The above description of well-preserved pit-structures facilitates the understanding of features representing an earlier ancestral form. Such features are now wide grassy hollows with little extant sign of stonework, often with slight depressions in the upper and lower margins. Excavation in two cases (Chapter 8: Nyangui G7/1 and Matinha) has shown the remains of a stone-lined pit and entrance passage (Plate 25) conforming to the plan and within the upper size-range of later pit-structures. There are however some consistent differences. In both excavated examples the passages do not appear to have been roofed tunnels and so would not have had houses over them. There are traces of possible house floors defined by single courses of stones on the upper side of the pit but stone-walled house-bays are absent. The presence of pottery and beads of glass and copper support domestic residence.

The poor state of preservation clearly indicates a date earlier than the well preserved pits and an age in the 16th and/or 17th century is indicated by the glass beads and radiocarbon determinations from Nyangui G7/1 and from Muozi midden, part of which is contemporaneous (Appendices E and F). (The Matinha radiocarbon determinations may be anomalous, only the very earliest end of the calibration range fitting into this bracket). The consistent collapsed condition may also be partly explained by the relatively poor quality of the stone revetting revealed in the two excavated examples. It is possible that some of these hollows could be rather later abandoned pit-structures from which the stone has been robbed, especially where single examples occur among groups of well-preserved pits.

Distribution appears to be limited to the northern highlands, and the Nyangui Block G survey detailed below shows an altitudinal separation above the later pit-structures, although at Matinha they occur together.

The pottery associated with these features is related to that of the early hilltop settlements (Appendix D) and an evolution of the pits from the sunken walled hollows of the latter may be postulated; this in turn would imply a similar livestock function for the walled hollows. There is less obvious direct resemblance to the pottery of the later pit-structures, but the structural affinities show a clear ancestral relationship.

As noted in Chapter 4, Summers (1958:15, 20) on the basis of surface examination interpreted these hollows as earthen dams for impounding water, following Finch (1949:53); this a likely secondary usage in some cases, supported by the conformation of old ditches. At his site in the "Nyamaropa Reserve", apparently south-east of Nyangui hill, he observed that: "usually an earthen pit can be found between each pair of stone-lined pits", implying contemporaneity. However this is hardly a consistent pattern, although the Matinha plan (fig. 64) also shows a couple of cases.

Size of well preserved pits
Pit diameters for well-preserved examples range between 3.5 and 11m and there is some correlation between average size and altitude, documented by an analysis of all recorded pits. This analysis considers a total of 260 pits, most of them from personal observation but some added from earlier accounts, notably Finch (1949) and Mason (1933). The majority are from the area from the National Park northwards, with 14 from Burnaby to the south-west and a few others scattered as far as Tanda to the west and Mkondwe to the south. Most of those below 1600m are from the Maristvale/Mwenje area and Burnaby. Areal coverage is thus uneven and while a substantial number of pits is considered they do not necessarily constitute a representative sample. In the present research, diameters were estimated by eye to the nearest half metre, with occasional recourse to a tape measure for control; most pits have heavy vegetation, much of it thorny, which inhibits descent into them and the manipulation of measuring tapes without laborious clearance. Ruined pits are not included.

Table 5.1 analyses the results by 100m intervals. While there is considerable size variation at all altitudes, the average diameter shows a clear increase above 1800m. The pattern is distorted by a couple of anomalies: a single line of six large more or less contiguous pits at 1610m five kilometres north-east of Chirimanyimo hill, and eight large pits between 1500 and 1600m far to the south at

Mkondwe near Penhalonga (recorded by Mason 1933). In view of the interpretation of the pits as cattle pens, the pattern suggests the greater importance of cattle above the upper limit of terracing at around 1700m.

Table 5.1.   Diameter of pit-structure pits by altitude

altitude (m)	no.	range	average	
> 2000	29	5 to 11m	7.14 ± 1.28m	
1901 - 2000	38	4.5 to 9m	6.52 ± 1.16m	
1801 - 1900	70	4 to 10m	6.10 ± 1.37m	
1701 - 1800	58	3.5 to 8m	5.35 ± 1.05m	
1601 - 1700	15	3.75 - 9.5m	6.75 ± 1.70m	- total
	6	7 to 9.5m	8.33 ± 0.98m	- 6 pits NE of Chirimanyimo.
	9	3.75 - 6.75m	5.69 ± 1.15	- remainder
1501 - 1600	30	3.5 - 9.75m	5.59 ± 1.90	- total
	8	6.4 - 9.75m	8.02 ± 1.12	- 8 pits at Mkondwe.
	22	3.5 - 8.5m	4.70 ± 1.21	- remainder
1401 - 1500	17	3 to 8.5m	5.04 ± 1.40	
1301 - 1400	3	5 to 6m	5.50 ± 0.50m	
Total	**260**			

As noted above, pit-structures occur consistently above 1400m and only three pit-structures are recorded below this altitude, two of them from near Maristvale; the third is the only fairly typical pit-*structure* at Ziwa ruins and, interestingly, appears to be the one excavated and described by Randall-MacIver (1906:17). None of the pit-*enclosures* or double-concentric enclosures described below occurs above 1400m and the reason for this dichotomy is unclear. This level more or less coincides with the foot of the western escarpment of the main highland range but there is no such sharp distinction further to the south-west.

Survey of pit-structures in Block G, Nyangui Forest
Nyangui Forest Reserve extends for some 27km along the narrowing spine of the Nyanga highlands, from Rukotso peak in the south, across the Bende Gap to just south of Chirimanyimo peak in the north. Most of the southern two-thirds of this area is now afforested with pine trees, *Pinus patula*, obscuring the archaeological features, mainly pit-structures, and the planting programme is extending rapidly northwards. In 1994 planting was taking place in Block G on the eastern slopes of the highland ridge. The aerial photographs show pit-structures in this area and a survey was undertaken to record these and study their distribution, since little systematic information is available on this for the Nyanga complex as a whole.

The area examined (fig. 31) covers approximately 6.5 square kilometres, situated on three parallel interfluves, from the road near the crest of the main watershed to the lip of the steep eastern escarpment, a distance of some 2.75 km with a vertical fall of around 420m.

The general topography is mainly controlled by the geological structure (Stocklmayer 1978). The spine of the highlands is formed by dolerite strata, intercalated with and often capped by old sedimentary sandstones, argillites and shales. These strata dip gently from west to east and overlie adamellite granites. The contact between the dolerite and the granites forms the lip of the escarpments to east and west. The western escarpment is close to the crest of the watershed, here declining gently northwards from 2160 to 2000m. To the east there are broad grassy, sometimes rocky, slopes to the lip of the escarpment at around 1680m, below which there is a precipitous drop of some 250m. Behind the eastern lip is a broad, relatively level plateau or shelf, best developed in the north of the area. A fairly narrow band of sandstones, argillite and shale, intercalated within the dolerite, forms a lesser step at around 1880m. The ground above this band of sedimentary rocks slopes relatively gently overall but with local steeper or flatter variations. Soils developed on the dolerite are red-brown and clayey and often deep. The more level areas show few stones apart from localised outcrops and hence have few stone-built features. Steeper slopes however have a fairly dense surface cover of stones and boulders of dolerite or sandstone.

Drainage tends to the ENE and is formed by tributaries of the Nyatungu river which have cut more or less deeply incised valleys separating broad spurs. Most of these valleys have at least some permanent flow of water. Current vegetation cover is predominantly open grassland, with few trees except in localised protected environments such as stream valleys and archaeological pit-structures. Many of the more level areas were settled by "squatters" in the 1980s, who were evicted by the Forestry Commission at the end of the decade.

Almost all stone-built structures were identifiable on the vertical aerial photographs at a scale of 1:25000 under the generally short grass cover and only a few were added from ground survey. The commonest features are typical pit-structures and terracing. Both well preserved and ruined pit-structures could be distinguished on the photographs by their morphology and vegetation cover. In the survey all well preserved pits were visited on the

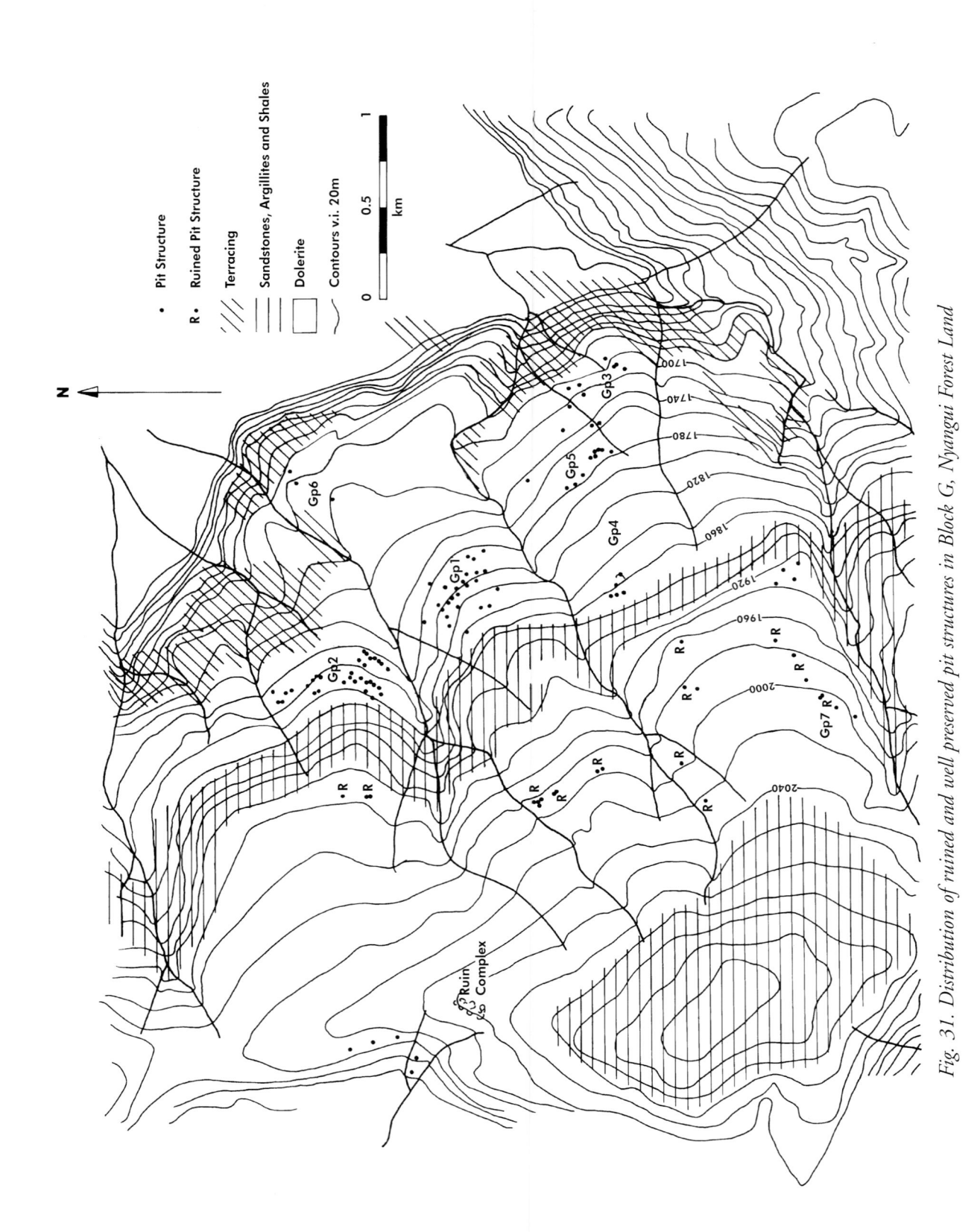

Fig. 31. Distribution of ruined and well preserved pit structures in Block G, Nyangui Forest Land

ground and estimates made of diameter and depth of the pits, and the number and size of house-bays on the platforms. Some ruined pits were examined on the ground and others plotted from the aerial photographs. Terracing was mainly plotted from the photographs with some observations on the ground.

The well preserved structures have pits up to 3m deep, and their entrance tunnels are largely intact and more or less unsilted for their entire length. Such structures usually support a dense woody vegetation of shrubs and creepers, often thorny and often with at least one large tree, typically *Cussonia* in this area. Such thickets are easily visible on the aerial photographs but make ground examination difficult and uncomfortable. Many of these pit-structures have a radial wall around one metre thick, 60cm high and five to 25m long, oriented approximately to south or north, and hence on these generally eastern slopes roughly on the contour. In pit group 1 at least (see below), many also have small basins around three metres wide, dammed by a stone wall immediately below the drain outlet from the pit; this feature was not systematically recorded for other groups. Tunnel entrances are curved and all except one curve to the right from the pit. House-bays defined by low stone walls are present on the platforms in varying numbers, though often difficult to trace in the dense thickets. There is invariably one such bay situated over the tunnel. Adjacent to this tunnel bay is often a small bay with raised floor as described above.

The ruined pit-structures form grassy hollows around 6 to 10m in diameter, often with bracken but little woody vegetation. These may have some visible remains of stone revetment and traces of a depression marking the position of the entrance passage. Rare examples are sometimes found among groups of intact pits but distribution of the two types is generally distinct. The marked difference in vegetation cover between the two categories is presumably due to the sheltering effect of the intact stone revetment from fire and wind. In areas affected by recent settlement, the natural vegetation has been disturbed and a very dense tall cover of grass and small shrubs has developed, especially on the platform around the pit, obscuring the structural features (which may have been disturbed anyway) even more than the normal woody growth.

Pit-structure distribution. (fig. 31). The well preserved intact pit-structures lie mostly in a fairly tight altitudinal band. They have been divided into six groups for reference purposes, but these groups also reflect the pattern of settlement in relation to the landscape.

Groups 1 and 2 form large relatively dense clusters on the two northern interfluves, between 1770 and 1830m, below the band of sedimentary rocks. Group 1 consists of 32 pits, three of them ruined, and covers about 11 hectares in an area some 500 by 300m. Group 2 has 29 pits, four of them partly ruined, and covers about 8 hectares in a band some 625m by 180m around the contour.

The small group 4, only five pits in c.0.6 ha, is on the next interfluve at around 1860-70m, again below the step of the sedimentary band on a broad gently sloping shelf; these have been affected by recent settlement. Group 5 is below another step on the same spur and consists of a single line of nine pits extending over c.350m at about 1770m. Below this, across a minor valley, is the more diffuse group 3, 10 pits in c.8 ha, between 1700 and 1740m, fairly close to the lip of the escarpment. Group 6 consists of only two double pit-structures, both somewhat collapsed, also just above the escarpment on the middle spur.

The altitudinal range of all these pit-structures is thus from 1700 to 1870m.

Above the sedimentary band, at least 23 further pits are identifiable, mostly from the aerial photographs but a few added from ground survey. All of these are ruined pit-structures, including G7/1, the excavation of which is described in Chapter 8. They range in altitude from about 1930 to 2020m. There is a strong implication that the upper slopes were abandoned at some point and settlement concentrated lower down; one might speculate on some change, perhaps climatic, which made the higher levels uninhabitable.

On the crest of the main range is the early hilltop settlement 1732DD27, and to the north-west of this on the western side of the ridge are a few intact pit-structures at around 2000m. That they occur higher than those on the eastern slopes may be explained by shelter from the easterly winds.

Terracing

Terracing occurs generally around the lip of the escarpment, extending down it where practicable. In stonier areas it may extend above the top of the escarpment up to around the 1760m contour. A few pit-structures of group 3 and group 6 (the latter all more or less decrepit) occur below this level but not in the immediate vicinity of terracing. Distribution of pit-structures and terraces is thus mutually exclusive, as it is further north in the Chirimanyimo area and apparently elsewhere in the upper altitudinal range of terracing.

Pit size. Diameters of the well preserved pits were estimated by eye to the nearest half-metre with occasional cross-checks by measuring to ensure reliability. In the case of oval pits, average diameter is used.

Average pit diameter by altitude is as follows:

Altitude	No. of pits	Mean diam	S.D.
1701 - 1750	14	4.6	1.0
1751 - 1800	39	5.56	1.02
1801 - 1850	28	5.6	1.19
1851 - 1900	5	6.5	2.07

The lowest pits appear to be significantly smaller, conforming to the general pattern of the much wider sample analysed above.

There is also some variation in the average pit diameter between the groups:

Group	No. of measurable pits	Range	Mean	S.D.
1	29	4.25 - 8.0	5.72	1.16
2	29	4 - 8.25	5.5	1.13
3	10	4 - 6.5	4.94	0.96
4	5	4.75 - 10.0	6.5	2.07
5	9	4.75 - 6.5	5.5	0.65
6	4	3.5 - 4.0	3.75	0.5

Here the larger size of the highest group 4 may be noted and the small size of the lowest group 6, which may again follow the general altitudinal trend, although the samples are small and the variation in group 4 large.

Groups 1 and 2. Some rough statistics may be given for the largest groups 1 and 2 to show general pit-structure characteristics and internal variation.

Group 1 has 32 pit-structures between 1770 and 1830m in altitude. Pit diameters range between 4.25 and 8m with an average of 5.72 ± 1.16. Two of the largest pits are at 1820m but three equally large at 1780m. Depth ranges from 1.80 to 2.90m with an average of 2.25 with little correlation between depth and diameter. Sixteen pit-structures have radial walls, the majority between west and south-west and only one east of the north/south line, reflecting the slope aspect. Twelve have clear basins below and another eight have possible basins, while the rest have none. Twelve of the pits with radial walls also have basins or possible basins, but three of them have none, while six of the structures with basins have no radial walls, so the association is not constant. There is no consistent correlation between pit size and presence of radial walls or basins.

Some provisional figures can be given for the number and size of house-bays with due allowance for dense vegetation. The number of observable house-bays per platform ranges from two to nine. Two of the largest pits have the largest number of bays (seven and nine), but otherwise there seems little relationship with pit size. Internal diameters of bays over the tunnel range from 2.75 to 7m, with most between 4 and 5m. Of the other bays, two are less than 2m, 28 between 2 and 3m, 42 between 3 and 4m and 10 between 4 and 5m, seven of the latter associated with larger pits more than 7m in diameter.

Group 2 has 29 pit-structures with an altitudinal range of 1780 to 1820m, the largest number at around 1810m. Pit diameters range from 4 to 8.25m with an average of 5.5 ± 1.13. The three largest pits, 7.5, 8 and 8.25m, are in the upper part above 1800m, but smaller pits also occur here as well as lower down. The largest pits are towards the southern side of the group. Depth ranges from 1.60 to 3m with an average of 2.38m; there appears to be no correlation of depth with diameter. Thirteen pit-structures have radial walls, six of which run north-east and only one is south-east of a NE/SW line, again reflecting the general slope aspect. No data was collected on the presence or absence of basins in this group.

The number of observable house-bays on the platforms ranges from one to seven with an average of 3.25. There is a tendency for the larger pits to have more bays, but the largest appears to have only one, while one 6m pit has seven. The main bay over the tunnel is generally around 4 to 4.5m in diameter and others range from 2 to 4.5m.

ENCLOSURES

Enclosures are here classified into a number of consistent forms: simple enclosures, pit-enclosures, double-concentric enclosures and split-level enclosures. All represent homesteads directly associated with or closely adjacent to terracing, and their areal distributions are distinct (figs 28 and 29). All except the split-level are found in the lowlands below 1400m. Also frequent in most lowland areas are occurrences of stone walls with no consistent configuration; these are probably also occupation sites but no description or classification has been attempted. In addition there are small enclosures four metres or less in internal diameter, probably individual houses, which occur singly or in small groups unassociated with a larger enclosure; these are especially common in the Maristvale/St Mary's area.

Pit-enclosures (fig. 32)
These are distinct from the highland pit-*structures*, although there are close affinities between the two types. They occur at and around Ziwa, while a few recorded in Tanda indicate that they extend westwards beyond the Nyangombe river. A slightly different form is found in the north-eastern lowlands. None was excavated during the recent research but the simple enclosure, Ziwa MSE17 described in Chapter 8, has many of the same features.

They are usually built on a gentle slope, from which an artificial revetted platform is built out as in the highland pit-structures, but here of lesser height, rarely more than a metre or a metre and a half. The entrance is on the upper side where the wall is around 1.20m high and usually greatly thickened, thicknesses of up to four metres being not uncommon. The entrance thus takes the form of a narrow passage, often lintelled, with dimensions comparable to those of the pit-structure tunnels, around 1.10m high and 50cm wide. The rest of the wall circumference is usually lower and thinner and it may be almost absent at the lower edge of the platform. The circumference is often interrupted by houses or raised platforms whose *dhaka* walls would have completed the enclosure perimeter. Fragments of baked *dhaka* with pole- and stick-impressions are often found on the wall.

In many cases there is provision for a horizontal wooden drawbar to close the entrance passage. The drawbar was built into a long socket on one side of the passage and could be slid across to engage in a shorter socket on the opposite side. There may be a hole in the top of the wall above the long socket into which a stone locking pin could be dropped to secure the bar in the closed position (described by Summers 1958:80). Above the bar is often a slot between the lintel slabs so that the closure could be reinforced with vertical poles. In some cases the wooden bar has survived; one such has been

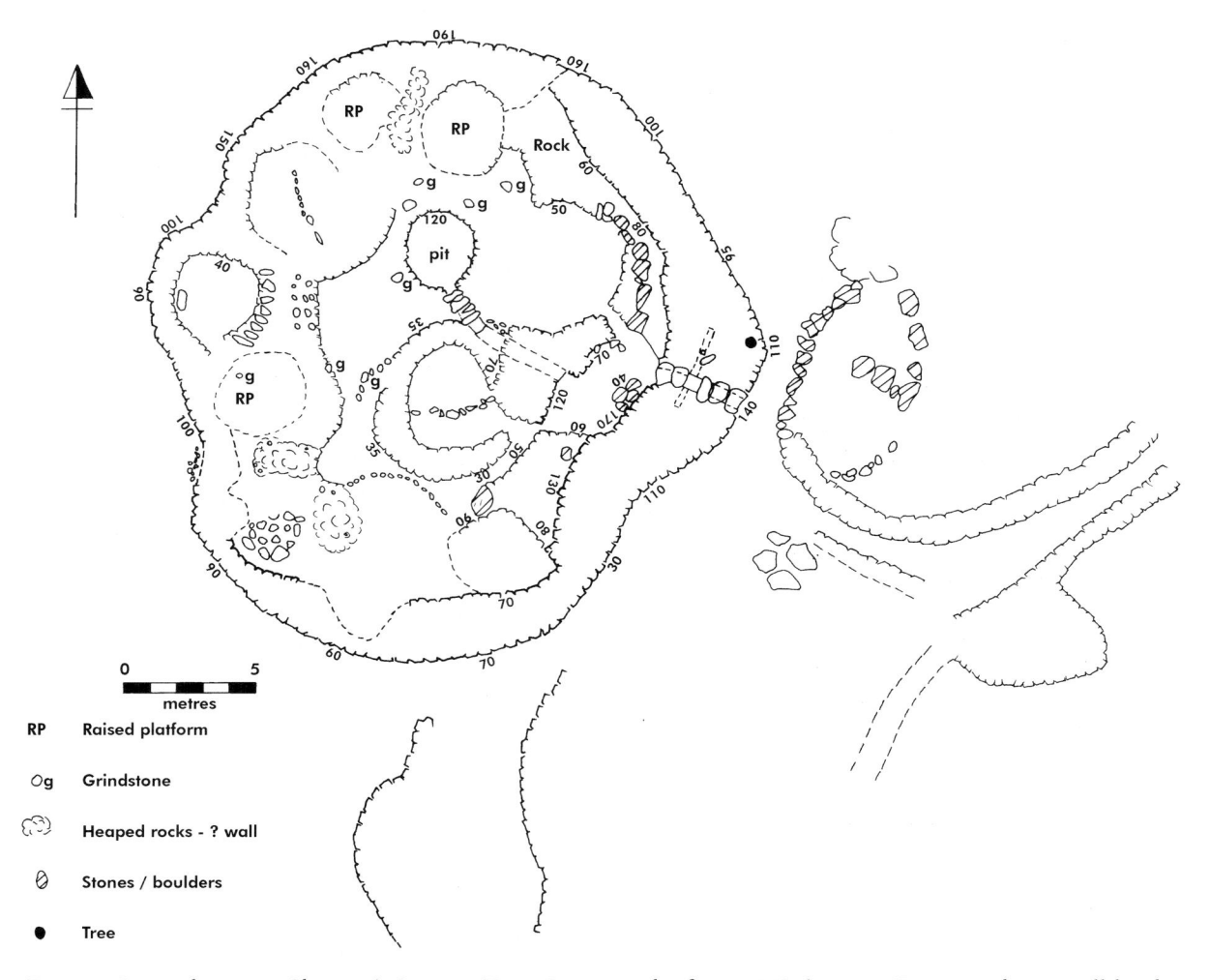

Fig. 32. Pit-enclosure at Chirawu's Site 12, Ziwa Ruins, grid reference VQ625959. Figures indicate wall heights

identified as a species of *Albizzia,* and another from a fort in Zimbiti in the same general area as *Azanza garkeana* (Huffman 1975).

The platform accommodates a more or less central stone-lined pit, usually 2.50 to 3.50m in diameter and around 1.50m deep, the floor paved if not on bedrock. Access to this is by a sunken passage, again often lintelled, starting from just inside the main enclosure entrance. This passage may also have drawbar sockets. In a high proportion of cases the passage has been deliberately blocked at one end or sometimes completely filled with stones. There is always a drain at the lower side of the pit leading out through the platform. Around the pit there may be raised platforms and house floors (often of the divided type discussed below), but in about 75% of cases these are not clearly observable and may have been absent (Chirawu 1999). Sometimes such a pit-enclosure without other structures is appended to a simple residential enclosure with raised platforms and divided houses (e.g. Summers 1958:84). Pits excavated by Summers at Ziwa yielded few finds beyond the odd potsherd. However at Chirawu's Site 12, a test trench in a pit at the mouth of the lintelled entrance passage showed up to 25cm of accumulated deposits with small sherds, bone fragments and charcoal flecks, extending into the passage and overlain by stones blocking the entrance. Twenty centimetres of humus had formed in the pit after the blocking, indicating that this took place at the time the homestead was abandoned (Chirawu 1999:96).

Many enclosures, both with and without pits, are linked by stone-walled pathways to longer arterial walled passages leading through the terraced fields.

A detailed study of enclosures was undertaken by Chirawu (1999) within the area designated as the Ziwa National Monument. In four sample blocks totalling 16.25 square kilometres, 92 pit-enclosures were recorded, of which 34 had clear signs of other structures. Measurable pit diameters ranged from two to nine metres with an average of 3.20m (n=73). Internal average diameters of enclosures ranged from 6.50 to 22m with a mean of 12.90m (n=76). In a separate sample of 53 pit-enclosures, 26% had old *dhaka* on the walls, and pottery and grinding stones were observed in 51% and 34% respectively. 72% of pit passages were deliberately blocked. Enclosure density naturally varies across the landscape according to the topography; the maximum density recorded was 12 pit-enclosures and 19 "simple" enclosures (without pits) in an area of 25 hectares, but it is uncertain how many were occupied simultaneously.

Dating of the Ziwa enclosures in general is probably from the 18th to early 19th centuries, although a greater spread is not ruled out. The bead evidence is consistent with this (Appendix E). There are only two radiocarbon determinations from an actual pit-enclosure, but there are six others from the Ziwa area, four from simple enclosures and two from forts; from other indications all may be considered to belong to the same cultural phase. Uncalibrated dates range from 140 ± 45 to 232 ± 12 BP, with the range of possible calibrations from AD 1670 to 1900 (Appendix F). A refinement of this range is offered by a surviving wooden locking bar from the entrance to a pit-enclosure, from which both the core and the outer rings were dated (Appendix F; Chirawu 1999). Juggling with the three possible calibrations for each indicates a date of AD 1738-1755 for the outer rings if the tree was around 80 years old, or 1798-1810 if about 35 years old; the number of growth rings supports the latter. This of course represents only one point in time within the Ziwa occupation. The area was almost entirely depopulated by the 1890s when the first European travellers passed through.

Pit-enclosures in the Kagore area, below the north end of the highland range to the east, differ somewhat from those in the Ziwa area in that entry to the pit is by a short sloping unroofed passage, while enclosure entrances are also generally unlintelled.

As with the pit-structures, it is deduced that the pit in each enclosure would have housed a few dwarf cattle while the divided houses included provision for small stock. The implications of this and of relative pit size here and in the highland pit-structures are discussed in Chapter 6.

Double-concentric enclosures (fig. 33)

In the northern lowlands, the double-concentric enclosures appear to be the local equivalent of the Ziwa pit-enclosures. Their distribution (fig. 28) extends from St Mary's northwards to the Ruangwe area where they occur both in the Chigura hills and along the foot of the eastern escarpment. They also extend west from Nyautare at least to the Nyangombe river, and probably across the latter into heavily terraced areas of Chikore and northern Tanda communal lands. These structures have an outer wall, often low and roughly built with one or more plain entrances, and a more solid inner enclosure. The inner enclosure, usually centred but occasionally abutting one side, is well built, the wall around 1.20m high and about a metre thick, with a plain entrance and internal diameter ranging from two to five metres, average 3.60m. The excavation of an inner enclosure at Chigura (Chapter 8) revealed a drain on the lower side and Summers (1958 fig. 42) shows a drain in a similar position in an enclosure in the Nyautare area. This could be a regular feature but has not been observed in other cases. There is occasional thickening of the walls around main enclosure entrances but this is not common and lintels are very rare.

Such enclosures are often built on level ground, but some built on slopes have the interior divided by a terrace. There may be houses or raised platforms between the inner and outer walls (e.g. Summers 1958: figs 42, 44), but these are often not observable, as is the case for the pit-enclosures. The divided houses described below have not been recorded in this area. One site near Chirangeni (Chapter 8; fig. 82) has a group of three double-concentric enclosures, with an adjacent group of stone-walled houses and raised platforms not enclosed by a wall. The Chigura example (fig. 89) is appended to a residential enclosure with numerous structures. (As noted above, Summers' Site V at Ziwa shows a similar association, with a pit-enclosure without other structures appended to a residential enclosure – Summers 1958:84.) As with the pit-enclosures, double-concentric enclosures may be associated with walled pathways.

Occupation of these structures continued well into the 19th century as shown by two recent radiocarbon determinations and the state of preservation at the Chigura site (Chapter 8; Appendix F). No glass beads were found in the excavations at that site. There is no indication as yet of when their construction started – 18th century may be suggested. The associated pottery shows affinities with the Ziwa sites (Appendix D).

A parallel function of double-concentric and pit-enclosures is suggested by the similar configuration and the mutually exclusive distribution of the two types. A few cattle would have been kept in the central enclosure, and perhaps other livestock within the outer wall where this area is not occupied by domestic structures. The absence of divided houses may indicate a different accommodation arrangement for small stock from that of the pit-enclosures or pit-structures.

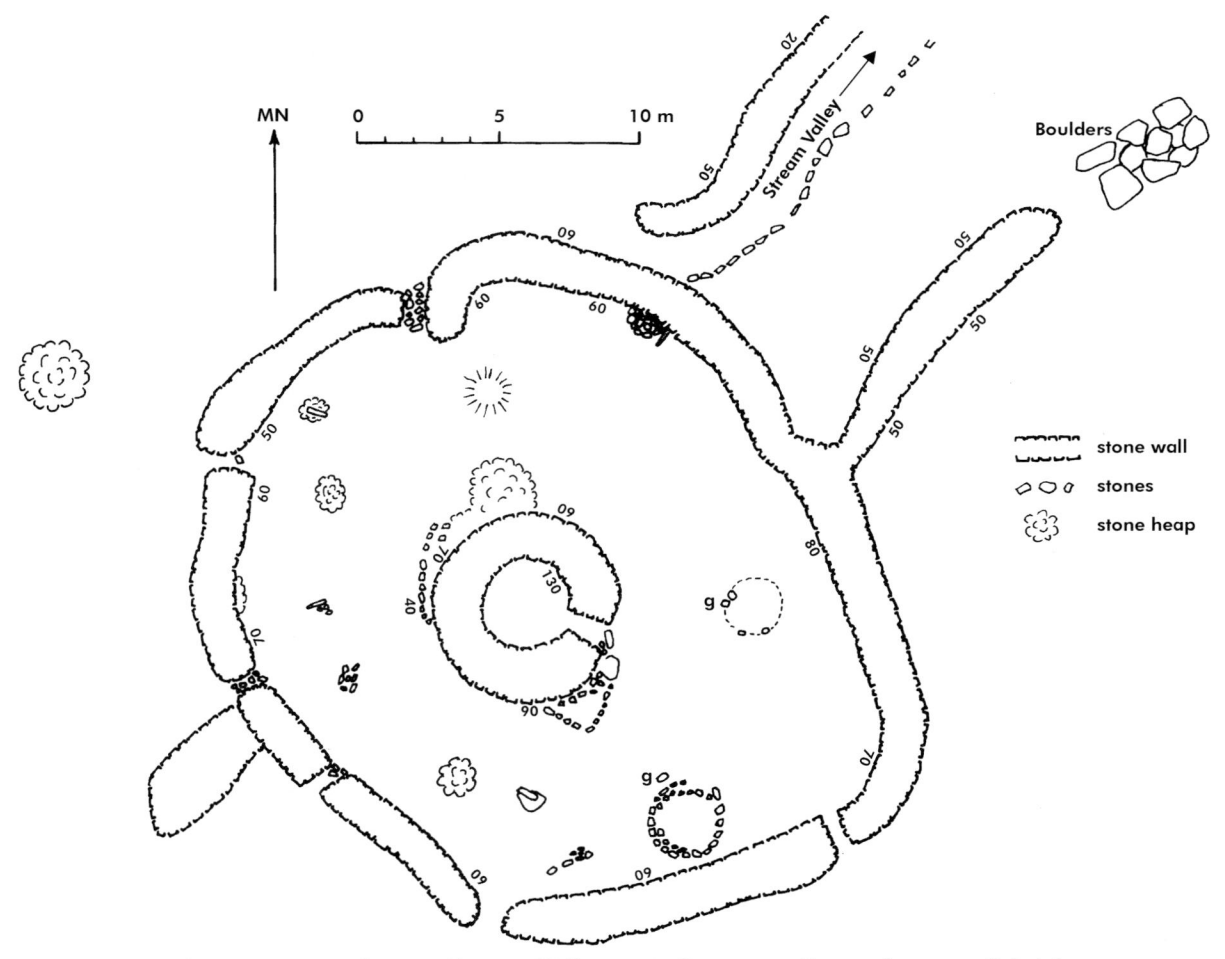

Fig. 33. Double concentric enclosure, Chigura Hills. g=grinding stone; figures denote wall height

Split-level enclosures (fig. 34)
This type, not recognised prior to the recent research, appears to be restricted to an area across the highland ridge north of Chirimanyimo hill. Nine examples were recorded, from Kumbu on the western escarpment, over the highlands, to the upper Nyarwaka valley at the foot of the eastern escarpment, with an altitudinal range of 1290 to 1700m.

They are oval to circular in plan, built on sloping ground, with a relatively massive outer wall up to about 1.80m high. The design varies to some extent but has common features. The lower end constitutes an oval pit-like chamber, the lower side formed by the outer wall and the upper side deeply revetted. This chamber is in most cases subdivided by internal walls or lines of vertical slabs and is entered from above by a short steeply-ramped passage. At different levels above it are house-bays, and the single main entrance is a tunnel-like passage through the outer wall to one such bay, from the side rather than the top of the enclosure. Internal size ranges from 8 by 8m to 20 by 17m and the number of house-bays from one to four. Several have small "cupboards" built into the walls of house-bays or lower chambers, a feature seen in the houses of the Chirangeni enclosure (see Chapter 8) but rare elsewhere; Summers however records two examples at Ziwa built into a wall within a residential enclosure (1958:85).

Minor excavation was undertaken at a site north-east of Chirimanyimo Madziwa School at the crest of the eastern escarpment. This showed the lower chamber to be paved with stones but few other clear details. The lower chamber of these enclosures was thus probably for livestock, perhaps cattle, calves and small stock, segregated by the dividing walls. These must have entered through one of the houses.

Dating of this enclosure type is unknown, as is the relationship to the pit-structures which occur in the same area of the highlands, in one case closely adjacent.

Simple enclosures
Simple enclosures lack a main central feature but are otherwise variable. They are found in all lowland

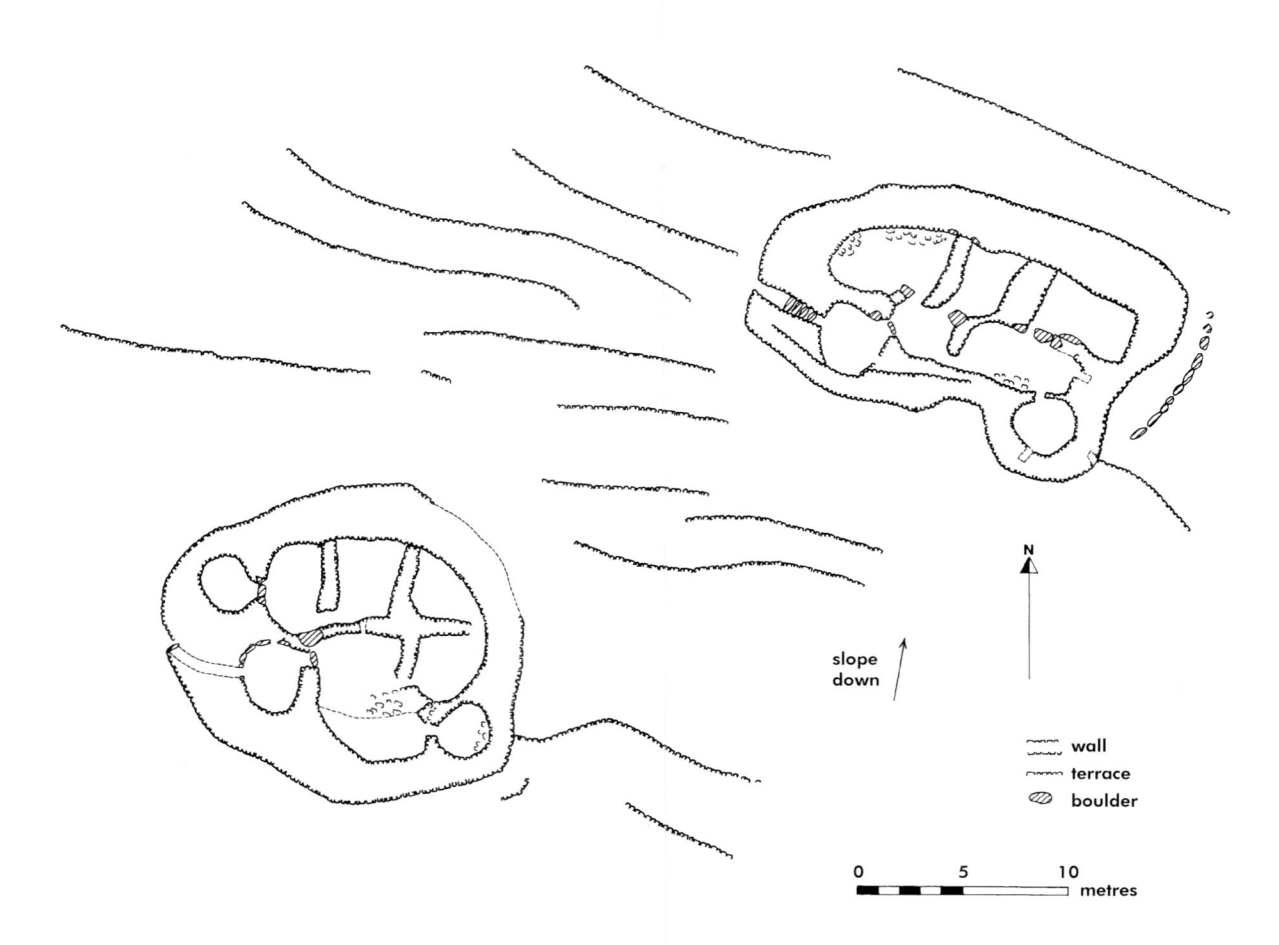

Fig. 34. Two split-level enclosures north of Chirimanyimo, grid reference VR768310

areas and take the form of the local pit- or double-concentric enclosure without the pit or inner enclosure. Thus at Ziwa, the enclosure wall is typically comparable to that of the pit-enclosures and has the same type of entrance, often lintelled, through the thickened wall on the upper side. Excavated examples, MSE17 and SN153 (figs 76, 80) are described in Chapter 8. Chirawu (1999) shows their overall frequency at Ziwa to be slightly less than for pit-enclosures, with internal diameter ranging from 5 to 28 metres, average 10.90m. About 45% have observable internal houses or raised platforms, a third have *dhaka* fragments on or in the wall, a third have grinding stones, 17% have drawbar sockets and 60% have recorded pottery. Thus with the possible exception of those apparently lacking internal features, both pit and simple enclosures represent standard homesteads, the latter lacking formal provision for cattle.

The simple enclosure at Ziwa Mujinga Area B (see Chapter 4; fig. 42, number 13) is atypical in some respects (fig. 35). This is around 22m in diameter and has a very irregular outline composed of short stretches of stone wall, most of the gaps between having the remains of *dhaka* structures. These include four houses with traces of dividing

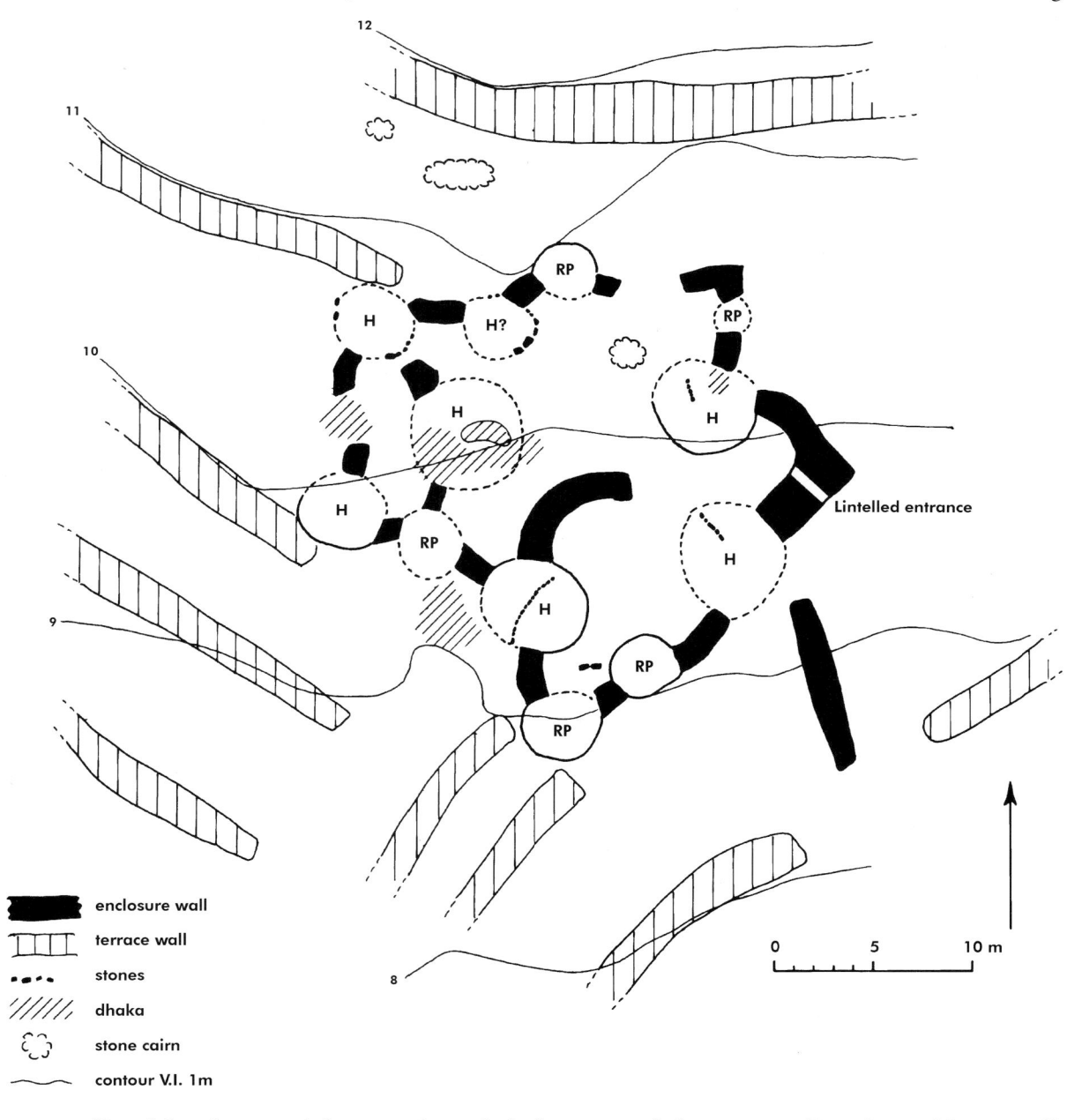

Fig. 35. "Simple" enclosure with houses and raised platforms around the perimeter. Ziwa Ruins, Munjinga. H = house floor; RP = raised platform

walls, two probable smaller houses apparently undivided, five probable raised platforms, and two plain gaps, one of which has *dhaka* remains. A patch of *dhaka* floor indicates another undivided house in the interior. The lintelled entrance of the enclosure faces downhill, a very unusual orientation.

In the northern lowlands, a parallel relationship between simple and double-concentric enclosures is apparent, although survey procedures were not sufficiently systematic to allow quantification. The Chigura site (Chapter 8, fig. 89) provides an example of a simple enclosure with an unusually large number of internal structures, with a double concentric enclosure appended on the lower side.

Other sites

The important site of Mount Muozi is described in detail here, with brief mention of a few other sites, some relatively large, which do not fit into any of the above categories.

Mount Muozi

Muozi is unique among known sites of the Nyanga complex in that it appears to have been occupied throughout most, if not all, of the span of the complex; there is also a substantial ash midden (see Chapter 8), a feature not observed at any other site. Part of the site is a stone-walled settlement which does not take the form of any of the standard homestead types and represents an elite residence (fig. 37). This has sacred significance for the Nyama people in addition to its archaeological interest and merits detailed description here. It was described by Soper and Chirawu (1997) and parts of that account are repeated here with some amendments, amplified by further work.

The site as a whole lies on the summit of Mount Muozi at grid reference VR 741154 and is designated 1732DD36 (fig. 42, no.5). This prominent summit, at an altitude of 2100m, forms a small isolated plateau at the end of a long spur projecting from the main western escarpment of the highlands above Maristvale Mission and Nyanga High School (Plate 16). Between the plateau and the main escarpment, the neck of the spur drops very steeply some 140m into a narrow saddle, while the plateau itself rises about 600m above the piedmont slope below.

The plateau (fig. 36) is about 275m long by 120m wide, and the stone-walled settlement (fig. 37) is on a further promontory which projects from the south-west corner with a slightly lower saddle between. Much of the plateau itself has evidence of occupation, including some walled hollows. Plateau and promontory are surrounded on three sides by inaccessible precipitous slopes, often sheer cliffs of dolerite, capped, at the western end at least, by sedimentary sandstone. The plateau normally has a dense cover of grass and shrubs and the southern edge and south-western promontory have a good stand of mature "mountain cedar" trees (*Widdringtonia nodiflora*) with thorny undergrowth beneath. These trees, up to 2m in circumference, form a belt up to 30m wide between the crest of the slope and the edge of the cliffs below; many of the upper trees are dead, probably killed by occasional fierce grass fires such as one which occurred in 1995.

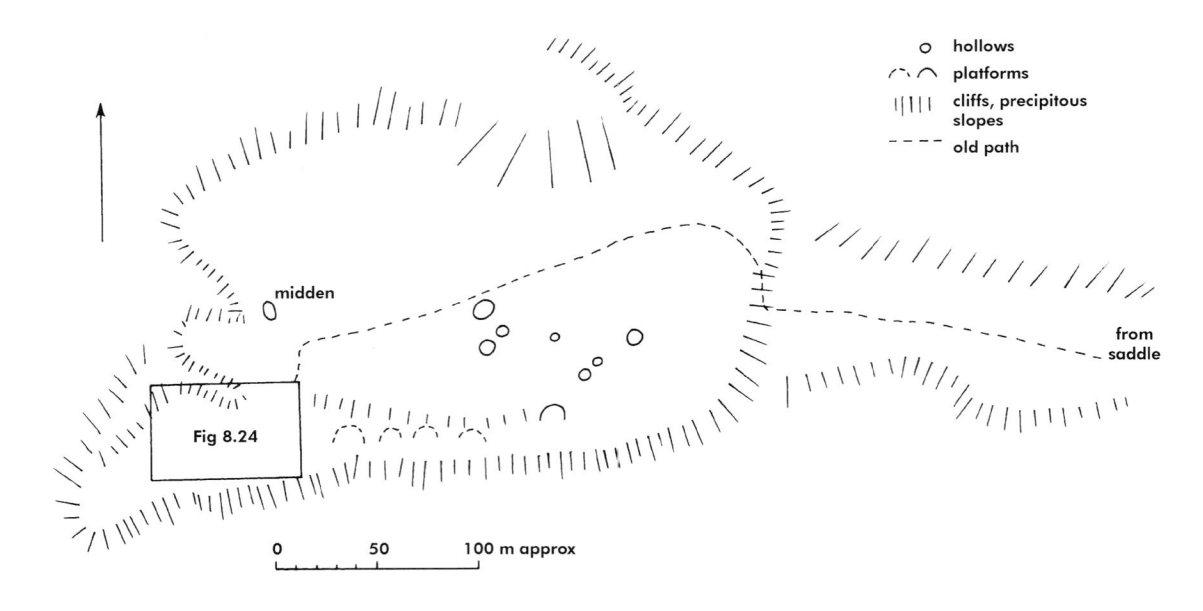

Fig. 36. Muozi. General plan of the plateau

The plateau can be approached by a steep two-hour climb from Maristvale Mission around the north side, culminating in a breakneck path to the top. Alternatively it can be reached from the east, from the Nyangui Forest road north from the Bende Gap; this involves a 40-minute descent/ascent across the neck from the nearest point attainable cross-country by Land Rover. Access is thus difficult and must always have been so.

In September 1995 the whole area was swept by a fire which — conveniently for archaeological purposes — cleared the plateau and most of the promontory of grass and undergrowth. A survey of the main ruins was then carried out and a small test pit dug in the large adjacent ash midden. A further trench was dug in the midden in 1997.

The description of the archaeological remains starts near the top of the spur of the main highlands, before the descent to the neck. Here at an altitude of just over 2000m, is an early hilltop settlement (here on the slope rather than the top of the spur) consisting of a number of sunken enclosures and walls. Below this on a slight rise at the eastern side of the saddle of the spur are at least seven conical stone cairns (Plate 16), the best preserved of which are about 1.50m in diameter and 1.20 to 1.60m high, with a single monolith set in the top; such cairns have not been recorded elsewhere in the Nyanga complex. About ten further cairns, larger and lower around 2m in diameter and 60 to 90cm high, are found beyond and below this point in the first saddle of the main neck, with about ten more on the subsequent low rise and second slight saddle.

The first part of the ascent to the plateau is extremely steep with broken pottery littering the slope. At the top of this are about five terraced house platforms with perhaps twelve more above on a relatively level shoulder, including some small circular enclosures two to three metres in internal diameter. Some of the walls are double-faced with a fill of rubble and earth. The second part of the ascent to the top is slightly less precipitous but still steep, and has another twenty or so platforms/stone circles.

The remains of a walled path can be traced for much of the ascent and this reaches the plateau around the eastern corner. From here it takes the

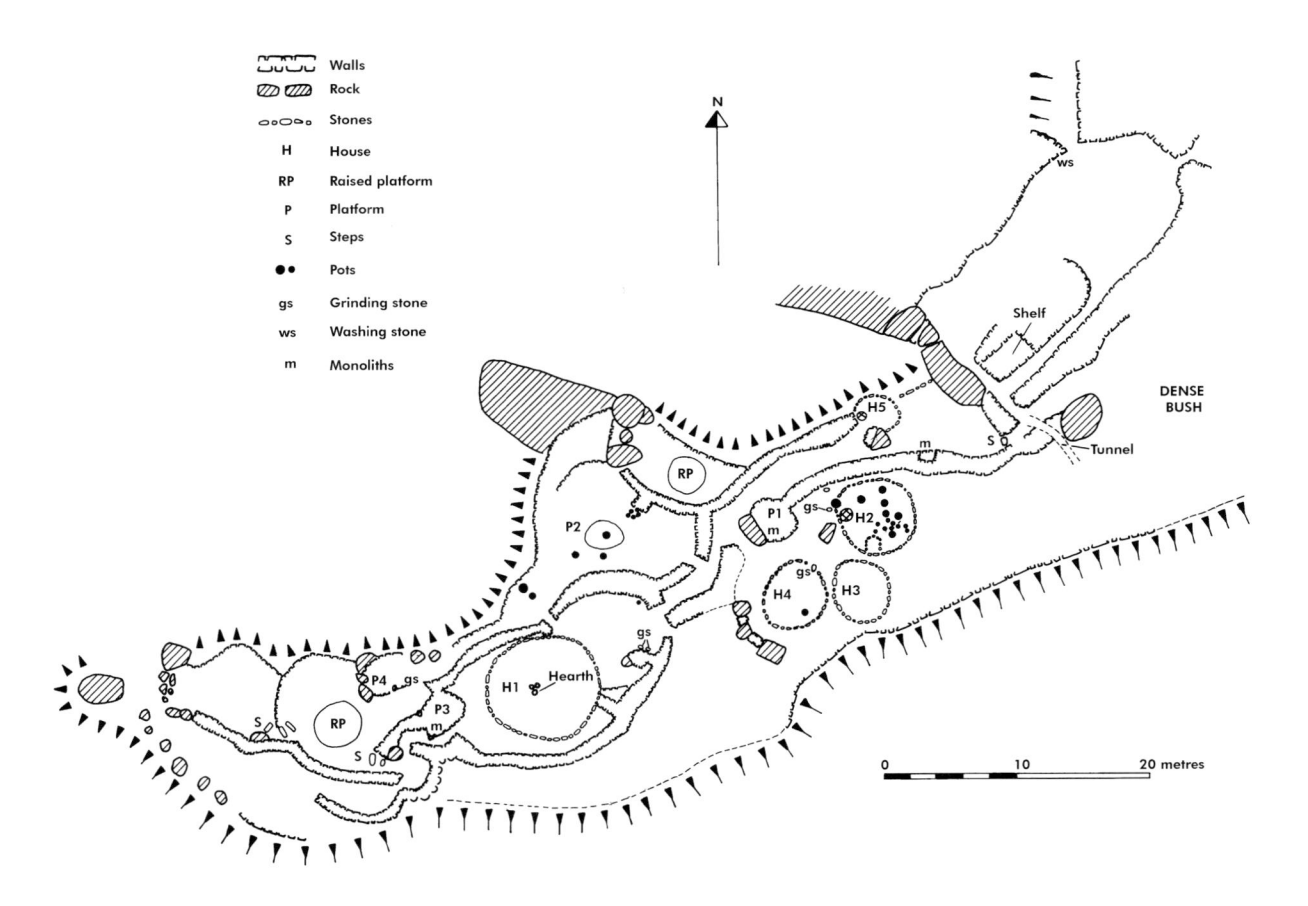

Fig. 37. Muozi. Plan of the stone ruins on the western promontory

form of a sunken pathway running diagonally across to the south-west corner, past a large boulder to the beginning of the main stone ruins on the promontory. Most of the southern side of the plateau either side of the path is covered with banks and hollows with some stone revetting; these are probably of different ages, none necessarily contemporary with the stone walls. Some of the hollows are comparable to the walled hollows of the early hilltop settlements such as 1732DD27 and Chirimanyimo, though there are no signs of the typical low-walled enclosures. Surface scatters of potsherds and bone fragments are common, but this area has not been examined in detail. A slight saddle across the middle of the plateau debouches to the south in a shallow reentrant in which there are a number of hollows 5 to 8m in diameter. All along the southern edge among the *Widdringtonia* trees a series of platforms is scooped out of the slope, the lower ones with retaining walls above the precipice. These have affinities to the western terraces of Chirimanyimo Hill; a large sherd of a deep straight-sided bowl was found on what appears to be a house platform in one of them. The north-western corner of the plateau shows no clear signs of any remains, but there is a single pot close to the edge of the spectacular precipice of the corner itself which could well have been moved there relatively recently from the promontory where other complete pots are found; it now has a few coins in it but these are of recent date, deposited since 1993.

Some 30m north of where the path meets the stone ruin complex and about 15m from the top of the main western cliff, is the large ash midden, about 14m long and 7m wide; there is further midden material to the north-east, apparently more weathered. A few glass and shell beads and a copper stud have been collected from the surface of the former, which also shows potsherds and bone fragments.

As the sunken pathway approaches the south-western corner of the plateau, it passes a big rock and turns south to descend into a large hollow with revetted walls, 20m long, 9m wide and around 1.50m deep. At the north-east end of this a narrow entrance leads to a second hollow, with stone walls to the south-east which were not surveyed due to lack of time; here there is at least one large wide-mouthed pot and one smaller pot with panels of punctates on the shoulder (fig. 38, nos 1, 36). A washing stone was found on the surface close to the entrance to the first hollow. (Washing stones are small flat stones with deeply incised cross-hatched grooves – (e.g. fig. 94)

At the southern corner of the first hollow, two sunken passages converge from its south-west and south-east sides and lead down to the south-east to the neck of the promontory which juts out to the west. This neck is divided by a low east/west wall. Access to the wider southern part appears to have been through a lintelled tunnel at the foot of the passage from the hollow, but the lower end of this is completely silted over and it is not clear where it emerged. An adjacent step down leads to the narrower northern section.

The whole southern edge of the promontory is revetted by a retaining wall along the top of the steep slope. The eastern part of the southern section is an open area about 8m wide with no apparent features, but there is heavy silting here behind the retaining wall. Further east there is still dense bush which was not surveyed. At the western end of this area are three low revetted house platforms of sub-circular shape, two of them 4 to 5m in diameter. The third is c.6m in diameter and has a collection of 17 complete and partly broken pots (Plate 17; fig. 38). There is no clear floor to the platform on which the pots stand, only red-brown clay loam beneath the leaf mould. A copper bracelet was collected on a rock ledge somewhere in the vicinity by Mr J.Stables and is described below with the finds from the midden excavation (fig. 60d).

The vessels from the house platform range from small bowls to large wide-mouthed pots up to more than 60cm in diameter and height, with a capacity of up to 140 litres. These and other more or less complete pots from the site are illustrated in Figure 38. Two of the large pots (nos 7, 12) have a raised rib below the neck with a discontinuous incised herringbone pattern; a graceful narrow-necked pot with flared rim (no. 17) has a lattice pattern of raised ribs on shoulder and body; one smaller necked pot has incised cross-hatched decoration on the shoulder (no. 11). The larger of these vessels and others elsewhere on the site are more reminiscent of the pottery associated with the lowland ruins than of the highland pottery of the pit-structures, but the bowls and punctate panel decoration would be more typical of the latter. The raised rib below the neck on both wide- and narrow-mouthed pots would seem to be more peculiar to this site on present evidence, while a gourd-shaped pot with short vertical flutes on the shoulder (no. 6) appears to be unique.

To the north-west of these house platforms is a high platform, partly formed by a natural rock and partly revetted to a height of at least 80cm. At least ten long thin stones up to 80cm long have fallen radially from this and seem originally to have stood on top, where a few slabs may have been part of a decking. Between the larger house and this platform

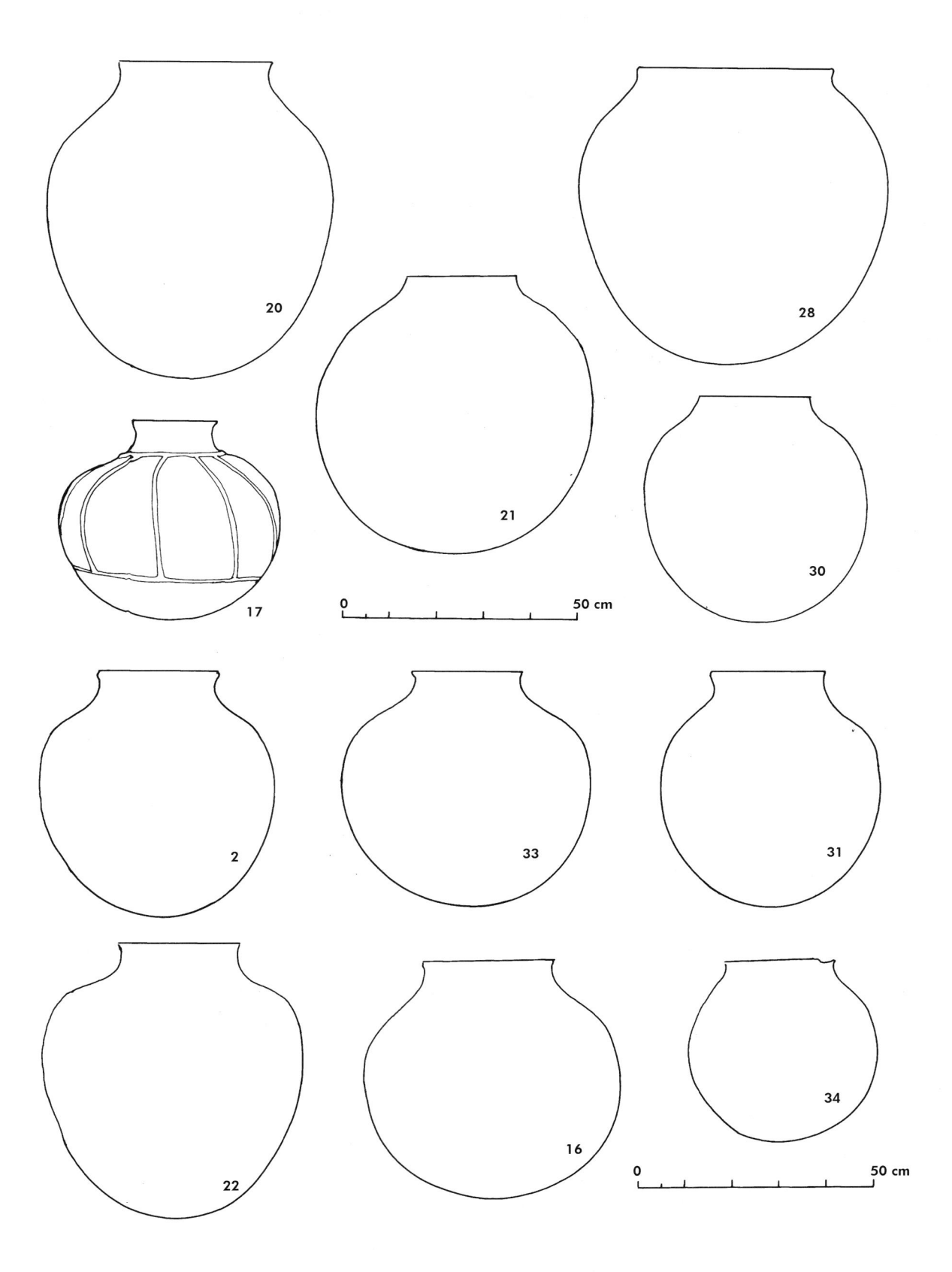

SETTLEMENTS, HOMESTEAD STRUCTURES AND OTHER FEATURES

Fig. 38. Muozi. Complete vessels from the surface

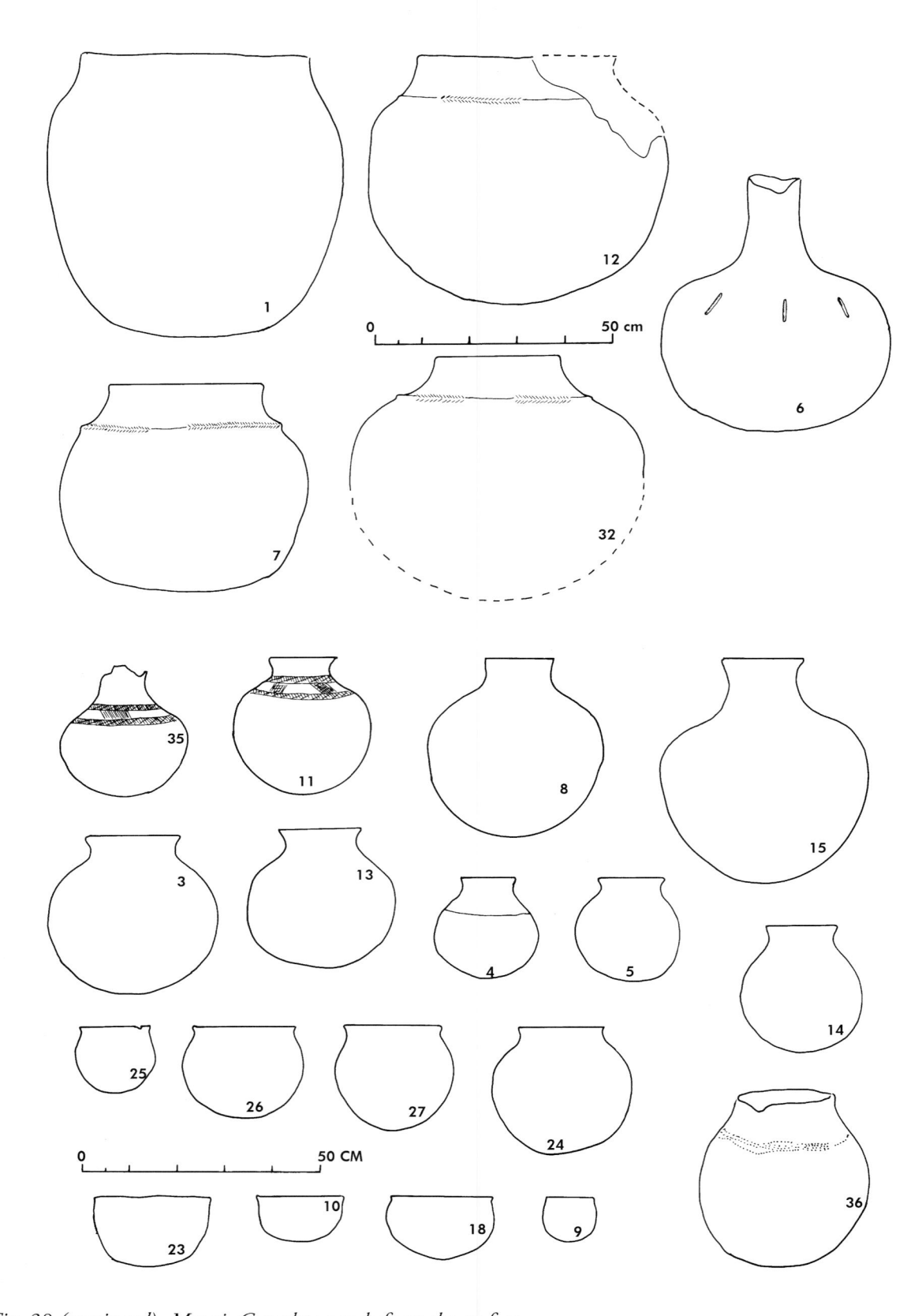

Fig. 38 (continued). Muozi. Complete vessels from the surface

is a large flat-topped rectangular rock which, to the imaginative, might conjure ideas of an altar. An entrance passes to the west of the platform.

On the northern side of the neck, the step down from the foot of the entrance passage leads into an open area bounded on the north by the edge of a steep slope down into a deep cleft between the promontory and the cliff at the end of the main plateau. This slope is a soft ashy scree littered with animal bones, including complete horn cores of cattle. On the south side is a seat-like alcove within the east/west wall, with a small fallen monolith in front which may once have stood on it. At the west end of the open space is a small house platform abutting a low circular platform, partly rock partly walled, leaving a passage between it and the east/west wall. This passage leads up behind the high platform where it is joined by the entrance from the south side of the neck.

The passage leads up to the south-west to the main enclosure of the complex. It opens into a semicircular courtyard neatly paved with flat stones, on the left of which is a high platform joined to the wall from which numerous grinding stones are spilling. The walls here are the best built in the complex, about 1.50m high. An entrance at the north-west corner of this court leads down to a broad terrace which can also be entered from the passage before the court. On this is a solid platform with a pot on top (fig. 38, no.23); other vessels scattered around include a group of four small bowls and a wide mouthed pot (nos 23-27) and two large pots with a raised ridge on the shoulder decorated with incised herringbone (no.32; the other is badly broken). A narrow entrance at the north-east side of this terrace leads to a small lower terrace on which is a typical raised platform above the scarp of the cleft.

In the main enclosure, most of the space to the south-west of the court is occupied by a large house some 8m in diameter with short blocking walls on each side. Three stones in the middle resemble a hearth but are loose on the surface. The surface is soft and ashy, apparently from the burning of a long accumulation of leaf mould, but with lumps of baked *dhaka* showing through. Beyond this house a narrow passage leads out of the enclosure past a solid platform on which is a group of small monoliths, a long barbed iron spearhead and a unique iron object consisting of four splayed iron strips bound in the middle with a spirally wound bar (Plate 18; described in Chapter 8 with the finds from the midden excavation. This piece and the spearhead are now in Mutare Museum for safe keeping). The passage twists down to a terrace walled on the south side, on which is another raised platform three metres in diameter.

Steps lead down from here to a final small terrace also walled on the south side, and beyond are rocks to the tip of the promontory.

It may be noted that access to the whole promontory complex is restricted to the single passage from the first hollow (unless there is a further entrance from the east hidden by the remaining dense bush). Access is further constricted to the main enclosure and large house, presumably that of the principal resident of the site. The houses on the south side of the neck where the main group of pots now stand might perhaps have been the wives' quarters, direct access to the main enclosure being along the north side of the E/W wall with the alcove, guarded by the single small house. The solid platforms indicate ritual functions – at the mouth of the path to the main enclosure, on the northern terrace, the high platform beside the passage, the grinding stone platform in the courtyard, and beyond the main house. The small terraces at the end would appear to be the principal resident's private preserve with his granary on the raised platform.

This part of the site, and by extension the whole mountain, is of sacred significance to the indigenous Nyama people of the surrounding district. The stone ruins are traditionally associated with an eponymous Muozi, who was a powerful figure among the Nyama people and lived here as a diviner and rain maker (files in the District Administrator's office). His riches, fame and popularity were not welcomed by others, including the Saunyama chiefs, and one of these is said to have organised an army to destroy him. His death brought a curse on the Unyama territory, so that the rains failed for many consecutive years, until Saunyama decided to pay compensation to appease his avenging spirit. *Rapoko* (finger millet) and beer were, and perhaps still are, sent up the mountain by the hands of members of a clan that had good relations with Muozi. Failure to do this would cause drought and other disasters, and Nyama people would not themselves dare to climb the mountain to this day. Matowanyika and Mandondo (forthcoming) record a current version of the same story.

Other traditions – with a rather conflicting message – say that all Saunyama chiefs used to be installed and buried on Muozi. Traditional procedures and rituals were laid down to be performed before they could approach the site. Some of these procedures have now been discontinued or forgotten and the last installation is said to have been in 1953. The reuse of the site and restoration of its traditional significance are now under consideration. In respect for this sacred aspect, no excavation has been undertaken on the promontory and the pots have been photographed but not disturbed.

Clearly the stone ruins on the promontory, situated in an easily defensible and symbolically prominent position, were the residence of an important person as recounted in the tradition recorded above. The bone remains on the ashy scree slope indicate fairly lavish meat consumption at this time, both of cattle and smaller animals. The more or less complete pots show relationships to those of both the later highland pit-structures and the lowland enclosures; some of the whole vessels however appear to be unique. The completeness of the pots and the generally fair state of the stone walls would suggest a relatively recent date, though the inaccessibility and sacred nature of the site would militate against much human disturbance. This part of the site may thus date from the 18th or early 19th century. As described in its final state it is unlikely to have been contemporary with the ash midden and other remains on the main plateau. Although the pottery from the top spits of the midden (Chapter 8 and Appendix D), including both punctate and incised cross-hatched decoration, has affinities with some of the complete vessels, the beads and radiocarbon dating suggest a rather earlier date for this material.

From the general historical and archaeological angle, this site on Mount Muozi presents a link between oral history and the remains of the Nyanga terrace complex. The traditional significance of the site clearly needs to be followed up with the assistance of Chief Saunyama and local informants, who can doubtless shed much more light on the interpretation of some of these remarkable remains.

Chirangeni
The excavated Chirangeni enclosure described in Chapter 8 is also atypical of any of the homestead or fort categories but has features of several. The partial banquette and entrance are reminiscent of forts in general (see below in this chapter), and the stone-walled houses recall those of the National Park forts, though here better built. The paved chamber attached to the central house, to which livestock entered through the house as in the split-level enclosures, has aspects of a pit and central enclosure, while the cupboards also form a link with split-level enclosures. A 19th century date is probable.

Haro (1732DD22; grid reference VR750288-751292).
This is an extensive complex of walls stretching for about 400m along and below the lip of the escarpment at the head of the Kumbu valley, 2300m NNW of Chirimanyimo Hill. Width down the slope is c.30 to 100m. The walls are rather roughly built and often tumbled and form a series of interlinked irregular enclosures up to about 15m across, with some roughly terraced platforms and smaller enclosures among them. They form a continuous irregular wall along the crest of the slope with a couple of enclosures extending on to the plateau above. There are at least two concentrations of slag, one associated with baked *dhaka*, but very few potsherds. The age and associations of this site are unknown.

Demera Hill. This site is on top of the large hill east of Nyanga Town (1832BB16, grid reference VQ740243). A few linear walls appear to divide the space between the twin peaks and there is a wall about 50m long above a steep rock face east of the northern peak. There are a few enclosures and revetted occupation platforms, with a scatter of small potsherds and at least one local occurrence of slag. The maximum dimension of the site is about 150m. This is not a typical fort nor does it resemble the early hilltop settlements. It can probably be attributed to the Manyika in the 19th or perhaps 18th century.

DOMESTIC STRUCTURES

Evidence for houses is best represented in the later phases of the complex – well preserved pit-structures and pit-enclosures. As described in Chapter 8 (e.g. Fishpit, MSE17, Chigura), house walls were built of relatively thin close-set vertical poles, plastered on the inside, within a low stone surround or wall. This construction is mirrored in the houses of the restored pit-structure in the National Park, which were modelled on traditional dwelling of the Nyama people (Plate 13). These have low walls of the same construction less than a metre high, and the eaves of the thatched roof, supported on the stone wall, extend almost to the ground. A similar superstructure may be envisaged for the archaeological houses. (It should be emphasised that the internal features of these restored houses, notably the semicircular *chikuva* platform at the back of the house, have not been identified in any of the excavated examples. They are a Shona feature of doubtful authenticity in this context.)

Divided houses
Houses with a low dividing cross-wall are found in virtually identical form both in the highland pit-structures and the lowland enclosures of the Ziwa area. Relatively well-preserved excavated examples are described in Chapter 8 in the reports for the Fishpit and Ziwa MSE17 sites (figs 73, 74, 77; Plate

28). The houses are normally around five metres in diameter with walls of close-set poles plastered on the inside. In the case of pit-structures they are surrounded by a roughly built stone bay wall. The cross-wall is often represented only by line of vertical stones, sometimes with traces of *dhaka* plastering, but intact *dhaka* walls survive in some cases in the highlands. They divide the house into approximately equal halves. One half has a plastered clay floor with a central hearth, a grinding stone set in the floor, and often small compartments formed by moulded *dhaka* kerbs. The other half, usually at a lower level, is roughly paved with stones. The height of the cross-wall may be from 15 to 50cm on the upper side and higher examples have a narrow central doorway. Better preserved examples have traces of separate entrances to each half of the house. Individual pit-structures or Ziwa enclosures may have several such houses; in the case of pit-structures one of them may be over the tunnel, with the tunnel slot opening into the paved half.

Such houses are common in pit-structures throughout their distribution, *pace* Summers (1958:83) who specifically states that he did not find them in the highlands. Examples in the National Park area are described or illustrated by Randall-MacIver (1906:11 and pl. IIIa) and by Hall (1905:99) who writes:

> One half of each floor is paved, the other half is a raised floor of *daga* (clay) with a raised rim of *daga*. The huts are thus divided into two parts, one for the family and the other for the goats.

Cases of surviving *dhaka* cross-walls also in the National Park area are reported by Garlake (1966:15) and by C.B.Payne (pers. comm.), while at least two pit-structures at Glenhead south of Troutbeck, investigated by Huffman but unpublished, have house-bays with similar *dhaka* cross-walls and have given two recent radiocarbon dates (see Appendix F). The presence of divided houses to the south at Mkondwe near Penhalonga is shown by Brand (1970). To the north, the example of Nyangui G1/21 is described in Chapter 8, while divisions of house-bays by vertical stones have also been observed in the Chirimanyimo area.

Divided houses are also common in the lowland enclosures of Ziwa ruins. Two examples have been excavated recently, MSE17 described in Chapter 8 and Chirawu's site 12 (Chirawu 1999). Similar structures were also excavated at Ziwa by Summers (1958:82), who notes that they are absent further north in the Nyautare area, an observation confirmed by the recent work.

Summers (1958: 79-84) interpreted these features as "grinding places", largely on the evidence of an example excavated at his site IV at Ziwa, some 1.5km SSW of the Site Museum. This is a circular enclosure 23m in internal diameter, enclosing five such "grinding places" and seven raised platforms. The excavated "grinding place" was the largest of the five, measuring some 6.75 by 5.90m in internal diameter, with one half stone-paved and the other at a higher level with a *dhaka* floor and grinding stone. Traces of a *dhaka* wall were detected around one quadrant only (though there was also a considerable quantity of loose *dhaka* in the lower half), suggesting to Summers that the structure was open, with no more than a protecting wall on the windward side. The other features of this type in the same enclosure were smaller, around 3 to 3.50m diameter. Summers based his argument for these being grinding places on their apparent openness and the consistent presence of grindstones, suggesting moreover that there might have been one such structure for each wife in a polygamous household. However, the function of the lower paved half of the structures was not considered, nor was the question why such a large proportion of the available homestead space should have been devoted to this particular activity, especially seeing that the large excavated example occupied a raised central position within the enclosure.

The excavations at MSE17 and at Chirawu's Site 12 cast doubt on Summers' structural and functional interpretation. In the first place they were almost certainly walled and roofed, not open-air as Summers imagined. Admittedly the excavation of MSE17 showed only slight traces of a complete wall circuit, but the similar feature excavated at Chirawu's Site 12 had carbonised stake bases around most of the circumference and a considerable amount of burnt wall *dhaka*. Certainly there is no positive evidence here or in Summers' excavation that they were *not* walled. House 2 at MSE17 in addition showed a solid wall of poles plastered with *dhaka* which would seem to be more than a simple windbreak but this wall forms part of the outer perimeter of an annexe and might be expected to be more substantial.

The interpretation of these houses by Hall, quoted above, is probably correct. The plastered rooms are clearly kitchens for the processing and preparation of food and doubtless other domestic activities. The lower rooms with their rough paved floors and separate entrances, from outside the platform in the case of the pit-structures, would make uncomfortable sleeping quarters and must have been for the penning of small stock at night; such stock could perhaps have been the personal property of the wife whose kitchen it was. However no surviving traces of dung deposition on or between the paving stones have been noted in the recent excavations and results of phosphate analysis were inconclusive.

If small stock were kept in the divided houses, it would support the view that the pits housed small cattle. Supporting evidence for both points comes from a recent interview with Claud Munditi, born on Rhodes Estate in 1922 and until recently village head at Chirimanyimo whither he moved in 1947. When asked if goats were kept in the traditional kitchen at night, he readily described without prompting that there used to be a low cross-wall dividing off a lower space for the goats. There were two doors, the back one only used in an emergency. He had moreover been told by his father that the pits were for small humped cattle whose horns were quite short but could be cut off if they grew too long to pass through the tunnel. Goats were not kept with the cattle.

Raised platforms

Raised platforms, usually about three metres in diameter, are a typical feature of lowland enclosures in all areas and also occur, though less regularly, in highland pit-structures. In these features a series of vertical stones from 20 to 50cm high supports a circular decking of slabs on which a *dhaka* floor is usually laid (Plate 19), though more rarely the slabs are bare. Considerable quantities of baked *dhaka* fragments with stick impressions are often associated indicating walls, but traces of such walls are rarely preserved in situ. Hall (1905:100) however observed "the sticks in some instances still standing upright in the *daga*". In some excavated cases remains of charcoal must represent a thatched roof and destruction by fire. These features are usually interpreted as storage granaries by comparison with such structures still in use in the area, which however are rectangular since the platform is made of logs. The raised floors provide ventilation beneath and some protection from termites.

On the other hand, Summers (1958: e.g. 82-4) consistently regarded these raised platforms as "huts", even though he acknowledged that comparable modern structures are normally for the storage of grain and other items. His interpretation seems to be supported by the example which he excavated at his Site IV. This was a large platform, some 4.50m in diameter, on the floor of which were found a *dhaka* potstand and a heap of white ash. There was some evidence that the *dhaka* walls might have continued right down to the ground around the platform, though such a device would seem to negate any ventilation function and give possible access to termites and other insects.

The recent work has produced no direct evidence of function. Excavation of such a feature at Chirawu's Site 12 in 1993 did show an area of plastered floor and a number of iron arrowheads but no other details. The ratio of raised platforms to house floors in Ziwa enclosures averages around three to one (Chirawu 1999) which might be thought rather high for storage huts. Summers may therefore have been right in thinking that at least some were sleeping huts. A dual purpose for sleeping and storage seems unlikely in the absence of evidence for internal partitioning. It may be mentioned in passing that further north in the Nyautare area the sizes of such platforms fall into two categories, some being around 3m in diameter and the others half that size; the smaller ones would certainly be too small for sleeping in but could well be bases for *dhaka* or basketry granaries or even poultry houses. The question of the function of raised platforms thus remains incompletely resolved for the time being.

HOMESTEADS AND SYMBOLISM

The Nyanga stone structures have been characterised as practical "folk architecture" serving the everyday needs of ordinary people (Whitty 1959). However there are aspects of the design of many homesteads which appear to go beyond the requirements of functional efficiency so that an important symbolic element among these everyday needs can be deduced. The only earlier writer to appreciate this element has been Bruwer (1965), albeit misled by his Phoenician preconceptions in interpreting the pits as symbolic representations of Astarte's womb. The ritual significance of monoliths associated with homesteads or in isolated situations, was suggested by Finch (1949) and Summers (1958) but they did not extend the discussion to features of the homesteads themselves. More recently Jacobson-Widding (1992) has developed an anthropological approach to the conception of some of the ruins by some current Manyika people.

The design of different categories of homestead may be examined from the point of view of efficiency of apparent function relative to economy of construction effort, in an attempt to identify features which appear to go beyond purely practical dimensions.

The highland pit-structures represent a massive investment of labour in the construction of the platform necessary to accommodate the central pit, and thus the pit itself assumes a central importance, with the houses and other structures conceptually secondary as well as peripheral. The relative elevation of the houses above the cattle in the pit could also have been significant. An ideological importance for pit and cattle may thus be suggested, but the depth of the pit also serves the practical purpose of shelter from the winter winds, while its position enhances the security of the cattle. The construction of the tunnel may also be seen as over-elaborate, but is an effective solution to the problem of access to attain the requisite depth, built to the minimum dimensions to admit dwarf cattle and supporting a house above to control access and security. The curvature from one side reduces the steepness incurred in a direct approach from above, but the fact that perhaps 95% of the tunnels curve *left* into the pit is doubtless significant, and an explanation of the exceptions not constrained by the configuration of local bedrock is an intriguing question. The tunnel access from outside the homestead facilitates entry and exit and may be noted for contrast with the internal passages of Ziwa pit-enclosures; also the tunnels were rarely deliberately blocked, contrasting with the frequency of this practice at Ziwa as mentioned above.

The ruined pit-structures provide rather less well preserved data for speculation. The basic pit is present but probably had an unroofed entrance passage, and the platform is less developed as the focus of settlement around it. Possibly the pit was still primarily functional and had not yet achieved all its symbolic connotations.

The lowland pit-enclosures of the Ziwa area show marked affinities to the pit-structures, such as the presence of the pit and the identical divided houses. However there are also consistent differences, some of which are also seen in the Ziwa enclosures without pits, and these differences often reflect less functional efficiency at Ziwa. Shelter from the wind cannot have been an important consideration in the warmer conditions of the lowlands and this may in part explain the smaller and shallower dimensions of the pits. Even so, the cattle in the pits were still below the level of the houses. From a functional point of view the penning of livestock could have been more economically accomplished by building a small walled enclosure, as in the double-concentric enclosures further north. As it is, the pits of the Ziwa enclosures entailed the massive effort of platform construction for little practical advantage and must reflect the same principles as the highland pits but divorced from their functional qualities, reinforcing the symbolic significance of both.

Again in these lowland enclosures it is hard to see any practical purpose for the lintelled passage entrance to most of the pits; an open passage could have served as well since no great depth is required. The entry to this passage from within the main enclosure entrance differs from the pit-structures but provides more security. The frequent deliberate blocking of many of the pit entrance passages at Ziwa (38 out of a sample of 53) has been mentioned above. This could have had a practical purpose reflecting changing circumstances during occupation of the homestead as suggested by Chirawu (1999), but it often consists of more than a simple blocking wall. Moreover the excavation at Chirawu's site 12 indicates that the blocking in that case took place at the time the enclosure was abandoned so that a symbolic purpose may be preferred. These considerations are less applicable to lowland pits outside the Ziwa area, where access is normally by a short sloping or stepped open passage.

The entrances to most enclosures at Ziwa, both with and without pits, take the form of a lintelled passage, usually with provision for a wooden drawbar. The wall around the entrance is normally greatly thickened up to four metres, apparently for the express purpose of lengthening the passage and again involving far more effort than consistent with a simple barrier. The wall is no higher than the lintel stones and little extra security is provided by the latter apart from constraining the entrant to a stooping and more vulnerable posture. There must be strong symbolism in the entry to the homestead through a restricted passage of significant length.

One may conclude that most of the Ziwa residents had surplus resources of labour beyond that required for subsistence, which afforded the luxury of indulging in expensive symbolism in their homesteads.

The double-concentric enclosures of the northern lowlands appear more practical in design. The solidly constructed inner enclosure is of the same dimensions as the Ziwa pits but built up from the ground, eliminating the need for a platform. Summers (1958:16) suggested that this was because they are built on level ground, but this is not always so, many of the enclosures being divided into two levels by a terrace. The outer wall of these enclosures is usually lower and often has multiple entrances. Lintelled doorways rarely occur in homesteads in this area, being restricted to forts. These structures are thus more consistent with the economical application of labour to functional needs. The people of the northern lowlands could have been more constrained by economic factors with less resources to spare, or may have directed their symbolic proclivities to less tangible or lasting effect.

The split-level enclosures of the northern highlands also seem to involve effort beyond the purely practical but expressed in rather different ways and avoiding the major investment of a full platform. The lower chamber, presumably for livestock, is formed by the high lower wall of the enclosure and entered from within it by a short open sloping passage. The wall at the entrance however is thickened and the entrance passage lintelled as at Ziwa. The passage opens into a house-bay and the cattle and other stock must have passed through this house, as with House A at the atypical Chirangeni enclosure (see Chapter 8).

While important symbolic elements may be deduced in many of the homestead structures, it is difficult to suggest interpretations for these. The features identified as requiring explanation beyond the purely functional concern mainly the pits and tunnels/passages. Among other approaches, sexual symbolism and fertility and the liminality of entrances might provide general analogies, but specific meanings can hardly be inferred and will not be pursued here. The symbolic significance of the pits for the present Manyika people of Matema in the highlands is in fact analysed and discussed by Anita Jacobson-Widding (1992) in the context of round structures and artefacts in general – pots, kitchens, circular enclosures – but the relevance of this to the builders of the pits is uncertain. Although she postulates a continuity of culture in the small-scale setting of the traditional village, which should preserve the meaning of symbols over many generations, no consistent explanation of the function of the pits was given even by elderly men, so that any remembered account of original symbolism is even less to be expected.

FORTS

These structures, usually on hilltops or prominent positions, are characterised by relatively massive walls around two metres in height and often two metres thick, forming a complete circuit, except in some cases where they crown a precipitous cliff and that side has been left unguarded. Walls often have a raised parapet on the outer side and a ledge (banquette) on the inner side. Most have "loopholes", squarish holes of uncertain function through the walls, particularly either side of main entrances. The entrances are lintelled (Plate 20), often with a horizontal drawbar slot and a slot in the roof through the banquette above. Most have two or more such entrances of the usual height and width for enclosure entrances (c.1.20m by 50cm), but in some cases, particularly the smaller forts, a second back entrance is very small and appears to have been concealed among boulders.

Distribution covers the western lowlands and the highlands from about the latitude of Troutbeck southwards (fig. 29). None however have been recorded north of Nyautare in the lowlands or in the northern highlands. It is not proposed to describe them in detail since they have not been investigated in any systematic way, but they have implications for the sociopolitical background of the complex and a general discussion is relevant.

The forts vary in size, design and probably function and a broad classification is suggested at the risk of conveying too great an impression of homogeneity:

- Small single enclosures usually less than 15m in diameter, often with outcrops or large boulders inside and no evidence of regular occupation (Plate 21). These may be interpreted as temporary refuges for the occupants of double-concentric and simple enclosures in their vicinity, although they could also have had other social or ritual functions. They are mainly found from south of Maristvale/St Mary's to south of Nyautare and westwards to the Nyangombe river. They often surmount small kopjes but some are in areas of relatively low relief. One built of white quartz south-west of St Mary's has some house or grain bin platforms outside.
- Larger forts with an inner enclosure of similar massive construction at one end. Both inner and outer walls have lintelled entrances and loopholes and the outer enclosure could be a later enlargement. There are two of these at Ziwa, one on a hill north of the Site Museum and the other on the opposite side of the valley to the west on the south end of the Mujinga ridge (fig. 39). These have traces of *dhaka* house floors showing regular occupation. Pit-enclosures and simple enclosures occur close by.
- Larger single enclosures on top of hills or kopjes in the National Park area. Many of these have small stone-walled houses around five metres in outer diameter more or less densely packed inside. Chawomera Fort (Summers 1958:62) measures 23 by 17m internally and has only four or five house circles, but a fort just east of the old Troutbeck road north of Chawomera is c.17m in diameter and has nine house circles within it, while another on a high bluff west of the upper Nyangombe valley has 29 houses within a size of c.40 by 30m. These are clearly defended settlements, more than temporary refuges for the inhabitants of neighbouring pit-structures. Their contemporaneity with the latter, while probable, has not been conclusively demonstrated and in any case there would have been little space to accommodate many pit structure occupants and their livestock in times of insecurity.

- Nyangwe Fort (Summers 1958: fig. 18) is a unique case. Here an original enclosure similar to the previous category has been extended by the addition of five abutting enclosures, the whole complex measuring c.70 by 58m internally. There is a total of at least 12 entrances and 54 loopholes. Only three of the appended enclosures have stone house circles. This could be a chiefly head quarters to which people and their livestock could retreat in time of danger.
- A number of defensive sites have been recorded west of the Nyangombe in Tanda. Several of these have a main enclosure with an outer crescentic enclosure added on one side (fig. 40; Barnes 1977) and have traces of house floors or raised platforms within both sections. Others

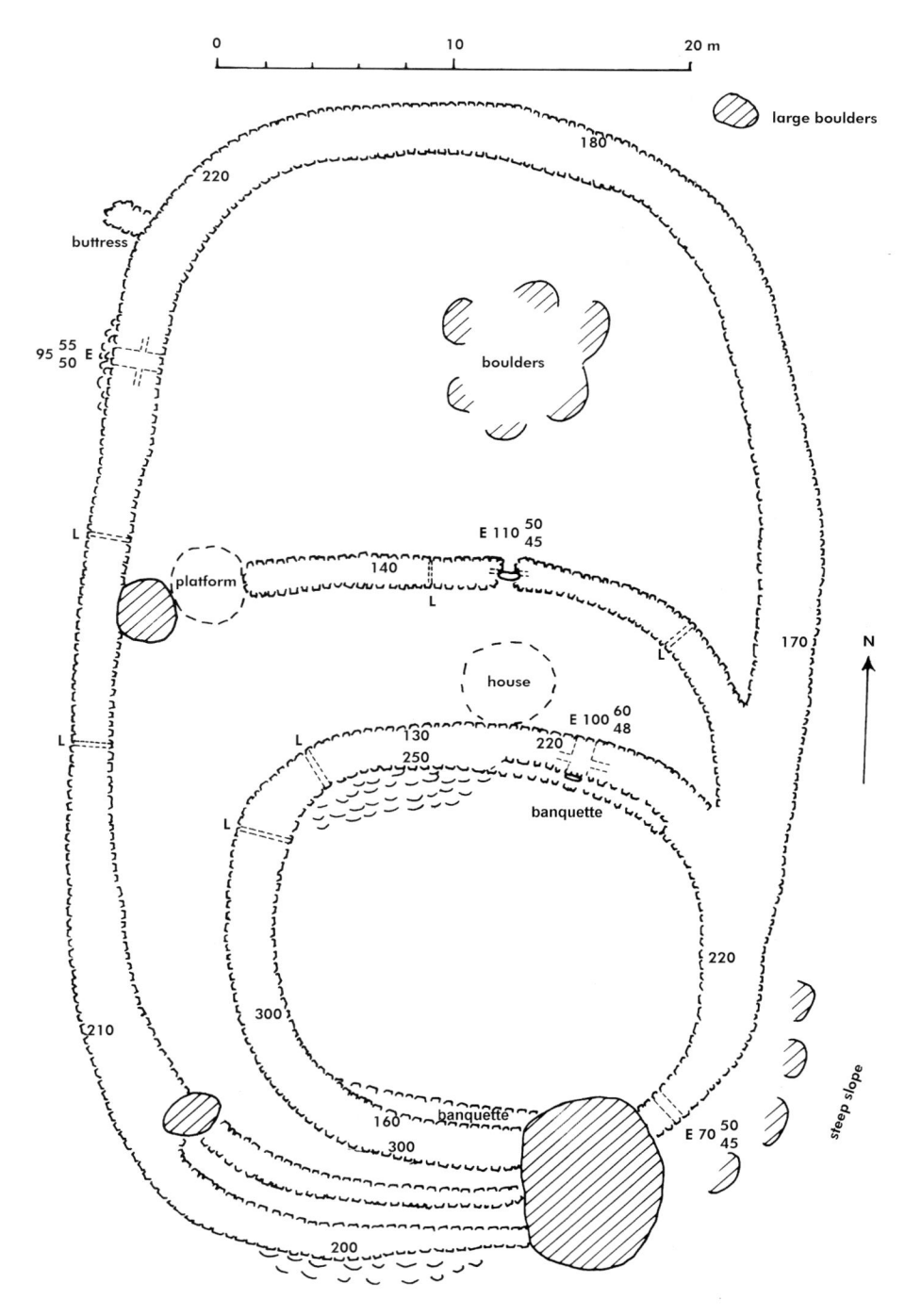

Fig. 39. Sketch plan of Mujinga fort, Ziwa Ruins. L = loophole; E = lintelled entrance with height and width at top and bottom. Other figures denote wall heights

are single enclosures 30m or more in diameter also with house floors. In one case several irregular enclosures are built among large boulders on the sides of a kopje.

The Ziwa forts and several of the National Park ones including Nyangwe are described by Randall-MacIver (1906), and Nyangwe and Chawomera by Summers (1958). Not included in the above classification are the less coherent ruins on top of Demera Hill above Nyanga town and forts well to the south near Penhalonga. Some at least of the latter are attributable to the Manyika (Martin 1940) (as some of the National Park examples may also be).

The forts carry implications for the security and social structure of their communities and their dating and associations are relevant to the interpretation of Nyanga settlement. The lowland forts may be assumed to be contemporary with the stone enclosures in their vicinity, supported by a radiocarbon determination on a wooden locking beam from "Zimbiti fort" in the Ziwa area which is consistent with other Ziwa dates – probably 18th to early 19th century. For Nyangwe Fort, beads from a midden below the wall of one of the appended enclosures suggest a 17th-century date (Summers 1958:54-5; Appendix E), giving a *terminus post quem* for this enclosure at least, though the midden could derive from the occupation of the original enclosure. How long these highland forts were occupied and when abandoned is uncertain. Some of them must have continued in use as late as the 19th century, assuming a connection with pit-structures in the general area, some of which are believed to be of that date as argued earlier in this chapter.

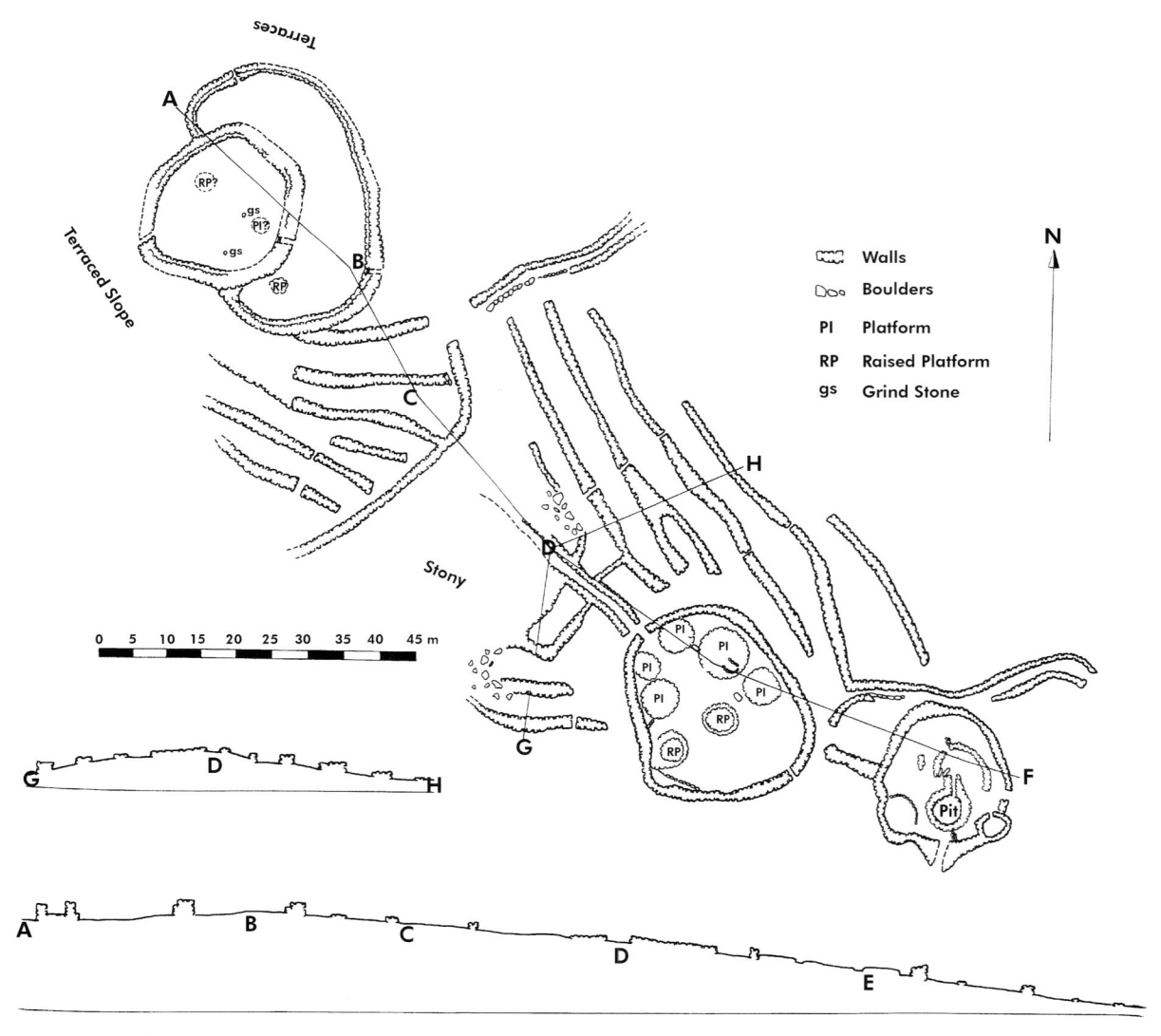

Fig. 40. Complex of fort, residential enclosure and pit-enclosure, with terraces and walled passages. Nyahava, Tanda, grid reference VQ321953

If they were even partly contemporary, the pit-structures and forts are contrasting types of features which imply some social distinction in the highlands. The forts were regularly occupied and thus were more than temporary refuges for dispersed villages of pit-structures. They could represent foci of local authority, in which case their distribution suggests relatively localised sociopolitical units, with perhaps a larger centre at Nyangwe. The Ziwa forts suggest a similar scale of organisation, perhaps with a more important, though hardly defended, centre nearby at Nyahokwe. In the St Mary's/Maristvale area the small forts without regular occupation suggest communal security measures, while north again the lack of forts indicates greater security or some other strategy for coping with aggression. A relatively late dating, probably within the 18th/19th centuries, indicates contemporaneity with the Manyika and Saunyama chiefdoms discussed by Beach in the Annex. If Beach is correct in thinking that the basic distribution of political units has remained generally stable, it follows that the National Parks forts would have fallen within the Manyika sphere of influence and the areas to the north under Saunyama. The forts would then represent local chiefs and headmen under these polities.

Minor inter-community raiding was probably endemic as Beach suggests, while larger scale events are illustrated by the major cattle raid by Manyika on Saunyama in the late 19th century (see Annex). Ngoni raiding as part of the wider historical effects of the *mfecane* also impinged on the area and is stressed in the recorded traditions, but Beach plays down the likelihood of any major disruption caused by that.

IRON WORKING

Iron tools must have been critical for the construction and cultivation of the terraces and ridges and for building activities. Evidence for iron production is relatively common in most of the areas examined and 26 sites were recorded during the recent work, ranging from slag scatters to quite well preserved smelting furnaces and smithing hearths. None was excavated but Summers (1958) excavated a number of furnaces and descriptions are also given by Bernhard (1962).

The furnaces and smithing hearths are almost always within small roughly built stone enclosures three to four metres in diameter, and most slag occurrences were also associated with these. The mouths of the furnaces are aligned with the enclosure entrances but this is not always the case for the smithing hearths.

Furnaces

Three different types of furnaces are represented among the better preserved examples:
1. Oval with mouth at one end and two tuyere holes at the other (fig. 41a; Plate 22);
2. Oval with mouth on one side flanked by low projecting walls, and tuyere holes at the ends (fig. 41b);
3. Circular, conical with one to three tuyere holes at the back (fig. 41c).

All three types are found within an area of a few square kilometres in the Nyahokwe area east of Ziwa, but elsewhere there is some hint of differing distribution. All the four furnaces seen in the National Park/Nyanga town area are of type 1 and Summers (1958:61, 114) adds another example a little to the west at Leaping Waters. The only furnace seen in the north-east was also of this type. Two furnaces seen west of Nyautare are of the type 3; Summers reports remains of other furnaces from this area but details are unclear. The only example of type 2 seen was at Nyahokwe; another good example from the same area was destroyed during the independence war (Bernhard 1962). Two of the furnaces of type 1 in the National Park area may be associated with water furrows D1 and NP10 (see furrows section in Chapter 4). No sites were recorded in the Burnaby area or west of the Nyangombe but fieldwork in these areas was relatively brief and evidence may have been missed.

A few well preserved examples may be described.

Large oval furnace of type 1 with mouth at end, on the south-east flank of Ziwa mountain, grid ref. VQ 634940. The enclosure is low-walled, 4m in diameter. Interior diameters of the furnace are 92 by 50cm, narrowing to the front; outside diameters 115 by 85cm; height 96cm; chimney c.65 by 15cm; mouth 37cm wide and c.30cm high facing west; two tuyere holes at the back, 12cm wide and 10cm high, 17cm apart and 23cm above the inside base; outside surface eroded. No slag or tuyeres were seen but there is thick leaf mould all around.

Oval furnace of type 1 with mouth at end, on the east side of the upper Pungwe valley, National Park, grid ref. VQ 778747, close to two pit-structures (fig. 41a; Plate 22). Enclosure 3.50m in diameter and c.50cm high. Interior of furnace 80 by 40cm; height 90cm; chimney 57 by 12cm; mouth 32 by 27cm; two tuyere holes at the back 8 to 10cm in diameter, 20cm above the inside base; breasts and navel on the front, with a raised belt all round. Very little slag was found in the vicinity.

Oval furnace of type 2 with mouth at the side, in the Nyahokwe area, grid ref. VQ 654948, at the foot of a granite kopje (fig. 41b). Enclosure 4 by 4.50m in diameter and up to 60cm high. Interior of the furnace measures 75 by 35cm, with a tuyere hole at each end; height c.80cm; chimney 56cm long, width incomplete; mouth 64cm wide and c.40cm high, facing north-west, flanked by two low broad projecting walls; inside surface coated with slag; much of the outside is eroded but there are traces of a raised belt. In front are two pieces of slag-coated *dhaka* slab pierced by round 3cm holes, which must be part of the blocking of the wide mouth during use. There is a considerable deposit of slag below the enclosure entrance but no tuyeres were seen.

Conical furnace of type 3, in Tsvitu area west of Nyautare, grid ref. VR 582302, near the top of a dolerite hill (fig. 41c). The enclosure is 4 by 3.50m in diameter with wall up to 1.20m high. Internal diameter of furnace c.85 by 70cm; height 105cm; mouth 65 by 50cm facing south-west; chimney oval 18 by 14cm; three tuyere holes at the back, 17cm wide and 35cm high, two of them blocked with stones; slag film on parts of the inner wall surface; outside eroded showing coil junctions of construction. There was little slag but some tuyere fragments with 30 to 34mm bore.

A number of other furnaces are sufficiently well preserved to show the remains of moulded features over the mouth. These were presumably female sexual symbols as in the National Park example above but are too eroded for clear identification.

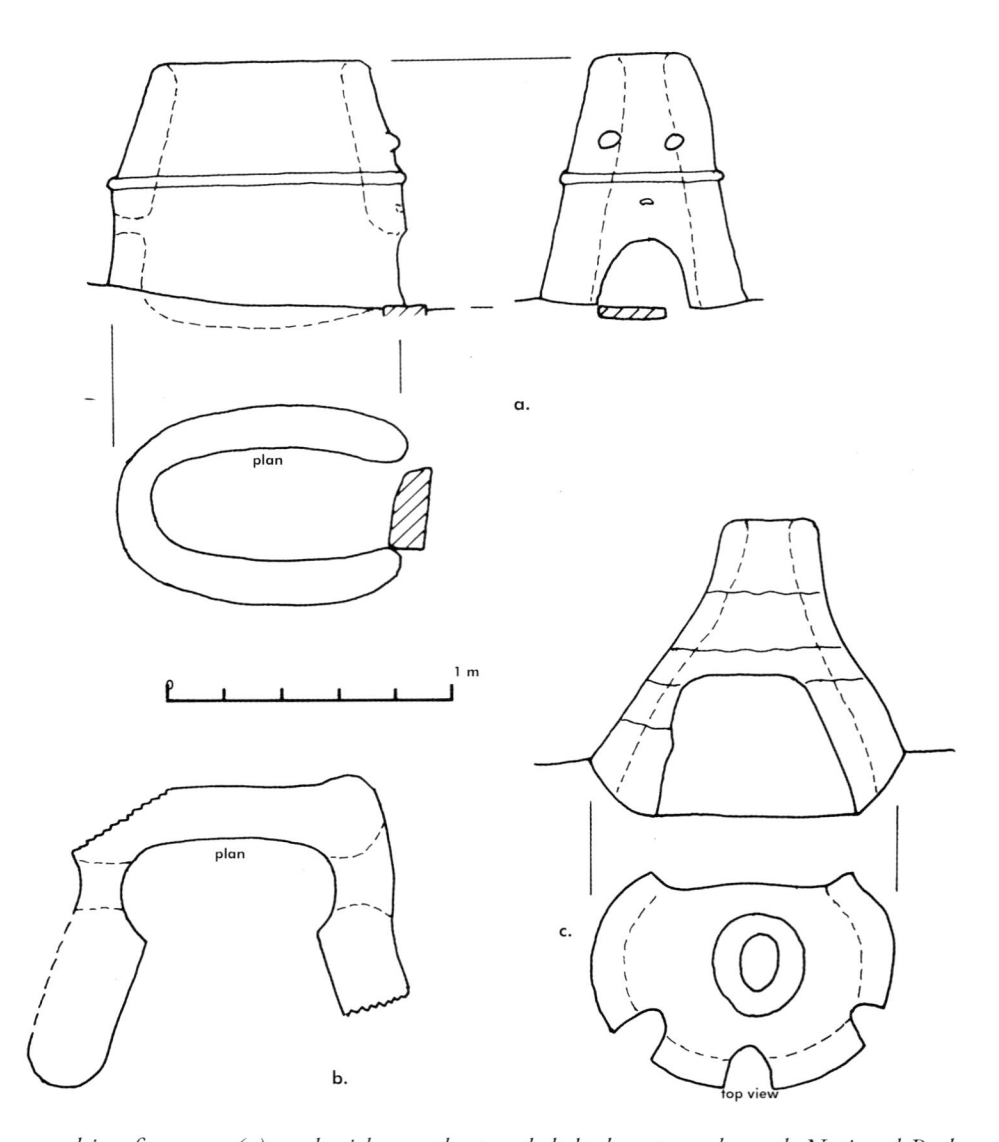

Fig. 41. Iron-smelting furnaces: (a) oval with mouth at end, belt, breasts and navel: National Park, upper Pungwe valley; (b) oval with mouth at side and projecting arms, Nyahokwe; (c) conical, Tsvitu north-west of Nyautare

Furnaces excavated by Summers were at Ziwa, Nyautare (one in a rock shelter) and at Leaping Waters above Nyangombe Falls (1958:61, 99-101, 114-123). Although his descriptions are not very detailed and most of the furnaces were poorly preserved, in several cases he found a hole in the floor 12 to 15cm in diameter and 35 to 55cm deep, in one case filled with charcoal. A deep cutting by an unknown recent excavator in the base of the furnace below Demera furrow D1 might have destroyed such a hole.

Smithing hearths

Four of these were recorded – at Nyahokwe, Kagore, Demera hill, and Tuscany Farm north-east of Troutbeck. The two former are immediately adjacent to furnaces of type 1 in the same enclosure, and the two latter in enclosures of their own; at Demera the enclosure with furnace of type 1 is within 20m. Summers (1958:61) records another at Ziwa, also in an enclosure. The hearths are small, relatively thin-walled, semi-cylindrical or horse-shoe shaped *dhaka* structures, 20 to 30cm wide internally and 25 to 30cm high, with traces of a tuyere hole at the back or side. They are associated with anvils of granite or dolerite and dolerite hammer stones.

Slag and ores

Slag deposits and tuyere fragments are often very sparse in the vicinity of furnaces but are sometimes more abundant, especially in the north-east. The slag is almost all very fine, most pieces 3cm or less in size and few more than 6 or 7cm. The ore in most areas was probably magnetite sand; this weathers from the dolerites and concentrations occur, for instance in the vicinity of Ziwa Site Museum. Laterite is mentioned in the geological report for some areas of the highlands but no substantial occurrences were seen during the present research. If used, laterite might be expected to produce greater volumes of slag.

In the north-eastern lowlands from Elim to Kagore and up the escarpment towards Chirimanyimo, slag occurrences are quite frequent but furnaces rare. Of 13 slag occurrences, only one has surviving furnace remains, though there is a report of another near Kagore. Some slag deposits in this area form substantial heaps. The largest is Madunje, high up on a shoulder of the highlands west of Kagore. Here there is a series of heaps up to about a metre in height in an area about 20 by 20m, enclosing two hollows where furnaces may have been located. If there was ever a stone enclosure it has been swamped by slag. The only furnace seen in this area was north-west of Kagore, within an enclosure 3.50m in diameter. This is a small example of a type 1 oval furnace with mouth at the end and probably a single tuyere, flanked by a small smithing hearth associated with anvils and hammer stones.

None of these iron-working sites is dated but all occur quite close to stone enclosures, pit-structures or other features of the complex and it may be assumed that they are associated. Judging by the amount of slag, the output of most individual smelting sites was not great, but the number of sites indicates a fair overall production which must have been adequate for the needs of the local communities. The concentration of sites in the Nyahokwe area suggests that there was some local specialisation. Iron artefacts from excavated settlement sites include a fair number of arrowheads of various shapes, small knives, *mbira* (thumb piano) keys and miscellaneous pieces. Few hoes appear to have survived; Summers (1958:109, 112) found a few fragments and there is a chance find of two complete specimens from Ziwa (Plate 23).

Plate 12. Low enclosure wall at Nyangui 1732DD27 early hilltop settlement

Plate 13. Pit-structure with restored houses, National Park

Plate 14. Grassy hollow of a ruined pit-structure. Nyangui G7/1

Plate 15. Pit-structure with two radial walls. Nyangui Block G, group 1, pit 13

Plate 16. Mount Muozi from the east side of the saddle. Two cairns in the foreground

Plate 17. Mount Muozi stone walled site. House circles with the main group of complete pots.

SETTLEMENTS, HOMESTEAD STRUCTURES AND OTHER FEATURES

Plate 18. Iron object from Mount Muozi

Plate 19. Raised platform with plastered floor surface. Ziwa, Chirawu's site 12

Plate 20. Lintelled entrance of a fort in Tanda. Grid reference VR360120

Plate 21. Small fort with aloes south of Nyautare. Site 1732DC44, grid reference VR662225

Plate 22. Furnace of type 2. Middle Pungwe valley, National Park

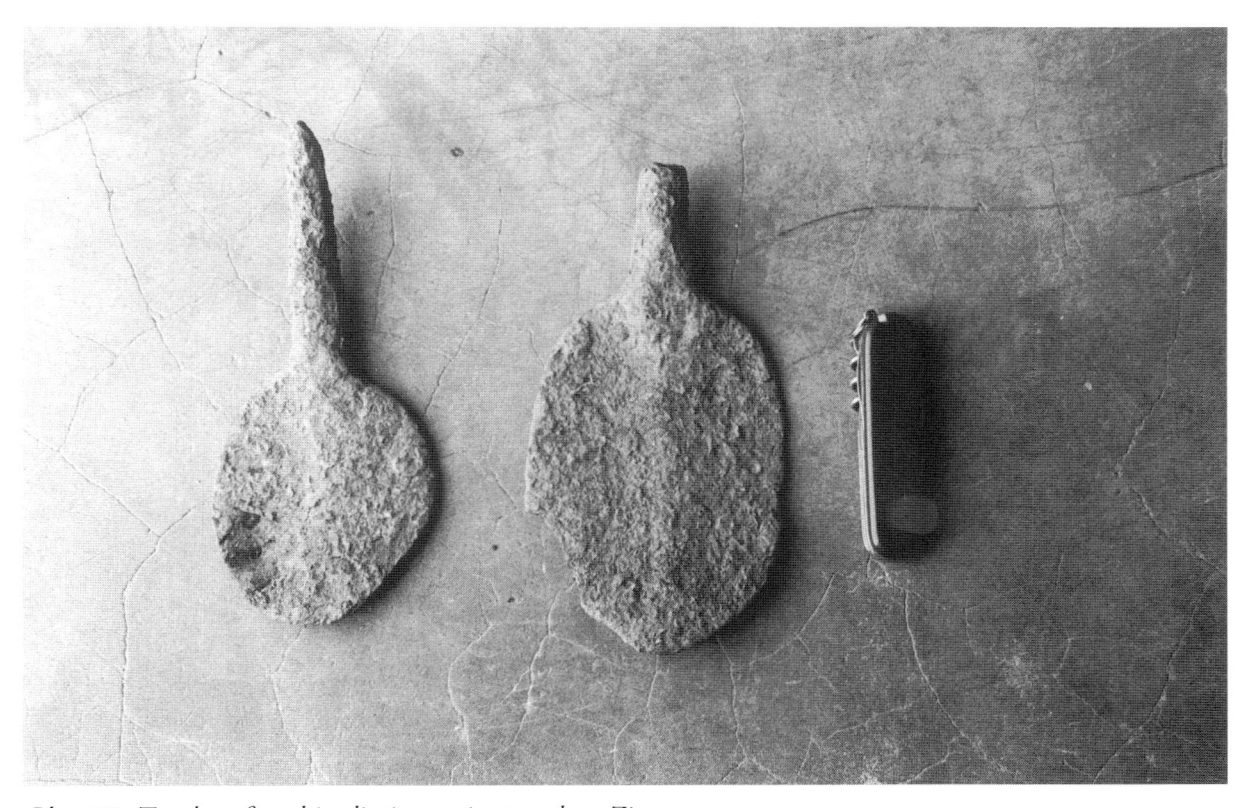

Plate 23. Two hoes found in digging a pipe trench at Ziwa.

CHAPTER 6

LIVESTOCK AND AGRICULTURE IN THE NYANGA COMPLEX

The range of environments within the Nyanga archaeological complex, arising from variations in altitude and rainfall, might be expected to have elicited a complementary range of agricultural adaptations. Basic options were rainfed cultivation with or without terracing, exploitation of more or less wet lands, and irrigation. The general response was the integration of livestock husbandry with cultivation; implementation must have varied with local circumstances.

Evidence comes primarily from the fields themselves – terraces, cultivation ridges, putative gardens – with deductions from homestead design as described in Chapters 4 and 5, amplified by rather sparse evidence of seeds and animal bones. Interpretation is assisted by ethnographic analogies at varying degrees of direct relevance. The general context within African agriculture and recent crops and cultivation practices in Nyanga are discussed in Chapter 3.

LIVESTOCK

Most of the direct evidence for livestock, with the exception of a few teeth and other fragments, comes from the Muozi ash midden described in Chapter 8, this being the only site offering substantial accumulation of domestic refuse and good alkaline conditions for preservation. Even here the sample is quite small and its main value is in showing the types of domestic animals present – dwarf cattle, sheep and goats. Even with a larger sample, this atypical mountain-top site could not be used to make reliable deductions on the general proportions of different animals, or on herd management practices, since the slaughter patterns may well have differed from those of the wider society. Further deductions about the livestock kept and their management are drawn indirectly from the evidence of the homestead structures described in Chapter 5.

It was argued in Chapter 5 that the pits of the highland pit-structures and Ziwa pit-enclosures were designed for the penning of cattle, and show the ideological as well as economic importance of these. The restricted entrance tunnels could only admit *dwarf* cattle and would have constituted an artificial selection on breeding, constraining any tendency to increasing size. This would not preclude the keeping of larger beasts elsewhere, and the constraint hardly applies to the northern double-concentric enclosures or the less typical pit-enclosures which lack lintelled entrances or passages.

The dwarf cattle now identified from Muozi appear to represent a hitherto undefined breed for southern Africa with relatively robust horns (Appendix B). Two estimates for horn spans of 49 and 52cm from Muozi are given by Plug *et al* (1997), which would be a tight fit for the entrance passages and tunnels. There is however a remembered tradition that horns could be polled if they grew too long (Claud Munditi, Village Head, Chirimanyimo). Munditi said that these cattle had humps, a point also noted by Machiwenyika, quoted in Appendix I to Annex. There are other allusions to dwarf cattle in the region. Beach (Annex) notes references to particularly small *kasiri* cattle in the Marondera area of Zimbabwe which were kept in the houses and could fit through the small doorways. Dwarf cattle were also documented by Selous (1881:313) in Zambia just north of the modern Lusaka:

> "I measured one of the largest cows (though they were all much of a size); she stood just 3ft. 4in. [1.02m] at the withers. Though so small, these little cows are capital milkers; they all had very small horns and were really beautiful little animals. [The horn size may indicate a different breed.]"

As noted in Chapter 2, the perennial grasses of the highlands constitute "sour" grazing and lose nutritional value as they mature from May or June onwards, so that cattle lose weight. This also applies to much of the lowlands. At the present time however cattle are kept year round by indigenous farmers in the highlands, often without artificial supplements, so this is not precluded in the past. Dwarf cattle might be expected to be less affected and more resilient, though nutrition as well as genetics may have contributed to their size.

Pit size and implications
If the pits were built to accommodate dwarf cattle, pit size should give an indication of the relative numbers kept in the homesteads and hence perhaps of family wealth. We may also consider here the central enclosures of the double-concentric enclosures of the northern lowlands, since they occupy an equivalent position within the homestead and are likely to have served the same function – though not necessarily for *dwarf* cattle as noted above.

The pits of the lowland pit-enclosures and the central enclosures have a restricted size range. The largest sample of measurements comes from Ziwa, for which Chirawu (1999) provides information on the diameters of 126 pits (using the average diameter for oval pits). The size range is from two to nine metres but very few are over four metres, and the overall average is 3.3m. A few pit-enclosures occur in the Kagore area east of the highland range; these have short sloping open entrance passages rather than the lintelled passages of Ziwa, but are also small. Three measured diameters are 3.75 to 4.5m. Occasional pit-enclosures also occur west of the Nyangombe river, also with open entrance passages; these are also small though the only estimate available is 3m (fig. 40). Central enclosures of double-concentric enclosures are little larger; a total sample of 42 have a range of two to five metres internal diameter, with an average of 3.58 ± 0.76.

Using the analogy of cattle kraals built of wooden posts in rural areas of Zimbabwe, some estimates of stock holdings can be attempted. Such kraals accommodate one beast to around three to four square metres. If we take the lower estimate as more appropriate to dwarf cattle, our sites represent one to 21 beasts for Ziwa pits with an average of 2.9, and one to six or seven for the double-concentric enclosures with an average of 3.5.

The small size of these lowland pits/central enclosures appears to reflect relatively low cattle ownership in the lowlands. However, even if the cattle were generally few, one might expect more variation in holdings between families, and the restricted size range could rather reflect a standard practice of keeping a few beasts in the homestead, perhaps for milk and manure, while more may have been kept elsewhere. Simple enclosures with house remains but no pit or central enclosure were presumably those of families without cattle.

The pits of the highland pit-structures, apart from being considerably deeper (usually two to three metres), show more variation in size which would suggest that they accommodated the whole family cattle herd. The range of pit diameters above 1700m (that is above the terracing) from the sample discussed in Chapter 5 is 3.50 to 11m with an average area of 30.3 square metres, representing a holding of three to 32 beasts with an average of 10. Below 1700m the range is 2.4 to 25 animals with an average of 9.4. To take a single community, the pit-structures of Nyangui Group 1 (see Chapter 5), the average number is 8.57 beasts with a range of about five to 17 and a total of 249 for the whole group if all complete pits were occupied. The carrying capacity of the high grassland for modern cattle, larger than "indigenous" breeds, was given in Chapter 2 as three to eight hectares per beast. If we reduce this by say a half for dwarf cattle, it would represent a pasture requirement of 3.75 to 10 square kilometres for this community; the interfluve on which it is situated, without other contemporaneous pits, covers some four square kilometres, or rather more if extended to the crest of the ridge, adequate if the pasture was in good condition.

It may be useful to consider these figures from a different angle in the light of a very rough estimate of the numbers of cattle and people in the Unyama area in the late 19th century. Beach (Annex) hazards a rough guess of 2000 cattle here before the rinderpest epizootic, apparently on the tenuous extrapolation of an 1895 estimate for Mutasa District (Manyika). This figure would presumably cover both highlands and lowlands, but the data do not permit more than a rough overall figure. A few calculations can be based on this figure to give a general picture of cattle/people ratios, even if subject to numerous uncertainties.

The data for all pit-structures in the sample give an average area of 29.8 square metres for the highlands, representing almost 10 cattle at three square metres each. For the lowlands we have an average diameter of 3.4m for pits and central enclosures, representing three beasts each. If we further assume for the sake of argument, equal numbers of highland and lowland homesteads and ignore the possibility of cattle kept outside these enclosures, 2000 cattle would represent 308 cattle-owning homesteads, divided between highlands and lowlands. Beach further estimates a total human population of about 5000 for Unyama. If, again for the sake of argument, we say that 20% of lowland homesteads had no cattle, we get a total of about 347 homesteads at an average of about 14 men, women and children each, which seems a little high. Given the number of highland pit-structures, it seems unlikely that only 154 were occupied at any one time, even for Unyama alone, which may suggest that the cattle estimate is too low. A larger number of cattle might be envisaged in the 18th to early 19th century than at the end of the 19th, when pit-structures had apparently been abandoned.

No attempt has been made to estimate the size of small stock holdings. These included both sheep and goats as identified at Muozi (Appendix B) and they may have been the only livestock owned by the occupants of the simple enclosures in the lowlands. They were accommodated in the divided houses of the highland pit-structures and Ziwa enclosures, incidentally implying some individual ownership within the homestead. Their accommodation in the northern lowlands where there are no divided houses is uncertain. Goats may have been favoured in the lowlands where more browse was available and where sheep might have been more at the mercy of several species of grasses with sharp barbed awns, especially *Heteropogon contortus,* as well as blackjacks (*Bidens pilosa*) on recently cultivated fields.

As with many African societies, sheep and goats were probably the main source of meat, while cattle constituted wealth and provided milk. The latter may only have been slaughtered and eaten in old age or on special occasions; certainly the very few beasts postulated for the lowland homesteads would not have allowed for regular slaughter. The central ideological role of cattle is emphasised by the powerful symbolic significance of the pits discussed in Chapter 5. However one of the prime economic functions of all livestock must have been the production of manure discussed below.

Soil fertility and manure
Soils are discussed in Chapter 2 where a distinction is made between the heavily weathered and leached soils of the highland plateaus and lowland valleys, and the younger, thinner, stony soils of the escarpments and hill slopes with greater inherent mineral fertility. The archaeological remains show that highland settlement was largely on the infertile plateaus, whereas lowland settlement – or at least the visible stone enclosures – is amid the stony terraced areas. The leached plateau soils could hardly have been effectively cultivated for fields or gardens without enhancement of fertility by manuring. The younger soils of terraced areas would have given better initial returns, but prolonging the fertility of at least a proportion of the exploited area was necessary to make the heavy labour demands of terracing cost-effective. Manure must thus have been essential.

There is no direct evidence for manure but the rarity of dung and rubbish deposits must be significant. Only Muozi and perhaps Nyangui G7/1 (Chapter 8) show any substantial accumulation of domestic rubbish, ash or dung, nor have remains of dung deposits been found in pits or divided houses. Some dried dung may have been burnt for fuel in the highlands as suggested by Summers (1958:238), but this would have been less necessary in the lowlands where wood would have been more easily available. It therefore seems inescapable that the dung was used for manure, and that domestic ash and other refuse were included with it.

There is little indication of how the dung was utilised, apart from the suggested use of cattle slurry at some of the pit-structures noted in Chapters 4 and 5 and discussed below. This was made possible by the use of furrow water, where available, to flush out the enclosed, paved highland pits. Where no water was utilised, removal would have to have been by hand. The bacterial decomposition of fresh dung, as with other organic matter, uses nitrogen and may actually reduce fertility temporarily if applied directly. Thus accumulation and rotting of dung and associated bedding material, within the pen or on a midden, is a general farming practice, to be spread or dug into the soil during preparation for planting. Such a midden outside an enclosure or pit-structure would have been removed to the fields or gardens at least once a year, leaving little or no trace unless left behind when the homestead was abandoned.

In societies where the collection of dung for manure is essential for intensive cultivation, stall-feeding is a common practice, and this has been argued for Nyanga by Sutton (1988). In this practice, livestock are kept permanently penned, at least during the growing season, and forage is brought to them. Dung is thus concentrated instead of being mostly scattered over the pastures and animals are only taken out for watering. At Nyanga in the case of pit-structures served by furrows such watering might not have been necessary. The dung and urine are mixed with surplus forage and bedding material to give fairly rapid accumulation. This process has been documented ethnographically, notably in parts of central and eastern Nigeria (Netting 1967; White 1941). Here among the Kofyar the manure mixture is allowed to collect to a considerable depth within the pen, with the added advantage of absorbing the urine which is rich in nitrogen and might otherwise be lost through drainage or seepage. In those parts of the Ethiopian highlands where cattle are stall-fed the information is less specific, but it appears that the stalls may be cleared out more regularly (Amborn 1989).

In the Nyanga case, such stall-feeding is plausible and is supported by the very solid nature of the pens. However deep accumulation in the pits is unlikely; in the small, shallow, lowland pits it would soon block the entrance tunnel and prevent animals being taken out for water, while in the larger highland pits, many of which have a steeper gradient to the floor, it would block the drain. Deep accumulation would also prohibit flushing for slurry. Regular clearance would thus have been necessary. Collecting and carrying forage to the pens would be laborious but compensated to some extent by the saving of labour for herding in the pastures. After the harvest, stock could be grazed on crop residues in the fields to give direct manuring for next season. Removal of the manure to the midden and eventual transport to the garden or fields could be accomplished with baskets assisted by some form of wooden pitchfork, and perhaps by animal carriage.

The lower floor of the small stock accommodation in the divided houses allowed for some accumulation, but again not to great depth.

Information from Dr I.Mpofu of the Department of Animal Science, University of Zimbabwe, permits some rough estimates of cattle manure production, excluding urine. Indigenous cattle in Zimbabwe consume forage containing around nine kilogrammes of dry matter per day in the wet season, of which 60 to 70% is digested and 30 to 40% voided as dung, say an average of 3.2kg per day. In the dry season, six to eight kilogrammes are consumed of which 40 to 60% are digested, say an average of 3.5kg of dung, or an average of 3.35kg per day for the year. Assuming these present-day Zimbabwe cattle to be about the same size as South African Nguni cattle (a sample of which was used by Plug *et al*, 1997, for comparison with the Nyanga osteological sample excavated at Muozi), and that the Nyanga dwarf cattle were on average 20% smaller in all dimensions, they would have been just over half the weight, so dung production may be reduced by this proportion – c.1.7kg/day for the year and c.1.6kg for the wet season.

Total annual production for an average homestead would then be:

    highland pit-structures @ 10 beasts - 6.2 tonnes
    Ziwa pit-enclosures @ 2.9 beasts - 1.8 tonnes
    double-concentric enclosures @ 3.5 beasts - 2.2 tonnes

Much of this production however would have been deposited during grazing in the dry season at least, so it may be more realistic to calculate wet season production, assuming stall-feeding for six months of the cropping season to harvest:

    pit-structures - 3.0 tonnes
    pit-enclosures - 0.86 tonnes
    double-concentric enclosures - 1.0 tonne

This is of course only dung dry-matter production and does not include rotted bedding material and surplus forage which would provide greatly increased bulk of organic matter. Allowing a guesswork factor of three for this, production could be assessed at 9.0, 2.6 and 3.0 tonnes respectively, available for spreading on gardens or fields. In addition, at least some proportion of the dry-season production might be expected to have been deposited directly on the fields during grazing of crop residues. It is difficult to assess if or how far the pit-structure figure should be adjusted for dung off-take as slurry, but nutrients from this would still be available. Cattle manure would also have been supplemented by a lesser but significant amount of manure from small stock, but there is insufficient data to estimate this.

Manure is an important source of nutrients, especially nitrogen, phosphates and potassium. It also reduces the acidity of the soil and raises the level of organic matter, improving water holding capacity and the infiltration rate. Most of the nitrogen in the organic matter, apart from ammonium nitrate or urea, is released by slow mineralisation and becomes available to crops only in seasons subsequent to application. At the present day, cattle manure in the rural areas of Zimbabwe tends to be of low quality due to trampling and aerobic decomposition in the kraal which results in a high sand content and major loss of nitrogen through volatilisation of ammonia (Murwira 1993:11). Better quality would be produced in the stone-paved or bedrock-floored Nyanga pits and enclosures, and stall-feeding would provide extra organic material for the absorption of urine which contains about half of the nitrogen excreted and 65% of the potassium, though very little phosphates. Regular removal to a dung midden would allow for some volatilisation from the surface of the midden, but with anaerobic conditions in the interior. Mugwira and Shumba (1986) found that kraal manure in two rural areas of Zimbabwe averaged 0.98 - 1.05% nitrogen, 0.13 - 0.19% phosphorous and 0.99 - 1.47% potassium. Values for Nyanga should have been higher, perhaps nearer to figures for Britain of 1.7 - 2.5% N, 0.2 - 0.5% P and 1.3 - 2.0% K respectively (Wild & Jones 1988:101).

The value of slurry should also be considered. This consists of faeces and urine diluted with washing water. Undiluted it has a dry-matter content of about 10% and nutrient content of c.0.5% N, 0.1% P and 0.4% K. The availability of P and K to crops is similar to that provided by farmyard manure, but in the case of nitrogen depends on the time of application in relation to plant growth and soil conditions. About half the total nitrogen is present in the form of ammonium – urea – which is readily available for crop uptake but subject to rapid volatilisation in storage or spreading, unless quickly incorporated in the soil (Wild & Jones 1988:102).

The relatively low ratio of carbon to nitrogen leads to less immobilisation of nitrogen in the decomposition of the organic matter than is the case for fresh manure or other organic material. Application of slurry would be advantageous for crop growth in homestead gardens in the highlands, but would be a laborious process with the use of gourds or pots of limited capacity, so that the collection source would need to be adjacent to the garden, as seems to have been the case for the basins or hollows below some pit-structures.

Mugwira and Shumba (1986) found that average application rates for kraal manure in the rural communities studied were 35 to 39 tonnes per hectare every three or four years, approaching the rates recommended by agricultural extension workers of 40 tonnes every four years. It is impossible to know how the Nyanga farmers scheduled their manure application, but an average of about 10 tonnes per hectare per year might be taken as a working figure, perhaps rather less in view of the probable better quality. Manure production in Nyanga homesteads has been discussed above, from which it may be roughly estimated that manure from the average highland pit could fertilise just under one hectare per year, and from the lowland pits and enclosures about a quarter to a third of a hectare. This could be increased slightly with the addition of small-stock manure which would presumably be all that was available to homesteads without cattle.

These amounts might be adequate for highland families but would probably not have sufficed for more than gardens and limited infields near the lowland homesteads. Here outer fields, terraced or ridged, would have been reliant on natural fertility apart from that provided by grazing after the harvest. If this fertility was a significant factor in subsistence, as the great extent of terracing and ridging implies, an adequate area of outfields would have been needed to sustain a long enough fallow cycle to restore some fertility. Failing this, it would have been necessary to move the community, leaving that whole settlement system "fallow", perhaps to be reoccupied and the capital infrastructure overhauled after a suitable interval. For the lowlands at least, with their minimal cattle numbers in the home area, this situation would have constituted a nutrient trap whereby insufficient fertility could be transferred from pasture to cultivated land.

Crops and cultivation

Food plants grown in the Nyanga area earlier in the 20th century were listed and discussed in Chapter 3 and the great majority of these would have been known to the inhabitants of the Nyanga terrace complex, representing a wide range of staples and subsidiary plants. Important staples, as elsewhere in the region, would have been grains (sorghum, bullrush and finger millet, some rice), legumes (cowpeas and ground beans), and root crops such as *majo* (taro), *tsenza* (*Plectranthus*) and the wild calla lily (*Zantedeschia*). Maize, known by at least the late 19th century, may have been present earlier as a minor crop. Subsidiary plants include cucurbits, oil seeds and a wide variety of leaf vegetables, some of them useful weeds of cultivation rather than actual cultigens.

Only a relatively small proportion of this suite of plants is likely to provide surviving traces in archaeological contexts – mainly those with hard seeds subject to carbonisation, which excludes the root crops and many of the leaf plants. Seeds identified from excavations during the recent project are listed in Appendix C. Cultigens are sparsely represented among these but the data may be considered together with that obtained from Summers' excavations (1958:176-7) to show sorghum, finger and bulrush millet, cowpeas, ground beans, cucurbits, castor oil and perhaps maize (apparently from a surface context at Summers' Site IV). The only seeds from highland sites are one cowpea and one sorghum grain from G1/21 and Fishpit respectively, both later pit-structures, so there are no data to distinguish any difference between highland and lowland crops – which in any case might be expected to be at the variety rather than the species level. These archaeologically attested plants are all within the traditional crops listed above as still grown in the area and it is safe to assume that the other traditional crops documented in Chapter 3 were also grown, together with the useful weeds of cultivation. The roots would have been especially important but no preserved traces have been identified. Among other seeds identified, the grasses, *Panicum maximum* and perhaps *Sporobolus*, may indicate deliberate collection for food, while the wild fruits would of course have been utilised.

Intercropping and rotation are not directly documentable archaeologically but are widely understood in African traditional cultivation and would undoubtedly have been practised in a context as complex as that of Nyanga. Attendant advantages are the fixation of nitrogen by legumes for accompanying grains, adjustment of appropriate crops to relative fertility, maintenance of ground cover to inhibit evaporation and erosion, and spreading of labour requirements for planting, weeding and harvesting. Different moisture requirements of crops and varieties gave some flexibility in coping with short term rainfall fluctuation. Manuring of gardens and infields would have enhanced the benefits of these practices.

It is probable that the outlying terraced fields were devoted to the main grain staples, especially sorghum. This is supported by the lack of any traces of subsidiary ridging or mounding which are associated with most other crops in recent cultivation practice. The outlying large cultivation ridges would be more suitable for root crops, *Colocasia* and *Zantedeschia*, along the wetter ditches, with grains and other crops on the drier crests, perhaps including maize and rice. Legumes and pumpkins would be interplanted with grains. *Tsenza* would also have been grown here, but as a monocrop. Gardens and infields would have been cultivated more intensively and had more variety, with vegetables, oil seeds, cucurbits and some grains and legumes in case of failure on the less secure outer fields.

Technology

Narrow terraces are workable only with hand tools (and in any case ploughs were unknown in this region in pre-colonial times). Direct evidence of the tools used is sparse. Iron hoes must have been imperative for terrace construction and ridging but few traces of these have been found, apart from two small but robust chance finds recovered in the digging of a pipe trench at Ziwa (Plate 23). The small strong blades and strong tangs of these would be appropriate for working among the stones of the terraces, but a broader blade might be considered more effective in the major movement of soil for the cultivation ridges. Hoes must have been valued possessions, wearing out quickly against the stones in terrace and homestead construction. They would have been carefully curated and the iron probably recycled. Wooden digging sticks may well have been used for some cultivation tasks and wooden levers would have assisted in shifting large stones.

Provision for storage was essential to span the long dry season from harvest in about June to the availability of fresh produce in December or January, even in situations where irrigation could prolong the growing season in either direction. The raised platforms described in Chapter 5 reflect substantial storage capacity for preservable crops such as grains, legumes and pumpkins, while certain root crops could be left in the ground until required.

Field systems

Agricultural options, as mentioned above, are rainfed cultivation with or without terracing, exploitation of more or less wet valley lands, and irrigation, and these are all represented in the remains of field systems as described in Chapter 4.

The application of these various options is related to basic soil fertility. Younger soils of the stony slopes with greater inherent fertility were exploited by terracing, and abandoned or fallowed as fertility declined. The deeply weathered and leached soils of the highland plateaus have little potential without manuring and may not have been generally exploited, apart from homestead gardens adjacent to pit-structures, manured with dung or slurry from the pits and irrigated where practicable. Any fields for these communities must have been on the terraced escarpments, and it is not clear how they, or outlying fields in general, may have been protected from animal depredation. However in the National Park area, where there is only localised terracing, these plateau soils were exploited with the aid of irrigation. Here fertilisation with accumulated manure would have been essential, while kraaling of livestock on the fields in the dry season could be envisaged. Lowland alluvial and colluvial soils were exploited by ridging, mainly for water control, and some were irrigated. With lower rainfall, leaching is less intense and fertility might be maintained by some local manuring, incorporation of organic material in the ridges and regular fallowing. Irrigation was practised where viable with considerable skill and ingenuity, but was largely devoted to gardens, with the vast majority of terraces dependent on rainfall.

Evidence for homestead gardens is reasonably clear in the radial walls of many pit-structures and in the walled plots found locally at Chirangeni (Chapter 8), but is less clear in the other lowland enclosures. Here gardens may have been located in vleis where the water-table was relatively shallow.

The above discussion takes its approach from the perspective of the terracing and assumes that valley lands were also exploited by terrace builders where available. However none of the cultivation ridges have been directly or even indirectly dated, and it is not certain that the large-scale ridging systems west of the highlands were contemporary or associated with the terracing. A large-scale simultaneous use of both terracing and ridging by the same community seems unlikely in terms of labour requirements. Lowland practice may have switched from a concentration on terracing to one on ridging (or vice versa), perhaps prompted by some climatic fluctuation. More probably, each local community emphasised one or the other system according to the predominant type of land available. Where both were available it would have offered alternative options in very wet or dry years. An indirect hint of this is given by Taylor (1924:43) who quotes a Saunyama informant as having heard that terraces were built because the low-lying land was flooded. It may be noted that ridging systems extend westwards to the Rusape/Headlands area where terracing becomes sporadic, concentrated mainly on the limited dolerite occurrences. Thus terracing and ridging probably represent parallel exploitation by related communities, each incorporating occurrences of the minor resource where it fell within its ambit.

Land holdings

The permanent capital works of the terraces, homesteads and ridging systems imply some degree of individual or family land tenure to realise the benefits of the labour invested. The size of land holdings however is uncertain. Some indication of terraced home fields is given by the Ziwa SN113 terrace survey (Chapter 4). In this case, the propinquity of the homesteads would not have given scope for consolidated holdings, implying more fields elsewhere, but there is no way of estimating their location or size. A sandy tributary valley of the Nyangombe with ridging lies a short distance to the north of the surveyed site, and homesteads on the surrounding hills would doubtless have had plots there to expand their agricultural options in terms of crops and climatic vagaries. The two hoes mentioned above were in fact found in this valley. The Maristvale survey, with fewer homesteads in the vicinity, suggests a more consolidated holding with ridged vlei land immediately adjacent. The Chirangeni survey again constitutes a larger area of terracing with the likelihood of subsidiary plots in the valley below. There must have been considerable variation in types of holdings and their distribution, according to the availability of different types of land and social factors such as local population density and family size.

In the highlands, terraced fields must have been at some distance below the homesteads on the escarpments, while the homestead gardens take the place of the lowland valley plots.

Grazing rights would have been more on a communal basis. In the highlands wide pastures were available on the grassland plateaus and on any fallowed terraces, while crop residues on the terraced fields would be used after the harvest in the dry season. In densely settled areas of the lowlands, such as Ziwa or parts of Nyautare, walled paths facilitated the passage of stock through the fields, but pasture may have been scarce apart from small unutilised pockets and fallow terraces. Main cattle herds, if any, may thus have been kept at a distance, as suggested by the small size of the pits or central enclosures. In both highlands and lowlands, stall-feeding may have eased pressure on pastures during the growing season, but forage and bedding material would still need to have been collected.

Intensification

Intensification in general was discussed in Chapter 3 where it was noted that elaborate landesque capital works, such as the terracing, ridging and permanent homesteads of Nyanga, have often been regarded by archaeologists as indicating intensive agriculture. Certainly they represent an intensification of effort over some previous hypothetical system, but how far can the Nyanga systems be regarded as actually "intensive"? A decrease in the intensity of cultivation from gardens to infields to outfields is suggested on the basis of almost universal farming practice. Within this framework some degree of almost continuous production from Nyanga gardens may be postulated and probably annual cultivation of infields. However the normal criteria for assessing intensification in living societies – population density and productivity in terms of yields – cannot be adequately estimated from our data, while even the occupation span of individual homesteads is uncertain. A more realistic criterion is the sustainability of the community as a whole in the same location for an indefinite period. Discussions above suggest this was not the case for the Nyanga lowlands, and that communities may have had to shift periodically, even if this may have been a cyclical process in the long term. We may thus, if definition is needed, fall back on Sutton's conception of a repertoire of specialised techniques which maintained the population as a whole for a few centuries but ultimately succumbed to overspecialisation or outside factors beyond its control.

Stimulus

What was the stimulus to the development of these specialised techniques? The conventional explanation of a community forced to take refuge in an isolated difficult environment hardly holds, except perhaps for the initial stage represented by the early hilltop settlements as considered in Chapter 7. The Nyanga lowlands at least are not easily defensible as a refuge area and do not constitute a remote or difficult environment, although the northern highlands might be seen in this light. Among other factors which have been considered as promoting intensification, external demand would not seem to have been operating at Nyanga on a scale to have stimulated production of a saleable surplus, while exaction of tribute by an elite or outside power seems improbable. Nor would overall population pressure have been a factor. We may hark back to Brookfield's emphasis on opportunities (see Chapter 3) in relation to the limited fertile areas of stony dolerite soils and wetlands, which required specialised techniques for their exploitation. These, once initiated, would have provided a "quantum leap" in productivity and concentrated local populations with the manpower and surplus resources to fuel further development.

CHAPTER 7

NYANGA SOCIETY IN THE LATER IRON AGE

Chronology and settlement patterns

A later Iron Age date for the Nyanga stone structures has been recognised since the work of Summers around 1950, if not before. This is apparent from the state of their preservation, the nature of the ceramics, and surviving traditions about some of the features. The recent work establishes a span from the 14th to the 19th century, thus extending Summers' estimate of 15th to 18th centuries, and it is now possible to construct a broad internal chronology of development with the help of 30 radiocarbon determinations from 15 sites (Appendix F), the ceramic and bead evidence (Appendices D and E), the evolution of homestead designs (Chapter 5) and their relative preservation. The combined evidence indicates a series of shifts in settlement focus in relation to altitude and area. That this is a single sequence of cultural development is demonstrated by the ceramic relationships between the early hilltop settlements and the early ruined pit-structures, and thence by the distinctive features of the homestead structures, demonstrating both evolution and continuity down to the latest phases in both the highlands and the lowlands in the 19th century. Consideration of the patterns of settlement at successive stages offers some preliminary deductions on relative population size and distribution, and on social and political organisation.

The development of the complex may be set out provisionally as follows:

	Highlands	Ziwa	Northern lowlands
1300	early		
1400	hilltop settlements	?	?
1500	↕		
1600	ruined pit-structures	?	?
1700	↕	↑	↑
1800	later pit-structures	pit-enclosures	double conc enclosures
1900	↓	↓	↓

This time-chart must be regarded as provisional, since the absolute and relative dating, especially of the later part of the complex, is not perfectly established owing to the imprecision of the ceramic and bead evidence and the alternative calibrations of radiocarbon determinations falling in the last four centuries. For the earlier phases, moreover, a closer definition of full time-spans needs more radiocarbon tests from reliable contexts than have been possible so far. The picture may also be incomplete in that of the lack of dated sites in any given area in a particular time range cannot be taken as conclusive negative evidence in the present state of knowledge, since other site categories may not have been recognised or dated.

The chronology and patterns of distribution of the successive stages discussed below may be considered, and perhaps partly explained, in relation to possible changes of climate which would have affected the viability of occupation and subsistence at different altitudes. Relevant factors would be temperature, rainfall and the wet-season cloud-base. The last of these would have been influential in determining the limits of effective settlement because of the dense mist which it occasions in the highlands, sometimes persisting for days at a time; nowadays the critical level is about 1900m, although some people have recently been attracted above this altitude by the favourable conditions for potato cultivation. The climatic history outlined in Chapter 2 indicates that cold and probably dry conditions prevailed between AD 1300 and 1500, followed by some amelioration to about 1675, and a further cooler/drier trend till about 1850. Most of the evidence for this climatic history derives from South Africa however; in north-eastern Zimbabwe the changes were probably less extreme and the colder phases more curtailed (Tyson and Lindesay 1992). While changing climatic conditions may well have influenced the zones preferred for settlement and the shifts which occurred over the centuries at Nyanga, it would be unwise to regard them as the only determining factor — doubtless undocumented human political and social factors played an equal or more influential role. Nevertheless, any sustained changes in temperature and especially rainfall or its seasonality would have affected cultivation practices and livestock husbandry in both higher and lower terrain, and may well have stimulated the adoption of different crops or varieties and adjustments of the prevailing combinations.

The full development of the stone architecture of the settlement structures may partly have been a response to a shortage of timber resulting from forest clearance in the highlands. If the highlands were originally forested and clearance was initiated from the first establishment of the early hilltop settlements, such a shortage of timber may have made itself felt in the course of a couple of centuries. Thus in the later phases available long timbers must have been reserved for roofing and relatively thin and short poles had to suffice for house walls. The culmination of the process is seen in the Chirangeni enclosure where house walls are of neatly built stone without wooden poles. While stone was extensively used from the first, it was only with the well preserved pit-structures and pit enclosures that full expertise was achieved. In this connection, it was noted in Chapter 5 that the revetment of the early ruined pits was of inferior quality and that any houses surrounding these pits lacked the low stone walls of the later house bays. The stone architecture is likely to have been perfected in the highlands and the techniques carried to the lowlands with the expansion of settlement, even though timber may initially have been more plentiful there.

Early hilltop settlements

The earliest stone structures that have been recognised are those of the early hilltop settlements distributed along the crest of the northern highlands from at least Worlds View in the south, to north of Chirimanyimo Hill (fig. 29). The lower part of the midden and some of the other features on Mount Muozi belong with these. These settlements of around the 14th to 15th centuries appear on present evidence to emerge spontaneously in their distinctive mountain-top situations without local antecedents, as discussed further below.

The hilltop sites often cover several hectares, representing relatively large nucleated settlements. Chirimanyimo Hill and Nyangui 1732DD27 are described in Chapter 8. The low-walled and probably hedged enclosures typical of these sites are likely to be residential, although this has not been established by excavation. Terraced platforms also supported houses at Chirimanyimo, with similar indications on Rukotso and Muozi. The walled hollows were probably for livestock and ancestral to the later pits, given the postulated cultural continuity.

Some such hollows were built within the low-walled enclosures as at Chirimanyimo VIII but this is not an invariable pattern. On the hilltop plateau at Chirimanyimo, the surrounding wall and rather different residential enclosures have a different character from the more typical structures and suggest a more elite settlement, an interpretation supported by the large size of the site as a whole. Some social stratification may thus be suggested, but evidence of relative wealth such as glass beads is lacking.

The hilltop locations lack ready access to surface water in most cases and are ostensibly very exposed; they must have been very cold in winter, the more so as their occupation spanned the first cold phase. However drier conditions may have raised the cloud-base and reduced the occurrence of unpleasant dense mist, and the hilltops may have attracted more of any available moisture. Exposure to the elements (and to any enemy) might have been mitigated by mountain forest if the highlands were originally forested as discussed in Chapter 2. However the presence of cattle bones at the excavated sites shows that at least some open pasture must have been available.

The subsistence base is still unclear beyond the few cattle bones. The location of fields for cultivation has not been identified; the nearest terracing is usually at some distance from the settlements and may not have been initiated by this time. Clearance of any climax forest by shifting cultivation, utilising and exhausting its accumulated organic fertility, probably started the process of conversion to short grassland. Seasonal occupation appears unlikely in view of the permanence of the structures and density of pottery remains in the excavated hollows, while related sites have not been recognised at lower altitudes.

It is uncertain why these high hilltops should have been selected for occupation at this stage. The varying size of the sites, the lack of evidence of obvious wealth and the apparent lack of contemporary sites at lower elevations, indicate that prestige was not a factor in site selection, although relative importance is apparent for Chirimanyimo Hill. The rarity or absence of glass beads or other recognisable imports indicates cultural isolation, and the tightly clustered nucleated settlement pattern contrasts strongly with the much looser dispersed groupings of the ruined and later pit-structures. This could suggest that refuge or concealment from some external threat was involved, although there is no sign of any communal defensive measures and there are no relevant historical records for this period to substantiate or rebut this. A possible threat, direct or indirect, could have been the Great Zimbabwe state which was extending its influence at around this time, as shown by a site of that tradition at Harleigh Farm near Rusape whose dating is broadly contemporary. However in subsequent unsettled times, for which there is more information, people were not driven so far. Threats from the east or north are also possible, but no information is available for these areas.

Pit-structures

These are divided into two categories as described in Chapter 5: "ruined pit-structure" reduced to grassy hollows, and well preserved examples with their stone revetment still largely intact. The ruined pit-structures (and the related upper part of the Muozi midden) date from the 16th and/or 17th century and the ceramic evidence shows development from the early hilltop settlements. The locations of the ruined pits are still at relatively high altitudes, though lower than the hilltop settlements. Distribution appears to be limited to the upper eastern slopes of the main highland range from Chirimanyimo Hill to the Troutbeck area; they could stretch somewhat further since they have not previously been recognised and reported as distinctive features. Frequency is less than for the later pit-structures, representing a more limited population.

The well preserved pits appear to have persisted well into the 19th century but their beginning is less certain. The design clearly derives from that of the earlier ruined pit-structures and continuity between the two types should be expected, but at Matinha (Chapter 8) and Nyangui Block G (Chapter 5) the rarity or absence of examples in an intermediate state of preservation suggests some hiatus in occupation in those areas at least. Further fieldwork is needed to identify areas where such intermediate states of preservation and design occur – perhaps south of the Bende Gap and north of the National Park, an area not yet examined in detail.

The distribution of the well preserved pit-structures is substantially wider than that of the earlier pits, extending from the northern end of the main highlands north of Chirimanyimo, at least to Mkondwe near Penhalonga in the south, and to beyond Triashill in the west, at altitudes above 1400m (fig. 28). This distribution clearly shows an expansion of the area occupied, while the greater frequency of sites in the landscape also indicates higher population density, assuming a significant proportion of them to have been in use at any one time. Site location is locally constrained by the availability of suitable stone, including large slabs for tunnel roofing.

The downward movement from the hilltop settlements to the ruined pit-structures may have coincided with the warmer, wetter intermediate climatic phase around the 16th century when a lower cloud-base may have influenced settlement. The succeeding cool phase from the late 17th century perhaps caused the further downward shift of the well preserved pit-structures, or even a temporary hiatus in highland occupation. It is conceivable that the transition to the well built and preserved later pit-structures took place in the lower part of their altitudinal range where they are directly associated with terracing.

Some indications of the social organisation of this phase can be discerned. The pit-structures, both ruined and well preserved, present a contrasting settlement pattern to the preceding early hilltop settlements. Interpreted as family homesteads, they are distributed in loose groupings, with spacing from 30 to 100m or more, which may be construed as villages; groups of up to 30 are noted in Chapter 5 for Nyangui Block G (fig. 31). This change in residence pattern may imply some relaxation of any constraints affecting the location of earlier settlement and must certainly reflect changes in social organisation. Pit size and number of houses in the well preserved pit-structures vary between and within groups or villages as noted in Chapter 5. Double pit-enclosures or satellite pits show relative wealth in cattle in some cases. There was thus variation in family wealth and consequent social importance. Extensions to the primary platform around the pit are quite common and probably represent expanding family size, but there is little to indicate whether or not duration of homestead occupation extended beyond a single generation. Water furrows serving groups of homesteads reflect community cooperation and management institutions for construction, maintenance and water allocation. These institutions probably operated within a kin-based social organisation, as with the ethnographic examples of irrigation systems described in Chapter 4. South of about Nyanga town, scattered walled forts with internal house circles are interspersed with pit-structures (Chapter 5; Adams 1988). These, if contemporary, may be interpreted as refuges in time of danger, but may also represent local authority. Forts of this type appear to be absent further north.

The interpretation of the pits as cattle pens in the centre of the homestead indicates the increasing importance of cattle, materially and doubtless ideologically. It also implies adequate pasture, showing that the highlands cannot all have been densely forested by this time – although stall-feeding of cattle in the pits for part of the year might have reduced the pasture requirement. The restricted size of the entrance tunnels of the later pits would only have admitted dwarf cattle, but the apparently open entrance passages to the early ruined pits would not have excluded larger beasts; however dwarf cattle were already present at Muozi contemporary with the early pits. The association of terracing with the lower well preserved pit-structures shows the parallel importance of cultivation. This may mark the introduction of terrace technology, although an earlier beginning contemporary with the ruined pits is not unlikely.

Lowland enclosures

The main distinctive forms of lowland enclosures comprise pit-enclosures and double-concentric enclosures as described in Chapter 5. Distribution of these is mutually exclusive (fig. 28), the former at and around Ziwa and the latter to the north, from St Mary's through Nyautare to Ruangwe. Both probably extend west across the Nyangombe river. Related simple enclosures in both areas lack the central feature. While both types are similar in size and basic plan, with the well built central pit or small enclosure interpreted as cattle pens, there are other consistent differences. The double-concentric enclosures lack lintelled entrances and divided houses and their outer walls are generally low, often with multiple entrances.

The pit-enclosures of Ziwa date from the 18th to early 19th centuries, although a greater spread is not ruled out. Their form indicates a development from the well preserved pit-structures with which they are at least partly contemporary. The northern enclosures, including the double-concentric type, also appear to continue well into the 19th century on the basis of recent radiocarbon determinations and preservation at Chigura and Chirangeni (see Chapter 8), but their beginning is uncertain. The radiocarbon date and derived pottery from the Chirangeni garden terrace suggest occupation contemporary with Ziwa but are not associated with any structure.

The split-level enclosures (Chapter 5; not strictly lowland) from a limited area across the highland range just north of Chirimanyimo Hill remain undated, the only excavation having yielded little cultural material. There is no impression of any great age and they could post-date or be contemporary with neighbouring pit-structures. Similarly undated are the pit-enclosures of rather different pattern to Ziwa in Kagore north-east of the highlands and across the Nyangombe in southern Tanda; these could be parallel developments to Ziwa.

Occupation of the lowland enclosures in general is thus contemporary with that of the well preserved pit-structures in the highlands, although the apparent development of pit-enclosures out of pit-structures would indicate that the latter started somewhat earlier. This occupation would have coincided with the last cold phase from the late 17th century, when drier conditions may have reinforced the terracing as a water conservation measure and perhaps stimulated the exploitation of lower, damper lands by cultivation ridges. Occupation of the lowlands might also have been expected during the preceding warmer phase, but has not been documented.

The distribution of lowland homesteads, like that of the pit-structures, displays loose clustering in village groupings and suggests that population was locally dense if all were occupied simultaneously. Homestead location avoids the valleys and may be on relatively gentle slopes or level ground. Stone for building is again necessary but is hardly a constraint, in dolerite areas at least. Homesteads in general show close integration with terracing being often linked to walled trackways negotiating the field systems and providing passage for livestock to grazing areas and water. Cross-terrace divisions, as revealed especially in the surveyed area at Ziwa (Chapter 4), delimit areas of home fields as land holdings, but their relatively small size implies extra cultivated land further afield, probably including a share in any available vlei land.

Homestead size again varies as with the highland pit-structures, to which can be added the presence or absence of pits or inner enclosures, with their implications for cattle ownership as discussed in Chapter 6. Relative wealth is thus again apparent, while for the Ziwa enclosures at least, the non-functional aspects of design reflect availability of labour surplus to subsistence requirements, showing that this was not an especially impoverished society in general. The discussion in Chapter 6 also draws attention to the standardised small size of the pits/inner enclosures and suggests that only selected beasts were kept in the homesteads; this in turn could imply that more were kept elsewhere.

The duration of homestead occupation is again hard to assess but there is little to suggest that it exceeded a single generation. Individual homesteads may have been abandoned, for instance on the death of the owner, and new ones built nearby within the same community. However baked *dhaka* fragments frequently incorporated in enclosure walls indicate more than one phase of house building, suggesting a cycle of abandonment and renovation of many homesteads. It is argued below that this could correspond to a fallowing cycle for the terraced fields in which the whole community temporarily shifted its location. The frequent blocking of pit entrances at Ziwa and some inner enclosures further north may have a practical explanation, but could equally well be a symbolic action on the abandonment of the homestead.

The differences in homestead design between Ziwa and the northern lowlands could reflect a chronological development from one to the other, since available dating (which is hardly conclusive) could indicate later occupation of the latter. If that were the case, the more strictly functional aspects of the northern homesteads could result from greater stress, perhaps linked to slightly lower rainfall, maybe exacerbated by the final cold dry phase. A more likely explanation of the differences, however, might be the development of variant and broadly contemporary cultural traditions.

Some of the lowland forts may represent some degree of social stratification. There are several categories of these as described in Chapter 5. Two examples at Ziwa ruins have inner "keeps" and evidence of regular occupation, suggesting a higher stratum of authority such as local chiefs. Most of those further north in the St Mary's/Nyautare area however are small single structures without regular occupation and must have been temporary refuges; further north forts appear to be absent. Westwards across the Nyangombe are larger defensive enclosures with more numerous house remains which may indicate more concentrated authority, perhaps coupled with greater concern for security towards the fringes of the complex.

What were the relationships between highland and lowland communities, given the contemporaneity of pit-structures and lowland enclosures ? The contrasting environments provided scope for different economic specialisations – emphasis on cattle in the highlands and cultivation on the escarpments and in the lowlands. The situation is most easily examined in the northern highlands where the escarpments are high and steep and the transition from lowlands to highlands more or less abrupt, although there is little significant impediment to movement between the two. Here the highland and lowland communities were relatively close to each other and must have had regular interaction. In addition the close affinities between the Ziwa pit-enclosures and the highland pit-structures demonstrate an intimate cultural relationship and surely a degree of direct kinship between the occupants. The northern enclosures show less affinities to the highland pit-structures, perhaps reflecting a less direct relationship but not ruling out connections or cooperation.

A general scenario of mutual exchange and cooperation can be envisaged whereby cattle products from the highlands were exchanged for agricultural staples and other produce from the lowlands. In addition some of the cattle of the lowlanders might have been boarded out with highland kin, at least in the wet season when it would be desirable to keep them away from the growing crops and when the highland pastures would be at their best. It may be noted that in the Ruangwe area at least cattle have in recent times been moved up and down, to and from wet-season grazing in the local highlands, where they were left largely unattended (stock theft has now put a stop to this practice or entailed closer supervision). However a full-scale seasonal transhumance of whole communities or parts thereof with their stock seems unlikely in the past in view of the permanence and elaboration of the homesteads in each area which imply more than seasonal occupation.

Further south where topographical differences are not so marked, lowland resources would not have been so conveniently available to the highlanders. It may be significant that it is here we see the development of unterraced irrigated cultivation in the highlands.

Complementarity and cooperation between highland and lowland communities is not uncommon in other parts of Africa. Widgren (1999), using the Iraqw of central Tanzania as a case study, has seen this as constituting a "geographical division of labour", prerequisite for the development of intensive cultivation. Whether or not Nyanga agriculture should be considered intensive was discussed in Chapter 6.

POPULATION SIZE AND DENSITY

It is evident from the expanding geographical extent and increasing density of sites that the overall population was increasing through the development of the complex, culminating in perhaps the 18th or early 19th century. However it seems unlikely that the total numbers were ever especially large in comparison with other parts of Zimbabwe. Beach considers the question of population size in the Annex. Arguing from early colonial figures, he estimates a very approximate total figure of only about 5000 for Unyama in the late 19th century , with an overall density no higher than other parts of the eastern side of the Zimbabwe plateau (the most densely occupied part of the country). A significantly larger population in earlier times is unlikely as it would surely have attracted the attention of Portuguese observers, even in the absence of any mineral resources in which they were primarily interested. Also any substantial out-migration, occasioned either by critical population density during the complex or by a catastrophic collapse, should have been reflected in a wider diffusion of the clan totems peculiar to this area.

Relative isolation from trading activities as well as from Portuguese observers is indicated by the rarity of exotic items on excavated sites, limited to sparse beads (Appendix E), with only Muozi and Nyangui G7/1 showing relative prodigality in this respect in the 16th or 17th century. Had agricultural production been on a large scale providing surplus for exchange, a greater quantity of exotic items would be expected.

The impression is thus of a relatively small and isolated overall population which would have been fully exploiting a fairly small proportion of the whole area at any one time.

There must however have been quite dense *local* concentrations of population to provide the labour for terraces and ridge systems and homestead construction. Just how dense is difficult or impossible to calculate. Within a concentrated area of terracing and settlement such as Ziwa ruins, a census of homesteads with their sizes and apparent number of houses could be taken and estimates of occupants made for each, but there are too many imponderable factors for even an approximate figure – Was the function of all the "houses" and enclosures the same, how many enclosures were occupied at any one time, and how much of the area was simultaneously exploited? Also an intensive agricultural system allowing the indefinite sustainable cultivation of at least a core area of fields might be expected to be reflected in long occupation, but as pointed out above, the duration of homestead occupation, or even less the life of the whole community, is uncertain and a long occupation sequence has only been identified at Muozi.

The conception of a few small densely populated communities can be reconciled with the wide extent of the terracing and other agricultural and settlement remains on the hypothesis that the fields had a more or less limited fertility span and that construction was therefore an ongoing piecemeal process, with new areas being brought into use as old ones were abandoned. Eventually all suitable land available to a local community would have been exhausted and it would have been necessary to move to new location. Over a century or more, even a relatively small local population could gradually have exploited quite large areas such as Ziwa or Nyautare. On this time scale however, one might expect that, if the same conditions persisted, it would have been possible to re-occupy earlier settlements after an adequate period of fallow. This would have been facilitated by the already established capital infrastructure of terraces and homesteads, further realising the value of previous labour investment. Evidence of such a rejuvenation process is seen in the broken *dhaka* incorporated in many enclosure walls, representing the debris of earlier structures cleared to make way for new construction.

THE WIDER CONTEXT

The data and interpretations presented in this volume have largely concentrated on the internal archaeological evidence for the Nyanga area, but they need to be understood in relation to the wider history of the region. A historical background derived from rather scanty documentary and oral tradition sources is provided in the Annex by David Beach, who stresses its significance to the interpretation of the archaeological evidence. However it will be seen that much of this concerns the history of the ruling dynasties of polities still extant in the 20th century, rather than the wider population represented by most of the archaeological evidence. The dynasties of Manyika and Maungwe and their general territories can be traced back to the 16th century and that of Saunyama well back into the 18th, within the span of the archaeological complex. They are obviously relevant to a full historical picture of the district, notwithstanding the lack of any close correlation between their territories and the archaeological distributions as discussed below. The earlier phases of the complex are beyond the scope of any historical evidence (in the narrow sense) and have to be viewed against available archaeological evidence for neighbouring areas which was discussed in Chapter 1.

The complex was preceded in Nyanga in the first millennium AD by Early Iron Age communities characterised by Ziwa ceramics. Such sites are found to east and west of the northern highlands but not on the main highlands themselves, the highest site being at about 1660m just south of the Bende Gap. The end of the Early Iron Age as generally defined was around the 12th century elsewhere in northern Zimbabwe but is not yet dated in the Nyanga area where a later continuation is not inconceivable. There must however be a hiatus of several centuries between it and the beginning of recognisable late Iron Age settlement with its stone structures in the lowlands. It seems improbable that the Nyanga lowlands would have entirely unoccupied during that intervening period, but any such occupation is not yet documented archaeologically.

In the highlands the initial phase of the Nyanga complex – the early hilltop settlements –

was closer to the end of the Early Iron Age, but lacks any known antecedents. The stone structures do not resemble any earlier remains known from this or neighbouring areas. The pottery bears none of the characteristics of Ziwa ware, nor does it relate in obvious ways to later Iron Age wares of the early to mid-second millennium in other parts of Zimbabwe, such as the Musengezi and Harare ceramic traditions of the 13th to 16th centuries found from the Harare region northwards to the Zambezi valley. If there are any connections, they are therefore more likely to lie in districts to the north or east (largely in Mozambique) which are poorly explored archaeologically. However, as outlined above, local cultural continuity is evident within the Nyanga complex from this initial phase onwards. What then may have been the identity of the original settlers?

The Nyanga stone structures as a whole were tentatively attributed by Summers (1958) and Beach (1980) to speakers of a language of the Sena group now found to the north-east in Barwe in Mozambique. They reasoned, probably correctly, that they were built by the ancestors of the Nyama people whose language was then classified as Sena by Doke (1930). This classification is now cast in doubt by Beach (Annex) and it seems that the Nyama language is better regarded as a branch of Shona, albeit of a distinctive form. However attribution of the initial phases of the complex to ancestral Shona speakers does not seem to be consistent with current archaeological interpretations. An origin of Shona speakers from south of the Limpopo was postulated by Huffman (1978), establishing themselves in southern Zimbabwe as the Leopards Kopje and Gumanye ceramic traditions at the beginning of the later Iron Age in the 10th or 11th century. Continuity is then traceable through the Great Zimbabwe tradition to the present day. Huffman (1978) also attributed the Musengezi and Harare ceramic traditions to early Shona speakers but revised this view in 1989 to derive the Musengezi tradition from north of the Zambezi, hence being non-Shona in origin. (This should also apply to Harare in view of its close affinities with Musengezi.) By the 16th century most of the people of northern Zimbabwe – or at least those with whom the Portuguese interacted – were speaking Shona (Beach 1980:21) with the exception of the Mbara kingdom which has been plausibly equated with the Ingombe Ilede archaeological tradition (Garlake 1970). They had thus become "Shonaized" in the course of a couple of centuries.

In the Nyanga case the pottery of the early hilltop settlements is unrelated to Leopards Kopje or Gumanye and is not accompanied by the characteristic terra cotta figurines of those traditions. On this basis there is little to associate these sites with ancestral Shona speakers. However the historically attested polities of Manyika and Maungwe were certainly Shona speaking, as it now seems was Saunyama. The founders of these dynasties are claimed to have come from "Nembire" in the Mutapa state, a successor to the Great Zimbabwe state, which ruled much of northern Zimbabwe from the 15th or 16th century; while these may be legitimising myths not to be taken too literally, they at least reflect Shona origins. Another "Shonaisation" process of the general population of the Nyanga archaeological complex – perhaps indeed originally Sena-speaking – would thus seem to be involved. The Manyika appear to have been speaking Shona by around the 16th century (Beach 1980:160) but the process could have taken longer in Saunyama, the core area of the complex for which there are no Portuguese records.

We may now consider the territories of these separate and rival polities in relation to the 18th century distribution of pit-structures, pit-enclosures and double-concentric enclosures and their associated terracing. Typical highland pit-structures are widely distributed in Saunyama and parts of Mutasa (Manyika). Both the closely related pit-enclosures and not so closely related double-concentric enclosures are also found within Saunyama extending west into parts of what is now Makoni (Maungwe) but which may earlier have fallen within Saunyama (Beach, Annex). The split-level enclosures also fall within Saunyama. Thus Saunyama in the late 18th century included all four types of archaeological settlement, while only parts of Mutasa are included in the complex. A simple correlation of archaeological evidence with political units is thus not evident, even allowing for some undocumented fluctuation in territories. It may therefore be proposed that the archaeological evidence represents an earlier substratum of communities persisting into the 19th century, on which the political superstructure and the process of Shonaisation had been imposed. The tradition relating to the Muozi site – the killing of the eponymous Muozi by Chief Saunyama (see Chapter 5) – would fit neatly into such an interpretation, while some of the forts, seen as representing a degree of social stratification or local authority, could equally represent this political control. Similarly the "walled village zone" extending west towards Rusape and Headlands (Whitty 1959, see Chapter 1), related to the Nyanga complex and with associations with a Makoni dynasty, may also be seen in this light.

Abandonment of the complex

The societies represented by the Nyanga archaeological complex survived and flourished in a modest way over a period of around 600 years by successive adaptations to a varied environment. This was achieved through the development of increasingly specialised techniques for the exploitation of the local potentials of soils, water and materials, perhaps influenced by climatic fluctuations. Such techniques included terracing, cultivation ridges, livestock husbandry, management of water and fertility, and skilful use of stone for construction. However, specialised systems depend upon a whole range of internal and external factors – social, political, economic, ecological and climatic – and are vulnerable to change in any of these.

How may circumstances have changed beyond the capacity of the society to adapt through further specialisation ? Change in average annual rainfall seems an improbable factor since the Nyanga communities seem already to have survived the possibly drier conditions of the last cold phase around the 18th century and the present rainfall of 700mm or more would seem adequate. An extended episode of dry years such as that on the lower Zambezi in the 1820s (Beach: Annex) could however have contributed to disruption. Ecological decline, even if ameliorated by the sort of cyclical fallowing suggested above, may well have led to diminishing returns in the long term. Social factors are difficult to assess on present archaeological data, but labour and its organisation is a critical resource in specialised peasant agriculture. This must have been affected in Saunyama by the extended political struggle for the chiefship between rival houses which began by the late 18th century and involved internecine strife which depopulated a substantial area of the lowland complex (Beach: Annex).

A combination of such adverse factors led, not to the total collapse of society and economy, but to a new adaptation which abandoned most of the specialised labour-intensive agricultural practices with their elaborate capital infrastructure, while parallel social changes must have eventually phased out the stone homesteads, equally laborious in construction. This may have been a gradual process continuing through the 19th century, leaving few active remnants to be observed by the first literate observers.

SECTION TWO

EXCAVATED SETTLEMENT SITES

CHAPTER 8

EXCAVATED SETTLEMENT SITES

This long chapter comprises detailed reports on the excavation of eleven settlement sites. Different categories of settlements and homesteads with varying date and distributions were synthesized in Chapter 5. Much of that synthesis relies on the detailed excavated data and the excavation reports are presented here for reference so that readers not concerned with the finer details may not be overwhelmed in the more general descriptions and discussions in Part One.

Samples of most categories of sites were selected for excavation and arrangement here is by a combination of chronology and site category — two early hilltop settlements (Nyangui 1732DD27 and Chirimanyimo Hill); Muozi midden (representing several phases of occupation); two ruined pit-structures (Nyangui G7/1 and Matinha I); two well-preserved pit-structures (Nyangui G1/21 and Fishpit); two simple enclosures at Ziwa (MSE17 and SN153); a unique enclosure (Chirangeni); and a double-concentric/simple enclosure (Chigura). The general location of these and the excavated terrace sites is shown in figure 42. The derivation of the site names was explained in Chapter 1. It is considered that these names are more easily distinguishable than the official site numbers based on map sheets allotted by the National Museums and Monuments; the latter are however given in each case.

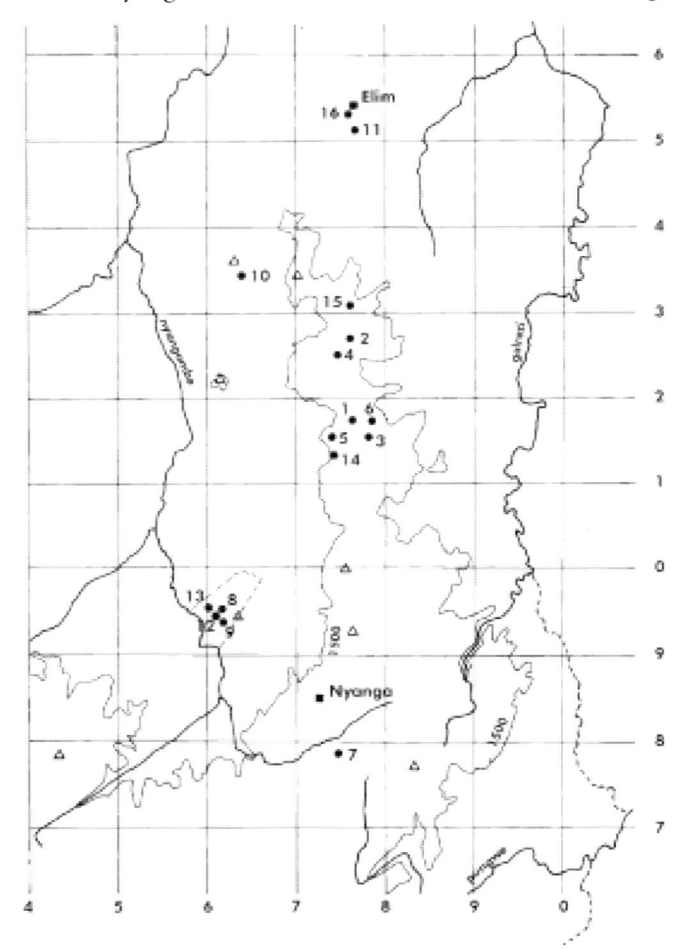

Fig. 42. Location of excavated sites. 10km grid. **Occupation sites**: *1 - 1732DD27; 2 - Chirimanyimo Hill; 3 - Nyangui G7/1; 4 - Matinha I; 5 - Mount Muozi; 6 - Nyangui G1/21; 7 - Fishpit; 8 - Ziwa MSE17; 9 - Ziwa SN153; 10 - Chirangeni; 11 - Chigura.* **Terrace excavations**: *12 - Ziwa SN113; 13 - Ziwa Mujinga; 14 - Maristvale; 15 - Chirimanyimo school; 16 - Elim*

NYANGUI HILLTOP SETTLEMENT 1732DD27

Site 1732DD27 was selected for the first investigation and dating of the early hilltop settlements, being more easily accessible than most of the others.

Measuring about 300m north to south and 120m east to west (fig. 43), it lies on the crest of the main range of the Nyanga highlands on Nyangui Forestry Commission land at an altitude of 2050m at grid reference VR 764174 (fig. 42, no.1). Here the crest declines gently northwards as a broad ridge, steepening slightly immediately north of the site. To the east the ground is fairly level for 150 to 200m with lines of sandstone boulders trending roughly north/south. (The eastern slopes beyond this are described in Chapter 5 under the Nyangui Block G pit-structure survey.) To the west the ground slopes more steeply to a permanent spring some 60m from the edge of the site. This spring is in a reentrant which broadens to the north-west where there are a number of pit-structures, the nearest being 200m away. The edge of the main escarpment is about 350m to the west. A recent water furrow runs north from the spring and curls across the ridge as it declines north of the site, to serve homesteads to the north-east occupied in the mid-1980s.

The site is situated on the western side of the ridge crest, where large boulders provide shelter from the bitter easterly winter winds, and on the westerly

Fig. 43. Nyangui 1732DD27. General plan of the site traced from an aerial photograph

slope below. Within this area are numerous small walled hollows or sunken enclosures about three to seven metres in internal diameter, and larger low-walled enclosures up to around 20m in diameter. The walls of the latter features often consist of a double row of large vertical stones with the remains of a earth fill between. On the western slope longer walls form terraces.

Walled hollows and larger enclosures are interspersed, the former tending to be among larger boulders and the latter in somewhat less rocky areas. The site plan (fig. 43) is traced from a section of a vertical aerial photograph, enlarged to c.1:2500 and checked against the features on the ground. Parts of the site are obscured by dense thorny thicket which makes observation impossible even on the ground. This doubtless conceals some of the most significant features!

Two walled hollows were partially excavated, the first, A, within the edge of a dense thicket in the north-central part of the site, and the second, B, one of a pair towards the southern end.

HOLLOW A (fig. 44)

This is a partly sunken enclosure of irregular oval shape, with internal measurements of 6.50m north-west/south-east and a maximum of 5.50m south-west/north-east. A large vertically faced boulder c.3m high forms the southern side, with a slightly smaller boulder 1.60m high at the ENE edge and a lower boulder to its south 1m high. The surrounding stonework is rather rough and includes stones up to 60cm in size. It is up to 50 or 60cm high but must originally have been higher, judging by the quantity of loose stones in the interior. On the west and north it appears to form an actual wall a metre or so thick, while on the higher eastern side it is more of a revetment. A narrow entrance passage, 35cm wide at the base, enters from the east, the lower eastern boulder forming its northern side; this passage is filled with earth and fallen stones to a depth of 70cm. The mouth of the passage slopes down to a floor which has a slight slope to the west. No signs of a drain through the wall were seen, but the lower western side was not excavated. The eastern side appears to have been dug out to level the floor prior to construction.

After clearance of the thicket within the hollow, the surface presented a litter of stones, many of substantial size, which could hardly have been distributed across the full width by natural agencies and must represent deliberate destruction of the walls. The north-eastern quadrant (Trench I) and the area in front of the entrance (Trench III) were excavated.

Stratigraphy was as follows (fig. 45):

Surface — matted roots and leaf mould, c.5cm
1. Loose dark grey-brown topsoil with numerous roots. Numerous sherds.
2. Dark brown friable loam. Numerous stones and sherds.
3. Lighter brown to reddish brown less friable loam with small disseminated charcoal fragments. Some stones, numerous sherds and a few animal teeth.
4. Red-brown firm clay-loam with charcoal flecks and some stones and sherds.
5. Cobbled floor on light brown natural clay.

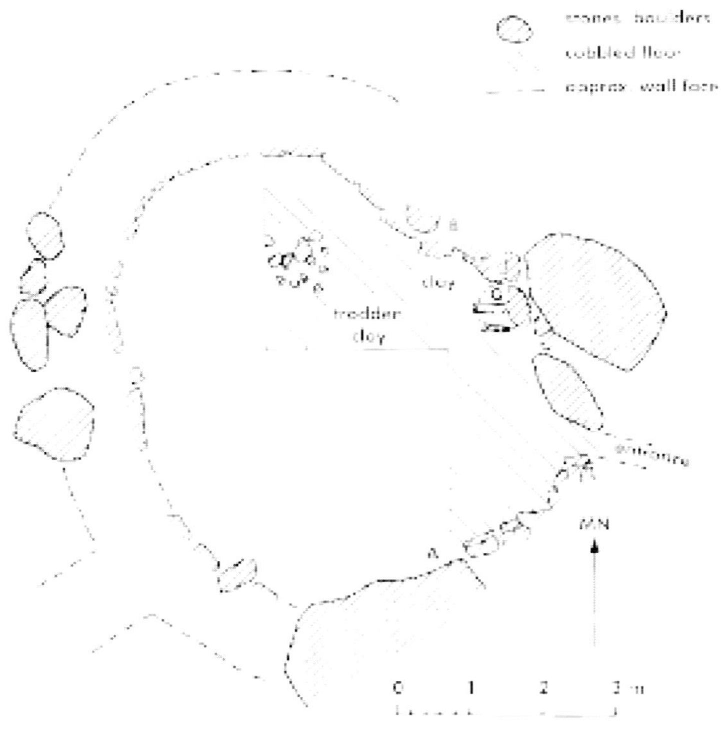

The cobbled floor is composed of small weathered fragments of dolerite around 5cm or less in size, pressed into the surface of the clay. A small area of these at the north-eastern edge of the floor was removed in error before the feature was recognised, but the stones are also missing towards the centre where there is a trodden surface of dirty clay, the cobbles having probably been dislodged by usage. Such cobbled floors have not previously been reported from Nyanga sites. At the western edge of the excavated area in trench I there is a patch of irregular larger

Fig. 44. Nyangui 1732DD27. Plan of hollow A. G = grave

stones which continue below the level of the surrounding floor; these may be natural but were not investigated further.

At the north-east margin of the hollow immediately below the boulder was an anomalous stone which did not appear to form part of a wall face. This measured 58 x 28 x 18cm and had a flat but nodular upper surface. Beneath it were two long

is made of the length from the greater trochanter which was not well preserved. The diameter of the head of the femur was 44mm.

It is clear from the bones exposed that the body was buried in an ultra-contracted position on its back, with its head to the WSW somewhere below the knees, towards the centre of the hollow. No sign of any grave goods was found in the limited

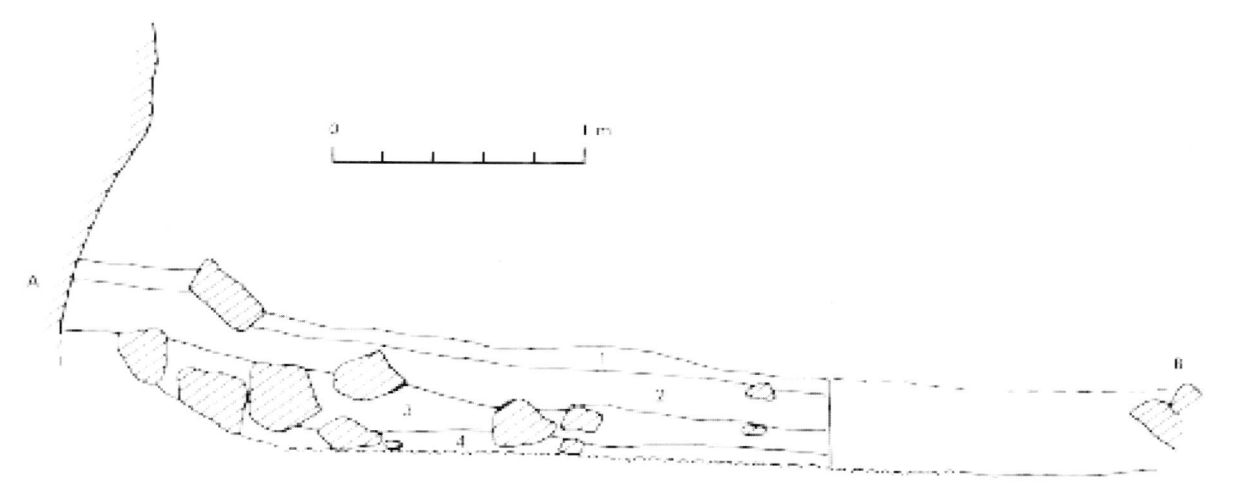

Fig. 45. Nyangui 1732DD27. Section of hollow A

thin horizontal stones set below the level of the cobbled floor. When the stones were removed, the outline of a small grave was detected (Plate 24). This was ovoid in shape, 65 x 55 cm, cut into natural clay and decomposed dolerite, with a fill of firm clay loam with rare charcoal flecks and sherds, browner and softer around the bones. The uppermost bones were encountered at 25cm below floor level on the north-east side and proved to be a pelvis. Extending south-west from this were firstly the two tibiae/fibulae and beneath them the femurs, articulated with the pelvis. The left patella and right astragalus were present in position and the left humerus sloped up from below under the left knee, its distal end in contact with the right knee and its proximal end missing. There was no sign of the lower arm or any other ankle or foot bones. The bones were not removed, partly because they were in soft condition and no consolidant was available, and also out of concern to leave the deceased undisturbed.

The inner width of the pelvis was 105mm and the left sciatic notch at least 35mm wide. The epiphyses of the proximal right femur and distal left tibia were well preserved and completely fused, indicating a mature adult. The maximum length of the right femur between the head and the medial condyle was 430mm, indicating a stature of 1.50 to 1.60m (Lundy and Feldesman 1987), if an estimate

excavation. This mode of burial appears similar to one recorded by Summers (1958:57) in a small stone enclosure near Nyangwe Fort. No other burials have been reported firmly associated with the Nyanga archaeological complex, apart from two slightly flexed burials in passages of a pit-structure at Mkondwe (Martin 1937), which appear to represent a different burial arrangement, and a few bones of a very young child beneath an upturned pot in the passage of a small pit-enclosure close to the present Ziwa Site Museum (Randall-MacIver 1906:28).

The function of the hollow remains uncertain. It is highly improbable that it was ever roofed, given the irregular shape and the high boulders on the periphery. Nor was there any trace of wall foundations or post-holes to indicate a house or other structure within it. Probably it was for livestock, perhaps sheep or goats, it being doubtful if the cobbled floor would have sustained the trampling of large stock such as cattle. Alternatively it could have been a meeting place. Subsequent to the burial, perhaps that of the owner, the hollow was abandoned and the walls partially dismantled, the red-brown clay-loam of layer 4 probably deriving from the earth fill of the walls. The site was then used for the disposal of rubbish, layers 3 and 2 representing midden accumulation between the loose stones. Any bones in this have disintegrated apart from a few teeth, probably of cattle, but a total of more than 4600 broken potsherds was recovered from the area excavated. Of these, 92% are plain body sherds and the remainder rims, necks and a very few decorated sherds.

Since only about 35% of the hollow was excavated, there were probably well over 12000 sherds in all. This midden accumulation shows that occupation continued in the surrounding area after the abandonment of the structure.

Samples were taken for phosphate analysis through the deposits and showed: layer 1 - 600 ppm; 2 - 5100 ppm; 3 - 8850 ppm; 4 - 3300 ppm; and 5 between cobbles - 2250 ppm. The high values for layers 2 and 3 reflect the midden accumulation subsequent to abandonment. The somewhat lower values for layers 4 and 5 could be consistent with the penning of livestock but cannot be conclusive.

Trench II, 2 by 1m, was sited 10m east of Hollow A in a gap in the thicket, below a rough wall of natural boulders and large stones. There was a shallow deposit of dark brown loam with decomposed dolerite fragments towards the base. This yielded some sherds, two iron fragments and a bovid tooth but no information on the possible function of the wall.

Hollow B

This is one of a pair of walled hollows towards the southern end of the site about 150m south of Hollow A (fig. 46). An excavation was first attempted in the larger north-eastern hollow (Trench IV) and showed many large stones, some apparently *in situ* on and embedded in clean red-brown clay, with an overburden of dark grey humus and roots with some loose stones. The base of the hollow sloped downwards in irregular fashion to the north-west. Since no coherent features or floor surface were detected and only a few plain sherds were found, the excavation was discontinued.

Hollow B is the smaller south-western hollow, most of the interior of which was excavated as Trench V. This hollow is sub-circular in shape, 4.80m in diameter. The stratigraphy showed (1) up to 50cm of dark grey matted humus and roots among loose stones up to 60cm or more in size, with a dense concentration of sherds at the base on the western side. Below this was (2) dark grey loam grading into brown loam with numerous potsherds and dispersed charcoal fragments. Large stones occurred within this, especially on the east side where some were not removed. Below this again was a cobbled floor similar to that in Hollow A, covering most of the floor area

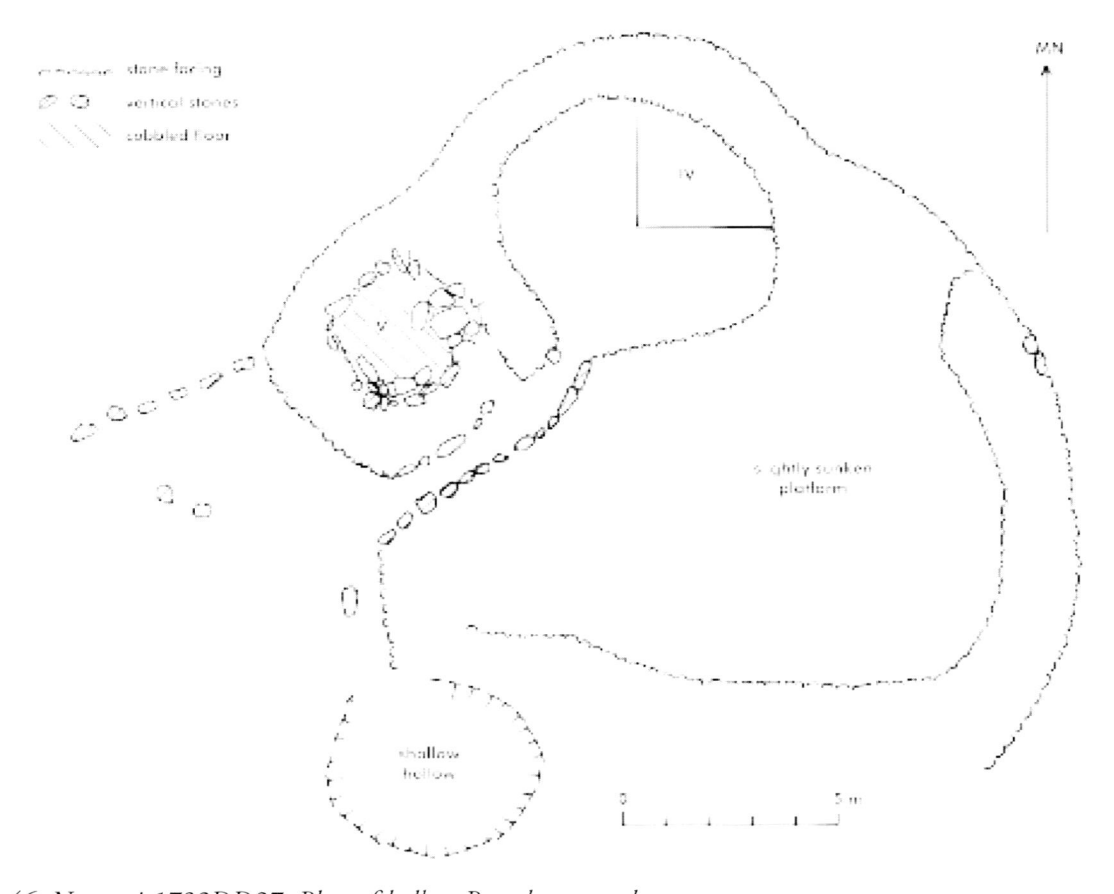

Fig. 46. Nyangui 1732DD27. Plan of hollow B and surrounds

and depressed in places beneath the weight of the larger stones. Around the south side a number of stones apparently *in situ* formed a rough bench about 40cm wide and the wall here is up to 90cm high. There is a rather poorly preserved entrance at the east side which opens on to a passageway c.70cm wide leading to the north-eastern hollow.

The general shape and size and the probable bench suggest a roofed house but no positive evidence was found to confirm this and no clear traces of a hearth were seen. As with Hollow A, there appears to have been deliberate destruction and deposition of rubbish. 805 sherds were recovered, of which 92 % were plain body sherds.

Dating

Samples were collected for radiocarbon measurement from the disseminated charcoal fragments in both hollows. Two of these, from Hollow A layer 3 and Hollow B layer 2, were submitted for dating. The results at one standard deviation are as follows:

Hollow A (Pta-7166)   650 ±20 BP, cal AD 1312(1331)1354; 1384(1392)1399
Hollow B (Pta-7174)   590 ±20 BP, cal AD 1405(1411)1417

These results indicate a dating for the site around the 14th to early 15th century. With the broadly comparable results subsequently obtained from Chirimanyimo Hill, they confirm that these hilltop settlements are the earliest identified component of the Nyanga stone structures.

In the present case, the nature of the samples, consisting of small fragments mostly measuring 10mm or less, is hardly as satisfactory as, for example, a carbonised post base *in situ* would have been, and it is possible that the charcoal derived from old trees. However the two results are in close agreement and the dating is expected to be older than that for the pit-structures and enclosures on the basis of the different structures and pottery. Unfortunately, no glass beads or other imported objects were recovered. The first occupation of Mount Muozi, visible only three kilometres to the south-west, is shown to be contemporary by the pottery and radiocarbon dates.

Finds

Pottery (fig. 47)
A total of 5663 sherds was recovered, made up as follows:

	Hollow A	Hollow B	Trench II	Total
Diagnostic rims	128	24	7	159
Undiagnostic rims	141	25	11	177
Plain necks	69	17	12	98
Decorated body sherds	10	-	1	11
Bases	1	-	-	1
Handle fragments	3	-	-	3
Plain body sherds	4291 (92%)	739 (92%)	184 (86%)	5214 (92%)
TOTAL	4643	805	215	5663

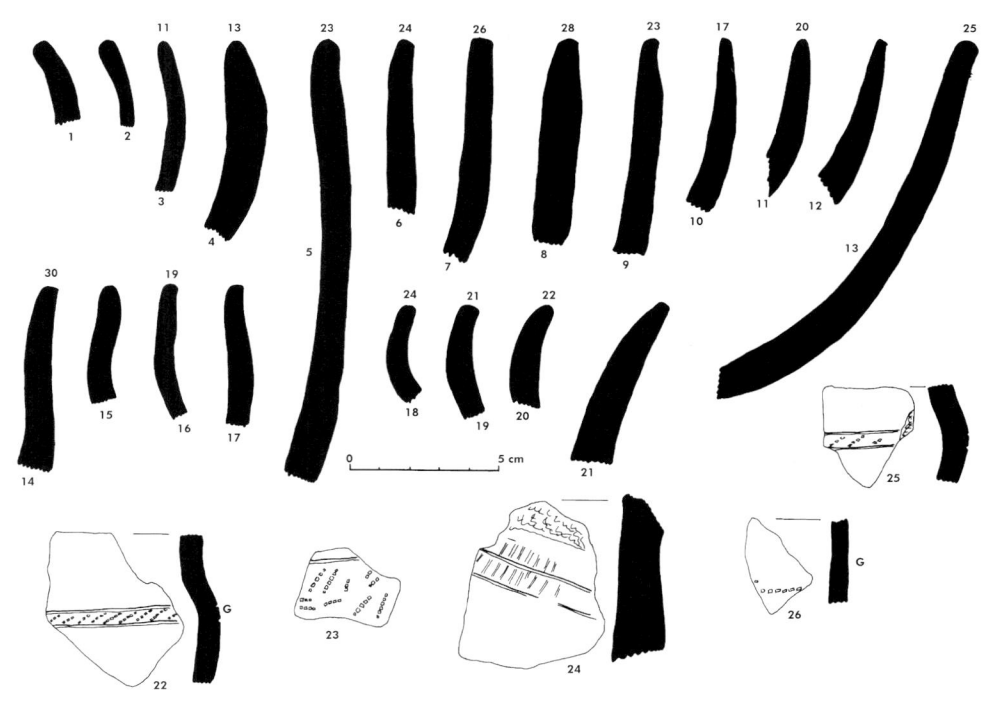

Fig. 47. Nyangui 1732DD27. Pottery. G = graphite; figures above sherds are rim diameters.

Colour varies from dark grey or black to light brown, showing considerable variation of oxidisation in firing. In addition there are a few sherds of whitish or light buff ware with biscuity paste and heavy temper of fine quartz. Paste varies from fine and hard to crumbly but is generally fairly hard, often showing a black unoxidised core. Inclusions are mainly quartz with the addition of feldspar or iron oxide concretions in some cases, and occasional fragments of rock; maximum grain size is often up to 3mm, with occasional fragments up to 10mm. Surface finish varies from relatively smooth to quite rough and seven sherds have graphite burnish (see below under decoration). Maximum sherd thickness ranges from 5 to 24mm with an overall average of 9.86 ±2.45mm, thin sherds of 5 or 6mm being relatively rare. Lip forms are roughly squared or rounded, the former rather more frequent at about 60%, there being little consistent correlation with vessel shape. In general the quality is not high, with the exception of one smoothly finished light brown constricted bowl.

Vessels are classified on the basis of rim sherds since there are few cases where an appreciable proportion of the profile is preserved. Types are as follows, with numbers based on rim sherds after reconstruction:
- Deep straight-sided or slightly waisted vessels (nos 5-9, 14-17): 36 (26 with smooth finish)
- Hemispherical bowls (4, 10, 11): 62 (43 with rough finish)
- Open bowls (12, 13): 2 (1 smooth)
- Constricted bowls (1-3): 5 (3 smooth)
- Wide-mouthed pots (18-21, 27): 21 (19 smooth)
- Narrow-mouthed pots (28,29): 2 (1 smooth)
- Undifferentiated necked pots: 4 (all rough)

The hemispherical bowls thus tend to be more roughly finished than the deep vessels and necked pots.

The diameters of measurable rims are as follows: deep vessels (9) 19 - 30cm, av. 24.3; hemispherical bowls (10) 13 to 30cm, av. 19.4; open bowls (1) 25cm; constricted bowls (2) 11, 12cm; wide-mouthed pots (7) 18 to 24cm, av. 20.9; narrow-mouthed pots (1) 14cm. The presence of 134 sherds (2.4% of total) over 15mm thick and some of them up to 24mm, suggests that there were some much larger pots (e.g. no.21). Ten such sherds in Hollow A were thickly encrusted with carbon inside indicating a cooking function; this could however be from the secondary usage of a large sherd after breakage of the original vessel.

The largest handle fragment (30) consists of a thick strap handle springing from the rim probably of a wide-mouthed pot with slightly out-turned rim. The other two fragments are of similar handles, possibly the same one though their sizes vary.

The only defined base (31) is somewhat thickened and roughly flattened, with finger impressions around the edge.

There are some minor differences in vessel frequencies and finish between the pottery from Hollows A and B:

	Bowls	Necked pots	Rough	Smooth	Burnish
Hollow A	54%	46%	38%	58%	4%
Hollow B	43%	57%	71%	29%	-

This could reflect different activities or perhaps social status.

There are only 13 decorated sherds, of which only four are large enough to show an identifiable motif. All come from or close to Hollow A. They are as follows:
- 3 graphite-burnished sherds from a small wide-mouthed pot or shouldered bowl, with a narrow band of oblique comb-stamping outlined by incisions on the shoulder (22,25). Thickness 9mm.
- 1 rough thick sherd with broad rather crude cross-hatching (24). Th. 17mm
- 1 body sherd with an incised line and random impressions of a short lenticular comb (23). Th. 9mm

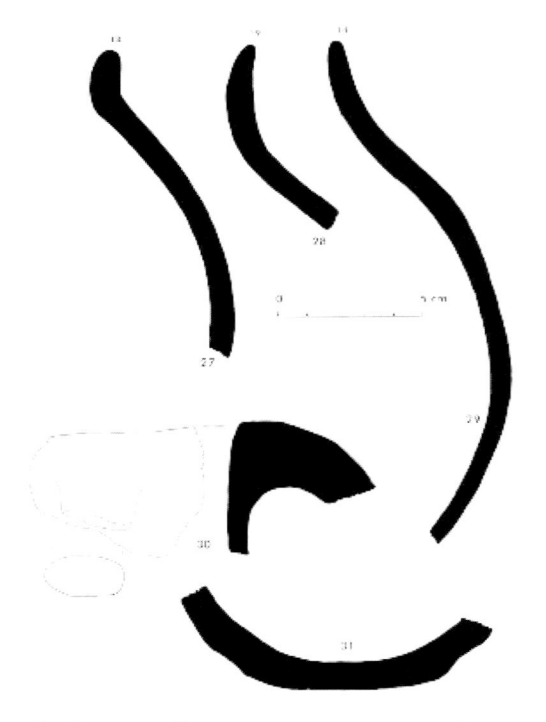

Fig. 47 (continued). Nyangui 1732DD27. Pottery

- 1 graphited body sherd with a single line of square-toothed comb impression (26). Th. 7mm
- 1 tiny graphited neck sherd with a single oblique incised line. Th. 9mm
- 1 tiny rim sherd with two oblique incised lines
- 1 rough body sherd with a single incised line
- 1 small rough rim with 2 converging lines of broad incision, possible accidental. Th.9mm
- 1 tiny body sherd with single horizontal and oblique incised lines. Th. 8mm
- 2 plain graphited sherds. Th. 10/9mm.

The rarity of decoration and handles suggests that the vessels represented come from elsewhere. Cross-hatching is characteristic of later Nyanga lowland pottery, especially in the Nyautare and Ruangwe area, though not on such a thick rough sherd. The graphited vessel with narrow comb-stamped band is foreign to the terrace complex but could perhaps be an Early Iron Age sherd picked up and brought to the site. No close parallels for the handle fragments are known. Graphite burnishing is very rare in contemporaneous material from Chirimanyimo Hill and Muozi but occurs as a small component of later assemblages, sometimes associated with hatching (Appendix D). The absence of any decorated pieces in the smaller assemblage from Hollow B may not be significant.

All plain body sherds were examined for traces of carbon with the following results:

	Hollow A	Hollow B	Trench II	Total
Carbon outside	6.5%	5.7%	4.7%	6.3%
Carbon inside	3.1%	7.5%	3.1%	3.8%

About 20% of those with carbon inside are quite heavily encrusted, one to two millimetres thick. In addition there are 37 sherds from Hollow A with a hard shiny black deposit on the inside surface which also appears to be carbon. Around 1.5% are black and heavily reduced inside but without a carbon crust.

Iron
Trench II: layer 2 – small irregular fragment of plate 19 x 21mm.
  layer 4 – tapered triangular fragment 38 x 11x 2mm ? tang of knife or razor.
Trench I: layer 2 – rod 117mm long. Square section 4 x 4mm in centre, one end tapers to c.5 x 2.5 mm, other end broken but one side splays outwards. ? arrowhead.
Trench III: layer 1 – semicircular plate, bent at corners, 63 x 31 x c.2mm.
  — fragment of small round rod, wound wire bangle or natural concretion, 6 x c.5mm.
  — subtriangular fragment 29mm long, butt c.4 x 2mm, splaying and thinning to c.10 x 1mm at other end. ? butt of small implement.
  — similar piece, length 33mm, butt c.3 x 2mm, end c.9 x 1mm.
  — 3 irregular broken fragments of thin plate, 31 x 15mm, 20 x 19mm and 17 x 17mm.

One small piece of slag 36gm in weight came from Trench III layer 3.

Teeth and bone (all from Hollow A)
- 7 molar teeth, 1 fragment of mandible, 1 fragment of femur shaft – cattle
- 2 skull fragments, fragments of tooth enamel, unidentified

Discussion

This and the other hilltop settlements, with their dating around the 14th century, clearly represent an early phase of highland occupation preceding that of the pit-structures or any known lowland sites of the Nyanga terrace complex. As the pottery comparison in Appendix D indicates, there is a relationship with the ruined pit-structures which are dated later, about the 16th or 17th century; further work may close this chronological gap. There is no direct relationship to the agricultural terracing. Possible reasons for the occupation of these exposed mountain tops are considered in Chapter 7.

The cobbled floors of the hollows examined on this site have not yet been found elsewhere. The only comparable hollow which has been excavated, at Chirimanyimo Hill, has a floor of decomposed dolerite where cobbling would have been unnecessary, while no walled hollows have been excavated on Muozi. Similarly the burial has no exact parallels but the same reservations apply. The occupants were certainly keeping cattle and were presumably cultivating, but signs of their fields have not been recognised.

CHIRIMANYIMO HILL

The Chirimanyimo Hill site covers an area around 700 by 500m, making it easily the largest known site of the Nyanga complex. It is centred on grid reference VR 760270 and is designated 1732DD22 (fig. 42, no.2). The hill itself is the northernmost of the high peaks of the Nyanga highland range, with a height of 2180m, rising north-east of the narrow saddle of Matinha. Although it is not a markedly salient feature, its forested crest is visible for many kilometres around. It stands about 100m above a more gently sloping base from which the land drops steeply to the south-east to the head of the Marozi valley, while high ridges extend to the east and north. Geologically it is formed of sedimentary sandstones, argillites and shales, overlying granite and capped by dolerite on the crest (Stocklmayer 1978). This crest is now largely covered by thick indigenous forest but more open land surrounds it, notably on a shoulder to the north-east. A rough track approaches nearly to the crest, dating from the war of independence in the 1970s when there was a Rhodesian military post on the hill.

The summit (fig. 48) is a fairly level plateau some 200m north-east/south-west and 120m north-west/south-east. This drops off steeply for a height of 20m or more to north, west and south but is more easily approachable from the east. At the east and north-east sides of this small plateau are fairly wide areas of bare rock interspersed with thickets of giant heather and aloes. The remainder is largely covered by dense growth around 5m in height, with thick thorny undergrowth slightly ameliorated in places by browsing cattle, while there is taller forest on the steep surrounding rocky slopes. All the forest is richly draped with Spanish moss and lianas, nourished by frequent mist and cloud, and the prevailing south-easterly winds make for a very inhospitable environment in winter. The very limited visibility and often painful access make it difficult to maintain one's orientation and hinder investigation and surveying, but a partial plan was made by threading a theodolite traverse through the undergrowth and relating this to an aerial photograph blown up to a scale of c.1:2050 (fig. 48).

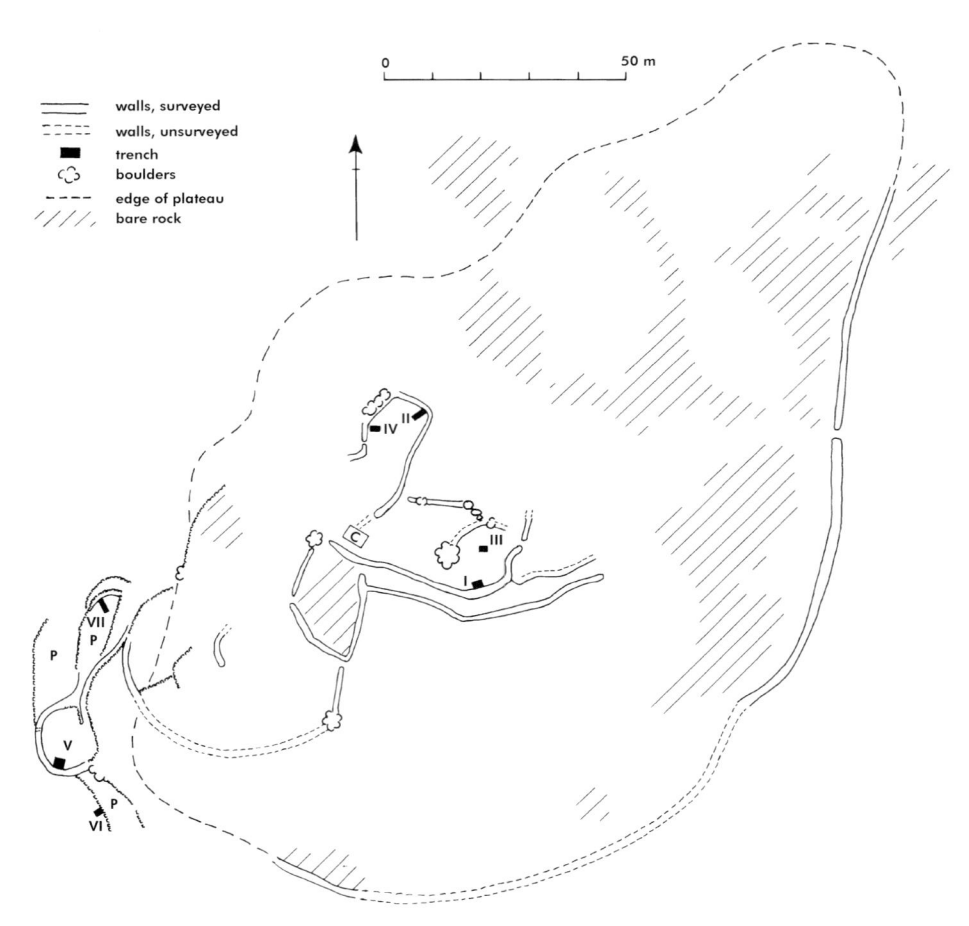

Fig. 48. Chirimanyimo Hill. Plan of the hilltop. P = terraced platform; C = cement floor

A stone wall around 1.50m in height and width surrounds nearly half of the summit plateau from near the north-eastern corner around the east side to the south-south-west. The east side of this is clearly visible on the ground and the aerial photographs, as is the south-west end; the south-east portion was traced but not surveyed through dense bush. There appear to be no structures in the bare rock areas but walls are frequently encountered in the forested west to south-west side.

A walled "avenue" 50m long and 2 to 4m wide leads west from the eastern open rock area to a smaller area of bare rock surrounded by walls; for convenience this is referred to here as the "*dare*" (meeting place in Shona). The avenue is in fact visible on the 1987 aerial photograph and must have been cleared during the war; (there is a cement floor of an old radio hut just north of the *dare*). There are low-walled enclosures to the north of the avenue and *dare*, two of which were investigated with test pits. South of the avenue is dense thicket in which there are also walls, though it was not possible to trace their configuration.

On the steep rocky slope sheltered below the western edge of the plateau is a complex of terraced platforms some 50m long with revetting up to 3m high, and an enclosure c.12 by 10m with a substantial wall, all stepping down some 7m. A diagonal walled path runs down from the plateau edge to the enclosure. This complex does not continue to north and south but similar features could possibly exist undetected elsewhere since the survey was not exhaustive.

On the shoulder of the hill to the north-east, in the open and emerging from patches of forest, is an extensive complex of low-walled enclosures and occasional walled hollows (fig. 49). Similar features can be seen on the other early hilltop settlements, and these examples are directly comparable to those already described at Nyangui 1732DD27. The walls of these enclosures are constituted by double rows of vertical stones, originally with an earth fill, and the enclosures are up to 25m in diameter, occasionally more. Traces of similar remains emerge all around the lower edge of the forest and there was a large complex outside the forest to the north-west

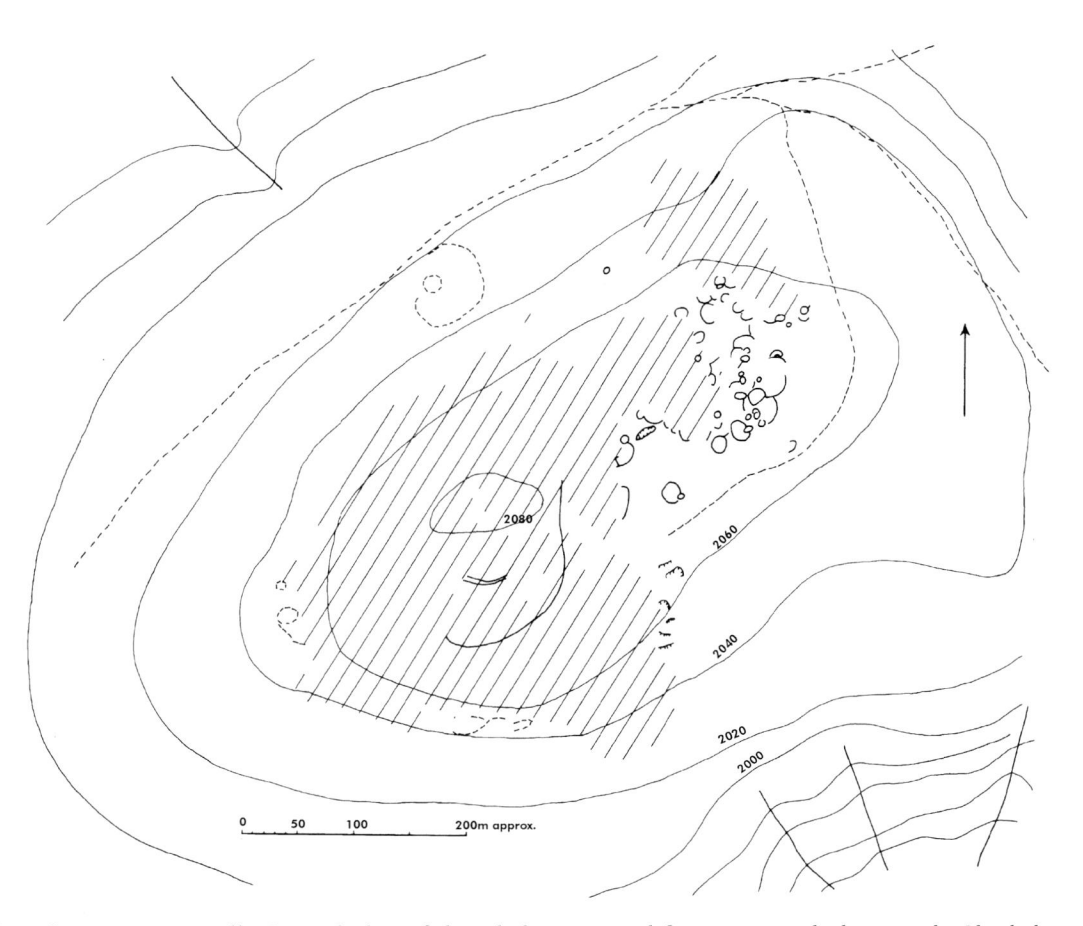

Fig. 49. Chirimanyimo Hill. General plan of the whole site traced from an aerial photograph. Shaded area is forest or dense bush

in the area now occupied and modified by the homestead of Claud Munditi, the village headman for the scattered occupants of the area around the hill and northwards. Figure 49 is traced from the enlarged photograph, checked and amplified by examination on the ground.

Excavations

From surface examination it could not be determined whether the enclosures in the open area were contemporary and related to the walled ruins on the forested hilltop, nor indeed whether the terraced platform area below the western edge was associated with them either. Exploratory excavations were undertaken to clarify this by obtaining samples of pottery and other cultural remains, samples for dating and some idea of function. On the plateau two test pits were dug in each of two enclosures (Trenches I to IV). Below the western edge trenches were dug across a probable house site on a terrace at the northern end (Trench VI), within the walled enclosure (Trench V), and below the terrace wall of a platform at the southern end where it was anticipated rubbish might have been discarded (Trench VII). Finally Trench VIII was dug across a walled hollow on the shoulder to the east, c.120m east of the main outer wall.

Enclosure A

This is a sub-oval enclosure c.12 by 19m in size. It is well defined to the south by the wall of the avenue up to 1m high on this side, and less well by a lower irregularly built wall on the north, while there are rocks on the west side.

Trench I, 2 by 1.50m, was excavated against the south wall. The stratigraphy showed:
1. Leaf mould and grey brown topsoil.
2. Brown gravelly loam with small stones which increase in number downwards to around 30cm below the surface. This layer rests on a rather uneven surface of firm light brown clay-loam at a distance of 60 to 100cm from the wall. Between this and the wall, and continuing beneath it, is softer brown loam with numerous stones, often densely packed. There is a feature of three vertical stones at the edge of the clay loam resembling a hearth but with no obvious signs of burning, and a large rock appears to be set within the clay loam. Pottery occurs throughout, a total of 215 sherds, and some small fragments of charcoal.

Trench III, 2 by 1m, was on a slight mound in the middle of the enclosure. This showed c.5cm of leafmould over 20cm of reddish brown gravelly loam containing a few sherds, a piece of iron slag and small charcoal fragments. Below this over about half of the trench was a probable floor of hard, light brown clay. There was a deeper disturbance c.50cm in diameter in the north-west corner; this was probably a tree pit with brown gravelly loam fill with a few ochreous lumps, possibly *dhaka* fragments. At the eastern end of the trench the floor level is less consolidated, and a probable fill of brown gravelly loam with small stones continues to at least 35cm below the surface.

Although the excavated areas were very limited, the floors and probable hearth indicate a residential enclosure.

Enclosure B

This a walled area north of the *dare*, about 30m long and 9 to 10m wide at the north end, apparently widening to the south. The walls are generally low, around 50-60cm high.

Trench II, 3 by 1m, was dug against the wall in the north-east corner. The stratigraphy shows:
1. c.5cm of grey brown leafmould
2. up to 15cm of red-brown gravelly loam with small stones sloping down slightly to the south-west.
3. fairly compact orange clay-loam, browner and more gravelly to the north-east, including fairly large stones. This contains pottery, several pieces of iron slag and small charcoal fragments. A line of three stones across the north-east end 60-80cm from the wall face appear to be in situ; smaller stones are packed behind and continue under the wall which is about 60cm high. This may be some kind of bench or the base of an earlier wall line. Outside these stones the surface of 3 is fairly dirty with ochreous lumps, being probably an old trodden surface graded to the line of stones.
4. Sterile brown loam with a fair number of medium-sized stones and lumps of decomposed dolerite. At the south-west end is a large flat stone and several smaller ones overlying 4 but not forming a convincing wall.

Trench IV was 2 by 1m east/west, one metre from the west wall on the western side of a low mound.
1. Leafmould c.5cm.
2. Brown gravelly loam, lighter at the east end and darker towards the wall, containing a fair amount of pottery and some charcoal towards the base.
3. An area of smooth floor across the centre of the

trench, especially smooth and burnt on the south side west of centre where it is 27cm below the surface. This surface continues to the north side where it is 20cm below the surface, without the smooth plaster. There appears to be an edge to the east running across the trench and this could be a step up or a cross-wall. The hard floor does not continue to the west end but there is an interface at the same level with flecks of charcoal, perhaps representing a trodden surface, which continues to the stone wall. There was a rough arc of stones in the north-west corner 25cm below the surface which may be a feature or possibly fallen wall stones. A single blue-green glass bead came from this layer.

This walled area also appears to have been residential, with possible industrial activity suggested by the slag.

The western terraced area
Trench V
This excavation measured 2 by 2m against the southern wall of the enclosure below the western edge of the plateau. This enclosure is approximately oval, 12 by 10m internally. There is a large tree towards the north end and thick undergrowth in the eastern side, the whole heavily draped with mossy lianas. The wall around the lower west side is substantial, around 1.50m high and 1.50 to 1.70m thick, pierced by a drain at the north-west side. The east side of the enclosure is a high revetment, somewhat tumbled. The only access appears to have been the walled path sloping down from the north. Below is a steep rocky slope and there are terraced platforms to north and south. Trench V showed only thick leaf mould and roots overlying solid, rather uneven bedrock. Probing indicated little deposit anywhere in the enclosure and it may be suggested that the enclosure was for livestock.

Trench VII
3 by 1m north-west/south-east across a probable house floor at the northern end of the terraced area. The platform here is c.5m wide, of which one metre is the outer terrace wall, slightly raised. At the east side is a revetment around 2m high to the next terrace above. On the west side the revetment drops 1.30m to a narrow subsidiary terrace below.

The section shows:
1. 7 to 8cm of leafmould and roots
2. 8 to 10cm of brown loam, gritty at the south-east end and more earthy to the north-west. At the south-east end this rests on a hard floor of light brown clay, its surface flush with a long flat stone slab.
3. up to 10cm of fine orange-brown loam in the north-west half of the trench, overlying a rather softer continuation of the floor up to the stone wall. There are some disturbances in the floor, probably from old tree roots. At the north-west end the floor surface curves up into an almost vertical face against the stones of the wall.

There was some charcoal in layer 2 and a very few plain potsherds throughout. The floor and base of the *dhaka* wall face confirm that this was a house site and suggest that the terraced platforms in general were residential.

Trench VI
1 by 1m against the base of the revetment of the lowest platform south of the enclosure. The revetment is 1.20m high. Below the usual leafmould there was up to 40cm of dark brown gravelly loam and stones, resting on more or less continuous stones and boulders which pass beneath the base of the wall. 81 sherds and a piece of iron slag were recovered, representing rubbish thrown from the probable residential platform above.

The walled hollow
Trench VIII investigated a walled/revetted hollow in the south-western edge of an isolated thicket about 110m east of the outer wall on the hilltop. The hollow is within the southern edge of an ovoid shaped enclosure 36 by 24m in diameter which surrounds and extends to the west of the thicket, and there is a second probable hollow at the north-east end (fig. 50). The vestige of a cross-wall in the edge of the thicket suggests that this was a double enclosure, the western half with the excavated hollow being appended to the eastern. The enclosure wall at the open west side is formed by a double line of stones of one or two courses around 40cm high and with an earth fill. There are large boulders within the thicket.

The hollow is sub-oval in shape, 5 by 4.50m, bounded by the enclosure wall on the south-east side and largely revetted/walled elsewhere. The west wall after excavation was c.90cm high, formed of large vertical stones with smaller stones on top. The east side was up to 1.30m high. The number of stones in the fill indicates that the walls were originally higher; this could have been a house, but no signs of *dhaka* facing or post-holes were detected. A total of over 650 sherds, some quite large, was recovered, as well as two granite rubbing stones and a little iron slag. Stone flakes were also quite common, together with a cleaver and a unifacial handaxe or core, and these must derive from a much earlier Stone Age occupation of the area.

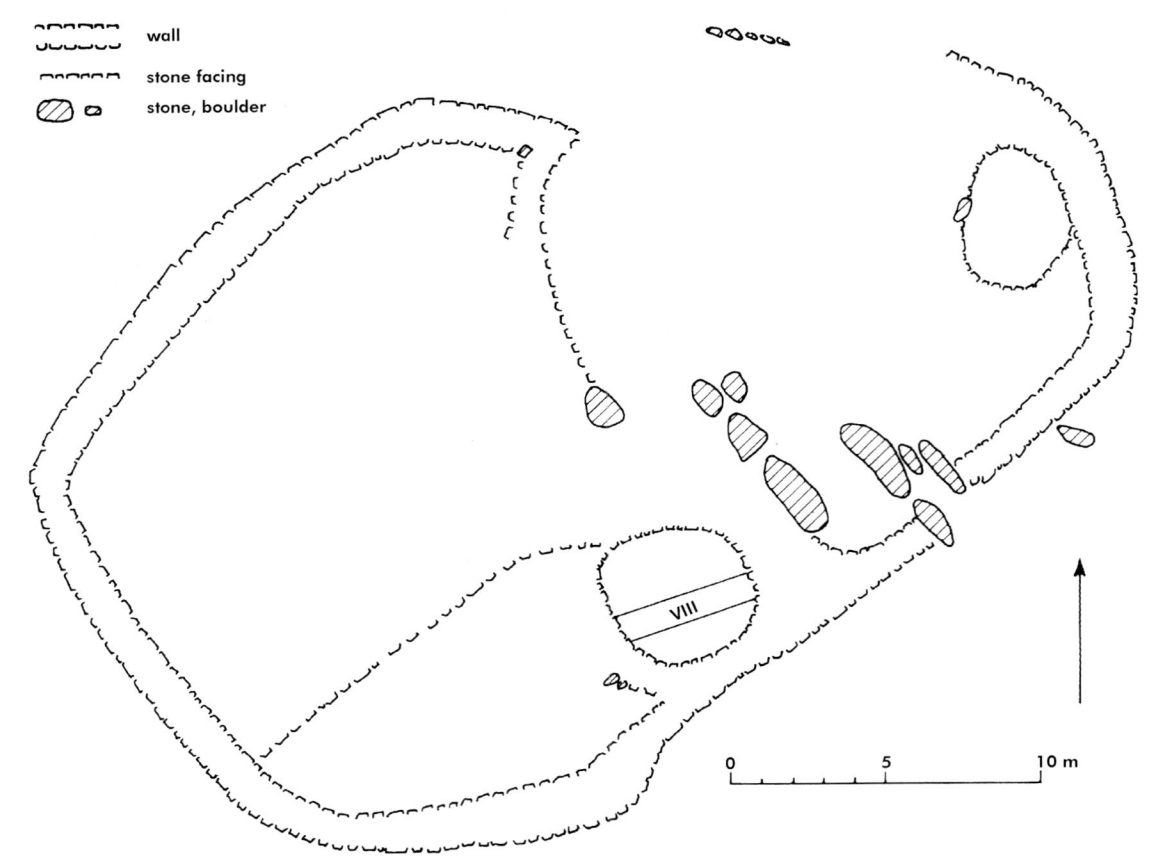

Fig. 50. Chirimanyimo Hill. Plan of enclosure with Trench VIII

Trench VIII was 4.90 by 1m across the hollow and showed the following stratigraphy (fig. 51):
1. Leafmould and roots 5 to 8cm thick.
2. Dark brown gritty loam with numerous stones, containing some pottery and small charcoal fragments towards the base. 10 to 15cm thick.
3. Brown to dark brown clayey loam c.20cm thick, gritty in places, with charcoal fragments and numerous potsherds and stones, mostly weathered dolerite. This rests on a fairly smooth surface of decomposing dolerite bedrock, sloping up slightly towards the western end. In the eastern half of the trench large stones are continuous and appear to form an uneven pavement around 20cm above the bedrock which reappears below the eastern wall.

It would appear that the walls were partly demolished after abandonment, and that the hollow then served for dumping domestic rubbish, of which only the pottery is preserved. This situation is similar to that at the comparable hollow excavated at Nyangui 1732DD27.

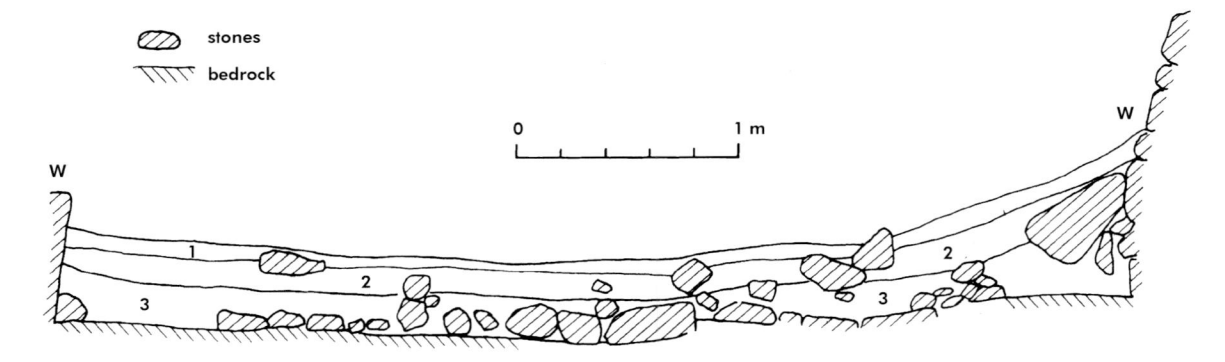

Fig. 51. Chirimanyimo Hill. Section of Trench VIII

Dating

Three radiocarbon determinations have been obtained:
Trench I, layer 2: 720 ±15 BP. cal. AD 1293 (1297) 1301 (Pta-7635)
Trench II, layer 3: 530 ±60 BP. cal. AD 1411 (1430) 1452 (Pta-7603)
Trench VIII, layer 3: 690 ±20 BP. cal. AD 1299 (1305) 1312; 1354-1384 (Pta-7618)

These indicate occupation in the late 13th to early 15th centuries and the contemporaneity of the walled hollow to the north-east with the enclosures on the summit plateau. They are consistent with those from Nyangui 1732DD27 and confirm the very early dating of the hilltop settlements within the Nyanga complex as a whole.

Finds

Pottery (figs 52 to 54)

The pottery from individual trenches was combined into three assemblages for comparison between the different areas of the site and to assess the likelihood of contemporaneity. These assemblages were from the summit enclosures (Trenches I - IV), the western terraces (Trenches VI and VII – there were no diagnostic sherds from V), and the walled hollow (Trench VIII). Sherd counts were as follows:

	I-IV	VI/VII	VIII
Diagnostic rims	35	20	17
Undiagnostic rims	25	-	22
Necks	31	5	59
Decorated body sherds	5	-	-
Plain body sherds	705	118	417
Total	*801*	*143*	*515*
Sherds with soot outside	62	-	18
Sherds with soot inside	1	-	34

Colour ranges from brown to grey-brown to grey, with more grey sherds and one apparently red-slipped sherd in I-IV and one or two reddish-brown sherds in I-IV and VIII. Temper is quartz with the regular addition of feldspar in I-IV. Maximum visible grain size is generally 1 to 3mm with a few up to 4 to 6mm, but tends to be finer in I-IV, while VII and VIII have more heavily tempered sherds. Average maximum sherd thickness is 8.44 ±2.12mm for I-IV, 8.63 ±2.48mm for VI/VII and 9.40 ±2.23mm for VIII.

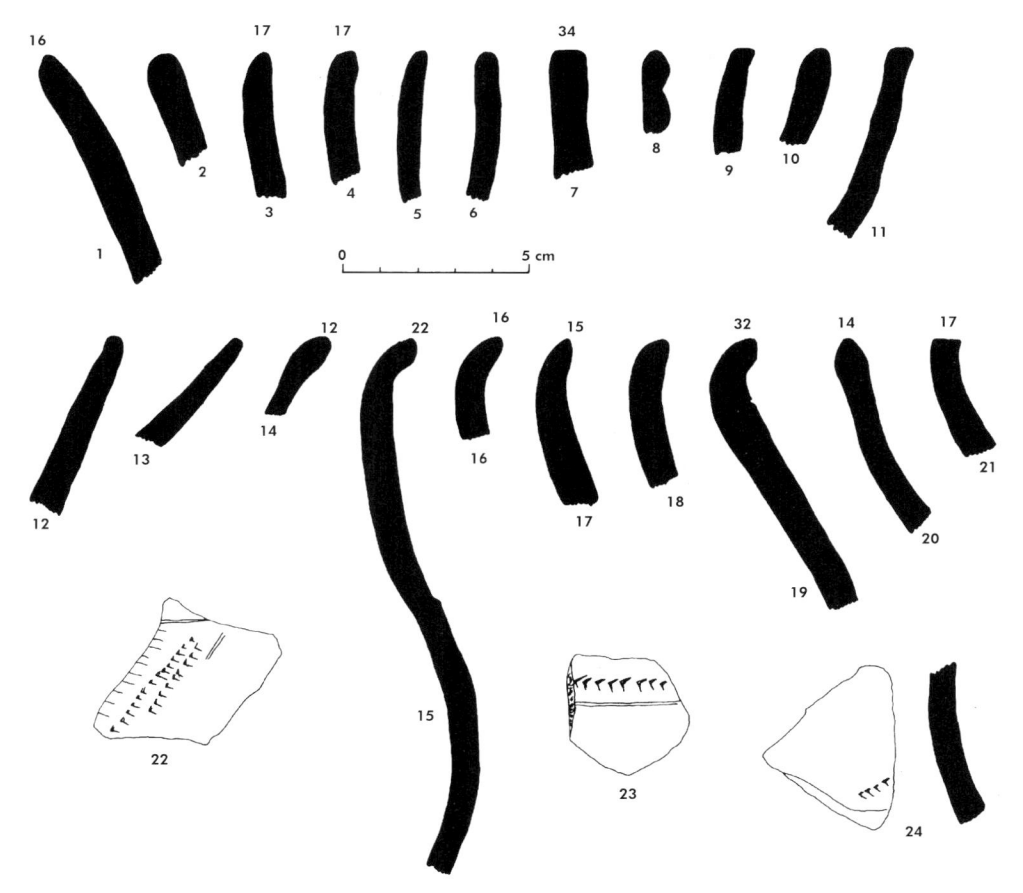

Fig. 52. Chirimanyimo Hill. Pottery from Trenches I to IV

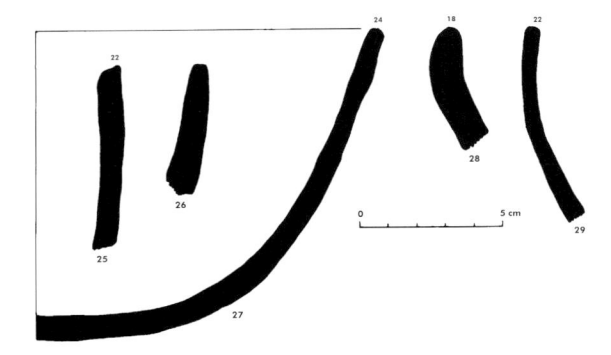

Fig. 53 Chirimanyimo Hill. Pottery from Trench VII

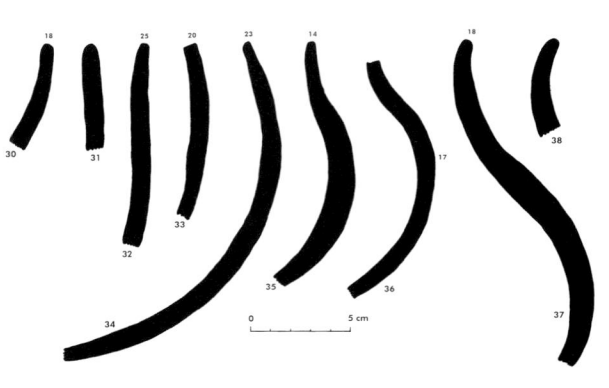

Fig. 54. Chirimanyimo Hill. Pottery from Trench VIII

Vessels, rims and finish are as follows (numbers in brackets refer to Figures 52 to 54):

	I-IV	VII	VIII
Deep/waisted vessels (3-5,25,31-2)	4	1	2
Hemispherical bowls (6,8,26,30)	2	1	3
Open bowls (9-14,27)	12	1	-
Constricted bowls (1-2,33-4)	2	-	2
Wide-mouthed pots (15-19,28-9,35-6,38)	7	3	8
Narrow-mouthed pots (20,37)	1	-	1
Undifferentiated necked pots	4	-	-
Total	**32**	**6**	**16**
Square lip	9	4	7
Round lip	15	2	5
Tapered round lip	8	-	1
Rough finish	10	5	7
Smooth finish	22	1	8

There are very few decorated sherds, all from I-IV. These comprise a single rough discontinuous incised line below the neck of a large pot (19); 3 sherds with triangular punctates, two of them with an incised line (22-24); and one plain graphited sherd.

Measurable rim diameters are: deep/waisted vessels (5) 17-34cm; hemispherical bowl (1) 18cm; open bowls (3) 12-24cm; constricted bowls (3) 16-23cm; wide-mouthed pots (9) 14-32cm; narrow-mouthed pots (2) 14, 18cm. There appear to be no consistent size differences between assemblages apart from two large vessels in I-IV, a deep vessel at 34cm and a wide-mouthed pot at 32cm. All other vessels do not exceed 25cm.

Although there is a broad similarity between the assemblages, there are some apparent differences between I-IV and VIII. These include the greater average thickness of VIII; some variations in temper and perhaps in colour; a higher proportion of open bowls in I-IV (which tend to have straight out-sloping rims as at 1732DD27); and a higher proportion of round/tapered round rims also in I-IV. The sample from VII is too small for any useful conclusions from the typological features, but temper and perhaps colour relate it more to VIII. The differences could reflect varying status or function which might be expected between the summit plateau and outlying areas of the site, but hardly suggest significant difference in date.

Slag
Trench I -   4 pieces, 253gm
Trench III - 1 piece, 26gm
Trench II -   11 pieces, 427 gm
Trench VII - 2 pieces, 11gm
Trench VIII - 24 pieces, 325gm

Glass bead
1 rounded blue-green bead, diameter 5mm, length 3mm. Trench IV.

Teeth
7 fragments, medium bovid. Trench IV.

Stone
- 1 small quartz pebble, translucent, 11 x 10 x 7mm. Trench VI.
- 1 piece of vesicular decomposed dolerite with a hollow in one side, 112 by 95 by 60mm (fig. 55c). Trench VIII.

Flaked artefacts from Trench VIII
- 1 cleaver, sandstone, 80 x 50 x 39mm (fig. 55b).
- 1 unifacial core or handaxe, 136 x 101mm (fig. 55a)
- 2 flakes sandstone
- 7 flakes grey quartzite
- 1 small quartz flake (? rough scraper)

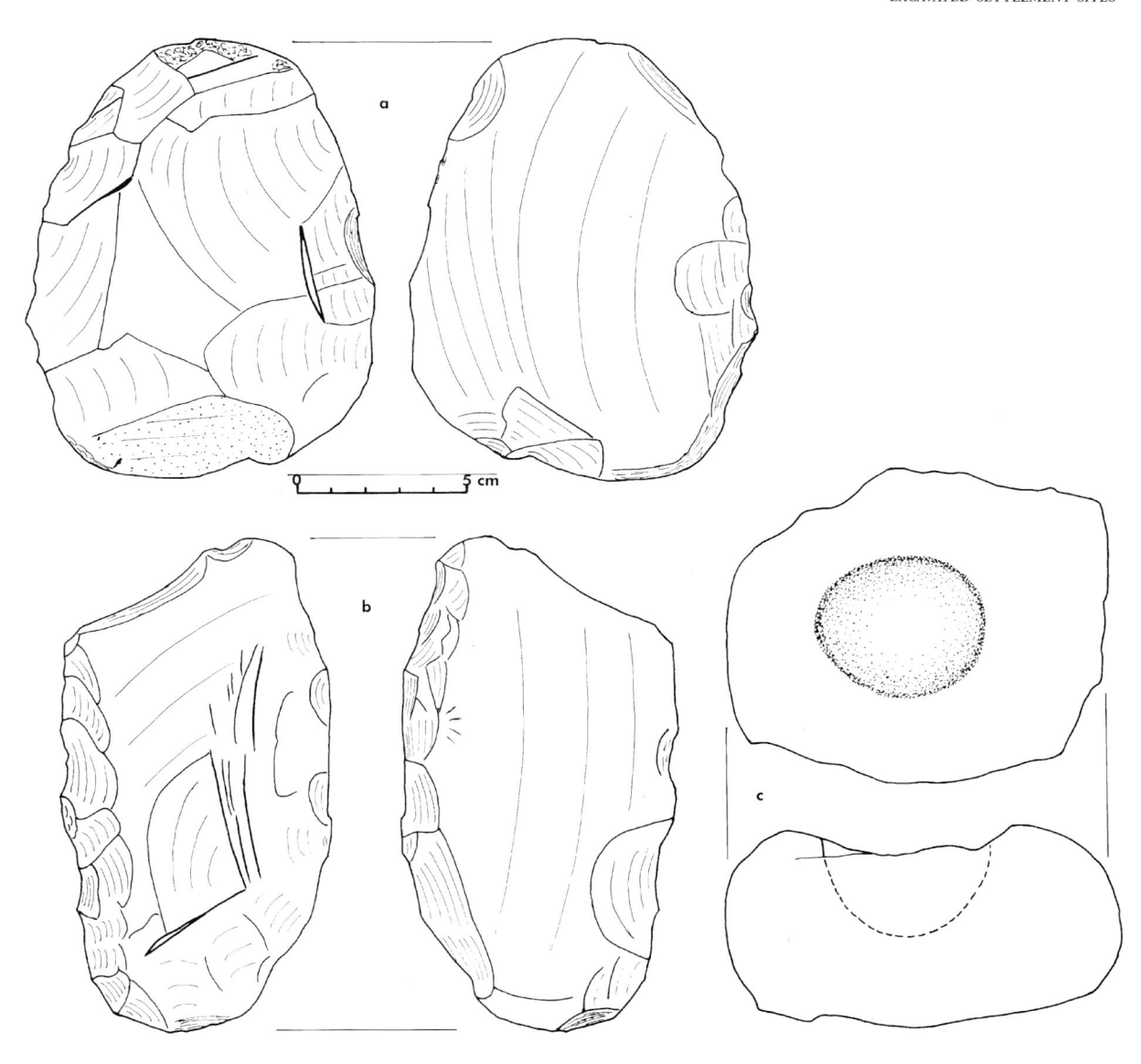

Fig. 55. Chirimanyimo Hill. Stone artefacts from Trench VIII

Discussion

The radiocarbon dating and, if less precisely, the consistent nature of the pottery, indicate that the various components of the site form a single related complex, the largest of the known early hilltop settlements. This and the walled enclosures on the hilltop with their perimeter wall — which is peculiar to this site — suggest that it was also the most important. It may thus be suggested that this was the residence of an important chief, surrounded by relatively numerous followers. The single glass bead indicates at least some external contact but this was clearly not well developed.

Other early hilltop setlements are listed in Chapter 5. The terraced platforms have parallels at Muozi and immediately below the north side of the peak at Rukotso, and possibly in the terraces on the west side of the 1732DD27 site. They appear to be residential, here with provision for livestock in the asociated enclosure. The low-walled open enclosures are common to all these early hilltop settlements except Muozi; they are likely to have formed the base of thick hedges and probably enclosed dwellings. The walled hollows are also common to all sites; the smaller examples may have been houses, but larger examples, such as Hollow A at 1732DD27, cannot have been roofed and were probably for livestock.

Reasons for living on exposed hilltops are discussed in Chapter 7.

MOUNT MUOZI

The Muozi site (1732DD36, grid reference VR 741154, fig. 42, no.5) and especially the stone-walled settlement on the promontory were described in Chapter 5. This report is mainly concerned with the excavation of the large ash midden, most of which relates to the first two phases of the archaeological complex, the early hilltop settlements and the ruined pit-structures.

The plateau (fig. 36) is about 275m long by 120m wide. Although it has not been systematically investigated much of the southern side either side of the path has evidence of occupation, including banks and hollows, some with stone revetting, and scatters of potsherds and bone fragments. Some of the hollows are directly comparable to the walled hollows of the early hilltop settlements such as 1732DD27 and Chirimanyimo described above, though there are no signs of the typical low-walled enclosures. Site 1732DD27 is visible from here on the crest of the main highlands 3km to the north-east, as is the similar site at VR 760155 at the eastern beginning of the Muozi spur. The platforms scooped out of the slope along the southern edge of the plateau among the *Widdringtonia* trees also have affinities to the western terraces of Chirimanyimo Hill; here a large sherd of a deep straight-sided bowl, a characteristic type of the early hilltop settlements, was found on what appears to be a house platform.

The main western cliff of dolerite north of the promontory extension is capped by sedimentary sandstone. Some 15m from the edge is the large ash midden, measuring about 14 by 7m. Augering suggests that it is about 70cm deep in the middle, thinning towards the south end and deepening to the north as the underlying ground surface slopes down. The surface has an ashy consistency and there are numerous sherds and bone fragments as well as occasional beads of glass and shell and metal objects including a copper stud.

A test pit (Trench I) one metre square was excavated to a depth of 60cm in October 1995 and a second trench (II), two by one metres, was dug adjacent to the north in May 1997, reaching a maximum depth of 1.40m. Trench I was excavated in 15cm spits and Trench II in 10cm spits, stratigraphy where visible being more or less horizontal.

The matrix of the upper 60cm when dry in October was homogeneous fine light grey ash of the consistency of dry cement, overlying a browner, earthier surface which was mistakenly thought to be natural soil in Trench I. The ash contained numerous sherds, bones and beads of glass, copper and shell. This deposit, dark grey when damp in May 1997, thins somewhat towards the north in Trench II, with browner lenses towards the base. Glass beads were relatively rare in this second trench, perhaps because the damp material would not pass through a fine sieve; it was however carefully examined and the local scarcity of beads is thought to be genuine.

The stratigraphy of the lower deposits in Trench II was:

Spit 7: 60-70cm. Fine brown ashy soil with lenses of burnt orange material up to 5cm thick.

Spit 8: 70-80cm. Fine grey-brown ashy soil. A large sandstone slab slopes steeply from the north end of the western section from 25 to 75cm below the surface, and a second slab projects 50cm horizontally into the trench from the southern end of the west section at a depth of 70cm. There are smaller stones beneath these and they form part of outcropping rocks around which the midden has accumulated.

Spit 9: 80-90cm. Uneven and discontinuous band of greyish-brown consolidated ash with small red or brown flecks and small fragments of charcoal. Soft grey-brown ash between the large stones.

Spit 10: 90-100cm. Grey-brown more earthy deposit with fairly numerous stones mostly up to 7cm in size, a few larger.

Spit 11: 100-120cm. Stony in a matrix which varies from soft grey between and below the larger rocks to a firm discoloured red-brown elsewhere, especially in the north-east corner. Bedrock at 110cm at the south end, sloping down slightly to north.

Spit 12: 120-140cm. Pocket in the north-east corner with fairly dense stones in grey ash, becoming soft brown earth at the base. Pottery and bones continue to the base.

Five human hand and foot bones from spits 5, 8 and 9 in Trench II, all apparently from the same individual, suggest that the trench may have cut the edge of an undetected grave. This cannot however have projected far into the trench and is unlikely to have caused any significant mixing of the cultural material.

Charcoal is present throughout, mostly in small fragments, and five samples have been dated giving results consistent with depth. Determinations at one standard deviation are:

depth	date BP	calibrated AD
15cm	265±25	1657(1664)1671; 1780-1795 (Pta-7399)
45-55cm	385±15	1507(1514)1525; 1560 (1586) 1596; 1618(1624)1632 (Pta-7060)
60-70cm	395±25	1485(1511)1525; 1560(1591, 1631) 1632 (Pta-7400)
80-90cm	520±25	1425(1434)1442 (Pta-7397)
100-110cm	570±20	1411(1417)1424 (Pta-7401)

While the alternative calibrations introduce some ambiguity, the lower part of the deposits is firmly dated to the early 15th century, that is contemporary with or slightly later than the results for Nyangui 1732DD27 and Chirimanyimo Hill (see above). The middle to upper deposits appear to date somewhere between the early 16th and early 17th centuries, thus contemporary with the ruined pit-structure Nyangui G7/1 (see below). The top of the sequence may be mid-17th or even late 18th century. These results do not in themselves indicate whether deposition was continuous or interrupted.

within unit 1 and the sherds from 0-30cm and 30-60cm are illustrated separately.

Raw sherd counts are as follows:

	Unit 3	Unit 2	Unit 1
Diagnostic rims	18	11	67
Undiagnostic rims	9	12	30
Plain necks	10	10	44
Decorated body sherds	-	-	21
Plain body sherds	184	202	865
Total	*221*	*235*	*1027*

Finds

Finds by spit:

Spit	Potsherds	Bone frags	Beads glass	Beads copper	Beads shell	Iron	Copper	Slag
Trench I								
Surf.	28	-	3	2	-	4	-	-
1	17	41	21	4	2	1	-	-
2	50	37	98	7	3	-	-	-
3	118	83	46	6	5	-	-	-
4	143	146	11	2	25	-	-	-
total	356	307	179	21	35	5	-	-
Trench II								
Surf.	39	78	13	1	-	1	-	-
1	108	413	-	-	1	2	-	-
2	69	471	2	-	1	-	-	-
3	66	295	-	1	-	-	-	-
4	113	249	7	1	1	1	-	-
5	102	157	1	6	55	-	4	-
6	174	204	-	-	15	-	2	1
7	88	149	-	-	27	-	3	1
8	60	120	-	2	19	-	1	1
9	87	102	-	-	15	1	-	-
10	67	73	-	-	-	-	-	-
11	120	114	-	-	16	-	2	-
12	34	30	-	-	-	-	-	-
Total	1127	2455	23	11	150	5	12	3

In addition a broken cowrie shell was found in spit 1 and a quartz crystal in spit 11.

Pottery (figs 56 - 59)

For purposes of analysis the midden deposit spits have been combined into three stratigraphic units on the basis of stratigraphy, radiocarbon dates, sherd thickness and the occurrence of glass beads. These units are: Unit 1: 0-60cm, Trench I spits 1-4 and Trench II spits 1-6; Unit 2: 60-90cm, spits 7-9; Unit 3: 90-140cm, spits 10-12. Surface material is included in Unit 1. This division gives larger samples for analysis, but it is difficult to decide exactly where the divisions should come. There is some variation

Colour of diagnostic sherds varies from light brown, through brown and grey-brown to grey, with a few red-brown sherds, most of the grey-brown sherds being unevenly coloured. There is a higher proportion of grey sherds in Unit 1. Temper inclusions consist of quartz, with fairly common additions of feldspar in Unit 1 and rare additions of iron concretions and rock fragments throughout. Maximum grain size is mostly 2 to 3mm with a tendency to finer sizes in Unit 1 and more coarse grains in Unit 3. Temper density is medium to heavy with more variation in Unit 1 which includes a number of lightly tempered sherds.

Vessels, lip form and surface finish are as follows (numbers in brackets refer to the illustrations):

EXCAVATED SETTLEMENT SITES

	Unit 3	Unit 2	Unit 1
Deep vessels (21-3,45-8,56-8)	7	7	5
Hemispherical bowls (14-5,34,59-61)	4	-	4
Open bowls (13,35-9,50,62)	3	4	8
Constricted bowls	-	-	-
Necked bowls (9-12)	-	-	4
Wide-mouthed pots (1-8,26-32,42-5,51-5)	4	3	29
Narrow-mouthed pots (24-5)	-	-	2
Undifferentiated necked pots	-	-	6
Total	*18*	*12*	*60*
Square lips	10	2	2
Round lips	5	6	30
Tapered round lips	3	3	44
Finish, rough	14	4	35
smooth	9	8	28
plain burnish (total sherds)	5	10	12
graphite burnish "	-	-	6
quartz burnish "	-	-	6

Bowl forms decrease in percentage frequency through the sequence, except for necked bowls which only occur in Unit 1, as do the only two narrow-mouthed pots. Most of the open bowls from Unit 1 have out-turned rims. Three of the wide-mouthed pots in Unit 1 are small smooth vessels with very short rims. Square lips decrease in frequency from over half in Unit 3 to very rare in Unit 1, while round lips, especially tapered ones, show the reverse trend. There is a fairly high proportion of rough finish and occasional plain burnish throughout. (Figures for burnish include plain body sherds, other figures applying only to diagnostic sherds.) The only cases of graphite and quartz burnish are in Unit 1, graphite sometimes combined with other decoration. There is no consistent association of lip form or finish with vessel types, except that three of the four necked bowls are burnished, one plain and two with graphite.

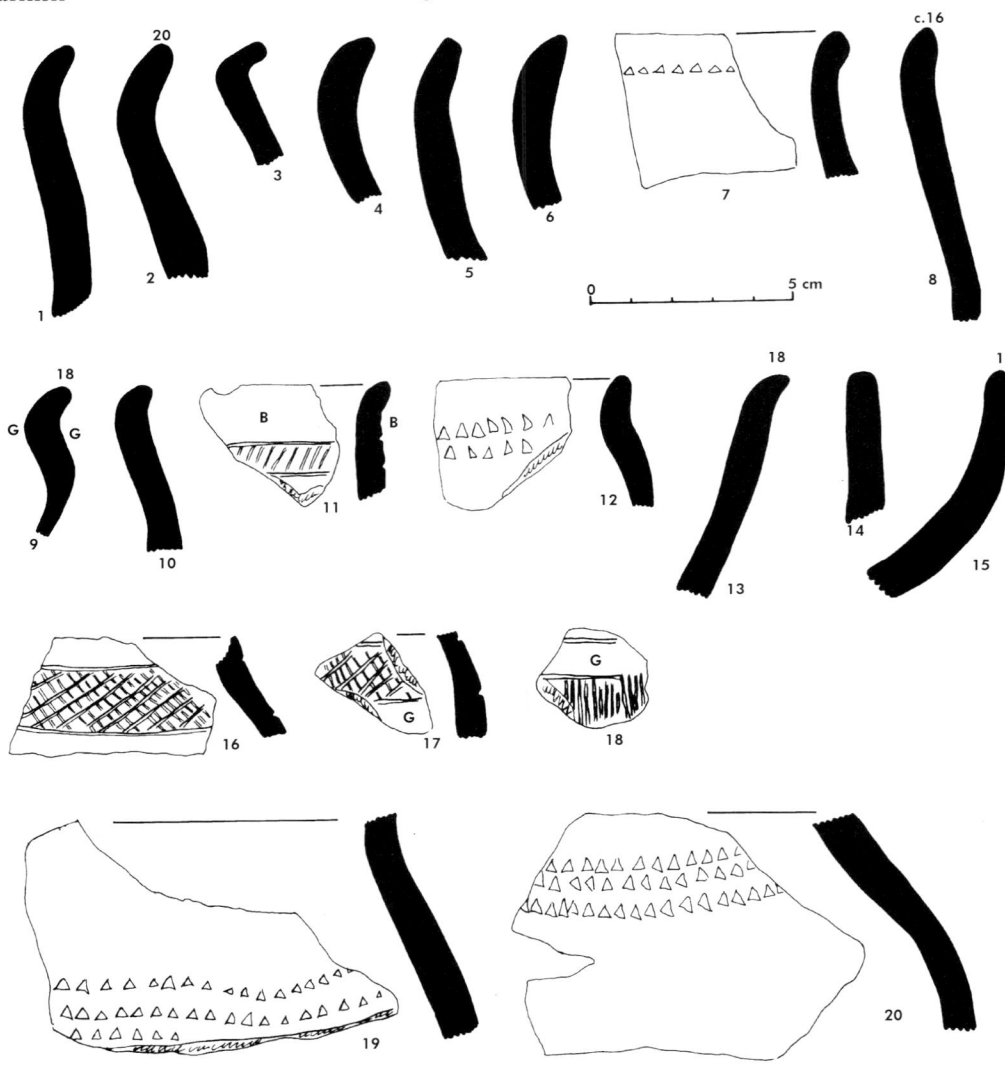

Fig. 56. Muozi midden. Pottery from 0 to 30cm below surface. G = graphite; B = plain burnish

Average maximum sherd thickness (all sherds) decreases from 11.07 ±2.56 in Unit 3, to 8.95 ±2.14 in Unit 2, to 8.46 ±1.96 in Unit 1.

Decoration is restricted to Unit 1, apart from a single shallow groove on the neck of a wide-mouthed pot in Unit 3 (51). The Unit 1 decoration comprises:

- 6 sherds with one to three rows of triangular punctates, one with rough burnishing (7,12,19-20,41);
- 4 sherds with incised cross-hatching, two in a band (one with graphite) and two uncertain (16-17);
- 2 sherds with an incised diagonally hatched band, one with graphite and one with plain burnish (11,18);
- 6 sherds with graphite burnish and 6 with quartz burnish.

The punctate and incised decoration occurs on the neck or shoulder of necked bowls or pots, with one single line of punctates on the rim of a wide-mouthed pot (7). All the decorated sherds were in the upper half of the unit (1a) except for one punctate, one graphite burnish and two quartz burnish. The quartz burnish is a slip of finely crushed crystal applied to the surface, giving a glittering effect which may be mistaken for graphite.

Bones

The bones from Trench I and the soft scree slope have been analysed by Ina Plug and published in detail (Plug, Soper and Chirawu 1997); results are summarised here.

In view of the relatively small samples, all were treated as a single assemblage. Domestic animals identified were cattle (13), sheep (4), goats (3), chicken (1) and dog (2). The house rat, a commensal of humans, is also represented (2). (Minimum numbers of individuals in brackets.) Only a few wild animals are represented, namely a monkey and

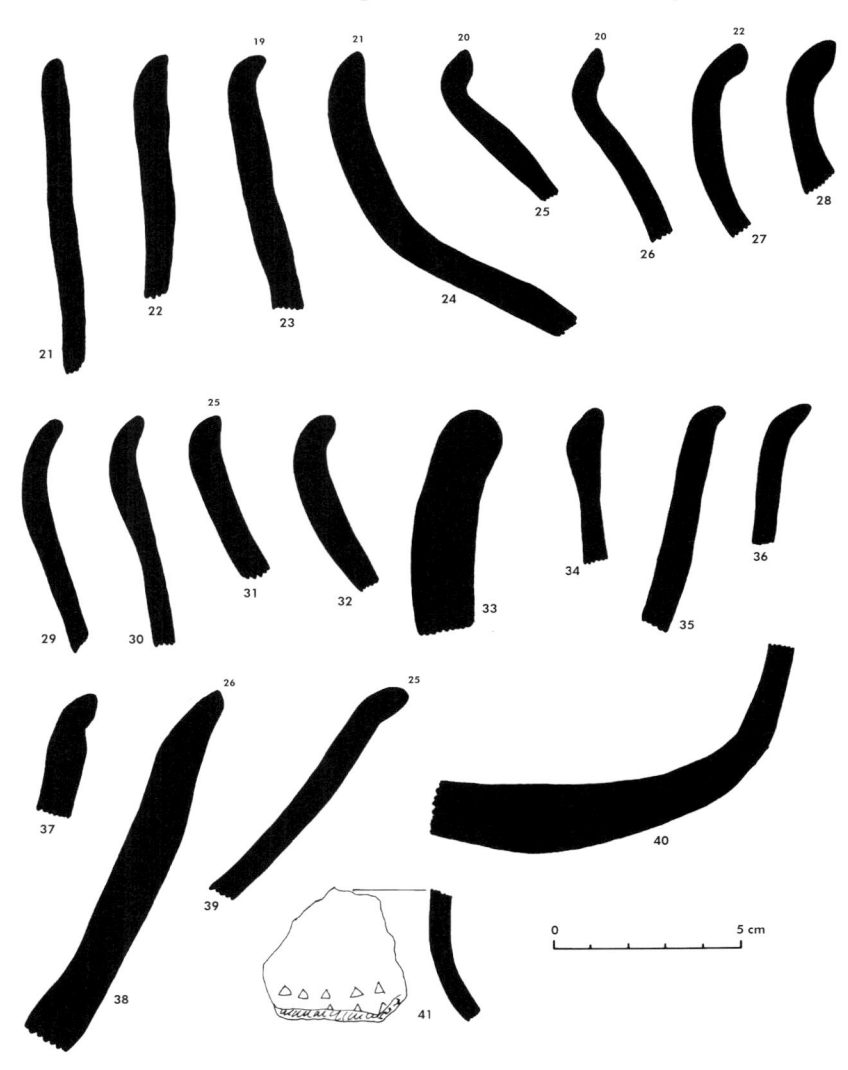

Fig. 57. Muozi midden. Pottery from 30 to 60cm below surface

a large mammal, probably a giraffe. The house rat, *Rattus rattus*, has been identified on South African Iron Age sites from the middle of the 8th century AD and chicken has been present there since Early Iron Age times. Cut and chop marks on many of the bones are consistent with carcass dismembering and reducing large bones to smaller portions. Traces

attach to the skull at an angle of 30° and point upwards and outwards. They are virtually straight with very little curvature. The horn cores are robust in comparison with the size of the skull. The occipital bone is particularly well developed in the area of the *squama occipitalis*. This would allow for strong musculature needed to support the heavy horns.

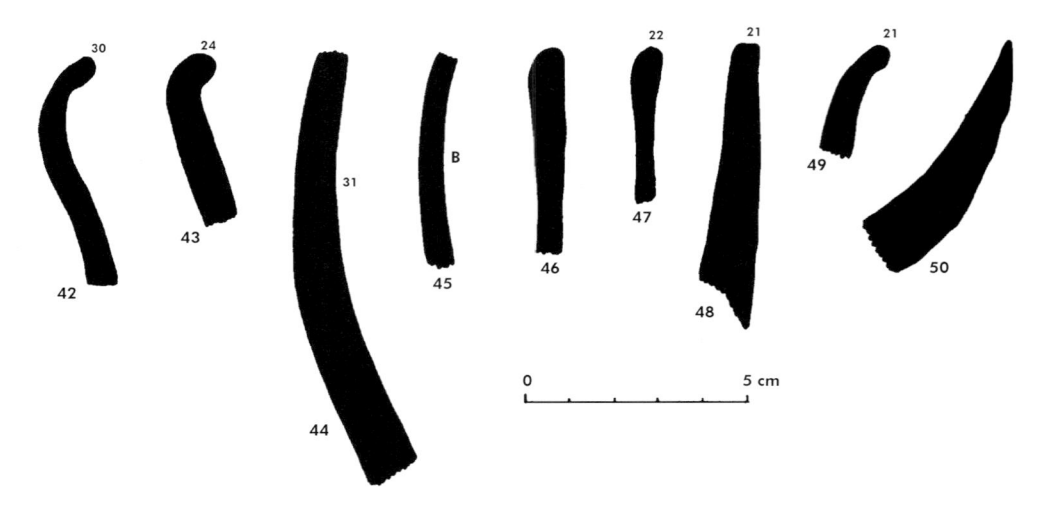

Fig. 58. Muozi midden. Pottery from 60 to 80cm below surface. B = burnish

of chewing by carnivores, perhaps dogs, is also common.

The most significant results relate to the size of the cattle. Measurements of complete limb bones (talus, calcaneum, phalanges) are compared with those of a control sample of modern unimproved Nguni cattle from South Africa:

> Seen in isolation, none of the bones present are reliable predictors of height. Nevertheless, on average, the lengths of virtually all the Muozi cattle bones are 20% to 30% smaller than those of the control sample. .... The average shoulder height of the control Nguni sample at the Transvaal Museum is 1.23m. The Muozi cattle, considering the small size of all measurable bones, are unlikely to have been more than 0.9-1m at shoulder height. .... The dimensions indicate that the Muozi cattle were of a dwarf variety. Whether this dwarfism is characteristic of a special breed, or due to environmental constraints, is at this stage uncertain. The configuration of the skull and horn cores, however, suggests the former.

The shapes of the skulls and horn cores show that the animals were flat faced. The horns

Almost all animals represented were adults.

This important osteological evidence from Muozi, therefore, confirms that there were cattle in Nyanga from at least the 16th century which would have been small enough to pass through the restricted

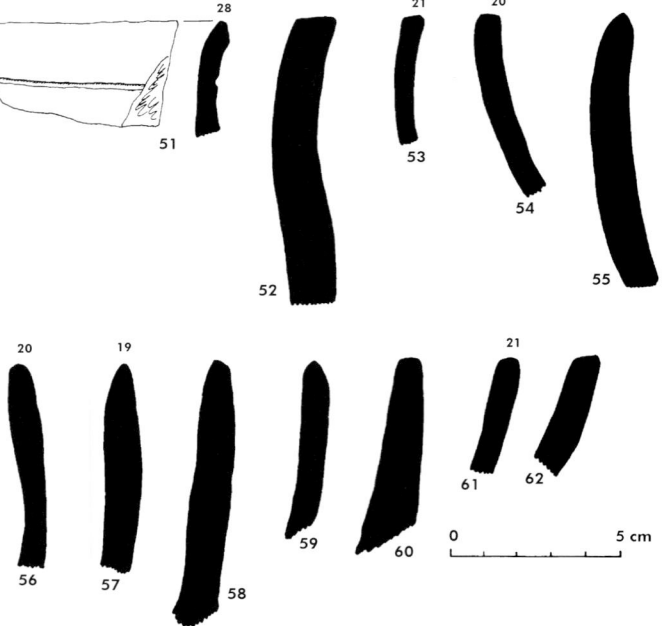

Fig. 59. Muozi midden. Pottery from 80 to 120cm below surface.

tunnels and entrance passages of the pit-structures and enclosures. The postulated function of the pits as cattle pens thus receives strong support, even though there are no such pits on the Muozi site itself.

The bone assemblage from Trench II has also been analysed by Dr Plug and her report is given in Appendix B. Additional species represented are human, genet or civet, wild bovid, hare, bushpig and suid, various large and small rodents, tortoise and land snail. Further metrical data is given which confirms the presence of dwarf cattle of a previously undocumented breed, while ovicaprids are also of relatively small size. The occurrence of the human bones is noted above.

Beads

Shell beads are well preserved in the alkaline conditions of the ash midden. These are not preserved, or at least have not been found, at any of the other sites excavated at Nyanga. Most of the shell beads are of snail shell, with significant numbers of ostrich eggshell in Units 2 and 3. Breakdown by total number and size of measurable specimens is as follows:

	0-30cm	30-60cm	60-90cm	90-140cm
Total no.	6	99	56	11
Size range	8.0- 13.0	3.4- 14.5	4.1 - 15.4	4.4 - 13.6
Av. diam.	6.88±3.27	5.99±2.87	9.56±2.78	9.25±2.54
No of o.e.s.	1.0	1.0	14	4.0
Range o.e.s.	8.0	9.0	6.4 - 13.5	6.9 - 11.5
Av. diam. o.e.s.	8.0	9.0	8.97±1.95	8.88±1.92

Size range is very variable throughout. There is some diminution in average size for the 0-60cm spits, but that for 30-60cm (unit 1b) is greatly biased by the presence of 41 beads of 4.2 to 4.3mm from a single concentration in spit 5. Ostrich-eggshell beads are almost restricted to Units 2 and 3. They are only slightly less variable in size and fall within the general range.

The "copper" beads are all manufactured by folding a strip of metal with the seam clearly visible, except for one more solid specimen from Unit 1b in which the seam has been entirely smoothed over. All appear to be of copper except for one small cylinder in Unit 1b whose yellowish colour may indicate brass. Shapes have been classified as biconical, barrel-shaped and cylindrical. The size ranges for the different types are:

	Diameter (mm)	Length (mm)
Biconical (12)	3.5-6.4 av. 4.77±0.9	3.0-5.0 av. 4.18±0.72
Barrel (7)	3.3-6.1 av. 4.80±1.22	2.0-4.1 av.3.19±0.73
Cylindrical (13)	3.3-6.0 av. 4.16±0.9	1.5-6.0 av.2.76±1.34

There is thus little difference in diameter but biconical tend to be longer and cylindrical shorter. There is no consistent correlation of size with depth. Distribution of types with depth is:

	Biconical	Barrel	Cylindrical
0 -30cm	10	3	2
30 - 60cm	1	4	10
60 - 90cm	1	-	1
90 - 140cm	-	-	-

There is some shift from cylindrical to biconical within Unit 1 and there are no copper beads below 80cm depth.

Glass beads are analysed with those from other sites in Appendix E. All come from the upper 60cm. Apart from a group of bi-coloured beads from the surface, the assemblage is essentially identical to that from the ruined pit-structure Nyangui G7/1 described below, four kilometres to the east. Both are consistent with a 16th or 17th century date, agreeing with the radiocarbon dating.

Iron

There are 10 iron objects, almost all from the surface or Unit 1; the surface objects are not necessarily from within the area of the trenches.
- 1 piece of curved rod, round section, probably part of a plain bangle, length 40mm, diameter 3mm. Surface.
- 1 straight rod, 101mm long and c.5mm in diameter, one end flattened to 2mm for a distance of 20mm. Surface.
- 1 arrowhead with barbed shaft, tapered butt and slightly broadened lanceolate head. The tang has a rectangular section 5 by 4mm, and the barbs are cut from opposite edges (fig. 60a). Length 144mm. Surface.
- 1 arrowhead tang, square section tapering from 5 by 4mm. Reversed barbs at the broken distal end cut from opposite edges (fig. 60b). Length 42mm. Surface.
- 1 rod tapered to one end, probably an arrow tang. Length 90mm, diameter c.5mm. Surface.
- 1 tapered rod, length 42mm, diameter c.4mm. 0-10cm below surface.
- 1 flat strip, tapered to one end, length 46mm, 4 by 2mm at broad end. 0-10cm b.s.
- 1 flat strip, tapering to one end, possibly an *mbira* key. Length 60mm, thickness 1 to 2mm, width 4 to 6mm. 0-15cm b.s.
- 1 rod, length 36mm, diameter c.3.5mm. 30-40cm b.s.
- 1 narrow triangular flat plate, heavily encrusted,

possibly a razor. Length 53mm, width 13mm at broad end. 80-90cm b.s.

The iron object from the platform beyond the main house in the stone ruins (Plate 18) was mentioned in Chapter 5. This consists of four curved iron bars splayed at each end, bound together in the middle by a spirally wound bar. The splayed bars are 290 to 295mm long, more or less round and 7 to 10mm in diameter in the middle. From the middle they are evenly flattened and splayed to rounded ends 29 to 33mm wide, thickness of the flattened part being 4 to 5mm tapering to the ends. At the narrower end of the piece the tips of the bars are bent outwards for 7 to 10mm. The spiral binding bar has 4 1/3 turns and is 8.5mm wide and 6mm thick, neatly tapering to the ends to give a regular barrel-shaped profile 37mm long and 32mm in maximum diameter. Iron pins have been driven into three of the interstices between bars and binding and into the centre to make the whole structure rigid. The curvature of the bars is not very symmetrical and one is notably twisted to make the narrower end of the piece approximately square. Diagonals at the narrower more symmetrical end are 154 and 140mm, and at the wider end 161 and 166mm. Maximum height standing on end is 250mm. The condition is excellent with very little corrosion. This is a remarkable example of a blacksmith's skill, well beyond the normal forging of single functional objects. Its purpose is not obvious nor have any parallels been discovered. Possibly it could be a stand for a very small pot or other object. A ritual or regalia function may be accepted, consistent with the find context and the sacred significance of this part of the site.

Slag

Three pieces, one from the base of Unit 1 (18gm), and two in Unit 2 (8, 79gm).

Copper (apart from beads)
- 1 stud, apparently identical to a "stud for the lip" collected from Mutoko and illustrated by Bent (1902:320). Conical head 9mm long and 12-13mm in diameter, hollowed underneath,

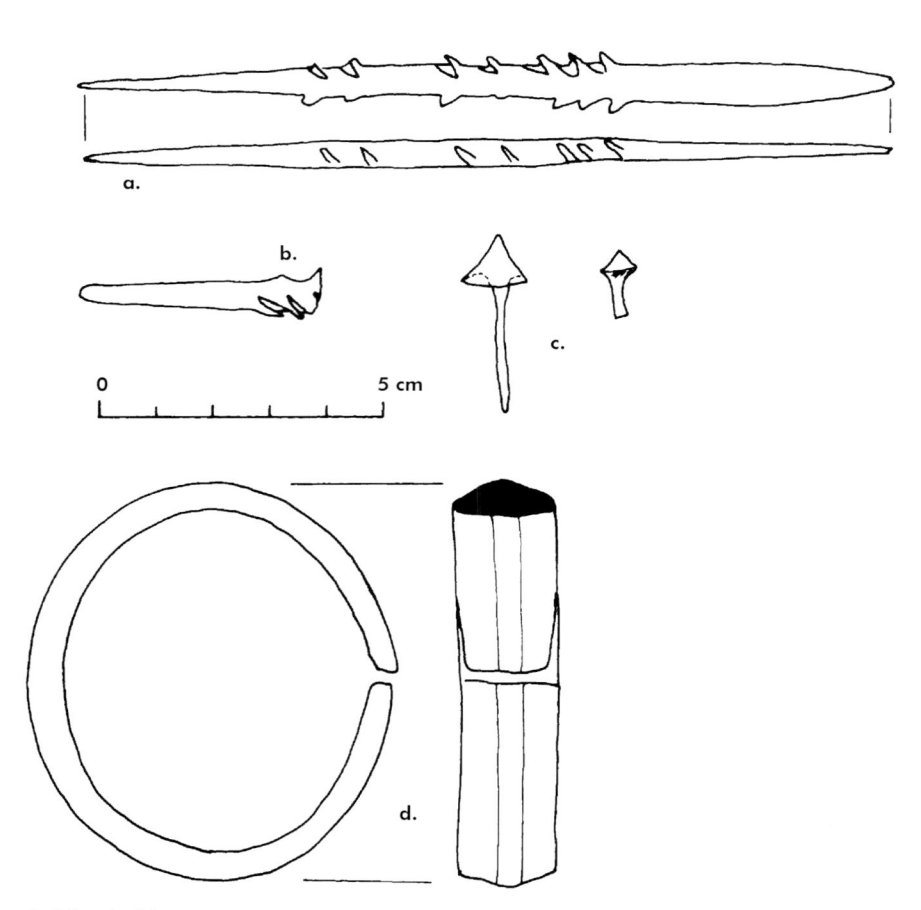

Fig. 60. Muozi. Metal objects

fused to a shaft tapering from 6 to 2mm in diameter, total length 33mm (fig. 60c). Unstratified, found in section cleaning.
- 1 stud, probably lip plug. Conical head 6mm in diameter grades into a broken shaft 2mm in diameter, total length 13mm (fig. 60c). Surface.
- 3 pieces of double, evenly twisted wire, lengths 42, 54 and 63mm, diameter 1 to 1.3mm. 40-50cm b.s..
- 1 single wire, partly roughly twisted, total length c.75mm, diameter 0.7mm. 40-50cm b.s.
- 1 piece of double evenly twisted wire, length 37mm, diameter 1.3mm. 50-60cm b.s.
- 1 piece of curved strip, length 18mm, width 3.3mm, thickness 0.7mm. 50-60cm b.s.
- 1 piece of double evenly twisted wire, length 40mm, diameter 1.3mm. 60-70cm b.s.
- 1 single wire, bent, length 66m, diameter 0.6mm. 60-70cm b.s.
- 1 single wire, length 40mm, diameter 0.8mm. 70-80cm b.s.
- 1 single wire, length 40mm, diameter 0.6mm. 100-120cm b.s.
- 1 section of spirally wound strip on a fibre core. Length 80mm, diameter 2.5 to 3mm, strip 1 by 0.4mm. 100-120cm b.s.

The "copper" bracelet from surface in the main ruins near the group of complete pots was also mentioned in Chapter 5. This is curved into an oval shape with a 2mm gap between the ends. Outside diameter 71 by 65mm. Section 17 by 6mm with the outside edges broadly bevelled (fig. 60d).

Other
- 1 ?stopper, ceramic. One side concave conical, other side convex. Diameter 33mm, thickness 21mm. 60-70cm b.s.
- 2 fragments of a hollow cylinder of chalky white ?ceramic, resembling the bowl of an imported clay pipe. Diameter c.16mm outside, thickness 1.7 to 2mm. 40-50cm b.s.

Discussion

Throughout the occupation of the site, the main animal herds must have been kept elsewhere, since grazing and water must have been very limited on the plateau. The main crops also must have been grown at a distance, perhaps on the stone terraces on the escarpment below. Water must have been a problem in the dry season. The nearest accessible water is probably 1500m distant on the northern side of the main spur where a stream descends from the highlands; there are traces of a path from the base of the saddle in this direction.

As discussed in Chapter 5, the whole midden perhaps with the exception of some of the surface material appears to be earlier in date than the stone walled site on the promontory, although the pottery from the top spits of the midden, including both punctate and incised cross-hatched decoration, has affinities to some of the complete vessels (fig. 38) and supports a cultural relationship.

Some of the remains on the plateau and along its southern edge, with their affinities to the early hilltop settlements, must be associated with the lower part of the ash midden and would date from the earliest known occupation of the highlands in the 14th/15th centuries. The absence of the low-walled open enclosures which are a prominent feature of other early highland settlements can probably be explained by the special and isolated nature of this site. If, for instance, such enclosures were designed as stock pens they would hardly have been needed at Muozi where there would have been little scope for the regular keeping of livestock.

The beads and pottery from the upper middle spits of the midden, as well as the radiocarbon dating in the 16th/17th centuries, show contemporaneity with the older ruined pit-structures, especially Nyangui G7/1. Presumably some of the plateau remains relate to this period and excavation is required to establish which ones. The continued use of the same midden supports a relationship with the earlier inhabitants, though the slight changes in stratigraphy and pottery could indicate an interruption in occupation.

Muozi is the only known site with stratified deposits which appear to span virtually the whole time range of the Nyanga archaeological complex. Comparable ash middens have not been located at other sites of the Nyanga complex, where ash was probably distributed with manure on the gardens and terraced fields – in this case the fields were perhaps too remote to be worth the transport. The midden has provided alkaline conditions for the preservation of bones and shell beads and this is the only good faunal collection to have been found. The evidence for dwarf cattle is significant for the interpretation of many of the stone ruins, although the specialised nature of the site limits any conclusions on herding practices within the complex as a whole.

NYANGUI G7/1 RUINED PIT-STRUCTURE

This site, designated 1732DD55, lies within Block G of Nyangui Forest land, the survey of which is described in Chapter 5. Pit group 7 is a rather diffuse group of grassy hollows above the edge of a deep valley at the southern edge of a broad and generally stoneless plateau. Large dolerite outcrops crown the steep valley side and scattered boulders extend some 50m further up as the gradient decreases. Site G7/1 is about 40m above the main line of outcrops, with a few emerging boulders nearby to the south-west. Altitude is 2000m and the grid reference is VR 781154 (fig. 42, no.3).

The feature (fig. 61) presents itself as a large grassy hollow some 12m in diameter and a little over two metres deep, with a linear depression on the upper north-west side and a slight saddle in the lower south-east side (Plate 14). A short section of stone revetment is visible in the north side of the hollow. In the base of the hollow is a confused concentration of stones around 3.50m in diameter, apparently relatively recently deposited as there is little silting among them; there is some impression of a collapsed very rough circular structure. A similar feature occurs in another pit of the group and these may derive from the "squatter" occupation of the area in the

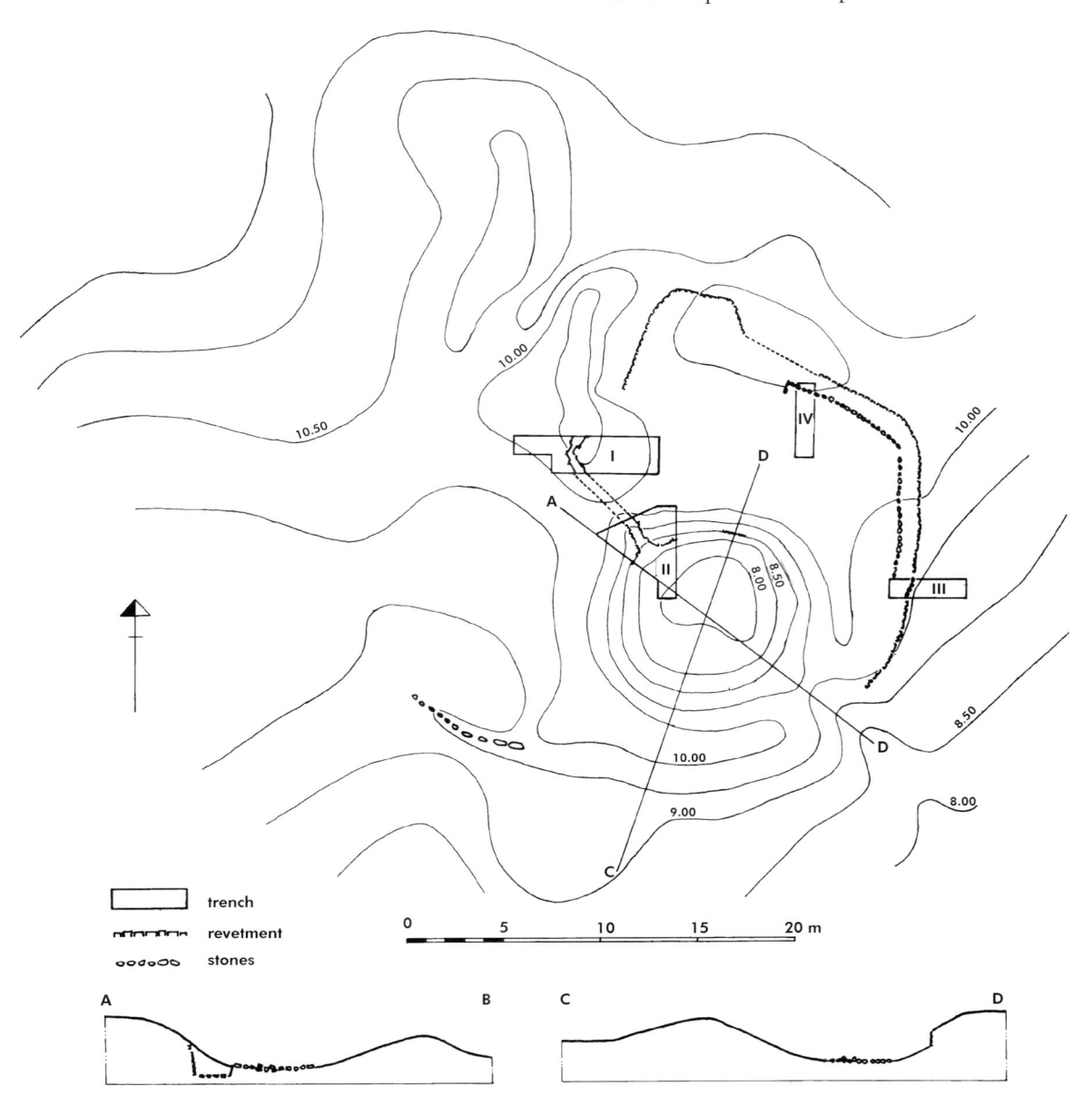

Fig. 61. Nyangui G7/1. Plan of ruined pit-structure

1980s. A broader depression to the north-west of the hollow was probably the source of the soil used as a fill to level up the platform around the pit, the lower side of which is now represented by a more or less rounded bank. The edge of the platform is defined on its east to north sides by a line of stones, partly a double line. To the south-west a natural boulder forms the beginning of a line of stones extending west-north-west, probably the remains of a radial wall from the platform.

From the surface features and excavation, it is deduced that the original stone-lined pit was eight to nine metres in diameter and at least 2.50m deep, and the platform some 24m in diameter.

Excavations were aimed at confirming the nature of the pit and entrance passage, identifying house floors on the platform and recovering cultural and dating material for comparison with the well preserved pit-structures at a lower level in Block G (see site G1/21 later in this chapter). Trench I was located across the north-western depression which, from the analogy of better preserved pit-structures, was likely to represent the entrance passage. Trench II was situated to section the side of the pit and was later extended to expose the mouth of the entrance passage. Trench III was placed outside the wall of the platform where surface sherds held out the possibility of midden deposits; and Trench IV was on the northern side of the platform where house structures might be hoped for.

Trench I

Trench I was 5.50 by 2m with an extension of 2 by 1m at the western end, designed to section the entrance passage and locate traces of any house on top of it. The stratigraphy showed:
1. Brown loam with grass roots around 4cm deep, rather darker in the passage depression.
2. Redder brown clayey loam, 12 to 18cm deep over the passage and around 10cm deep either side.
3. Red-brown clay-loam with ochreous lumps, possibly *dhaka*, at the level western end of the trench.
4. Finer more orange clay-loam with numerous fallen stones forming the fill of the passage.

On either side of the passage, Layers 2 and 3 rest on a surface of red-brown clay-loam with yellow lumps of decomposed dolerite. This is the artificial fill of the platform, eroded away on the slopes either side of the passage and continuing down behind the stone passage revetments. Potsherds and beads occur in all layers, with a greater concentration of sherds among the stones in layers 2 and 3 at the western end.

The passage runs north-west from the pit and takes a sharp bend to the north-east through a cleft in the underlying dolerite bedrock. Here the base is constricted to a width of only 25cm in the lower 35cm. On the south side of this cleft the width is around 45cm at the base and to the north of it it widens to 70cm, presumably near the passage mouth which was not exposed. The maximum depth of the stone facing is 1.10m where best preserved, but the fallen stones in the fill indicate that it was originally rather deeper. The base of the passage is fairly level in this section. There is some batter to the walls of the passage, the width at the surviving top being a minimum of 60cm, and presumably more at its original height. The quality of the stonework is somewhat irregular. The largest stone recovered from the fill measured 65 by 32 by 16cm, which would be hardly large enough to span the top.

In the western part of the trench outside the passage are a number of stones lying within layers 2 and 3, on or above the surface of the platform fill. A line or arc of these running NNW/SE could mark the wall of a house to the west but is not sufficiently regular to be entirely convincing. There is no clear trace of any floor either side of this.

From the surviving evidence, it is considered unlikely that the passage was originally roofed, with a house over the top. It is however conceivable that larger roofing slabs were present but were robbed for reuse elsewhere, and that any house remains were thus destroyed or subsequently eroded into the passage.

Trench II

Trench II was initially five by one metres, running north/south in the north-western quadrant of the hollow, sited to section the wall of the pit east of the entrance passage. A triangular extension was then made to the west to expose the lower part of the passage. Stratigraphy (fig. 62a) was:
1. Grey to grey-brown humus among the loose stones at the bottom of the hollow, humic topsoil with roots on the side of the pit.
2. Reddish brown sandy clay-loam with numerous tumbled stones, 30cm to 1.40m deep.
3. Thin yellowish sandy deposit on and between small stones which form the floor paving of the pit. This seems to derive from decomposed dolerite.

In the south-west section, layer 2 appears to show three phases of collapse represented by deposition of soil followed by collapse of stones from the wall. The matrix however was homogeneous and no surfaces were detected between the phases. Small potsherds and a few glass beads were found throughout.

EXCAVATED SETTLEMENT SITES

The lower walls of the pit were exposed either side of the mouth of the passage, that to the east having slumped somewhat from its original position. The western side was still in place preserved to a maximum height of 1.40m. The quality of the stonework is generally rather poor with no regular flat face.

The walls of the passage have spaced vertical stones at the base up to about 50cm high, interspersed with horizontal stones. The full height may be preserved only at one point on the western side where it measures one metre. The minimum span at the "top" is 60cm and there is again no indication that it was ever roofed. The base of the passage has six steps, the lower five formed by large stones with worn surfaces and the top one formed of four smaller stones. Riser heights from the floor of the pit are 30, 20, 12, c.25 and c.12cm, a total rise of 1.24m in 2.60m.

From this point there is no further rise, even a slight fall, in the 3.50m to Trench I.

Trench III

Trench III measured 4 by 1m, to section the eastern edge of the platform and recover cultural material, as numerous potsherds were present in the topsoil at this point. Stratigraphy (fig. 62b) was:
1. Grey-brown topsoil with roots, 3 to 6cm.
2. Darker brown loam with a few tumbled stones, 10 to 20cm.
3. Redder loam, 10 to 24cm, becoming sterile and more clayey at the base.

Layers 2 and 3 are banked against the outer face of the platform wall which is 55cm high. The inner wall-face reaches the north-west corner of the trench but does not continue. Layer 2 is also present within the top of this wall.

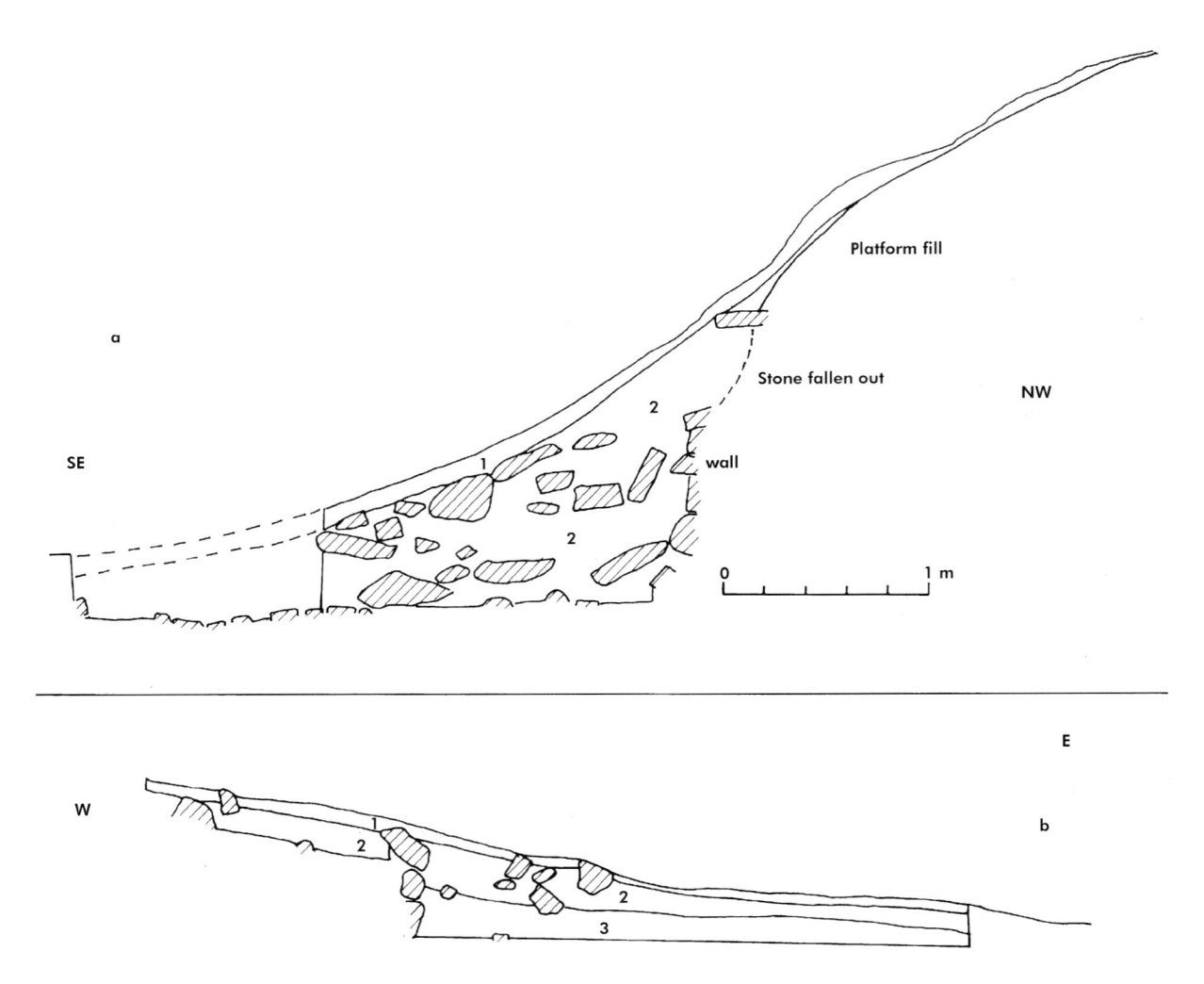

Fig. 62. Nyangui G7/1. a. Section of Trench II. b. Section of Trench III

Potsherds and beads were numerous in all three layers, this trench producing 65 of the 133 beads from the whole site and 30% of the sherds. It would seem that rubbish was discarded here outside the platform. No bone is preserved beyond a few tooth fragments. An iron arrow head was found in layer 3.

A charcoal sample from layer 3 has given a date of 340 ±15 BP (Pta-7069), calibrated to AD 1525(1540)1560 or 1635(1642)1645 at one sigma.

Trench IV

Trench IV also measured 4 by 1m, at the north-eastern side of the platform within the inner face of the platform wall, here represented by a single course of stones. Stratigraphy was:
1. Thin brown soil with roots.
2. Dark brown loam, c.12cm.
3. Orange-brown loam with ochreous lumps, possibly *dhaka*. At the southern end of the trench was softer red-brown loam with a spread of potsherds, some with thick soot inside, at 28cm below the surface, and bedrock beneath at around 40cm.
4. In the rest of the trench, red-brown sandy clay loam with rare sherds and ochreous lumps to around 40cm. Lumps of yellow decomposed dolerite at base.

There was no clear evidence for structures such as detectable floors or indications of walls.

Phosphate samples

Nine samples were taken.

Trench I:
platform fill	8500 ppm
4 - fill of entrance passage	16500
5 - crack in bedrock passage floor	9500

Trench II:
2 - 10-15cm above floor of pit	18000
3 - between small floor stones	17000
3 - between small floor stones	19500
3 - on floor of pit	22000

Trench III:
2 - 5 to 7cm below surface	13500
Trench IV, 4 - base of deposits	18500

The lowest value of 8500 ppm is from the platform fill and provides the nearest approximation to background levels, no samples having been taken from outside the limits of the site. Within the pit high values were obtained from the floor and just above it and are consistent with its use for livestock. The relatively high value for trench III is again consistent with the rubbish midden interpretation. There would have been little deposition in the entrance passage during use, and the fill would derive from occupation deposits on either side. Trench IV also indicates human deposition of uncertain nature.

Finds

Pottery (fig. 63)

A total of 1812 sherds was recovered, weighing 16,380gm. These are made up of 148 rims, 49 necks, 3 decorated body sherds and 1614 plain body sherds. 82 have soot outside and 30 have carbonised residues inside up to a millimetre or more thick. Most sherds are small and often weathered, but those from Trench III are larger. Colour is mostly grey or grey-brown with a few brown or light brown. In a fair number of sherds the inner surface is black, heavily reduced and partly eroded. Temper is quartz, often plus feldspar, with maximum visible grain size often up to 4 to 6mm. Firing is generally poor and the texture often crumbly. Sherds are generally thick, with maximum thickness ranging from 4 to c.15mm and a mean of 8.76 ±1.86.

Vessels comprise one deep vessel with slightly out-turned rim (no.7), one hemispherical bowl, two open bowls (3,4), one small constricted bowl (1), 21 wide-mouthed pots (5,6,8-16), three narrow-mouthed pots (17) and six undifferentiated necked pots. Lips are round, the majority tapered, and finish is predominantly rough. Rim diameters are 20cm for the deep vessel, 16cm for the constricted bowl, 14 to 24cm for the wide-mouthed and undifferentiated pots and 15cm for two narrow-mouthed pots.

Decoration occurs rarely on the rim and/or the neck/shoulder and consists of six cases of one or more bands of triangular punctates, sometimes with vertical panels of punctates between (1, 17-20). One punctate vessel is also graphited (18) and there is one plain graphited sherd.

Iron

- Fragment of heavily corroded rod, length 91mm, diameter ?5mm. Trench I.
- Arrowhead with long tapering tang and barbed head broken on one side. Total length 167mm, head length 25mm, original head width c.18mm, maximum tang diameter c.5mm. Trench III (fig. 63 no.21).

Stone

- Rubbing stone of sandstone, both sides smooth, 150 x 130 x 55mm, three edges rough and pitted from hammering. Trench II.
- Smooth quartz pebble 34 x 12 x 12mm. Trench I.

Teeth

- 1 third lower molar, large bovid. Trench IV.
- broken fragments from trenches I and III.

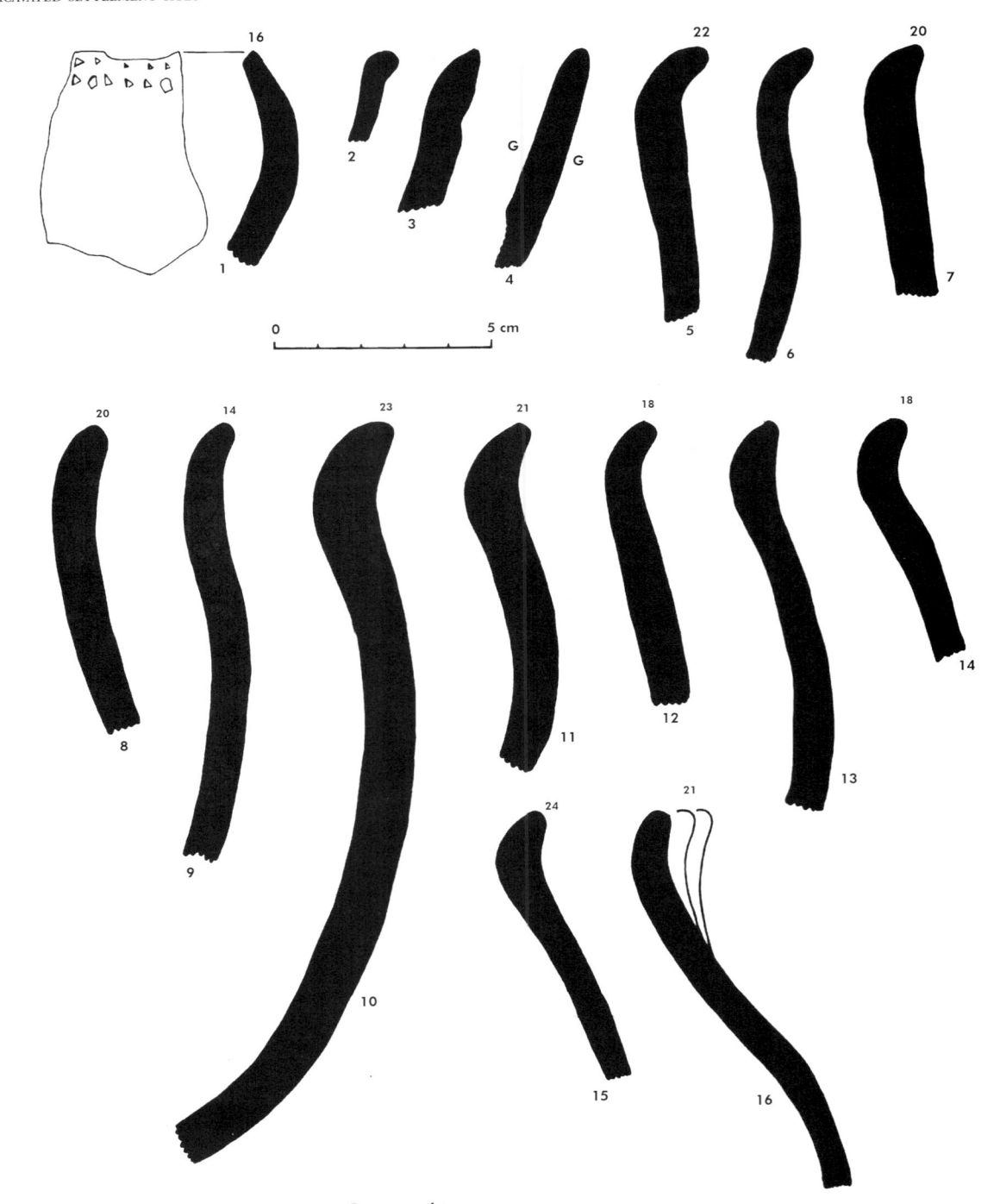

Fig. 63a. Nyangui G7/1. Pottery. G = graphite

Beads

The distribution by trench was as follows:

	I	II	III	IV	Total
Glass	38	2	60	19	119
Copper	5	7	1	3	16

The glass beads are analysed in Appendix E. The assemblage is very closely comparable to that from Muozi midden and consistent with a 16th/17th century date

The copper beads are all manufactured by folding a relatively thick strip to a circular shape, the seam being usually visible, but in the case of the larger solid bicones well smoothed over. Most are quite corroded. They have been classified as at Muozi into biconical, barrel-shaped and cylindrical. Size ranges in millimetres are:

	Diameter (mm)	Length (mm)
Biconical(8)	6-13 av.8.41±2.83	3.8-12 av.6.79±3.32
Barrel(1)	10	5
Cylindrical(7)	5.8-9 av. 7.06±1.14	2.8-8 av.4.27±1.71

Three larger bicones are 12 x 10.6, 13 x 12 and 7 x 9.2mm, accounting for the large standard deviations. The whole series is substantially bigger and more solidly made than that from Muozi (see above), suggesting a different source, which is puzzling in view of the similarity in the glass bead assemblages.

a roofed tunnel, an almost invariable feature of the well preserved pits. Had it been roofed, the slabs large enough to span the passage might have been sufficiently valuable to be robbed for reuse in later structures; however the nearest well preserved pit is well over one kilometre distant and it seems unlikely that they would have been carried that far. Nearer ruined pits have similar depressions marking their entrance passages with no clear traces of tunnels. It is thus probable that in these ruined pits the passage was never roofed; this could be a general characteristic of earlier pit-structures or may reflect

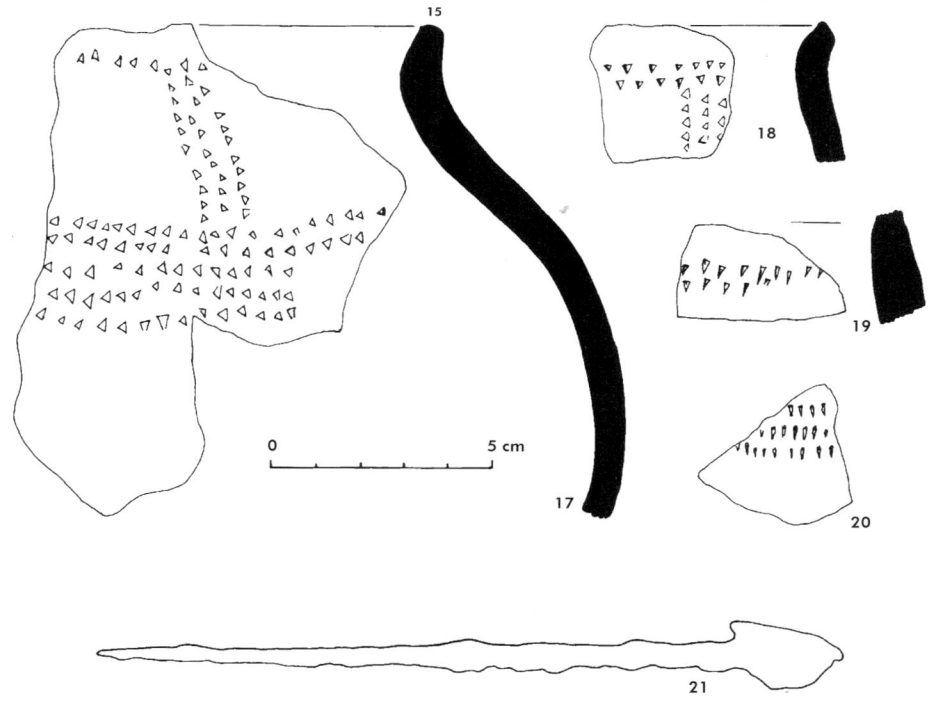

Fig. 63b. (continued) Nyangui G7/1. Pottery and iron arrowhead

Discussion

This site presents most but not all of the features typical of the well preserved pit-structures at the lower level of Nyangui Block G and elsewhere. The pit diameter of eight to nine metres is at the upper end of the size range and the depth is about average. The floor of the pit is paved with small stones in contrast to the fine paving of G1/21 (see below), which may reflect the rarity of flat slabs in the immediately available dolerite as compared with the sandstones of the latter. The passage length of around eight metres is fairly typical, as is the right-hand bend from the pit, here forced into a sharper angle by the conformation of the bedrock. The initial stepped rise from the pit is much steeper than in most pits but may again be necessitated by the bedrock. However, this passage was probably never

the dearth of suitable roofing slabs within a practicable distance.

Clear stone walls defining house-bays are absent on the platform, and any clear floors or lesser stone alignments which might have indicated house walls were not detected in the limited excavations, though they might well be found in a larger area excavation.

The probable radial wall from the south-western edge of the platform is a typical feature of the later pit-structures.

The number of beads recovered is definitely atypical of any other known pit-structure and is parallelled only by the contemporaneous assemblage from the Muozi midden. This question of relative bead frequency is discussed in Appendix E.

MATINHA I: PIT-STRUCTURES AND EXCAVATION

The site of Matinha I (fig. 64), designated 1732DD11, comprises a group of 16 ruined and 13 better preserved pit-structures, situated towards the northern end of the main highland range just within the Nyangui Forest reserve at an altitude of 2000m at grid reference VR 747251 (fig. 42, no.4). It is on the south side of a narrow saddle separating the heads of the Nyabomwe and Marozi rivers which flow to west and east respectively. The major hill of Chirimanyimo (2180m; described above) rises beyond the saddle to the north-north-east.

The site is on a fairly level plateau sloping down very gently to the east and northwards to the saddle. The north-eastern and eastern edges of the plateau drop quite steeply to the head of the Marozi valley. Geologically the immediate area is dolerite with red clay-loam soils; ferruginous argillites occur nearby to north and south, overlain a little further afield by sandstones and shales (Stocklmayer 1978). The vegetation is short grassland with a belt of exotic wattle along the crest of the ridge and saddle at the western edge of the site.

There are numerous pit-structures along the northern side of the plateau, continuing at a decreasing altitude along a spur to the east-south-east (Matinha II/III).

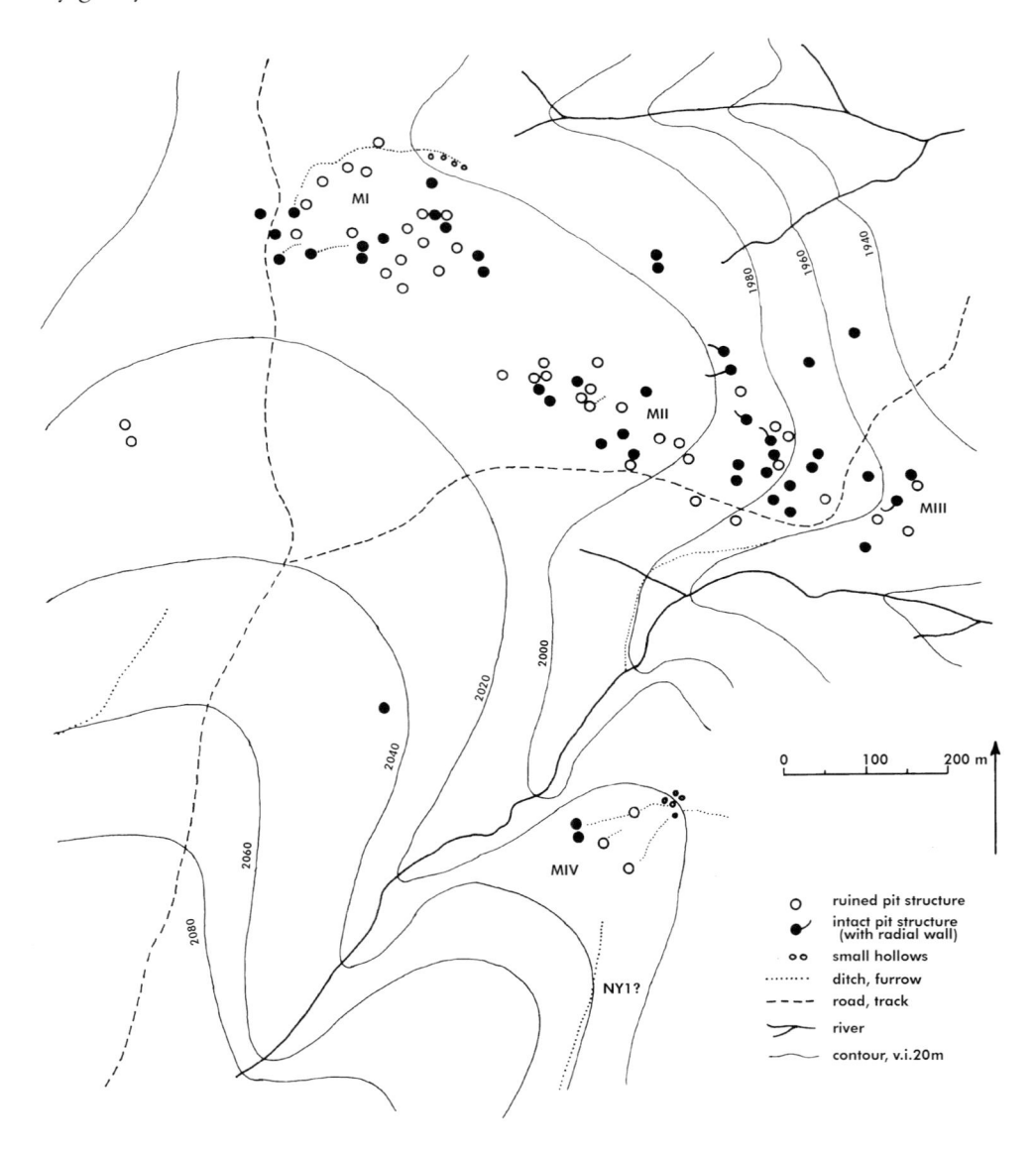

Fig. 64. Matinha. Map of ruined and well preserved pit-structures, with ditches and furrows. Traced from an aerial photograph

Both ruined and well preserved pit-structures are represented, here interspersed and often closely adjacent. This contrasts with the situation in Nyangui Block G, eight to ten kilometres to the south, where the distribution of the two types is mutually exclusive and altitudinally distinct (see Chapter 5). From this Block G evidence it is likely that two separate phases of occupation are represented at Matinha, each favouring the same general location, and specific localities within it where suitable stone was available for construction. Some of the final destruction of the ruined pits may have been occasioned by stone robbing for the later ones.

Some of the Matinha pit-structures, mainly the later ones, have ditches running from their drain outlets, but these do not appear to run to small hollows, nor are there impoundment dams below the drains as in many cases in Block G. Similarly only a few pit-structures lower down the eastern spur have radial walls. Here many of the ditches can be explained by the very gentle gradient, in which the pits have been excavated below the general ground surface so that ditches also need to be dug to ensure drainage. There is however one largish ditch from the north-western edge of the plateau, cut into the valley side below the site to the north, and this does have a series of about eight small hollows along its upper side, too small to have been old pit-structures, but which could have been fed from the ditch and represent impoundment for some purpose.

This raises the question of whether there was a water supply to some or all of the site. There is in fact a recent furrow, probably from the 1980s, traceable both on the aerial photographs and on the ground, which runs from a good spring c.1500m to the south-west. This takes a circuitous course around a spur and the head of a valley and disappears into the dense wattle thicket. The traceable length to this point is c.1700m and an extension of 600 to 700m could have carried it down the crest of the ridge to the site. A similar furrow would have been within the capabilities of the pit builders. The lack of radial walls and impoundment dams however suggests the absence of irrigated homestead gardens, nor does there appear to be a suitable site for gardens in the valley to the north in the vicinity of the ditch and small hollows.

Excavation

Excavation of one of the grassy hollows was undertaken to confirm that it was a ruined pit-structure, for comparison with Nyangui G7/1 and, if possible, to obtain dating evidence.

The hollow selected, Matinha I/1 (fig. 65), is towards the eastern end of the site about 40m from

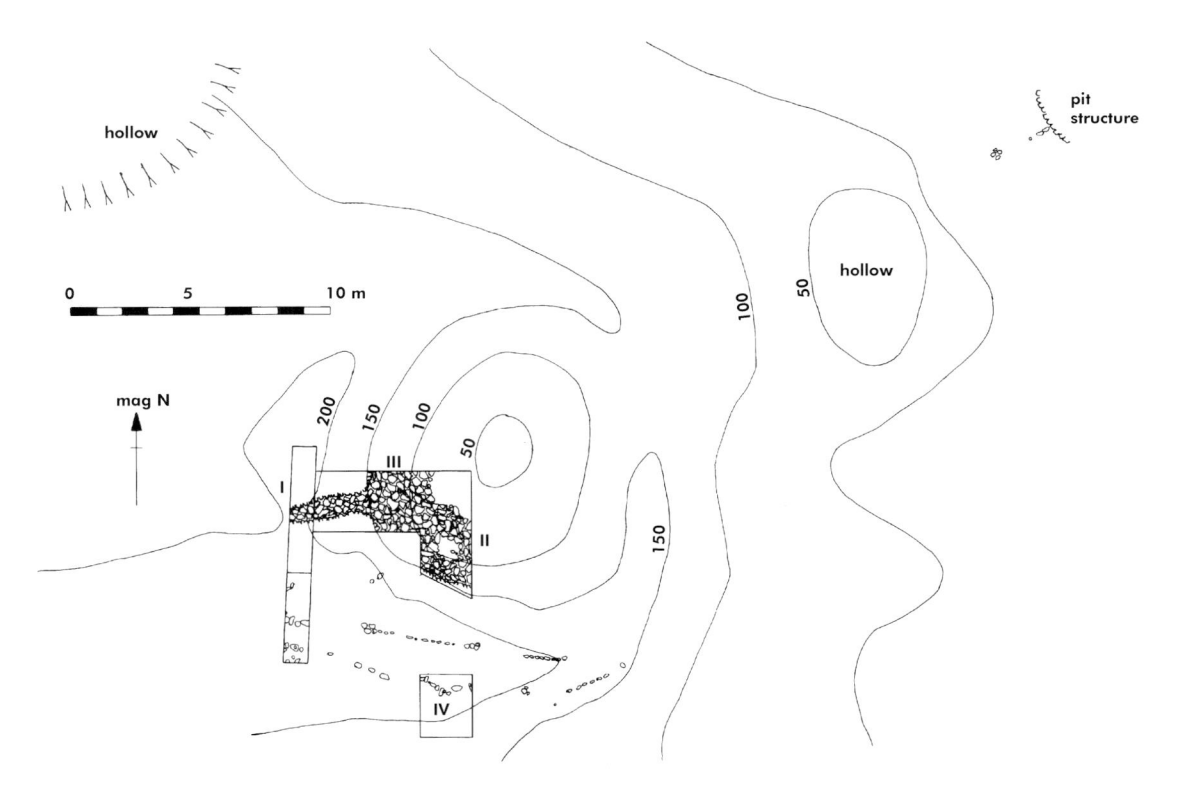

Fig. 65. Matinha I/1. Plan of ruined pit-structure. V.I. of contours 50cm

the edge of the plateau. Two well-preserved pit-structures and two adjacent ruined hollows crown this crest 20m to the north-east; there are other hollows 12 and 25m to the north-west and south-west and another well-preserved pit-structure 38m to the west with a ditch below.

The pit presents itself as an open grassy hollow about 13m in diameter and 2.10m deep below its higher southern edge. Two discontinuous lines of stones mark the rim of the platform on this side and the only other visible stones were rare and more or less loose on the sides of the hollow. A very slight depression on the west side suggested the position of an entrance passage, and a slight reentrant to the east may be the position of the drain. The contours on Figure 65 show the ground surface before excavation. There is a subsidiary hollow about nine by six metres in diameter and 60cm deep on the north-east side between the main hollow and the nearest well preserved pit-structure. This was not investigated.

Trench I was placed across the presumed line of the entrance passage and later extended to the south as Trench V in the hope of finding a house structure. Trench II sectioned the south-west side of the hollow, and Trench III joined I and II to expose the passage and west side of the pit. Trench IV was dug outside the south edge of the platform where it was thought there might be midden deposits. Much of the south-west quadrant and entrance passage were thus exposed and the remains of a stone-lined pit were uncovered.

The pit thus revealed (Plate 25) is roughly paved with stone slabs and the passage more neatly paved. The sides of pit and passage are revetted with stones, rather less well constructed than is the norm for the later pits. The pit revetment survives up to 60 or 70cm high, and numerous loose stones in the fill suggest an original depth of around two metres up to the rim of the hollow. Some of these fallen stones are up to 60 by 20cm and 10 to 15cm thick, suggesting large coping stones as in many well preserved pits. The curvature of the pit wall exposed and the configuration of the hollow indicate an original diameter of around nine metres, not necessarily circular. The walls of the passage are up to 1.15m high; the width at the base varies between 45 and 60 cm and the top is up to 78cm wide.

The paving is missing from the centre of the pit in the north-east corner of Trench II. Here the pit fill rests on natural subsoil of red-brown clay-loam with numerous lumps of pale yellow decomposed dolerite, grading down to more solid decomposed dolerite at a depth of 30cm. Since the pit fill had accumulated from the sides, the paving in the centre would have been exposed for longer and may have been robbed out.

The revetting of pit and passage is backed by similar red-brown clay-loam with yellow lumps which may be natural subsoil or artificial fill for the platform excavated from the pit or elsewhere.

The sections of Trenches II and III (fig. 66) show the following sequence of deposition:

6. deposition of red-brown clay-loam against the base of the wall by siltation
5. red-brown clay-loam with pale yellow lumps and numerous loose stones from the initial collapse of the upper part of the wall and platform fill
4. grey earthy loam in the eastern section, probably representing a halt in the collapse, with soil formation
3/2. grey-brown to brown gravelly loam with some yellow lumps and loose stones from continuing slower collapse and deposition
1. grey-brown humic topsoil.

The passage section (fig. 67) shows a soft grey deposit (6) on the paving stones, overlain by numerous fallen stones in a soft red-brown gravelly loam matrix with some charcoal (5). This matrix is

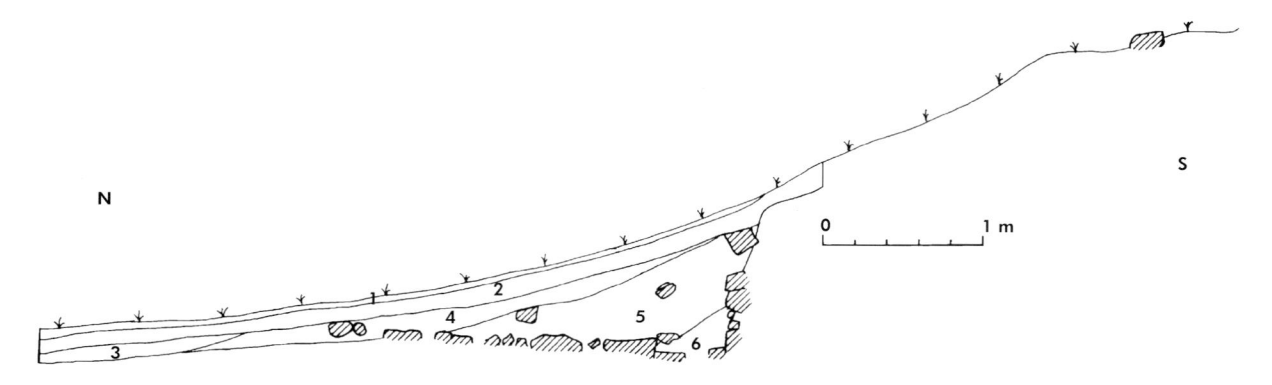

Fig. 66. Matinha I/1. Section of pit

softer and cleaner than that in the pit and may represent siltation down the passage from the upper west end. Over the top of the surviving revetment are lenses with decomposed dolerite (4) from the sides of the platform fill, and the remaining concavity is filled first with reddish brown gravelly loam (3) and then by less gravelly grey-brown loam (2) under a thin topsoil (1). The extent of aggradation, leaving only a very slight depression over the passage, supports a long period of deposition. The largest stones in the fill, 50 to 60cm long, would not have been big enough to bridge the passage. Any larger lintel stones could have been robbed for reuse in later pit-structures, but the batter of the walls and width at the top imply that it was never roofed.

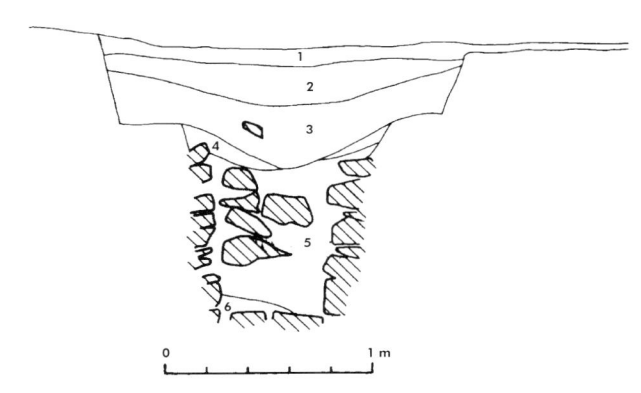

Fig. 67. Matinha I/1. Section of the entrance passage

Trench IV showed the outer rim of the platform to be a single course of stones up to 30cm high against the usual platform fill. The section showed grey-brown gritty topsoil thickening from c.5cm at the upper northern end to c.15cm at the lower side. Beneath this and banked against the stones is brown gritty loam grading into redder brown and sloping down to the south, containing red ochreous lumps, probably *dhaka* mud daub. This overlay clean red-brown clay-loam and contained a fair number of sherds, one Indian red bead and a cow tooth.

Trench V spanned the end of the two lines of stones marking the platform edge. There was a thin brown gravelly topsoil deepening on the south side of the northern stones. Beneath this was brown loam with numerous red ochreous lumps of ?*dhaka*. These lumps were continuous in the centre of the west side of the trench but showed no smooth surface; some occurred beneath the southern stones. The underlying deposit was clean brown loam. The ochreous lumps probably represent a collapsed mud structure, but there was no clear floor or any trace of walls.

The double line of stones at the southern side of the hollow appears to constitute a platform rim around 1.50m wide. The space between this and the southern pit edge is c.2m, widening to the west to c.4m to the entrance passage, leaving room for a smallish house. The space south of the pit was not excavated but would have been largely eroded away with the collapse of the upper pit revetment.

Dating

Insufficient charcoal for dating was obtained from the midden deposit of Trench IV and resort was made to two samples from Trench III, layers 6 and 5 of the pit fill, representing early stages in the collapse. Results were respectively:
190±40 BP, cal.AD 1673(1686,1738)1777; 1797(1810)1881 (Pta-7593) and 140±40 BP, cal.AD 1689-1733; 1813(1884,1920)1939 (Pta-7613).

Calibration brackets are very wide but even the early ends of the ranges are later than the dating of G7/1. However their context postdates the use of the pit and they may best be considered as indicating a minimum age. The later calibration ranges are improbable, given the supposed time gap between the ruined and better preserved pit-structures.

Finds

Pottery (fig. 68)
The pottery assemblage totals 2581 sherds, of which 192 are rims (94 undiagnostic), 23 necks, 10 decorated body sherds and 2356 plain body sherds. Colour ranges from brown through grey-brown to grey. 236 have soot outside and 83 have some carbonised residue inside. Temper is quartz, often with feldspar, and maximum visible grain size is mostly from 1 to 3mm, occasionally up to 5 or 6mm. Temper density is usually medium to heavy, rarely light; there is no consistent correlation between density and vessel shape, although most of the few decorated sherds are heavily tempered.

Among the diagnostic rims there are 5 deep straight-sided vessels (1-5); 25 hemispherical bowls (7-9, 13, 14); 9 open bowls (16-21); 1 constricted bowl (15); 3 necked bowls (10-12); 31 wide-mouthed pots (22-38); 3 narrow-mouthed pots (39, 40); and 2 undifferentiated necked pots. Many of the bowls have slightly out-turned rims, intermediate between the straight out-sloping rims of the other ruined pit-structure G7/1 and the more markedly out-turned rims of the later pit-structure G1/21. Measurable rim diameters are: deep vessels (3) 17-22cm; hemispherical bowls (5) 15-22cm; open bowls (1) 18cm; constricted bowl (1) 15cm; necked bowls

(2) 20, 24cm; wide-mouthed pots (14) 16-21cm; narrow-mouthed pots (3) 14-19cm. Vessel size is thus medium to small. Rim height for 27 necked pots ranges from 7 to 28mm with an average of 17.5mm.

Lips are almost all round, about a third of them tapered. Surface finish is almost all rough, only 8% of diagnostic sherds being smooth.

3.5 to 4.5mm, lengths 3 to 5mm. Trench I.
- 1 large bead of square section slightly tapered to the ends. Ends 6mm square, middle 7.5mm square, length 24mm, diameter of hole 4mm. There is the trace of a seam on one side, indicating that it was folded and probably hammered smooth. Trench III.

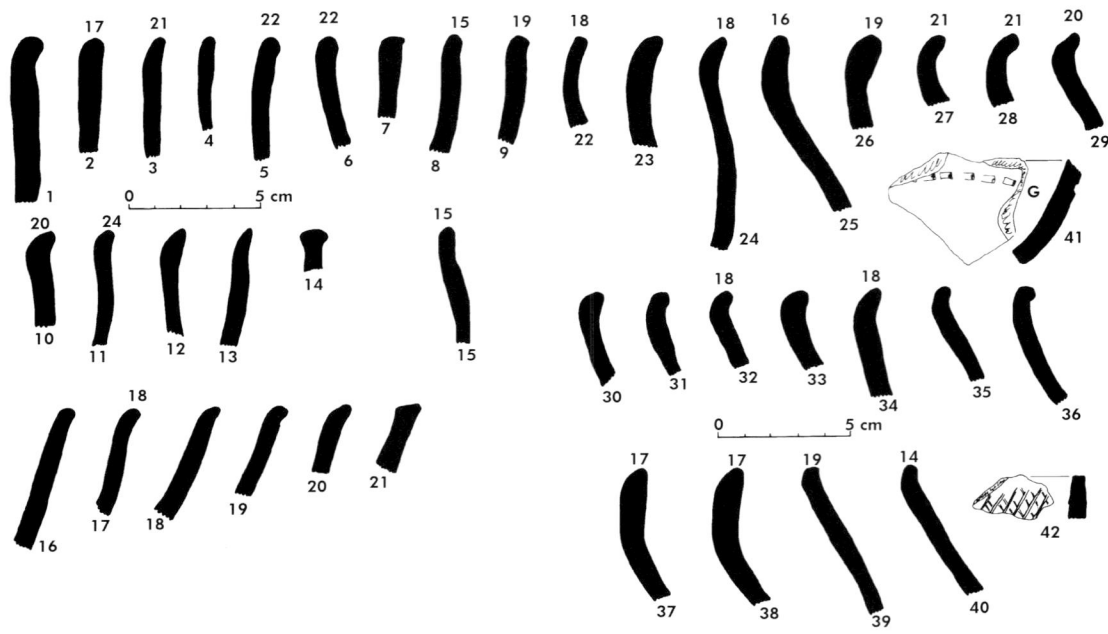

Fig. 68. Matinha I/1. Pottery. G = graphite

Decoration is rare. There is one incised cross-hatched sherd (42); one body sherd, probably from an open bowl, with a line of rectangular punctates outside and graphiting inside (41); and three sherds with two rows of rough triangular punctates probably from the same vessel. Two sherds have plain graphite outside, two inside and one inside and out.

Maximum sherd thickness ranges from 4 to 15mm with an average of 7.99 ±1.62mm.

Beads
12 beads were found, 4 of glass and 8 of copper.
Glass:
- 1 dull turquoise cylinder, diameter 6mm, length 4mm. Trench II
- 1 opaque white cylinder, diameter 4mm, length 3.5mm. Trench III
- 1 Indian red cylinder, diameter 4mm, length 3mm. Trench IV
- 1 turquoise oblate, diameter 3mm, length 1.5mm. Trench IV

Copper:
- 7 beads strung together on fibre string. These are slightly barrel-shaped and folded with small gaps showing in the seam. Diameters

Iron
- 1 corroded rod 83mm long and c.6mm in diameter. Trench IV

Stone
- 1 washing stone, unifacial, on irregular subtriangular piece of argillite, 85 x 80 x 24mm. Trench III.
- 1 smooth hammer stone, irregular ovoid dolerite pebble, 70 x 67 x 58mm, weight 362gm, light pitting on most of surface except broad end. Trench I.
- 1 flat trapezoidal rubbing stone, sandstone, smooth on both faces, 112 x 100 x 32mm. Trench I.
- 1 lump of magnetite, 50 x 47 x 45mm, weight 237gm

Teeth (Trench IV)
- 2 upper molars, cattle
- 1 broken tooth, small/ medium bovid.

Discussion
The excavation confirms that this hollow — and by inference the others of this type — had indeed been

stone-lined pit-structure. It is directly comparable to Nyangui G7/1 described above, except that the latter lacked continuous paving in the floor of the pit and had a steeper stepped entrance passage constrained by the configuration of bedrock. The quality of the stone revetment is similar. In neither case did the entrance passage appear to have been roofed. This observation may indicate that the earlier pit-structures in general lacked the tunnel so typical of almost all well preserved pits; and it would moreover rule out the presence house with a floor slot over the tunnel. An important difference is the rarity of copper and glass beads at Matinha compared with their relative profusion at G7/1, although the few found are consistent in type. Careful surface search of exposures and mole-hills around this and other hollows at Matinha revealed no beads. This may indicate wealth differences between the inhabitants of the two sites or perhaps some chronological variation in bead availability if the two are not exactly contemporaneous.

The question of the relative dating of ruined and well preserved pit-structures – whether they represent two distinct phases or continuous occupation – is not answerable with certainty without more extensive excavations. There does not appear to be much variation in the state of preservation of the well preserved pit-structures, though detailed assessment is difficult under the thick and often thorny vegetation cover. A few of the ruined pits are more clearly defined with some visible stonework and could be intermediate in date, but most are smoothly contoured and there must be a considerable time lag to account for this, even if robbing by later inhabitants hastened destruction. Thus two phases separated by a significant interval may be suggested, which is consistent with the clearer evidence from Block G (Chapter 5). The available dating evidence for the complex in general would put the ruined pits in the 16th or 17th century and the later pit-structures in the 18th or 19th.

It is not clear why the later inhabitants chose to live at 2000m at Matinha but only below 1870m in Block G. Matinha does not appear to be more sheltered than the upper areas of Block G. One could suggest that the inhabitants of Block G wanted to be closer to their terraces, or wanted water to irrigate their gardens which was not available higher up – although there are few radial walls and no basins below pits at Matinha to suggest gardens here.

NYANGUI G1/21 PIT-STRUCTURE

Pit-structure 21 is one of the largest and highest of Group 1 of the Nyangui Block G survey described in Chapter 5. It is situated at grid reference VR 786173 at an altitude of 1830m and is designated 1732DD54 (fig. 42, no.6). It lies on a relatively level shoulder of a broad spur, about 60m from the foot of a steep rocky slope formed by the band of sandstone and argillite, and the slope drops again quite steeply about 25 metres below the platform. About 30m to the north-west is a higher rocky knoll with a small walled structure on the crest. Pit 20 is at about the same level 120m to the north-west beyond the knoll and Pit 24 is 80m to the NNE at a lower level. Vegetation in the general area is grass and small shrubs, with dense thicket in and around the pit-structures.

There is a recent water furrow, used in the 1980s by "squatters" who occupied the more level area below Group 1, which runs from a permanent stream some 500m to the south-south-west and probably follows an old alignment. The recent furrow passes well south of G1/21, but there are traces of an old line crossing the head of a gully to the north, whence it could have been led to the site, although it cannot now be followed that far.

The platform of G1/21 (fig. 69) is somewhat irregular in outline, a maximum of 25m in east-west and north-south diameters. A radial wall abuts the southern side and runs south for about 25m, then turns to the west for another 25m, enclosing a level area. Three metres beyond the corner of the wall is Pit 22, c.6.50m in diameter with a relatively small platform; the mouth of its tunnel opens from within the radial wall, suggesting that it is ancillary to Pit 21.

Both pit and tunnel are well preserved. The pit is sub-oval, 8.60 by 7.30m in diameter, 2.25m deep at upper and lower sides, the sloping floor having a fall of one metre from west to east. There is a sump at the mouth of the drain on the lower east side. The walls are generally vertical and flush-faced in spite of being built of very irregularly shaped stones; there is a fair amount of wedging between the stones. The coping stones are more regular, large and mostly horizontal, the largest measuring 137cm long, 53cm wide and 40cm high. Rock material is sandstone. The tunnel from the upper west side is just over 8m long and curves to the right from the pit. There is the usual slot in the roof 3m from the pit and the outer end opens into a sunken revetted passage outside the platform at its upper edge. The tunnel is well built, nicely walled, roofed and paved (Plate 26), and generally clear of debris. The outer passage however was partially filled with large stones lying at haphazard angles; this could have been a deliberate blocking, although a gap was left through which it was possible to pass.

The irregular outline of the platform suggests a process of accretion and expansion, and two lobes at a lower level on the eastern side were shown to abut the main platform. Over the tunnel is a walled house-bay 5m in diameter, and south-east of this is a smaller bay 3m wide at a higher level, with a lower bay 5 by 4m to the east. These three bays open on to the edge of the pit. East of this again is a another small bay in which is a low mound of stones, and from here a walkway one metre wide exits to the north-east around the pit, walled on its eastern side. On the other side of this wall is a less well defined enclosure 5 by 3.60m. On the northern side of the pit are various walls but no clearly defined bays, but there are the remains of a raised platform 2.40m in diameter on a revetted plinth, with an entrance behind to the north-west leading down off the platform. To the north-west of the main platform is a double enclosure with entrances to north-west and south. Access to the whole complex appears to have been from the north, through the house-bay over the tunnel, with a second entrance north-west of the raised platform as already mentioned.

Below the main platform the drain from the pit debouches into a basin 4 by 4.50m in diameter, dammed by a low wall, as described below (Trench I).

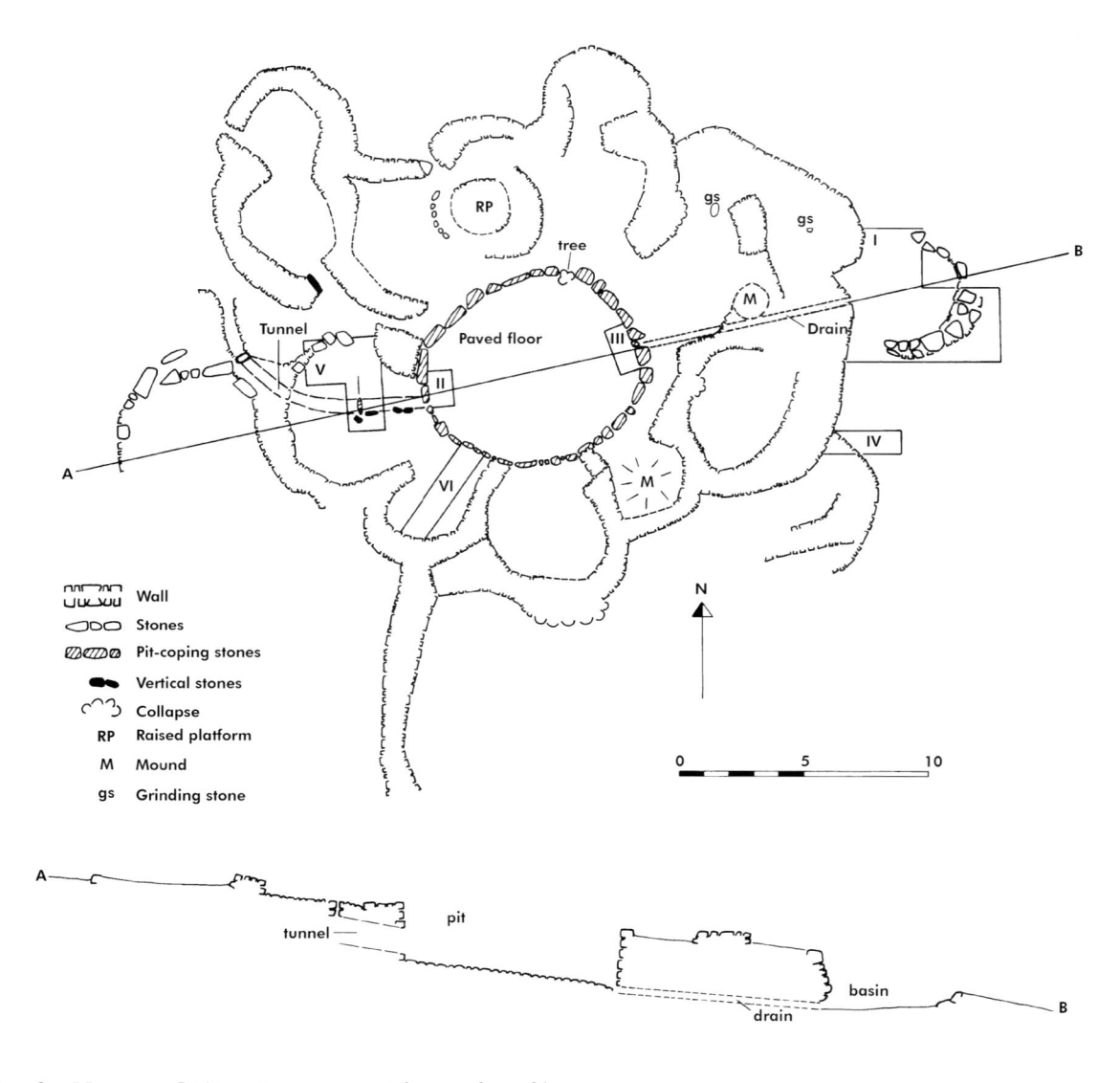

Fig. 69. Nyangui G1/21 pit-structure. Plan and profile

South-west of the platform is the area enclosed by the radial wall. Augering here showed 30 to 40cm of fine brown sandy clay-loam over redder clay-loam which becomes redder and more clayey with depth. The total depth to decomposed dolerite bedrock is 65 to 80cm near the wall, but further back is over 1.20m, the length of the auger. These deposits wedge out towards the north-west to only 20cm at 13m from the wall. The upper brown clay-loam represents silting behind the wall since abandonment, supported by the higher free Fe in the basal soil samples, the opposite of what would be expected from *in situ* soil formation. Otherwise these are typical leached plateau soils (Appendix A). This area is conjectured to have been a homestead garden, probably manured from the pit and basin below, and watered from the probable furrow.

Excavations

Five trenches were excavated, Trench I in the basin, II and III at the upper and lower sides of the pit, IV below the platform on the south-eastern side, V in the house-bay over the tunnel, and VI in the small raised bay.

Trench I (fig. 70) was 6 by 3m east/west with an extension 3 by 2.50m to the north. Most of the basin was excavated with the exception of the north-east corner. The excavation shows that, prior to the construction of the platform, a ditch one metre deep, around 60cm wide at the base with sloping sides, was dug into the natural soil which consisted of 50 to 60cm of red-brown clay-loam over red clay-loam with gravelly lumps of decomposed dolerite. The stone-lined drain from the pit was laid in this ditch, its base unpaved, and the platform wall built over it, the base of the wall rising over the sloping sides of the ditch (Plate 27). The mouth of the drain is 30cm high and 25cm wide. The wall above the drain is 2.30m high above the base and has bulged dangerously outwards. Fallen stones within the ditch fill show that it was originally higher. The outer lower lobe of wall north of the ditch abuts the main wall and must be of later construction.

The basin broadens away from the platform wall to a maximum width of 4m at a distance of 3m from it. The basin has also been dug through the red-brown clay-loam into the gravelly layer and the base rises slightly to the wall at the lower end, the centre having a floor of small stones. The outer wall forms an arc starting 1.50/2m from the platform wall and extending 4.50m from it. It is roughly built with up to four courses of irregular stones, the top 80cm and 60cm above the base at the sides and end respectively. The drain is 9m long through the platform and has a fall of 68cm. The top of the lower end of the basin wall is 6cm above the level of the base of the inner end of the drain, so that if the basin were full, water would back up through the drain to the pit sump.

Deposits in the basin (fig. 70) showed a wedge of red-brown clay-loam (5) up to 40cm deep against the platform wall, overlain by grey-brown loam (2) with lenses of red clay-loam (3). The outer side of the basin has similar grey-brown loam banked against the wall, while the central to eastern area has grey-brown silts (4) resting on the base. There is around 5cm of humic topsoil (1) over all. There were fallen stones and a fair number of potsherds in the narrower western end and one glass bead was recovered from the southern side of the basin.

Trench IV was 3 by 1m below the main platform wall, taking in the end of a lower platform wall abutting it. This was dug in the expectation of finding midden material. The deposits consisted of up to 15cm of grey-brown topsoil and 30cm of reddish brown clay-loam with small stones, banked

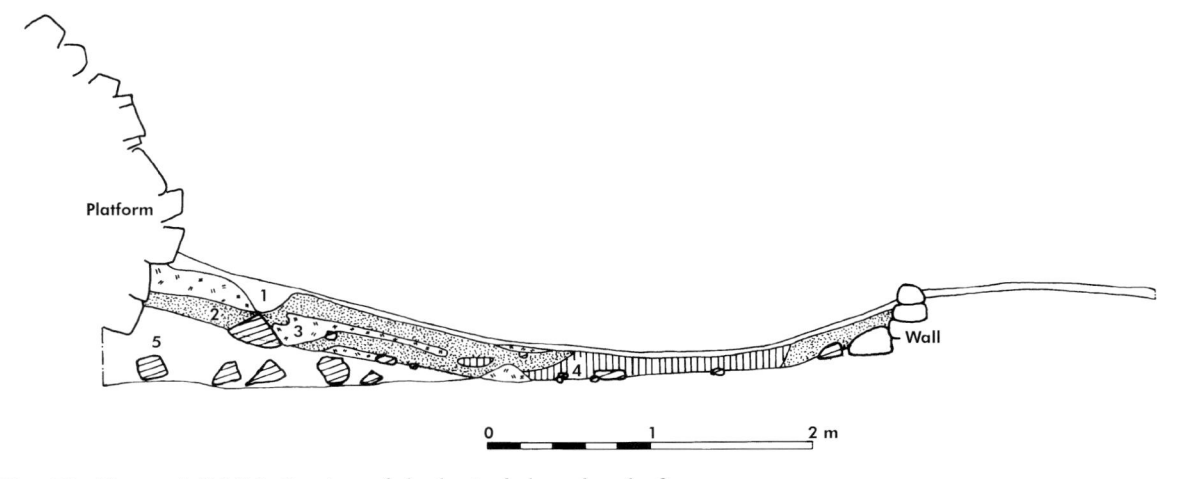

Fig. 70. Nyangui G1/21. Section of the basin below the platform

against the lower wall and main platform wall. This overlies the natural red-brown clay-loam. The reddish brown clay-loam contains quite numerous sherds but no beads or charcoal, and the base, with some sherds, continues beneath the stones of the lobe of the lower platform. There was a large section of a pot broken in situ near the base of this wall. The siting of the trench did not give sufficient scope to trace the base of the main wall, but it is assumed to have been built on the natural soil, the lower wall having been built after the deposition of at least 7cm of midden material. The height of the lower wall was 62cm and that of the main platform wall was 165cm above the north-west corner of the trench.

Trench III, 2 x 1m, was dug at the lower side of the pit across the probable position of the drain entrance. Deposits consisted of around 10cm of leafmould with matted roots, with some red clay-loam beneath this in the centre to east side. These rest directly on the paving stones of the pit floor, which slope down into a sump 90cm wide and 33cm deep at the mouth of the drain. The latter is 15cm high and 22cm wide, possibly narrowed slightly by a large root growing into the wall. The mouth of the drain was covered by a loose vertical, rather irregular slab 36 by 29cm in size.

Trench II was 1.50 by 1m across the mouth of the tunnel (plate 26) and again showed 10cm of leafmould and roots, over brown loam with roots resting on the neat floor paving. The brown loam was 20cm deep at the mouth of the tunnel, extending into it, and thinned to only 6cm at the lower side of the trench; it represents material washing or blowing through the tunnel. There is a low step, 8 to 10cm high, 15cm inside the tunnel mouth. The mouth is 1.20m high, 60cm wide at the top and 55cm at the middle and bottom. The pit wall rises 98cm above the top of the tunnel.

Probing shows that the general depth of leafmould over the paving of the pit is around 12cm or less. The paving is neatly laid without gaps between the stones, and individual slabs may measure up to at least 60cm in length. The sides of the pit were examined for traces of wear which could have resulted from its presumed use for housing cattle, in the hope of gaining some indication of the size of such cattle. Possible wear was identified on a very few wall stones at heights of 50 to 68cm above the floor; on the south side of the tunnel entrance at 70 to 76cm; and on the north side of it at 45 to 65cm and 98 to 102cm. These signs of wear are not easily identified and are frequently doubtful; they show only on stones which were weathered before inclusion in the wall. The sandstone is very hard and no suggestion of wear was detected on fresh breaks, even where these project in tempting positions for scratching against. Evidence for rubbing is thus unconvincing.

Trench V. This was designed to investigate the house-bay over the tunnel; it measured 4 by 1.50m initially, extended by 2 by 1.50m to the north-west. Most of the area shows 15 to 20cm of leaf mould and roots over rather rough stone paving. At the south end a line of vertical stones coincides with the line of the south side of the tunnel beneath, and the slot in the roof of the tunnel, measuring 60 by around 20cm and largely blocked by stones, adjoins this line. South of this line, much of the area is occupied and disturbed by the broad bases of flourishing bushes and small trees, but there are traces of a compact dark red rather gravelly surface representing a clay floor about 10 cm above the level of the slab floor to the north.

At the north end of the trench were fallen slabs of the bay wall, overlying red-brown clay-loam. Three white glass beads were found here. A line of lower vertical stones covered by the fallen slabs converges with a more substantial wall to the east; this wall is 70cm high, 2m long and up to 2m wide, the east end abutting the coping stones of the pit edge. The line of lower stones should mark the house wall and a patch of red clay just within them could be the remains of a fallen *dhaka* wall. A worn flat slab near the higher wall represents a door step.

This house is a typical divided dwelling, with a low cross-wall separating the clay-floored living area in the south half from the paved northern half which was probably for small stock. Better preserved examples were excavated at Fishpit in the National Park and MSE17 at Ziwa ruins (see below).

Trench VI was 4.50 by 1m, across the small raised bay adjoining the tunnel bay to the south-east, to the edge of the pit. Leafmould with roots overlay a slightly crumbly red-brown clay-loam, fairly clean to the south-west but looser and dirtier towards the pit. Beneath this for 1.50m from the edge of the pit is an unevenly paved surface, and this ends at a raised edge of stones about 20cm high which continues the curvature of the north-west end of the bay wall. Above this edge is a hard floor of red-brown clay, the eroded edge of which shows stone slabs with cavities beneath; the whole floor appears to be hollow underneath with a clearance of around 20cm. Two glass beads were found just above the floor.

At the south-west end of the trench there is a clear edge to the floor 17 to 24cm from the base of the bay wall, and between this and the wall are lumps of hard clay similar to the floor material but rising above the floor in places. This represents the remains of a *dhaka* wall, built against the stone wall, whose collapse produced the crumbly clay-loam overburden.

Similar small raised bays at the same relative position were noted in a number of other pit-structures in Nyangui Block G. A comparable raised enclosure, 3.20m in diameter in the same position relative to the pit and tunnel, was excavated by Storry (1974) in a pit-structure on the side of the Pungwe Gorge in the National Park. This had a *dhaka* floor up to 10cm thick resting on a platform of larger stones, but he did not excavate beneath to test if it was hollow. Such structures may be thus more common than has been recognised. It may be conjectured that they represent storage huts somewhat similar to the raised platforms. The purpose of the hollow floor is unclear since there would have been no passage of air from outside, nor would it have isolated the hut from termites or other pests. One informant linked it to an old practice of hiding an emergency reserve of food beneath the floor in case of enemy attack which destroyed the homestead or rifled its contents.

Phosphate samples
These were taken from different locations in an attempt to document the possible presence of dung and the use of manure in the garden. They gave the following results:

Trench I:
- old soil beneath platform wall, 5000 ppm
- centre of basin, 8500
- base of ditch in front of drain, 9000

Trench III:
- pit, between paving stones above drain, 12000

Trench II:
- pit, between paving in front of tunnel, 8500

Trench V:
- tunnel bay, between paving stones, 8000
- SE corner of garden, 5 samples at various depths from 10 to 80cm below surface, 291 to 789
- 50m west of pit-structure on slope, 789

The garden samples were obtained by augering. Very low values come from the accumulation of slope wash behind the radial wall, and slightly higher ones from the basal samples from the original soil, the same as the reference sample from the slope above. There seems to be little here to confirm manuring of the garden. The other samples show very much higher values and would be consistent with the keeping of livestock both in the pit and in the paved side of the divided house, and also with the flushing of slurry into the basin.

Finds

Pottery (fig. 71)
1437 sherds were recovered of which 89 are rims, 66 necks, 15 decorated body sherds and 1267 plain body sherds. The majority came from trenches I and IV, that

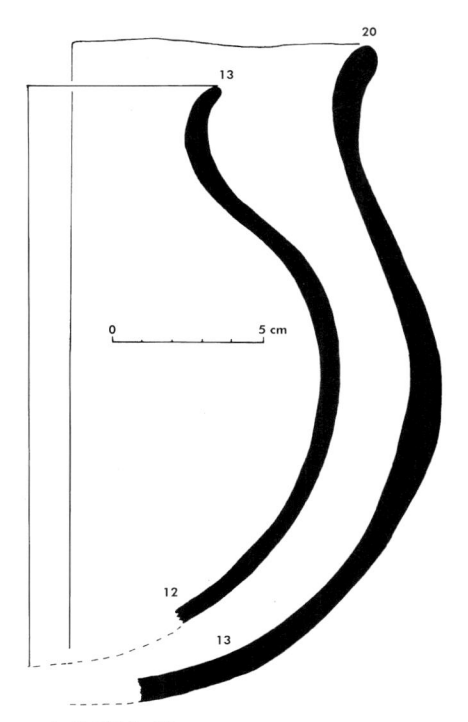

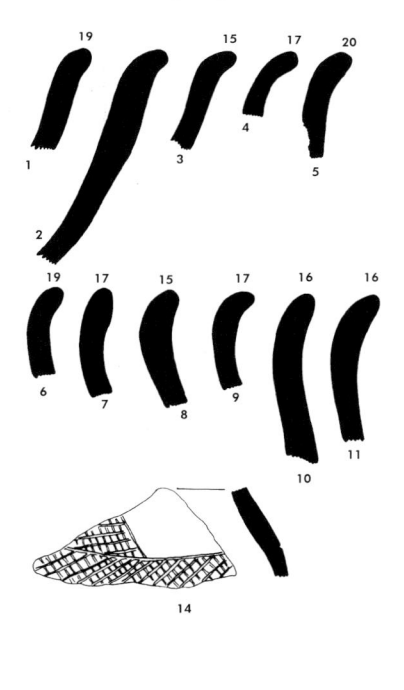

Fig. 71. Nyangui G1/21. Pottery

is the basin below the drain and outside the lower edge of the platform. Colour is grey or grey-brown, with a few brown examples. 200 have traces of soot on the outside and 24 have carbonised residues inside. Temper inclusions are quartz, often with feldspar, with maximum grain size mostly 2mm and a few of 3 or 4mm; density is medium or heavy in equal proportions.

Diagnostic sherds comprise six open bowls with out-turned rims (nos 1-5), two necked bowls, 11 wide-mouthed necked pots (6-11, 13) and one narrow-mouthed necked pot (12). Rims are round with a few also tapered. Rather more than half have smooth finish; open bowls are mostly rough and one necked bowl is graphite-burnished inside and out. One neck has plain burnish (and soot). Rim diameters are 15-20cm for four open bowls, 15-20cm for nine wide-mouthed pots, and 13cm for the narrow-mouthed pot.

Apart from the graphited necked bowl, there are three sherds with graphite inside and out, five with graphite outside and one with graphite inside. The only other decorated sherds are three with incised cross-hatching probably from the same vessel (14) in a band with panel above on the shoulder.

Thickness ranges from 3 to 15mm with a mean of 7.80 ±1.49

Beads
Only six glass beads were found, all of them drawn cylinders. Two of these are Indian red over a pale green translucent core. These are 4mm in diameter and 3 and 4mm in length. The other four are opaque white, three of them 4.5mm in diameter and 4mm long and the fourth 5mm by 3mm. The shorter Indian red and three of the whites have rounded edges.

The only other finds were two quartz crystals in trenches I and V and a tooth fragment from V.

Discussion
Insufficient well stratified charcoal was found for dating. The beads however indicate a later date than that for the ruined pit-structure G7/1, since neither of the types found here occurs in the much larger sample from that site. Both types have been found in stone enclosures at Ziwa ruins, in our own excavations and those of Summers (1958). Radiocarbon dates from three of those enclosures fall around the 18th or early 19th centuries. A similar date is feasible here though bead evidence, especially with such a small sample, is hardly conclusive.

This site is typical of the better preserved pit-structures of the eastern side of the northern highlands, many of which also have radial walls. Such radial walls seem to be less common further south and west, though Finch (1949:51) in the area east of Troutbeck, notes "a number of small walled enclosures or gardens" below a pit-structure and fed by a furrow from the drain of another pit above. She also describes stone-faced "dams" below several pits and linked to their drains, which sound similar to the basin of G1/21 but rather larger (Finch 1949:54, figs III and V). Basins to catch the effluent from pits imply a water supply, and Finch's pit-structures were also served by furrows.

"FISHPIT" PIT-STRUCTURE

The pit-structure here described is located in Nyanga National Park at grid reference VQ 747785 at an altitude of 1860m, c.700m north of the road to Mare Dam and c.400m north-east of the Fisheries Staff Township, on the west side of a valley descending from the ridge on which stands Nyangwe Fort (fig. 42, no.7). It is labelled "Fishpit" for convenience and is designated 1832BD78. It is the eastern one of a pair of such structures on the southern side of a reentrant valley below the Fisheries Township, and there is a third example 100m to the south-east on a shoulder of the main valley immediately above the old water furrow NP1 (see Chapter 4). These pit-structures were first observed in the course of recording the furrow whose source is some 300m to the south-east and which passes 25m below Fishpit. The structure was selected for excavation due to the presence of two surviving *dhaka* walls which appeared to be cross-walls dividing houses. These suggested good preservation of house structures and a relatively recent date, offering the possibility of dating a late phase of the Nyanga terrace complex.

This is a relatively small pit-structure (fig. 72), the pit itself being slightly oval with diameters of just over and just under five metres. The platform is approximately 22m across and 18m from the upper wall to the top of a series of three stepped tiers supporting the lower side. The upper wall is low, only a single course on the uphill side, but is set above the general level of the platform. The lower side has a combined height of 1.80m. There are two clear house-bays, A and B, with *dhaka* cross-walls, A over the tunnel and B to the right of the pit viewed from above. A third probable house-bay is at a lower level on the lower left side of the pit and 2.60m from it. Passageways lead from outside the platform through the low stone walls, one from the east to House B, and one from the west dividing so that one branch leads to House A and the other to the pit surround. No other structures are currently discernible on the platform, though there is ample space.

The tunnel entrance is outside the platform to the south-west and the tunnel itself curves down to the left under House A to reach the pit. There is a slot into the tunnel from the paved half of House A, 3.5m from the edge of the pit. A section of the tunnel roof one metre long has collapsed or been destroyed, taking with it part of the paved floor of House A. This collapse partly blocks the tunnel, while the lower end is silted to a depth of 40cm, graded to deposits in the pit. The pit end of the tunnel is 136cm high, 44cm wide at the bottom and 60cm wide at the top. The drain from the pit is not visible. There is no basin below to impound effluent from the drain as occurs in other pit-structures further north.

A section of the pit wall 1.20m long has collapsed or been destroyed on the south-western side, but the remainder is solidly built and in good condition. Much of the top course of coping stones has fallen or been pushed into the pit. These stones are up to 1.20m long and 15 to 25cm thick and it is hard to see how they could have fallen by any natural force when the wall beneath is still intact. The two coping stones which originally crowned the broken section are still above the pit but have been swivelled outwards, so that it appears as if the break and the casting down of the coping stones was deliberate, either at the time of abandonment or at some time subsequently. Perhaps relevant to this is a comment by Stead (1949:81):

> "Several natives of the Inyanga District have said that their fathers kept their cattle in the 'pits'. When the tunnel-like entrance is removed they make excellent cattle kraals, the exit being closed by means of poles in the gap in the wall."

Probably the hole in the roof of the tunnel represents an abortive attempt to open an entrance, abandoned in favour of breaking the pit wall, through which access can be gained relatively easily across the collapsed material. No other traces of recent occupation have been observed, but the whole area is densely covered with high grass which makes observation impossible. The third pit immediately above the furrow does have evidence of secondary use — two small raised platforms, two almost complete pots and some sherds.

Search was made around the outside of the platform for any traces of a rubbish midden but none was found. A test pit was also dug above the upper wall but with negative results.

The neighbouring furrow NP1 is described in

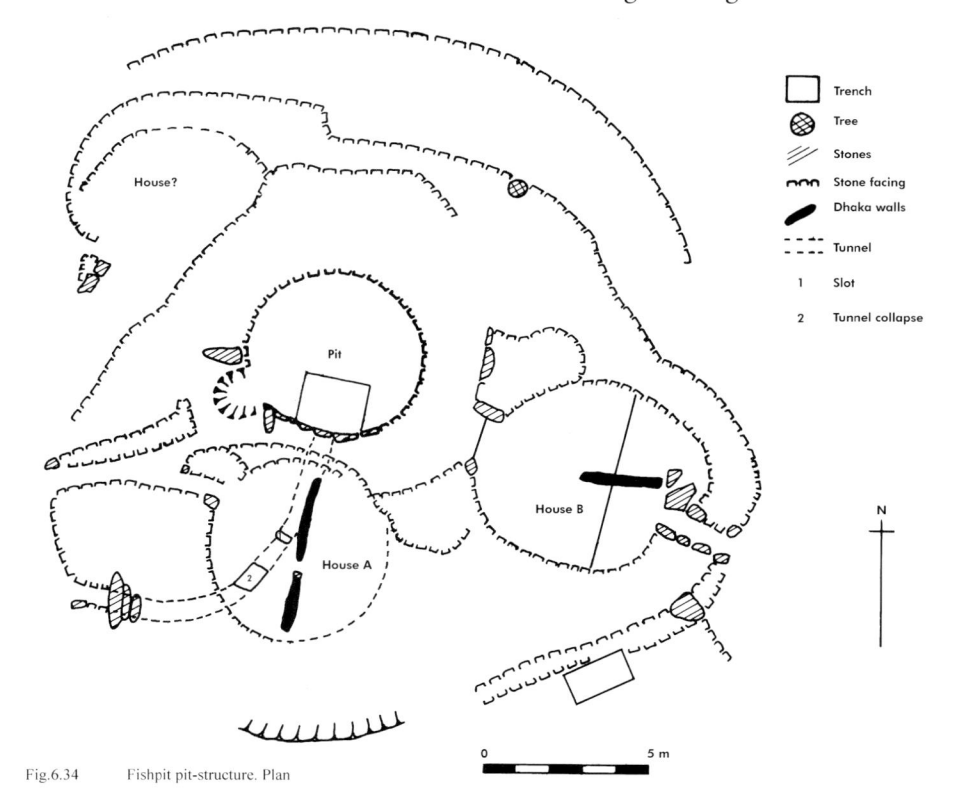

Fig. 72. Fishpit pit-structure. Plan

Chapter 4. The pit is 25m from the nearest point of the furrow, the base of the platform being about 4m above it. It would have been possible to bring water to the lower base of the platform from a point 75m further up the furrow, but not to the level of the platform itself. However no clear trace of any such branch furrow was detectable. There is thus no positive association of the furrow with the pit-structure.

Excavations

House A (fig. 73)

House A is five metres in diameter, divided across the centre by a *dhaka* wall around 35cm high running approximately north/south. This wall was probably never much higher; although there is no smooth top, there are no substantial deposits of broken *dhaka* in the immediate vicinity. It is around 30cm wide at the base and 20cm at the top. There is a gap 55cm wide in the middle; the ends of this gap do not show any smooth surface, but it must have been a doorway as the two halves of the wall are not aligned. A flat stone forms a step on the south side of the gap, with a vertical dolerite slab closing the space to the north wall, indicating a door width of just over 30cm.

The western half of the house is relatively neatly paved with irregular granite slabs which have broken away in part of the southern section around the tunnel collapse. The surviving floor level rises towards the upper southern wall. Some of the floor slabs pass beneath the base of the *dhaka* wall. The paving was covered by up to 10cm of grey-brown sandy loam soil with numerous grass roots. Just north-west of the doorway is the slot into the tunnel, showing three courses of stone slabs and measuring 55 by 8-14cm. The tunnel below this point is 1.10m high with little silting.

The edge of the paved floor is marked in places by carbonised remains of small posts, and by occasional long stones laid inside and parallel to the

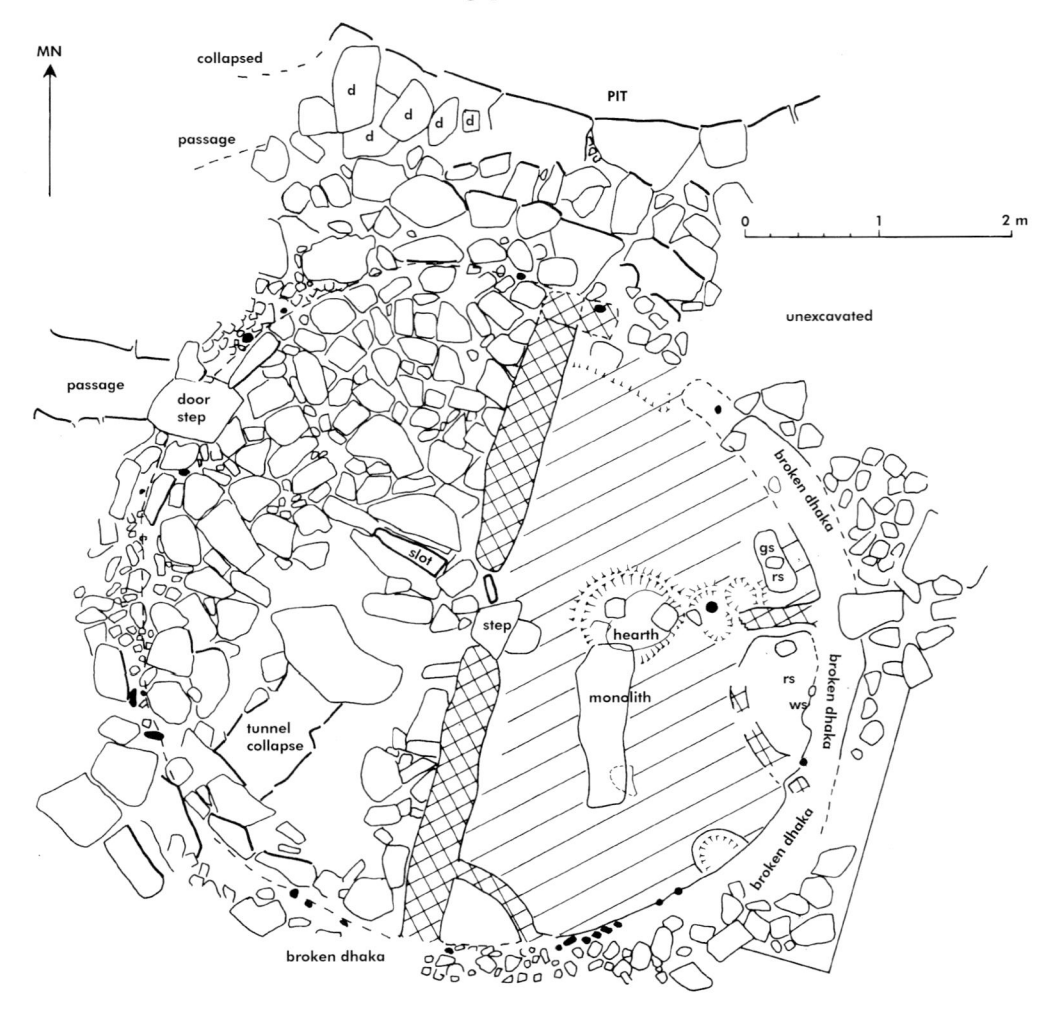

Fig. 73. Fishpit. Plan of House A. gs = grinding stone; rs = rubbing stone; ws = washing stone; d = displaced stone

wall line and standing proud of the stone paving. Occasional pieces of baked *dhaka* with pole impressions suggest that the outer house wall was formed by close set wooden poles with some internal plastering; behind this there appears to have been a packing of smallish stones, backed by larger stones to a height of perhaps 50cm, though the stone wall is not well preserved. The passageway from outside the platform leads into the north-west side of this paved room, the doorway being 40cm wide, floored by a broad stone slab. There was a relatively dense concentration of potsherds near the wall east of the doorway.

The eastern half of the house has a well preserved *dhaka* floor, slightly above the level of the paved western half. Over this was around 10cm of dark grey sandy loam with some small stones and *dhaka* fragments, with grey-brown sandy loam topsoil with grass roots above. The floor slopes down slightly from south to north. Adjoining the stone step of the central doorway is a semi-circular scar in the *dhaka* floor with a raised lip, probably the remains of a small *dhaka* step, since anything higher would have blocked the entrance. Just north of centre is a hollow with a slightly raised lip around its lower edge and two stones in the interior, the western one of which at least is set within the sloping *dhaka* surface. This *dhaka* surface does not continue across the middle of the hollow where there was a fill of orange-brown sandy loam resting on flat stones at a depth of c.18cm below the rim. This fill could represent burnt material but there is no ash and few charcoal fragments. This hollow is best interpreted as a hearth with one hearth stone missing, but could conceivably be the setting for a large granite monolith 1.25m long whose northern end overlaps the hollow. This however is more likely to be one of the missing capstones from the break in the tunnel, although it is hard to see why it should have been lifted carefully over the cross-wall and deposited here.

East of the hearth are a couple of minor depressions in the floor, one of which surrounds the carbonised base of a post 8cm in diameter. East of this again is the end of a low short radial *dhaka* wall. In the angle between the north side of this and the line of the outer wall is a grinding stone, 48 by 20cm, set in a raised *dhaka* surround, with a small raised *dhaka* basin between it and the end of the radial wall. Resting on the grinding stone were a rubbing stone and a piece of carbonised wooden shaft 12cm long. Another rubbing stone lay 20cm to the north-west, and another on the other side of the radial wall where there were also a number of potsherds. The grinding surfaces of these rubbers and of the grinding stone itself were deliberately pitted. To the south of the radial wall the plastered *dhaka* floor is missing and there are parts of a raised *dhaka* kerb indicating some kind of basin about one metre long and 50cm wide. Further to the south a smaller basin, 40cm long and 28cm wide, abuts the line of the outer wall. In the angle of the outer wall and cross-wall at the southern end is an arc of *dhaka* wall, 12cm thick and 20cm high, enclosing a quadrant-shaped bin.

At the northern side adjacent to the cross-wall, the *dhaka* floor dips to a doorway to the pit surround, abutted on the western side by the base of a possible buttress or jamb c.30cm wide with a carbonised post within it. A similar scar of rough *dhaka* on the east side of the doorway, also with a carbonised post, would give a door width of 60cm.

The line of the outer wall is again marked by occasional carbonised poles just outside the edge of the floor, best preserved as a close-set line towards the southern end. Only in a few places is there any *dhaka in situ* but there is a consistent band of small broken *dhaka* pieces and stones which resemble more a packing of reused material than the remains of a solid wall.

To the south of the house the ground rises, with roughly piled smallish stones behind the wall line. To the north-east is an area of rather poorly preserved stone walling between Houses A and B. To the east, between these, the ground is flat with no defining wall; excavation here showed an area of close-set rounded stones in a grey sandy loam matrix.

House B (fig. 74)
Some two-thirds of this house were excavated, the eastern side being left due to lack of time.

The bay is divided from House A by the area of raised walling to the west. To the north-west is another area of walling, east of which is a section of low stone revetment for the house platform. To the east is again a stone wall, pierced by a passage 40 to 50cm wide, leading east-south-east to the outside of the platform. To the south the ground rises and is faced by an irregular series of large stones behind the line of the house wall.

The floor was again covered by 10 to 15cm of grey-brown sandy loam topsoil with grass roots.

The diameter of the house is 5m and the standing *dhaka* cross-wall, 2.50m long, extends halfway across from the east, up to 80cm high on the south side and 65cm on the north side. There is no sign of any *dhaka* wall to the west, but the alignment is continued by a line of irregularly laid stones which complete the partition of the house. The inner end of the *dhaka* wall has a smooth rounded face, contiguous to which is a flat stone forming a step in an entrance through the partition.

The southern half of the house is largely paved with stones except for a *dhaka* feature at the southern edge. This is subtriangular in shape, 80cm across, and rises slightly from floor level to a shallow hollow in the top, with a raised rectangular stone behind against the wall. This feature could have been a small hearth or a potstand.

On this side the *dhaka* cross-wall has a foundation of flat stones raised about 8cm above the level of the paved floor. The bases of the irregular stones of the western partition continue below floor level. The line of the outer wall in both halves of the house is again marked by occasional carbonised pole bases and is similar in construction to House A — probably a line of close-set poles plastered on the

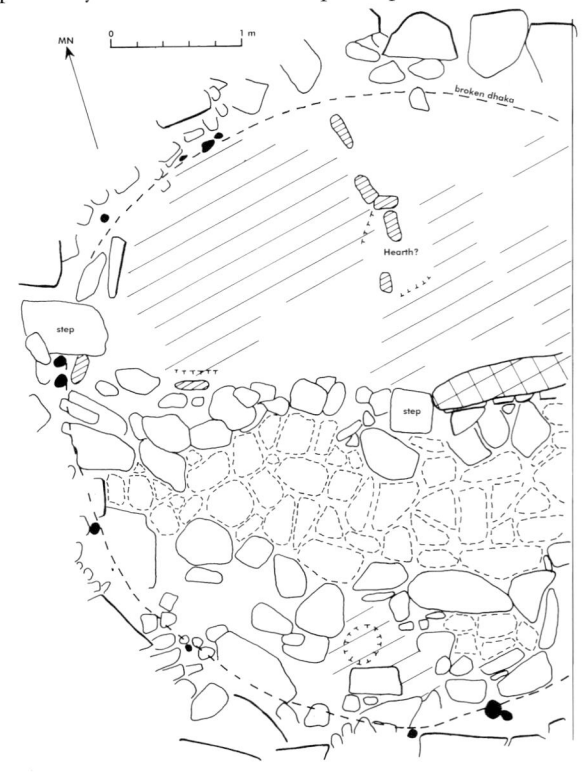

Fig. 74. Fishpit. Plan of House B

inside. The eastern passage gives access to this paved room from outside the platform, as in the case of House A.

The northern half of the house has a *dhaka* floor less well preserved than in House A, around 10cm higher than the stone paving of the southern half. One section of this floor extends to the rough stone partition, the edge dipping slightly towards it. There is a poorly preserved hollow about 70 by 50cm in size, 80cm from the doorway of the cross-wall; this has two vertical stones within it and is likely to have been a hearth. A discontinuous line of vertical slabs extends from here to the outer wall. At the western side a doorway gives access to the pit surround, with a broad stone slab 40cm wide as a threshold. Carbonised post bases to the south of this and a large stone to the north show that the doorway was not much wider than this. No grinding stone was found in the excavated part of this house.

The pit

A trench 2m by 1.50m was excavated across the mouth of the tunnel. This showed the following stratigraphy:

1. Soft dark grey sandy humus topsoil
2. Brown sandy loam with some smallish stones at the west side, sloping down to the south-east: platform fill derived from the broken pit side.
3. Lens of loose sand in the north-east corner 10 to 15cm below the surface, similar to the surface deposit near the lower end of the tunnel. Represents a storm event of material washed through the tunnel.
4. Grey-brown sandy loam to bedrock at 42cm below the surface in the south-east corner.
5. Grey-brown to brown sandy loam with charcoal fragments and lumps of *dhaka*, mainly around the mouth of the tunnel but extending outwards below 4 on bedrock.

The base of the pit is formed by softish granite bedrock which slopes down for about 60cm from the mouth of the tunnel and then levels out. Several large coping stone slabs from the rim of the pit were found within and covered by layers 1 and 2. Two of these were 85 and 90cm long and 15 and 20cm thick. The height of the tunnel mouth is 1.36m from bedrock, with 50cm of walling above, which with the thickness of the fallen coping gives an original pit depth of two metres at this point. The lower edge of the pit is 1.40m high above an unknown depth of fill.

A phosphate sample from cracks in the bedrock of the pit floor gave 618 ppm, a relatively low value but considerably higher than the 220 to 250 ppm for samples from 40m below the pit-structure (and below the furrow). However a sample from 15m above the pit-structure gave 770 ppm.

Dating

A charcoal sample from the door post of House B was dated to 330 ±20 BP, cal.AD 1638(1645)1651 (Pta-7402). As this seemed improbably early in view of the preservation of the *dhaka* walls, a second sample from the post at the end of the radial wall in House A was submitted for dating. This gave a date of 95 ±15 BP, with a "most probable" calibrated date of around AD 1900 (Pta-7599). This is consistent with two similarly recent dates from pit-structures with similar *dhaka* walls at Glenhead near Troutbeck obtained by Huffman (Appendix F). Pit-structures in this area were clearly unoccupied in the 1890s when they were first described by European travellers, but Hall (1909:179) observed much surviving woodwork, some still with the bark, so that they could not have been long abandoned. Some date in the 19th century is thus indicated. The 17th century radiocarbon date might perhaps be explained by the use of heartwood from an old tree.

Finds

Pottery (fig. 75)

A total of 822 sherds (after some reconstruction) was recovered, the great majority from Houses A and B with a few from the pit. Of these 33 are rim sherds, 70 are necks or shoulders and 719 plain body sherds. 14% have traces of soot on the outside, sometimes thickly encrusted, and 1.1% have soot inside. Many sherds, around 30% at a rough estimate, have an eroded inside surface.

Colour varies from light brown, through grey-brown to dark grey, many examples of the last probably due to secondary reduction over the fire. Surface finish is generally fairly smooth, occasionally rougher, and at least one vessel shows horizontal smoothing strokes. There are two brown burnished sherds from a single vessel. No graphite was seen.

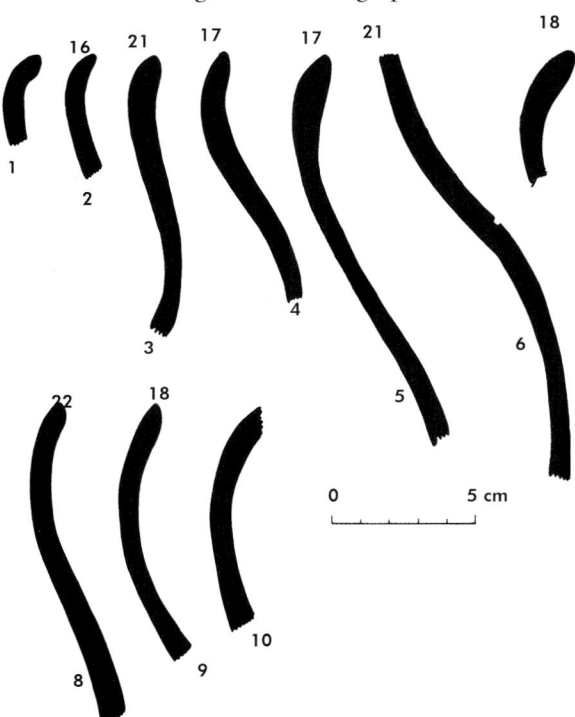

Fig. 75. Fishpit. Pottery

Temper is typically of angular quartz grains in medium to heavy concentration, with occasional pieces up to 5mm in size, and there are rare inclusions of granite fragments or iron concretions. Firing is generally good with an even grey or sometimes brown core.

Shapes are remarkably standardised, all the rim and neck sherds representing pots with out-turned rims and rounded necks. Lips are evenly rounded, sometimes tapered. Eleven diameters were measurable at 11, 13, 16, 17(x3), 18(x3), 21, 22. Body diameters were rarely measurable but vary somewhat relative to rim diameter. At least one vessel appears to be a necked bowl, whereas the majority are deeper globular pots. A few large thick body sherds indicate the presence of some larger vessels.

Only two vessels have any decoration, in both cases a single horizontal incised line on the shoulder.

Iron

A rectangular-sectioned rod with tapered ends, length 107mm, middle c.6 by 3mm, from House B

Beads

From the pit:
- 1 opaque white oblate, diameter 4mm, length 2.3mm.
- 1 dark blue oblate, diameter 3.5mm, length 2.6mm.

From House B:
- 1 opaque white cylinder, diameter 5mm, length 4mm.

Washing stone

Sub-quadrilateral piece of dolerite, thickness tapering to one side, 133 x 68 x 16mm. Crudely incised on both faces, with an apparent attempt to drill small holes through both ends, in one case from both sides. At edge of floor in House A.

Bones/teeth

Two deciduous molar teeth and a fragment of radius of cattle, 3 unidentifiable rib fragments and 9 other fragments, all from the south side of House B.

Carbonised stick

Section of carbonised wooden shaft, oval section 20 x 15mm, length 120mm. Lying on the grinding stone in House A.

Discussion

The main value of this excavation is in revealing the nature and construction details of the houses attached to a late pit-structure. The two houses show the following common features: a dividing cross-wall with a central entrance; one half paved and the other half smoothly floored with *dhaka* at a slightly higher level; a probable hearth in the middle of the floored side opposite the central entrance; access to the paved area from outside the platform, and to the floored area from the pit surround; a radial feature between the hearth and the outer wall. The *dhaka* features of House A are not present, or not preserved, in the excavated area of House B, where there is also no grinding stone (though some of these could be present in the unexcavated portion). The triangular *dhaka* feature of the paved half of House B is not seen in House A. Parallels for these divided houses are discussed in Chapter 5.

This pit-structure represents an average-sized homestead probably occupied by a single family and their livestock. The presence of two almost identical houses, each with kitchen, suggests that there were two wives, although it does not reveal if they were married to the same man. The paved areas may have accommodated their personal goats. The third possible house on the other side of the pit remains to be investigated and could be a sleeping house for other family members. Ancillary structures such as granaries may also have been present on the platform but cannot be detected without further excavation in the present condition of the site. The small family cattle would have been stalled in the pit which gave them shelter from the cold easterly winds in winter. Dung from the pit and houses would have been regularly removed with the domestic rubbish and used to fertilise a neighbouring garden and fields; some may have been dried for fuel as Summers suggests (1958:238).

The furrow passing below may well have been built by the inhabitants of the pit-structures and used for a convenient domestic supply, but mainly for irrigating fields below, where there is over a hectare of suitable land, more if the further side of the reentrant was also used.

After the site was abandoned, the houses were burnt and some *dhaka* from the house walls fell into the pit. At some subsequent time, part of the pit wall and tunnel were destroyed, perhaps for penning the larger cattle of later inhabitants. If this was the case, no sign of their homestead has been found. The furrow could equally well have belonged to these later inhabitants – or have been used by both groups.

ZIWA MSE 17 STONE ENCLOSURE

This excavation was occasioned by the need to open a homestead structure for display to visitors in the vicinity of the Ziwa Site Museum. It was a joint operation of the project and the National Museums and Monuments of Zimbabwe with the late Steve Chirawu of Mutare Museum as assistant director. The aim was to investigate the nature and construction of domestic structures, to expose samples of these for the benefit of visitors to Ziwa Ruins, and to try to recover seeds representative of the crops grown by the inhabitants. The excavation has been published by Soper and Chirawu (1996) and that report is included here in amended form.

This stone enclosure lies some 250m north-east of the Museum at grid reference VQ 618952 and is officially designated 1832BA91 (fig. 42, no.8). It is situated on ground sloping down gently to the north-west, in a slight saddle with higher ground to the east. A walled passage runs south-east/north-west immediately contiguous to the eastern side. There is terracing below to the north-west and at the same level to the south-west, though not immediately adjacent to the excavated enclosure. Thirty metres to the south-east and slightly above is a larger enclosure containing an unusually large but apparently shallow pit nine metres in diameter

The main enclosure (fig. 76) is roughly oval with internal diameters of about 20 by 11 metres, oriented NNE/SSW. The entrance is on the upper, south-eastern side and consists of a passage three metres long and 50 to 70cm wide, originally lintelled though only one lintel stone remains approximately in place; there are sockets for a drawbar towards the inner end. (Drawbars and their sockets are described in Chapter 5)

On the north-western side are three raised platforms (RP1-3), each three to four metres in diameter, with sections of walling between them forming the main enclosure wall on this side. About two metres below is a low outer wall. On the eastern side opposite the entrance is a slightly oval house floor with central division (H1); a stone wall blocks the space between it and the outside wall, flush with the north-eastern side of the entrance passage. There is a drain through the base of this blocking wall inside the lower facing stones, parallel to the edge of the house. Details of this house are given below. There are traces of a second such house at the southern end of the enclosure (H3).

At the eastern side of the enclosure is an open entrance c.1.15m wide leading to a small annex. This has a divided house floor (H2) on the south side and a poorly preserved raised platform (RP4) on the north, linked by an arc of wall to the east and joined to the main enclosure wall to form a complete sub-enclosure. Above the main enclosure to the south, and south-west of the outside of the entrance, is a similar annex, again with one divided house (H4) and a raised platform (RP5), with walls between them and connecting to the main wall; access to this annex was probably also from the main enclosure by an open entrance now collapsed.

The stone walls are in a generally poor condition, rising to a maximum height of about 1.15m around the entrance. Where collapsed stones interfered with excavation, walls were rebuilt on the original line using the adjacent stone, with the dual purpose of clearing the obstruction and restoring the appearance for the benefit of visitors. Larger stones were used for facing and smaller stones for the core, as in the intact walls. This applies to the end of the blocking wall between H1 and the entrance, the south side of the open entrance to the eastern annex and part of the end and south-eastern side of the wall north-east of RP1.

Excavation

Excavation included part of the western raised platform, RP1, the central house, H1, and a small part of the house in the eastern annex, H2.

RP1

RP1 is a rather large example of the circular raised platforms typical of Ziwa ruins and much of the rest of the Nyanga complex, being four metres in diameter. Before excavation, the upper surface consisted of light brown *dhaka* with a thin scatter of loose gravelly stones, with the edges of horizontal

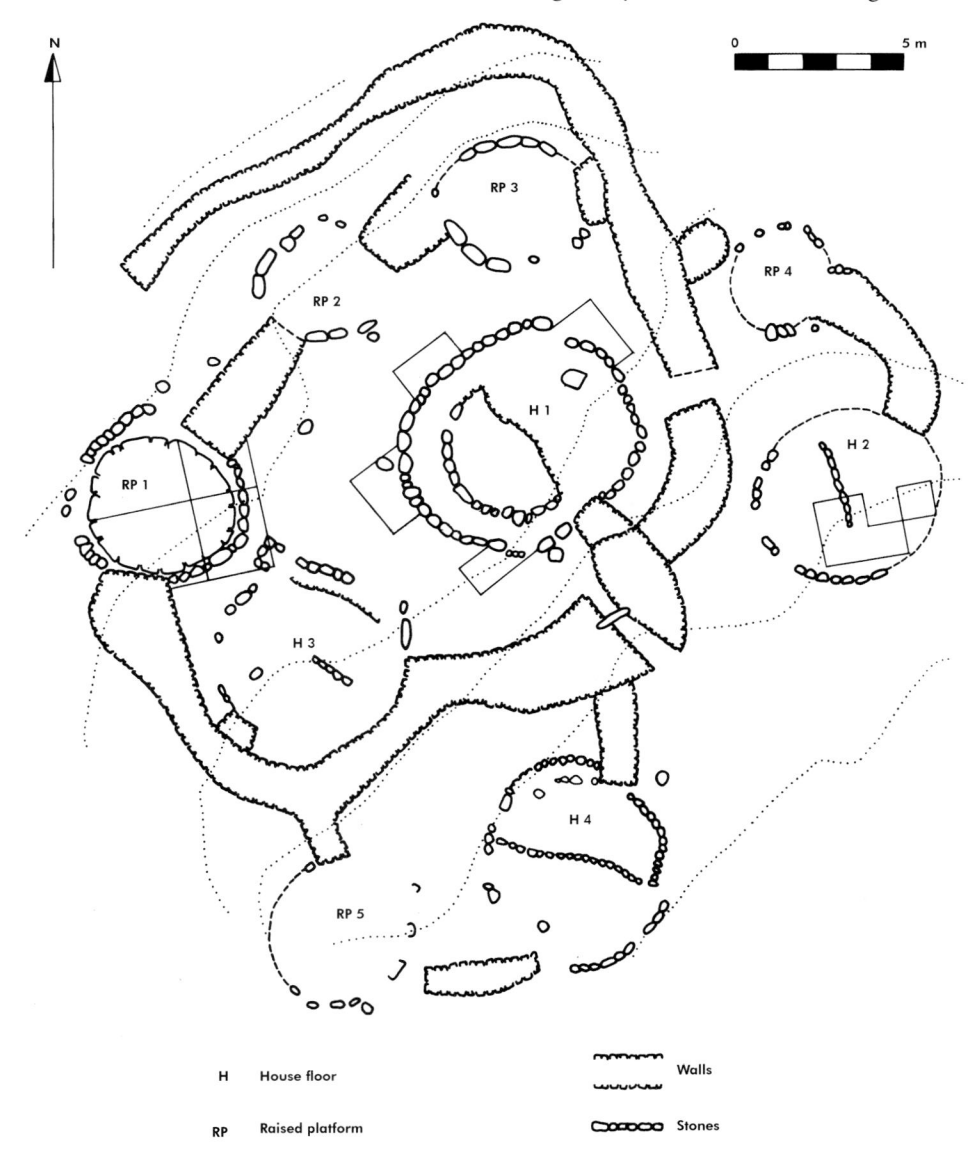

Fig. 76. Ziwa MSE17. Plan of the enclosure

stones exposed round the circumference except where occasional slabs had been displaced. The decomposed *dhaka* of the original walls and part of the floor had been redeposited round the edges so that no clear space was visible below the horizontal stones. There was a narrow gap between the edge of the platform and the ends of the adjacent walls to south and north-east, and a lower outer tier of revetment or protecting stones lines up with these wall ends.

The circumference of the platform was excavated to expose the outer ring of stones and clear the edges of the horizontal slabs. It became apparent that some of the platform slabs had slipped off their supports so that their inner edges had subsided together with the *dhaka* of the floor above. Accordingly an area c.1m wide at the eastern side was cleared of *dhaka* and the slabs relaid to demonstrate the construction for display. Where the slabs remained undisturbed, there was hollow space beneath; the thickness of the overlying *dhaka* was around 8cm. No trace of an original floor surface was identified and it is clear that this had been eroded away. Excavation revealed the following layers:

(1) loose surface material
(2) grey-brown earth outside the whole structure, silted in since abandonment, mostly on the enclosure side.
(3) brown soil with some small stones and burnt *dhaka* fragments between the edge of the platform and the outer ring of stones. On the east side there is a surface with much charcoal at the base of this, presumably from the burning of the roof.
(4) red-brown clay-loam, floor *dhaka* partly *in situ* and partly redeposited around subsided slabs and beneath the edge of the platform.

The construction of the platform started with the building of a solid foundation retained by the outer tier of stones. On this, vertical supporting stones were set at appropriate intervals and the whole was covered by a layer of horizontal slabs, leaving a clear space of around 20cm below; the subsidence of some of the edge slabs suggests that the supports were not well tailored to their irregular shapes. The slabs were then plastered with a thick layer of *dhaka*. Presumably a *dhaka* wall was constructed around the circumference and topped with a thatched roof. Summers (1958:83) who excavated a similar structure, records that "there was some evidence that the walls of the hut had been continued down round the edge of the stone substructure", although he does specify the nature of this evidence. In the present case, the charcoal between the edge of the platform and the outer stones indicates that this was an open surface prior to destruction and could not have supported a wall. No trace of any wall structure however was preserved around the eroded outer edge of the platform itself, an observation which also applies to the rather better preserved platform excavated earlier at Chirawu's Site 12 (Chirawu 1999). Hall (1905:99) however, commenting on examples in the National Park area of the highlands, describes raised platforms with *dhaka* floors, "with the sticks in some instances still standing upright in the *daga*". It is not clear whether the stone walls abutting platform RP1 were built before or after the platform and its *dhaka* superstructure.

Finds consisted of 301 sherds, 3 copper and 5 glass beads, 5 iron objects including a probable *mbira* (thumb piano) key, a small bundle of copper wire, 2 quartz crystals, 5 bone fragments, one carbonised seed (? cowpea) and 15 uncarbonised marula nuts from beneath the platform.

H1

H1 (fig. 77, Plate 28) represents a house floor with central division, typical of the divided houses commonly found associated with enclosures at Ziwa ruins and highland pit-structures (see Chapter 5). The internal diameters of the house itself would have been 5.50 by about 5.00m. An outer foundation 7.25 by 6.50m in diameter is formed by a single course of large stones around 25cm high. The house is divided along its north-west/south-east axis by a south-west facing step, 30 to 35cm high, built of horizontally laid stones originally faced and capped by *dhaka*; some 1.50m of this *dhaka* facing survives at the north-western end, baked but slightly displaced, while the south-eastern end survives unburnt. From these remains and some large loose fragments, together with a slight lip to the surviving plastered floor on the north-eastern side, the division would seem to have consisted of a low *dhaka*-faced wall 40cm wide, with a maximum height of 15cm on its north-eastern side and 50cm on its south-western side, and a slightly bevelled top sloping to the south-west.

The higher north-eastern half of the house has a *dhaka* floor sloping down to the north-west, on which parts of the rather rough plastering survive. In the middle, close to the dividing wall is a large hearth about one metre in diameter, formed by a shallow hollow with a low kerb at the lower edge. In the centre is a deeper, smaller hollow with an ashy fill, the total depth being about 20cm; two heat-spalled stones at the north-west edge may be part of a pot support. At the north-eastern edge of the floor is a small *dhaka* kerb 65cm long, perpendicular to and abutting the line of the wall, with a further arc of kerb forming a small quarter-circle in the angle between this and the wall to the north. There was no clear surface within this, but the floor surface outside it and to the south-west appears burnt. North-west of this kerb the floor surface dips some 5cm to the edge of a large granite grinding stone set in the floor, its eastern edge some 2cm proud of the floor level and its western edge some 10cm proud.

There are a number of carbonised post or pole bases, mostly quite small around 3 or 4cm diameter, outside the edge of the floor, while remains of the *dhaka* wall face itself survive at the south-eastern end and north-eastern side. Small stones form the wall foundation around the eastern quadrant but the lower northern quadrant is poorly preserved; here there were relatively numerous fragments of burnt broken *dhaka* in a grey brown soil matrix. At the south end the wall *dhaka* is burnt red, around 12 cm thick, and the rear side forms a vertical interface with a fill of loose small stones between the *dhaka* and stone blocking wall, though there is no smooth *dhaka* face.

The lower south-western half of the structure has a rather uneven pavement of stone slabs, again sloping down to the north-west. This paving extends under the line of the *dhaka* facing of the step and must have been laid first. The paving becomes more uneven at the higher south end where some of the stones seem to be exposed bedrock. The circumference of this section is formed by a single course of large stones similar to the outer foundation, the space between these two rings of stones having a loose fill of small stones. It was not possible to identify post bases or post-holes in this fill, but there were a couple of short lengths of *dhaka* wall face behind the inner line of stones at the WSW side and south end; two of these show small niches, perhaps the impressions of partly exposed posts about 10cm in diameter. The inner foundation would thus have been exposed forming a low narrow bench.

A large flat slab at the south end of the south-western side was probably a doorstep leading up towards the main enclosure entrance. A second door to the north-eastern half might be expected but was not clearly identifiable. There were no surviving traces of an entrance through the cross-wall which was too low to need one.

Before excavation, the top of the *dhaka* facing of the step, the *dhaka* kerbs, part of the *dhaka* floor and the large grindstone in the north-eastern half were visible, as were most of the large stones of the

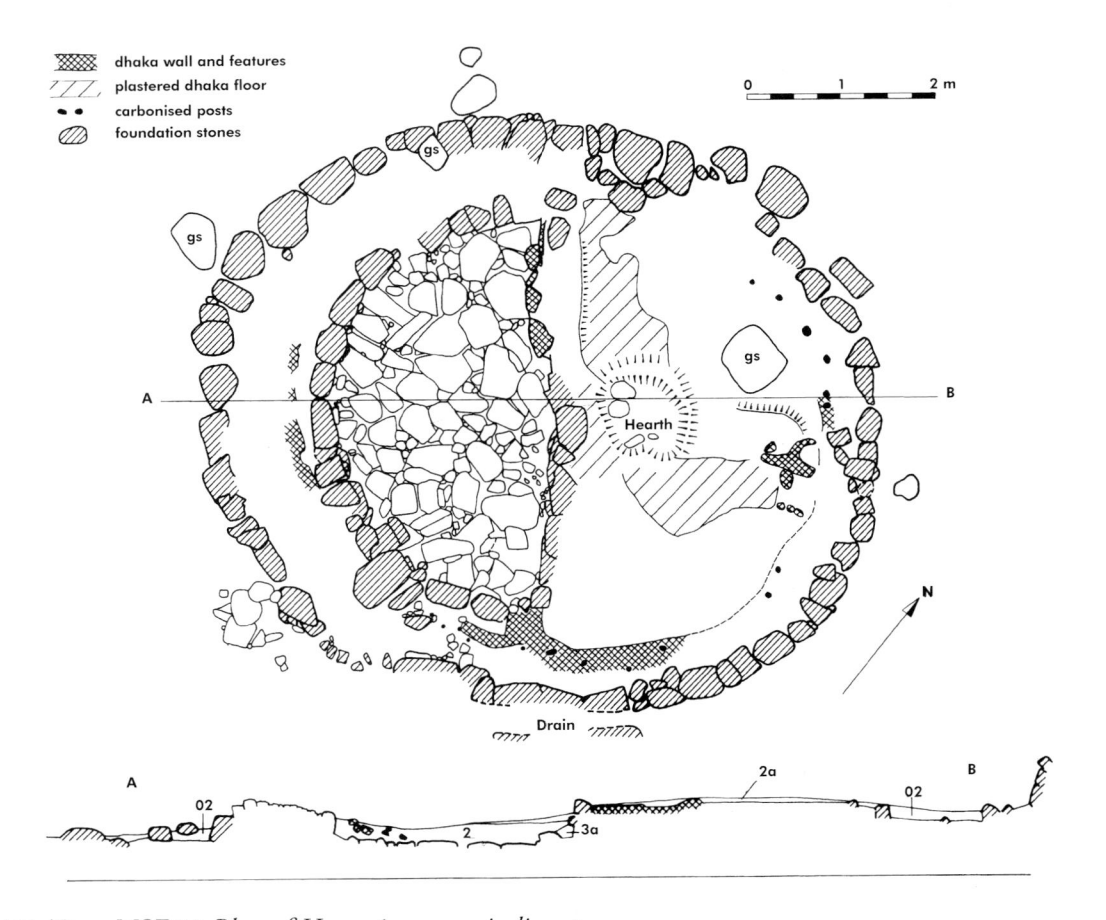

Fig. 77. Ziwa MSE17. Plan of House 1. gs = grinding stone

outer foundation and the inner foundation of the south-western half.

The north-western half of the structure was excavated first, providing the cross-section which is shown reversed in Figure 77. Trenches two metres long and around one metre wide were also excavated outside the outer foundation to the south-west, north-west and north-east to the original ground surface. The south-eastern half was then excavated and the area between the eastern quadrant and the outer stone wall was also cleared.

The stratigraphy was as follows:

South-west half:
1. Surface material, including loose grey-brown earth at the north-western end.
2. Firm dark grey soil, looser with burnt *dhaka* fragments in the northern corner. This rests on the stone paving over much of its area. A lens of browner material silted from the north-eastern half spreads across part of the surface of this layer and represents natural siltation since abandonment.
3. Along the north-western side, firmer grey-brown matrix with numerous small *dhaka* fragments: destruction layer resting on the paving.
3a. Light brown mainly fine deposit against the centre of the step, with body sherds of a single vessel broken in *situ*. This also rests on the paving.

In the south-eastern corner, brown gravelly clay subsoil is exposed in the step face below the stones. Some of this must have been dug away during construction to bring the floor more nearly level.

North-east half:
1. Loose surface material
2a. Grey-brown slightly gritty deposit, greyer nearer the dividing wall and looser with *dhaka* fragments at the north end. This is mainly a destruction layer, there having been little or no deposition since abandonment. At the southern end a burnt deposit with small charcoal fragments lies on the floor surface at the base of this layer, extending around 50cm out from the wall face.

Outside outer foundation:
1. Surface material
02. Dark grey soil similar to (2) above with some stones, 12 to 20cm thick, largely sterile with some sherds at the base. This represents natural siltation since abandonment and rests on an old ground surface of light brown gravelly clay with some stones protruding through. The stones of the outer foundation rest on the latter but at a slightly higher level, indicating some wear or erosion of the surrounding surface during habitation.

Finds comprised 759 sherds, one tiny fragment of blue-on-white porcelain, 3 glass beads, 7 iron objects, some small droplets of slag, 14 quartz crystals, 15 bone fragments and one carbonised seed.

Bulk samples for floatation were taken as follows: the whole of layer 3a; the base of layers 2 and 3 between the paving stones; the burnt deposit on the floor around the southern edge; the contents of the central hearth; loose soil from around the edges of the large grinding stone set in the floor. These were floated by a simple process of stirring and skimming in a large bowl; the seeds thus recovered are listed in Appendix C. The remaining soil was wet-sieved with negative results. All other deposits were dry-sieved through coarse and fine mesh, with the exception of some surface material from outside RP1. Samples were taken for phosphate analysis but values are low and not very informative – 600 ppm from the *dhaka* floor, 540 and 435 ppm between and below the paving stones, and 600 ppm from the old surface outside the house wall to the west. Two reference samples from outside the enclosure gave 424 and 640 ppm, but the analyses are from a different laboratory and are not necessarily comparable.

H2

H2 is the house floor on the southern side of the eastern annex. On the south edge of this a line of *dhaka* wall-face was visible on the surface, together with stones indicating a central step division similar to HP1. An area of 5 square metres was excavated to obtain more information on *dhaka* wall construction.

The outer side of the wall bears the impressions of close-set posts, leaving a thickness of around 2cm of *dhaka* behind the inner face; two of these posts are large, 14 and 15cm in diameter, the others smaller around 7 or 8cm but down to only 4cm; the spacing varies between 2 and 6cm. The inside face of the wall was preserved to height of up to 18cm over a length of c.2m, with a rounded junction between wall and floor. A strip of plastered floor surface survives at the base of the wall, continued by a hard surface of brownish gritty clay. There is a small arc of *dhaka* kerb in the corner between the wall and the presumed line of a low wall along the central step; the outer radius of this is 30cm and it is plastered within to form a small quadrant-shaped basin similar to that in HP1.

No trace of the raised wall along the central

division survives *in situ*, but the face of the step and some of the wall face of this lower half of the house are rendered with *dhaka* and there is a probable carbonised post base 12cm in diameter behind the line of the lower wall face. The fill of the lower half again consisted of dark grey soil with some stones; this was excavated to a harder brown gritty surface c.30cm below the step. Excavation was not continued below this and it is not clear whether this was the original floor.

Finds comprised 152 sherds, 1 copper bead, 7 quartz crystals, 1 dolerite pounding stone, 2 bone fragments and a carbonised seed.

Dating

A charcoal sample from H1 NW layer 3 has provided a radiocarbon determination of 160 ±20 BP, cal. AD 1689-(1698,1721)-1733; 1813-(1820,1860)-1884 (Pta-7067).

Potentially datable objects are the fragment of Chinese porcelain and the glass beads. Blue-on-white porcelain first appears in the archaeological record at Great Zimbabwe in the 16th century and it continued to be imported until recently. While different types are datable within this time range, this fragment is too small for specific identification. This tiny piece is the first case of imported ceramics to be firmly associated with the Nyanga complex.

The nine glass beads listed below are discussed in Appendix E. They are generally consistent with samples from Summers' excavations of lowland sites (Schofield in Summers 1958) and with an 18th or early 19th century date.

The evidence from this site is thus consistent with other dates from Ziwa ruins.

Finds

Pottery (fig. 78)
985 sherds were recovered, of which 61 are rims, 36 necks, 25 decorated body sherds and 863 plain body sherds. The sherds are mostly small with a few notable exceptions.

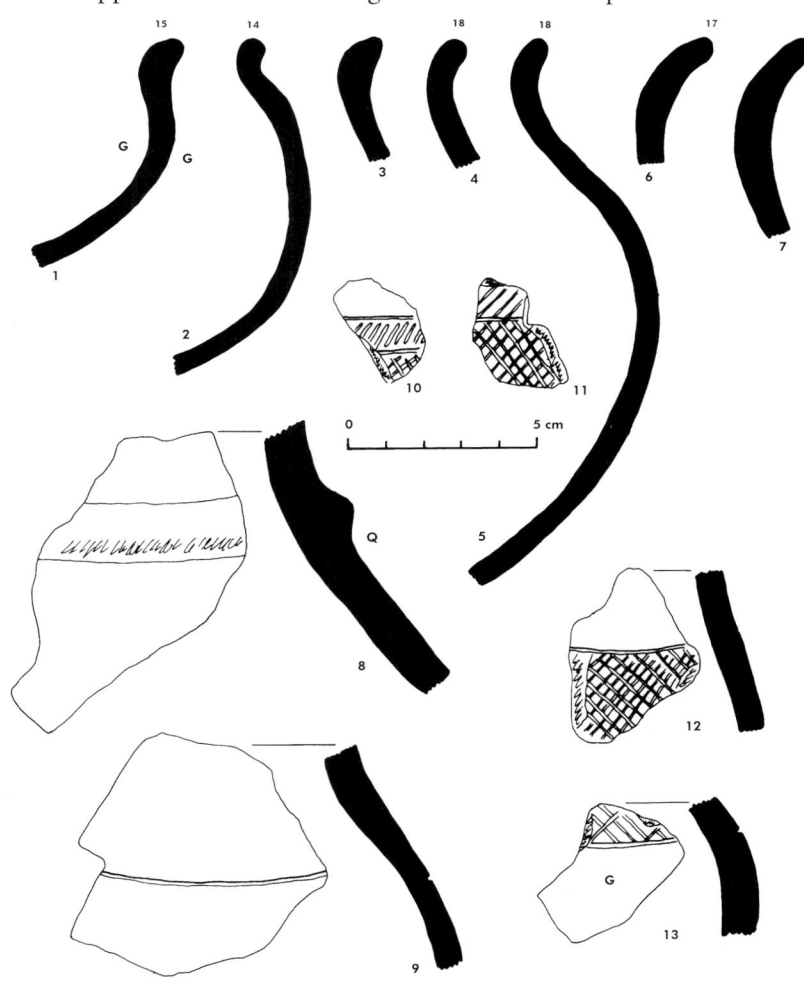

Fig. 78. Ziwa MSE17. Pottery. G = graphite; Q = quartz burnish

Diagnostic rims represent four necked bowls (nos 1,2), seven wide-mouthed pots (3-5) and nine undifferentiated necked pots. Rims are generally short, but there are two higher flared rims (6,7). Rim diameters are 17 to 19cm for four necked pots and 14 and 15cm for two necked bowls. There is one perforated round base sherd with two holes 2.5mm in diameter widening to the outside.

Temper is mostly quartz with occasional feldspar, often abundant, with maximum grain size generally 2 to 3mm, but some up to 5mm and in one case 11mm (no.8). Colour is light brown to grey-brown to grey. Finish is all smooth with rare plain burnish. 36 sherds have some thin soot outside.

Maximum sherd thickness ranges from 4 to 22mm with a mean of 7.74 ±1.64 (n=824).

Decoration after reconstruction is as follows:

Incised cross/diagonal hatching (10,11)	2
Incised cross-hatching (12)	5
Cross-hatching + graphite burnish (13)	2
Diagonal hatching	2
Diagonal hatching + graphite	1
Single incision (9)	8
Ridge + quartz burnish (8)	1
Plain quartz burnish	3
Plain graphite burnish	1

All incised decoration appears to be on the shoulder/body. The quartz burnish consists of finely crushed crystal applied to the outer surface to give a glittery finish. It is usually found on the rather rare vessels with raised ridges and the other sherds with this finish probably come from the same vessel as no.8.

Porcelain A tiny fragment of Chinese blue-on-white came from H1 layer 3. This measures only 15 x 10mm and it is doubtful if it can be further classified or dated.

Iron
- Long curved rod with square section 4 x 3mm and flattened tip, 315mm long. This resembles a key of an *mbira*, the traditional thumb piano, though it is much longer and thinner than those of present-day instruments in Zimbabwe, the longest of which reach around 25cm (D.Maraire, pers.comm.). From RP1, layer 1. (Fig. 79b)
- Broken triangular fragment of plate 56 x 55mm, tapered to one edge. Part of a wide blade. From RP1, layer 2. (Fig. 79c)
- Fragment of rod, rectangular section 4 x 2mm, 23mm long. From RP1, layer 2
- Square rod, 3.5 x 2.5 mm, 95mm long, one end flattened. From RP1, layer 3. (Fig. 79e)
- Small tanged double-edged knife (?) with leaf-shaped blade and end of tang bent into a loop. Max width 15mm, length 82mm. From between stones of wall near RP1 (Fig. 79g)
- Long rod, 5 x 5mm diameter, length 335mm, one end flattened with a small hole c.1.5mm diameter. This is somewhat similar to the "*mbira* key" from RP1, but the straightness and irregular cross-section are not consistent with *mbira* keys: perhaps it was unfinished. From H1 (2a)SE. (Fig. 79a)
- Arrow tang (?), square section 5 x 6mm, length 71mm, notches down one edge. From H1 (2a)NW. (Fig. 79h)
- Arrowhead (?), straight, twisted, double tapered. Length 145mm, max diam. 5.5mm. From H1 (2a)NE. (Fig. 79d)
- Rod 5 x 3mm section, length 96mm. From H1 (2a)SE. (Fig. 79f)
- 3 fragments of plate. From H1 (02), (02) and (2a)NE

Slag: small droplets from H1 (2)NW and (3)NW

Copper wire: 1 small bundle, 1.1mm thick. From RP1 (3)

Copper beads, folded to a circular shape. From RP1 (2), H2 (2)
- 2 biconical, 5.4mm in diameter by 7.3mm long, and 5.7 x 5.5mm

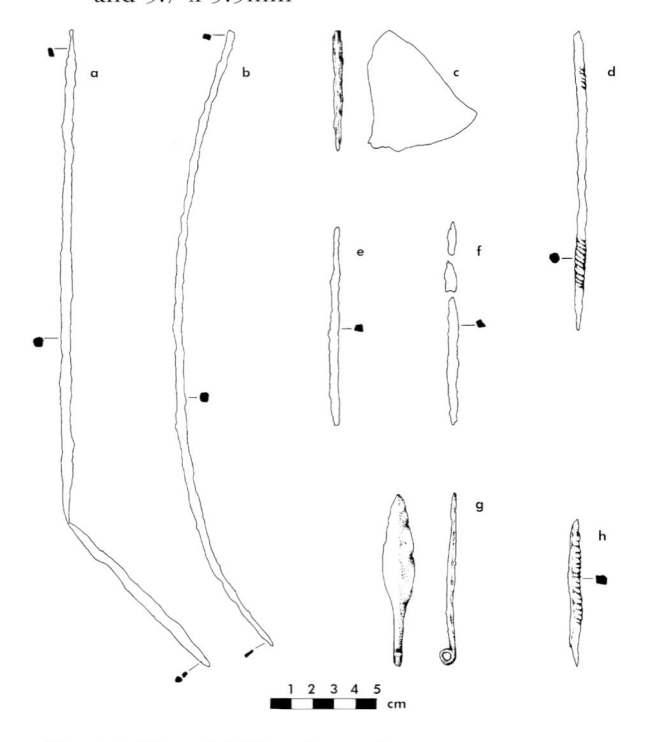

Fig. 79. Ziwa MSE17. Iron objects

- 1 barrel, 5.7 x 5.5mm
- 1 cylindrical, 5 x 4mm

Glass beads
These are all cane beads:
- 1 medium snapped black opaque – from RP1 (3)
- 1 small black oblate – from H1 (2a)SE
- 2 small rounded Indian red – from RP1 (3)
- 1 small rounded Indian red on a pale green translucent core – from RP1 (2)
- 2 small rounded yellow – from RP1 (2), H2 (2)
- 1 small rounded opaque white – from H1 (02) SW

Stone
- 23 quartz crystals, 2 from RP1, 14 from H1 and 7 from H2.
- Dolerite pounding stone from H2.

Bone
- proximal end femur, distal end humerus, fragment of astragalus, all small, probably sheep/goat
- 1 fragment large mandible
- 19 unidentifiable fragments from (2)

Seeds: See Appendix C.

Discussion

The excavation provided useful information on the nature and possible function of the divided houses and raised platforms as discussed in Chapter 5. These are relevant to the occupancy, organisation and economy of this site.

The raised platform provides details of the base and floor construction but sheds little light on function owing to its eroded floor and superstructure. Excavation of H1 and H2 clarifies the construction and function of the divided houses as dwellings with accommodation for small stock, refuting Summers' interpretation of these features as open "grinding places" (see Chapter 5). The three raised platforms incorporated in the wall of the main enclosure are probably storage huts, though one or more could be sleeping huts for unmarried children such as were provided in traditional Shona homesteads. The two divided houses in the main enclosure may well indicate the presence of two wives, each with her own small stock, though whether married to the same man is not possible to determine. The two annexes may have housed married sons or daughters; here the raised platforms are likely to have been storage huts, as the families concerned might be expected to have set up independent establishments if they had children.

The lack of a pit suggests that this family unit possessed no cattle, unless they were kraaled elsewhere, while the low ratio of probable storage huts to houses also suggests modest wealth. Each wife however seems to have had an average holding of small stock. The presence of a much larger enclosure a short distance up-slope, with the largest pit in the Ziwa National Monument, indicates wealthier neighbours.

ZIWA SN153 STONE ENCLOSURE

Ziwa SN153 is a simple enclosure designated 1832BA82. It is built of granite and lies some 250m west of Hamba hill at grid reference VQ 619938 (fig. 42, no.9). It was selected for excavation in the hope that it might illustrate the earlier chronological spread of the Ziwa ruins, since it is relatively poorly preserved in comparison with other enclosures which have been excavated. In the event however the radiocarbon dates obtained were not significantly different from those for other Ziwa enclosures, with a calibrated bracket of late 17th to early 19th centuries.

The site is situated on a gentle westerly slope which suffers from sheet erosion, the surface all around being light brown gritty or gravelly material derived from decomposed granite, with little topsoil and a thin grass cover with scattered *msasa* trees. On the site itself are a few trees and bushes, including *muchecheche* (*Ziziphus mucronata*) and *muchakata* (*Parinari curatellifolia*).

The enclosure (fig. 80) is relatively ill-defined, of irregular sub-oval shape with north/south axis, 25 by 20m outside and about 17 by 15m inside. It is on two levels, separated by a rather rough terrace c.40cm high, the wall of which has one course of stones on the upper side and is mostly tumbled below. The south end of this central terrace wall abuts a low granite outcrop which is extended on the west side by an ill-defined wall. Between this and the south outer wall, two lines of stones two metres long form shallow steps in the gentle slope. Three curved bays form projections in the lower west to south-west wall, which is around 60cm high and also mostly tumbled outside. The surface of the bays is more or less flush sections of wall between. There is another semi-circular bay in the north-east corner with a low single course wall. Elsewhere the terraces are more or less level, with no obvious features apart from a flat stone on the upper terrace. At the south end, a sub-circular feature three metres in diameter occupies a space in the outer wall, joined to the wall on either side by low lines of vertical stones. This feature could have been a raised platform from which most of the horizontal slabs have been removed. The enclosure wall on the upper eastern side is tumbled and ill-defined on its lower side. A gap towards its northern

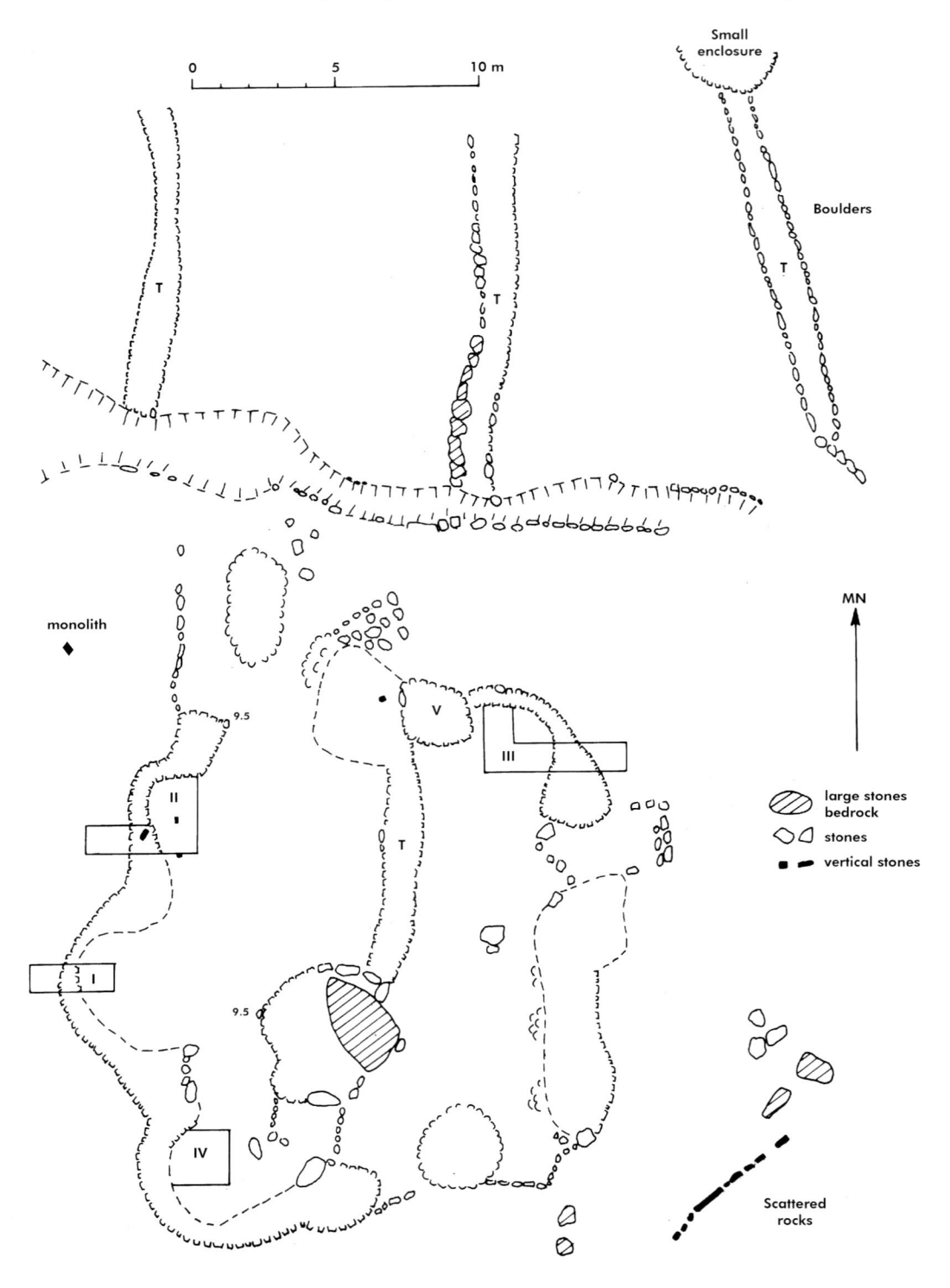

Fig. 80. Ziwa SN153. Plan of the enclosure. gs = grinding stone; T = terrace wall

defined on its lower side. A gap towards its northern end is partly closed by an outer feature of vertical stones. The lower western wall is extended to the north by a line of stones, and east of this is an oval heap of stones measuring four by two metres and 70cm high. East of this again, and separated by a gap, is another broad heap of stones about four by three metres, abutting a rather better defined squarish feature 2.50m square, in turn abutting the north-eastern bay. Two grinding stones were visible on the surface, one at the north end of the west wall and one below the west side of the south-central bedrock/wall feature.

Immediately north of the enclosure is a sunken drain (or possible path) formed by a shallow east/west gully with traces of stone lining, especially on the south side. Three terrace walls abut this gully on the northern side, about 10m apart, often with massive vertical stones on the lower side and a fill of quartz fragments. 24m to the north-north-east of the enclosure, the eastern terrace wall abuts a small enclosure, the lower wall of which is 1.80m high. To the south-east of the main enclosure is a line of boulders including a massive vertical slab. Seven metres north-west of the enclosure is a monolith 1.14m high and c.25cm square, with no other stones around it. Summers (1958:17) notes that monoliths are rare at Ziwa, but records one rather less than five feet high on the south slopes of Mt Hamba. The position and size would suggest that this is probably not the same one, though Summers is not always entirely accurate in his directions and distances.

Excavations

Trenches were dug in the four wall bays, and the squarish feature at the north end was partly dismantled.

The northern feature – Trench V

The west face of this feature is fairly straight and the other three sides slightly curved. It is built with larger stones around the base and a fill of smaller stones. Within the feature, just south of centre, was a square horizontal cavity, the top and bottom formed of flat stones and the sides in two courses. This cavity measured c.27cm square and 1.40m long, opening into the western face. It is clearly a partially collapsed drawbar slot, showing that this feature represents the eastern side of the original enclosure entrance. It appears that the western side has been at least partly demolished and the entrance itself filled with piled stones to the extent that it was not recognised. There is however a square vertical stone projecting 40cm above the stone heap which may well mark the outer western corner of the entrance passage, giving a width of 50cm.

Beneath the feature was a thin dark grey soil lens over sterile, unconsolidated red-brown gritty sandy loam, the original soil now largely eroded from around the site. One white bead was found on the old surface and a few sherds in the stone fill. The feature and beam slot were reconstructed.

The central western bay – Trench I

This trench was 3 by 1m across the wall. The outer wall face is here about 50cm high and rests on red gritty decomposed granite. The inner face was c.30cm high and has the remains of a probable *dhaka* facing. Deposits against the wall were:
1. Grey-brown topsoil around 10cm thick with a few sherds; probably mostly silted in behind the wall since abandonment.
2. Brown gritty matrix with broken burnt *dhaka* and charcoal fragments, 15-20cm thick.
3. Red-brown grit similar to the outer natural surface.

The *dhaka* may be the remains of a burnt collapsed structure or could be a deliberate fill to level up the platform, but no trace of any floor surface was found above or below it.

The north-western bay – Trench II

This was originally 4 by 1m across the wall, but was extended to the north by c.2 x 1.80m to cover the north-western quadrant of the bay. The outer face of the wall was neatly built, 45cm high with some higher stones, resting on sloping bedrock. The inner face was rougher and no signs of *dhaka* facing were seen. Deposits inside were:
1. Grey-brown topsoil with some sherds, around 15cm thick.
2. Red-brown gritty sandy loam with pieces of burnt *dhaka*, charcoal fragments and some sherds, becoming cleaner and apparently sterile at around 30cm below the surface. Most of the stones of the wall face rest on this but there was no clear floor or trodden surface on top.
3. Brown gritty sandy loam with sand lenses, with rare sherds.

There were four square or rectangular orthostats, two in the wall face and two 40 and 80cm from it and 1.10m apart. These have their bases 7 or 8cm below the top of layer 3 and their tops project above the surface; layers 2 and 1 must have accumulated around them, while no sign of excavated sockets in layer 3 could be detected.

Layer 3 appears to be the original ground surface graded to the bedrock outside the wall, the sherds being probably Early Iron Age material derived from a previous occupation. There is no sign of an old topsoil or trodden surface. Layer 2 seems best interpreted as a deliberate fill with rubble from some previous structure, prior to building the wall, though there is no clear sign of any floor on top. The orthostats form no regular pattern and no convincing interpretation suggests itself.

A charcoal sample from layer 2 gave a date of 220 ±25 BP, calibrated to AD 1678(1686)1695; 1724(1738)1763; 1803(1810)1817 (Pta-7155).

North-eastern bay – Trench III
This was 5 by 1m across the low eastern wall and 1.50 by 1m to the north wall, forming an L-shape. Deposits were:

Outside the wall:
1. Grey-brown humic sandy topsoil, 10cm
2a. Light brown clean sandy grit with a few sherds to bedrock at c.25cm below surface. The sherds are again probably derived Early Iron Age material.

Inside the wall:
1. Grey-brown humic sandy topsoil, 10cm.
2b. Greyish brown sandy grit with some sherds and charcoal, around 5cm thick. This rests on a redder surface, 3, over most of the trench, locally compacted. The low east wall appears to be built on the surface of 2a which has been cut away within it, so that 2b rests against a sloping interface with 2a. Layer 3 should be a floor surface, though it is mostly unconvincing. Two small concentrations of charcoal in 3 well away from the stone wall could be remains of posts. No sign of any *dhaka* walls was detected.

South-western bay – Trench IV
This was 2 by 2m within the bay against the wall. Deposits were:
1. Grey-brown sandy humic topsoil, browner and earthier towards the base, up to 15cm thick.
2. Brown gritty sandy loam matrix with much burnt *dhaka*, especially in the north-western half of the trench, up to 20cm thick. The surface of this shows as a clear interface in the north section but there was no sign of a floor in plan.
3. Discontinuous red-brown sandy lens up to 3cm thick, with some sherds and a piece of slag but little charcoal or *dhaka*. Continues under the base of the wall.
4. Red grit from decomposed granite.

At the base of layer 2 in the centre of the trench was a small concentration of stones, including two rubbing stones: one of quartz, single-faced, 120 x 90 x 50mm; and one of granite, double-faced, 140 x 130 x 40mm. A third rounded rubbing stone, 132 x 95 x 67mm, was found in a similar position near the northern side of the trench. Layer 3 is largely absent in the north part of the trench where layer 2 rests on the uneven surface of red grit. The stone wall on the west side has no large facing stones and the small quartz stones of the wall core are retained by a *dhaka* facing, 4 to 6cm thick, which rests on layer 3 where present. The *dhaka* retains little trace of any smooth surface. In the centre of the eastern section is a pit cut from the base of layer 2. The top of this is irregular in plan, 66cm wide, but it narrows rapidly to 46cm with the sides more or less vertical below this, to a total depth of 45cm. The lower fill is soft brown and sandy, and layer 2 with *dhaka* lumps dips into the top. The purpose of the pit is uncertain but the contents were collected for flotation, yielding a few grass seeds identified as *Panicum maximum*.

The top of layers 3/4 is likely to represent a living surface, although there is no formal floor. Layer 2 would then represent the collapse of a burnt house structure, perhaps roughly levelled up and the space reused.

A charcoal sample from layer 2 was dated to 190±25 BP, calibrated to AD 1670(1677)1684; 1741(1768)1784; 1792(1802)1808 (Pta-7161).

Finds

Pottery (fig. 81)
846 sherds were recovered, of which 58 are rims, 27 necks, 18 decorated body sherds and 743 plain body sherds. Some of the material is very weathered and represents Early Iron Age Ziwa ware in secondary context, as indicated by one internally thickened open bowl rim (no.14) and one pot rim with a diagonally hatched thickened rim band (11). There is an Early Iron Age site at the foot of Mount Hamba within 200m of SN153, from which Summers excavated prolific "Z2" pottery (1958:43; site XI).

The better preserved diagnostic sherds represent four necked bowls (nos 1-3), 10 wide-mouthed pots (5-10) and four undifferentiated necked pots. Lips are rounded, about half of them tapered. Rims are generally fairly short but there is one reconstructable pot profile with a higher flared rim and a single incised line on the shoulder (17). Measurable rim diameters are 16 to 20cm for eight necked pots and 17cm for two necked bowls. No. 4, a finely burnished graphited rim of a necked pot or open bowl, is reminiscent of Great Zimbabwe pottery. There is one flattish base, thickened outside

Temper is mostly quartz and feldspar, usually abundant, with maximum visible grain size of 2 to 3mm. Colour is brown to grey-brown to grey. 33 sherds have some soot outside and five have carbon residues inside. Finish is smooth and firing generally good. Maximum sherd thickness ranges from 3 to 15mm, with a mean of 7.46 ±1.82; this may be a little inflated by the Early Iron Age component.

Decoration appears to be invariably on the neck/shoulder and is as follows (excluding the obviously Early Iron Age rim):

Incised cross-hatched (15)	1
Incised cross-hatched + graphite (1)	1
Diagonal hatched + graphite	1
Single incision (13,17)	6
Plain graphite burnish (2,3)	7
Ridge + plain burnish (12)	1

The necked bowls are all graphited, one with an incised hatched band (1).

Beads
- 1 opaque white cylinder, diameter 6mm, length 5mm. Trench V.
- 1 dark blue translucent oblate, diameter 4.5mm, length 3mm. Trench II.

Iron
- 1 piece of rod, one end possibly tapered, length 104mm, diameter c.5mm. Trench II
- 1 piece of rod, rectangular section, width tapered to end, length 88m, middle 4 x 2.5mm. Trench II
- 1 piece of rod, one end ?thickened then pointed, length 57mm, thickness c.6 x 4 to 7mm. Trench IV.
- 2 sub-rectangular pieces of plate with possible asymmetrical broken tangs. 39 x 26 x c.2.5mm, tang 10mm wide; 57 x 4-6 x c.2mm, tang 4mm wide. Trenches II and IV.

Slag
Five fragments from four different trenches, total weight 335gm.

Quartz crystals
- 1 cloudy. 56 x 25 x 19mm. Trench V.
- 1 clear, 40 x 18 x 15mm, broken. Trench IV.

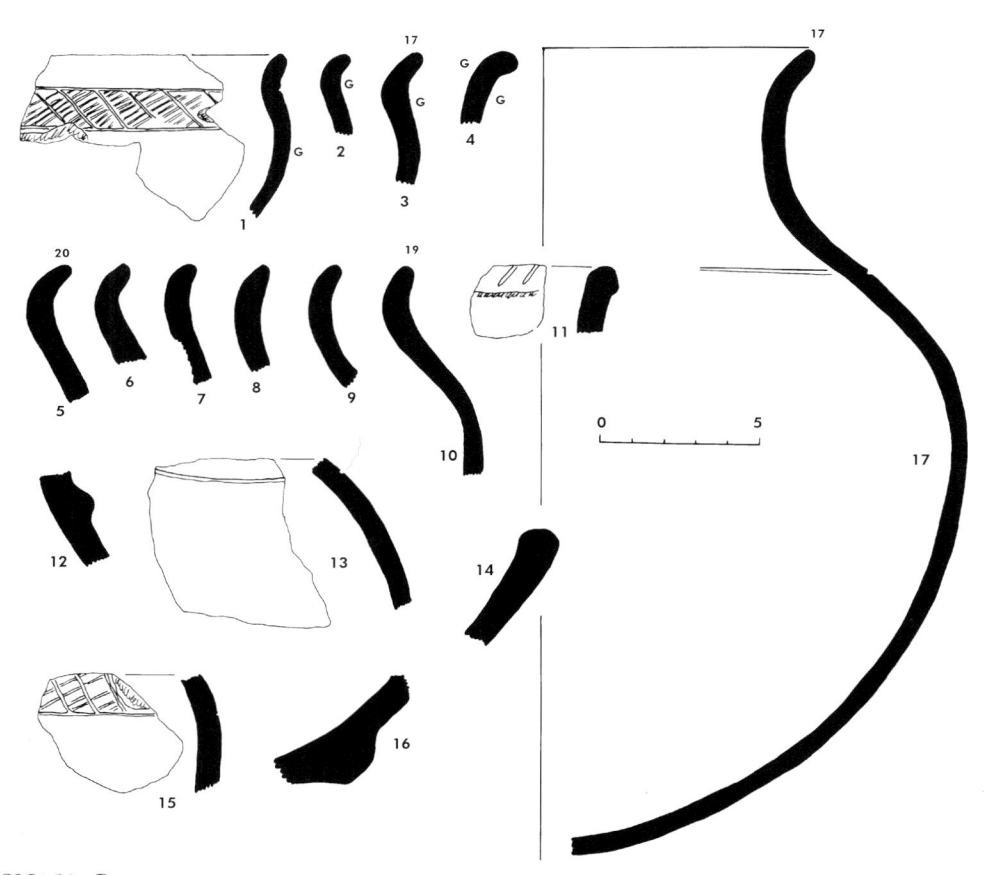

Fig. 81. Ziwa SN153. Pottery

- 1 clear, 40 x 18 x 15mm, broken. Trench IV.

Seeds
- 5 *muchakata* (*Parinari curatellifolia*) seeds from Trench V.

Bones/teeth
- Fragments of a large bovid tooth from Trench III.
- 11 unidentifiable bone fragments from Trenches II (1), IV (8) and V (2)

Discussion

This is a residential enclosure, with a typical entrance passage with drawbar socket which has been deliberately blocked and partly destroyed. In the absence of any clearly defined house floors or walls in the limited areas excavated, no clear information is forthcoming on the structures; however the *dhaka* facing of the inside face of the enclosure wall in Trenches I and IV suggests that these bays contained houses. If this is the case, there would have been three or four houses within the enclosure. None of these is of the divided type found in many Ziwa enclosures, while the lack of floors is also in contrast to other excavated sites. There are thus some minor peculiarities which may imply some difference from the better known enclosures. This difference could be chronological, or due to some cultural distinction between the granite areas/structures in the south-eastern part of the Ziwa Monument and the dolerite (and granite) areas/structures to the west and north. The granite structures in this south-eastern area are in general less well preserved. This is pointed out by Chirawu (1999), who attributes it to the inferior building properties and lesser profusion of granite stones, since at least some contemporaneity is indicated by a case where both granite and dolerite enclosures are linked to the same main walled passageway.

The radiocarbon determinations, with a broad calibration bracket of late 17th to early 19th centuries, are not significantly different from those from other excavated Ziwa sites. There is scope within the alternative calibrations for age differences of a century or more, but other evidence such as pottery and beads does not as yet offer sufficient refinement to establish an effective internal chronology. The age of SN153 relative to other enclosures thus remains uncertain.

STONE ENCLOSURES IN MAZARURA AND NYAUTARE AND THE CHIRANGENI EXCAVATION

The Chirangeni site lies at the foot of the western escarpment some 53km north of Nyanga town at grid reference VR 675344 (fig. 42, no.10). The geographical situation is described in Chapter 4, where the terracing is considered in detail.

Most of the slopes on both sides of the Hambuka valley, with the exception of Chirangeni hill itself, are heavily terraced (Plate 1), with numerous stone enclosures on slight shoulders or more level ground above or below the terraced slopes. Enclosures have been recorded in several areas.

To the west of the upper Hambuka valley, on the opposite side of the flanking ridge and close to the track, is a group of three double-concentric enclosures and a cluster of small house circles (fig. 82; the third enclosure is just off the plan to the west). The eastern enclosure is divided by a terrace, has bays within the outer wall at north and south sides, two circles of stones, possibly house foundations west of the central enclosure, and a ring of five vertical stones with a sixth in the middle to the south-east; the latter appears to be a storage bin support. There is scattered baked wall *dhaka* in the north-eastern area. The middle enclosure is also divided by a terrace but has no other obvious features. Between the two is a smaller irregular enclosure with a wide opening at one side. In the western enclosure, not shown on the plan, the inner enclosure in fact abuts the upper side rather than being central, and within this were a washing stone and a complete vessel, a deep wide-mouthed pot with slightly out-turned rim, 44cm high and 29cm in rim diameter. To the south of the eastern enclosures is an unwalled occupation site on a broad low terrace. Three probable house circles, around 3m in internal diameter with walls around 60cm high, and two smaller circles about 2m in diameter face inwards in a semi-circle. The other side of the circle is partly closed by two raised platforms, one with a vestigial circle of stones, partly paved within, in front of it. There are two patches of broken *dhaka* within the cluster. A radial low stone wall extends south from the remaining gap, and terraces c.80cm high step up to the east. A pathway lined with low stones skirts the north side of the cluster. This group clearly forms a tight-knit settlement and there are other enclosures within a couple of hundred metres to north and south-east.

To the north of the Chirangeni enclosure described below, and 60 to 80m above it in altitude, is a gently sloping plateau with a variety of enclosures. One has an inner enclosure, almost a pit, abutting the outer wall on the lower side. Another consists of three small enclosures two to three metres in diameter linked by a loop of wall forming a fourth enclosure. Another is oval, 19 by 17m in diameter with four open entrances, a bay within the wall on one side, several grinding stones and four raised platforms with outer rings of stones similar to the storage houses of the Chigura site (see below). Further to the north-east is a double-concentric enclosure with substantial inner enclosure and exiguous outer wall, but with 11 small and 5 large raised platforms, many with baked *dhaka*. Some of the large ones are again likely to have been storage houses and are associated with thick coarse vessels as at Chirangeni and Chigura.

There is thus a variety of stone enclosure designs with little standardisation apart from the double-concentric enclosures which form a regular component. In addition there are scattered examples of small enclosures three or four metres in diameter not associated with larger enclosures; these may be isolated houses or stock pens. The double-concentric enclosures are found westwards along the western range at least as far as the Nyangombe river. Several examples in which the inner enclosure abuts the outer wall appear to be a variant of these. There are a number of cases of deliberate blocking of either inner or outer enclosure entrances. Along the western range are also a number of loopholed "forts" which have not been observed in the Chirangeni area, although the excavated Chirangeni enclosure has some

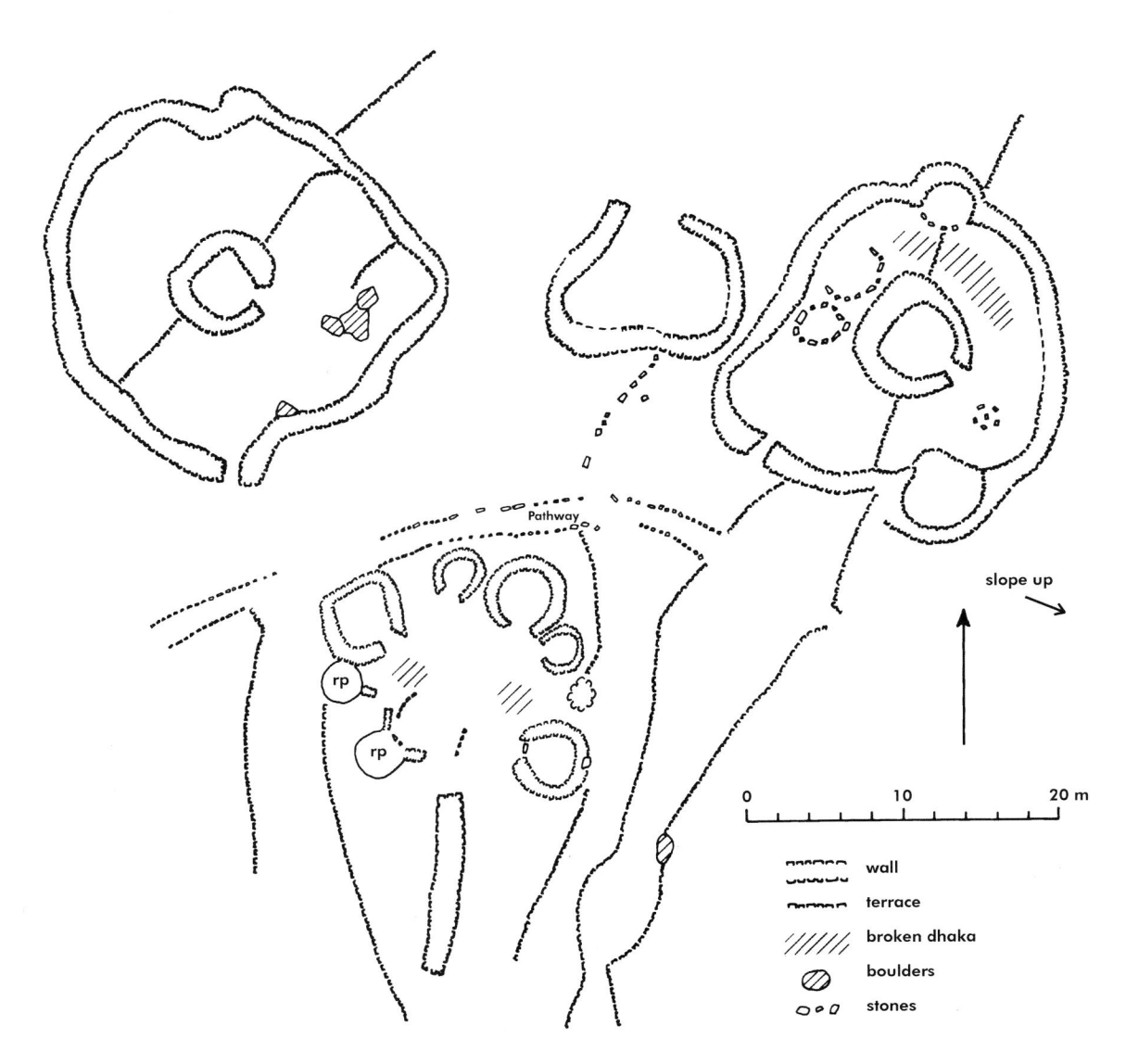

Fig. 82. Chirangeni area, west of Hambuka valley. Double concentric enclosures and an unwalled homestead. rp = raised platform

affinities as discussed below. These forts have lintelled entrances which are not present in the other enclosures. It is uncertain whether all these structures are associated and broadly contemporary. A general time range of 17th to 19th century, broadly similar to that of Ziwa, may be suggested on the basis of incised cross-hatched pottery associated with some of them.

Chirangeni Enclosure   1732DC47a

This large enclosure in the surveyed area described in Chapter 4 is at grid reference VR 675344 at an altitude of 1350m, about 70m above the valley watershed (fig. 42, no.10). It is different in character from any of the enclosures described above; the outer wall has some affinities with forts in general but it is larger in size than most, while the internal residential structures are of a type not yet recorded elsewhere.

The enclosure (fig. 83) is heart-shaped, measuring 28m from east to west and 34m from north to south internally. There is a vertical fall of 6.60m from south-east to north-west within it. The thickness of the outer wall varies, being up to 2.50m on the lower side but mostly around 1.50m. Wall height also varies; at the lower western side it is around 2.00m high outside and as little as 60cm inside, while at the upper, eastern edge it is only 70cm inside and 40cm outside. Some silting behind the upper sides is probable in each case. The only entrance is on the north-east side and is lintelled; the wall here is 1.70 to 2.00m thick and 1.80m high, the doorway itself being 1.25m high with a minimum width of 50cm. The walled pathway shown in Figure 13 comes across the valley from the north, curves past the entrance and continues uphill through the terracing to the north-east to a small plateau.

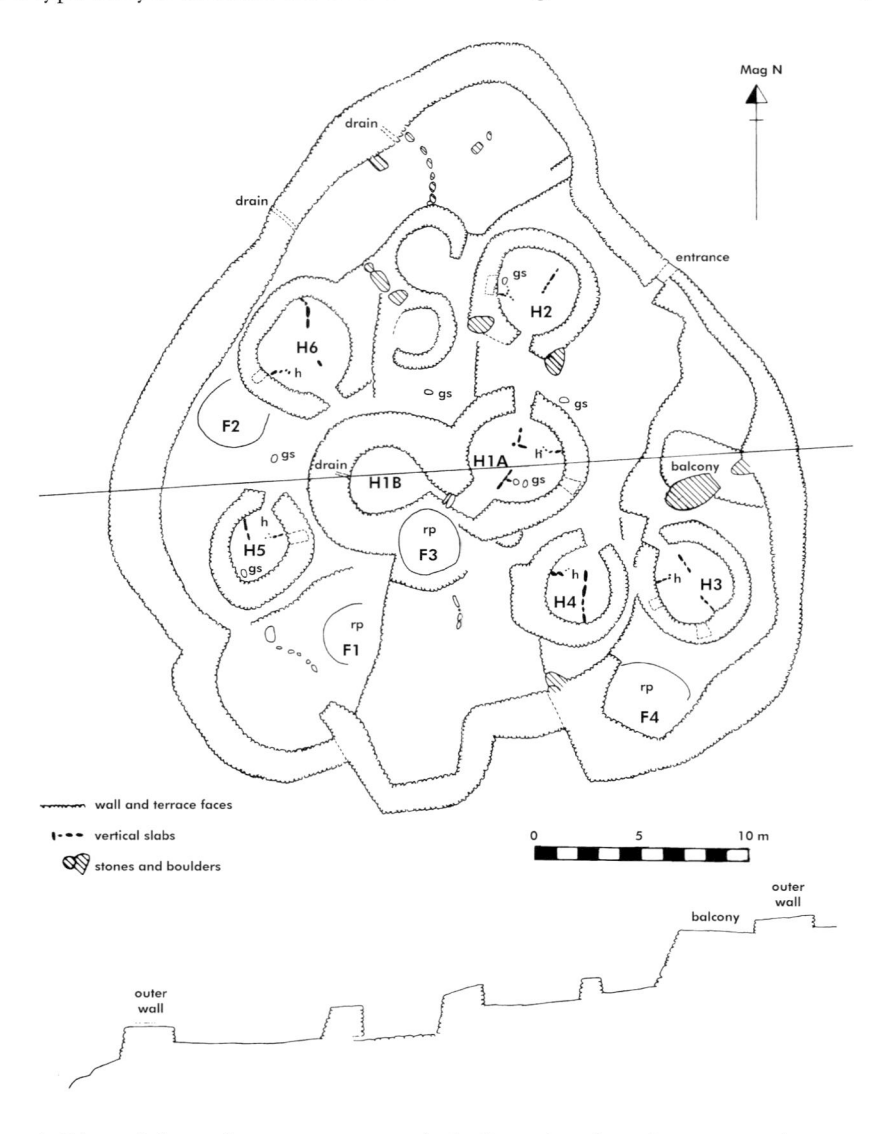

Fig. 83. Chirangeni. Plan of the enclosure. rp = raised platform; h = hearth; gs = grinding stone

Internal features

The most notable features are six stone-walled houses, the walls around 1.00m high and thick, well built with fairly flush faces. The smallest of these measures 3.60 by 2.70m internally and the largest, in the centre of the enclosure, 4.60 by 4.25m. Only the latter is approximately circular, the others being mostly sub-oval. Doorways are plain with no lintels. All have internal divisions formed by lines of vertical slabs up to 60cm high, usually a discontinuous transverse line from one side of the doorway and a shorter radial line from one side. Each house has a small hearth at the end of the radial division, four of these on the left-hand side from the entrance but in the two upper south-eastern houses on the right side. The hearths are marked by a pair of stones about 20cm apart, while a third stone, present in house 1A, would appear to have been movable. In each case there is a smooth concave *dhaka* base to the hearth.

All houses except one have a "cupboard" (in one case two) built into the thickness of the wall. Some of these are at floor level, others up to 50cm above the floor. These cupboards are 60-100cm in depth and around 40cm wide at the front, usually widening to 70 to 100cm at the back. A storage function may be suggested and a few animal bones and sherds were found within them in Houses 1 and 2.

The central house, H1A, is part of a double feature. At the back of the house a lobby steps down and from here a narrow stepped passage with two lintel stones leads down to a smaller second enclosure (H1B) with a fairly massive wall up to 2m thick and 1.90m high. The floor of this enclosure is paved with stones throughout and slopes down to a drain in the western wall. It thus resembles the pit of a highland pit-structure or a lowland pit-enclosure, but with walls built up from ground level.

Other features within the enclosure include:
- two small enclosures 2 to 2.50m in diameter north of the central double feature.
- four raised platforms, one (F3) on the south side of the double feature, one (F4) in a bay of the outer wall in the south-east corner, and two in the lower west section (F1 and 2, see below). The latter two have broken burnt *dhaka* on them.
- partial arcs of stones at the south/south-west sides, probably denoting structures such as houses without stone walls.
- larger standing stones in the lower north section, of uncertain function.
- at least two drains through the lower north-west outer wall.
- a "balcony" at the highest point on the eastern side overlooking the whole enclosure. This is a flat platform with no visible signs of structures, with a stone revetment 2.60m high around natural boulders.

Excavations

The central double feature, H1A and B, and one other house, H2, were excavated, as well as parts of two of the raised platforms. In addition a trench was excavated outside the lower outer wall in the hope of finding a midden deposit; the results of the latter were largely negative apart from a few sherds and a piece of rubbed soapstone.

H1A (fig. 84; Plate 29)

Excavation involved the removal of around 15cm of overburden consisting of 5 to 10cm of grey sandy humic topsoil over firmer grey-brown sandy loam.

The walls are 1.10 - 1.20m high, generally well preserved except for the eastern side of the doorway and the western corner of the lobby to H1B. Most of the wall construction is of irregular stones laid more or less horizontally, but there are five larger vertical slabs in the base of the wall on the eastern side, one of which fronts the cupboard. Large lumps of baked *dhaka* are incorporated in the outside wall face on the north-east side, indicating a previous *dhaka* structure, perhaps a house which the stone walling has replaced.

The doorway on the north side is c.80cm wide with a slab c.15cm high as a threshold at the inner end. From here two low vertical slabs divide the entry to east and west and this line is carried to the centre of the house by a line of higher slabs up to 57cm high. After a gap of 60cm, the line is continued to the south side by further vertical slabs up to 64cm high. The west side thus defined is partially paved with flat slabs, some of which are laid over a *dhaka* floor covering part of the north-western quadrant, the *dhaka* being worn away in front of the door. This paving terminates at the first step down to the lobby.

A small compartment at the north-east side is defined by a vertical slab 60cm high joining the central line and two slabs from the eastern wall (Plate 30). Beyond the end of the latter is a small hearth, around 40cm in diameter, of smoothed *dhaka* with a raised rim. Two vertical hearth stones are set in the edge of the *dhaka* and a third stone rests on it. Two flat stones to the south and north-west may have been for sitting close to the hearth. There was a quartz rubbing stone 30cm inside the eastern door jamb.

There is no smooth floor in the eastern half of the house, but a rather uneven surface of hard light brown sandy clay, gravelly in places, sloping up to the east where it appears to be laid against the base of the wall.

At the southern end of the eastern half were two grinding stones and parts of a broken pot lying on its side. The eastern grinding stone is shallowly concave with an oval grinding surface 46 by 28cm, 27mm deep longitudinally and 8mm laterally. The western one has a flat grinding surface 35 by 28cm. The pot has incised cross-hatched decoration (fig. 86, no.22).

The cupboard is within the wall on the east side. The opening is 37cm high and around 40cm wide, 48cm above floor level. It is 1.05m deep and the width splays to 1.00m at the back, which is formed by a large single vertical slab, part of the outer wall face. The upper fill was a brown sandy deposit with loose stones and pieces of broken *dhaka*, containing a few animal bone fragments and sherds, including the rim of a thick coarse vessel. There was a finer greyer fill below, also with loose stones. The total depth of fill was around 20cm and it rested on an uneven floor of gritty light brown clay. A lump of charcoal was found in the back corner c.10cm below the surface and has been dated to 300 ±20 BP, cal.AD 1648(1654)1660 (Pta-7590). This result is inconsistent with other indications of the age of the enclosure which suggest a more recent date as discussed below.

This eastern, left side of the house appears to have been a kitchen and living area, with hearth, storage cupboard and grinding facilities.

The lobby to the lower enclosure H1B is at the south-western side, about 1.70m square, paved with stones, with a step 26cm high within it. From here a passage 1m long and 50 to 60cm wide runs down in four steps to H1B, spanned by two lintel stones with head room of 1.30m.

H1B

This enclosure is sub-oval, 3.60 by 3.20m internally, with solid walls 1.60 to 1.90m high. The whole floor is neatly paved and slopes down from east to west with a fall of 45cm. At the lower side is the mouth of a drain 23 by 24cm, the base on decomposed granite. The paving was overlain by grey loose sandy humus and leafmould, with some lighter brown sandy loam at the sides, a total depth of less than 5cm in the centre and up to 20cm at the edges.

Fig. 84. Chirangeni enclosure, plan of House 1A. gs = grinding stone; p = pot

There is no indication that H1B was ever roofed and the drain would have allowed the escape of rainwater. The paving and the resemblance to true pits elsewhere suggest that it was for livestock, probably a few small cattle, either penned overnight or stall-fed on a more permanent basis. Access for these stock must have been through the western side of the house, which may also have accommodated small stock. There is no other obvious accommodation for cattle within the enclosure, or indeed outside it, but small stock may have been kept in some or all of the houses.

H2 (fig. 85)

This house lies immediately north of H1A, separated by about 1.50m, the doorways almost opposite each other. It has an irregular sub-oval plan, with internal diameters of 4.40 by 3.80m and walls 90cm to 1.15m high. Wall construction is similar to H1 with vertical slabs at the base around most of the north side. The doorway at the south side is around 90cm wide, paved, with a vertical slab 18cm high forming the inner threshold. The collapsed eastern side of the doorway was reconstructed. Deposits in this house were up to 15cm deep, loose grey sandy humus over brown to grey soft sand.

The east, right-hand side is again partly divided off by vertical slabs, one from just inside the doorway and a line extending 1.70m SSW from the back wall. Within this eastern side were uneven horizontal slabs which did not appear to have fallen from the wall but which did not constitute regular smooth paving. These lay in, and in some cases on, a grey sandy soil. They were planned and mostly removed, but no convincing surface was found. Beneath them was a boulder 25cm high in the middle, a few stones which appeared to be outcropping bed rock, and decomposed granite under the east wall. It thus seems that the uneven slabs must have been a rough paving, perhaps uncompleted.

On the west side, the floor is again a hard light-brown gritty surface similar to H1A. There is a cupboard within the wall, in front of which is a radial slab 46cm high, with a series of lower slabs to the north forming a small alcove. At the end of the first slab is a small hearth with two vertical hearth stones and a smooth hollowed *dhaka* base preserved to 40 by 30cm; the third hearth stone is missing. In

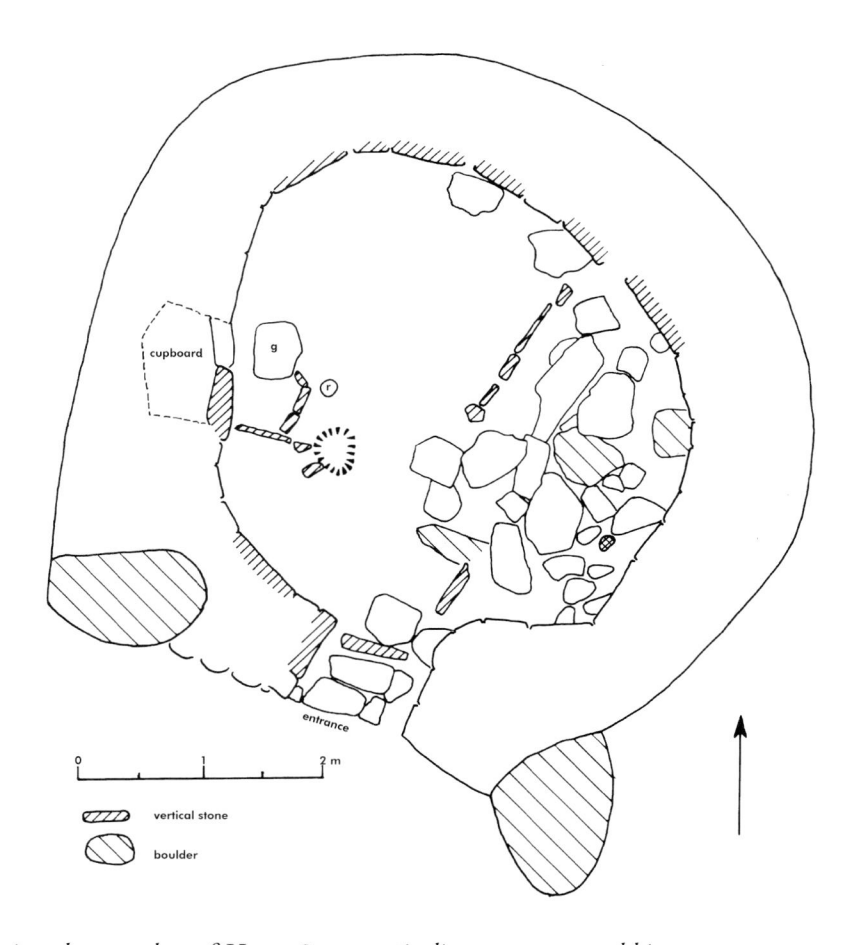

Fig. 85. Chirangeni enclosure, plan of House 2. g = grinding stone; r = rubbing stone

front of the cupboard and alcove is a grinding stone with grinding surface c.35 by 30cm and a 10mm concavity, sloping slightly towards the alcove. Two rubbing stones of granite and quartz lay close by.

The cupboard is roughly rectangular within the thickness of the wall. It is 45 to 60cm cm deep and about 90cm wide, the south half closed at the front by a vertical wall slab. The mouth is 42cm wide and 49 to 53cm high, the base only a few centimetres above floor level. A loose slab leaning against the larger alcove slab would have served to partially close the mouth. Inside there was around 10cm of light brown gritty soil over a hard red-brown uneven surface. Within this fill were a few sherds and bone fragments and a small perforated shell whorl, probably a bead.

The general configuration of H2 is comparable to H1A, but lacks the lobby and passage to H1B. The right side could again have housed small stock, the east side being the kitchen and living area, with hearth, storage cupboard and grinding stone.

F1

This feature, towards the south-west corner of the enclosure, appeared to be a small platform 3m wide with a low stone revetment and much broken *dhaka* on the surface. It was only partially excavated. Below loose grey sandy humus was a hard grey-brown sandy matrix containing lumps of broken *dhaka* and stones. Within this were a series of solidly based stones, forming a broken arc at the lower edge but otherwise with no regular pattern. These are interpreted as the foundation of a raised platform with *dhaka* superstructure which had been destroyed by fire, the horizontal slabs having been subsequently robbed for use elsewhere. Within the matrix were charcoal fragments, sherds and a few bones. Part of a thick coarse vessel was found in place against one of the stones. A sample of charcoal has been dated to 60 ±25 BP (Pta-7582), with a most probable calibrated date around AD 1900.

F2

This is a clearer example of a raised platform with broken *dhaka*, abutting the wall of House 6 at the lower western side of the enclosure. Vertical foundation stones were exposed around the southern edge where some of the horizontal slabs had fallen away. There was much broken *dhaka* in dark grey-brown humic soil. A patch of smooth *dhaka* floor c.80 by 40 to 60cm was preserved on the eastern side and the floor had subsided in places elsewhere, probably as a result of slippage of the underlying slabs. A short section of probable vertical *dhaka* wall was present near the south-east side. This was badly crumbled and may have been only 12cm thick at the base tapering upwards, with thin horizontal stick impressions. It does not seem to be at the edge of the platform and may have been an internal division. Sherds were relatively numerous and included fragments of thick coarse vessels, one a base.

All of the four raised platforms are approximately 3m in diameter. They are likely to have been storage houses for grain and other products, and the thick coarse vessels found with them have also been found in association with storage structures elsewhere, notable at Chigura (see below). F3 is clearly associated with House 1, F2 with House 6 and F4 with House 3 or 4. The lack of *dhaka* on F3 and F4 may indicate that there was never a *dhaka* superstructure or that any such structure was not burnt and has disintegrated and been washed away.

Finds

Pottery

The pottery from the enclosure (fig. 86) and from the "garden" terrace described in Chapter 4 (fig. 87) was analysed separately for comparison.

Sherd counts were:	*Enclosure*	*Garden*
Diagnostic rims	61	32
Undiagnostic rims	5	17
Necks	24	7
Decorated body sherds	28	9
Plain body sherds	639	472
Thick coarse sherds	80	-

The sherds from the garden terrace were more weathered and considerably smaller, with an average weight of 6.4gm compared with 23gm for the enclosure (excluding the thick coarse sherds). They are thus consistent with having been reworked in cultivation, either with manure from the enclosure or from a pre-existing site.

Colour of both assemblages ranges from brown to grey-brown to grey, with a higher proportion of grey-brown from the enclosure and of brown from the garden. Temper inclusions are mostly quartz and feldspar in both, maximum visible grain size being generally 1 or 2mm, occasionally up to 5mm, with the garden sherds tending to have smaller grains. Temper density is medium to heavy, heavy predominating in the garden and medium in the enclosure. Average maximum thickness, excluding thick coarse sherds, is 8.42 ±1.98mm for the enclosure and 7.66 ±1.76mm for the garden. The thick, coarse sherds are more or less identical to those described for Chigura (see below).

Vessels, lip form and finish are as follows:

	Enclosure	Garden
Deep/waisted vessels (31,33,34)	-	3
Deep perforated bowl (3)	1	-
Hemispherical bowls (29,30,32)	3	8
Constricted bowls (26-28)	-	3
Necked bowls (9-13)	5	1
Wide-mouthed pots (1,2,4-7, 14-17,35-39)	27	9
Narrow-mouthed pots (18,21)	2	-
Undiff. necked pots	1	-
Thick, coarse vessels (23-24)	2	-
Total	*39*	*24*
Square lips	-	1
Round lips	23	22
Tapered round	15	1
Rough finish	19	20
Smooth finish	21	4

Decoration in both assemblages shows a high proportion of punctates (8,19-21,28,35-37,39-40). These are triangular or rectangular in both cases, usually in bands of two or more rows. In the enclosure, panels and/or incised lines are occasionally combined with the bands (8,21), but their absence in the garden is of doubtful significance in view of the small sherd size. One punctate sherd from the garden is also graphited, the only graphited sherd from the site. Two vessels from the enclosure (9,22) have an incised cross-hatched band and diagonal panels respectively, and there are four sherds with single incised lines from the garden.

Thus the sherds from the garden tend to be thinner, lighter in colour, with finer, heavier temper. The rougher finish and greater frequency of bowls, including deep forms, may suggest an earlier date, but the lesser average thickness would not be consistent with general trends for the complex as a

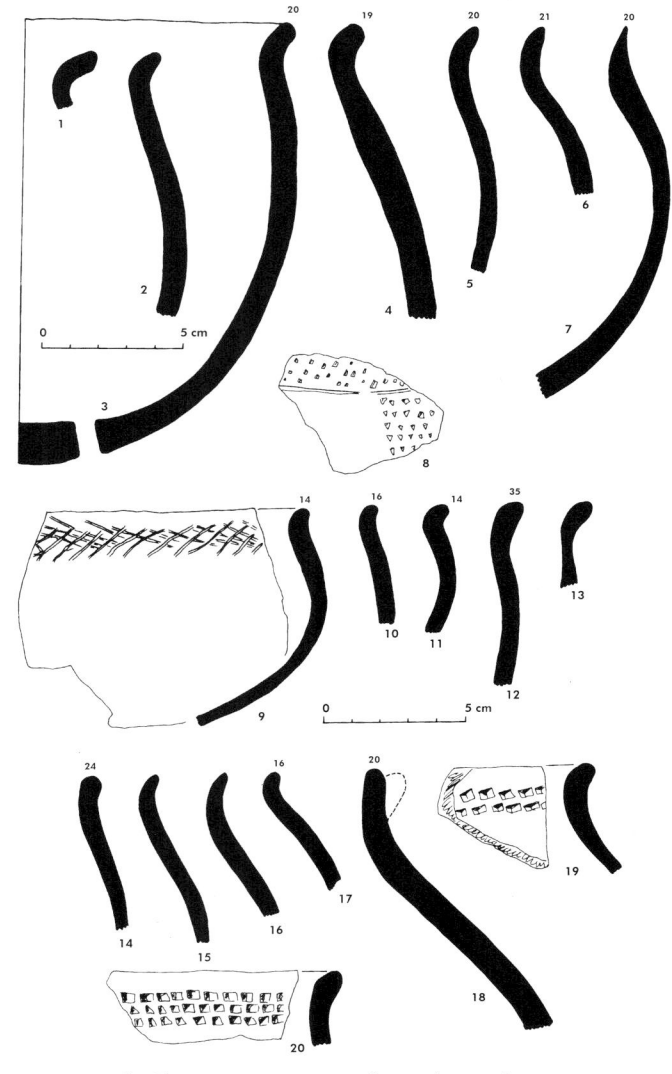

Fig. 86. Chirangeni. Pottery from the enclosure

whole. The general impression is that the two assemblages are related, especially in decoration, but that there are sufficient differences to make it doubtful that the garden terrace sherds are derived directly from the enclosure as a constituent of manure. There are too few sherds from the supposed earlier terrace phase to detect any possible differences from the upper deposits. The frequency of punctate decoration contrasts with the other excavated northern lowland enclosure of Chigura, which however has very similar thick coarse vessels.

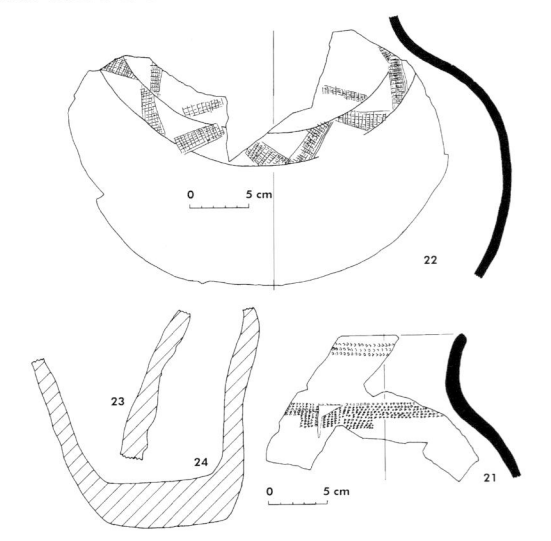

Fig. 86. (continued) Chirangeni. Pottery from the enclosure

Iron

From the floor of House 2:
- broken blade of a large arrowhead or double-edged knife with lenticular section, tapered to a rounded end; 78mm long, 15mm wide and 4mm thick in the centre (fig. 88c).
- axe with heavy rectangular-sectioned tang and splayed edge; 156mm long, blade width 40mm, centre of tang 20 x 13mm, weight 200gm. (fig. 88a)

From the floor of the raised platform F2:
- triangular piece of broken plate, 54 x 44 x 3mm.
- piece of rod with square section, one end tapered, length 57mm, middle 5 x 4.5mm.
- flat bar, widened then tapered at one end, with a small perforation through the wide part; length 123mm, width 7-10mm, thickness c.3mm (fig. 88b). Dr Maraire, a musicologist of traditional music, considers it unlikely that this was an *mbira* key (pers. comm.).

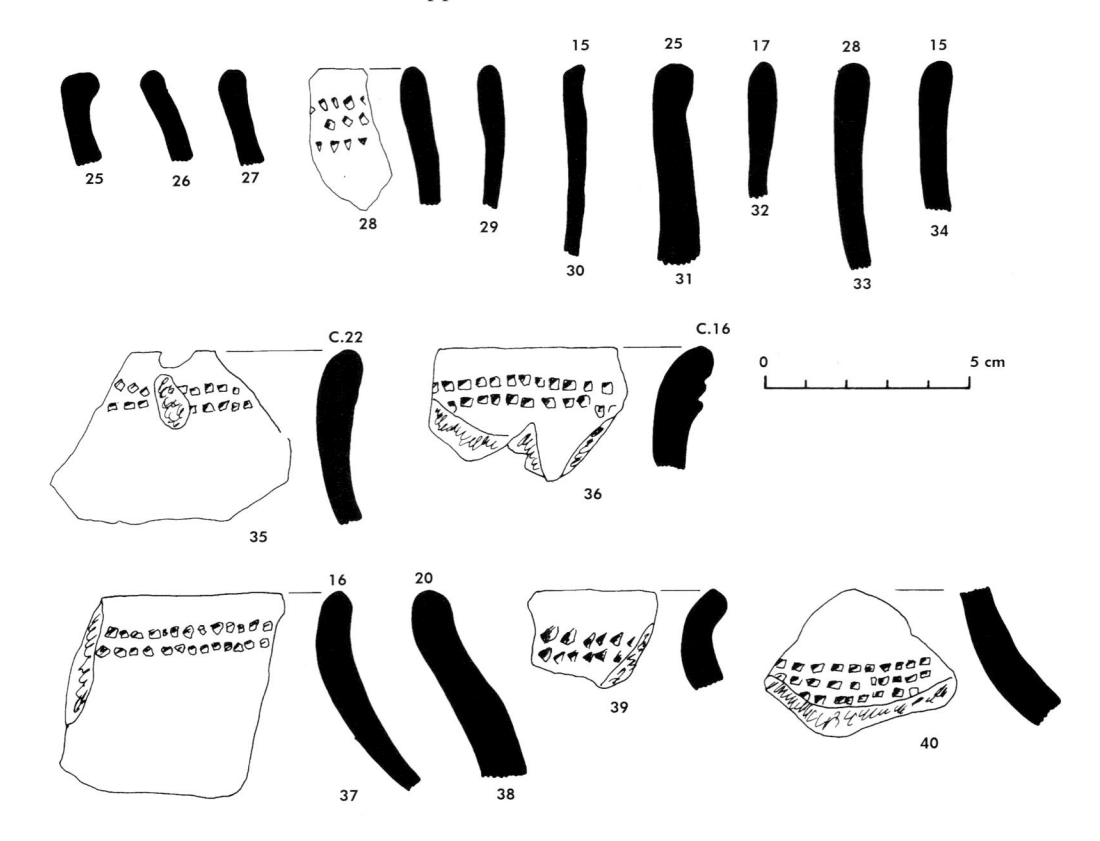

Fig. 87. Chirangeni. Pottery from the garden terrace

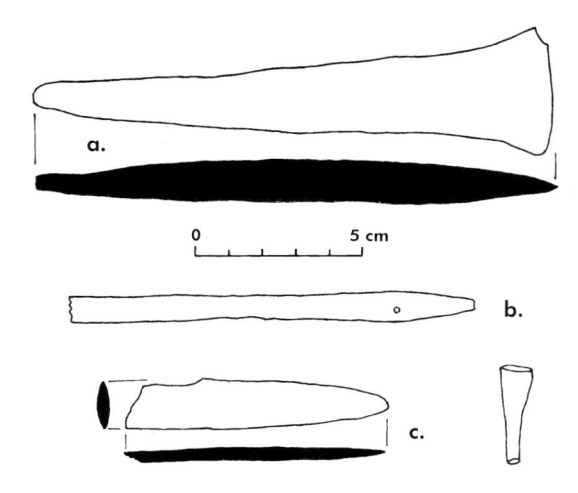

Fig. 88. Chirangeni. Iron objects and soapstone stopper from the enclosure

Beads (from House 2)
- 1 glass bead, a short cylinder of Indian Red on pale green translucent core, 5mm diameter and 3.5mm long.
- 1 thin perforated whorl of snail shell.

Bone
From Houses 1 and 2:
- cattle: 2 3rd phalanges and single fragments of scapula, radius/ulna, mandible, metacarpal and metapodial
- large bovid: fragments of a mandible and of a 1st or 2nd phalange
- unidentifiable: 37 rib fragments, 5 vertebrae fragments, 19 flakes and 5 miscellaneous

From raised platform F1:
- cattle: 1 lower 3rd molar, 2 mandible fragments
- large bovid: single fragments of molar tooth, pelvis, carpal and 3rd phalange
- medium/large bovid: 1 fragment of sesamoid
- unidentifiable: 2 enamel fragments, 3 skull fragments, 8 rib fragments, 14 flakes

A number of specimens show cut or chop marks or have traces of burning

Other finds
- small stopper of soapstone, perhaps for a snuff bottle, showing knife marks from shaping. Shallowly tapered with concave longitudinal section, length 30mm, diameters 10 and 4.5mm at ends. From the floor of F2 (fig. 88d).
- piece of light grey soapstone 57 x 25 x 23mm, quadrilateral section, rubbed on three sides, from outside the west wall of the enclosure.
- basalt hammer stone, quadrilateral section, one edge smoothed, ends smoothed from hammering; 130 x 52 x 49mm, weight 582gm, from House 2.
- Small core of clear quartz crystal, 23 x 20 x 12mm, from the floor of House 2.

Dating
The state of preservation would suggest a relatively recent date, probably nineteenth century, with which the radiocarbon date from F1 would be consistent, as would the later calibrated range from the garden terrace. The other radiocarbon result, that from the cupboard in H1A, is inconsistent with these and the state of preservation, and is improbably early. The sample may have come from the burning of an old tree. That the site must predate AD 1900 is borne out by Carl Peters (1902), who must have passed fairly close to the west in 1901 and gave the impression that the whole area was depopulated. He was told by a guide from Katerere: "Men are afraid to dwell here, even to wander alone through this land: it is the country of death". This must reflect a vivid memory of the struggle between the rival dynastic houses for the Saunyama chiefship in the 19th century (Beach Annex).

Discussion
The general picture is that of a substantial social unit, controlling a relatively large area of terraced fields incorporating a large garden. The head of the unit is likely to have occupied House 1A in the centre, with his cattle closely protected in 1B. Five other households of lesser but approximately equal status occupied the other houses. Whether these households were those of wives of a polygamous family or separate nuclear families of close relatives is not possible to say. The function of the high balcony overlooking the whole enclosure can only be speculated on. The central raised platform incorporated in House 1 may be the granary of the principal, while the other raised platforms appear to be related to particular houses. House 2, which has no platform, does have the two small enclosures adjacent to it. Small stock of individual households were probably kept within the houses. Manure from livestock and domestic rubbish was almost certainly used in the walled garden and perhaps on the terraced fields. The walled passage provided access to neighbours to the north and to the plateau above and would have kept people and livestock off the fields

This enclosure is somewhat anomalous for this area in a number of respects. The size and quality of the outer wall and the lintelled entrance set it apart from normal homesteads in the northern lowlands, which are typically double-concentric enclosures or simple enclosures with lower walls and house floors. These characteristics show some affinities with "forts", examples of which occur to the west and south-west, but there are no loopholes and no banquette except perhaps immediately on the south-east side of the entrance, though this is hardly typical; the wall on the upper side is hardly high enough to be defensive.

The configuration of the central double feature has no known parallels, though the resemblance of H1B to pits has been noted above and indicates a similar function. The stone-walled houses have their closest parallels in forts in the National Park, though the Chirangeni ones are more substantial and neatly built and no direct relationship is suggested. Small stone enclosures, usually around 3m in internal diameter, do occur singly or in groups unassociated with enclosures in this and many other areas, but again are less neatly built and substantial. It is the neat construction of the house walls which facilitates the insertion of the cupboards, and hence these have been hardly noted on other sites with rougher walling; examples have however been recorded in the lower chambers of split-level enclosures at the head of the Kumbu valley about 9km to the south-east.

Also apparently unusual are the small hearths and the internal division of houses by vertical slabs, but such features may have been missed in surface examination of less well preserved structures. There is some parallel with the internal low cross-walls which are common in the divided houses in the highland pit-structures and at Ziwa ruins (Chapter 5; MSE17 above). These divide the house into a kitchen/living area and a paved half, probably for small stock as may be the case here, but such houses appear to have had two entrances. Nor have they been recorded in the northern lowlands, either in the recent research or by Summers (1958) in his work in the Nyautare area.

Other features such as the raised platforms are more typical of the Nyanga complex.

The pottery relationships are discussed in Appendix D. The assemblages fall within the general range of later Nyanga complex ceramics but show some differences from both Ziwa to the south and Chigura to the north-east. Differences between the enclosure pottery and that from the garden have been noted above. The thick coarse vessels occur at other sites in and around the Chirangeni area and also at sites in the Chigura hills above Elim Mission/Ruangwe. Their consistent association with storage structures such as raised platforms has been noted above. The single glass bead is an 18th or 19th century type (Appendix E).

The size and quality of the structures, the number of houses and the extent of the associated terracing and walled garden suggest a locally important social unit, perhaps that of a chief or headman, although the rarity of exotic items such as beads does not indicate any great relative wealth. The house wall construction could be an experiment in new techniques, perhaps following the destruction of more traditional houses by fire. The internal configuration of the houses however might be expected to be more conservative; the paucity of comparable excavated data makes it difficult to assess how typical this may be for this area.

CHIGURA ENCLOSURES

The Chigura area is part of the Ruangwe Range which forms a lower northward extension of the main Nyanga highlands, separated from the latter by a relatively low gap. The Ruangwe range is some 25km long, with crests at around 1200m rising to a maximum of 1500m towards the southern end. The topography consists of a number of subparallel ridges striking NNW, between which are the valleys of the headwaters of the Musurudzi and Manjanja rivers, tributaries of the Matisi and ultimately the Gairezi. The ridges are formed by folded sedimentary argillites, sandstones and calc-hornfels, interspersed with dolerite sheets (Stocklmayer 1980). The eastern scarp is precipitous, around 300m high, rising from the plains of Katerere which extend eastwards broken by large granite inselbergs. To the west is more broken granite country beyond the Duza river, dominated by the spectacular peak of Nani rock. Average annual rainfall at Elim mission at the eastern foot of the scarp is around 700mm (see Chapter 2), but declines northward to 640mm at Avila Mission (Brinn 1987).

Terracing is common in the upper parts of the southern half of the range (Chigura) and along the base of the escarpments as far north as Ruangwe business centre, but is apparently absent further north and to the east of the range. It occurs mostly on the argillites and dolerites. The excavation of a terrace transect above Elim Mission has been described in Chapter 4.

Stone-walled homestead sites are common among the terracing in certain areas, particularly around the headwaters of the Manjanja river, though rare or absent in other equally terraced areas. They include simple enclosures with house floors and raised platforms, and double-concentric enclosures. Some of the enclosures on steeper slopes are divided by a terrace up to 70cm high, not continuous with terraces outside. In both types of enclosure the outer wall is relatively rough and low, usually with multiple entrances. The inner enclosure of the double-concentric type is better built with a thick wall around 100 to 120cm high and 3 to 5m in internal diameter. Similar double concentric enclosures are also found along the foot of the eastern escarpment for some distance south of Elim Mission, where there is also an iron-smelting site with a large accumulation of slag.

Almost all walls in this area have facings of stone with a core of gravelly earth. Type of stone naturally varies with the local geology, dolerite and clay- or siltstone being commonest. Facing stones of argillite or silt stone may be very small, down to 5 or 6cm square, though generally larger.

These enclosure types and at least some of the associated pottery (incised cross-hatched decoration and thick coarse vessels) are similar to those of the Nyautare area 15-20km to the south-west, but the more massively walled "forts" found in parts of Nyautare are apparently lacking here. Also lacking from both areas are the typical pit-structures of the main highlands and the pit-enclosures of the Ziwa area.

The site the excavation of which is described below, is a residential simple enclosure with an appended double-concentric enclosure, both enclosures having a number of terrace walls abutting them on both sides (fig. 89). It is in the hills some 2.5km south of Elim Mission at an altitude of

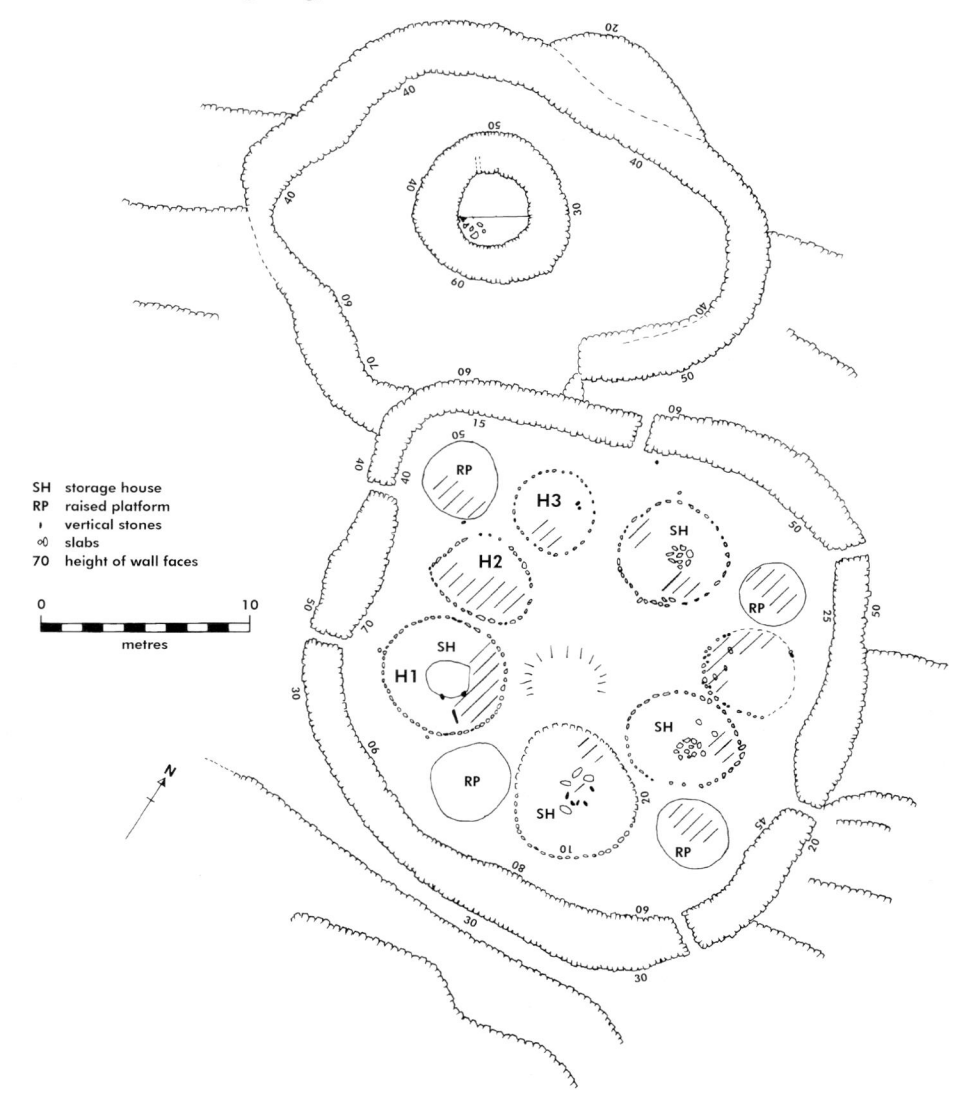

Fig. 89. Chigura. Plan of the double concentric and residential enclosures

1100m at grid reference VR 767513 (site number 1732DB8; fig. 42, no.11). It lies on a gentle slope on the south side of a slight saddle between two small hills, both of which are terraced and crowned with stone structures.

The residential enclosure is sub-circular, 22 to 27m in internal diameter, with a low outer wall with six entrances. The interior is fairly densely packed with circular structures, comprising four raised platforms, four 'storage houses' and three house floors, with an open space in the middle approximately 9 by 6m. Most of these features have varying quantities of burnt pole-impressed *dhaka* on the surface. Nine grinding stones and a number of rubbing and pounding stones were observed on the surface and four more grinding stones were found in excavation.

The raised platforms are all more or less ruined and/or silted up but appear to be typical of their type, 3 to 3.50m in diameter. The storage houses (see H1 below) are 5 to 6m in diameter, marked by an outer ring of stones and a ruined central structure of slabs. The house floors are 3.50 to 4m in diameter and lack the central slabs. The grinding stones were associated with both house floors and storage houses.

The double-concentric enclosure is appended to the residential enclosure on the lower north-west side. The outer wall of this is an irregular oval about 21 by 15m internal dimensions; it is in poor condition and no entrances are visible. The inner enclosure is 3.20 to 3.50m in internal diameter, the wall being up to 2m thick, well faced where unbroken, with an earth core. Before excavation the height of this wall reached a maximum of 60cm, but the interior proved to be deeply silted so that the actual height is around 1m. On the higher side of the inner enclosure, the inside face of the wall and parts of the outer face are somewhat collapsed, but the line of the outer face is traceable all the way round and no entrance is apparent; it is probable that the entrance had been deliberately blocked, as seemed to be the case with at least one other similar structure in the vicinity.

Excavation in the double-concentric enclosure

The lower north-western half of the inner enclosure was excavated (Plate 31). The stratigraphy showed 10 to 12cm of grey humic topsoil over 20 to 35cm of red-brown loam with fallen wall stones. This overlies decomposed dolerite bedrock, on which the wall was built and which forms the floor. The red-brown loam would appear to be wall fill from the upper side of the enclosure which has silted down following the collapse of the inner wall face on this side. No original deposits were detected on the floor.

At the lowest side of the enclosure was a drain outlet 28cm wide and 40cm high; since the outside of the inner enclosure was not excavated, the other end of the drain was not found and it is not clear if it simply penetrated the inner wall or debouched through the outer wall as well. No features were visible between the inner and outer walls but this area is also heavily silted.

Finds comprised only nine potsherds and four fragments of bone. Phosphate samples gave 500 ppm for the earth fill of the wall, 1000 ppm for 15cm below the surface of the deposits, 3000 ppm for the enclosure floor and 1000 ppm from the mouth of the drain, consistent with the penning of livestock. A value of 14000 ppm from 2 to 5cm below the surface of the topsoil appears anomalous but could result from recent dung of cattle which are grazed in the hills in the rainy season.

Excavations in the residential enclosure

Two structures were completely cleared, H1 (storage house) and H2 (house floor). In addition a trench was dug across a slight mound at the upper side of the central open space, but this proved to be a natural formation of sterile red loam over decomposed bedrock.

H1 (fig. 90; Plate 32)

This was visible before excavation as an outer ring of stones 5.70 by 6.00m in diameter. In the centre was a confused heap of stone slabs, some set vertically, about 2m in diameter, with more to the south-east. There was a quantity of burnt pole-impressed *dhaka* on the eastern side.

The stratigraphy showed:
1. Crumbly grey humic earth among the central slab structure with some pottery.
2. Brown silt among red-brown decomposed *dhaka* with varying amounts of burnt *dhaka* fragments. 7 to 15cm thick: wall destruction with some subsequent silting.
3. Burnt layer of soft grey ashy material up to 3cm thick, with charcoal and carbonised grass in places: from the burning of a thatched roof.
4. Discoloured grey floor. A plastered surface survives on the western side where there is a particularly heavily burnt area.

The *dhaka* fragments in layer 2 are of two kinds. The first kind is relatively massive with impressions of close-set vertical poles 4 to 8cm in diameter, and must derive from the house wall. The second type is 1.5 to 2.5cm thick over close-set horizontal thin stick impressions which often interlock and occasionally have traces of vertical elements; it is clear that this type represents the outside plastering of a woven wickerwork storage bin which must have stood on a platform represented by the central slab structure. Most of this type of *dhaka* was recovered from the eastern edge of the slab structure, suggesting that this side had been more thoroughly baked, helped perhaps by an east wind at the time of destruction by fire.

sedimentary series.

The uprights consist of a rough hexagon of six pillars with a central pillar, and a number of vertical radial slabs on the northern and western radii. Diameters of the hexagon are 190, 186 and 176cm. Four of the outer pillars were more or less broken off, but the two south-eastern ones and the central one were complete and measured 57, 60 and 45cm

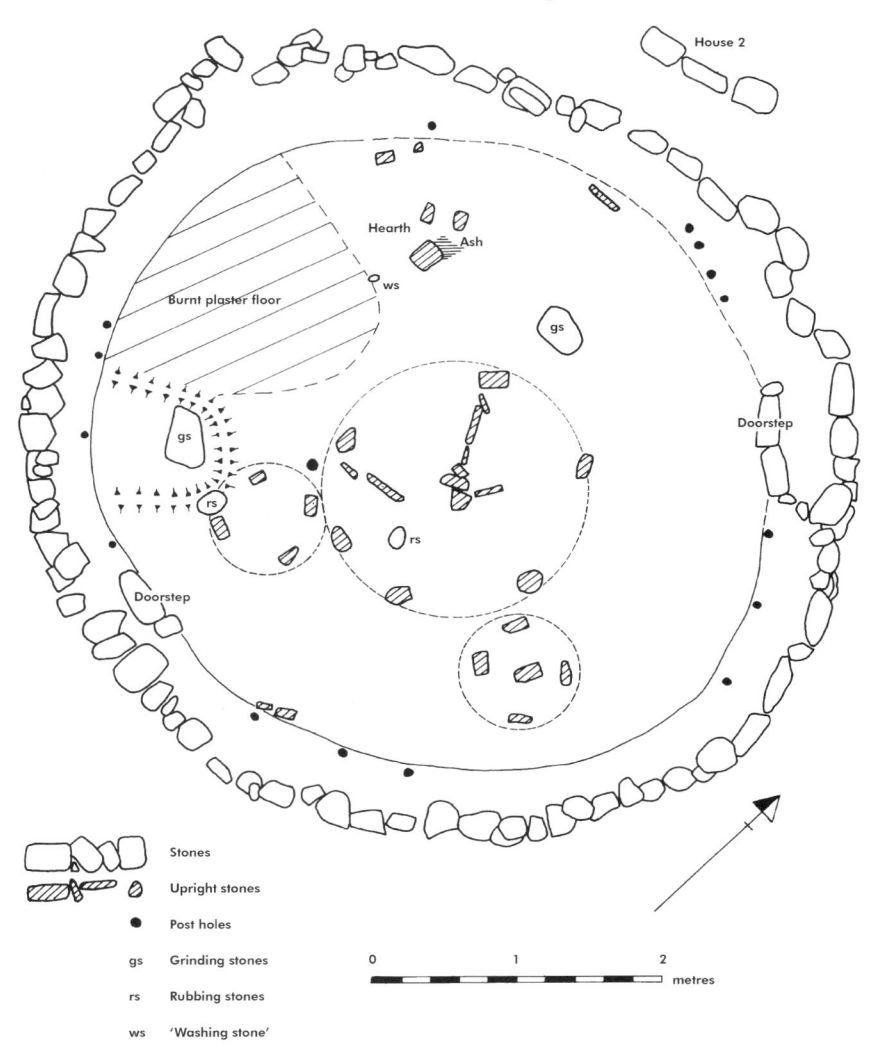

Fig. 90. Chigura. Plan of House 1

Central structure. This represents a high platform decked with stone slabs. The fallen slabs were cleared, measured and removed until only vertical stones set in the floor were left. The floor here is a relatively smooth surface of yellowish grey clay. Some pottery was found among the slabs, including pieces forming much of the upper half of a single pot with incised lines on the neck and shoulder (fig. 92, no.12). The slabs and vertical stones are of a fine-grained laminated slate-like argillite from the local

respectively above the floor. Two of the radial slabs were 51 and 55cm high and the others rather less, so the platform would have stood 50 to 60cm above the floor (substantially higher than the standard raised platforms described in Chapter 5). The pillars are mostly around 20 by 10cm in cross-section, with one 20 by 15; several show signs of rough dressing, as do some of the loose slabs. The positions of the pillars suggest a platform about two metres in diameter, allowing for a slight overhang. The total area represented by the loose slabs was approximately 5.1 sq.m. Some of these may be fallen radial support slabs and some are doubtless from the small platform immediately to the south-west (c.0.5 sq.m), but even so there must have been considerable overlapping of the decking slabs, given that the area of a two metre circle is only c.3.14 sq.m. The two largest slabs have one edge chipped to a curve and measure 85 x 28/34/27 and 86 x 24/36/22cm, giving respective edge curvatures of c.140 and 80cm radius. The length of the loose slabs ranges from 28 to 92cm with an average of 58cm, and width from 11 to 38cm with an average of 24cm.

An attempt was made to estimate the curvature of the fragments of *dhaka* plastering and measurements were taken of a sample of 20 fragments from 8 to 17cm in length. Diameters ranged from 0.52 to 2.20m, with an average of 1.28 ±0.48. Clearly the plastering was uneven and it is doubtful if this average represents the true diameter.

Thus this central structure seems to have been a platform 50 to 60cm above the floor which supported a plastered wickerwork bin up to 2m in diameter and of unknown height. It may be conjectured that this was for storage of grain, perhaps millet or sorghum heads.

Immediately to the south-east and south-west of the central structure were two smaller platforms which must have been around 80cm in diameter. Each has four outer pillars and the south-eastern one has a central pillar as well, the height of all being between 26 and 31cm above the floor. The decking slabs of the south-eastern feature were lying among the pillars, but those of the south-western one were not separable from those of the central structure. There was no clue to the nature of the superstructure of these features which may have supported unplastered baskets.

To the west of the south-western small platform, between it and the wall, is a grinding stone set in the floor, surrounded by a low *dhaka* kerb which abuts the wall at each end. A thick rounded upper rubbing stone lay on this kerb against one of the platform pillars, and another was found beneath the central structure. A second grindstone lay on the floor to the north of the central structure. Within the NNW side of the house is a hearth formed by two short pillars set in the floor and a heavier square stone resting on the floor; fine grey ash lay between the stones. Immediately south-west of this hearth, stratified in the burnt layer on the floor, was a "washing stone", a flat piece of dolerite scored with deeply incised cross-hatching on one side (fig. 94).

The wall of the house is of rather crumbly red-brown *dhaka*, which survives up to about 15cm above floor level on the higher south-east side. This wall was mainly traced by following the edge of the burnt floor and removing the pieces of broken baked *dhaka* whose matrix is very similar to the material of the wall itself. The inner wall face thus traced is 5.00 by 4.50m in diameter, and is some 20 to 40cm inside the ring of dolerite stones which surrounds the house. The outer face of the wall was not detected and it is not known whether it covered these stones. On the SSW and north-east sides of the house, the line of the inner face is interrupted by pairs of stones (with smaller stones flanking them in the latter case) which stand 15 to 18cm above the floor. These must form the raised thresholds of doorways. Just within the wall face it was possible to detect charcoal concentrations representing the carbonised bases of small posts; these rarely penetrated deeply into the *dhaka* of the wall, and it is likely that many more have been eroded out and lost. Certainly the baked *dhaka* wall fragments suggest spacing of only a few centimetres between vertical posts. The base of a semi-carbonised post 7.8cm in diameter was found resting on the floor in the angle between the central platform and the small south-western platform; this could have been the butt of a fallen roof timber. Pairs of stones are set weakly in the floor against the wall on the south and NNW sides, with a small slab in a similar vertical position on the north side.

As noted above, potsherds were found among the loose slabs of the central structure; many of these come from a single vessel which must have stood beneath the south-east edge of the platform. Sherds of a number of very thick coarse vessels were also found here, in one case crushed on the floor inside the SSW doorstep. Other sherds of one or more relatively thin necked pots with incised cross-hatched decoration came from outside H1 and H2 on the north-east side.

The grinding stones are relatively light, ranging in outer dimensions from 28 x 24 to 44 x 28cm, and 8 to 14cm thick, with a longitudinal concavity of 20 to 35mm. One exceptionally large example broken in three pieces measured 51 x 36 x 11cm and 65mm deep. Upper rubbing stones are relatively thick, sub-oval, somewhat asymmetrical, made on smooth granite pebbles; size from 16 x 13.5 x 9 to 24 x 17 x 11cm.

H2 (fig. 91)

H2 is a house floor immediately to the north of H1, there being only 45cm between their stone surrounds. It is roughly oval in plan, giving the impression of being squeezed into the space between H1 and H3, another house floor 70cm to the north. The outer dimensions of the stone surround are 4.50

by 3.90m. The base of the *dhaka* wall is similar to that of H1 but less well preserved; it is traceable around the western side where there is a similar doorstep. A plastered floor survives in the centre and north-west side. On the west side a grinding stone is set in the floor only 14cm from the wall and has a low rounded *dhaka* kerb around its lower side, with a plastered surface lipping up at this end. This grindstone is 45 x 25cm in size and 45mm deep longitudinally, though only 8mm deep laterally.

There is a second possible doorstep at the eastern side of the house, but the stones are irregularly placed and patches of baked clay and a burnt grey area of floor in front suggest that this was possibly a hearth. On the north side a small vertical slab and a *dhaka* surface could also have been a hearth, but this again is not certain. The internal dimensions of the house would have been about 3.60 by 2.90m

There was much loose baked wall *dhaka* on the surface showing close-set poles, mostly around 5cm in diameter but up to 8cm. Soil cover on the floor was a crumbly brown matrix with lumps of burnt *dhaka*, up to 15cm deep at the upper, south side but wedging out to the north. There were a few sherds on the floor, a rounded asymmetrical granite pounding stone 22 x16 x12 near the northern possible hearth, and a smooth dolerite spheroid 85 x 75 x 75 by the hearth/doorstep.

Dating

Two charcoal samples from the floor of H1 have been dated to 85 ±25 BP (Pta-7068) and 100 ±15 BP (Pta-7066), calibrating to a "most probable" calendar date of around AD 1900. This can be no more than a broad approximation but is consistent with a 19th century age such as might be expected

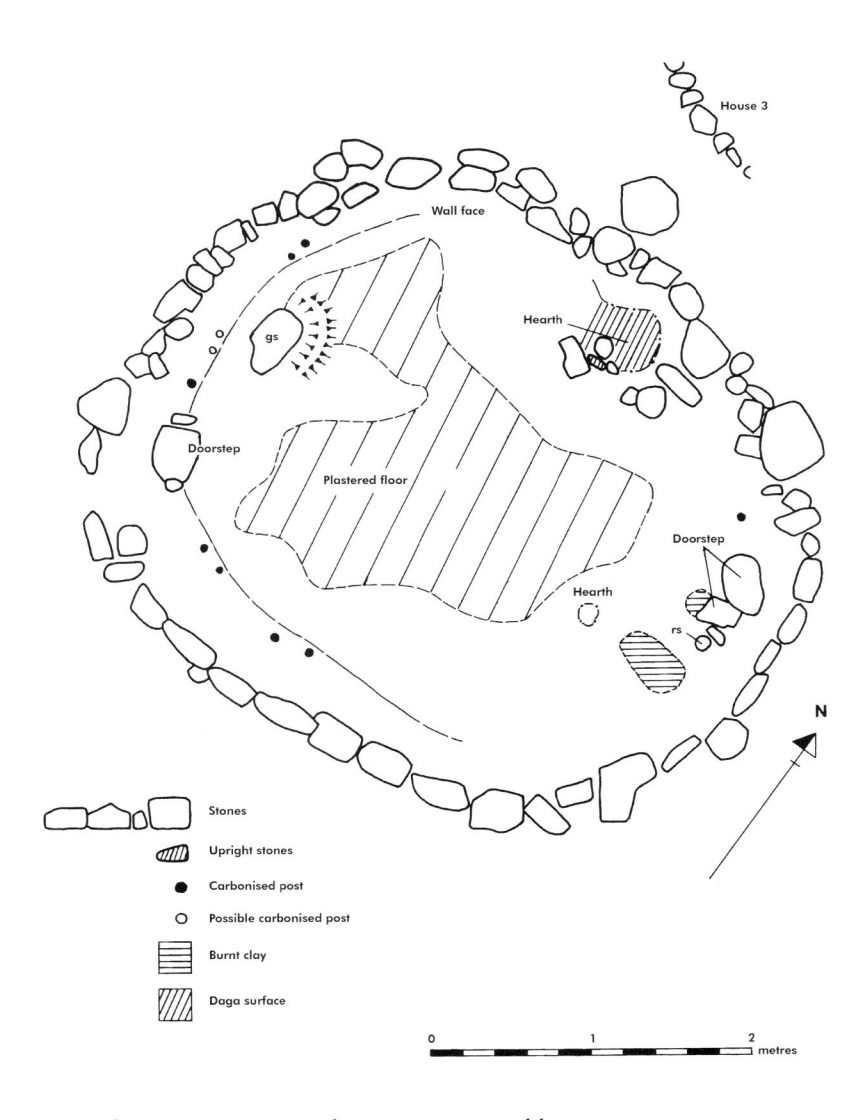

Fig. 91. Chigura. Plan of House 2. gs = grinding stone; rs = rubbing stone

EXCAVATED SETTLEMENT SITES

from the state of preservation of the structures and the large size of many of the potsherds. The date is unlikely to be quite as late as 1900 because a nearby site, 500m to the north-west, is reported to have been occupied by one Tambare, a diviner who died in the 1970s. This latter site has no stone enclosing wall and the pottery is very different, implying a considerable time interval between it and the excavated site.

Finds

Finds were as follows:

	Pottery				Bone frags	Iron	Washing stone
	Rims	Dec	pbs	Coarse			
H1	25	14	251	60	-	1 ring	1
H2	11	4	161	-	5	1 plate	-
Double encl.	1	-	8	-	4	-	-
Mound surface	-	-	48	-	5	-	-
H6 surface	-	-	-	-	-	1 ?axe	-

No glass beads were found.

Pottery (fig. 92)

The pottery sample is relatively small in terms of vessel numbers (16), but there are several reconstructable vessels and the sherds are often relatively large. Vessels comprise six wide-mouthed pots 18-21cm in diameter, with one of 27cm (nos 3-6); five narrow mouthed pots, two of them 18 and 19cm in rim diameter, and one rimless neck only 9cm in diameter (1,2,12,13); three necked pots (unspecified); and two necked bowls, one a roughly finished specimen 21 cm in diameter (7,8). There are no hemispherical or open bowls. Lips are all rounded, about a quarter of them also tapered. Colour is light brown to grey-brown to dark grey; there is occasional sooting of outside surfaces and one vessel has a carbonised residue inside. Firing is generally good and temper is of quartz with occasional feldspar, maximum grain size commonly up to 4mm. Finish is mostly smooth with a few roughly burnished, while graphite burnishing is relatively common. At least two narrow-mouthed pots have graphite burnish on the upper half (2,13), and one of the necked bowls is graphited inside and out. Decoration is all by relatively bold incision, consisting of a cross-hatched or diagonally hatched band on the shoulder, in one case with a second

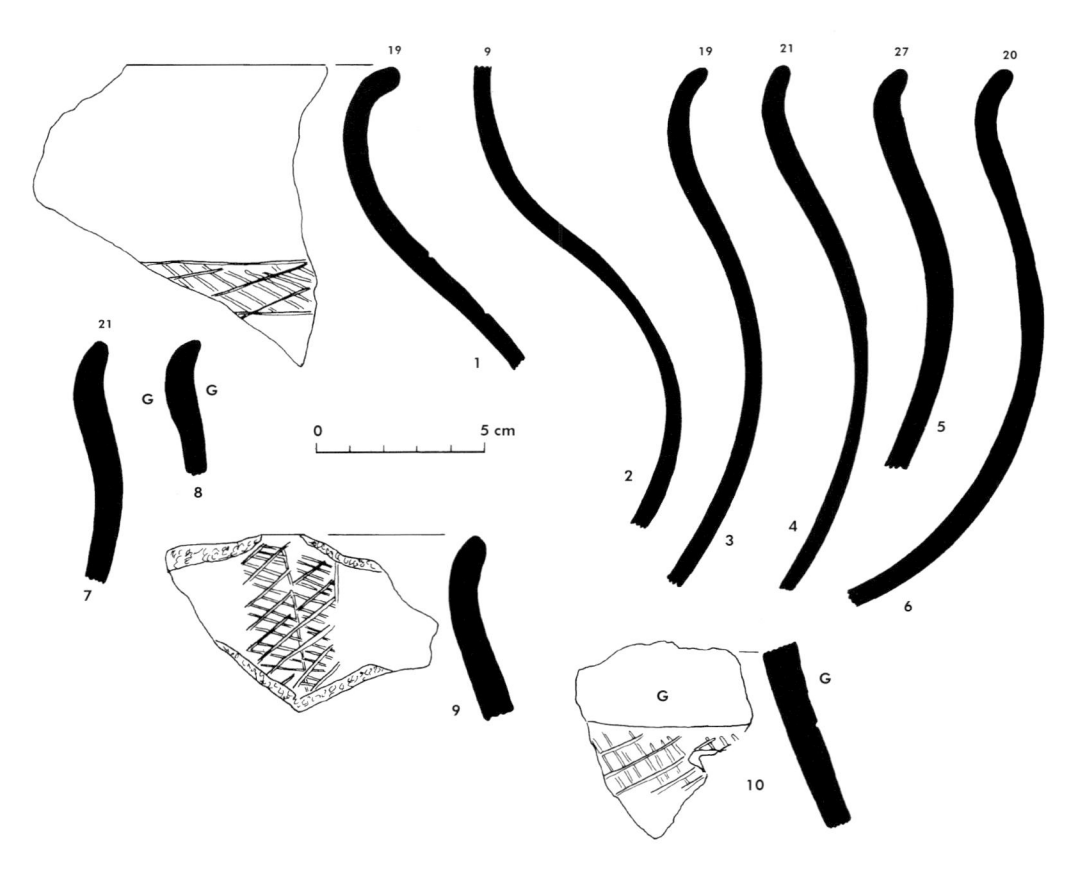

Fig. 92. Chigura. Pottery. G = graphite

band on the rim with vertical panels between (9-11,13,14). Two narrow-mouthed pots have single incised lines on neck and/or shoulder (12). One narrow-mouthed graphited pot with a cross-hatched band has been punctured at least twice on the lower body (13).

- 21 x 2mm from just outside the wall of H2
- a piece of wire c.3mm thick, bent in a ring 20mm in diameter with overlapping ends, on the wall of H1.
- a light axe or heavy hoe tang from the surface

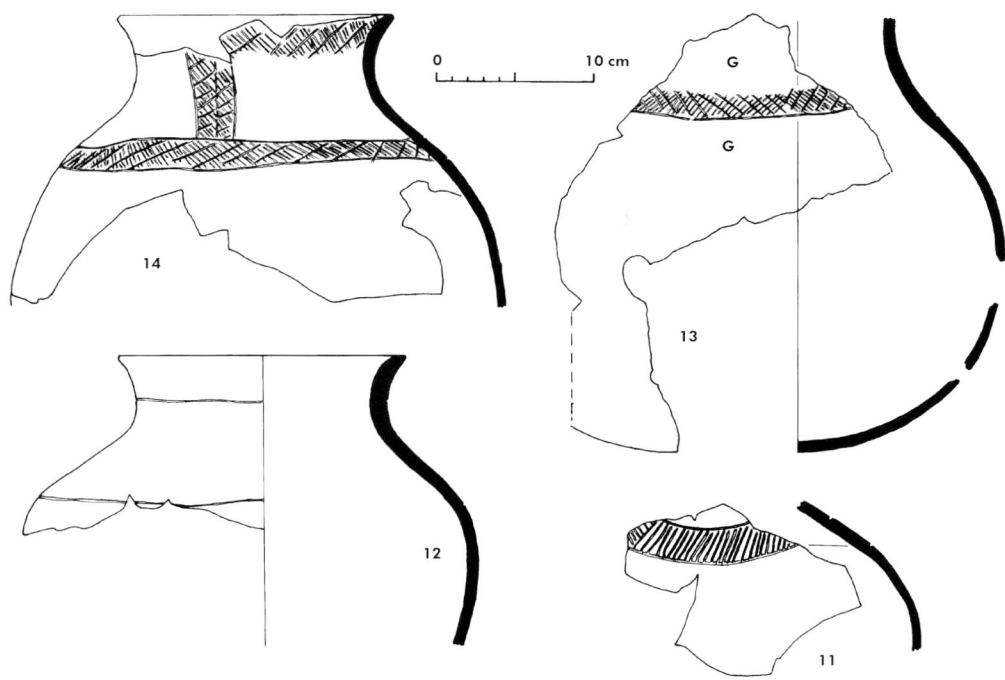

Fig. 92 (continued). Chigura. Pottery. G = graphite

Thick, coarse vessels (fig. 93)

Most vessels are deep, fairly narrow, and sub-cylindrical, sometimes with crude pedestal bases. They are made in a poorly fired orange-brown paste with little temper of quartz and occasional rock fragments. They are very unevenly modelled with walls up to 20mm or more in thickness and bases considerably thicker. Two reconstructed vessels (16,18) give more or less complete profiles, 27cm and 14cm high and around 19cm and 10cm in diameter respectively. One complete rim is somewhat constricted (15) and one base (17) may be a complete bowl profile or possible the base of a taller vessel. Similar vessels have been observed as surface finds at a number of sites in Chigura and also in the Mazarura area as at Chirangeni. They are consistently associated with storage structures, the storage house here and raised platforms at Chirangeni, and are likely to have had some storage function themselves, probably for dry material. No carbon residues have been noted.

Iron

The iron objects consist of:
- a flat fragment of plate with a curved edge 38 x

of H6 on the eastern side of the enclosure. This is V-shaped, 119mm long and 6mm thick, 23mm wide at the broad end which tapers to a sharp roughly curved edge. The iron at the end appears flaked by rust (fig. 94).

Bone
The bone fragments are unidentifiable.

Washing stone
A sub-rectangular piece of dolerite 90 x 59 x 24mm with rather irregular cross-hatched scoring on one side (fig. 94).

In addition there was one small piece of slag (6gm) from the mound and a piece of what appears to be leather from the floor of House 1.

Discussion

This site must represent the homestead of a relatively wealthy family, with three households/kitchens and four storage houses. As with MSE17 at Ziwa, the raised platforms may represent sleeping huts or further storage. Livestock would have been housed in the adjacent double-concentric enclosure, probably a few cattle in the central enclosure and

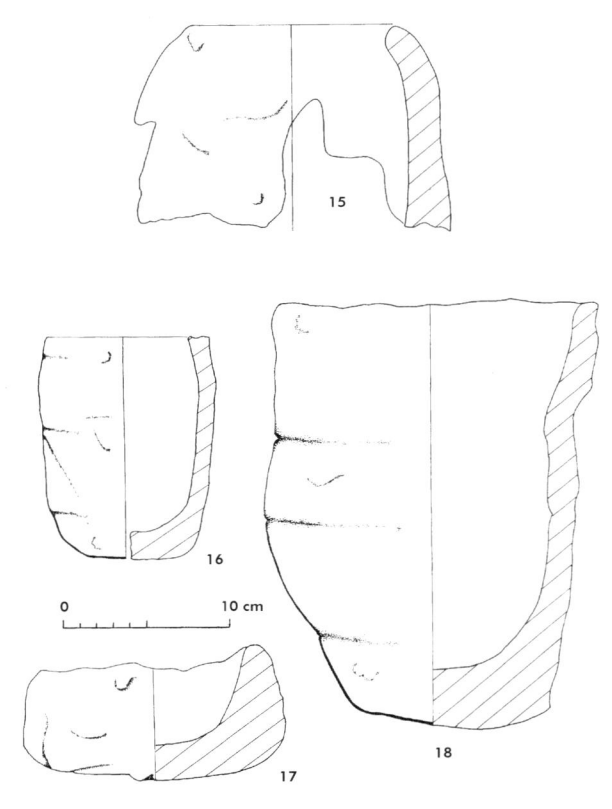

Fig. 93. Chigura. Thick coarse ware

possibly small stock in the outer. There seems to be no special provision for small stock in the houses, a feature of many other sites of the Nyanga complex.

or perhaps after its abandonment.

Parallels for the structures are mainly found in the northern lowland areas of the complex, though the raised platforms are ubiquitous. Double-concentric enclosures extend from Ruangwe to Mazarura, with some examples southwards to St Mary's (Chirawu 1999). In this northern area the central structures are well built with solid walls, while the outer wall is lower and rougher; internal dimensions of the central structures are comparable to those of the pits of pit-enclosures further south but generally smaller than those of highland pit-structures. Multiple enclosure entrances are common in the Ruangwe area but less so elsewhere. The storage houses are not common but at least one, also associated with the thick coarse vessels, was observed in Mazarura, a few kilometres north of and above Chirangeni. In addition, there appear to be several similar structures in Summers' plan of his Site XXII just north of Nyautare, although he did not excavate them (1958:104), as well as a number of smaller "stone tables". The incised cross-hatched pottery and thick coarse ware also form a link with Chirangeni; the former was relatively common in Summers' (1958) excavations in the Nyautare area.

The recent radiocarbon dates from here and from Chirangeni indicate that at least some of the occupation of these northern lowland ruins belongs to the 19th century and postdates the occupation of Ziwa. This could represent a shift of habitation northwards with concomitant cultural developments in homestead design and domestic structures, but it

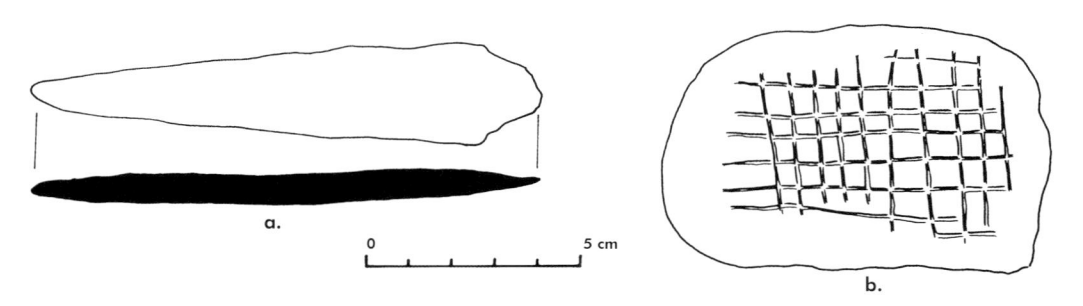

Fig. 94. Chigura. Iron axe and washing stone

The probable deliberate blocking of the double enclosure has a parallel in the common blocking of pit entrances at Ziwa ruins. As discussed elsewhere, this may have a functional explanation or be a symbolic action on the abandonment of the homestead. The homestead was destroyed by fire at,

seems more likely that these more northerly lowland sites represent a separate though related set of communities. Other sites, including less well preserved examples, need to be excavated to give a better idea of the chronological range of the northern ruins.

Plate 24. Nyangui 1732DD27, Hollow A. Grave cut through the cobbled floor

Plate 25. Matinha I, 1. Pit and entrance passage with stone paving and revetment

Plate 26. Nyangui G1/21. Mouth of the tunnel at the upper side of the pit

Plate 27. Nyangui G1/21. Lower revetment of the main platform over the drain. Appended platform to right

Plate 28. Ziwa MSE17. House 1 from the south

Plate 29. Chirangeni enclosure. House 1A with H1B behind

Plate 30. Chirangeni enclosure. East side of House 1A.

Plate 31. Chigura. North half of the inner enclosure of the double concentric enclosure

Plate 32. Chigura. Storage house H1 after excavation

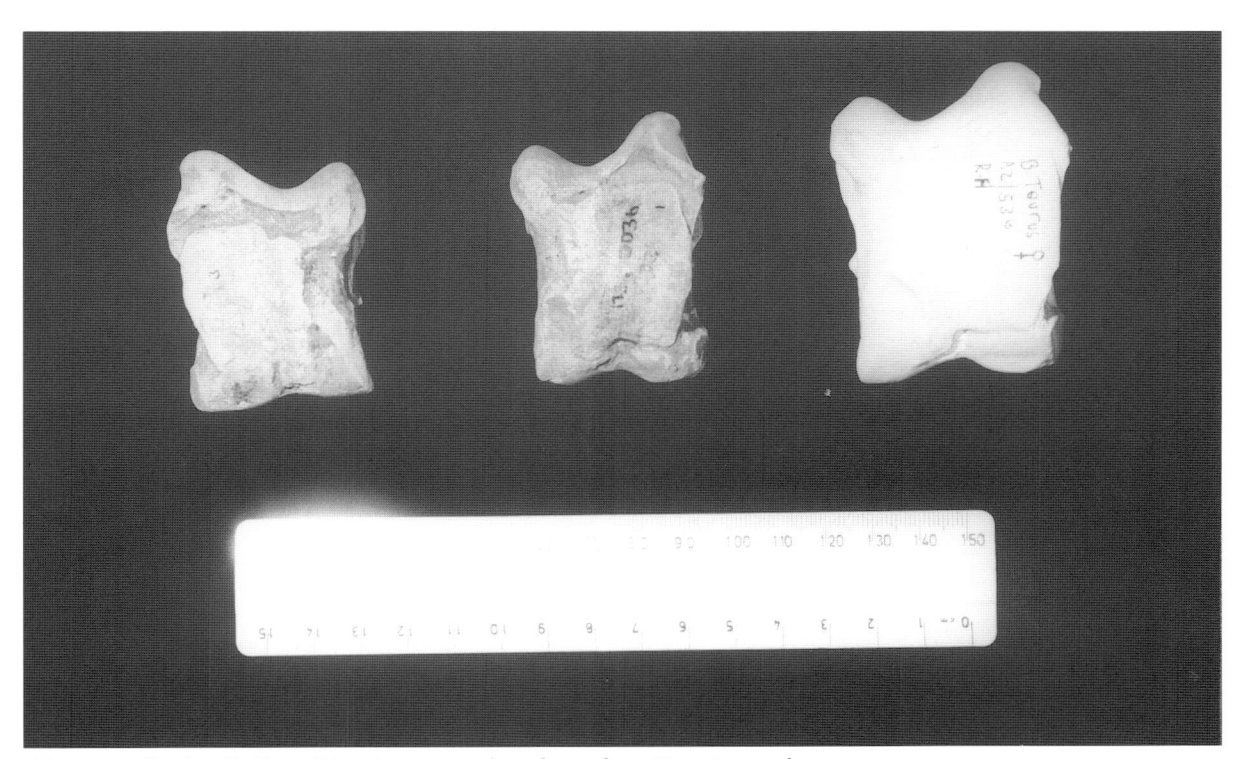

Plate 33. Cattle tali from Muozi compared with modern Nguni sample

ANNEX

HISTORY AND ARCHAEOLOGY IN NYANGA

by David Beach

This Annex reproduces a paper written by the late Professor Beach for the PanAfrican Congress of Prehistory which met in Harare in 1995, although in the event only a very summary version was presented and published in the proceedings (Beach 1996). He had previously included a brief consideration of the history of the Nyanga area in several books (1980, 1994a,b) and was undertaking a more detailed study of the pre-colonial history of northern and eastern Zimbabwe and adjoining Mozambique as part of his comprehensive enquiry into the history of the Shona people. The paper was thus presented as a preliminary assessment while the research was still in progress. The work was sadly terminated by his untimely death early in 1999 and the paper was never revised as he intended, to incorporate further reflection and to take account of the results of the recent archaeological research. Certain conclusions suggested in Chapter 7 on the basis of the archaeological evidence differ in some respects from his interpretations and it is to be regretted that these differences cannot now be reconciled. Such points include the correlation of the archaeological evidence with documented political (as opposed to social) units and whether the initial stages of the complex (beyond Beach's time frame) should be ascribed to ancestral "Shona" peoples.

Nevertheless the paper provides an important historical and linguistic background to the archaeological complex and publication here is a small tribute to his life and work. There has been some minor editing of the original, notably the reduction of end-notes by bracketing in the text those references which are duplicated in the main list of references.

Introduction

The 'Nyanga' archaeological complex, comprising terraces, channels or furrows, pit-structures, enclosures and stone strongholds, covers much of the modern Nyanga district of Zimbabwe. It is also found in the northern half of the Makoni district, and in Dowe, the eastern border area between the Mutasa and Mutare districts. Apart from reported terraces and fortifications on the eastern side of the Chimanimani range and two pit-structures in the Nyamakwarara valley, it does not seem to occur in Moçambique.[1]

Since their 'discovery' by Europeans in the 1890s, the ruins of the Nyanga complex have attracted much attention from amateur and professional archaeologists, but relatively little from historians. One of the reasons for this has been the fact that the Nyanga complex lay largely outside the main area of activity of Portuguese traders from the early sixteenth century onwards. Only in 1857 was there a brief reference to a gold mine in Nyanga (Beach 1988:7; 1994a:126-9). Another reason was that literate observers were not necessarily interested in terraces or pit-structures, and did not always report them. The outlying cluster of stone structures in Dowe was within 15 km of the historical capital of Manyika at Bingaguru, and may well have been seen by traders using the Honde or Nyamakwarara valleys to reach Manyika from Sena. Yet neither the 'Descripcão Corográfica' of c.1794 [2] nor the J.C.Paiva de Andrada - H. Kuss expedition of 1881 noted them.[3] Andrada in 1889 passed right through the terraces on both banks of the Nyangombe, but reported none of them.[4] The 1892 border commission was probably too far east to see ruins, but that of 1898 must have done so but did not mention them.[5] Neither did a survey report of 1897 which covered the entire 'ruins' area.[6] In short, the ability of written sources to record aspects of the Nyanga complex depended entirely on the interests of the writers. This factor was to persist in the colonial period.

The same limitations were true of collections of oral traditions. As far as Europeans were concerned, some were prejudiced in advance and did not believe that traditions could be relevant:

> "There are many native traditions regarding the ruins, but they are too long to tire you with" (Rossiter 1938:101).

However, as will be shown, some Europeans

did make enquiries. These were affected by the fact that most but not all of the complex was no longer functional by the 1890s. Consequently, not enough of an effort was made to collect traditions or oral histories. Those that were collected were not often treated sufficiently seriously. African historians began to consider the problem in the 1920s, and obtained better results. None of these efforts were able to benefit from modern approaches to oral tradition and history, in particular the analysis of different types of tradition and the reasons why people recalled some aspects of the past and forgot others.

Historical sources on the Nyanga complex

Documents
These cover the earliest direct observations of the complex from 1872 to 1905 and then cases where parts of it were still functioning up to the 1940s.

1872: C.Mauch observed terraces in Tsangura near the Nyangadzi. He apparently assumed that they were recent (Burke 1969:231).

1891: F.C.Selous and W.L.Armstrong found three deserted strongholds close to Mount Dombo.[7]

1894: G.D.Fotheringham and others reported that, whereas the Manyika in the upper Nyangombe valley were occupying hedged (rather than stone) enclosures, some of the furrows were still in use for irrigation. North of the Nyangombe and west of the main Nyanga escarpment, the complex was apparently disused.[8]

1894: M.J.C.Jeffreys recorded ruins and complete depopulation all the way from Nyakanga to Nani on the west side of the escarpment.[9]

1894: N.MacGlashan reported ruins in the same area. Some, especially 'forts', were well preserved.[10]

1897: Harding's patrol reported abandoned and apparently ancient fortified villages and terraces, and complete depopulation, all through Tanda and Rathcline until Ruchera was reached.[11]

1897-8: H.Schlichter distinguished between the inhabited area south of modern Nyanga town and the depopulated area to the north. He also distinguished between 'old negro cultivators' of rice and terraces and 'ancient' forts, pits and furrows (Schlichter 1899).

1898: T.Edwards recorded abandoned buildings and terraces in the same area as the 1894 reports (Hall and Neal 1904:353-60).

1899: L.G.Puzey reported the same abandoned buildings and terraces and a disused furrow, but not pit-structures (Hall and Neal 1904:360-5).

1899: C.Peters reported the same ruins between Nani and Nyanga town and then pit-structures, often partly filled in with trees growing inside (Peters 1902:155-183).

1901: J.G.McDonald reported the same buildings as abandoned (Hall and Neal 1904:365-7).

1904-5: R.N. Hall (1904, 1905) reported the strongholds in the Rhodes estates as abandoned, but thought that the house foundations inside were of recent African origin. He then added to his first report that, whereas most pit-structures were partly filled in and had trees growing inside, Africans still used some as kraals for goats and sheep, living in houses around them. He repeated this in Hall (1909).

1905: D.Randall-MacIver (1906) reported that the entire complex was abandoned, except that one village apparently lay within the Ziwa-Nyahokwe group of structures.

1949: E.M.Finch (1949) reported that people on the upper Tsanga were still using furrows for irrigation.

1949: W.H.Stead (1949) reported that terraces were still in use in the Nyamaropa area, and obtained second-hand evidence on small cattle still in the area.

1949-51: R.Summers and K.R.Robinson saw recent irrigation furrows in use in the Zimbiti area. (Summers 1971:174)

Oral traditions and histories
1897-8: Schlichter (1899:378), referring to the "northern plateaux", apparently north of the upper Nyangombe valley and west of the main Nyanga escarpment and thus in Unyama, was told that the buildings there were abandoned (i) because it was too cold and (ii) because there had been a big battle there and that the people were afraid of ghosts.

1899: Puzey was told that the people had no opinion on the ruins, which had always been there (Hall and Neal 1904:365).

1899: Peters, entering Unyama from Hwesa, was told by his Hwesa carriers that the depopulated area south of Nani was 'the country of death' and that ghosts had done the stonework (Peters 1902:159).

1904: Hall (1904:521-2) was told that the loopholes in the Rhodes estate strongholds were in fact functional for arrows, and that they had been in use in recent times as refuges from the Gaza.

1905: Randall-MacIver (1906:91) collected a second-hand 'tradition' from a Bulawayo European that the terraces had been built to keep rhinos from destroying the crops.

1923: J.Machiwenyika recorded the tradition in Appendix I between 1908 and his death in 1924. He does not appear to have travelled north of his family's home in Nyamhuka, and may not have seen much of the complex. He noted that the pit-structures were used for the keeping of very small cattle safe from thieves, but was inaccurate on their design. Ngoni raiders removed the cattle, but herds recovered. Furrows were used for the irrigation of winter crops until very recent times, and Nyanga people were used for the Mutare river Premier Estate irrigation furrow of 1905 because of their known expertise.[12]

1926: S. Muhlanga heard from a Nyanga centenarian that the pit-structures were built against Rozvi and other cattle-thieves who used rufimbi medicine to stupefy villagers and steal very small cattle. Each entrance was controlled from a house by vertical locking bars. Nguni raids removed the herds, and famine and pestilence led to depopulation (Lloyd 1926).

1932: R.D.S.Gwatkin (1932) reported that uneducated people had no explanation for the pit-structures, but that educated people stated that they had been used for very small cattle.

1938: E.Rossiter reported 'many' traditions but recorded none.

1940: C. Martin (1940:21) recorded that one Dowe stronghold was built by an ancestor of the local Muponda dynasty.

1949: Stead (1949:81) recorded that Nyanga informants claimed that their ancestors kept cattle in pit-structures and (now) use them for this, but with the tunnels broken down to allow easy access.

1988: C.Mukaronda (1988:11.3) recorded from both Manyika and Unyama informants that the stone structures were built by their ancestors, both against the Nguni and because of timber shortages. It was not clear whether details of hillside cultivation included terracing.

1988: G.Nyabadza (1988:5.7) recorded from Makoni informants that, whereas some stone structures in the Tanda area were built by their ancestors, others were already there when the people arrived.

1989: C.Chiro (1989) recorded Nyamaropa traditions on the use of terraces, stone strongholds and pit-structures by the local people.

1994: D.Maxwell (1999:19) reported that Hwesa informants stated that the terraces were already there when their ancestors arrived, and could offer no information on their use.

These historical sources on the Nyanga complex itself are only a tiny fraction of the documents and traditions of the region, and the fact that they are relatively scanty indicates that the majority of historical evidence had priorities that were quite different from those of archaeologists. It will be shown that, in fact, the rest of the historical evidence is of great relevance to the problem, but in the meantime it should be noted how important it is to locate both the area and the people involved in each piece of evidence.

The early population of the Nyanga region

District populations

The overall population of Zimbabwe in the early twentieth century is now relatively clearly known. Estimates collected by officials, either from a direct count or, more commonly, a calculation of adult male tax-payers x 3.5, give us a minimum population for each district, and I have indicated that I believe that the latter figure for the early 1920s can be raised by 20 percent, but not more, to allow for the undercounting of children. Whereas estimates up to about 1913 usually show a sharp increase in each district, this was a result of undercounting of tax evaders. By the early 1920s this factor had declined, and any apparent increases more probably reflect the very beginning of the major demographic explosion of this century. Consequently, early 1920s estimates are probably close to the late pre-colonial reality. There is so far no reliable evidence that the precolonial population had ever been higher, whereas this was not true for countries north of the Zambezi. District figures spaced according to the known distribution of population from contemporary documents fit into a formation I have called the "Great Crescent" of population, an area of preferred settlement along the eastern side of the main watershed of the Zimbabwean plateau that appears to have a history of over 1500 years.

The area under discussion falls within the Great Crescent, and the Nyanga district in the early twentieth century was neither more nor less populated than most others in the Crescent. However, in 1917 there was a considerable influx of refugees from Mozambique, and in that year the indigenous population was estimated at 17 539. Allowing a 20 percent increase for undercounted children, which is probably on the generous side in view of higher than usual infant mortality, we have a population of 21 047. Obviously, this is not a precise figure and, again obviously, it includes parts of Nyanga outside the Nyanga complex area. Makoni and Umtali districts in 1917 had populations arrived at by the same method, of 28 829 and 25 169, but very few of their people lived within the Nyanga complex area.[14]

Local populations (fig. 95)
The next stage is to look at population distribution within the Nyanga and northern Makoni districts. Here, it is necessary to use the earliest sources available. The reason for this is that very large parts of both districts were alienated for European settlement in the 1890s and 1900s. A surprising number of individual farms and land company estates were never effectively established and the inhabitants have continued to live on them to the present. Others however were taken up. Evictions had begun by at least the early 1920s, and continued at varying tempos until the 1970s. A peak period for evictions in Nyanga was the late 1940s. Consequently, a survey has been made of population estimates for sub-regions within each part of the Nyanga complex area in the 1890s and 1900s for the most part. These estimates, made by surveyors, officials and other observers, are obviously well below the real figures, but there is no special reason to expect exaggeration. The figures and their sources are given in Appendix II to this chapter.

Although the figures do not cover every area – the Lucan/Sawunyama, Mayo-Weya and an irregular block from Mhembere through Domba to Bonda are cases in point – enough of the ground is covered to present a fairly clear pattern. It falls into two parts, a depopulated and a populated zone.

The depopulated zone starts just north of Nyanga town, and covers the entire area just west of the main Nyanga escarpment as far north as Nani. However, there were small settlements in western Castle Nock/Zimbiti and St Swithin's, close to the Nyangombe. West of the Nyangombe, Rathcline and Tanda were virtually depopulated, though there was a small Unyama community in Tanda not observed in the 1890s.

Outside this depopulated zone, population seems to have been relatively even. On the map (fig. 95), polygons mark groups of 100+ people by 1890s-1900s estimates, spaced out evenly within the property in question. Inyathi Block, the Rhodes estate and Scotsdale/Nyamaropa come out with slightly higher densities and Inyanga Block with a slightly lower one, but I doubt if this is particularly significant. The Holdenby/Honde valley area was heavily wooded but had a significant number of villages, and Manga a greater number. From Dowe right round to Nyamhuka settlement seems to have been fairly even. There may have been a small patch of thinly-occupied land just west of St Triashill/southern Nyamhuka, but otherwise settlement in Makoni district seems to have been continuous along the watershed to Weya and Headlands. Population between Weya and Tsangura seems to have been sparse. Most of the population of Hwesa/Nyanga North was in its southern and south-eastern end.[15]

The existence of very marked differences of population density within the Nyanga complex area is striking. It is even more striking when it is realised that the depopulated areas lie almost entirely within Unyama, or where Nyama people lived west of the Nyangombe until the late nineteenth century. In fact, it will be shown that the oral traditions of the Sawunyama dynasty go far to explain them. Indeed, although there are significant areas of the Nyanga complex that lie outside the Sawunyama territory, that territory is so central to the complex that, given the time depth of Sawunyama traditions, it would be remarkable if there turns out to be no connection between them. But before turning to traditional history, the ethnographic and linguistic background must be outlined.

Totems and languages

Totems
One of the fundamental ways in which Shona-speakers have identified each other is through the *mutupo* (plural, *mitupo*) or totem, typically multi-purpose elements of Shona culture. Inherited through the male lineage, the totem is variously a

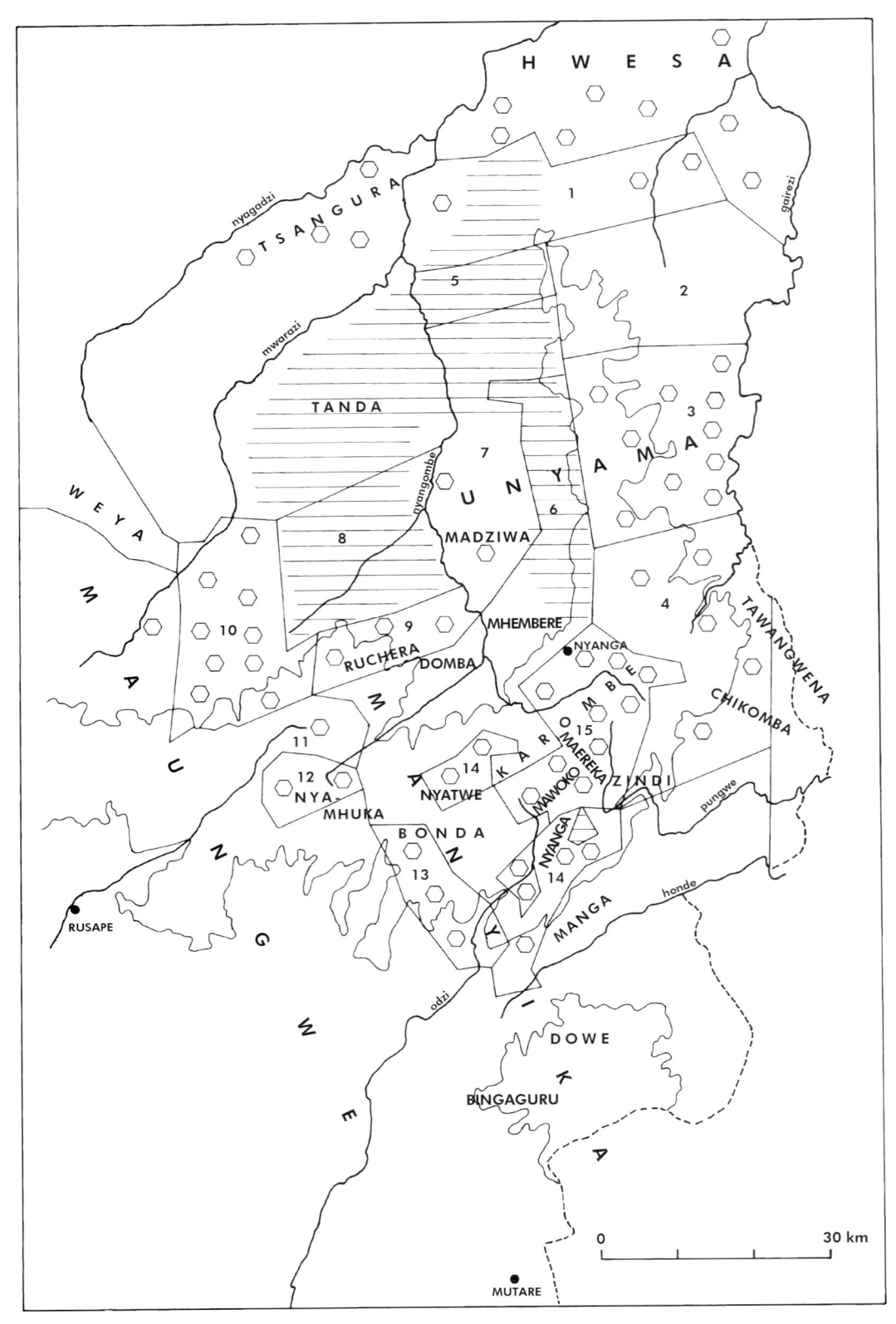

Fig. 95. Nineteenth century polities and population in the 1890s. Shaded areas were unpopulated. Each polygon represents approximately 100 people spread evenly within the property in question. Numbers refer to Appendix II. The 1500m contour is shown. Black dots are modern towns

badge of identity, a marker that indicated a limit to inter-marriage and a guide to token abstinence and morality. Thus a person of the *shumba* (lion) totem inherits it from his/her father, recognises other members of the *shumba* group as close or more remote relatives according to circumstances, may not normally marry another *shumba* person or eat lion (!) or from a lion's kill. Nearly all northern, central and southern Shona seem to be restricted to a rather limited set of totems, and these, especially *shumba*, *tembo* (zebra), *moyo* (heart) and *tsoko* (vervet monkey) are also to be found among the eastern Shona, east of the Nyangadzi, Macheke and Save rivers. However, the eastern Shona also have totems that are relatively rare west of these rivers, and when they do occur there, there is usually a tradition of immigration from the east. The general impression given by a combination of totems and traditions is of an early population partly interpenetrated by northern/central/southern totem groups through migration.

Typically eastern totems include *humba/nguruve* (wild pig - Makombe dynasty, Barwe), *mhara/guzho* (impala - Chikore dynasty, Tsangura), *shonga/nyati* (buffalo - Makoni and Chipunza dynasties, Maungwe, and Chirara dynasty, Bvumba), *shato/mheta* (python - Sawunyama dynasty, Unyama), *mhoni/chiwambu* (fieldmouse - Katerere dynasty, Hwesa), *newa/ingwe* (leopard - Tawangwena dynasty), and *ishwa* (termite).[16] In the Nyanga district the three main dynasties of the north – Sawunyama, Katerere and Tawangwena – have totems of this type, distinct from the *shumba* totem of the Manyika in the southern part of the district. Given that Katerere and Tawangwena at least have fallen within the political orbit of the *humba/nguruve* Makombe dynasty of the Barwe territory in recent times, it is understandable that the Manyika should have regarded the northern Nyanga peoples as being rather 'foreign', even before the Barwe immigration of 1917.

Languages and dialects

We know now that the Shona language covers the whole of the Nyanga district, and extends into the western and southern parts of Barwe in Mozambique, eventually reaching the sea between Beira and the Zambezi (Beach 1994a: 26). Beyond these limits is the Eastern Bantu language group labelled 'Sena' though in fact it extends up the Zambezi. Its precise border with Shona is complex, still unclear and complicated by migrations. Unfortunately, for a long time the confusion has been compounded by undue reliance on the work of C.M. Doke in 1929.

Doke spent four days around Mutare and another five in Nyanga and Makoni, collecting word lists and recording pronunciation. He also recorded from migrants in Harare but he never went north of Nyanga town. He also recorded from very few informants. The result for what is now called the Nyanga dialect cluster of Shona was a chain of dialects at short intervals along the Rusape-Nyanga road within a 20 km radius: Nyamhuka at Triashill, Nyatwe, Domba, Karombe at Juliasdale and Bunji in the Rhodes estate. Unyama was recorded at Nyanga (Doke 930:114-5). Subsequent studies seem to have confirmed that Nyanga Shona was and is distinctive, even affecting the speech of Shona-speakers in the emigrant Chirimuhanzu dynasty in 1854, but studies have been complicated by the passage of time and the eviction of people from their old areas into Zimbiti.[17] However, Doke never visited Hwesa or Tawangwena, and classified their speech as "Sena" on the basis of interviews in Mutare. (As both areas had Barwe immigrants from 1917, his data may well have been Sena – Doke1930:27). Consequently, these far northern and eastern Nyanga people were marked as "Sena" speakers on linguistic maps,[18] archaeologists were influenced by this (Summers 1958:265; 1975:247) and so was I (Beach1980:185). As some Sena and Shona-speakers have been called "Tonga" (Beach 1980:158), it was possible to write of north Nyanga being occupied in the past by Tonga *people* akin to those of the Barwe *territory* who spoke the Sena *language* either building or influencing the Nyanga *archaeological complex* and affecting the Nyanga Shona *dialects*. It would probably be safer to examine the question afresh.

Local histories

These six case studies cover all of the major and minor dynasties in and around the Nyanga complex area, starting in the west and proceeding in a decreasing clockwise spiral until the Unyama area is reached. Each history relies upon a mixture of documentary and oral sources, and must be regarded as a preliminary summary.

Maungwe

The history of the Makoni and Chipunza dynasties of Maungwe, of the *shonga* totem, pre-dates 1633 when Makoni was mentioned as ruling Maungwe by Fr Gaspar de Macedo. As the related Chipunza dynasty is apparently genealogically senior to that of Makoni, the dynasty has to be very old indeed (Beach980:166). However, in spite of an article that stretches the genealogy to fit the documentary dates

(Abraham 1951), a close examination shows that in fact it does not predate the first half of the eighteenth century, at least a century too late.[19] Nevertheless, there has never been any serious doubt that the *shonga* dynasties built the stone structures such as Chitakete that post-dated the Great Zimbabwe culture in the valleys of the Rusape river system; even those in favour of exotic origins for the Great Zimbabwe culture conceded this (Bent 1896:354). Just how far the *shonga* effectively occupied the northern parts of the modern Makoni district is not totally clear. Documents and traditions are positive that there was more or less continuous occupation of the Inyathi Block-Weya-south-eastern Mayo area for at least a century before 1900, where there are terraces and pit-structures.[20] But Tanda, northern Mayo and Tsangura present complications.

Makoni told Andrada in 1889 that he ruled all the land west of the Nyangombe opposite Sawunyama and Katerere.[21] This included Tsangura, which was practically independent, though in no position to resist Maungwe forces. The Mwendazviuya and Machorokoto *shonga* houses are thought to have been in Weya in about 1900,[22] while those of Makumbe and Maparura only moved into Tanda recently, the former in 1949.[23] The Sagovakova house claims to have occupied the terraced area of south-western Tanda between Nyahowe and Hwadza until Nguni raids drove it into exile in Nhowe, only to return in this century (Nyabadza 1989). As we saw, in 1897 Tanda and Rathcline were apparently empty, but Unyama traditions state that the major Nyoka house was in Tanda from the late 18th to the late 19th centuries.[24] In short, while Makoni claimed the land between the Nyangadzi and the Nyangombe, actual occupation seems to have been thin and not all by *shonga* houses, which fits traditions that Makoni rulers saw the area as a hunting reserve.[25]

Tsangura

The Chikore dynasty of Tsangura is of the rare *mhara* totem, best known through the Mashayamombe-Maromo dynasties of the west-central Shona area (Beach 1994b: 68-72). Consequently, some traditions claim that Chikore came from the much greater Mashayamombe dynasty.[26] But Mashayamombe-Maromo traditions claim, in much more detail, that the *mhara* dynasties came from Dzete, only some 15 km west of the Nyangadzi in Nhowe (Beach 1994b: 68-72). Chikore genealogies are short, but Mashayamombe-Maromo traditions put their emigration from Dzete in the last half of the 18th century, at the time of the documented Hiya raids, which are also reported in Nhowe traditions.[27] These, or the expansion of the Nhowe, whose traditions do not mention Chikore, might have led to this move.[28] A Bunjira group claims to have preceded Chikore, but after colonial rule began. As Chikore was in Tsangura by 1872 and Makoni tradition supports Chikore for its own reasons on this issue this claim is probably untrue.[29] Tsangura contains terracing.

Hwesa

The Katerere *mhoni* dynasty claims origins in "Mbire", which in this case and in others from Manyika to north of the Ruenya seems to mean the Mutapa state area. The earliest ancestor, Dembwetembwe Muriga, is said to have found Nyakasapa in Hwesa, a typical autochthone-figure ignorant of fire. Muriga's death-date is 1769± 36 and, as with most eastern Shona generational dates, this is probably late. Thus the dynasty was probably established in Hwesa by at least the middle of the 18th century.[30] Hwesa consisted of the entire area between Nyangombe-Ruenya and the Gaeresi north of a well defined frontier with Unyama that fringes the northern slopes of the Nyanga highlands. However, only a scattering of terracing seems to have lain within Hwesa itself, in the south.

Tawangwena

The Tawangwena *newa* dynasty originally held a territory that ran from the upper Gaeresi to an unknown limit in modern Mozambique to the south-east, apparently bordering the Chikomba house of Manyika along a line from Mataka peak to the Ruera river. In the 1890s the main stronghold of Tawangwena was on the mountain of the same name east of the Ruera, but there were at least 70 houses (huts) of Tawangwena on the west side of the river. In August 1902 the ruler of the dynasty crossed the river and colonial frontier in advance of the Portuguese forces attacking Barwe from the south. However, another branch of the dynasty continued in Mozambique.[31] Stone structures are noted in the Tawangwena area in Zimbabwe.

Manyika

The history of Manyika is exceptionally well known because its gold mines attracted Portuguese observers from 1512, the earliest known date for the territory's existence. Its dynasty's title of Chikanga was recorded as early as 1573, changing to Mutasa from 1822 (Bhila 1982:10, 157). It seems that its totem changed from *tembo* to *shumba* from about that time, both changes making it difficult for descendants of earlier rulers of the dynasty to succeed to the title. However, oral traditions and genealogies trace the dynasty only as far back as the late 17th century. It is possible that a refugee ruler of the Mutapa dynasty, with practically the same name and totem as those of the founding ancestor of the Chikanga-Mutasa traditions, was established as the new holder of the ancient Chikanga title after the Changamire-Portuguese wars of the 1690s (Beach1980:167). If this is so, the identity of the pre-1690s Chikanga dynasty remains open. It has been suggested that this earlier dynasty was of the *humba/nguruve* totem, related to the Makombe dynasty of Barwe.[32] However, traditions generally agree that the predecessor of the recent (*tembo-shumba*) Chikanga-Mutasa dynasty was the Muponda dynasty of the rare *nyere* or *nzvidzi* totem.[33] This gives us two possibilities: either the Muponda dynasty ruled Manyika before 1573, or it was the 1570s-1690s Chikanga dynasty. Either way, we have a political history of central Manyika that is relatively clear, though it is only from the 1790s that documents record the same names of rulers as those in oral traditions. An important point, related to the pit-structures, terraces and strongholds of Dowe, concerns the location of the Muponda dynasty. Traditions state that it ruled the whole of Manyika before the *tembo-shumba* Chikanga-Mutasa dynasty, and that its capital was at Nyaruhwe about 10km north-north-east of Bingaguru and 10km west of Mount Ruuinji in Dowe, whence it moved after it lost Manyika and where it lived until very recently.[34] In Manyika history these local distinctions are crucial. The history of northern Manyika is covered in detail by the traditions collected by Machiwenyika, and these have been the basis of most studies of the area.[35] The picture that they present is one of the gradual expansion northwards of branches of the Chikanga-Mutasa dynasty up to the frontier as it was in the 1890s. Since the dynasty was more or less at war with Sawunyama then, the impression has been left that it was not just the houses of Chikanga-Mutasa that were expanding, but the frontiers of Manyika as well. In particular, the names of two members of the dynasty – Nyamandoto and Nyarumwe – who triggered off this process, with the latter giving rise to the spread of his sons Mandeya, Saruchera, Sakarombe and Zindi into the northern border areas, seemed to correspond to "Inhamutota" (1813-18) and "Inharugue" (1796-1807, 1818 -22), rulers recorded by documents.[36]

It therefore seemed possible that this northern expansion of Manyika was relatively late. Moreover, those sub-rulers who were in the area first – Dumbwi of Nyamhuka, Mandigora of Bonda and two others who also held the titles of Saruchera and Sakarombe (of Bunji) – might have been connected to the Nyanga complex structures in northern Manyika. It also seemed possible, from Doke's work, that they had non-Shona connections.[37] In other words, it might have been this recent Manyika expansion that brought the Nyanga complex to an end in northern Manyika.[38]

On looking at the evidence more closely, another political and "ethnic" picture is much more probable. Firstly, the "Nyamandoto" and "Nyarumwe" of the Machiwenyika traditions cannot be the rulers of 1796-1822. The Nyamhuka geneaology is much too long to allow for this, Mandeya I having a death-date of *1735 ± 40. (It is not uncommon for personal names within a dynasty to be used more that once.[39]) Secondly, it is much more likely that the northern frontier of Manyika in the early 18th century was just where it was in the 1890s, and that the sub-territories such as Nyamhuka, Ruchera, Karombe and Bonda were simply re-allocated to emigrant houses from central Manyika on different occasions. This is what the 'Descripcao Corografica' of c. 1794 claimed, what happened in Bonda in the 1890s, and what J.G.Storry suggested.[40] The support given to a Chikanga claimant in 1795-6 by Saruchera would also confirm this.[41] Thirdly, there is no longer any need to suggest any non-Shona population in northern Manyika at any time, following the re-evaluation of Doke's work. Indeed, the evicted ruler of Bonda of the early 18th century, Mandigora, had a descendent sub-ruler only a few kilometres away in Shitowa, east of the Odzi, in 1921, and there has been no suggestion that he was non-Shona.[42] This gives us a northern frontier of Manyika in the 18th century that includes Nyamhuka, Ruchera, Mhembere, Karombe and most of the Nyangani range as far as the Ruera.[43] It includes part of the Nyanga complex.

Unyama

Our spiral tour of the territories around the Nyanga complex finally reaches its centre, Unyama territory under the Sawunyama *shato/mheta* dynasty. Like most dynasties from Manyika to beyond Hwesa, it claims to have come from "Nembire" in the Mutapa state. The founder is said to have been Mudziwepasi, and the genealogy gives him a death-date of *1760 ± 32. He may in fact have had predecessors in the area, because the traditions are primarily concerned with the civil war that broke out on his death. His capital was at "Madziwa", one of the most important sites of the Nyanga complex. A subordinate title, Sanyahokwe, survived in the dynasty until at least 1930.[44] Two of Mudziwepasi's sons founded outlying wards, Ganje and Sanyamaropa, on the Gaeresi frontier. On his death, his son Nyoka lured another son, Hata, into visiting their married sister in Makoni's territory, where he was murdered. However, Hata's house won the ensuing civil war, and Nyoka's house was expelled into Tanda. One member had the title Sanyabaku, which suggests that it also covered the whole of Rathcline.[45] Nyoka house and Hata house raided each other over the Nyangombe for five generations. On the death of Sawunyama Nyazema (or Nyakayi Samauzi) of Hata house, no later that the mid-1880s,[46] Nyoka leader Dzimbiti I struck a temporary alliance with Mutasa of Manyika. A preliminary cattle raid by the two was made on Madziwa.[47] The Hata house retreated to a loopholed stone stronghold, up a mountain called "Tani", but below a cliff. A Manyika hero penetrated the stronghold by descending from the cliff in a basket on a rope, panicking the Hata people into leaving their position, only to be routed by the allies.[48] A final two-day battle in eastern Unyama gave the area its name of "the place of blood", Nyamaropa. The two senior Hata leaders died with many of the house, and Kadzima led the survivors first to Maungwe, then into modern Mozambique and finally, ironically, to seek refuge under Mutasa, settling in Manga.[47]

The reason for Mutasa's change of policy was that, very quickly, he had fallen out with the new Sawunyama, Dzimbiti I. There are suggestions that he intended Unyama to become a tributary area.[49] Expansion was now his policy, and it was Manyika raiding that helped to persuade Katerere to make a submission to the Portuguese in 1886.[50] In practice Sawunyama remained independent, but with Dzimbiti I living near the Nyangombe,[51] most of his people living east of the Nyanga escarpment,[52] and a zone that was depopulated between them, from Nyamakanga to Nani. This was probably because it was the area most vulnerable to Manyika raiding, just as it was the easiest and most used route for European travellers in the 1890s. Almost all of Nyoka house abandoned its lands west of the Nyangombe except for the Saturo group that is still there.[53] Nevertheless, its weakness did not stop the Sawunyama dynasty from preying on those even weaker, such as a community on the Gaeresi in 1894.[54]

On the death of Dzimbiti I in 1902, Kadzima claimed the title, but the Rhodesians gave it to the next Nyoka leader, Samkambwa Dzimbiti II, and apart from a temporary union in 1951-68 the two houses have remained separate, with Nyoka rulers taking the Sawunyama title and Hata the Bonde, Gwidibira or Hata titles. However, it is important to note that both houses in this century have had members on both sides of the Nyanga escarpment, just as they had each done during their separate tenures of Unyama before 1902. (Hata house returned after 1902, leaving only a few members in Manga.)[55]

The foregoing history explains much that was mysterious in the earlier sections of this paper. It shows why some areas of terracing on both sides of the Nyangombe were deserted in the 1890s. It explains the legends of ghosts in the ruins area. It suggests why the Unyama people, at least, should have found it hard to keep the Nyanga complex going, and at the same time it explains why their oral traditions have said far more about the civil wars than about terraces or water furrows: land and the right to inherit it were more important than the details of how it was used. However, although Unyama and its temporary extension west of the Nyangombe together cover much of the Nyanga complex area, they do not cover it all, and other factors have to be considered before a general discussion can begin.

Mfecane raiding, famine and the Nyanga complex
The historical sources on the Nyanga complex listed above offer some contrasts. The documents show that, while much of the complex was no longer functional by the 1890s, elements of it – terracing, irrigation and pit-structures – continued in some areas into this century, while oral histories (rather that oral traditions) reported the use of stone strongholds as late as the 1880s. Oral sources, however, tended to offer explanations for the end of the complex. Apart from the implied climatic change suggested by Schlichter's informants, both he and Peters were told of the Unyama civil war. But Machiwenyika and Muhlanga laid stress on the notorious *mfecane*, blaming Zwangendaba's Ngoni for both the removal of cattle and for a war-induced famine caused by the interruption of agriculture. Machiwenyika at least was well aware that not all famines resulted from raiding.[56] Both raids and famines need examination. In both cases, documents give us precise dates for events within the range of Portuguese establishments' sources of information, but areas such as Nyanga outside that range remain hazy. Moreover, by the 1890s there was already a tendency for oral sources to lump together under the names "Zwangandaba" and "Swazi" what were in fact at least five groups of Ngoni invaders led by Nxaba, Mpanga, Ngwana Maseko (and his son's regent Magadlele), Zwangandaba and Nyamazana. (The last-named was technically only "Nguni" and not "Ngoni" as she never crossed the Zambezi.)[57] From the 1820s when the first of these groups

arrived, they were known by the Shona as *madzviti*, a term that was also used for the Ndebele and Gaza Nguni who arrived in the late 1830s. As the Gaza emigrated from the region in 1889, the Ndebele in this century have increasingly been blamed in oral traditions for raids that were in fact the work of the Ngoni and Gaza.

The first and best dated group to enter the region was that of Nxaba. His raiders conquered Sanga, between the Chimanimani range and the Save, in 1827, but it was not until 1830 that he raided the *feira* of Manyika, as well as Teve. In 1832 the Portuguese *feira* was raided again, and in 1833 the eastern Manyika route to Sena was cut by Nxaba and the exiled Mutasa Nyamandoto. Nxaba's main base was Sanga, but his group also had bases in Jindwi and Barwe. In 1836 he attacked Sofala and shortly afterwards was driven from Sanga by Soshangane's Gaza. He then went towards Zumbo and crossed the Zambezi.[58]

The Maseko Ngoni touched Manyika on their route from the Changamire state to the central Shona area before 1835, operated with Nxaba until his defeat by the Gaza, and seem to have been based in Barwe from 1835. In 1836-7 they were raiding on the Ruenya north of the Nyangombe-Gaeresi confluence as far as Tete, and in late 1838 or early 1839 they crossed the Zambezi. However, after the Nxaba-Maseko defeat by the Gaza there were scattered groups of Ngoni in several places, including Cheringoma and the Sena area.[59] There seems to be no contemporary evidence that the Zwangendaba Ngoni ever came close to Manyika.

This is a very brief summary of a complicated situation, but in essence the Nxaba and Maseko Ngoni seem only to have been in the Manyika-Barwe area from 1830 to 1838 at the outside. Whereas they certainly attacked central and eastern Manyika, at Bingaguru and the *feira*, Teve, Sofala, Barwe, Sena, Tete, Budya and the eastern part of the Mutapa state, there is no contemporary evidence that they attacked northern Manyika and Unyama. Obviously, it is possible that they did, but equally their wide dispersal during eight years may have meant that the Nyanga complex escaped.[60]

A much more serious threat was that of the Gaza. They were in the Sanga area from c.1836 to some time between 1838 and 1840, when they returned to the lower Limpopo region. In 1862, under Mzila, they re-established themselves at the extreme southern end of the Eastern Highlands, and were there until 1889 when Ngungunyana led them back to the Limpopo valley.[61] There is no doubt that the Gaza did raid northern Manyika and Unyama, with Mutasa allegedly being pursued to a forest near Nyangani in 1873. However, their last raid on Manyika in 1888 ended in defeat at Bingaguru, and no further raids occurred.[62]

Although Manuel Antonio de Sousa 'Gouveia' was operating from Gorongosa from 1863 onwards, and his conquest of Barwe from 1879 to 1883 led to his occupation of Hwesa in force from 1886 to 1891, there is no strong evidence that his forces were in Unyama or northern Manyika, except in the 1873 war when he was supposedly on Mutasa's side.

In short, if any external raiding did lead to the virtual but not complete abandonment of the Nyanga complex, the most likely villains were the Gaza first, Nxaba and the Maseko Ngoni second, but certainly not Zwangendaba. However, there are serious grounds for doubting whether external raiding had any such effect. We know that from the 1850s to 1893 the Ndebele raided the southern Shona more frequently than anyone else, yet that part of the Great Crescent had more people and cattle than anywhere else in the independent Shona country. Only in the flat country of Sunga and to a lesser extent in Chinhota and Rimuka did they cause any depopulation in the central Shona country.[63] Moreover, from the 1860s to the 1880s the Gaza raided the Duma confederacy, only some 150 km west of their capital. They broke up the political cohesion of the confederacy, but they were no more successful than the Ndebele in depopulating Duma, which apparently had relatively large cattle herds up to 1890.[64] If they had no serious effect so close to home, they are unlikely to have been any more effective far to the north in Nyanga. It is true that in central and eastern Manyika the people concentrated in mountainous areas, and Mutasa's attempt to occupy a low-lying capital on the banks of the Odzani in the 1880s had to be abandoned, but the overall picture for the nineteenth century was not one of collapse.[65]

If we have to suggest a prime contender for the overall decline of the Nyanga complex – and we do not have to do so – then famine is a better candidate than external raiding. Independent studies have shown that a truly catastrophic drought struck the lower Zambezi and the Sofala-Inhambane coast from 1823 to 1831, before the *mfecane* had any serious effect.[66] Clearly Machiwenyika and Muhlanga, in blaming the Ngoni nearly a century later, were confusing the sequence of events. Another great famine that covered the entire region from the Ndebele state to Inhambane – and southwards – also affected the lower Zambezi in 1858-63. It is possible that, once again, the Nyanga complex escaped, for a drought that affected northern Nyanga and the central Shona country in 1871-2 does not appear to have troubled the lower Zambezi, but it seems hard to believe that this was so.[67]

Drought in the Nyanga complex is a complex subject. It falls within a range of climatic zones from exceptional high – and reliable – rainfall to relatively low. Moreover, the mountains create their own local effects, so that even within Unyama the eastern slopes of the Nyanga highlands have much better rainfall than the rain shadow area to the west. Thus, drought in the normally wetter areas could reduce the value of agricultural and pastoral practices that made the most of an already favourable environment, whereas drought in drier areas would severely affect practices that made farming only just possible.

Cattle and the Nyanga Complex

The shortest possible summary of our knowledge of cattle in precolonial Zimbabwe and central Mozambique is that some people had many, some few and some none, but that everybody regarded them as being exceptionally important, and did their best to increase their herds by breeding, trading, theft and raiding.[68] As with the human population, statistics are crucial and problematic. Two complicating factors are the rinderpest panzootic that swept the region in 1896 with dire effects on herds, and the fact that those whose duty it was to count livestock were also those who, in 1894-6, were taking cattle, sheep and goats as part of the Hut Tax system. For both of these reasons, early estimates of cattle numbers were bound to be on the low side.

In July 1895 the Native Commissioner Umtali estimated that there were the following numbers of livestock in the five sixths of Mutasa's area that he had visited: 1150 cattle; 1000 sheep and 3000 goats. However 321, 127 and 843 respectively had already been paid for tax, making a total of 1471 cattle, 1127 sheep and 3483 goats as a basic pre-rinderpest figure. The NC had not yet visited Unyama or Hwesa, which latter area was then under the NC Mtoko who supplied no figures.[69]

The rinderpest struck the central area and the rest of the Umtali District severely, an exceptionally low cattle figure for 1900 of 175 rising to 780 the next year. However, northern Manyika, Unyama and Hwesa in the new Inyanga District had 958 cattle reported in 1900, 1450 in 1901 and then a fairly steady rise to 6400 in 1910.[70] It seems probable that northern Manyika escaped the worst of the rinderpest, because it was off the main transport routes that spread the disease. Harding was able to buy cattle, sheep and goats cheaply from Sakarombe in 1897.[71] As with the human population, it is not certain just when the apparent increase in Nyanga cattle ceased to represent undercounting and began to reflect reality. Probably it was quite early, as cattle ceased to be taken for tax after 1896, while they were harder to hide than taxpayers. But the increase was staggering: although Umtali District overtook Inyanga in cattle numbers in 1929 (19,538 : 18,600), the latter's herds had reached 28,578 by 1938.[72] This kind of increase was general over most of the country, and it is thought to be due in part to the increased grazing available when it was no longer necessary for people to keep their cattle close to places of security.

An intriguing aspect of the Nyanga complex was that of the very small cattle noted by E.A.Nobbs, Machiwenyika, Muhlanga, Gwatkin and Stead. In 1927 Nobbs reviewed the state of Shona cattle and made it clear that, though they were relatively small with the smallest being found in Mutoko, they were not as small as the *kasiri* breed, which was by then virtually extinct except in Marondera.[73] Had cameras been more in use before the rinderpest, the matter of the size of *kasiri* cattle would be known for certain. What is certain is that some Shona cattle were small enough to fit through the doorway of an ordinary Shona house (hut), where they were kept for extra security. There were too many observations of this for it to be a delusion. One good observer, an ex-Native Commissioner and cattle rancher, considered that the very small cattle were deliberately bred in order that they could fit through doorways, and because they fattened faster on limited grazing than large breeds.[74]

On the other hand, *kasiri* cannot have been common, or there would have been far more examples noted. The three cases of *kasiri* definitely being kept in houses all occurred in the central Shona country, as do nearly all of the notes on "tiny" cattle. Evidently, most Shona cattle were small, but only some really small. Other locations for keeping cattle included enclosures between rocks, gullies in the sides of hills or even in the centre of a village in one case.

It has to be stressed that, whatever their size, cattle were part of a complicated set of social and economic values. Like goats and sheep – whose numbers in relation to cattle in Manyika were typical of most of the country – they were valued for meat, but they were also units of account in bride-price transactions. Indeed, sometimes bride-prices were calculated in head of cattle when none were actually exchanged, just as the thousands of *milreis* in the accounts of the Portuguese on the Zambezi were often bales of cloth rather than coinage. For some families, cattle scarcity made actual slaughter uncommon: gold washers from Rupire, west of Hwesa, used to trade gold dust for cloth in Tete, trade the cloth for a cow on the upper Mazowe, butcher it and sell the meat for more gold dust to those who had no other access to beef.[75]

In short, cattle existed in a class situation within a generally poor society, with the owners of a few very small cattle lying between those with only goats and those with several smallish cows. Theft by the not entirely legendary *gororo* semi-professional cattle thieves was a perpetual worry to smaller families without the numbers to mount a full time cattle guard or retaliatory raids to recoup losses. Raids, of course, affected everybody and would lead to all cattle being kept in places of greater safety, people and animals being jammed together until the raiders had gone. But the *gororo* might well be one's own neighbour, and was always a danger (Beach 1994b:262). This picture is based on evidence from the whole independent Shona country, but it is of significance in interpreting the Nyanga complex.

Discussion, argument and interpretation

Dating
Unless the Nyanga archaeological complex entirely predates the historical evidence, the latter has to be admitted to the question. In fact, available radiocarbon dates suggest an overlap with the history, which begins in the eighteenth century. At least, the historical evidence suggests a useful model for consideration of the archaeology.[76]

Historical evidence
Oral traditions, as has already been shown elsewhere, vary in type. Shona "political" oral traditions tend to have a much greater time depth than "economic" or "social" traditions because they are of more relevance to the present than the latter. It is not surprising that oral history/tradition on terracing in Nyamaropa was still available in 1989, as it was still in use in the 1940s. But it is also not surprising that traditions on the complex in northern Manyika were recalled in the 1920s but had virtually faded by the 1980s. The same is true for northern Maungwe and Dowe. Documents are perhaps best for the insight they give into human and animal population numbers and distribution, but they also do much to confirm oral traditions on political boundaries.

Technology
It is worthwhile using a truism here: people are inventive, people borrow ideas, but invention and borrowing do not spread universally. It is quite likely that the people of the Nyanga complex visited Tete, Sena or the *feira* of Manyika, selling gold and ivory or trading surplus food for a few slaves. The "loophole" idea could well have come from the Portuguese, but the Nyanga complex is primarily a triumph of invention. However, the inventions' spread had its limits: it did not spread to any significant extent south of central Manyika.

It seems obvious that the centre of innovation was Unyama, including the temporary Unyama occupation west of the Nyangombe, but invention spilled over into Hwesa, Tawangwena, northern Manyika and parts of Maungwe and Tsangura. This was not a political event, but an economic and social one, which is why traditions say so little of it. The central Manyika cluster of pit-structures in Dowe is unlikely to have been linked to the Muponda dynasty, or it should have covered all of central Manyika and not just a part. It looks very much like am emigrant Unyama house settling in Dowe, perhaps a long time ago in view of the re-use of some pit-structure passages for burials. Such temporary re-settlements of emigrant groups were common in the area.[77]

Interpretation
i. It seems sensible to look for multiple causes and effects rather than single ones.
ii. It is important to bring in the population figures. As Summers (1958:257) warned, the complex, impressive as it is, might well have been the work of a small, locally shifting population. However, if the Nyanga district in the late pre-colonial period had a population like that of 1920, and if Hwesa had about 5000 men, women and children, and northern Manyika 10000, then that leaves Unyama only around 5000. This would explain why so much of the complex was abandoned by the 1890s, in any case: so few people could not possibly have used more than a small proportion of the terraces, furrows, strongholds and pit-structures in any part of Unyama, and it is not surprising that so many pit-structures were abandoned, with trees growing in them. Unless the Unyama civil war's culmination was quite exceptionally bloody, which seems unlikely, the Unyama population cannot have been very high beforehand, or we would have far more emigrant groups of the rare *shato/mheta* totem than is the case today. At a very, very rough guess, Unyama might have had 2000 cattle before the rinderpest, but I am inclined to think that this would have been on the high side. All in all, the Nyanga complex in Unyama was an amazing achievement for so few people, even over two or three centuries, but I find it very hard to see historical support for the idea of a larger population.

iii. Political boundaries matter. If it is true that there was no major change in them over the 1700-1900 period, then archaeological models must take politics into account. Summers' idea of a move from the 'Uplands' to the 'Lowland' is not workable in the Rhodes estates area, unless that was once Unyama territory, because of the boundary, but it might apply inside Unyama, with a shift from the northern Inyanga Block/ Nyamaropa /Sawunyama Communal Area to Zimbiti and the lowlands. However, I doubt even this. From the historical evidence, I would expect the Nyanga complex in northern Manyika to have been run as a chain of semi-autonomous economic and social units, as the northern lands under Mutasa from Nyamhuka to Zindi and Chikomba were obviously operating in the nineteenth century, and probably earlier.[78]

Unyama tends to present a different picture in the historical sources. Only Sanyamaropa and Ganje seem to have been distinct wards, and both Hata and Nyoka houses, when in control of Unyama, seem to have seen the entire territory as theirs. Consequently, a division between 'Upland' and 'Lowland' wards seems unlikely, and transhumance of some kind seems possible. It is interesting that officials and surveyors in the 1890s, thinking of potential European farming but also looking at African settlement, also considered transhumant farming. They thought in terms of summer cropping and winter grazing in the eastern valleys of the Gaeresi system and summer grazing on the high ground, while they saw the main Nyanga escarpment as no barrier to human or cattle movement.[79]

iv. Oral traditions probably deserve a lot more credence than they have tended to be given, when linked to the picture from the rest of the independent Shona country. Terraces and furrows are not clearly explained, and in any case probably had different functions in different parts of the complex. Strongholds are not difficult to explain, remembering that raids were both intermittent and often launched by neighbours within the same territory, rather than by foreigners. As in the rest of the independent Shona country, in areas largely untouched by the *mfecane*, defensive strongholds were only occupied occasionally. Pit-structures seem in effect to be a local equivalent of central Shona house-stalling, by the poorer cattle-owners. Like the enclosures with locking bars in the lowlands, they were primarily against theft by *gororo*, but perhaps also for shelter from the weather. Small cattle and house-stalling, it must be recalled, were apparently not to be found among the (relatively) cattle-rich southern Shona. The argument that small cattle were hard to get into pit-structure tunnels seems to miss the point: it was supposed to be hard to get them out! Larger cattle, obviously, would not fit into tunnels, but in any case they would tend to be owned by the richer families who did not face the same problem.

v. The end of the complex, in one sense, did not occur, as Summers pointed out (1971:174). Again, multiple causes and effects for the decline are likely. The ordinary passage of time with a small population automatically brought many parts of the complex to an end, in each area. The big droughts must have had some effect. The Unyama civil war probably did far more to damage the complex inside Unyama than any external raiding, with whole houses moving in and out of the territory – and it helps to explain the Tanda-Rathcline abandonments, in that case because Nyoka house won its war. The northern Manyika had no reason to fear the Gaza after 1888, nor did they join the 1896 rising, so strongholds were simply not used again, except possibly on the Nyamhuka frontier with Maungwe. Much the same applied to Unyama after the Tani and Nyamaropa battles. Pit-structures and small cattle ceased to be necessary, partly because of the colonial police force and especially because of the great increase in cattle wealth in the 1900s. The last pit-structures were abandoned, and very small cattle were bred out in favour of larger breeds.

Conclusion

This paper does not claim to have "solved" the problem of the Nyanga complex: much of the latter is not explicable by historical evidence. However, it does claim that historical evidence is of value in interpretation, even though more research is required.

Acknowledgements

The author thanks Robert Soper and the British Institute in Eastern Africa/University of Zimbabwe Nyanga project for discussion and, especially, the base map of terracing supplied. I am also indebted to the Research Board of the University of Zimbabwe for grants making possible the archival research in Mozambique, and to the National Archives, Zimbabwe; the Ministry of Local Government; the Arquivo Historico Ultramarino, Lisboa, and the Arquivo Historico de Mocambique, Maputo.

APPENDIX I TO ANNEX

Hist. Mss. MA 14/1/1-2 "History and customs of the Manyika", Lesson 57. "How the cattle kraals were built".

by Jason Takafa Machiwenyika, c.1889 - 1924

Many hundreds of years ago, the people in this country used to dig underground pits which they called *hunza* similar to European mines. These underground pits were built with stones along the walls, in order to keep the earth from falling in, just as is done in the mines. The walls after stone-work were then smeared with mud and the doorways were left at the either [sic] ends of the pits for cattle to go in and out. Thus the way the cattle kraals were built. They were not built of timber or barbed wire as they do nowadays.

When all the cattle kraals were built as explained in the above paragraph, they then built huts on the surfaces of the pits in which the head-men of the villages stayed. Their work was to keep the enemies and robbers off the kraals. These kinds of kraals were secretly built so that neither foe nor thief would easily discover the mouths of the pits during the absence of the keepers. The head-men's huts were linked with the pits mouths, so that the cattle entered through their huts into the kraals. Within the kraals there were passages for letting out the dung. The types of these ancient cattle kept in pits can be easily imagined than described: that is they were very small and funny to look at. They had long horns and the bulls had a huge hump on their necks.

In course of time there came a raid of Zvungendaba. This occurred because Zvungendaba had fought with Mzilikazi and was driven from his country called Shengwe and with him came many followers. He went through the north and killed many people in this country, and others were taken captives. Zvungendaba with his followers took nearly all the cattle in this country. During this period there was great misery in this country, because the people stayed in the mountains fearing Zvungendaba raid. During this miserable time many people were also killed by wild animals in particular – lions, hyenas and tigers. The people had no cattle nor cultivated crops because the people of Zvungendaba speared them mercilessly. They hunted for their food in the forest along rivers and mountains, there again they met with unfriendly animals which greatly multiplied their troubles. After Zvungendaba's raid there came peace in this country and nearly all the people were rich and happy. People began to move westwards where they bought more cattle in exchange with hoes, which were made by old people. If you travel around Umtali and district, you will wonder to see the remains of the ancient buildings built centuries ago before the arrival of Europeans.

When the Europeans came in this country they were very much astonished by discovering old African ruins. The Land-Surveyor Mr. Fairbridge was very much surprised when he discovered ancient ruins, and he thought that they were European because of their magnificence. He asked from old Africans who built them and they answered him that they were built by our grandfathers. He asked whether or not they had wagons to carry the stones, and the answer was 'No, Sir.'

There is also something interesting which used to be done by Manyika people in the north. They used to hoe their fields early in winter, in places where they knew that water can reach easily. The fields were hoed along the rivers, and from these rivers they dug small furrows, which aided them in leading the water to the fields. Some of the furrows came a long distance to their fields. Thus irrigation began before the coming of Europeans. They carefully irrigated their fields in which they sowed these crops: peas, beans, pumpkins, mealies and other roots. The water ran through them rapidly and in a great volume. The countries in which irrigation was carried on are these: Nyatwe, Karombe, Nyamhuka, Bonda, Nyanga and the surrounding countries.

When the Europeans came in this country they settled at Old Umtali in the year 1895 and there they began system of irrigation. They asked from Chief Mutasa whether his people knew how to dig furrows and the chief said 'Go to Inyanga, there you will find people who know how to make furrows.' So the Europeans went to Inyanga where they got some men to do the digging for them. The furrow was dug along the river Umtali which flows towards Premier Estate. That is the first furrow in this country and it passes near Old Umtali Mission. There are many Africans who died during digging that furrow. They were forced to work hard and even beaten to death if they showed any sign of fatigue or laziness. The manager of that furrow was called by Africans Mudabura which means one who beats, and by Europeans he was called Wilson. The other supervisor was called Kaneresi whose nationality was an Indian. It was he who used to beat the people with the foot of the gun, so that many died. That great furrow irrigates the fields of lemons, oranges and many other fruit trees of the Premier Estate under the government control.

APPENDIX II TO ANNEX

Population distribution in the Nyanga complex area 1890s-1920s

Numbers of sub-areas correspond to those on the map.

1. St Swithin's
Part Hwesa, part Unyama: Charterland Goldfields, now Communal Land.
About 200, 1899,[80] but Hwesa (the southern and more populous half of which is on the map) had 1084 taxpayers (x 3.5 = 3 794) (Maxwell 1994:37)

2. Lucan/Sawunyama
Unyama and small strip of Hwesa in north-east: White's Consolidated, now Communal Land.
No figures yet.

3. Scotsdale/Nyamaropa and Nyangui
Unyama: Scottish Africa, now Communal and Forest Land.
100 families (x 3.5 = 350) in 1908,[81] 1028 in north-eastern part in 1921.[82]

4. Inyanga Block
Unyama and part of Tawangwena and Chikomba section of Manyika: Anglo-French Matabeleland/Matabeleland Exploration Syndicate.
500 in 1898.[83]

5. Inverness/St Swithin's
Unyama: French South African Development, now Communal Land.
Unoccupied.[84]

6. 'Dutch Settlement' and Nyanga Communal Land
Unyama: 23 farms of which 8 became Reserve.
25 on New Hanover, 50 on B4 in 1898-9,[83] remainder deserted except for one village on Ziwa (Randall-MacIver 1906)

7. Castle Nock and Carlow/Zimbiti
Unyama: Paulet's Mashonaland/White's Consolidated, now Communal Land.
20 in 1898-9, rest deserted except for Sawunyama Dzimbiti I's village on Nyangombe.[85]

8. Rathcline
Maungwe, Unyama occupation: Rathcline Syndicate/White's Consolidated, now State Land.
Deserted in 1900.[86]

9. Bannockburn North
Ruchera section of Manyika: Scottish African/French South African Development.
300 in 1898-9.[83]

10. Dartmoor/Inyati Block
Maungwe: Inyati Syndicate/White's Consolidated now partly State Land.
252 houses, 1000 people in 1899.[87]

11. Mount Dombo group
Nyamhuka section of Manyika: Cheira-Lesapi Source-Cheira Source-Mount Dombo-Dombo Mission-Silveira.
150 in 1898-9.[83]

12. Michell's group
Nyamhuka section of Manyika: Timaru-Omaruti-Dunedin-Invercargill-Otago-Wick and also Harewood.
350 in 1898-9.[83]

13. Bannockburn South
Bonda section of Manyika: Scottish African/Austro-African Estates, now part of Manyika Communal Land.
300 in 1898-9.[83] All farms between there and areas 14 and 15 thickly populated in 1922, but no actual figures.[88]

14. Manhattan group and Outspan Reserves
Sanyatwe section of Manyika: Manhattan Syndicate, London-Liverpool-York; Sanyanga-Mandigora-Muredzwa section of Manyika, Manhattan Syndicate, Pungwe Falls-Sanyanga's Garden-Iron Cliffs-Minnehaha-Frobisher-Nyamusomoka-Shitowa-Nyawari-Rupangu-The Downs-Hondi Gorge.
In 1922 the Syndicate was planning to evict 600+ people, not necessarily all.[88] Enclaves within this block, first outspans, then reserves, now farms, held: Matiza (Muredzwa) 103, Shitowa (Mandigora) 115 and Musinyanga none (no sign of occupation) in 1921.[89]

15. Rhodes estates group
Karombe section of Manyika: Inyanga Valley-Inyanga Slopes-Inyangombe-Gaeresi-Pungwe Source-Erin-Placefell-Bideford-Fruitfield-Wicklow, now National Park, Forest Land and Nyanga town.
250 householders in labour tenancy (x 3,5 = 1 050?) in 1902.[90]

Estimates for remaining areas fringing the complex are largely found in the references in Note 15.

END NOTES

Unless otherwise stated, all archival references refer to the National Archives, Zimbabwe.

1. Octávio Roza de Oliveira, 'Zimbáuès de Moçambique (Proto-história Africana), *Monumenta*, 9, 1973, 47, 54; Peters (1902: 352).
2. Arquivo Histórico Ultramarino, Lisboa, Moçambique Caixa 17 (série velha), 'Descripção Corográfica do Reino de Manhica, seus custumes e leis ... c. 1794.'
3. H. Kuss, 'Notes sur la géographie de quelques régions voisines du Zambèze,' *Bulletin de la Societé de Geographie*, Paris, vii, 3, 1882, 376-9, and map.
4. J. Renato Baptista, *Africa Oriental, Caminho de Ferro da Beira a Manica*, (Nacional, Lisboa, 1892), map; 1:1 000 000 Carta de Moçambique, Ministério da Marinha e Colónias, Comissário de Cartográfia, 1911, Folha 'Macequece; D.N. Beach, 'As origens de Moçambique e Zimbabwe: Paiva de Andrada, a Companhia de Moçambique e a Diplomacia Africana, 1881-91,' *Arquivo*, 13, 1993, 5-80.
5. J.J. Leverson, 'Geographical results of the Anglo-Portuguese Delimitation Commission in South-East Africa, 1892,' *Geographical Journal*, 6, 1893, 505-18 and map; L 2/2/6/6, Secretary of British South Africa Company, London, to Administrator, Salisbury, 19 November 1898, enclosing J.J. Leverson to Foreign Secretary, Morro's, Gaeresi, 10 August 1898.
6. L 2/1/38, O.H. Ogilvie, Mining Commissioner, Umtali, Report, 28 June 1898.
7. Hist. Mss. AR 4/1/1, Diary of W.L. Armstrong, 15 February 1891.
8. *Rhodesia Herald*, 26 October 1894.
9. Hist. Mss. Misc/JE 1/1/1 'A journey from Manica to Tette, August 1894'; Hist. Mss. Misc/JE 1/2/1, Map.
10. A 15/1/1, N. MacGlashan, MC, Manica, to Mines Office, Salisbury, 10 December 1894.
11. LO 5/4/6/1, C. Harding, OC Native Contingent BSAP, to DSO, Salisbury 9 October 1897.
12. Hist. Mss. MA 14/1/1-2, 'History and customs of the Manyika', Lesson 57.
13. Taylor (1924). This battle was also described, in more melodramatic terms, in Hist. Mss. MA 14/1/1-2, 'History and customs of the Manyika,' Lesson 25.
14. D.N. Beach, 'Zimbabwean demography: early colonial data,' *Zambezia*, xvii, 1, 1990, 31-83; D.N. Beach, 'First steps in the demographic history of Zimbabwe: the colonial period from 1895 to 1922,' in *Demography from Scanty Evidence, Central Africa in the Colonial Era*, ed. B. Fetter, (Lynne Rienner, Boulder, 1990), 47-59; Beach (1994a: 16-23)
15. Kuss, 'Quelques régions', 379; Leverson, 'Geographical results,' map.; L 2/2/117/26, Native Commissioner, Umtali, to Chief NC, 16 January 1908; L 2/1/38, MC, Umtali, Report, 28 June 1898; L 2/1/247/1, CNC to Administrator, 19 January 1897, NC, Rusape, to CNC, 21 November 1899, CNC to Chief Secretary, 5 April 1900 and 8 June 1900; N 3/24/16, Acting NC, Rusape, to CNC, 3 January 1901; N 3/24/1/2, CNC to NC, Rusape, 6 December 1917.
16. R.H. Baker, 'The *Mutupo* among the Wamanyika,' *NADA*, 3, 1926, 48-54; Fernando de Sousa Ladeira, 'Usos e costumes dos Manicas - ensaio etnográfico,' obra não publicada, Beira, 1957; C. Bullock, *The Mashona*, (Juta, Cape Town, 1927), 96-115; Beach (1980, 1994b)
17. K.D.Mkanganwi, 'Notes on the dialects of Inyanga,' unpubl. paper, Salisbury, 1970; Mukaronda (1988:20); G. Fortune, '75 years of writing in Shona,' *Zambezia*, i, 1, 1969, 57.
18. 1:2 500 000 Map of African Tribes and Languages of the Federation of Rhodesia and Nyasaland, Director of Federal Surveys, Salisbury, 1964.
19. P. Carbery, 'Maungwe traditions,' unpubl. MA Oral Tradition paper, University of Zimbabwe, 1986, 18; Beach (1994b: 276).
20. See the last six references under 15 above, and Nyabadza (1989: 5.15).
21. Arquivo Histórico de Moçambique, Governo Geral, Caixa 38 M1(2), J.C. Paiva de Andrada ao Governador Geral, Toue, 19 de agosto de 1889.
22. Ministry of Local Government, Division of District Administration, Harare, Per/5/HM/Chiendambuya, 'Chiendambuya' by A.B.N. Beale, August 1972.
23. MLG, DDA, Per/5/MH/Makumbe (Makoni), Delineation Report, Tanda, 2 December 1965.
24. MLG, DDA, Per/5/Sawunyama, District Commissioner, Inyanga, to Provincial Commissioner, Manicaland, 10 April 1963 and District Administrator, Inyanga, to Provincial Administrator, Manicaland, 2 April 1987.
25. MLG, DDA, Per/5/Chikore, DA, Makoni, to PA, Manicaland, 21 September, 1984.
26. N 3/33/8, NC, Rusape, to CNC, 2 December 1903.
27. MLG, DDA, Per/5/Chikore, Acting DC, Makoni, to PC, Manicaland, 4 October 1966; Beach(1994b: 68-72).
28. N 3/33/8, NC, Mrewa, to CNC, 11 December, 1903; W. Edwards, 'The Wanoe', *NADA*, 4, 1926, 13-28.
29. MLG, DDA, Per/5/Chikore, DA, Makoni, to PA, Manicaland, 21 September 1984; Burke 1969: 229).
30. Maxwell (1994:45-53, 408-9, 414) and my own dating based on Beach (1994b: 275-8).
31. N 1/1/4, NC, Inyanga, to CNC, 23 July and 26 August 1902; AHM, Arquivo da Companhia de Moçambique, Secretário Geral, Relatórios das Circunscrições, Caixa 223, Manica, Campanha do Barué, Columna de Operações por Manica, Relatório de Joâo d'Oliveira Amaral ao Secretário de Negócios Indígenas, 12-9 de setembro de 1902.

32. D.P. Abraham, 'The early political history of the kingdom of Mwene Mutapa, 850-1589', *Historians in Tropical Africa, Proceedings of the Leverhulme Inter-Collegiate History Conference, September 1960*, (UCRN, Salisbury, 1962), 83.
33. N 3/33/8 NC Umtali to CNC, 19 January 1904; Baker, 'Mutupo', 51. *Nyere* is usually translated as 'snuff container', and Baker adds the alternative *nzvidzi*, 'badger' – actually, 'otter.'
34. Hist. Mss. MA 14/1/1-2, 'History and customs of the Manyika,' Lesson 68; L 2/1/147/2 NC Umtali to CNC, 20 January 1899; Martin (1937)
35. Hist. Mss. MA 14/1/1-2, 'History and customs of the Manyika,' Lessons 1-133.
36. *Ibid.*, Lessons 45, 89; Bhila (1982: 150-60).
37. Hist. Mss. MA 14/1/1-2, 'History and customs of the Manyika,' Lessons 89, 103-5; Beach (1980: 186); Storry (1976).
38. This my initial interpretation, but it was based on insufficient familiarity with the sources. There was a good deal of interaction between myself and both Hoyini Bhila and the late Guy Storry in the 1973-4 period, and in fact they were much more cautious.
39. Hist. Mss. MA 14/1/1-2, 'History and customs of the Manyika,' Lessons 89-102; MLG, DDA, Per/5/HM/Mandeya I, Notes by R.E. Reid, 10 December 1975. His translation of Machiwenyika's Nyamhuka history shortens the genealogy by one generation. In fact, Machiwenyika *also* makes the definitely nineteenth-century Mutasa Mudemberwa a son of Nyarumwe (Lesson 44), while N 3/33/8 NC Umtali to CNC 19 January 1904 makes Nyarumwe a son of Pfete, generally considered to have been the Chikanga who died in 1795.
40. AHU Moçambique, Caixa 17 (sério velha), 'Descripção Corográfica ... c. 1794; Hist. Mss. MA 14/1/1-2, 'History and customs of the Manyika,' Lesson 107; Storry (1976).
41. H.H.K. Bhila, 'The Manyika and the Portuguese, 1573-1863', unpublished Ph.D. dissertation, University of London, 1971, 132-3.
42. N 3/24/12, NC Umtali to Superintendant of Natives, Umtali, 7 April 1921.
43. MLG, DDA, Per/5/Mutasa Vol. 2, 'Samembere Headmanship' by R.E. Reid, 10 June 1975. This gives the location on each modern farm of Manyika headmen in Nyanga, and the location of their descendants.
44. MLG, DDA, Per/5/Sawunyama, NC Inyanga to PNC Manicaland 30 April 1951, DC Inyanga to PC Manicaland 10 April 1963, Delineation Report, Sawunyama, September-October 1965.
45. See note 44, and 1986 genealogy.
46. See note 9 and MLG, DDA, Per/5/Bonde-Hata, DC Inyanga to PC Manicaland, 17 November 1967.
47. MLG, DDA, Per/5/Sawunyama, DC Inyanga to PC Manicaland 10 April 1963. Chief Mpatsi, son of Mutasa Tendai, who died in 1965, stated that he had taken part in this raid as a teenager.
48. Taylor (1926: 43-6); Hist. Mss. MA 14/1/1-2, 'History and customs of the Manyika', Lesson 25. The hero was still alive in the early 1920s, aged c.75. 'Tani' remains unlocated so far. However, J. Renato Baptista's map (note 4) shows Nani in Hwesa at 'Tani', which is not unusual for Portuguese sources influenced by Sena as far back as the seventeenth century. (Note that Andrada, in note 21, spelt 'Nhowe' with a 'T'.) Is it possible that the Hata house retreat went as far as Nani? This might explain why Jeffreys found people near Nani in 1894, but Maxwell (1994: 84) reports Hwesa re-occupying Nani in 1901. But, if the story is true, the fort should not be hard to find. [However C.Payne was told by Johannes Chitewo of the "Tanhi Collective Cooperative Farming Society" that "Tanhi", a closer alternative spelling, is either synonymous with or close to Rukotso (pers.comm.). RS]
49. N 3/33/8, NC Umtali to CNC, 19 January 1904; Jeffreys was told by the northern Manyika that Unyama was 'neutral' ground: see note 9.
50. Beach, 'Origens de Moçambique e Zimbabwe', 26.
51. L 2/1/38, MC, Umtali, Report, 28 June 1898; Peters (1902: 166).
52. L 2/1/38, MC, Umtali, Report, 28 June 1898.
53. MLG, DDA, Per/5/Sawunyama, DA Nyanga to PA Manicaland, 2 April 1987.
54. AHM, ACM, Secretário Geral, Processos, Barué, Caixa 179, Mario Barreto ao Governador da Companhia de Moçambique, Beira, 15 de janeiro de 1895.
55. MLG, DDA, Per/5/Sawunyama, DC Inyanga to PC Manicaland, 4 June 1964; MLG, DDA, Per/5/Mutasa Vol. 2, H.K. Saunyama and T.N. Shato to *Rhodesia Herald*, 23 December 1968.
56. Hist. Mss. MA 14/1/1-2, 'History and customs of the Manyika people,' Lesson 115.
57. A re-examination of the *mfecane* period in Zimbabwe is probably overdue. Liesegang (1970) established the parameters by securely dating Ngoni groups' movements into and out of the region, but more evidence – some of it contradictory – has emerged since, on developments in the interior (Beach 1980:264-6, 308-9; Bhila 1982:169-95; J.D. White, 'Esitshebeni', unpublished book, Shabani, 1974, 252-85). The issue is not whether it happened – that is indisputable – but what happened where and when.
58. Liesegang (1970:317-29); Bhila (1982:169-82)
59. Liesegang (1970:329-35)
60. Bhila (1982:175-6) cites two interviews, carried out

in 1972 and 1974, to the effect that the Ngoni raided northern Manyika in 1830. I am a little sceptical about this because (a) I wonder how definitely Bhila's Manyika informants distinguished this raid from the subsequent ones up to 1888 and (b) I wonder whether they tended to put it in the pre-Gaza period because Bhila himself is descended from the people of the Gaza state, and they wished to spare his feelings. Part of their account, concerning the poisoning of Nguni raiders, is actually a common myth in the Eastern Highlands and not specific to northern Manyika.

61. Liesegang (1970:328-9); G.J. Leisegang, 'Aspects of Gaza Nguni history,' *Rhodesian History* 6, 1975, 1-14; Beach, 'Origens de Moçambique e Zimbabwe', 36-8.
62. Paiva de Andrada, *Manica ... Report ... to the Minister ... Lisbon 24 January 1891*, (Philip, London, 1891), 7-8.
63. Beach (1994a:20)
64. R.M.G. Mtetwa, 'The "political" and economic history of the Duma people of south-eastern Rhodesia from the early eighteenth century to 1945', unpublished DPhil. dissertation, University of Rhodesia, 1976, 147-206; Beach, 'Origens de Moçambique e Zimbabwe', 64.
65. *Ibid.*, 49-52.
66. G.J. Leisegang, 'Agricultural change and population growth in Mozambique, 1880-1980', *SSRC/Third World Economic History and Development Group Conference*, Leicester, September 1984, 15; M.D.D. Newitt, 'Drought in Mozambique 1823-1831', *Journal of Southern African Studies*, xv, 1, 1988, 16-35.
67. Liesegang, 'Agricultural change,' 15; J. Iliffe, *Famine in Zimbabwe*, (Mambo, Gweru, 1990), 13-20.
68. R.S.Roberts (1980); R.M.G.Metwa, 'Myth or reality: the "Cattle Complex" in South East Africa, with special reference to Rhodesia,' *Zambezia*, vi, 1, 1978, 23-36.
69. F 4/1/1, Secretary, Native Department to Statist, Salisbury, 21 September 1895; A 15/1/1, Hut Tax 1 August 1894 - 30 June 1895, list by M. Lingard, Salisbury, 19 July 1895.
70. T.T.J. Jamu, 'The re-birth of African cattle herds, 1895-1910', unpubl. BA Honours dissertation, University of Zimbabwe, 1985, Table 1.
71. LO 5/4/6/1, C. Harding, OC Native Contingent BSAP, to DSO, Salisbury, 9 October 1897.
72. T.T.J. Jamu, 'The growth and control of African cattle herds, 1910-1955,' unpubl. MA dissertation, University of Zimbabwe, 1987, Tables 1-12.
73. Nobbs (1927).
74. F. Oates, *Matabele Land and the Victoria Falls*, (Kegan Paul, London, 1889), 226; W.M. Kerr, *The Far Interior*, (Sampson Low, London, 1887, 2 vols), i, 183; W.H. Brown, *On the South African Frontier*, (Sampson Low, London, 1899), 200; F.C. Selous, *A Hunter's Wanderings in Africa,* (Bentley, London, 1881), 36; Bent (1896:318); *Gold and the Gospel in Mashonaland 1888*, eds. C.E. Fripp and V.W. Hiller, (Chatto and Windus, London, 1949), 65; Hist. Mss. WE 3/2/6, Reminiscences of M.E. Weale.
75. J.C. Paiva de Andrada, *Relatório de uma viagem ás Terras do Changamira* (Nacional, Lisboa, 1886), 24.
76. T.N. Huffman, 'Corrected radiocarbon dates for the Iron Age in Rhodesia' in Beach, 1980:325.
77. Hist. Mss. MA 14/1/1-2, 'History and customs of the Manyika,' Lessons 64-6, 72-4, 120-33; C. Martin (1937).
78. Hist. Mss. MA 14/1/1-2, 'History and customs of the Manyika,' Lessons 89-102.
79. N 3/24/12, NC, Umtali, to CNC, 12 October 1900; L 2/2/117/26, NC, Umtali, to CNC, 16 January 1908, W.J. Atherstone to Under Secretary to Administrator, 26 March 1908.
80. L 2/1/38, Resident Magistrate and Civil Commissioner, Umtali, to Surveyor General, 2 and 3 March 1898, Survey Report by H.J. Pickett, 1899, MC Umtali, Report, 28 June 1898.
81. L 2/2/117/26, NC, Umtali, to CNC, 16 January 1908.
82. N 3/24/12, NC, Umtali, to Superintendant of Natives, Umtali, 9 March 1921.
83. L 4/4/16, Reports by H.J. Pickett, 1898-9.
84. *ibid.*; L 2/1/86/1, NC, Umtali, Report, c.1904; L 2/1/86/2/2, NC, Umtali, to CNC, 20 January 1899.
85. L 4/4/16, Reports by H.J. Pickett, 1898-9; L 2/1/38, MC, Umtali, Report, 28 June 1898; Peters, *Eldorado*, 166.
86. L 2/1/247/1, CNC to Chief Secretary, 8 June 1900 and Reference 14.
87. L 2/1/247/1, NC, Rusape, to CNC, 21 November 1899.
88. A 3/18/39/16, NC, Inyanga, to CNC, 31 August 1922.
89. N 3/24/12, NC, Umtali, to SN, Umtali, 9 March and 7 April 1921.
90. N 1/1/4, Memorandum of agreement between J.B. Michell and Sakarombe, Zindi, Maereka, Mawoko and Sanyanga, 8 December 1902.

APPENDIX A

Soil Analyses

The following analyses were carried out by the Chemistry and Soil Research Institute of the Department of Research and Specialist Services of the Zimbabwe Ministry of Agriculture. They provide the detailed data for the general description of soils in Chapter 2 and the comments on soils from individual terrace and ridge excavations in Chapter 4.

Site	*Ziwa SN113 T6*			*Ziwa Mujinga A T2*			
Layer	2	3	4	1	2	2a	3
Texture	cSaL	cSaL	cSaL	cLS	cLS	mLS	cSaL
Clay %	12	18	21	8	7	8	14
Silt	14	14	13	8	7	8	7
F.sand	31	31	24	33	34	36	16
M.sand	22	20	20	30	26	28	22
C.sand	22	17	22	22	25	20	41
pH	5.4	5.8	5.4	4.9	4.9	4.4	4.6
Ex Ca	11.0	10.9	10.6	7.3	3.1	2.2	2.7
Ex Mg	3.2	5.1	5.0	2.0	1.8	1.9	2.6
Ex Na	.06	.06	.12	.03	.02	.04	.05
Ex K	.00	.00	.00	.35	.11	.18	.23
CEC	15.8	15.7	15.8	8.9	4.1	4.2	5.7
Base sat	91	100	100	100	100	100	98
E/C	131.2	86.6	75.1	117.6	59.0	49.5	40.9
Org C	2.76	1.34	1.06	2.63	.41	.47	.32
Free Fe	13.95	12.53	11.77	.70	.73	.84	.93

Site	*Maristvale T20*				*Chirimanyimo A T2*			
Layer	1	2a	2b	3 s/s	1	2	3	4 s/s
Texture	mSaCL	mSaL	mSaCL	C	C	C	C	C
Clay %	29	18	29	47	50	56	57	61
Silt	11	10	9	14	18	19	17	13
F.sand	30	31	30	19	22	16	17	11
M.sand	19	26	22	12	7	7	6	7
C.sand	11	15	11	8	3	3	3	8
pH	4.4	4.5	4.1	4.7	4.9	4.2	4.2	4.3
Ex Ca	4.6	3.9	.34	5.7	5.5	2.1	1.5	2.5
Ex Mg	2.0	1.8	1.4	3.4	3.1	.9	.9	1.3
Ex Na	.07	.09	.05	.08	.04	.03	.05	.04
Ex K	.24	.21	.10	.08	.95	.08	.05	.09
CEC	7.9	6.6	5.6	9.0	9.8	4.7	3.9	3.9
Base sat	88	92	88	100	98	65	64	100
E/C	27.6	37.2	19.4	19.1	19.6	8.4	6.9	6.4
Org C	2.01	1.68	.83	.95	2.89	3.27	2.66	2.56
Free Fe	4.88	6.01	5.02	7.35	11.90	10.98	11.10	5.04

Site	Elim T3			Maristvale cultivation ridges			
Layer	1	2	3 s/s	4	5	6	8
Texture	mSaL	mSaCL	CL	mSaCL	mSaCL	mSaCL	mSac
Clay %	19	21	38	20	23	24	43
Silt	20	20	20	11	11	9	12
F.sand	35	33	22	32	29	31	19
M.sand	15	14	9	25	24	25	17
C.sand	12	11	12	13	13	13	10
pH	6.4	6.1	5.4	5.3	5.0	4.8	5.1
Ex Ca	15.8	12.0	16.4	5.5	5.4	5.1	7.5
Ex Mg	5.1	3.7	7.1	3.3	2.3	2.2	4.2
Ex Na	.05	.06	.06	.12	.09	.09	.18
Ex K	.49	.48	.33	.03	.06	.00	.03
CEC	22.7	17.9	25.7	8.3	7.4	6.7	11.7
Base sat	95	91	93	100	100	100	100
E/C	121.2	83.2	67.4	42.1	32.8	30.6	27.3
Org C	2.43	.96	.58	.93	.61	.45	.93
Free Fe	2.53	2.92	3.72	3.37	2.57	4.00	3.98

Site	Nyangui G1/21 garden			National Park, below furrow NP1		
Depth cm	10-20	35-45	70-80	10-15	40-50	65-75
Texture	fSaCL	fSaCL	C	mSaCL	mSaCL	mSaCL
Clay %	32	34	50	20	33	24
Silt	16	12	11	6	12	5
F.sand	48	46	35	26	28	25
M.sand	3	4	2	40	19	38
C.sand	2	4	2	9	9	10
pH	3.9	3.9	4.2	3.8	3.8	3.8
Ex Ca	.4	.1	.2	.4	.2	.1
Ex Mg	.3	.2	.3	.4	.2	.1
Ex Na	.04	.02	.02	.06	.02	.04
Ex K	.13	.02	.02	.04	.02	.02
CEC	3.5	2.3	2.6	1.8	1.4	1.6
Base sat	26	15	20	46	35	14
E/C	11.1	7.0	5.1	9.3	4.2	6.7
Org C	2.27	1.41	.89	.98	.63	.62
Free Fe	3.49	5.53	7.17	.77	.82	.92
Total P	2911	316	789	316	419	770

APPENDIX B

Bones from Muozi Midden Trench II

Dr Ina Plug and Shaw Badenhorst

Transvaal Museum, P O Box 413, Pretoria 0002
plug@tm.up.ac.za

Introduction

The site, situated on top of an isolated spur of the highlands, is described in Chapter 5. Excavations of Nyanga complex sites have seldom yielded any faunal material worth analysing and the Muozi midden was the first where a substantial faunal sample was recovered (Plug *et al.* 1997). The most important result from the analysis of material from the first excavation was the presence of dwarf cattle remains in the deposits. As these were the first evidence of such small cattle from southern African archaeological sites, it was important to confirm and extend the findings.

During 1997 a new test trench of 2m x 1m to a maximum depth of 1.40m was excavated in the same midden (Trench II). Charcoal samples show that the midden dates from the 14th to 17th centuries AD, the pottery and other finds being consistent with material from contemporary sites on the main highlands. The faunal remains were submitted to the Transvaal Museum for analysis and form the basis of this report.

The faunal sample

Trench II was excavated in 12 arbitrary layers and yielded a total of 2 480 bone fragments with a total mass of 10 495g (Table 1). 12.6% of these were identifiable to species or animal size class. This new sample is therefore considerably larger than the previous one where a total of 402 fragments were recorded, with 33% identified to species or size class (Plug *et al.* 1997). Although the new sample is larger, the bones are more fragmented than those of the earlier sample. Hence the relatively larger number of unidentifiable fragments.

The remains from each level were analysed separately, but for the purpose of this paper levels were combined as suggested by the excavator, namely the surface, levels 1-3, 4-6, 7-9 and 10-12 (Soper personal communication). The samples from the surface and from levels 10-12 are small, but those from the other combined levels are more or less of equal size.

Species present

Table 2 presents the species identified in the combined levels. The wild animal species represented occurred, or still occur, in the region today. The human foot and hand bones are from an adult person and were found in levels 5, 8 and 9. It is possible that the suid remains in the upper levels are from a domestic pig, but there are no diagnostic features to prove this.

Domestic animals identified are dog, cattle, sheep, goat and chicken. The house rat, *Rattus rattus*, although not a domestic animal in the conservative sense of the word, is a commensal of people and forms part of the human habitation profile. Of all the domestic animal remains, those of cattle are the most common. The majority of the cattle remains were those of small animals. The two frontal fragments present are flat, indicating that the cattle were flat-faced. The frontal fragment with a horncore shows that the horn was relatively robust and straight, leaving the skull at an angle of ca 35°. The area of the *squama occipitalis* on the occipital bone is well developed, suggesting strong musculature.

Domestic animal sizes

Table 3 gives the sizes of the cattle bones and the percentage difference from those of modern small to medium unimproved Nguni cattle in South Africa. The measurements of cattle published in Plug *et al.* (1997) are not repeated there except where the new identifications increased the samples. In those instances the formula was recalculated to incorporate the additional data.

The measurements of sheep and goat are listed in Table 4. The modern Pedi sheep and "unimproved" indigenous goat measurements are based on a few South African specimens only as access to material is limited at present. The results should therefore been seen as showing a possible trend only.

Comparisons between livestock sizes of animals from archaeological sites are a current project of the Archaeozoology Department of the Transvaal

Museum and will include the Muozi data. Table 5 compares the average measurements of the *tali* of cattle and sheep from some Late Iron Age sites from the northern parts of South Africa with the Muozi samples (see Plate 33 for the Muozi and modern *tali*). These measurements reflect the general size ranges of livestock at the time. Goat measurements are not included in this table as not enough measurements are available. A single goat *talus* comes from Molokwane and is over 20% larger than the Muozi specimen. Molokwane, Riekersdam and Rietfontein are Tswana sites and Thulamela is attributed to the Venda.

Domestic animal slaughter ages
Table 6 presents the ages of domestic animals at death. The results show that neither very young nor very old animals were slaughtered. The very young cattle and sheep/goat (classes 1 and 2), and older animals (classes IX in cattle and VI in sheep/goat), are not represented. For the rest the samples are too small to determine any particular trends.

Taphonomy
Many of the bones were gnawed by carnivores and rodents, 116 and 65 respectively. Some of the fragments have large incisor damage corresponding to porcupine teeth. A total of 455 bone fragments have been burnt. Almost half of these are calcined, an indication that they were submitted to high temperatures (Brain and Sillen 1988).

Butchering damage in the form of cut and chop marks is common and visible on 183 fragments. These include a cattle skull frontal fragment with cut and chop marks. The marks are not deep enough to suggest that they were incurred when the animal was killed and they were probably caused during skinning and preparations for distribution and cooking.

With the exception of a polished rib fragment, no other worked bone was present in the submitted sample.

Discussion and conclusions
Animals identified include contributors as well as non-contributors to the subsistence economy of the site. Determining these two categories is often problematic as the position of many species may be ambiguous. The house rat, small rodents, mole rat and the giant land snail could well have been self-introduced. The house rats would have become incorporated within the deposits while the site was still inhabited, as these animals only occur in close association with people. The other small rodents, the mole rat and the giant land snail could have been introduced during habitation or at any time thereafter.

The possibility that some of the supposed non-contributors could have been utilised in one way or another should also be considered. Traditional medical practitioners in Zimbabwe use rat dung to treat new born infants and snail shells to treat ulcers for example (Gelfand *et al.* 1985:310-311). Although it may not be valid to draw analogies from the present to the past, it does emphasize the wide variety of uses that many animals may have for many different purposes, not always obvious from present day perspectives. Animals such as the felid and the genet/civet were most likely hunted or trapped. They could have been used for food, but their skins and probably teeth and other body parts were most likely used for other purposes as well.

There is a marked reduction in the number of identifiable bone fragments from the upper to the lower spits. Nevertheless, there is no significant change in the species representation as the smaller number of species in the lower spits seems to be an artefact of the sample size rather than of human choice.

Comparisons between the new sample and that from the earlier excavation show much species overlap. The old sample has remains of a vervet and a giraffe size mammal extra, whereas the new sample adds human, genet or civet, felid, wild bovid, hare, bushpig and suid, various large and small rodents, tortoise, and land snail to the species list of the site.

The human remains come from levels 5, 8 and 9, but the structure, the state of the cortex and the general appearance indicate a single individual. The bones are a medial phalanx of the right thumb (level 5), a left medial tarsal and scaphoid carpal (level 8), and two right first phalanges (Levels 8 and 9). Judging by the skeletal parts present, namely hand and foot bones, there is a strong possibility that the excavation touched on the edge of a grave. It would be advisable to extend the trench to determine whether there was indeed a grave and its possible effect on the integrity of the deposits.

The cattle sizes again support the previous finding of dwarf cattle as the measurements fall within the parameters of the previous sample. It is interesting to note that the breadth of the distal (but not of the proximal) metacarpal does not differ much from that of the modern so-called unimproved Nguni. The horncore diameters are also very similar. Nevertheless, the Muozi skull frontals are markedly smaller, indicating small skulls with robust horns. It may be argued that the well developed distal metacarpals and equally strong sculpture of the *squama occipitalis*, are structured to support the relatively heavy horn load.

Preliminary results on cattle size comparisons with Late Iron Age samples show that the cattle of the Muozi herds were significantly smaller than those from any other Late Iron Age site thus far examined. This includes cattle from the Venda sites (De Wet 1993). The average greatest lateral length of the *talus* varies at the Venda sites from 65 mm for Tavhatshena to 68mm each for Dzata and Tshirululuni.

The sheep and goat measurement comparisons show that the small stock of Muozi were also generally smaller than their Iron Age and present-day counterparts. Whereas the Muozi cattle skull and horncores differ morphologically from other Iron Age and modern cattle, no morphological differences could be detected in the small stock.

Based on the morphological differences of the cattle it may be argued that we are dealing with a hitherto undefined breed for southern Africa. However, it is less clear whether this was the case of the small stock. Reduced stature due to environmental constraints should also be considered as a possible factor for the smallness of both cattle and small stock.

Generally the material from the 1995 samples is less fragmented, hence the larger mass, although the fragments are fewer in number than the more recent sample. Based on the large number of carnivore gnawed bones and the morphology of the tooth marks it can be assumed that domestic dogs were responsible for the damage. The calcined bone fragments suggest that they were tossed into the fire or glowing coals first, before being deposited in the midden. Slaughter patterns indicate that very young and very old animals were not slaughtered. Although the sample is too small to draw any particular conclusions, it does nevertheless indicate that the herds were probably well managed and that only adult or near adult animals were slaughtered. Unfortunately the material was not suitable to determine gender, so no conclusions can be drawn on gender slaughter ratios.

In conclusion the new sample corroborates earlier findings of the presence of dwarf cattle and that these are of a previously unknown breed, based on skull and horn morphology. However, the presence of unusually small sheep argues for environmental constraints as an additional factor to be considered when interpreting the Muozi livestock.

We are grateful to Mr Wulf Haacke who photographed the specimens in Plate 33.

Table 1 Muozi Trench II, total faunal sample of all spits combined.

Skeletal part	No
Identifiable fragments	313
Unidentifiable fragments	
Enamel fragments	7
Skull fragments	64
Vertebra fragments	219
Rib fragments	609
Miscellaneous fragments	767
Bone flakes	501
Total unidentifiable fragments	2167
Total sample	2480
Mass identifiable fragments g	4470
Mass unidentifiable fragments g	6025
Total mass g	10495

Table 2 Muozi Trench II: Species present per combined units expressed as number of fragments. (Numbers in brackets in the Total column are minimum numbers of individuals)

Species	Surface	Level 1-3	Level 4-6	Level 7-9	Level 10-12	Total	Mass g
Homo sapiens sapiens human	0	0	1	4	0	5(1)	12.5
Canis familiaris dog	0	0	1	0	0	1(1)	6.2
Genet or civet	0	1	0	0	0	1(1)	1.2
Felid large	0	0	1	0	0	1(1)	0.4
cf *Potamochoerus porcus* bushpig	0	0	0	0	1	1(1)	39.7
Suid	0	2	0	0	0	2(1)	15.0
Bos taurus cattle	3	26	46	32	15	122(12)	3152.1
Ovis aries sheep	0	8	3	4	0	15(6)	50.5
Capra hircus goat	2	7	2	1	0	12(5)	48.7
Ovis/Capra sheep or goat	3	18	5	2	1	29(9)	59.4
Bovid small	0	5	3	0	0	8(2)	11.9
Bovid medium indeterminate	0	6	9	6	1	22(0)	108.4
Bovid large indeterminate	1	15	18	15	12	61(1)	884.1
Bovid large non-domestic	0	0	0	1	0	1(1)	65.3
Rattus rattus house rat	0	6	1	4	0	11(3)	2.7
Hystrix africaeaustralis porcupine	0	0	0	1	0	1(1)	2.9
Cryptomys sp mole rat	0	0	0	11	0	11(2)	3.4
Rodent indeterminate	0	0	0	3	0	3(1)	0.4
Lepus saxatilis hare	0	0	1	0	0	1(1)	1.5
Gallus domesticus chicken	0	3	0	0	0	3(1)	0.3
Tortoise	0	0	0	1	0	1(1)	2.1
Achatina sp giant land snail	0	0	0	1	0	1(1)	1.4
TOTAL	9	97	91	86	30	313	4470.1

Table 3 Muozi: measurements of Bos taurus from Trench II expressed in mm, and % smaller than average Nguni (including Muozi Trench I)

Skeletal part	n	$\bar{x}$	sd	min	max	% smaller
Horncore						
DB: diameter at base	4	53.4	3.4	49.0	57.0	10.0
Os frontale						
Horn base to midline	2	69.2	-	-	-	34.6
Os occipitale						
Condyle length	1	24.5	-	-	-	31.9
Radius						
DP: proximal breadth	2	29.2	-	27.8	30.5	26.5
BFp: breadth of *facies proximalis*	2	60.2	-	59.1	61.3	13.5
Bp: proximal depth	2	66.9	-	64.4	69.5	16.4
Bd: distal breadth	1	56.9	-	-	-	10.0
BFd: breadth of *facies distalis*	1	52.6	-	-	-	6.0

Talus
GL l: greatest length lateral	7	56.9	5.4	45.5	62.6	21.6
GL m: greatest length medial	8	52.1	3.9	45.0	57.5	21.7
DL: greatest depth of lateral half	7	31.0	2.1	29.0	34.6	29.6
Bd: greatest depth of distal end	7	35.8	3.7	29.3	39.1	20.6

$2^{nd} + 3^{rd}$ carpal
GB: greatest breadth	2	27.5	-	27.4	27.6	11.7

4th carpal
BFd: breadth of *facies distalis*	2	20.5	-	18.4	22.6	24.9
GH: greatest height	2	16.9	-	16.1	17.7	27.8

Ulnar carpal
GL: greatest length	1	26.1	-	-	-	36.2

Radial carpal
GD: greatest width	1	26.0	-	-	-	34.3
GH: greatest height	1	26.0	-	-		7.3
BFd: breadth of *facies distalis*	1	25.8	-	-		1.7

Tibia distal
Bd: distal width	6	54.6	4.7	46.5	59.9	15.3
Dd: distal thickness	6	39.4	2.4	36.7	43.0	23.5

Os malleolare
GD: greatest thickness	1	28.3	-	-	-	15.5

Metacarpal
Bd: distal breadth	1	54.3	-	-	-	4.3
DD: distal depth at condyles	1	19.6	-	-	-	12.9
dd: distal depth above condyles on shaft	1	28.3	-	-	-	9.8

Metatarsal
BP: proximal breadth	1	38.3	-	-	-	23.7
DP: proximal depth	1	37.2	-	-	-	9.4
Bd: distal breadth	1	45.0	-	-	-	15.7

Phalanx media
GL: greatest length	3	34.5	1.2	33.4	35.7	18.1
Bp: proximal breadth	3	22.9	2.4	20.1	24.6	24.4
Bd: distal breadth	3	19.2	1.3	18.7	19.9	18.3
Sd: shaft thickness	3	21.3	0.6	20.2	22.7	24.0

Phalanx distalis
DLS: diagonal length of sole	4	53.9	6.4	46.7	60.7	25.3
Ld: length of dorsal surface	5	43.3	4.1	37.6	46.8	22.3
HP: height at extensor process	6	36.1	6.1	27.4	39.8	14.3
BFp: breadth of *facies articularis*	4	18.2	2.7	14.8	21.1	24.5

APPENDIX B

Table 4 Muozi: Capra hircus and Ovis aries measurements expressed in mm and % smaller than Pedi sheep and indigenous goat

Capra hircus

Skeletal part	n	x̄	sd	min	max	% smaller
Scapula						
SLC: smallest length of collum	1	17.7	-	-	-	31.7
Radius						
Sd: smallest breadth of diaphysis	1	15.7	-	-	-	39.7
Bd: greatest breadth of distal end	1	25.9	-	-	-	29.6
Talus						
G Ll: greatest length lateral	3	25.3	1.0	24.3	26.3	17.2
G Lm: greatest length medial	6	23.4	1.7	21.2	25.0	18.9
Dl: greatest depth of lateral half	2	14.0	-	13.3	14.8	10.8
Dm: greatest depth of medial half	6	13.8	1.1	12.2	15.2	16.4
Bd: greatest breadth of distal end	5	15.5	2.4	11.3	17.2	17.4
Calcaneum						
GL: greatest length	2	46.4	-	45.3	47.4	30.0
GB: greatest breadth	2	16.5	-	15.2	17.7	29.8
Metatarsal						
GL: Greatest length	1	116.7	-	-	-	10.0
Bp: greatest breadth of proximal end	1	19.8	-	-	-	21.2
Dp: greatest depth of proximal end	1	18.8	-	-	-	22.7
SD: smallest breadth of diaphysis	1	12.2	-	-	-	30.3
DD: smallest depth of diaphysis	1	13.3	-	-	-	24.9
Bd: greatest breadth of distal end	1	23.5	-	-	-	23.5
Dd: greatest depth of distal end	1	15.6	-	-	-	17.0
Phalanx media						
GL: greatest length	1	27.5	-	-	-	9.1
Bp: greatest breadth of proximal end	1	11.3	-	-	-	18.2
SD: smallest breadth of the diaphysis	1	7.7	-	-	-	26.5
Bd: greatest breadth of distal end	1	8.9	-	-	-	20.9

Ovis aries

Skeletal part	n	x̄	sd	min	max	% smaller
Radius						
BP: greatest breadth of proximal end	1	23.4	-	-	-	23.5
Bfd: breadth of proximal *facies articularis*	1	23.1	-	-	-	17.5
Dp: depth of proximal end	1	12.8	-	-	-	17.0
Talus						
G Ll: greatest length lateral	1	23.4	-	-	-	18.5
G Lm: greatest length medial	1	22.4	-	-	-	19.0
Dl: greatest depth of lateral half	1	12.5	-	-	-	22.8
Dm: greatest depth of medial half	1	13.5	-	-	-	19.5
Bd: greatest breadth of distal end	1	14.9	-	-	-	24.3

Table 5 Comparison between the average sizes of the Muozi tali and those of other Late Iron Age sites from the north of South Africa (Dm measurement is not listed as this measurement is not standard)

Bos taurus	Muozi	Thulamela	Riekersdam	Molokwane
G Ll: greatest length lateral	56.9	66.0	71.3	70.1
G Lm: greatest length medial	52.1	59.0	65.9	64.7
Dl: greatest depth of lateral half	31.0	37.0	38.2	39.2
Bd: greatest breadth of distal end	35.8	43.0	41.6	44.4
Ovis aries	Muozi	Thulamela	Rietfontein	Molokwane
G Ll: greatest length lateral	23.4	25.4	29.2	29.6
G Lm: greatest length medial	22.2	23.5	28.2	28.4
Dl: greatest depth of lateral half	12.5	14.1	17.2	17.0
Bd: greatest breadth of distal end	14.9	16.8	19.8	19.1

Table 6 Muozi: Domestic animal age classes

	Bos taurus				Ovis/Capra			
Age Class	Level 1-3	Level 4-6	Level 7-9	Level 10-12	Level 1-3	Level 4-6	Level 7-8	Level 10-12
III	0	2	1	1	2	1	1	0
IV	1	1	0	0	1	0	0	0
V	0	1	0	0	1	1	0	0
VI	0	1	1	1	0	0	0	0
VII	0	0	1	0	n a	n a	n a	n a
VIII	1	0	0	0	n a	n a	n a	n a
TOTAL	2	5	3	2	4	2	1	0

APPENDIX C

Report on the identification of plant macrofossils

Jimmy Jonsson

Department of Archaeology and Ancient History, Uppsala University

Identification of the plant macrofossils was undertaken in consultation with R.B.Drummond, formerly of the National Herbarium, Harare, and with Dr S.Kativu of the Botany Department, University of Zimbabwe, whose assistance is gratefully acknowledged. Identifications are as follows:

Site	Provenance	Number	Species
Ziwa MSE 17	RP1	1	*Vigna unguiculata*
		17	*Sclerocarya birrea* (Marula)
		1	*Ziziphus abyssinica*
	H1	54	*Vigna unguiculata*
		2	*Cucurbita* sp.
	H2	1+1?	*Cucurbita* sp.
Ziwa Chirawu site 12	H5	1	*Eleusine corocana*
		1 frag	*V. unguiculata* or *Phaseolus*
		2	*Cucurbita* sp.
		2	unident.
	H4	37	*Eleusine corocana*
		1	*Vigna (Voandzeia) subterranea*
		1	*Phaseolus vulgaris*
		1	*Vigna luteda*
		2	unident.
Ziwa SN153	IV pit	3	*Panicum maximum*
		4	unident.
Chirangeni	H1A	25	*Panicum maximum*
		4	*Sporobolus pyramidalis*
		1	*Eragrostis lehmannia*
		1	*Dactyloctenium aegyptium*
		1	*Cyperus* sp.
		33	*Diospyros* ?
		25	unident.
	H2cupboard	1	*Sorghum bicolor* var. *guinea*
		2	*Panicum maximum*
		16	*Diospyros* ?
		8	unident.
Nyangui G1/21		1	*Vigna unguiculata*
		3	unident.
Fishpit	Hse A	12	*Panicum maximum*
		1	*Eragrostis lehmannia*
		7	unident.
	Pit	1	*Sorghum bicolor* var. *guinea*
		23	*Panicum maximum*
		1	*Eleusine indica*
		1	*Eragrostis lehmannia*
		43	unident.
Muozi	midden	5	unident.
1732DD27		8	unident.

The cultigens, *Vigna unguiculata* (*nyemba*, cowpea), *V. subterranea* (*nyimo*, ground bean), *Eleusine corocana* (*rapoko*, finger millet), *Sorghum bicolor* (*mapfunde*) and various cucurbits are all indigenous crops reported to be grown in the Nyanga area at the present day (see Chapter 3). The sorghum is tentatively identified as belonging to the guinea variety, adapted mainly to the higher rainfall areas of Zimbabwe. Beans (Phaseolus) however are a recent introduction and their presence at Ziwa, probably early in the 19th century, requires confirmation from larger samples.

Most of the wild plants identified belong to the *Gramminaea* such as grains and grasses. Several fruit species were also present, most of which could not be identified. The grass *Panicum maximum* grows on well drained soils and is commonly an indicator for good fertile soil. *Sporobolus pyramidalis* is found in open woodland and wet areas such as river banks. *Eleusine indica* is the most common weed infesting maize and finger millet in Zimbabwe, but it also grows on disturbed ground in drier areas. *Eragrostis lehmannia* grows close to water courses and river banks. *Panicum maximum* and another species of *Sporobolus* (*panicoides*) are reported to be eaten as famine food, while *Sclerocarya birrea*, *Ziziphus abyssinica* and several species of *Diospyros*, especially *mespiliformis*, are popular wild fruits (Tredgold 1986). The edible species may have been brought to the homesteads as food and the other wild plants as weeds associated with cultigens.

APPENDIX D

Comparison of pottery assemblages from Nyanga excavated sites

The pottery from the eleven sites excavated in the recent research is here analysed in an attempt to detect consistent typological variation within the complex. In general, the Nyanga pottery is undistinguished, often unprepossessing, with rare decoration and few clearly separable shapes, while few vessels are entirely regular and symmetrical. Samples of diagnostic sherds thus tend to be relatively small. Nevertheless, the analysis does reveal consistent trends corresponding to the chronological and geographical outline of the complex presented in Chapter 7, although the data does not permit a detailed seriation which could provide more precise relative dating.

Some chronological control is provided by Muozi midden, the only site which provides a stratified sequence, but the latest part of the complex is probably not represented there. Some approximate independent ordering of the structures characteristic of different periods or areas is offered by the radiocarbon dating and other indications. The Muozi sequence is here divided into three stratigraphic units, while Chirangeni is divided into two assemblages, from the enclosure and "garden" terrace. For Chirimanyimo Hill, assemblages from three areas are considered separately since they are characterised by different structural remains and are not necessarily directly contemporary; the combined assemblage is also included. The other sites are treated as single assemblages. Seventeen assemblages are thus analysed.

These assemblages are also grouped by a combination of site type, apparent date and geographical area:
(1) early hilltop settlements: Nyangui 1732DD27, Chirimanyimo Hill and the lower Muozi units;
(2) highland ruined pit-structures: Nyangui G7/1 and Matinha. Muozi upper unit is included with these since the dating and bead assemblages show it to be contemporary with G7/1;
(3) later pit-structures: Nyangui G1/21 and Fishpit;
(4) lowland enclosures at Ziwa Ruins: MSE17 and SN153;
(5) northern later lowland enclosures: Chirangeni and Chigura.
(6) the garden terrace at Chirangeni.

It can be seen that this grouping largely follows the different types of settlements and homesteads described in Chapter 5, and the categorisation discussed at more length in Chapter 7. The aim is to provide larger combined samples in order to distinguish general trends, but some variation between sites of the same group may be obscured. These variations or apparent anomalies are identified in the discussion; they may be due to inadequate samples, possible minor differences in dating, or social/functional differences. Number 6, the Chirangeni garden terrace, has been kept separate since it lacks diagnostic structural associations and the assemblage level analysis shows inconsistencies with Group 5 in which it fits geographically.

In the analysis, vessel types, lip forms, finish and decoration are compared, as well as average maximum sherd thickness and rim height. Maximum thickness of all sherds was measured before any reconstruction. Other attributes exclude plain body sherds and apply only to diagnostic sherds after reconstruction; they may be taken to represent the minimum number of vessels.

Shapes are divided into a number of general classes. However these classes often grade into one another, so that attribution in some cases is subjective, particularly for the smaller rimsherds. No attempt was made to classify the very smallest rims. These classes are as follows:
- Deep vessels with vertical sides/rims or slightly waisted
- Hemispherical bowls with vertical rims
- Open bowls with out-sloping rims, sometimes out-turned
- Constricted vessels with in-sloping rims
- Necked bowls — relatively shallow vessels with slight necks and out-turned rims, often finely finished but with some rough examples
- Necked pots — globular vessels with out-turned rims. Narrow-mouthed pots have a rim diameter less than about two-thirds of body diameter (often subjectively estimated) and the remainder are wide-mouthed pots, or are classified simply as necked pots where the slope below the neck is uncertain.

Lips are usually unevenly finished and may vary around the circumference. They are divided into roughly squared, round, tapered round, and thickened round, the last rare and perhaps not deliberate. Finish is classified as rough or smooth, rough indicating a granular and/or uneven surface. There is a small amount of graphite burnishing in many assemblages and some rare plain burnishing; another rare finish is quartz burnish, in which crushed crystal is applied to the surface to give a glittering effect.

Rim height was measured for out-turned rims of wide-mouthed and undifferentiated necked pots. This measurement is the vertical distance from the lip to the vertical tangent point of the outside neck curvature. Since this curvature is usually shallow, and since the often irregular rims make the precise orientation of smaller sherds difficult to determine, this measurement is usually an approximation, while even on larger sherds the rim height may vary around the circumference.

The data are tabulated by assemblage in Table 1 and combined into the above six groups in Table 2. The following observations summarise the distinguishing attributes of each group and draw attention to apparent anomalies within groups.

Group 1. *Early hilltop settlements* are characterised by common deep/waisted vessels and hemispherical bowls, with occasional open and constricted bowls but no necked bowls. Square lips predominate, rough and smooth finish are more or less equal and there is some plain burnish. Decoration is rare, with a few examples of graphite burnish, rough incised hatching, punctates and single incision. Within the group, 1732DD27 has more frequent square lips and hemispherical bowls and only one open bowl, while there are no constricted bowls from Muozi. Smooth finish and plain burnish become more frequent between the lower and middle units of Muozi, but samples are small and this may not be significant.

Group 2. In the early *ruined pit-structures*, deep/waisted vessels, hemispherical, open and constricted bowls still occur but in decreasing numbers, and rare necked bowls appear. Almost all the open bowls of this group have out-turned rims, in contrast to the straight rims of the first group. Narrow-mouthed pots are consistently present. Rims are almost all round, many being tapered, and rough finish totals 74% with rare plain burnish. Graphite burnish is present, and quartz burnish at Muozi. Incised hatching is rare, punctates rather less so. Within the group, hemispherical bowls are far more common at Matinha, and there is a higher proportion of smooth finish and plain burnish at Muozi upper unit. Rims are higher at Matinha with an average of 17.8mm (n=23), compared with 13.9mm (n=22) at G7/1, and 12.9mm (n=24) at Muozi.

Group 3. The assemblages from *later pit-structures* have a few necked bowls, with open bowls at G1/21, but other types of bowls are absent. Wide-mouthed pots predominate. Lips are almost exclusively round or tapered round, the latter more common at Fishpit. Decoration is very rare, apart from graphite burnish at G1/21; there is one case of incised hatching at G1/21 and three of single incision at Fishpit.

Group 4. The *Ziwa enclosures* have the smallest samples but are relatively homogeneous. Bowl forms are absent apart from necked bowls, as are narrow-mouthed pots. Rims are again all round, with tapered forms considerably more common at SN153. Graphite and quartz burnish occur and incised hatching and single incision are comparatively common, but punctates are absent. There are two ridged sherds and one wide-mouthed pot with perforations in the base.

Group 5. The assemblages from the two *northern enclosures* are less homogeneous, but a common feature is the thick coarse vessels which do not occur in the other assemblages. Necked bowls and narrow-mouthed pots are relatively common, while hemispherical bowls occur at Chirangeni. Lips are round and finish generally smooth, though less so at Chirangeni. Graphite burnish occurs on narrow-mouthed pots as well as bowls at Chigura. Incised hatching is the commonest technique at Chigura. Punctates occur only at Chirangeni; hatching is rare from the excavations at this site, although several examples occur on the surface in the vicinity of the enclosure. Rims tend to be very short at Chirangeni with an average of 10.8mm (n=27), as against 15.3mm (n=6) at Chigura.

Group 6. The assemblage from Chirangeni "garden" terrace has not been included with that from the enclosure as it exhibits some anomalies. Hemispherical bowls predominate, and deep vessels and constricted bowls also occur, with a few necked bowls and relatively few necked pots compared to other assemblages. Lips are round but rough finish predominates. Punctate decoration is common, as in the enclosure, and there is some single incision but no hatching. Intuitively one might regard this assemblage as earlier than, but related to, that from the enclosure.

A number of general trends can be identified. For vessel shapes, deep/waisted vessels and most bowl forms, except the necked variety, are characteristic of earlier highland sites (groups 1 and 2), while necked bowls are present on all later sites in both highlands and lowlands. Squared lips largely die out after the earliest group, in which tapered round lips are relatively rare. A rough finish is also more typical of the early groups. For decoration, incised hatching is found mainly in the lowland enclosures (the single example from 1732DD27 being atypical), while punctates are more typical of the highlands, apart from the anomalous case of Chirangeni. There is a fairly consistent decrease in average sherd thickness through time, declining from 9.65mm for the early hilltop settlements, to 8.32mm for the ruined pit-structures, to 7.52mm for the later pit-structures; the figure for the Ziwa enclosures is 7.60mm and for the northern enclosures 7.95mm, the last boosted by the rather high figure for Chirangeni. Thinner sherds are however also present on the earlier sites as shown by the high standard deviations for individual assemblages. With the thinness on the later sites goes better firing. The size range of measurable rims is generally comparable throughout, suggesting that the decreasing average thickness does not reflect decreasing average vessel dimensions. Few very large pots over about 40cm diameter are represented, apart from very occasional body sherds.

The main trends thus appear to be chronological, though minor contemporaneous geographical differences are discernible, such as between later highland pit-structure and lowland enclosures, and between southern and northern lowland enclosures. Unfortunately no early lowland sites have been identified contemporary with the highland groups 1 and 2. There is a clear relationship between the pottery of the early ruined pit-structures and that of the preceding early hilltop settlements, indicating direct cultural continuity. The pottery of the later highland pit-structures relates more to the lowland enclosures in vessel frequencies, but has very little decoration (a characteristic of highland sites in general). Among the lowland enclosures, the Ziwa sites have affinities with Chigura in most attributes, with Chirangeni being anomalous in some respects. Overall, there is sufficient consistency and continuity to assign the different groups to phases or facies of a single tradition. Individual sites however exhibit idiosyncrasies; certain of these may be attributable to sampling effects, but some individuality is also indicated.

There is no obvious relationship in form, decoration or technical attributes to the Ziwa Early Iron Age pottery of the first millennium AD. A cultural discontinuity is thus evident. The collection of more or less complete vessels among the stone ruins on Mount Muozi, briefly described in Chapter 5 and illustrated in Figure 38, shows similarities to and differences from the excavated assemblages. The necked bowls and smaller necked pots are similar though undistinctive; the one vessel with punctate decoration can be paralleled from highland sites and Chirangeni; and two with incised hatching can be paralleled from lowland sites. However, the larger necked pots have few counterparts among the excavated material, while a number of vessels are peculiar to this site as far as present evidence goes. The large pots are over 50cm in height, the largest being 69cm high, while maximum diameters range from just over 50cm to 65cm; the capacity of the largest is estimated at around 140 litres and several others would hold just under 130 litres. Other special vessels are: one medium-sized narrow-mouthed pot with a graceful flared rim (no.15); one gourd-shaped pot with cylindrical neck and vertical flutes on the shoulder (no.6); three rather squat large pots, one narrow- and the others wide-mouthed, with a raised ridge on the shoulder decorated with herring-bone incision (nos 7, 12, 32); two rims of very narrow-necked pots with a raised collar at the base of the neck; and a complete spherical pot with out-turned rim with a pattern of vertical and horizontal ridges on the body (no.17). The last vessel does in fact have parallels. Summers (1958:143) found ridged sherds of this type both in a highland pit-structure and in lowland enclosures, while single examples were recovered at MSE17 and SN153; such vessels commonly have quartz burnish (which may indeed be peculiar to them), but this is not detectable on the Muozi example. All these vessels appear to reflect the special status of the site and some may have been carried up in relatively recent years (? late 19th/early 20th century) in connection with rituals.

Table 1. Pottery analysis by site

	1732DD27		Ch.Hill I-IV		Ch.Hill VII		Ch.Hill VIII		Ch.Hill all		Muozi 10-12		Muozi 7-9		Matinha		G7/1	
Deep bowls	38	28%	4	13%	1	17%	2	13%	7	13%	7	39%	5	42%	5	7%	1	3%
Hem bowls	62	46%	2	6%	1	17%	3	19%	6	11%	4	22%	-		23	30%	1	3%
Open bowls	2	1%	12	38%	1	17%	-		13	24%	3	17%	4	33%	9	12%	2	6%
Constr bowls	5	4%	2	6%	-		2	13%	4	7%	-		-		1	1%	1	3%
Necked bowls	-		-		-		-		-		-		-		2	3%	-	
Wide-m pots	21	16%	7	22%	3	50%	8	50%	18	33%	4	22%	3	25%	31	41%	21	62%
Narrow-m pots	2	1%	1	3%	-		1	6%	2	4%	-		-		3	4%	2	6%
Necked pots	4	3%	4	13%	-		-		4	7%	-		-		2	3%	6	18%
Total vessels	134		32		6		16		54		18		12		76		34	
Square rims	99	63%	9	28%	4	67%	7	54%	20	39%	10	56%	2	20%	3	4%	-	
Round rims	40	26%	15	47%	2	33%	5	38%	22	43%	5	28%	5	50%	48	63%	13	39%
Tap.rnd rims	15	10%	8	25%	-		1	8%	9	18%	3	17%	2	20%	23	30%	20	61%
Th.rnd rims	2	1%	-		-		-		-		-		1	10%	2	3%	-	
Total rims	156		32		6		13		51		18		10		76		33	
Rough finish	73	46%	10	31%	5	83%	7	47%	22	42%	12	55%	4	19%	65	92%	26	81%
Smooth finish	84	54%	22	69%	1	17%	8	53%	31	58%	6	27%	8	38%	6	8%	6	19%
Plain burnish	-		-		-		-		-		4	18%	9	43%	-		-	
Total	157		32		6		15		53		22		21		71		32	
Graph burnish	2		1		-		-		1		-		-		4		1	
Quartz burn	-		-		-		-		-		-		-		-		-	
Cross-hatch	1		-		-		-		-		-		-		1		-	
X-hatch +Graph	-		-		-		-		-		-		-		-		-	
Diag hatch	2		-		-		-		-		-		-		-		-	
Diag + Graph	-		-		-		-		-		-		-		-		-	
Punctates	-		3		-		-		3		-		-		2 (1+Gr)		6	
Single incision	-		1		-		-		1		-		-		-		-	
C-st + Graph	2		-		-		-		-		-		-		-		-	
Ridge	-		-		-		-		-		-		-		-		-	
Perforation	-		-		-		-		-		-		-		-		-	
Av. Thickness	9.86±2.45		8.44±2.12		8.63±2.48		9.40±2.23		8.84		11.07±2.6		8.95±2.14		7.99±1.62		8.76±1.86	
av. Rim height	22.3 (10)		11 (9)		25 (1)		21 (5)		15.3 (15)		25 (2)		11.5 (2)		17.5 (27)		13.9 (26)	
Total sherds	5663		810		166		646		1622		201		199		2581		1787	

Table 1 (continued) *Pottery analysis by site*

	Muozi 1-6		G1/21		Fishpit		MSE17		SN153		Chirang enc		Chirang gdn		Chigura	
Deep bowls	7	12%	-		-		-		-		-		3	13%	-	
Hem bowls	4	7%	-		-		-		-		4	10%	8	33%	-	
Open bowls	8	13%	6	30%	-		-		-		-		-		-	
Constr bowls	-		-		-		-		-		-		3	13%	-	
Necked bowls	4	7%	2	10%	1	4%	2	11%	4	22%	5	13%	1	4%	2	13%
Wide-m pots	29	48%	11	55%	10	36%	7	39%	10	56%	27	69%	9	38%	6	38%
Narrow-m pots	2	3%	1	5%	2	7%	-		-		2	5%	-		5	31%
Necked pots	6	10%	-		15	54%	9	50%	4	22%	1	3%	-		3	19%
Total vessels	*60*		*20*		*28*		*18*		*18*		*39*		*24*		*16*	
Square rims	2	3%	1	5%	-		-		-		-		1	4%	-	
Round rims	30	52%	15	79%	13	54%	14	82%	8	47%	21	55%	19	79%	9	75%
Tap.rnd rims	25	43%	3	16%	11	46%	3	18%	9	53%	15	39%	1	4%	3	25%
Th.rnd rims	1	2%	-		-		-		-		2	5%	3	13%	-	
Total rims	*58*		*19*		*24*		*17*		*17*		*38*		*24*		*12*	
Rough finish	32	48%	8	42%	9	32%	5	29%	-		19	48%	20	83%	2	13%
Smooth finish	26	39%	10	53%	19	68%	12	71%	14	100%	21	53%	4	17%	14	88%
Plain burnish	9	13%	1	5%	-		-		-		-		-		-	
Total	*67*		*19*		*28*		*17*		*14*		*40*		*24*		*16*	
Graph burnish	9		10		-		1		7		-		-		10	
Quartz burnish	6		-		-		4		-		-		-		-	
Cross-hatch	3		1		-		5		2		2		-		3	
X-hatch +Graph	1		-		-		1		-		-		-		4	
Diag hatch	1		-		-		3		1		-		-		1	
Diag + Graph	1		-		-		1		-		-		-		-	
Punctates	6		-		-		-		-		13		15 (1+Gr)		-	
Single incision	-		-		3		7		5		-		4		2	
C-st + Graph	-		-		-		-		-		-		-		-	
Ridge	-		-		-		1		1 burn		-		-		-	
Perforation	-		-		-		1		-		1		-		-	
Av. Thickness	8.46±1.96		7.80±1.49		7.01±1.40		7.74±1.64		7.46±1.82		8.42±1.98		7.66±1.76		7.64±1.51	
av. Rim height	16.2 (38)		19.2 (11)		17.3 (11)		16.4 (13)		14.8 (17)		11.6 (30)		20.3 (6)		17.0 (11)	
Total sherds	*942*		*1439*		*770*		*824*		*845*		*717*		*536*		*615*	

Table 2. **Pottery analysis by groups.** Group 1, Early hilltop settlements — 1732DD27, Chirimanyimo Hill, Muozi 7-12; Group 2, Ruined pit-structures — Matinha, Nyangui G7/1, Muozi 1-6; Group 3, Late pits — Nyangui G1/21, Fishpit; Group 4, Ziwa enclosures — MSE17, SN153; Group 5, Northern enclosures — Chirangeni Enclosure, Chigura; 6, Chirangeni Garden

	Group 1		Group 2		Group 3		Group 4		Group 5		Chirangeni Gdn	
Deep bowls	48	21%	13	8%	-		-		-		3	13%
Hem bowls	72	32%	28	16%	-		-		4	7%	8	73%
Open bowls	21	9%	49	11%	6	17%	-		-		-	
Constr bowls	8	4%	2	1%	-		-		-		3	13%
Necked bowls	-		6	4%	3	6%	6	17%	7	13%	1	4%
Wide-m pots	67	30%	81	47%	21	44%	17	47%	33	60%	9	38%
Narrow-m pots	3	1%	7	4%	3	6%	-		7	13%	-	
Necked pots	8	4%	14	8%	15	31%	13	36%	4	7%	-	
Total vessels	*227*		*170*		*48*		*36*		*55*		*26*	
Rims square	132	55%	5	3%	1	2%	-		-		1	4%
Rims round	73	31%	91	55%	28	65%	22	65%	30	60%	19	79%
Rims tap.rnd	31	13%	68	41%	14	33%	12	35%	18	36%	1	4%
Rims th.rnd	3	1%	3	2%	-		-		2	4%	3	13%
Total rims	*239*		*167*		*43*		*34*		*50*		*24*	
Finish rough	111	45%	123	72%	17	36%	5	16%	21	38%	20	83%
Finish smooth	125	50%	38	22%	29	62%	26	84%	35	63%	4	17%
Plain burnish	13	5%	9	5%	1	2%	-		-		-	
Total	*249*		*170*		*47*		*31*		*56*		*24*	
Graph burnish	3		14		10		8		10		-	
Quartz burnish	-		6		-		4		-		-	
Cross hatch	1		4		1		7		5		-	
X-hatch + graph	-		1		-		1		4		-	
Diag hatch	2		1		-		3		1		-	
Diag Hatch +Gr	-		1		-		2		-		-	
Punctates	3		14		-		-		13		15	
Single incision	2		-		3		12		2		4	
Comb-st + Gr	2		-		-		-		-		-	
Ridge	-		-		-		2		-		-	
Perforation	-		-		-		1		1		-	
Av. Thickness	9.65mm		8.32mm		7.52mm		7.60mm		7.95mm		7.66mm	

APPENDIX E

Glass and copper beads

Beads constitute virtually the only specific material evidence from Nyanga excavations for contacts with other areas. A total of 346 glass beads, 60 copper beads and 185 shell beads were recovered during the present research. The majority of these come from two sites only, Muozi midden and Nyangui G7/1; samples from other sites are very small and some excavated sites yielded none. The source of the copper beads is unknown but is probably within the broader region. The glass beads are certainly exotic and would have derived directly or indirectly from the east coast of Africa through the Indian Ocean trade. The generally small numbers may reflect sporadic exchange with neighbouring peoples rather than any direct organised trade. The beads are all from dwelling sites or rubbish deposits and must represent casual loss. Large bead samples in other parts of Zimbabwe are usually deliberate deposits in hoards or accompanying burials; since no hoards have been found in Nyanga and few burials (and even those lacking beads), it would be unwise to assume that the relatively few beads found are representative of a genuine overall rarity. Relative abundance between sites is discussed below.

Glass beads

Glass beads were recovered from nine excavated sites, of which only Muozi midden and Nyangui G7/1, both relatively early in the Nyanga complex, yielded relatively large samples. Muozi alone has a stratified sequence; the others are treated as single component assemblages. No beads were found at the early hilltop settlement of 1732DD27 and only one from Chirimanyimo hill, while they are again rare or absent at the apparently late sites of Chigura and Chirangeni.

All beads recovered are reheated drawn canes and most have well rounded ends. Most are rounded "oblates" but in some cases the cylindrical shape is still recognisable; a few of the latter have relatively angular ends but not sharp snap fractures. Shape frequencies are given in Table 1. The differences of shape would seem to be due to vagaries of manufacture and are unlikely to be significant, although rounded cylinders are relatively more common at Nyangui G7/1 and in the earlier material at Muozi. Diameter is greater than length in all cases, except for a very few long cylinders, notably two Indian Reds from Nyangui G7/1. There appears to be little consistent correlation of shape with colour, apart from a tendency for most Indian Red on Pale Green and the later Whites to be cylindrical and relatively large.

Table 1 Bead shape

	Oblate		Angular cyl		Rounded cyl		Total
Muozi surface	13	81%	1	6%	2	13%	16
0 - 15	16	70%	5	22%	2	9%	23
15-30	75	77%	6	6%	17	17%	98
30-45	29	55%	5	9%	19	36%	53
45-60	7	58%	1	8%	4	33%	12
Total	140	69%	18	9%	44	22%	202
Nyangui G7/1	67	56%	8	7%	44	37%	119
Matinhal	1		-		3		4
Chirimanyimo	1		-		-		1
Nyangui G1/21	-		2		4		6
Ziwa MSE17	5		2		1		8
Ziwa SN153	1		-		1		2
Fishpit	2		1		-		3
Chirangeni	-		-		1		1

Eight colour categories were distinguished within which there are some variations of hue: Indian Red (IR), Indian Red on Pale Green translucent (IRGR), Sky Blue translucent (SBL), Royal Blue (RBL), Black (BLA), Yellow (YEL), Olive Green (OGR) and White (WH). All are single coloured except for IRGR, and all are opaque except for SBL, the inner core of IRGR and one RBL from Ziwa SN153. Colour frequencies are given in Table 2 and percentages for Muozi and G7/1 in Table 3.

GLASS AND COPPER BEADS

Table 2 Colour frequencies

	IR	IR GR	SBL	RBL	BLA	YEL	OGR	WH	Total
Muozi Surf	6	9	-	-	-	-	-	1	16
0-15	18	-	1	3	-	-	-	1	23
15-30	61	-	20	13	3	1	-	-	98
30-45	36	-	10	5	-	1	1	-	53
45-60	8	-	3	-	-	1	-	-	12
Total	129	9	34	21	3	3	1	2	202
Nyangui G7/1	70	-	18	12	8	3	8	-	119
Matinha I	1	-	1	-	-	-	1	1	4
Chirimanyimo	-	-	1	-	-	-	-	-	1
Ziwa MSE17	2	1	-	-	2	2	-	1	8
Ziwa SN153	-	-	-	1	-	-	-	1	2
Nyangui G1/21	-	2	-	-	-	-	-	4	6
Fishpit	-	-	-	1	-	-	-	2	3
Chirangeni	-	1	-	-	-	-	-	-	1

Table 3 Percentage frequency of colours for Muozi Midden and Nyangui G7/1

	IR	IR GR	SBL	RBL	BLA	YEL	OGR	WH	Total
Muozi surface	38	56	0	0	0	0	0	6	16
0 - 15	78	0	4	13	0	0	0	4	23
15-30	62	0	20	13	3	1	0	0	98
30-45	68	0	19	9	0	2	2	0	53
45-60	67	0	25	0	0	8	0	0	12
Total	64	4	17	10	3	1	0.5	1	202
Nyangui G7/1	59	0	15	10	7	3	7	0	119

There is a striking coincidence of colours and frequencies between the samples from Nyangui G7/1 and the middle levels of Muozi. Both have high frequencies of IR, fair quantities of SBL and RBL, minor occurrences of BLA, YEL and OGR and an absence of IRGR and WH. IRGR must thus be a relatively late type, and its only appearance at Muozi is on the surface, where a cohering group of nine small oblates with signs of heating subsequent to manufacture was found. WH also appears to be generally late, especially relatively large cylinders at G1/21 and SN153, although there is a small rounded cylinder at the ruined pit-structure of Matinha I. The small samples from the other sites allow few firm conclusions but it may be noted that SBL occurs only on the early sites of Chirimanyimo Hill and Matinha, and the rarity or absence of IR on later sites contrasts with their high frequency in the large early assemblages. The RBL from Ziwa SN153 differs from the earlier examples in being translucent but there is a more typical specimen from Fishpit. Yellow is rare but generally early except for the two at Fishpit.

Size

Length and diameter were measured in one millimetre categories by colour, a few specimens being too broken to measure. Averages are given in Table 4. Sample sizes can be taken from Table 2.

Table 4 Average glass bead lengths and diameters in millimetres by colour and site

	IR		IRGR		SBL		RBL		BLA		YEL		OGR		WH	
	L	D	L	D	L	D	L	D	L	D	L	D	L	D	L	D
Muozi, surf.	2.3	3.7	2.0	2.9	-	-	-	-	-	-	-	-	-	-	2.5	3.5
0 - 15	2.4	3.2	-	-	2.2	3.5	-	-	-	-	-	-	-	-	3.5	3.5
15- 30	2.6	3.6	-	-	2.5	3.7	2.5	3.8	2.3	3.2	3.5	4.5	-	-	-	-
30-45	2.5	3.5	-	-	2.6	3.7	2.2	3.3	-	-	3.5	3.5	1.8	4.5	-	-
45-60	3.0	4.1	-	-	2.3	3.5	-	-	-	-	3.5	4.5	-	-	-	-
Nyangui G7/1	2.8	3.5	-	-	2.6	3.4	2.4	3.5	2.4	3.3	3.2	3.8	2.1	3.2	-	-
Matinha I	2.5	4.5	-	-	2.6	3.4	-	-	-	-	-	-	-	-	3.5	4.5
Chirimanyimo	-	-	-	-	2.5	4.5	-	-	-	-	-	-	-	-	-	-
Nyangui G1/21	-	-	3.5	4.0	-	-	-	-	-	-	-	-	-	-	3.8	4.2
Ziwa MSE 17	2.5	3.5	2.5	4.5	-	-	-	-	3.5	4.5	3.0	4.0	-	-	1.8	3.5
Ziwa SN153	-	-	-	-	-	-	2.5	4.5	-	-	-	-	-	-	5.5	6.5
Fishpit	-	-	-	-	-	-	2.5	3.5	-	-	-	-	-	-	3.5	4.0
Chirangeni	-	-	3.5	5.5	-	-	-	-	-	-	-	-	-	-	-	-

There is not much pattern to be made out here, except that most of the OGR tend to be smaller than other types and YEL to be slightly larger.

Dating
The above data show some chronological differences in the bead assemblages and these may be compared with the beads from Summers' excavations (Schofield, in Summers 1958:222-7). The latter were recovered from six sites at Ziwa ruins; three in the Nyautare area; Nyangwe Fort and a pit-structure near Chawomera fort in the National Park; and a pit-structure at Leaping Waters near Nyangombe Falls. Sample sizes range from one to 24 glass beads. Four of the Ziwa sites and one at Nyautare include IRGR, and at most of these there are also high proportions of WH, which is consistent with our later assemblages. Ziwa site XV, the "Acropolis", has the largest sample of 24 which includes 7 WH, 2 IRGR and 1 IR, corresponding with our later assemblages, but also 4 pale blue translucent, 2 pale blue-green t/l and 4 grey-blue t/l, all of which might be comprised within our SBL. The assemblage of 17 glass beads from Nyangwe fort comprises 13 IR, 2 YEL and two "opaque green" (? = OGR), and lacks both IRGR and WH. 12 copper or brass beads came from the same context. This sample is thus similar to Muozi and G7/1 and indicates a similar relatively early date. It does not however necessarily date the fort itself as it comes from a substantial midden underlying the wall of one of the subsidiary enclosures. The pit-structure near Chawomera fort also yielded 2 IR, 1 opaque green, 1 pale blue translucent and 1 blue-green and lacks WH or IRGR, but this may not be significant in such a small sample. Thus only the last two compare with Muozi and G7/1 and the others correspond with our later samples.

Absolute dating of bead assemblages is more difficult and imprecise, but comparisons can be made with some major collections from northern Zimbabwe and elsewhere.

The Baranda site near Mount Darwin, a Mutapa-Portuguese site thought to be the historically documented *feira* of Masapa and dated by imported ceramics to the 16th/17th centuries, yielded 18174 glass beads (Pikirayi 1993:155). Of these 74.6% were IR, 5% green, 6.7% yellow, 8% dark blue, 3.6% light blue and 1.8% black, while there was only a single example of IRGR and 15 (0.1%) white. In contrast, there is an almost total switch of types in assemblages from three loop-holed stone enclosures in the same area which gave 832 beads: 38.9% white, 37.9% red-on-white, 12.5% IRGR, 3.4% red, with only 3 (0.4%) IR, 0.5% green, 1.1% light blue, 0.1% dark blue and 0.5% black. These sites are poorly dated but are probably 18th or 19th century. The Baranda sample compares closely with Muozi and G7/1 in the high proportion of IR and rarity of WH and IRGR as well as in some of the minor elements. The late assemblages have high levels of WH and IRGR but also include types not present in Nyanga such as red-on-white, red-on green and red. Red-on-white is a late type, as Martin (1940) records it and white opaque cylinders among old Manyika beads in the Penhalonga area; a collection of red-on white was also found by C.Payne (pers.comm.) on the surface of a path near the summit of Mount Nyangani. Martin also notes IR and IRGR among beads from middens at hill-forts near Penhalonga occupied within living memory.

A firmly dated late 16th to 17th century assemblage of beads comes from the Portuguese site of Dambarare near Mazowe (Garlake 1969:41-44), from the original ground surface and from burials associated with the first building phase. Garlake divided the beads into four classes, of which Class 1 are shell beads and Class 4 miscellaneous. Class 2 are "normal 17th century Portuguese trade beads", comprising irregular oblate and cylindrical opaque reheated canes, 2 to 4mm in diameter and 1.5 to 4mm long. Class 3 are also reheated canes but are smaller, more regular and transparent or translucent. Class 2 is directly comparable to the Nyanga beads and consists of 250 specimens: 3.6% royal blue, 1.2% blue-grey, 3.6% light blue, 1.2% blue-green, 2.4% green, 7.2% yellow, 71.6% Indian red, 0.4% white and 8.8% black. 133 Indian reds came from a single group in a child's burial. The high proportion of Indian red, relatively common black, yellow, royal blue and light blue, the absence of IRGR and single example of white, compare closely with the Muozi and G7/1 assemblages.

Mupira (1991) includes some beads from the Great Zimbabwe tradition of which 57 beads from Ruanga north-east of Harare are the closest geographically. Here IR constitute 39 %; frequencies of other colours are not separated from those from the Hill Ruins at Great Zimbabwe, but yellow are said to be relatively common and blue relatively few, while IRGR and white are absent. Schofield (Summers 1958:202) notes IRGR cylinders and oblates as relatively common from an excavation in the Renders Ruin area of Great Zimbabwe, but says that such had only previously been recorded from southern African sites later than the first quarter of the 19th century - although he says on page 198 that they are of 18th century date in most circumstances.

Beads from 15th to 17th century deposits at the Great Zimbabwe tradition site of Manekweni near the coast in Mozambique are listed by Garlake (1976). These are reheated cane beads of similar size and shape to the Nyanga ones. Of 643 glass beads, 26 % are Indian red, 35% yellow, 10% white, 8% green, 5% royal blue, 5% black and 11% blue-green/ grey-blue/ pale blue. The range is thus similar to Muozi and G7/1 apart from the whites, but the predominant yellow provides a marked difference.

The apparently numerous beads from rich 14th/15th century burials at the site of Ingombe Ilede, on the Zambian side of the Zambezi below Kariba, were analysed by du Toit (in Fagan et al 1969) but his report is not very useful. He divided the beads into four series on the basis of glass texture and composition and says that these have no chronological significance, but proceeds to treat them as representing different periods. No quantification is given. "... the more common forms were red, yellow, small green and turquoise beads; later they were joined by the royal blue form." Here red may perhaps be assumed to be Indian red.

Data on beads from Kilwa, the major trading port in southern Tanzania (Chittick 1974:460-495), do not provide any more precise dating. More types of beads are present there, notably beads of wound glass not found in Nyanga, but the drawn cane beads are similar. Allowing for uncertainties of colour terminology, the Muozi and G7/1 assemblages could be consistent with periods IIIa, IIIb or IV, anywhere between the late 13th and 17th centuries. However in period V, 18th/19th centuries, the percentage of Indian reds falls markedly, as it does on our later sites.

Earlier beads from the Harare and Musengezi traditions in northern Zimbabwe were analysed by Mupira (1991). Almost all came from two burial sites, Monk's Kop for Musengezi c.220km WNW of Nyanga, and Graniteside in Harare c.180km to the west. Both are dated to around the 13th century. Virtually all beads in both cases are reheated canes with high proportions of cylindrical but a fair number of oblates. The vast majority are between 2 and 4mm in diameter and in most cases diameter is greater than length, so that shape and size correspond to the Nyanga beads. Broad colour percentages are as follows:

	IR	White	Green	Black	Blue	Grey	Yellow	Total
Muse-ngezi	43	-	47.2	6.1	2.7	0.1	0.4	1924
Harare	11.2	0.2	73.9	0.02	8.8	-	5.9	4571

The Indian reds from Harare include a single IRGR. Shades of blue are difficult to correlate with Nyanga from his detailed colour terminology, but the majority from Harare are "cobalt blue" and from Musengezi "turquoise blue". The range of colours appears to be broadly the same as Muozi and G7/1 but frequencies vary, especially the high proportions of green and relatively low blue. Both white and IRGR however are very rare. It may be concluded that the 17th century Nyanga beads are of types which had been in circulation for several centuries and do not help in establishing a *terminus post quem* date.

The Muozi and G7/1 assemblages are thus consistent with a 17th century or earlier date, while those samples with IRGR or significant numbers of white must be later, 18th or 19th century.

Discussion

The presence of relatively abundant glass and copper beads on two sites (Muozi midden and G7/1) and their rarity or absence on others implies some special circumstances affecting the former sites. These could be: a short-lived period of bead affluence into which the two sites happen to fall; a special social or economic status of these two sites, bestowing preferential access to beads, or relative wealth with which to acquire them; or different depositional processes from other sites where beads, if in equally frequent use, were more carefully conserved or disposed of away from the site.

On the first possibility, the two sites are shown to be broadly contemporary by the beads themselves, supported by the radiocarbon dates, but there is nothing ostensibly to distinguish G7/1 from the other ruined pits; of these, Matinha yielded few glass beads, while careful surface search of several others yielded none. While the ruined pits are presumably culturally related and should fall within a single poorly-defined time bracket, the dating and other evidence from the excavated examples does not allow precise relative age to be established. The accumulation of the relevant part of the Muozi midden however, might be expected to have spanned an appreciable period, certainly more than the brief episode of bead availability implied.

Equally, there is no indication of a special status for G7/1, apart from the beads, but Muozi is certainly different in character owing to its isolated and relatively inaccessible location. A special, perhaps elite, status could be postulated for this site and it is conceivable that G7/1, four kilometres away and one of the closest ruined pits, could have been a direct satellite settlement. However this is unsupported speculation.

Muozi does exhibit peculiar deposition practices, represented by the large ash midden, the only such feature recorded thus far for the whole of Nyanga. This may be accounted for by the isolated position which precluded the removal of ash and other refuse to the fields for manure. Thus if beads were regularly lost and swept up with other debris, they would end up in the midden. The general sparseness of rubbish deposits at other, especially later, sites has been noted and might account for the rarity of beads. At G7/1 however, while beads were more frequent in the midden deposit of Trench III, they were also common in the other trenches. This contrasts with Matinha and it is difficult to explain why the inhabitants of G7/1 should have been more lax, unless beads were in greater abundance and less carefully conserved. But the Matinha occupants were hardly indigent as they had copper beads, including a unique large specimen.

It is thus difficult to provide a convincing, consistent explanation for these two larger samples on present data. The almost total lack of beads from the early hilltop settlements indicates their isolation from trade networks — or exceptionally good curation. The radiocarbon dates of 14th to early 15th centuries show that they precede any Portuguese trade, but beads were certainly entering Zimbabwe at this time from the Islamic coastal trade. The late sites of Chirangeni and Chigura are unlikely to have been so isolated, and perhaps the lack or rarity of beads here may reflect good housekeeping and the careful removal of domestic rubbish with manure to the fields.

Copper beads

Copper beads were also recovered mainly from the 16th or 17th century sites of Muozi upper midden, Nyangui G7/1 and Matinha I and have been described in the site reports in Chapter 8. There are also four examples from MSE17 at Ziwa ruins. The G7/1 examples are substantially larger and more solid than those from Muozi, as shown by the weights below, indicating a different source. The seven barrel-shaped beads from Matinha, strung together, fall within the size range of Muozi.

Relative weights are as follows:

Cylindrical
Muozi   0.025 to 0.3g av. 0.12 ± 0.1 (13)
G7/1   0.2 to 1.4g av. 0.46 ± 0.47 (7)
Matinha   7 beads + string 1.0gm (7)
MSE17   0.2g (1)

Biconical/barrel
Muozi   0.05 to 0.7g av. 0.26 ± 0.18 (19)
G7/1   0.4 to 6.0g av. 1.65 ± 1.92 (9)
Matinha   Sq. section bead 6.0g (1)
MSE17   0.35 to 0.5g av. 0.45 (3)

In his Nyanga excavations, Summers (1958) found a total of 16 copper or bronze beads: eight from Nyangwe Fort, one from Chawomera Fort, six from the pit-structure near Chawomera, one from a pit-structure at Leaping Waters and two from Ziwa "Acropolis". These were classified as beads of "segmental wire" and "rectangular wire" (Schofield in Summers 1958:222-7). Examination of these specimens shows that the former correspond to our barrel-shaped beads and the latter to our cylindrical. Seven of the Nyangwe beads and the Chawomera specimen are segmental and their size range is: diameter 5 to 9.5mm, average 7.12 ± 1.36; length 3.5 to 5mm, average 4.88 ± 0.58. They are thus substantially larger than the Muozi bicones or barrels and compare better with G7/1, being also made of thicker metal than the thin sheet of Muozi. There are two smaller segmental beads only 4mm in diameter from the pit-structure near Chawomera. The four rectangular wire beads from this pit-structure and the two from Ziwa Acropolis have diameters of 3 to 5mm, average 4.43 ± 0.73; and lengths of 1.5 to 4mm, average 3.2 ± 1.04, thus smaller than the G7/1 cylinders but again with thicker metal than Muozi. A number of both segmental and rectangular are well preserved, regular in shape and smoothly finished, with the join smoothed over. One large square-section bead from Leaping Waters appears directly comparable to the Matinha specimen, though slightly larger and more tapered at the ends (5 to 8.5mm diameter, 29mm long); this is the only one which Schofield lists as cast, but a seam is just evident on the Matinha specimen

Of these beads, Summers (1958:127) reports:

> Our labourers called them *gengejaia* and said they came up from Portuguese territory, a likely explanation for their most un-Bantu name. Large numbers of similar bronze beads had been dredged out of the Revue river near Macequece during alluvial gold workings. Although not accurately dated, they would seem to belong to the sixteenth to eighteenth centuries.

It seems unlikely that copper beads were imported to the coast from overseas, since they are very rare on east-coast trading sites which have been extensively excavated. At Kilwa, Chittick (1974) mentions none, while at Fort Jesus in Mombasa, Kirkman (1974) found only a single cylindrical example, in an 18th century context. Inland origins are thus indicated. Major copper sources occur in the region. Pre-colonial copper mining is documented from the Chinhoyi area of north-central Zimbabwe (Garlake 1970), from the Copper Belt of Zambia/Shaba (Bisson 1975), and from Messina, just south of the Limpopo (van Warmelo 1940). It was also mined until recently closer to Nyanga at Inyati mine, north-east of Headlands, although no old workings appear to be recorded.

Copper beads have been recovered from a number of archaeological sites in the Zimbabwe region. Copper working is firmly associated with the Ingombe Ilede tradition of about the 14th to 16th century, of which the type site, on the north bank of the Zambezi below Kariba, has rich burials with copper ingots and wire and the tools to work them. (The cross-shaped ingots are identical to those from the Chinhoyi area to the south.) Manufacture of wound wire bangles was practised but beads are very rare, only five being listed as found with one burial but not described (Fagan *et al* 1969:72). Test excavation at the related site of Chedzurgwe in Urungwe found only one possible copper bead but this was of spirally twisted wire (Garlake 1970:31). Beads from the 17th century Portuguese site of Dambarare, north of Harare (Garlake 1969:44), appear to be different in character, described as short lengths of wire clipped round a fibre core, 1 to 2mm in width (length) and 2 to 4mm in diameter. Six copper beads from the Great Zimbabwe tradition midden at Ruanga, north-east of Harare (Garlake 1973), included one small cast cylinder and five folded butt-jointed cylinders 1.5 to 7mm in diameter. Gerharz (1973) cites three bronze beads from the Khami phase site of Niamara, east of Nyanga in Mozambique; these are spherical, two of them 5mm in diameter but one very large, 22mm in diameter.

At the Great Zimbabwe tradition site of Manekweni in Mozambique, Garlake (1976:41) found 24 copper beads, mostly folded thin strips of copper 2 to 3 mm long and 4 to 6mm in diameter, presumably cylindrical, the largest 7mm long and 12mm in diameter. There were also three cast truncated bicones. Pikirayi (1993:155-7) found only 5 copper beads of "folded wire" at Baranda near Mt Darwin, but had a total of 52 from the later loop-holed structures, constituting 5.8% of all beads. Most of these are short biconical, made of short lengths of triangular section wire around 1.5 to 2mm thick, roughly bent so that the squared ends do not meet flush, with diameters around 4 to 6mm.

None of these occurrences appear to be directly comparable to the Nyanga assemblages. The variety of types suggests multiple places of manufacture, probably using metal traded from the mining areas. The more regular beads of thicker metal imply more specialised craftsmanship than the simple folded cylinders of thin sheet metal. No traces of local manufacture have been noted in the Nyanga area, but such work would have been on a relatively small scale and could easily have escaped notice.

APPENDIX F
Radiocarbon dates for Nyanga sites

Early hilltop settlements   calibrated ranges

Pta-7174	Nyangui 1732DD27 Tr.V	590 ± 20 BP	1405 (1411) 1417
Pta-7166	Nyangui 1732DD27 Tr.III	650 ± 20 BP	1312 (1331) 1354; 1384 (1392) 1399
Pta-7603	Chirimanyimo Hill II	530 ± 60 BP	1411 (1430) 1452
Pta-7635	Chirimanyimo Hill I	720 ± 15 BP	1293 (1297) 1301
Pta-7618	Chirimanyimo Hill VIII	690 ± 20 BP	1299 (1305) 1312; 1354-1384

Ziwa enclosures

Pta-7161	SN153 Tr.IV	190 ± 25 BP	1670 (1677) 1684: 1741 (1768) 1784; 1792 (1802) 1808
Pta-7155	SN153 Tr II	220 ± 25 BP	1678 (1686) 1695: 1724 (1738) 1763; 1803 (1810) 1817
Pta-1191	Zimbiti Fort	200 ± 50 BP	1669 (1683/1745/1807) 1878
Pta-1595	Ziwa Fort	140 ± 45 BP	1683 - 1745; 1807 (1854) 1900
Pta-7067	MSE 17	160 ± 20 BP	1689 (1698,1721) 1733; 1813 (1820,1860) 1884
Pta-6410	SC12 rim of log	210 ± 20 BP	1674 (1680) 1686; 1738 (1755) 1775; 1798 (1804) 1810
Pta-5158	SC12 core of log	232 ± 12 BP	1671 (1674) 1677; 1768 (1775) 1780; 1794 (1798) 1801

(note: most likely felling date is 1804 if tree c.35 years old, 1755 if c.80 years old)

| Pta-7720 | Mujinga | 150 ± 20 BP | 1693-1727; 1816-1888 |

Pit-structures

Pta-7069	Nyangui G7/1 Tr.III	340 ± 15 BP	1525 (1540) 1560; 1635 (1642) 1645
Pta-7593	Matinha I Pit 1	190 ± 45 BP	1673 (1686,1738) 1777; 1797 (1810) 1881*
Pta-7613	Matinha I Pit 1'	140 ± 40 BP	1689-1773; 1813 (1884,1920) 1939*
Pta-7402	Fishpit Hse B, 2.	330 ± 20 BP	1638 (1645) 1651**
Pta-7599	Fishpit Hse A	95 ± 15 BP	(1900)
Pta-1412	Glenhead	75 ± 40 BP	(1900)
Pta-1549	Glenhead	60 ± 45 BP	(1900)

Other sites

Pta-7399	Muozi midden 15cm	265 ± 25 BP	1657 (1664) 1671; 1780-1795
Pta-7060	Muozi midden 45-55	385 ± 15 BP	1507 (1514) 1525; 1560 (1586) 1596; 1618 (1624) 1632
Pta-7400	Muozi midden 60-70	395 ± 25 BP	1485 (1511) 1525; 1560 (1591,1621) 1632
Pta-7397	Muozi midden 80-90	520 ± 25 BP	1425 (1434) 1442
Pta-7401	Muozi midden 100-10	570 ± 20 BP	1411 (1417) 1424
Pta-7068	Elim Chigura	85 ± 25 BP	(1900)
Pta-7066	Elim Chigura	100 ± 15 BP	(1900)
Pta-7601	Chirangeni garden	200 ± 50 BP	1669 (1682,1745,1807) 1825; 1834-1878
Pta-7590	Chirangeni cupboard	300 ± 20 BP	1648 (1654) 1660**
Pta-7582	Chirangeni R-plat	60 ± 25 BP	(1900)

* only the very earliest part of the calibration range appears consistent with the probable age of the structure
** too early for the probable age of the structure and inconsistent with other determinations

REFERENCES AND ANNOTATED BIBLIOGRAPHY

The following list comprises both references from the text of this book and a full bibliography of published sources on Nyanga archaeology. The latter are annotated but not all are quoted in the text. A number of letters to the press are included, for some of which I am indebted to C.Payne; doubtless others have been missed.

Abraham, D.P. 1951. The principality of Maungwe its history and traditions. *Native Affairs Department Annual* 28: 57-83

Adams, L. 1988. The archaeology of the Nyanga uplands, Zimbabwe. Unpublished BA dissertation, Univ. of Southampton
    Description and discussion of pit-structures, fort and other features in an area of the National Park east of the Pungwe valley

Adams, W. 1989. Definition and development in African indigenous irrigation. *Azania* 24:21-27

Adams, W., Potkanski, T. and Sutton, J. 1994. Indigenous farmer-managed irrigation in Sonjo, Tanzania. *Geographical Journal* 160,1:17-32

Adams, W., Watson, E. and Mutiso, S. 1997. Water, rules and gender: water rights in an indigenous irrigation system, Marakwet, Kenya. *Development and Change* 28:707-730

Allan, J. 1965. *The African husbandman.* Edinburgh, Oliver and Boyd

Amborn, H. 1989. Agricultural intensification in the Burji-Konso cluster of south-western Ethiopia. *Azania* 24:71-83

Anderson, D. 1989. Agriculture and irrigation technology at Lake Baringo. *Azania* 24:85-97

Archer, J. 1988. *Crop nutrition and fertiliser use.* 2nd edition. Ipswich, Farming Press

Aylen, D. 1941. Who built the first contour ridges? *Rhodesia Agricultural Journal* 38, 3:144-148
    Describes terraces of earth and stone in the area of Rhodes Hotel and Pungwe gorge and mentions water furrows and erosion gullies.

Barnes, J. 1977. Survey of a ruin in Tanda Purchase Area, Rhodesia. *Rhodesian Prehistory* 7, 15:19-20
    Description and plan of a fort with crescentic abutting outer enclosure, loopholes and lintelled entrances with drawbar holes.

Bassett, W.J. 1963. *A preliminary account of the vegetation and land use of the Inyanga Intensive Conservation Area.* Salisbury, Federal Dept of Conservation and Extension Tech.Mem. No.14

Beach, D. 1980. *The Shona and Zimbabwe.* London, Heinemann.
    Brief summary of Nyanga history on pp.185-6.

_____. 1988. "Refuge" archaeology, trade and gold mining in nineteenth-century Zimbabwe: Izidoro Correia Pereira's list of 1857. *Zimbabwean Prehistory*, 20: 3-8

_____. 1990. Zimbabwean demography: early colonial data. *Zambezia* XVII,1:21-83
    Relevant parts reviewed by Beach, this volume, Annex

_____. 1994a. *The Shona and their neighbours.* Oxford, Blackwell

_____. 1994b. *A Zimbabwean past.* Gweru, Mambo Press

_____. 1995. Archaeology and history in Nyanga, Zimbabwe. History seminar paper, University of Zimbabwe, April 1995. (Reproduced as Annex, this volume.)

_____. 1996. Archaeology and history in Nyanga, Zimbabwe: an overview. in Pwiti, G. and Soper, R. (eds) *Aspects of African Archaeology*: 715-718. Harare, University of Zimbabwe Publications. (Summary of Beach, 1995).

_____. 1997. Oral tradition in eastern Zimbabwe: the work of Jason Takafa Machiwenyika. c.1889-1924. History seminar paper No.99, University of Zimbabwe.
    Relevant parts of Machiwenyika's account are quoted in Annex.

_____. 1998. Zimbabwe's south-eastern highlands in 1891-92. *Heritage of Zimbabwe* 16:1-36.
    References to old stone terracing and structures near Chimanimani.

Bent, J.T. 1896. *The ruined cities of Mashonaland.* London, Longmans.

Bernhard, F.O. 1959. A "Ritual Z2 pit" on Ziwa Farm, Inyanga. *South African Archaeological Bulletin* 14,55:104-5.
    Excavation of a cylindrical Early Iron Age pit with a small pot containing a lump of iron bloom.

_____. 1961. The Ziwa ware of Inyanga. *Native Affairs Department Annual* 38:84-92.
    A rather rambling description with illustrations.

_____. 1962. Two types of iron smelting furnaces on Ziwa Farm (Inyanga). *South African Archaeological Bulletin* 17, 68:235-236
    Describes well preserved conical and oval furnace types.

_____. 1963. A Bambata type pot from Inyanga. *South African Archaeological Bulletin* 18, 72:185
    Brief note and illustration. No description.

_____. 1964. Notes on the pre-ruin Ziwa culture of Inyanga. *Rhodesiana* 11:22-30
    General description and discussion with cursory description of several sites, including two burials.

Bhila, H. 1982. *Trade and politics in a Shona kingdom*. Harlow, Longmans

Bisson, M. 1975. Copper currency in central Africa: the archaeological evidence. *World Archaeology* 6:276-292

Blench, R. 1994-5. Linguistic evidence for cultivated plants in the Bantu borderland. *Azania* 29-30:83-102

Bolding, A., Manzungu, E.and van der Zaag, P. 1996. Farmer-initiated irrigation furrows: observations from the Eastern Highlands. in Manzungu, E. and van der Zaag, P. eds *The practice of smallholder irrigation: case studies from Zimbabwe*. Harare, University of Zimbabwe Publications:191-218

Bordini, M.A. 1974. Excavations of two graves in a cemetery near Bonda Mission. *Rhodesian Prehistory* 6,12:15-16
    Excavation of two graves in an old Christian cemetery.

Boserup, E. 1965. *The conditions of agricultural growth: the economics of agrarian change under population pressure*. London, Allen and Unwin.

Brain, C.K. and Sillen, A. 1988. Evidence from Swartkrans Cave for the earliest use of fire. *Nature* 366:464-466

Brand, W. 1970. Further observations on the Pit Ruin M4, Mkondwe Farm, Penhalonga, Rhodesia. *South African Archaeological Bulletin* 25,98:59-64
    Report on the clearance of a pit-structure in the group investigated by Mason (1933), amending Mason's plan and adding some details.

Brinn, P.J. 1987. *Communal land physical resource inventory: Nyanga District*. Harare, Chemistry and Soils Research Institute, Soils Report No.A539,
    Little reference to ruins but useful environmental background.

Brookfield, H.C. 1972. Intensification and disintensification in Pacific agriculture. *Pacific Viewpoint* 13:30-48

_____. 1984. Intensification revisited. *Pacific Viewpoint* 25,1:15-44

_____. 1986. Intensification intensified. review article of Farrington, I.S. (ed) *Prehistoric intensive agriculture in the tropics*, (BAR 1995). *Archaeology in Oceania* 21, 3:177-180

Bruwer, A.J. 1965. *Zimbabwe: Rhodesia's ancient greatness*. Cape Town, Keartland: pp15-23, 108-112
    Narrative description of the ruins with the fixed preconception that they were built by Phoenicians.

Burke, E.E. (ed). 1969. *The Journals of Carl Mauch ... 1869-1872*. Salisbury, National Archives

Challenger, G. 1964. The relationship of land use to ecology in the Inyanga area of Southern Rhodesia. In *The ecology of man in the tropical environment*. IUCN Pub. n.s. No.4:295-302
    Largely on potential for modern agriculture.

Chauke, C. 1996. Water furrows in the Nyanga archaeological complex: description, function and relationship to other features. Unpublished BA Hons Archaeology dissertation, University of Zimbabwe
    Deals with furrows, mainly in the National Park. Gives some detailed data not included in this volume (Chapter 4)

Chipunza, K.T. 1993. Those pits at Nyanga. Letter to *The Herald* 23rd Sept. 1993 (with reply by Soper 4th October)
    Suggests water furrows are erosional features and questions the use of pits for cattle.

Chirawu, S. 1994. Terraces built to create space: Research on Nyanga forts continues. *Manica Post* 29th July/5th August 1994
General account.

_____. 1999. The archaeology of the ancient agricultural and settlement systems in Nyanga lowlands. Unpublished MPhil dissertation, University of Zimbabwe.
    Detailed description and analysis of settlement structures at the Ziwa National Monument and in the St Mary's/ Maristvale area, including two excavations

Chiro, C. 1989. Iron Age stone structures in the Nyamaropa area of Nyanga District and their significance for the Nyanga Iron Age. Unpublished BA Archaeology dissertation, University of Zimbabwe
    Describes, not very clearly but with sketch plans, a number of varied stone enclosures in Nyamaropa at the foot of the eastern escarpment. Reports modern localised terrace building to poorer standards than the old terraces.

Chittick, H.N. 1974. *Kilwa: an Islamic trading city on the East African coast*. Nairobi, British Institute in Eastern Africa, Memoir 5

Clark, J.D. 1959. *The prehistory of southern Africa*. London, Penguin. pp.301-302
    Includes a brief conflated account of the Nyanga remains based on Summers (1958).

Collett, D. 1982. Excavations of stone-walled ruin types in the Badfontein valley, Eastern Transvaal, South Africa. *South African Archaeological Bulletin* 37,135:34-43

Crawford, J.R. 1967. Report on an excavation at

Harleigh Farm, near Rusape (National Monument No.72) 1961-1962. *Arnoldia* 3,6

Crawford, O.G.S. 1950. Rhodesian cultivation terraces. *Antiquity* 24:96-9

   Brief general discussion heralding Summers' fieldwork of 1949-51, with impressive air photographs.

Davison, S.L. 1993. Idea from the past. Letter to *The Herald* re pit-structures. 1st Sept. 1993 (with reply by Soper 8th September)

   Suggests that pits were water storage dams, echoing van Hoffen (1966).

Denevan, W. and Turner, B. 1974. Forms, functions and associations of raised fields in the Old World Tropics. *Journal of Tropical Geography* 39:24-33

De Wet, E. 1993. Methodological considerations of Late Iron Age fauna from the Soutpansberg. Masters dissertation, University of the Witwatersrand, Johannesburg

Dodshon, R. 1994a. Rethinking highland field systems. In Foster, S. and Smout, T. *The history of soils and field systems*. Aberdeen, Scottish Cultural Press:53-65.

_____. 1994b. Budgeting for survival: nutrient flow and traditional Highland farming. In Foster, S. and Smout, T. *The history of soils and field systems*. Aberdeen, Scottish Cultural Press:83-93

Doke, C.M. 1930. *Report on the unification of the Shona dialects*. Hertford, Austin

Dunwiddie, P. and LaMarche, V. 1980. A climatically responsive tree ring record from Widdringtonia cedarbergensis, Cape Province, South Africa. *Nature* 286:796-797

Edwards, T. 1898. Wonders of Mashonaland. *Rhodesia Herald* 20 December. Quoted in Hall and Neal 1902:353-358

   Calculates the manipulation of 261,773,750 tons of stones and earth in the construction of terraces in that part of the complex which he saw.

Elwell, H. 1977. *Open channel design*. Harare, Institute of Agricultural Engineering

Fagan, B. 1965. *Southern Africa during the Iron Age*. London, Thames and Hudson. pp.136-142

   Includes a clear summary account of Nyanga based on Summers (1958).

Fagan, B, Phillipson, D. and Daniels, S. 1969. *Iron Age cultures in Zambia II: Dambwa, Ingombe Ilede and the Tonga*. London, Chatto and Windus

Farrington, I. 1985. The wet, the dry and the steep. Archaeological imperatives and the study of agricultural intensification. in Farrington, I. ed. *Prehistoric Intensive Agriculture in the Tropics*. Oxford BAR 232:1-9

Finch, E.M. 1949. Pit people of the Inyanga Downs. *Proceedings of the Rhodesia Scientific Association* 42:38-59

   Very perceptive description and discussion of a wide range of archaeological features including "forts", pit-structures and furrows, in the area north-east of Troutbeck, based on field survey.

Fleuret, P. 1985. The social organisation of water control in the Taita Hills, Kenya. *American Ethnologist* 12:103-118

Fortune, G. 1974. The dialects of Shona and their relation to the standard language. Paper to Social Sciences section of the 3rd Rhodesia Science Congress.

Fricke, W. ed. 1996. Aspects of terrace farming in the western Sudan: geo-ecology, economy and culture. In *Kulturentwicklung und Sprachgeschichte im Naturraum Westafrikanische Savanne*. Berichte des Sonderforschungsbereichs 268, Band 8. Frankfurt-am-Main: pp.87-177

Fripp, C. and Wells, L.H. 1938. Excavations in a pit circle at Inyanga, S.Rhodesia. *South African Journal of Science* 35:399-406

   Excavation of a trench across a pit in the National Park, with evidence for reflooring of lower half. Comparison of pottery with Mason (1933).

Frobenius, L. 1931. *Erythräa: Länder und Zeiten des heiligen Königsmordes*. Berlin, Atlantis Verlag. pp254-8

   Description of Nyanga terracing and pit-structures and discussion of interpretation, including irrigation.

Gale, C.L. 1980. Vukutu. *Rhodesian Prehistory* 18:10-13

   Brief report of three sets of ruins, probably "refuge", on Vukutu Hill near Sanyatwe/ London Store. No description..

Galloway, A. 1937. A report on the skeletal remains from the pit-circles, Penhalonga, Southern Rhodesia. *South African Journal of Science* 33:1044.

   Technical description of three skeletons found by Martin (1937). Identifies a preponderance of Bush-Boskopoid features with minor Negroid features, hence representing an early phase of Bantu settlement. (Galloway's (1959) classification of Mapungubwe skeletons as Bush-Boskopoid has been revised as typical Negroid so that little weight should be given to this diagnosis).

Galloway, A. 1959. *The skeletal remains from*

Bambandyanalo. Johannesburg

Garlake, P. 1966. *A guide to the antiquities of Inyanga.* Bulawayo, Historical Monuments Commission

    Still the most useful guidebook, competently written, mainly covering typical structures in the National Park and Ziwa (Van Niekerk) ruins. Some of the directions may be difficult to follow due to changes in the road system.

_____. 1967. Value of wide discussion on Inyanga theories. Letter to *Rhodesia Herald* 3rd Jan. 1967 (see under van Hoffen 1968)

    Reply to van Hoffen (1966), countering the use of pits as water storage.

_____. 1969. Excavations at the seventeenth century Portuguese site of Dambarare, Rhodesia. *Proceedings and Transactions of the Rhodesia Scientific Association* 54:23-61

_____. 1970. Iron Age sites in the Urungwe district of Rhodesia. *South African Archaeological Bulletin* 25:25-46

_____. 1973. Excavations at the Nhunguza and Ruanga ruins in northern Mashonaland. *South African Archaeological Bulletin* 27:107-143

_____. 1976. An investigation of Manekweni, Mozambique. *Azania* XI: 25-47

Gayre, R. 1972. *The origin of the Zimbabwean civilisation*. Salisbury, Galaxie Press.

    On page 126 claims the Nyanga terracing to be an agricultural complex supporting the "urban industrial agglomerations" of Great Zimbabwe etc. Misquotes Summers to show the ruins are not "African".

Gelfand, M., Mavi, S., Drummond, R. and Ndemera, E. 1985. *The traditional medical practitioner in Zimbabwe*. Gweru, Mambo Press.

Gerharz, R. 1973. Niamara: Funde und Befunde aus eine eisenzeitlichen Ruine Sudostafrikas. *Acta Praehistorica et Archaeologica* 4.1973/1:199-233

    A detailed description of a Khami phase ruin in Mozambique not far east of Nyanga. This site was excavated and described by Wieschoff (1941) and the report is an amplification based on Wieschoff's records. A few potsherds are of Nyanga type.

Gilges, W. 1956. Mysterious slave pits of the Inyanga ... *The Rhodesian and Central African Annual*:31-33

    A brief article mainly on pits, favouring slave labour for construction.

Gilliland, H.B. 1938. The vegetation of Rhodesian Manicaland *Journal of South African Botany* IV,3:73-99

    Considers that the high grasslands were originally forested. Refutes claim that any non-indigenous plant species grow in the pits.

Greenland, D.J. and Lal, R. (eds). 1977. *Soil conservation and management in the humid tropics.* Chichester, Wiley

Grigg, D. 1982. *The dynamics of agricultural change: the historical experience.* London, Hutchinson.

Grove, A.T. and Sutton, J. 1989. Agricultural terracing south of the Sahara. *Azania* 24:114-122

    General review with references to Nyanga

Gwatkin, R.D.S. 1932. The ancient forts of Penhalonga, Southern Rhodesia. *Rhodesian Mining Journal* Part I 6, 65:513-514; Part II 6, 66:553-554; Part III 7, 68:693-695

    Interprets the pit-structures as forts or block houses of an integrated defensive system built by foreign immigrants.

Håkansson, T. 1989. Social and political aspects of intensive agriculture in East Africa: some models from cultural anthropology. *Azania* 24:12-20

Hale, G. 1966. *Cultivation terraces in western Darfur*. PhD thesis (Geography) UCLA .UMI Ann Arbor

Hall, R.N. 1904. Inyanga fort: a report on the examination of these ruins. *South African Journal of Science* 2:519-525

    Description of Nyangwe fort, with plan.

_____. 1905. Stone fort and pits on the Inyanga Estate, Rhodesia. *Journal of the Royal Anthropological Institute* 35:92-102

    Describes Nyangwe fort (duplicating Hall 1904 with minor omissions) and pit-structures on Rhodes Estate (National Park).

_____. 1909. *Prehistoric Rhodesia*. London, Unwin

    Convincingly refutes Randall-MacIver's (1906) claim that the Nyanga ruins are identical with the Great Zimbabwe tradition. Some inaccuracies and exaggerations. Descriptions of Nyangwe fort and stone-lined pits duplicate Hall (1904/5).

Hall, R.N. and Neal, W.G. 1902. *The ancient ruins of Rhodesia*. London, Methuen. pp.350-367

    Includes a second hand account preceding Hall's field work, quoting Edwards (1898) and other early observers, with some information from Schlichter (1899).

Hallpike, C.R.. 1970. Konso agriculture. *Journal of Ethiopian Studies* 8,1:31-43

Hoepen, E.C.N. van. 1939. A pre-European Bantu culture in the Lydenburg District. *Argeologiese Navorsing van die Nasionale Museum, Bloemfontein* II,5:47-74

Hudson, N. 1973. *Soil conservation*. London, Batsford

Huffman, T. 1975. A radiocarbon date from Zimbiti ruin, Inyanga. *South African Journal of Science* 49:247-248

    Date of 200 +/- 50 BP on a surviving wooden drawbar from the entrance of a fort near Ziwa ruins. Some superficial discussion of the language of the builders.

_____. 1978. The origins of Leopard's Kopje: an 11th century difaquane. *Arnoldia* 8, 23:1-23

_____. 1989. *Iron Age migrations: the ceramic sequence in southern Zambia*. Johannesburg, Witwatersrand University Press

_____. 1996. *Snakes and crocodiles: power and symbolism in ancient Zimbabwe*. Johannesburg, Witwatersrand UP

Jacobson-Widding, A. 1992. Pits, pots and snakes: an anthropological approach to ancient African symbols. *Nordic Journal of African Studies* 1, 1:5-27

    Explores the symbolic meaning attached to pits and various other features and objects by the present Manica, and by implication the Shona in general, although the pits are rather peripheral to the argument.

Jones, T.R. 1935. Prehistoric stone structures in Magaliesberg valley. *South African Journal of Science* 32:528-536

Kirkman, J. 1974. *Fort Jesus: a Portuguese fortress on the East African coast*. Oxford, Clarendon

Lampkin, N. 1990. *Organic farming*. Ipswich, Farming Press

Liesegang, G. 1970. Nguni migrations between Delagoa Bay and the Zambezi, 1821-1839. *African Historical Studies*, III, 2:317-37

Lloyd, E.M. 1926. In the early days. *Native Affairs Department Annual* 4:107-110

    A circumstantial account of pit-structures and their use for protecting cattle from raiders in Muponda (?Penhalonga), derived from a very old man reputed to be over 100 years old in 1924.

Locke, P.G. 1991. A review of ancient and medieval coins found in Zimbabwe. *Heritage of Zimbabwe* 10:51-60

    Includes a number of coins of uncertain provenance from the Nyanga/Mutare area, ranging back to Roman and early Indian.

Lundy, J.K.and Feldesman, M.R. 1987. Revised equations for estimating living stature from the long bones of the South African Negro. *South African Journal of Science* 83:54-55

Madya, M. 1989. Crops grown by Africans in east and north-east Southern Rhodesia in the period 1895-1922. Unpublished BA History dissertation, University of Zimbabwe.

Maggs, T. 1995. Neglected rock art: the rock engravings of agricultural communities in South Africa. *South African Archaeological Bulletin* 50, 162:132-142

_____. 1997. Stone-walled agricultural communities of South Africa and Botswana. In Vogel, J. ed. *Encyclopedia of precolonial Africa*. Walnut Creek, AltaMira Press:231-235

Mandipa, C. 1989. Organisation of space: the case of Nyanga. Unpublished BA Archaeology dissertation, University of Zimbabwe

    Considers the layout of "traditional" kitchens in the Nyautare area but relates to communities resettled from c.1950. Few parallels to any excavated houses but notes that some (rectangular) sleeping huts may have been raised from the ground.

Manyanga, M. 1995. Nyanga pottery: the relationship between the pre-ruin wares, upland and lowland wares. Unpublished BA Hons Archaeology dissertation, University of Zimbabwe

    Analyses museum collections of pottery from excavations preceding the present project. Notes little continuity between Early Iron Age and "Ruin" wares.

Marker, M. and Evers, T. 1976. Iron Age settlement and soil erosion in the eastern Transvaal, South Africa. *South African Archaeological Bulletin* 31:152-165

Martin, C. 1937. Prehistoric burials at Penhalonga. *South African Journal of Science* 33:1037-43

    Two burials from passages to hut circles in a pit-structure and a third from a cairn excavated by Mason (1933). Suggests that the former are secondary.

_____. 1940. Manyika beads of the XIXth century. *Native Affairs Department Annual*:18-26

    Describes old beads current among the Manyika and some from middens of hill forts occupied within living memory.

_____. 1941. Manyika pottery. *Proceedings of the Rhodesia Scientific Association* 38:52-62

    Describes current Manyika pots and their manufacture.

Mason, A.Y. 1933. The Penhalonga ruins, S.Rhodesia. *South African Journal of Science* 30:559-581

    Describes stone structures at Mkondwe, including ancient and recent forts, terracing, water furrows and especially pit-structures, through one of which a complete cross-section was excavated. Further work on this group of pits was done by Brand (1970) and burials described by Martin (1937).

Mason, R. 1962. *Prehistory of the Transvaal.* Johannesburg, Witwatersrand U.P.

Matowanyika, J. 1991. *Indigenous resource management and sustainability in rural Zimbabwe: an exploration of practices and concepts in commonlands.* PhD thesis, Waterloo, Ontario.

    A study in Kagore below the highlands to the north-east. Includes customary prohibition of settlement and cultivation on terraced areas.

Matowanyika, J. and Mandondo, A. (forthcoming). *In the shadow of Mount Muozi: indigenous knowledge systems, as ecological prudence, in the sustainable management of a local common property resource comprising terraced mountain slopes in Nyanga District, Zimbabwe.* Harare, IUCN Regional Social Policy Series. (Draft)

    Parallel study to Matowanyika (1991) in three areas on the west side of the highlands, analysing current practices in the use and conservation of areas of old terracing. Includes traditions concerning Mount Muozi and its significance in local beliefs.

Maxwell, D. 1994. A social and conceptual history of north-east Zimbabwe, 1890 - 1990. Unpublished DPhil dissertation, Oxford

_____. 1999. *Christians and chiefs in Zimbabwe: a social history of the Hwesa people c.1870s-1990s.* Edinburgh UP, International African Library 20

Mears, M. 1969. Inyanga slave pits were play pens. *Rhodesia Herald* 23rd Aug. 1969

    Amusing tongue in cheek interpretation.

Morgan, R.P.C. 1986. *Soil erosion and conservation.* London, Longmans

Mugwira, L. and Shumba, E. 1986. Rate of manure applied in some communal areas and the effects on plant growth and maize grain yields. *Zimbabwe Agricultural Journal* 83,3:99-104

Muhlanga, S. 1926. In the early days. *Native Affairs Department Annual* 4:107-111.

    see Lloyd (1926). The account seems to have been actually recorded by Muhlanga.

Mukaronda, C. 1988. The late pre-colonial and early colonial history of Nyanga. Unpublished BA History dissertation, Univ. of Zimbabwe

    Sometimes muddled treatment of archaeological evidence. History mostly derived from Storry (1976) and Machiwenyika, but has a first-hand reference to old cultivation, including long ridges in vleis.

Mullan, J.E. 1969. *The Arab builders of Zimbabwe.* Umtali, J.E.Mullan

    Attributes the Nyanga ruins to Yemeni Arabs, with a confused understanding of the archaeological evidence.

Mupira, P. 1991. A classification of imported glass beads from some Iron Age traditions in Zimbabwe. Unpublished BA Hons Archaeology dissertation, University of Zimbabwe

_____. 1995. The archaeological agricultural landscape in Nyanga, Zimbabwe: local attitudes and their implications for protection and preservation. Unpublished MPhil dissertation, Cambridge.

    Considers heritage management, mainly of Ziwa ruins, and how it can be integrated with the attitudes and welfare of the local population.

Murwira, H.K. 1993. Nitrogen dynamics in a Zimbabwean granite derived sandy soil under manure fertilisation. Unpublished DPhil dissertation, University of Zimbabwe

Nehowa, O. 1994. GIS application in archaeology using MGE PC-1 from Intergraph. Unpublished BSc (Surveying) project, University of Zimbabwe.

    An attempt at a computerised correlation of terrace distribution with geology. Final correlation was not achieved due to inadequate computer memory for the chosen software.

Netting, R.M. 1968. *Hill farmers of Nigeria: cultural ecology of the Kofyar of the Jos Plateau.* Seattle, Univ.of Wisconsin Press

Nobbs, E.A. 1927. Native cattle in Southern Rhodesia. *South African Journal of Science* 24:328-342

Norton, E.A. 1926. Inyanga, Southern Rhodesia: some remains of ancient civilisation. *Journal of the Africa Society.* 25:237-44

    Describes an ancient road ascending the north side of the Bende Gap and running north along the eastern side of the highland crest before dropping eastwards down a spur (?Nyambarawanda). Also describes enclosures below the eastern escarpment. Length of road (c.40 miles) appears exaggerated, but most of the area is now heavily afforested.

Nyabadza, G. 1989. Land settlement in northern Makoni (Maungwe) from the precolonial to the early colonial period (c.1625 - c.1940). Unpublished BA History dissertation, Univ. of Zimbabwe

    Makoni immigrants to northern Makoni District found stone ruins on arrival, but also themselves built stone refuges and associated cattle enclosures.

Nyamapfene, K. 1991. *Soils of Zimbabwe.* Harare,

Nehanda Publishers.

Owen, R., Crossley, R., Johnson, T., Tweddle, D., Kornfield, I., Davison, S., Eccles, D. and Engstrom, D. 1990. Major low levels of Lake Malawi and their implications for speciation rates in cychlid fishes. *Proceedings of the Royal Society of London* B240:519-533

Owen, R., Verbeek, K., Jackson, J. and Steenhuis, T. (eds). 1995. *Dambo farming in Zimbabwe: water management, cropping and soil potentials for smallholder farming in the wetlands.* Harare, Univ. of Zimbabwe Publications

Paver, B. 1957. *Zimbabwe cavalcade: Rhodesia's romance.* London, Cassell, 2nd edition

Secondary description and discussion of Nyanga ruins. Air photos of Chirangeni, Pungwe gorge, and Nyangwe and Little Nyangani forts.

Peters, C. 1902. *The Eldorado of the ancients.* London, Pearson.

Peters passed down the western side of the highlands in August 1901 when the area from Nhani to Inyanga Police Camp was apparently totally depopulated. He mentions or describes, not very clearly, terraces, enclosures, furrows and pit-structures, speculating that the latter were mine shafts and for gold washing, and that all show Semitic influence.

Petheram, R.W. 1974. *Inyanga with special reference to the Rhodes Inyanga Estate.* National Trust of Rhodesia.

Mainly on European settlement in the 1890s but devotes three pages to a chatty account of the ruins and their varying interpretations.

Pikirayi, I. 1993. *The archaeological identity of the Mutapa state: towards an historical archaeology of northern Zimbabwe.* Uppsala, Societas Archaeologica Uppsaliensis, Studies in African Archaeology 6

Plug, I., Soper, R. and Chirawu, C. 1997. Pits, tunnels and cattle in Nyanga: new light on an old problem. *South African Archaeological Bulletin* 52, 166:89-94

Identifies bones of dwarf cattle from the Muozi ash midden and discusses their significance for the interpretation of the pits.

Public Relations Department 1950. *Inyanga - the highlands of Rhodesia* (brochure). Salisbury.

Includes a competent summary description of the ruins, perhaps written by Summers.

Randall-MacIver, D. 1906. *Mediaeval Rhodesia.* London, Macmillan. pp.1-37

Includes the first archaeological investigation of the ruins. Describes four forts, a pit-structure and water furrows on Rhodes Estate (National Park) and the stone ruins and Early Iron Age "Place of Offerings" at Van Niekerk (Ziwa) ruins (thought to be contemporary). Photographs and plans of sites and finds.

_____. 1927. Rhodesia. *Antiquity* 1:103-104

Brief note commenting on Norton (1926) and retracting his previous interpretation of Ziwa terraces as defensive "entrenchments".

Rattray, J.M. 1957. The grasses and grass associations of Southern Rhodesia. *Rhodesia Agricultural Journal* 54,3:197-234

Reij, C., Scoones, I. and Toulmin, C. 1996. *Sustaining the soil: indigenous soil and water conservation in Africa.* London, Earthscan

Rhodesia Herald. 1894. Article on Inyangombe valley. 26th October

The first published report on the stone ruins (with *Umtali Avertiser* 1894)

Rhodesia Herald. 1962. Iron Age site to be opened at Nyanga. 25th December.

Notes the opening of Nyahokwe and the small site museum, since destroyed.

Roberts, B.K. 1996. *Landscapes and settlement: prehistory to the present.* London, Routledge

Roberts, R.S. 1980. African cattle in precolonial Zimbabwe. *Native Affairs Department Annual* 12:84-93

Robins, P. and Whitty, A. 1966. Excavations at Harleigh Farm, near Rusape, Rhodesia. *South African Archaeological Bulletin* 21 (80):61-80

Rossiter, E. 1938. Prehistoric Inyanga: data and conclusions. *Proceedings and Transactions of the Rhodesia Scientific Association* 36:95-101

A fanciful description and interpretation of the ruins. Many ruins are attributed to a military group from Egypt overseeing indigenous slaves.

Rudd, S. 1984. Excavations at Lekkerwater ruins, Tsindi Hill, Theydon, Zimbabwe. *South African Archaeological Bulletin* 39 (140):88-105

Ruthenberg, H. 1976. *Farming systems in the tropics.* Oxford UP

Schlichter, H. 1899. Travels and researches in Rhodesia. *Geographical Journal* 13, 4:376-396

Like Peters, Schlichter passed southwards through the western lowlands to Nyanga Police Post. He enthuses about, but does not describe, terraces (regarded as recent), and ancient forts, slave pits, large aqueducts, smelting furnaces, extensive citadels and an "ancient Semitic inscription". The whole paper is full of unsubstantiated assertions. His idea of a direct analogy is that Great Zimbabwe and Solomon's temple were both built of unhewn stones.

Schofield, J. 1942. A survey of the recent prehistory of Southern Rhodesia. *South African Archaeological Bulletin* 38:81-111

    Rather brief section on "the Eastern Complex". He regards the pits as cattle pens with similar arrangement to a Zulu kraal, with the cattle in a central position. Some relevant comments on beads.

Scoones, I. and Toulmin, C. 1995. Socio-economic dimensions of nutrient cycling in agropastoral systems in dryland Africa. in Powell, J.M. *et al* (eds) *Livestock and sustainable nutrient cycling in mixed farming systems of sub-Saharan Africa.* Addis Ababa, ILCA

Selous, F.C. 1881. *A hunter's wanderings in Africa.* London

Shaw, J. 1994. Manuring and fertilising the Lowlands 1650-1850. in Foster, S. and Smout, T. (eds) *The history of soils and field systems.* Aberdeen, Scottish Cultural Press:110-118

Shell Farmer. 1960. The ancient agriculture of Inyanga. May/June 1960:1-5

    Article based on Summers (1958).

Soper, R. 1981. A survey of the irrigation systems of the Marakwet. in Kipkorir, B., Soper, R. and Ssenyonga, J. (eds) *Kerio Valley: past, present and future.* Nairobi, Institute of African Studies:75-95

_____. 1993a. New light on Nyanga pits. Letter to *The Herald* 8th Sept.

    Reply to Davison 1993 refuting the water storage interpretation.

_____. 1993b. Nyanga pits. Letter to *The Herald* 4th Oct.

    Reply to Chipunza (1993).

_____. 1994. Ancient fields and agricultural systems: new work on the Nyanga terrace complex. *Nyame Akuma* 42:18-21

    Summary of results of the first two years of the present project, with an introductory note by John Sutton.

_____. 1995. The mystery of the "slave pits". *The Zimbabwean Review* 1,3:20-21

    Discussion of pit-structure function.

_____. 1996. The Nyanga terrace complex of eastern Zimbabwe: new investigations. *Azania* 31:1-35

    Full interim report of research from 1993 to early 1955.

_____. 1997. Eastern African terraced-irrigation systems. In Vogel, J. ed. *Encyclopedia of precolonial Africa.* Walnut Creek, AltaMira Press.

    Describes terracing of Nyanga and Engaruka.

_____. 1999. Water furrows in Nyanga National Park. *Zimbabwean Prehistory* 23:3-14.

    Shortened version of "Hydraulic works" in Chapter 4, this volume.

Soper, R. and Chirawu, S. 1996. Excavation of a stone enclosure at Ziwa Ruins, Nyanga District. *Zimbabwea* 4:34-43

    Detailed site report of excavations in an enclosure near Ziwa Site Museum (MSE 17), including a discussion of the significance of divided houses.

_____. 1997. Ruins on Mount Muozi, Nyanga District, Zimbabwe. *Zimbabwean Prehistory* 22:14-20

    Description of the Muozi site and excavation of a test pit in the ash midden.

Ssennyonga, J. 1981. The Marakwet irrigation system as a model of a systems-approach to water management. in Kipkorir, B., Soper, R. and Ssennyonga, J. (eds) *Kerio Valley: past, present and future.* Nairobi, Institute of African Studies, pp 96-111

Stead, W.H. 1946. Succeeding to the name Mandeya. *Native Affairs Department Annual* 23:11-12

    Describes a stone-built seat used in sub-chiefs' inauguration in Makoni District.

_____. 1947. Types of clay pots found in Inyanga District. *Native Affairs Department Annual* 24:100-102

    Gives Manyika names of traditional pots.

_____. 1949. The people of early Rhodesia. *Proceedings of the Rhodesia Scientific Association* 42:75-83

    Reasoned interpretation of terraces and pits, concluding not too dogmatically that they were built under Arab influence to grow wheat for Sofala, the pits being either to protect grain-bins or as sheltered dwellings. Records the current cultivation of narrow terraces in Bende in the 1940s and the reuse of pits as cattle kraals.

Stocklmayer, V.R. 1978. *The geology of the country around Inyanga.* Rhodesia Geological Survey Bulletin 79

_____. 1980. *The geology of the Inyanga North - Makaha area.* Zimbabwe Geological Survey Bulletin 89

Storry, J.G. 1974. Pungwe pit-structure: a preliminary report. *Rhodesian Prehistory* 13:10-13

    Description and minor excavation of a pit-structure in the Pungwe gorge.

_____. 1975. Preliminary dendrochronology study in Rhodesia. *South African Journal of Science* 49:248

Experimental coring of a number of tree species in the National Park, of which *Widdringtonia whitei* gives promising results, though the oldest sample was only 26 years old.

_____. 1976. The settlement and territorial expansion of the Mutasa dynasty. *Rhodesian History* 7:13-30.

Discusses the terracing but does not succeed in relating it to Manyika history, although the distribution overlaps and it should be contemporary.

Straube, H. 1967. Der agrarische Intensivierungs komplex in nordost Afrika. *Paideuma* XIII: 198-222

Summers, R. 1950. Iron Age cultures in Southern Rhodesia. *South African Journal of Science* 47:95-107

Synthesis of evidence available at that time, mainly pottery. Little on Nyanga which is tentatively regarded as distinct from the rest of the Iron Age.

_____. 1952. Inyanga: a preliminary report. *Antiquity* 26 (102):71-75

Preliminary summary of the work of the Nyanga Research Fund and some conclusions. Equates the "Upland culture" with Manyika, apparently on the basis of the pottery.

_____. 1958. *Inyanga: prehistoric settlements in Southern Rhodesia*. Cambridge UP

Definitive monograph on his and Robinson's research from 1949 to 1951, with sections on beads (Schofield), bones (Cooke) and botanical notes (Wild). Describes the structures, excavations and finds, with perceptive interpretation and synthesis

_____. l971. *Ancient ruins and vanished civilizations of southern Africa*. Cape Town, Bulpin.

Seeks to integrate Nyanga ruins into a general classification of stone structures in southern Africa, making for an often disjointed treatment. Discusses dating, cultural interpretation and influence, and climatic correlation.

Sunday Mail. 1976. Pottery jar found in remote Nyanga area (with photo). 5th December

Report of a pot spotted by an Air Force pilot and deposited in Mutare Museum. Location not given.

Sutton, J.E.G. 1969. "Ancient civilizations" and modern agricultural systems in the Southern Highlands of Tanzania. *Azania* 4:1-13

_____. 1983. A new look at the Inyanga terraces. *Zimbabwean Prehistory* 19:12-19

A thoughtful description and discussion of the terraces from the point of view of an extensive agricultural system, with consideration of the role of irrigation.

_____. 1984. Irrigation and soil conservation in African agricultural history. *Journal of African History* 25:25-41

A general discussion of "specialised" techniques in African agricultural systems calling for more attention to surviving field systems, with a section on Nyanga derived from Sutton (1983).

_____. 1985. Irrigation and terracing in Africa. in Farrington, I.S. (ed) *Prehistoric intensive agriculture in the tropics*. Oxford, BAR 232: 737-64

Considers terracing and irrigation in the broader context of African agricultural systems and argues against their being taken as evidence for agricultural intensification rather than degrees of specialisation. Summarises their distribution, mainly in eastern Africa, including Nyanga.

_____. 1986. The irrigation and manuring of the Engaruka field system. *Azania* 21:27-51

_____. 1988. More on the cultivation terraces of Nyanga: the case for cattle manure. *Zimbabwean Prehistory* 20:21.24

Reconsiders the terraces as possibly a more intensive agricultural system using manure from stall-fed cattle.

_____. 1989a. Fields, farming and history in Africa. *Azania* 24:6-11

_____. 1989b. Towards a history of cultivating the fields. *Azania* 24:99-112

Wide ranging review of "specialised" agricultural techniques with frequent references to Nyanga on aspects of terracing, ridging, irrigation, manuring and settlement patterns.

_____. 1998. Engaruka: an irrigation agricultural community in northern Tanzania before the Maasai. *Azania* 33:1-37

Swan, L. 1994. *Early gold mining on the Zimbabwean plateau: changing patterns of gold production in the first and second millennia A.D.* Studies in African Archaeology 9. Uppsala.

Fig. 6.11 and p.94 demonstrate the lack of correlation between Nyanga complex sites and gold mining.

Talma, A.S. and Vogel, J. 1993. A simplified approach to calibrating 14C dates. *Radiocarbon* 35 (2):317-322

Taylor, G.A. 1924. The genealogical method of

anthropological enquiry. *Native Affairs Department Annual* 2:33-48
   Includes the description of a battle between Sawunyama and his brother Kadzima in c.1875, involving a "fort" with stone walls and loopholes at "Tani" (not identified).

"Tilian" 1972 Of slave pits, figs and sweet peas. *Rhodesia Herald* 30 December.
   Association of fig trees with pits and of aloes with forts. No mention of lemons and vines !

Tomlinson, R.W. 1973. *The Inyanga area. An essay in regional biogeography*. University of Rhodesia Series in Science, Occasional Paper No.1

Tredgold, M.H. 1986. *Food plants of Zimbabwe*. Gweru, Mambo Press.

Trevor, T.G. 1930. Relics of pre-European culture in Rhodesia and South Africa. *Journal of the Royal Anthropological Association* LX:389-399
   Only reference to Nyanga is passing mention of furrows on p.392.

Tyson, P.D. and Lindesay, J.A. 1992. The climate of the last 2000 years in southern Africa. *The Holocene* 2, 3:271-278

Umtali Advertiser. 1894, 6th December.
   First brief mention of stone ruins to be published (with *Rhodesia Herald* 1894)

van der Zaag, P. (forthcoming). Steep slopes, stubborn stones and a determined people: notes on the bench terrace technology in Biriwiri, Chimanimani District.

van Hoffen, P. 1966. The Inyanga "slave pits" were probably built for the retention of water. *Rhodesia Herald* 19th Dec.
   Replied to by Garlake (1967).

_____. 1968. Were "slave pits" really for water storage ? letter to the *Rhodesia Herald* 4th Oct.
   Ignoring Garlake's reply !

van Warmelo, N.J. 1940. *The copper-miners of Musina*. Pretoria, South African Department of Native Affairs

Vogel H. 1988. Deterioration of a mountainous agro-ecosystem in the third world due to emigration of rural labour. *Mountain Research and Development* 8, 4:321-329

Wandera, J.G. and Soper, R. 1986. Agriculture and animal husbandry. in Soper, R. (ed) *Taita-Taveta District Socio-cultural Profile*. Nairobi, Ministry of Planning and National Development. and Institute of African Studies, pp 80-97

Watson, E., Adams, W. and Mutiso, S. 1988. Indigenous irrigation, agriculture and development, Marakwet, Kenya. *Geographical Journal* 164,1:67-84

Watt, J.M. and Breyer-Brandwijk, M.G. 1962. *The medicinal and poisonous plants of southern and eastern Africa*. Edinburgh and London, Livingstone

White, S. 1941. The agricultural economy of the hill pagans of Dikwa Emirate, Cameroons(British Mandate). *Empire Journal of Experimental Agriculture* IX:65-72

Whitlow, R. 1980. The morphology of two different vleis in the highveld of Zimbabwe Rhodesia. *Zimbabwe Rhodesia Agricultural Journal* 77 (2):71-80

_____. 1983. Vlei cultivation in Zimbabwe: reflections on the past - a play with a difference. *Zimbabwe Agricultural Journal* 80 (3):123-135

Whitty, A. 1959. A classification of prehistoric stone buildings in Mashonaland, Southern Rhodesia. *South African Archaeological Bulletin* 14,54:57-71
   A classification for Mashonaland in general. Also rather general on Nyanga but recognises a "surprisingly sophisticated" and realistic attitude to building compared to the "conceptually primitive" stone architecture of Great Zimbabwe.

_____. 1961. Inyanga. reprinted from *The Central African Examiner* Jan. 1961
   Summarises parts of Summers (1958) but postulates a further, probably later, component to the west, with defensive walled villages on kopjes with some of the characteristics of Nyanga architecture.

Widgren, M. 1999. Islands of agricultural intensification in eastern Africa: the social, ecological and historical contexts. *Environment and Development Studies Unit Working Papers* No. 43:3-14, Stockholm University

Wieschoff, H.A. 1941. *The Zimbabwe-Monomatapa culture in south-east Africa*. Menasha (Wisconsin), G.Banta. pp 23ff
   Belated publication of work on Frobenius' expedition in 1929. Describes terraces, furrows and pits, not always entirely accurately, interpreting the pits as dwellings. Gives the first description of "double concentric enclosures". Excavation of the Khami phase site of Niamara east of Nyanga in Mozambique (republished by Gerharz 1973), and description of ruins in Maungwe north-east of Rusape.

Wild, A. and Jones, L. 1988. Mineral nutrition of crop plants. In Wild, A (ed), *Russel's soil conditions and plant growth*. 11th edition:69-112. London, Longmans

Index

Adams,W 22, 24, 25, 78
African agriculture 2
agricultural intensification 23, 25, 26, 80, 130
Agricultural practices 2
Agriculture 2
Avila 15, 19, 208

Baranda 12
Barwe 3, 137, 227, 228, 229, 231
Beach,D
   3, 8, 10, 12, 115, 125, 135, 136, 137, 138, 207, 222, 227
Bende 4
Bende Gap
   9, 13, 15, 19, 33, 34, 54, 93, 103, 133, 136
Bernhard,F 10, 115
British Institute in Eastern Africa 4, 234
Brookfield,H 22, 23, 26, 130
Bruwer,A 11, 92, 110
burials 9, 143
Burnaby 13, 73, 92, 115

cairn 47, 67, 103
calibration 12
cattle 10, 21, 89, 91, 93, 99, 100, 107, 110, 111,
   124, 125, 128, 130, 132, 133, 134, 135, 143,
   147, 159, 174, 178, 181, 185, 186, 193, 203,
   207, 210, 215, 230, 231, 232, 233, 235,
   242; dwarf 9, 10, 91, 98, 110, 111, 124, 125,
   134, 160, 161, 163, 223, 224, 232, 242, 243
Chawomera fort 112, 114, 259, 262
Chigura 7, 13, 35, 98, 99, 102, 134, 140, 199,
   204, 206, 208, 215, 251, 252, 253, 257, 261, 263
Chimanimani 2, 54, 74, 222, 231
Chinese porcelain 190, 191, 192
Chirangeni 15, 33, 46, 99, 100, 112, 129, 130,
   132, 134, 140, 198, 208, 215, 216, 249, 251,
   252, 253, 257, 261, 263
Chirawu,S 10, 42, 98, 101, 102, 109, 110, 111, 125,
   159, 186, 188, 198, 216
Chirimanyimo hill 13, 18, 20, 21, 28, 31, 33, 49, 58,
   62, 74, 76 , 86, 89, 92, 93, 95, 100, 104, 109, 110,
   117, 132, 133, 134, 140, 145, 147, 148, 156, 157,
   170, 240, 251, 257, 258, 263
Chitakete 10, 12, 228
climate 4, 17, 18, 21, 131
copper 15, 92, 104, 156, 161, 162, 168, 174, 188,
   191, 192, 257, 259, 261
cowpeas 31, 128, 188, 250
crop rotation 22, 26, 128
cultivation ridges 2, 4, 5, 7, 10, 12, 22, 24, 28, 31, 42,
   55, 58, 63, 72, 73, 75, 124, 129, 134, 138, 241

dam 9, 61, 62, 63, 65, 74, 76, 78, 79, 92, 180
Darfur 23

dhaka 47, 67, 91, 97, 98, 101, 107, 109, 110, 112,
   116, 117, 134, 136, 150, 151, 165, 167, 173, 178,
   179, 180, 182, 183, 184, 186, 187, 188, 190, 195,
   196, 198, 199, 201, 202, 203, 210, 212, 213
divided houses 86, 90, 98, 99, 108, 110, 111, 126,
   127, 134, 178, 179, 186, 188, 193, 208
Doke 2, 137, 227, 229
double concentric enclosures 86, 93, 96, 98, 99, 101,
   102, 111, 124, 125, 127, 134, 137, 198, 199, 208,
   209, 210, 215
drains 33, 36, 43, 45, 46, 47, 50, 53, 76, 90, 95,
   98, 99, 127, 151, 171, 175, 177, 178, 179, 180, 181,
   186, 195, 201, 202, 210

early hilltop settlements 11, 53, 86, 92, 103, 130,
   131, 132, 133, 136, 137, 140, 149, 155, 163,
   251, 252, 253, 261
Early Iron Age 3, 8, 9, 10, 33, 136, 147, 160, 195,
   196, 253
Elim 15, 18, 19, 33, 52, 117, 208, 209, 241, 263
Engaruka 25, 78, 79
erosion 18, 22, 37, 45, 53, 68, 69, 71, 76, 193

Farrington,I 26, 27
Finch, E 9, 62, 72, 75, 76, 92, 110, 180, 223
Fishpit 8, 67, 75, 89, 91, 108, 128, 140, 178,
   180, 249, 251, 252, 258, 263
floatation 7, 190
forts 2, 9, 12, 39, 42, 64, 86, 98, 108, 111, 112,
   115, 133, 135, 137, 199, 208, 209, 223, 238, 260
Fripp,C and Wells,L 9, 91
Frobenius,L 9, 33

Gaerezi river 228, 230
Gairezi Facies 20, 34, 15
Gairezi river 13, 15, 20, 208
Galloway,A 9
gardens 26, 28, 32, 47, 49, 55, 62, 71, 72, 74, 76,
   77, 78, 89, 124, 126, 127, 128, 129, 130,
   171, 175, 177, 179, 180, 186, 204, 205, 207,
   208, 241, 263
Garlake, P 10, 109, 260, 262
Gayre, R 11
glass beads 7, 89, 92, 99, 151, 154, 156, 161, 165,
   167, 168, 174, 180, 185, 188, 190, 191, 193,
   197, 207, 214, 257
goats 91, 109, 110, 124, 126, 143, 159, 186, 193,
   223, 232, 242, 244
gold 15
Great Zimbabwe 8, 9, 10, 11, 12, 133, 137, 191,
   196, 228, 260, 262
grinding stones 98, 101, 107, 195, 199, 202, 210, 212
ground beans 31, 128, 250
Gumanye 11, 137

Gwatkin,R 11

Hall,R 8, 21, 61, 74, 109, 110, 185, 188, 223
Harare tradition 11, 12, 137, 260
Harleigh Farm 10, 11, 12, 133
Headlands 2, 13, 15, 55, 130, 137, 225, 262
Honde river 13, 32, 222, 225
Huffman,T 10, 11, 98, 109, 137, 185, 227
Hwesa 54, 224, 225, 227, 228, 229, 231, 232, 233, 236

Ingombe Ilede 260, 262
intercropping 22, 26, 28, 31, 32, 128
interfluve 12
Inyanga Downs 9, 62
Inyanga Facies 34, 15
iron objects 68, 107, 110, 129, 144, 147, 161, 167, 174, 185, 188, 190, 192, 197, 206, 215
iron slag 15, 115, 116, 117, 147, 150, 151, 154, 162, 190, 192, 196, 197, 209, 215
iron working
   2, 15, 65, 68, 71, 86, 115, 117, 209
irrigation 22, 23, 24, 26, 27, 60, 61, 62, 63, 64, 67, 68, 69, 71, 73, 74, 75, 78, 79, 124, 129, 133, 223, 224, 230, 235

Jacobson-Widding,A 110, 112

Kagore 4, 15, 98, 117, 125, 134
Khami phase 9, 11, 262
Kofyar 22, 25
Konso 23, 25, 78, 79

Leopards Kopje 11, 137
Little Ice Age 13
Lloyd,E 9
loopholes 2, 12, 112, 113, 208, 224

Machiwenyika,J 28, 32, 62, 124, 224, 229, 230, 231, 232, 235, 238
Maggs, T 23
maize 27, 31, 32, 54, 55, 128, 129, 250
majo 28, 32, 55, 128
Makaha Gold Belt 15
Makoni 2, 3, 28, 32, 222, 224, 225, 227, 228, 230
Mandondo,A 4, 28, 32, 107
manure 10, 17, 18, 22, 23, 25, 26, 28, 49, 54, 72, 91, 125, 126, 127, 128, 129, 177, 179, 204, 206
Manyika 3, 9, 10, 28, 55, 62, 75, 80, 86, 110, 112, 114, 115, 125, 136, 137, 222, 224, 227, 228, 229, 230, 231, 232, 233, 234, 235, 236, 260
Marakwet 74, 78, 79
Maristvale 10, 13, 18, 19, 20, 33, 41, 49, 51, 53, 56, 58, 62, 63, 64, 92, 93, 96, 102, 112, 115, 130, 240
Martin,C 9, 114, 143, 224, 260
Masapa 12

Mason,Y 9, 21, 62, 72, 91, 92
Matinha 62, 64, 76, 78, 92, 133, 140, 148, 170, 171, 175, 251, 252, 254, 258, 261, 263
Matowanyika,J 4, 107
Maungwe 3, 10, 12, 136, 137, 227, 230, 233, 234, 236
mihomba 24, 28, 31, 55, 67, 69
millet 27, 32, 107, 128, 212, 250
Mkondwe 2, 9, 11, 62, 75, 92, 109, 133, 143
Mount Darwin 2, 12, 259
Mozambique 2
Mukaronda,C 10, 32, 55, 224
Mullan,J 11
Munditi,C 110, 124, 150
Muozi 4, 7, 10, 13, 42, 58, 63, 86, 89, 102, 107, 126, 134, 137, 140, 145, 147, 155, 161, 163, 242, 249, 251, 253, 259, 260, 261, 263; midden 7, 91, 92, 124, 126, 132, 133, 136, 156, 168, 169, 242, 251, 252, 257, 258
Musengezi tradition 11, 12, 137, 260
Mutapa state 11, 12, 137, 228, 229, 231, 259
Mutare 11, 13, 32; museum 7, 107, 186, 272
Mutasa 2, 3, 10, 125, 137, 222, 228, 230, 231, 232, 234, 235
Mutoko 11, 15, 32, 162, 232
Mwenje 58, 63, 92

Nani rock 13, 208, 223, 224, 230, 238
National Museums and Monuments of Zimbabwe 5, 8, 86, 140, 186
Ngoni 115, 224, 230, 231, 238
Nguni 28, 160, 224, 228, 230, 242
Niamara 9, 11, 12, 262
Njemps 25, 78, 79
Norton,E 9
Nyabadza,G 10, 224, 228
Nyahokwe 10, 15, 115, 117, 223
Nyama people 3, 10, 107, 137
Nyamaropa 4, 15, 19, 54, 92
Nyanga National Park 4, 5, 13, 15, 17, 20, 21, 61, 63, 65, 69, 73, 7 5, 76, 78, 89, 91, 92, 108, 109, 112, 114, 115, 129, 133, 178, 180, 188, 208, 236, 241, 259
Nyanga town 3, 4, 11, 13, 15, 62, 63, 64, 65, 73, 86, 114, 115, 133, 223, 225, 227, 236
Nyangani mountain 13, 19, 20, 21, 65, 229, 231, 260
Nyangombe river 3, 13, 15, 20, 35, 46, 65, 67, 68, 71, 72, 97, 98, 112, 115, 117, 125, 130, 134, 135, 199, 222, 223, 225, 228, 230, 231, 233, 236
Nyangui 4, 13, 19, 20, 58, 63, 64, 74, 86, 92, 93, 103, 125, 133, 141, 169, 170, 179, 236
Nyangui 1732DD27 8, 64, 86, 95, 104, 132, 140, 149, 152, 154, 155, 156, 157, 249, 251, 252, 253, 257, 263
Nyangui G1/21 8, 17, 76, 89, 91, 109, 128, 140,

165, 169, 173, 175, 180, 241, 249, 251, 252, 258
Nyangui G7/1 8, 76, 92, 95, 126, 136, 140, 157, 161, 163, 164, 171, 173, 175, 180, 251, 252, 254, 257, 258, 259, 260, 261, 263
Nyangwe Fort 8, 9, 11, 71, 76, 113, 115, 143, 180, 259, 262
Nyautare 4, 9, 46, 62, 74, 98, 109, 110, 112, 115, 116, 130, 134, 135, 136, 147, 198, 208, 209, 216, 259

Payne,C 21, 68, 76, 109, 238, 260
Penhalonga 2, 9, 62, 75, 89, 93, 109, 114, 133, 260
Peters,C 8, 61, 63, 92, 207, 223, 224, 230, 237
phosphate samples 7, 77, 110, 144, 167, 179, 184, 190
Pikirayi,I 11, 12, 259, 262
pit-enclosures 35, 37, 54, 86, 89, 93, 96, 98, 99, 101, 111, 124, 125, 127, 131, 133, 134, 135, 137, 143, 201, 209, 216
pit-structures 2, 3, 4, 7, 8, 9, 13, 20, 26, 42, 50, 53, 58, 62, 63, 64, 65, 67, 68, 69, 71, 72, 75, 76, 78, 86, 89, 91, 92, 93, 95, 96, 97, 108, 109, 110, 111, 112, 115, 117, 124, 125, 126, 127, 128, 129, 131, 132, 133, 134, 135, 137, 140, 141, 143, 145, 161, 165, 169, 170, 171, 172, 173, 175, 179, 180, 182, 184, 185, 188, 201, 208, 209, 216, 222, 223, 224, 228, 229, 230, 233, 234, 235, 251, 252, 253, 259, 262
Plug, I 10, 91, 124, 159, 161, 242
Portuguese 11, 12, 135, 222, 228, 230, 232, 233, 259, 261, 262
pottery 3, 7, 11, 12, 24, 37, 49, 50, 89, 92, 98, 99, 101, 103, 104, 108, 132, 134, 137, 144, 145, 147, 150, 151, 152, 153, 155, 156, 157, 163, 165, 166, 167, 173, 177, 179, 183, 185, 190, 191, 196, 198, 200, 204, 208, 209, 210, 212, 214, 216, 251
pumpkins 32, 62, 129, 235
Pungwe river 2, 10, 13, 20, 32, 65, 71, 76, 115, 179, 236

radiocarbon determinations 8, 10, 12, 21, 91, 92, 98, 99, 109, 114, 131, 145, 153, 156, 167, 173, 184, 191, 193, 196, 198, 202, 204, 207, 213, 216
rainfall 4, 13, 17, 18, 20, 39, 46, 50, 51, 62, 78, 129, 131, 138, 208, 232
raised platforms 67, 71, 86, 91, 97, 99, 101, 107, 110, 113, 129, 176, 179, 186, 187, 188, 193, 194, 198, 201, 204, 206, 207, 208, 209, 210, 211, 215
Randall-MacIver,D 3, 8, 61, 74, 93, 109, 114, 143, 223, 224, 236
reservoirs 65, 70, 71, 74, 78, 79
Rhodes Estates 5, 9, 61, 91, 236
Rhodes estates 223
Rhodes Trustees 4
rice 9, 28, 31, 32, 76, 128, 129, 223
Robinson,K 9, 223

Rossiter,E 11
Ruangwe 13, 15, 28, 35, 52, 98, 134, 135, 147, 208, 216
Ruenya river 2, 13, 15, 228, 231
ruined pit-structures 53, 75, 76, 78, 89, 92, 93, 95, 111, 131, 133, 134, 140, 147, 157, 161, 163, 164, 169, 171, 173, 175, 180, 251, 252, 253, 258, 261
Rukotso mountain 13, 15, 86, 93, 132, 155, 238
Rusape 11, 12, 19, 31, 55, 130, 133, 137, 227, 228, 239

Saunyama 3, 4, 80, 107, 108, 115, 136, 137, 138, 207, 225, 230
Schlichter,H 8, 61, 223, 230
Schofield,J 10, 191, 259, 260, 262
Selous,F 124, 223
Sena 137, 222, 227, 231, 233, 238
Settlement patterns 2
sheep 25, 124, 126, 143, 159, 193, 223, 232, 242, 244
shell beads 104, 156, 161, 163, 204, 207, 257, 260
Shona language, people 3, 11, 28, 32, 108, 137, 193, 222, 225, 227, 228, 229, 231, 233, 234
slave pits 86, 89, 92
slurry 26, 72, 77, 78, 91, 126, 127, 129, 179
soils 5, 9, 17, 18, 33, 35, 37, 39, 41, 46, 47, 51, 53, 54, 57, 58, 73, 93, 126, 129, 170, 177, 240
Sonjo 78, 79
Soper,R 10, 58, 74, 78, 102, 159, 186, 234, 242
sorghum 27, 31, 32, 78, 128, 129, 212, 250
split-level enclosures 50, 86, 96, 100, 108, 111, 134, 137, 208
stall-feeding 10, 25, 91, 126, 127, 133
Stapleford Forest 2, 4, 13
Stead,W 9, 54, 92, 181, 223, 224, 232
Stidolph,P 15, 61, 63
stone artefacts 43, 151, 154
storage houses 199, 204, 210, 215, 216
Storry,G 10, 179, 229, 238
Summers,R 2, 3, 4, 7, 8, 9, 10, 11, 12, 13, 28, 33, 46, 62, 76, 91, 92, 97, 98, 99, 100, 109, 110, 111, 112, 114, 115, 117, 126, 128, 131, 137, 143, 180, 186, 188, 191, 193, 195, 196, 208, 216, 223, 227, 233, 234, 253, 259, 262
Sutton,J 4, 8, 10, 22, 23, 24, 25, 26, 31, 62, 73, 78, 91, 126, 130

Taita 78, 79
Tanda 13, 92, 97, 98, 113, 134, 223, 224, 225, 228, 230, 234
taro 28, 128
terracing, terraces 2, 3, 4, 5, 8, 11, 12, 15, 18, 22, 23, 24, 25, 26, 33, 35, 42, 46, 49, 53, 54, 58, 61, 63, 64, 68, 72, 89, 91, 93, 95, 96, 124, 125, 126, 128, 129, 130, 132, 133, 134, 136, 137, 138, 147, 186, 198, 200, 208,

222, 224, 228, 230, 233
thick coarse vessels 199, 202, 204, 206, 208, 209, 212, 215, 216, 252
Troutbeck 4, 9, 63, 72, 73, 109, 112, 117, 133, 180, 185
tsenza 10, 28, 31, 128, 129
Tsindi 10, 11

University of Zimbabwe 4, 7, 234
Unyama 75, 125, 135, 223, 224, 225, 227, 228, 229, 230, 231, 232, 233, 234, 236, 238

Van Niekerk Ruins 3
Verbeek,K 17, 39, 40, 46, 51, 53, 54, 58
vleis 24, 27, 42, 44, 53, 55, 56, 57, 60, 129, 130, 134

walled hollows 86, 92, 102, 104, 132, 142, 144, 147, 149, 151, 153, 156
walled village zone 12, 137
washing stone 12, 104, 174, 185, 198, 212, 215
water furrows 2, 4, 7, 9, 10, 25, 60, 61, 63, 69, 72, 78, 91, 115, 133, 171, 175, 180, 186, 230, 235
Whitty,A 10, 11, 12, 110, 137
Widgren,M 135
Wieschoff,H 9, 11, 62, 74, 91, 92
Worlds View 13, 86, 132

Ziwa: mountain 3, 13, 33, 115, 236; National Monument 3, 4, 98; pottery 3, 10, 136; ruins 3, 8, 9, 10, 12, 33, 93, 97, 98, 101, 109, 111, 117, 125, 130, 134, 135, 136, 208, 216, 259; Site Museum 15, 19, 33, 35, 39, 53, 112, 117, 143, 186
Ziwa Acropolis 12, 259, 262
Ziwa MSE17 101, 108, 109, 140, 178, 186, 249, 251, 253, 261
Ziwa Mujinga 18, 33, 39, 101, 112, 240, 263
Ziwa SN113 8, 18, 33, 35, 39, 40, 46, 130, 134, 240
Ziwa SN153 8, 101, 140, 193, 196, 249, 251, 252, 253, 257, 258, 263

1